POLITICAL BOOMS

Local Money and Power in Taiwan,
East China, Thailand, and the Philippines

Series on Contemporary China   (ISSN: 1793-0847)

Series Editors: Joseph Fewsmith *(Boston University)*
Zheng Yongnian *(East Asian Institute, National University of Singapore)*

Published*

**To view the complete list of the published volumes in the series, please visit:
http://www.worldscibooks.com/series/scc_series.shtml*

Series on Contemporary China – Vol. 16

POLITICAL BOOMS

Local Money and Power in Taiwan,
East China, Thailand, and the Philippines

by

Lynn T. White
Princeton University, USA

World Scientific

NEW JERSEY · LONDON · SINGAPORE · BEIJING · SHANGHAI · HONG KONG · TAIPEI · CHENNAI

Published by

World Scientific Publishing Co. Pte. Ltd.

5 Toh Tuck Link, Singapore 596224

USA office: 27 Warren Street, Suite 401-402, Hackensack, NJ 07601

UK office: 57 Shelton Street, Covent Garden, London WC2H 9HE

British Library Cataloguing-in-Publication Data
A catalogue record for this book is available from the British Library.

Series on Contemporary China — Vol. 16
POLITICAL BOOMS
Local Money and Power in Taiwan, East China, Thailand, and the Philippines

ISBN-13 978-981-283-681-6
ISBN-10 981-283-681-0
ISBN-13 978-981-283-682-3 (pbk)
ISBN-10 981-283-682-9 (pbk)

Typeset by Stallion Press
E-mail: enquiries@stallionpress.com

For
Jeremy, Kevin, and Fekade

"No. I could never have survived as a lawyer. I am a man of honor.... I would have to bribe judges out of responsibility to my client. But judges are venal and may sell the case to the other side if it intervenes with a higher bid. Then I would have to kill the judge.... It is well that I used my talents otherwise."
— Grasing de Guzman
(a "Godfather" in Nueva Ecija, Philippines)

"When I hear the word culture, I reach for my gun."
— Hermann Göring

"Comparative analysis is no substitute for detailed investigation of specific cases."
— Barrington Moore

"We have had difficulty perceiving change because we have looked for the wrong kind of conflict (conflict within the government) and have underestimated the extent to which the government itself as a whole has been in conflict with other power systems."
— E. E. Schattschneider

"Generally speaking, our rural reforms have proceeded very fast, and farmers have been enthusiastic. What took us by surprise completely was the development of township and village industries.... This is not the achievement of our central government. Every year, township and village industries achieved 20 percent growth.... This was not something I had thought about. Nor had the other comrades. This surprised us."
— Deng Xiaoping

Contents

Abbreviations

AFP	Armed Forces of the Philippines
CCP	Chinese Communist Party
CD	*China Daily*, Beijing
Comelec	Commission on Elections (Philippines)
CPI	Corruption perception index
CR	Cultural Revolution
CYL	Communist Youth League (China)
DPP	Democratic Progressive Party (Taiwan)
EPZ	Export Processing Zone (Taiwan)
FDI	Foreign direct investment
FEER	*Far Eastern Economic Review*, Hong Kong
GMRB	*Guangming ribao* (Bright Daily), Beijing
GNP	Gross national product
ISI	Import-substituting industrialization
IRRI	International Rice Research Institute (Los Baños, Philippines)
JFRB	*Jiefang ribao* (Liberation Daily), Shanghai
KBL	*Kilusang Babong Lipunan* (New Society Movement)
KMT	Kuomintang (Nationalist Party; a.k.a. Guomindang)
LSYFZ	*Lüshi yü fazhi* (Lawyer and Law), Hangzhou
MFN	Most favored nation (whose exports enjoy low tariffs)
Namfrel	National Citizens Movement for Free Elections (Philippines)

NGO	Non-governmental organization
NIC	Newly industrializing country
NMRB	*Nongmin ribao* (Peasants Daily), Beijing
NP	New Party (Taiwan)
OFW	Overseas Filipino Worker
PFP	People First Party (Taiwan)
PC	Philippine Constabulary
PLA	People's Liberation Army (China)
PSB	Public Security Bureau (police, China)
PRC	People's Republic of China
ROC	Republic of China (Taiwan)
RMRB	*Renmin ribao* (People's Daily), Beijing
SAO	Subdistrict Administrative Organization (Thailand)
SEZ	Special Economic Zone (China)
SHKXB	*Shehui kexue bao* (Social Science News), Shanghai
SJJJDB	*Shijie jingji daobao* (World Economic Herald), Shanghai
SMEs	Small and medium-sized enterprises
SOEs	State-owned enterprises (China)
TRT	Thai Rak Thai (Thaksin's party, 'Thais Love Thais')
XMWB	*Xinmin wanbao* (Xinmin Evening News), Shanghai

Romanizations

TAIWAN

For romanizations of Mandarin Chinese, the *pinyin* system despite its mainland imprimatur is sometimes used on Taiwan. It is employed in all parts of this book's bibliography, except for names. Taiwan's people and places are normally romanized in the Wade–Giles system, which was once standard there. Often the apostrophes and hyphens are omitted, and some variance (e.g., *yi* or *i*) is common. Some islanders mix systems (e.g., Lee Teng-hui), and their own preferences are followed when known. A few use *gwoyeu romatzyh*, a romanization that incorporates tones into the orthography (e.g., in the personal name Ying-jeou). A version of *pinyin* called *tongyong pinyin* makes changes (e.g., *zh-* to *jh-*, *x-* to *s-*, *q-* to *c-*, *-i* to *-ih*) that reflect southern pronunciations of Mandarin that are more common even on the mainland than Beijing accents are. *Tongyong pinyin* appears on street signs in Taiwan but would confuse most readers who know Chinese if it were used here. Standard romanizations also have political roots.

EAST CHINA

Putonghua — "the common language," formerly the imperial bureaucrats' Mandarin (*guanhua*), but now with a more democratic name — is spoken by more than twice as many people as the planet's next most frequent language, English. So some effort to acquaint non-China readers with it may be appropriate here. Its standard romanization in the People's Republic (except Hong Kong and Macau) is *pinyin*. For place names, *pinyin* has superseded "post office" spellings (e.g., Beijing for Peking, Xiamen for Amoy, but still Hong Kong rather than Xianggang).

Pinyin at first seems odd to English speakers because it uses *c*'s, *q*'s, *x*'s, *z*'s, and *zh*'s with unexpected sounds. It is even more counterintuitive than the Wade–Giles system. A brief table can help readers gain confidence when saying words in *pinyin*. New readers would benefit especially from memorizing the five consonants on the table that is presented below.

The basic unit of Chinese is a syllable (always written with a single character). When you see a romanized word, it is usually two syllables long. The division between syllables is ordinarily obvious in the spelling, so each of them can be pronounced separately, but dipthongs within syllables are frequent.

Tones (pitch changes within syllables) are not covered by most romanization systems. The aim here is to give people who know other languages sufficient accuracy so that they will be brave enough to cite Chinese names. Here, below, are just the letters that most differ from what general English speakers expect. The first five are consonants, always occurring at the beginnings of syllables. After these, four endings of syllables are listed. A reader who follows this table — and says all other *pinyin* as if it were English — will have a pronunciation that is close enough for normal purposes.

Pinyin = <u>SOUND</u>

five sounds to start syllables:

> *c-* = <u>ts</u>- (a hard, plosive <u>ts</u>- sound)
> *q-* = <u>ch</u>- (also plosive, as in "<u>ch</u>ime")
> *x-* = <u>sh</u>- (a soft "<u>sh</u>-," almost an "s")
> *z-* = <u>dz</u>- (as in "a<u>dz</u>e," but initial)
> *zh-* = <u>j</u>- (a hard sound, as in "<u>j</u>am")

four sounds to end syllables:

-*ian* = -<u>ien</u> (have a "<u>yen</u>" for this)
-*ong* = -<u>ung</u> ("Acht<u>ung</u>!" as in German)
-*ui* = -<u>way</u> (as in "<u>way</u>")
-*i* = -<u>ee</u> (but sometimes "-<u>r</u>," or "-<u>uh</u>")*

Pronounce all other letters as in English (and when they are vowels, use the Latin long forms that are also frequent in English). The most problematic symbol in this system is -*i*. A viable policy for English readers is simply to ignore its irregularities, although these are described in a note below for anybody who is interested.

THAILAND

Thai romanizations of personal names present an unusual problem, because often the individuals owning them prefer to go by romanized forms that reflect Sanskrit-Pali etymology and national orthography, rather than actual pronunciations in spoken Thai. A surprising number of words appear for this or more random reasons in varied romanized spellings: Prapass/Praphat, Dhanarajata/Thanarat, *jaopho/chaopho/ chaopho*, Kamnan Bo/Kamnan Poh, or even the unofficial name of

---

* Variance of the romanized -*i* might be skipped by English readers who do not know Chinese. This vowel in *pinyin* stands for the English sounds

"-ee" after *b-*, *m-*, *p-*	(labials) (vowel as in "sk<u>i</u>")
and *d-*, *l-*, *n-*, *t-*	(dental stops and liquids) (e.g., L<u>i</u>)
and *j-*, *q-*, *x-*	(palitals) (say *qi* as "ch<u>ee</u>," *xi* as "sh<u>e</u>")
"-r" after *ch-*, *r-*, *sh-*, *zh-*	(retroflexes) (say the vowel in "sh<u>ir</u>t")
deep "-uh" after *c-*, *s-*, *z-*	(dental sibilants) (as in "<u>uh</u> huh")

This -*i* is a technical flaw of *pinyin*. It is the most frequent case in which a single symbol does not map to a unique sound. Because *pinyin* is praised for its distinction between palitals and retroflexes (*j-* vs. *zh-*; *q-* vs. *ch-*; *x-* vs. *sh-*), such blitheness about the -*i* is odd. However, English readers who do not know Chinese can be confident if they will just take the trouble to learn the table above for the *c-*, *q-*, *x-*, *z-*, and *zh-* initials that seem most fearsome, and (less important) the four syllable ends as noted. Then they can respectably neglect further problems, including this bothersome -*i*.

the widely revered King Rama IX, which is variously latinized as Bhumibol Adulyadej to follow the Thai spelling, or else Pumipon Adunyadet or other attempts to invoke the sound. Although a standard romanization for spoken Thai exists, many do not follow it. For Thailand as for other countries in this book, the spelling preferences of individuals are followed whenever these are known, and commonly seen standardized romanizations are followed in other cases.

THE PHILIPPINES

Philippine typesetting often omits accents that appear in words of Spanish origin (thus Jose rather than José, Corazon rather than Corazón), but it is also usual to include the tilde in words such as Malacañang, the name of the presidential palace. This book follows conventions that have been most commonly read in print from Philippine publishers. The official Tagalog/Pilipino language is already romanized.

Acknowledgements

The list of institutions and people to whom I owe thanks for help with this project is so long, there is no way to record it fully. To begin with individuals: I could never have written this book without the loving encouragement of my wife, Barbara-Sue White. The book is dedicated to Jeremy White, Kevin White, and Fekade Sergew, our sons and foster son who have been constant joys to both of us.

Warm thanks go also to many scholars, some anonymous and many honored in a list below, who have read parts of this manuscript or helped me by discussing the ideas in it. I am thankful to Wong Siu-lun of Hong Kong University's Centre of Asian Studies and to Peter Cheung of that University's Department of Politics and Public Administration. They and their colleagues have provided not just office space but also intellectual friendship. I am grateful to the East-West Center, and to Charles Morrison and Chris McNally, for providing a useful office there too. I enjoyed a brief stay in Singapore at the East Asian Institute of National Singapore University and the Institute of Southeast Asian Studies. Barbara-Sue and I also thank Hao Yufan and Hao Zhidong of the University of Macau, and many of their colleagues, especially Miranda Lei and Newton and Romy Lam, for similar help during a short period in their fascinating city.

Particular thanks go to my sometime co-authors Li Cheng and Kate Xiao Zhou, as well as to my other former students at Princeton, notably Zheng Yongnian for his help in Zhejiang during the summer of 2006. It has been my lucky honor to teach these and other scholars who were born in China (Yang Dali, Huan Guocang, Wu Guoguang, Peng Dajin, Wang Hongying, Wang Xu, Ye Min, Miao Yanliang, Zhang Yue, Chen Jing, David Dahua Yang, Wu Xiaohui, and others), as well as Americans, Canadians, Singaporeans, and Koreans who study the four places of central interest in this book and who are included in a list below. I have learned a lot from each of these. I owe debts likewise to many former teachers and current colleagues whose contributions to this book have been crucial.

Extremely generous logistical help has come from Priscilla Roberts in Hong Kong. Michael Share in that city, Gong Wei and Catheling Qing in Zhejiang, John and Penny Lawton in Australia, and Helen Braverman, Walter and Linda Blue, Vicky and David Harding, and Audrey and Brian Peach in Britain have also been generous in their help as this book was prepared. Tony Diller, founder and former head of the Thai Studies Center at the Australian National University, has given invaluable advice on Thai aspects of the project, especially those relating to language. I have known Tony since we were students at the same public primary school in Oakland, California. Rita Alpaugh and Tim Waldron helped with clerical work at Princeton. These friends, like others listed below, have been patient with the many questions that I have put to them during the course of this research.

Editors at World Scientific Press, especially K.K. Phua and Yvonne Tan, have helped this project immensely. I also owe great thanks to Douglas Merwin, to my text editor Chean-Chian Cheong, to the indexer Jim Farner, and to the artist Azouri Bongso.

Tsering Wangyal Shawa is a wizard at making digital maps, and I am immensely grateful to him for the cartography that appears inside this book's covers. Readers of the book will soon catch my view that many political scientists' lack of attention to locations and languages is an implicit form of American liberal exceptionalism. This inhibits objective study especially of democracies. Mainstream political science and economics have too blithely ostracized geography, as well as anthropology not to mention history, from the social sciences, so they now cover actual politics and economies less well than they could. Wangyal's maps, which show all major places (not cases) to which the text refers are integral to the inductive approach that the book takes.

It is a real pleasure here to express my warm gratitude to all of those mentioned above and to: Ammar Siamwalla, Aileen Baviera, Lowell Bennett, Nancy Bermeo, Mayling Birney, John P. Burns, Chai-anan Samudavanija, Chan Kam-wing, Chang Mau-kuei, Jo Ern Chen, Chen Weiyi, Cheng Xiaonong, Megan Chiao, Eun-Kyong Choi, Ja Ian Chong, Gregory and Paula Chow, Chu Yun-han, Roger Cliff, Alison Conner, Tom Christensen, Valerie Cropper, Josephine C. Dionisio, Audrey Donnithorne, Michael Dowdle, Gregory Felker, Mario C. Feranil, Trina Firmalo, Leizl Formilleza, Mary Gallagher, John Gershman, Linda Luz Guerrero, Chad Hansen, David Hodson, Ian Holliday, Carsten Holz, Hsiao Hsin-huang, Jean Hung, Carmen Jimenez, John Kamm, Kau Ying-mao, Katie Ko, Atul Kohli, Kuah Khun Eng, Erik Martínez Kuhonta, Reginald Y. W. Kwok and his family, Leslie and Ivy Lam, Lang Youxing, Lam Wai-fung, Pierre-François Landry, Carlos Lazatín, Carol Leiggi, Li Yanhui, Liao Nien-fu and Chen Lu-ning, Evan Lieberman, Liu Gang, John Londregan, Susan McEachern, Alexander R. Magno, Lubna Malik, Ma. Melanie R.S. Milo, Erik Mobrand, John Montague, Alex Mutebi, Nittaya Vairojanavong, Orapin Sopchokchai, Gerald Osborn, Norman Owen, Pasuk Phongpaichit and Chris Baker, Christina Paxson, Pei Minxin, Elizabeth Perry, Pranee Thiparat, Shelley Rigger, Joel Rocamora, Steven Rood, Stanley Rosen, David Shambaugh, Michael Shapiro, Elizabeth Sinn, Ronald Skeldon, Sombat Chantornwong, Su Chi, Sukhum Chaleysub, Eric Thun, Jeanette Ureta, Geoff Wade, Wang Cangbai, Wang Chongfang, Wang Gungwu, Philip Wickeri, Nailene Chou Wiest, Linda Wong, Stan Wong, Wu Chong, Wu Jauhsieh, Wu Nai-teh, Xiao Hanxiang, Yang Jun, Deborah Yashar, Henry Yee, and several PRC citizens who prefer not to be listed.

My debt to my home institution is heavy: Princeton University made leave time available. Special thanks for summer research support go to Princeton's Woodrow Wilson School.

I remain solely guilty as the perpetrator. This book contains many strongly stated views. The paradigms and definitions used in parts of the book are different from those employed by many other scholars. I have tried to take alternative paradigms to task only for the sake of suggesting that it is difficult to make exclusive claims about valid ways of conceiving matters that can actually be seen in many ways. This is a comparative study about long-term development in four complex places of East and Southeast Asia. Its aim is to make what happened in each of them clearer by attempting inductions from similarities and contrasts with what happened in the others. In such a project, I had to rely on both primary and secondary sources (including Wikipedia, whose myriad writers and editors deserve thanks from practically all contemporary authors). I am in debt to the many scholars cited in footnotes, from whose varied and wonderful works I have learned a great deal.

Lynn T. White III
Princeton
July 2008

Introduction: What Politics Aids Booms?

Why have the development experiences of Taiwan, East China, Thailand, and the Philippines been so variant? If readers approach this book through its title, they may be surprised because they have never heard of a boom in the Philippines. "Boom" refers to a quick economic or political change that is welcomed by most citizens. Politics for these purposes is not just governmental. One of the main ideas to be developed here, even as regards the Philippine case, is that both the origins and results of quick economic growth or stasis depend on specifically political incentives among the most effective social elites. These are often the leaders of businesses, including small manufacturing and service enterprises that sell to domestic markets.

These leaders are local, not national. In the Philippines, regional leaders have usually been able to keep rivals from founding firms that might change the power structures in areas that one or a few families have long dominated.[1] In Taiwan, East China (meaning southern Jiangsu and Zhejiang), and Thailand, the most effective local leaders

---

[1]There are bases for predicting that a future Philippine boom is possible as that country nears a level of GDP/cap at which others have expanded quickly. The 1950s moderate growth of the Philippines is discussed in chapter 5.

during periods of fast growth had political incentives to encourage entrepreneurship. In the Philippines, traditional politicians in most localities have often been able to prevent the arrival of new business elites. So the Philippine anomaly in the book's title, when taken together with evidence on the bases of booms in Taiwan, East China, and to some extent in Thailand, raises questions along several dualistic dimensions: to what extents were the origins and results of change political or economic? Local or national? Official or unofficial? Based on coercive sanctions or money? If money, land rents or business profits?

A single, unified political-economic framework can explain what has happened, and also what has not happened, in the four places under study. Several findings can be summarized, although the reader need not believe them separate from documentation later in this book:

— Both the origins and results of booms are more political, and less narrowly economic, than many writers have suggested.
— They are more parochial and less national (at least in these four places, if not others) than most reports say.
— They are more frequently nonstate-political, as distinct from official, than is suggested by cadres or by many scholars who must rely on national government sources.
— Booms are not just shaped by incentive policies that encourage change, but also by preventive policies (either national or local) aimed to avoid the competition that wealthy new elites would bring against previous systems of leaders. Booms occur when effective local elites want to be bosses in their own firms, rather than upholders of an *hidalgo* culture that actively disdains economic-political entrepreneurs as alien and uncultivated.[2]
— Monetary capital is a factor for growth, but violence and threats of physical coercion often substitute for the local effects of

---

[2]An *hidalgo* was a lower Spanish nobleman, defined by ancestry. The word shortens *filho de algo*, "son of somebody." Family, not enterprise or wealth, was the referent for pride. In parts of the Philippines, such as Bikol, this existential identity is documentably strong.

money. Force trumps other political factors in developing East Asian localities more often than most English-speaking readers of this book may yet realize.

— It matters whether the money that goes into politics comes originally from land rents or instead from industrial-commercial profits. If it comes largely from land, the resulting politics tends to be fragmented according to those tracts. If it comes from factories, the resulting politics begin to normalize political cleavages along a modern policy division between workers and capitalists, regulations and markets, left and right.

Another theme here, related to each of these two-part dimensions, is a challenge from this liberal author to other liberals. Why are all the main parties in Taiwan or Thailand, and even China's ex-communist party, so business-oriented and relatively uninterested in workers? How can democratic theories, as constructed thus far, account for a polity like the Philippine one, which has had free competitive elections with very high turnouts for most of a century, since 1907, except for relatively short interruptions, but still lacks a government that can do much for the people? Philippine politics highlights the need for a better theory of democratic institutions that actually serve democratic values, rather than disserving them. Any advocate of voting must also think hard about Thailand under Thaksin Shinawatra, an enthusiastic democrat who had populist policies and who loved elections because he could use money from office to buy any poll that was held.[3] Neither a junta nor a Leninist party solves all problems, but these cases might show liberals that elections alone do not solve them either. Overly sharp distinctions between democracies and dictatorships, which enable quantitative studies of politics, ignore these issues.

Taiwan, China, Thailand, and the Philippines all have a great deal of money politics, regardless of their regime types. Many political scientists, especially Americanists, tend to suggest that all politics might be reducible to a matter of voting. Even in countries such as the U.S.,

---

[3]Such thinking has begun. See Larry Diamond, "The Democratic Rollback: The Resurgence of the Predatory State," *Foreign Affairs* (March–April 2008), 36–48.

however, half the news about elections is about candidates who have or lack rich campaign war chests. When liberals take more seriously the influence of money on all kinds of regimes — as they have scarcely begun to do — they may need to specify less flaccidly their ideas about the kinds of institutions that they expect to promote fair justice.

Neoclassical economic theories have also failed to predict long-term development. Several countries in East Asia have experienced record-breaking, pell-mell rates of economic growth, at first locally in some areas and then more broadly. Other countries have remained unexpectedly stagnant or have revealed unforeseen fluctuating results. Neoclassical approaches did not predict that Taiwan would turn in a world-class economic performance, especially during the 1960s. Apparently no major economist predicted that China would start to thrive in the 1970s — or would prosper in such a remarkably sustained fashion for so many decades thereafter. Economists have not shown why slow growth remained such a stubborn Philippine problem for so long until recently, or why Thailand's economy grew so fast for several decades before 1997 although its rate since then has varied. Development economists tend to explain economic development retrospectively. They point out that governments which "get the basics right" by intervening minimally, increasing saving rates, and encouraging exports over relatively short periods often enjoy spurts of development.[4] But they scarcely try to show why officials adopted those policies rather than others. Minimal central state intervention may not be a government policy so much as a counterpolicy of local economic elites to make their own decisions. Saving rates may reflect family traditions as much as official policies. Especially for large countries, domestic markets are also important in growth, even though export data are more available.

Political factors of economic development, as distinct from official policy factors, have often been neglected by development

---

[4]W. Scott Thompson, "Observations on the Philippine Road to NIChood," in *The Philippine Road to NIChood*, W. Scott Thompson and Wilfredo Villacorta, eds. (Manila: De la Salle University and Social Weather Stations, 1996), 54, quotes World Bank, *The East Asian Miracle: Economic Growth and Public Policy* (New York: Oxford University Press, 1993), on "getting the basics right."

economists. Theorizing with government-supplied data is easy, and many jobs for development economists are in officially funded institutions. So politics as economic factors deserve more attention, as do political results of booms. What are the interactions of quick economic growth and regime change both in nations and localities? Is there a link, for example, between Taiwan's boom and the island's later vibrant democracy? What caused Shanghai Delta industrial growth rates to begin rising very quickly in the early 1970s, especially from rural factories selling then to domestic markets, and what have been the effects on politics of this rampant expansion of suburban and rural industries? Did domestic, not just international, spurs for Thailand's growth from the late 1970s affect the 1990s' increasingly civilian (rather than military) dominance of that country's politics by Sino-Thai ex-businessmen? What has caused the Philippine problem with progress, and what is likely later to improve that performance?

The Philippine test place is important in this study, although none of the three places that have enjoyed more recent booms is identical with any of the others. The archipelago shortly after World War II had a per-capita income that was approximately double that of Thailand then. Half a century later, this relationship was reversed; Thais, on average, had become almost twice as rich as Filipinos. If the standard economic recommendations of foreign investment, technology, and linkage to institutions such as the World Bank was the golden key to development, why did so relatively little happen in the Philippine market economy?

Taiwan, just to the north, showed obvious contrasts. As late as 1959, per-capita income in the Philippines was higher than on Taiwan. In the 1960s, and at a somewhat reduced pace after the oil crisis of 1973, Taiwan's economy soared ahead. By century's end, the average wealth of a Taiwanese (measured in purchasing parity terms) was six times that of a Filipino.[5] What caused this divergence?

---

[5]The "purchasing power parity" measurement of this relationship gives the poorer economy a better showing than other means of assessing it would. A United Nations Development Programme estimate of the Philippines PPP GDP/capita was US$3,971, and a Taiwan government parallel estimate for the island (on which the UNDP does not report) was US$22,186, both for the year 2000.

Most economists have no long-term response to such questions. They try to explain economic development over short time horizons, such as venture capitalists use when allocating funds — just a few years at the longest, certainly not the decades in which sustained economic change or stasis actually takes place. Most neoclassical economists are content to give, to any government, good general market advice. If an economy runs into problems, they can usually note that such advice was not taken. They do not inquire why the gospel was not received, or whether other factors caused or prevented growth over periods exceeding half a decade.

Labor prices have been relatively low by global standards during the periods of fastest growth in Taiwan, East China, and Thailand; but they have also been low in the Philippines. Filipinos have some obvious advantages that might aid development. Their domestic market is very large, now numbering between 90 and 100 million potential customers. By population, they have one of dozen largest nations on earth. Unlike the people of any other major country in East Asia, many of them converse easily in English, the most important single language of export markets. Yet scant foreign capital has arrived in the islands. For agriculture, which absorbs most Philippine labor, foreigners have sponsored the highest-profile technology research program in the world, the International Rice Research Institute (IRRI) at Los Baños on Luzon. Why has such aid not made more Philippine farmers richer, better educated, and more likely to set up as entrepreneurs in industry or commerce? Why have the higher rice yields not been sold as capital for industrial expansion?

Growth in the other three traditional rice economies under study here has come especially from small and medium-size enterprises (SMEs). These local firms were founded in Taiwan and China (but not Thailand) after agrarian reforms, whose trajectories national leaders lacked enough local information fully to monitor. Leaders of SMEs have, in the three places that have boomed recently, made many profits by evading controls designed by other local or national leaders who wanted no rivals on their turfs. Violence has been common in these political booms, along with money. Development has occurred only when national or local leaders who could benefit from it were sufficiently strong to effect it. When they did not see potential gain or did not want it, growth was scant.

LIBERAL MONEY POLITICS

Elections, where they are held, can become purchasable economic factors. They have contributed in democracies to problems of political corruption like those in authoritarian regimes, because elections are easier to acquire than elected ideologists in the West have interests in publicizing. The money to purchase them comes largely from government contracts that the elected representatives arrange after they get into office. This is a problem in most electoral democracies. It is especially salient in a political economy that enjoys an economic boom because labor is still priced near agricultural subsistence levels, while capital-managing elites can use modern production and marketing methods to reap a windfall from the sold value of the labor for which they paid little.

Boom periods are eras in which agriculture still provides a practically unlimited supply of labor willing to work at low wages.[6] Many of these laborers in either domestic or export jobs are female, and almost all are relatively poor ex-peasants. A crucial aspect of the growth of business power in Asia has been the flexible ease with which SME managers can lay workers off, when markets are slow.[7] Economies with these traits become very prosperous at great speed, when local and national elites cooperate to maximize the returns to labor.

Institutions to reduce corruption and coercion may foster fairness, but local and state leaders often lose profits by creating them.

---

[6]This relies on W. Arthur Lewis, "Economic Development with Unlimited Supplies of Labour," *The Manchester School of Economic and Social Studies* (1954), 139–91.

[7]For more documentation and a related argument, see Hsiung Ping-Chun, *Living Rooms as Factories: Class, Gender, and the Satellite Factory System in Taiwan* (Philadelphia: Temple University Press, 1996), 32–34.

Voting can become a popular habit. Elections can legitimate klepto-crats, while also providing later means to remove them.[8] Juntas that overthrow democracies, citing corruption, often become vulnerable to the same charge. If wealth and education levels rise, elections become somewhat less manipulable. Taiwan, the richest of the four places under study here, has become an island of business politics. Proletarian resistance to this trend has been hard to express in a place where many people have security reasons to fear communism. So the Democratic Progressive Party has sought votes by trying to present its basically leftist side of the left-right cleavage, which is normal for an industrial society, in terms of a Taiwanese-mainlander cleavage instead.[9] Separations of power on Taiwan are now cleaning up money politics, which remain major issues in elections. Of the four places under study here, Taiwan has by far the most mature electoral system. In Thailand and East China, local businesses deeply influence politics in alliance with either soldiers or officials. The Philippines has just about the longest experience of free elections in the developing world — yet this voting has not done much over many decades for the quality of governance there.

Money is scarcely less crucial in Philippine politics than in the other three places, but election winners there tend to be local hege-monists (often with their own militias). Democratically elected gov-ernments have met in Manila for about ten decades, except during the three-year Japanese occupation and the martial law period in the second half of Marcos's presidency. The U.S., running a colonial regime, had sponsored elections at every administrative level in the Philippines since the twentieth century's first decade. Most elections

---

[8]Compare Bolivar Lamounier, "Authoritarian Brazil Revisited: The Impact of Elections on the Abertura," in *Democratizing Brazil: Problems of Transition and Consolidation*, Alfred Stepan, ed. (New York: Oxford University Press, 1989), 43–79.

[9]Election surveyors at National Cheng-chih University and elsewhere have shown that the main DPP constituency is workers, fisherfolk, and less-educated peasants. This analysis of the industrial cleavage does not deny the importance of "identity" issues on Taiwan or of north-south differences. But see David D. Yang, "Classing Ethnicity: Class, Ethnicity, and the Mass Politics of Taiwan's Democratization," *World Politics* 59:4 (July 2007), 503–38.

have been highly competitive. Citizens have enjoyed a choice of different candidates, both locally and nationally. Voter turnouts have often exceeded 80 percent — and have done so for years. Speech has been free (although speakers have not always been safe from unofficial violence). There is a keen national culture of care about cleanness in counting ballots — as Ferdinand Marcos discovered, when he failed to steal the 1986 presidential election from Corazon Aquino.[10] Yet Philippine democracy, despite the particularly enthusiastic cult of civil society in politics, does little for most people. Elections do not produce governments that have made them much richer, better educated, better housed, or healthier.

Political parties are supposed to be means that help voters express their views; yet Filipino parties are ephemeral and weak. Robert Dahl defines democracy as "a political system one of the characteristics of which is the quality of being completely or almost completely responsive to all its citizens."[11] If so, many so-called democracies are far from this ideal. What factors can explain this pattern?

This book makes two suggestions. First, opportunities for political support by networks with effective power — sometimes mostly in the state, but often mostly in local business elites — cause economic growth or its lack. Second, such growth, if they can arrange it, strengthens those elites' capacities as against rivals, in whatever type of regime they have.

LOCAL NONSTATE AUTONOMIES IN FOUR RICE COUNTRIES

Japan was the first major Asian economy to develop. Even now, most studies of Asian politics concentrate on the formation of economic policies in the central state rather than in local nonstate firms, because that was an important Japanese pattern. It was followed with minor variation later in South Korea, where *chaebol* copied *zaibatsu* and links

---

[10]The vote checkers, finding fraud, walked out on Marcos and thereby legitimated in public the decision of a close election that he had narrowly lost to Aquino.

[11]Robert Dahl, *Polyarchy* (New Haven: Yale University Press, 1971), 2.

of exporting combines with the state have also been close.[12] The explanandum of such studies is the effect of official economic policies as footnoted by government documents. The explanandum here is different, and it can best be understood by three ways to seek it:

— a search for "policies" based in intentions and situations at all sizes of collectivity that are causally effective (not just national governments, and not just conceived as hierarchal 'levels'),
— a search for the histories of habits and institutions, over long (not short) lengths of time that are needed for factors to have lasting even if inconsistent cultural results, and
— a search for the effects of industrial-commercial change on politics (not just the effects of political structures on growth, although these processes are mutually interactive over time).

From this perspective, two factors in the prosperous places under study have been the most salient spurs to economic boom. First, the most effective political groups did not stymie opportunities to set up autonomous new firms, especially small factories and stores. Where these opportunities were taken, wealth and education spread to somewhat larger parts of the population. This syndrome was contagious; it moved among towns by demonstration effect. It created more middle-income people. They could, if their slowly changing cultural identities allowed this possibility, take up the option to become entrepreneurial.

Second, the previous existence of import-substituting industries aided the boom syndrome — if the managers were not so strong vis-à-vis the state that they could maintain high tariff walls against

---

[12]Chalmers A. Johnson, *MITI and the Japanese Miracle: The Growth of Industrial Policy, 1925–1975* (Stanford: Stanford University Press, 1982) offers an historical and political treatment of the evolution of economic guidance by government in Japan over a half century. This book does not neglect time or institutions — and for just that reason, it is not a general description of the ways in which all countries of Asia have developed even though some of them (especially South Korea) show patterns resembling Japan more than others do. On that point particularly, see Atul Kohli, *State-Directed Development: Political Power and Industrialization in the Global Periphery* (Cambridge: Cambridge University Press, 2004).

imports. Low tariffs were demanded by external markets (notably the U.S. and Europe) that received the exports.

Taiwan, East China, and Thailand have met these two conditions more fully than the Philippines. Both factors depended on the state being partly "autonomous" from other social organizations, while also being sufficiently "embedded" in them to gather information and resources.[13] The most important embedded autonomy was that of local managers, not bureaucrats. "All politics is local," according to Speaker of the House Tip O'Neill. The top of any government is a small collectivity, which may or may not control others. A great variety of leaders make states rich or poor, and most policy is not national. Quick economic growth, at least in the East Asian places studied here, increases the portion of the economy that is outside the control of the central government.

Gillian Hart coined memorable acronyms for three explanations of Asian booms: CC, MM, and SS ('Confucian culture,' the 'magic of the market,' and the 'strong state.')[14] None of these alone is a sufficient account. Anthropologists have predictably stressed the cultural one that economists regularly reject in favor of the market one. Political scientists, again predictably, suggest that strong states create booms — but they might just as well look also at local power networks.

The main discourse on East Asian successes has covered different kinds of "developmental states" by Johnson, Gold, Amsden, Wade, Evans, Kohli, and others.[15] Various analysts, ranging widely from

---

[13]This expands on works by Peter Evans, including "Predatory, Developmental, and Other Apparatuses: A Comparative Political Economy Perspective on the Third World State," *Sociological Forum* 4:4 (1989), 561–87.

[14]Reported as a personal communication from Hart in Ruth McVey, "The Materialization of the Southeast Asian Entrepreneur," in *Southeast Asian Capitalists*, Ruth McVey, ed. (Ithaca: Southeast Asia Program, Cornell University, 1992), 9.

[15]See Johnson, *MITI and the Japanese Miracle*, Thomas Gold, *State and Society in the Taiwan Miracle* (Armonk: M.E. Sharpe, 1986), Alice H. Amsden, *Asia's Next Giant: South Korea and Late Industrialization* (New York: Oxford, 1989) and Amsden, *The Rise of the Rest,: Challenges to the West from Late-Industrializing Economies* (New York: Oxford, 2003), Robert Wade, *Governing the Market: Economic Theory and the Role of Government in East Asian Industrialization* (Princeton: Princeton University Press, 1990), Peter Evans, *Embedded Autonomy: States and Industrial Transformation* (Princeton: Princeton University Press, 1995), and Kohli, *State-Directed Development.*

Paul Krugman to Yoshihara Kunio or Linda Grove, have suggested problems with this growth model.[16] These researchers do not all have the same theory. In general, however, many stress links between states and big businesses that trade internationally. Such institutions have received most of the credit for the economic booms in several Asian countries. In Japan and S. Korea, as well as most other countries after growth was well under way, much of that credit is deserved. Yet especially during the initiations of booms, small businesses and medium-sized domestic businesses have less often been studied as political networks. Some historians and Europeanists have noted their importance in the past and outside Asia, but developmental nonstate agents deserve more attention.[17]

The modern economic sectors in all four countries studied here are largely led by ethnic Chinese. Equivalents of Johnson's MITI or the overall guidance systems of other "tigers" are absent in Thailand, the Philippines, or most other Southeast Asian countries. As Danny Unger observes, "Most studies of Southeast Asia's political economies do not offer state-centered explanations."[18] Researchers who seek

---

[16]See Paul Krugman, "The Myth of Asia's 'Miracle'," *Foreign Affairs* (November–December 1994), 62–78. More attention to history is in Yoshihara Kunio, *Building a Prosperous Southeast Asia: From Ersatz to Echt Capitalism* (Richmond, Surrey: Curzon Press, 1999), and especially in Linda Grove, *A Chinese Economic Revolution: Rural Entrepreneurship in the Twentieth Century* (Lanham: Rowman and Littlefield, 2006), which shows that traditions among Chinese SMEs are linked to the contemporary boom.

[17]The main exceptions are about Japan rather than any place further south: Richard J. Samuels, *The Business of the Japanese State: Energy Markets in Comparative Perspective* (Ithaca: Cornell University Press, 1987), and Thomas C. Smith, *Native Sources of Japanese Industrialization, 1750–1920* (Berkeley: University of California Press, 1988). The most cited theoretical case for flexible SMEs as distinct from "Fordist" production is by Michael J. Piore and Charles F. Sabel, *The Second Industrial Divide: Possibilities for Prosperity* (New York: Basic Books, 1984). This is Western, as is David S. Landes, *The Unbound Prometheus: Technological Change and Industrial Development in Western Europe from 1750* (Cambridge: Cambridge University Press, 1969).

[18]Danny Unger, *Building Social Capital in Thailand: Fibers, Finance, and Infrastructure* (Cambridge: Cambridge University Press, 1998), 5.

strong states do not find what they want in these countries. The economic engines of growth in that part of the planet have received exceptionally odd labels: Yoshihara calls Southeast Asian capitalism "ersatz."[19] Bernard and Ravenhill find prosperity there "derivative."[20] Doner suggests that strong political guidance, even in market economies there, can fail to produce growth.[21] Krugman notes the lack of research and development that might sustain long-term development. Part of the Southeast Asian or Taiwanese or Chinese difference lies in analysts' presumptions derived from tigers to the northeast.

Many writers, following Johnson's seminal work on Japan, have offered state-institutional narratives on "miracle" growth. Some, such as Krugman, have argued that the miracle was mostly a "mirage": good results, as long as they lasted, came from tendencies (whose roots still call for explanation) to have high savings rates and apply wise macro-economic policies. Both the miracle and mirage explanations tend to detach "cultural" factors from "structural" ones with more assertive confidence than this book does.[22] Fast growth has occurred in many East and Southeast Asian places where the Confucian heritage is important to a sizeable part of the population. This is true historically in Japan, as in Taiwan, Hong Kong, Singapore, Korea, and mainland China.[23] In Thailand too, most of the residents of Bangkok, and

---

[19]Yoshihara Kunio, *The Rise of Ersatz Capitalism in Southeast Asia* (Singapore: Oxford University Press, 1988).

[20]Mitchell Bernard and John Ravenhill, "Beyond Product Cycles and Flying Geese: Regionalization, Hierarchy, and the Industrialization of East Asia," *World Politics* 47 (1995), 171–209.

[21]Richard Doner, "Politics and the Growth of Local Capital in Southeast Asia: Auto Industries in the Philippines and Thailand," in *Southeast Asian Capitalists*, Ruth McVey, ed. (Ithaca: Southeast Asia Program, Cornell University, 1992), 191–218.

[22]An often-cited, nervous warning about this distinction is David Elkins and Richard Simeon, "A Cause in Search of its Effect, or What Does Political Culture Explain?" *Comparative Politics* 11 (January, 1979), 127–46; but Elkins and Simeon offer a crucial backtracking apology on 136, and it applies to more situations than most who cite them have suggested.

[23]On Japan, see Robert Bellah, *Tokugawa Religion* (New York: Free Press, 1957), which treats a very complex topic in this way.

notable pluralities in provincial capitals have paternal Chinese genealogies, although they are also loyal Thais.

In Southeast Asia, the portion of ancestral Chinese in national populations rank-correlates with growth performances: 77 percent in Singapore, 33 percent in Malaysia, 13 percent in Thailand, 3 percent in Indonesia, and only 1.5 percent in the Philippines.[24] A sample of five is too small to make any sure proof, and self-identification of Chinese with the local nation may be more important than patrilineal ancestry, but this match is at least suggestive. Ways can be found of finding institutional mechanisms in lineages that produce such a result. Local political hierarchies as small as families are important among these.

The problem with cultural explanations is analytic and epistemological; it is not practical. Specifiable cultural traits support high savings rates, hard work, and fiscal discipline that have aided growth — even though opposite traits of the same cultures sometimes support opposite behaviors. Any culture shapes the range of options that people socialized into it see as available. Individuals' intentions are affected, in a probabilistic way, by the collectives in which they grow up, and these norms are restricted, rather than just generic to all actors anywhere. Habits in people's heads shape behavior, even if they do not determine it monocausally. The main chance for understanding is not just to identify cultural factors, but to show the contexts of concurrent causes in which they are activated or not.

Variance among cultures comes in many forms, as Michèle Lamont's comparative research shows. Nations vary in their habitual proclivities, but so do classes, status groups, and localities.[25] Individuals naturally search among their various traditions to find the normative options that best serve them in situations of the moment. Often the available choices are diametrically opposite to each other. As many

---

[24]These 1981 estimates are in Jamie Mackie, "Changing Patterns of Chinese Big Business in Southeast Asia," in *Southeast Asian Capitalists*, Ruth McVey, ed. (Ithaca: Southeast Asia Program, Cornell University, 1992), 163.

[25]Michèle Lamont, *Money, Morals, and Manners: The Culture of the French and the American Upper-Middle Class* (Chicago: University of Chicago Press, 1992).

social scientists emphasize, "culture" does not produce events in a fully deterministic way. Culture can be causal, but it acts as a co-factor with other catalysts in some situations, while it is latent or other aspects of it may act oppositely if those further non-cultural catalysts are not present. Clifford Geertz, for example, described Bali's cockfight as being a symbol that echoes formally with Balinese cultural ideas about kinship, the material world, ritual, and varying depths of personal commitment — but then he also suggested he could just as easily have written another essay based on the Balinese brahmana ordination ceremony. This is just as "like Bali," but it is quietistic rather than violent, unrelated to kin commitments, and in other ways a diametric opposite of the cockfight.[26] Any culture is a path-dependent sets of norms; and if it were completely coherent, it would not have been so useful to its adherents for so long.

Cultures constrain options that seem live to actors, without surely determining which will be chosen. Predictions about the causal constraints imposed by a culture can nonetheless be made, especially when it is taken as one co-cause (catalyst) among others. Weber, for example, thought that Chinese families tended to foster values of natural harmony and parochialism so strongly that they would inhibit Chinese economic growth — as arguably they did for centuries, before he died (in the early 1920s).[27] Now that these same Chinese family habits are combined with new technologies and opportunities for global market access, rural Chinese family firms in Taiwan, East China, and Thailand have used the same norms of small group solidarity to create organizations that exploit cheap labor brilliantly. Rejection of

---

[26]Clifford Geertz, "Deep Play: Notes on the Balinese Cockfight," in *The Interpretation of Cultures* (New York: Basic Books, 1973), 412–53.

[27]Max Weber, *The Religion of China: Confucianism and Taoism* (Glencoe: Free Press, 1951). The possibility of joint causation, and of causes becoming active or latent depending on the presence or absence of other causes, is as available in social affairs as in chemistry or physics. But essentially different epistemologies should not be needed for social and natural truths, except to note that social researchers are like their subjects. Physicists have the scientific disadvantage of being unable to get inside the "heads" of their atoms.

"culture" as causal is just rejection of the intellectually bothersome fact that events can have multiple concurrent causes.[28]

RICE REFORMS

Paddy cultivation was for centuries the main economy in all four places this book compares.[29] This agriculture in most years produced high calorie yields per unit of land. It required intensive applications of labor, during the relatively short seasons of transplanting and harvesting. The high food yield supported large populations for such work. Man-made paddies required maintenance but were self-refertilizing. Algae on the water surface used solar energy to fix nitrogen from the air, very efficiently per unit of land, thus making nitrogenous compounds available to the rice plants. Soft paddy soil also made a standard, malleable, easy-to-weed, sustainable, and productive platform for rice agronomy.

At the times during the crop cycle that require intensive labor, especially the periods when rice seedlings are transplanted from nursery fields into large fields and the periods of harvest, almost everybody had to go work in the fields. If, in traditional China for example, there was insufficient local political solidarity or coercion

---

[28]Peter M. Swire, "The Onslaught of Complexity: Information Technologies and Developments in Legal and Economic Thought" (Senior Thesis, Woodrow Wilson School, Princeton University, 1980) shows parallels between twentieth century intellectual trends in the statistics of multiply caused events, in courts that increasingly allowed no-fault verdicts, and in post-theoretical inductive econometrics. Positivist procedures, as in early rather than late Wittgenstein for example, resist such trends.

[29]This generalization is less true of peripheral areas than of flatlands. One reason why the Philippine examples in this book are seldom from Mindanao is the importance on that island of large-plantation agricultural exports other than rice, although some similar plantations are also on islands further north. Rice countries are studied here for the same reason that the logic of "case selection" is rejected here: The aim is to use insights from each of the four places (not cases) to see more about the others, and this is helped because they all grow rice. The aim is not to generalize over all of them — they differ in ways the main chapters stress — much less to find universal laws that would apply even to places that do not happen to grow wet rice.

to guarantee that this transplanting and harvesting were accomplished within relatively short time windows, there was less rice to eat. If that happened over many years running, there would be fewer people. So the highly artificial paddy environment that predominated in China or Taiwan tended to provide high harvests, dense populations, and a requirement of local coordination or tyranny. In much of Thailand, slash-and-burn (rather than paddy) agriculture fed more of the people, whose density was traditionally reduced by malaria.

Wet rice culture has traits that are unusual among economic sectors: paddy agriculture can absorb many workers with scant effect on productivity, allowing "agricultural involution."[30] After flat rice fields and the canals to irrigate them have been dug, they use non-human factors more efficiently than labor. Traditional rice agriculture allows few economies of scale. It thus perpetuates small farms tended by humans and animals (rather than machines so long as the calorie yield per land unit remains traditionally high). The "green revolution" changed that, as did the crop commercialization that accompanied the adoption of costly chemical fertilizers and high-yield seeds. Results varied, however, in accord with the local distribution of political and economic capacity. Genetic engineering or hybridization of rice seeds, combined with government pressure for higher grain tax collections, changed traditional patterns. The effects of the new ways to grow rice depended not just on novel technologies and seeds, but also on local structures of power and enterprise.

The new agronomy had different effects in each of the four countries studied here. It was, in each case, crucial for later developments in their local political economies, despite these differences. Taiwan's

---

[30]Clifford Geertz, *Agricultural Involution: The Process of Ecological Change in Indonesia* (Berkeley: University of California Press, 1963), and Francesca Bray, *The Rice Economies: Technology and Development in Asian Societies* (Berkeley: University of California Press, 1986). These are the starting points in *Agrarian Transformations: Local Processes and the State in Southeast Asia*, Gillian Hart, et al., eds. (Berkeley: University of California Press, 1989), 1.

land reform, which the mainlander government initiated in order to garner some Taiwanese political support after KMT losses in 1947 and 1949, predated scientists' development of most new seeds. So Taiwanese farmers decided independently, and later, whether they would profit from planting them. In East China, the peak of the "Green Revolution" in the late 1960s and early 1970s deserves more study (it has been overshadowed by a 'Cultural Revolution' then). It combined with post-Great Leap alienations of rural power networks, and with Cultural Revolution decimations of the urban offices that had monitored the countryside earlier, to allow rural leaders in small collectivities new autonomies. These local bosses set up machine shops and then factories.

Thailand's experience was more like Taiwan's, but for a different reason: the Bangkok bureaucracy's ancient habit was to avoid meddling in Thai farmers' decisions about what to plant. High-end rice export markets also favored the tasty Thai varieties. So Thailand had no Green Revolution — but the selfsame bureaucratic reticence also allowed Sino-Thai businessmen the autonomy to found new enterprises easily. Marcos in the Philippines, by contrast, inadvertently proved that high-yield rice could become, for its tillers, an unprofitable crop. This was one of East Asia's oddest economic developments ever. As analysts on the political left have documented, the Green Revolution has bred inequality, at least in the Philippines.[31] Most economists suggest that Philippine relative poverty is instead the result of insufficient technology and insufficient reverence for neoclassical economic policies.[32] The influence

---

[31]Brian Fegan, "Accumulation on the Basis of an Unprofitable Crop," in *Agrarian Transformations: Local Processes and the State in Southeast Asia*, Gillian Hart, *et al.*, eds. (Berkeley: University of California Press, 1989), 159–78, parallels other work, especially based in central Luzon, by Ernest Feder, *Perverse Development* (Quezon City: Foundation for Nationalist Studies, 1983). Ingrid Palmer wrote about this problem early, in *The New Rice in Indonesia* (Geneva: UN Research Institute for Social Development, 1977).

[32]This is expanded in the editors' "Introduction" to *Agrarian Transformations*, 2 and passim.

of politics, especially local enterprise leadership, is an element that the economists miss.[33]

New technologies — agrarian, industrial, and commercial — are adopted only if their users profit directly (as they usually did in Taiwanese, East Chinese, and Thai industries) or are forced into them (as was the case with high-yield rice varieties in Marcos's time). Wise economic policies are always potentially available. They are not applied unless leaders at the politically relevant sizes of collectivity choose them.

There are two schools of thought about the Green Revolution: that it raises rural wealth on average, and that it further impoverishes poor peasants. These two schools argue with each other — but the bulk of evidence suggests they are both right. High yield varieties live up to their name in most years. They also produce, especially in years of bad typhoons, net losses of wealth for poor farmers.

"Top-down" agricultural programs give strong financial incentives (or orders) to farmers concerning the type of seeds and technology they use. "Bottom-up" approaches stress the need to see first what farmers want to do, and then to help them do it.[34] Later chapters will detail the political conditions under which autonomous rural networks emerged from either of these policies. Countries in which entrepreneurs could set up new factories and stores tended to boom. Under other political conditions, peasants were saddled with debts

---

[33]Whole books by economists, when they bother to mention the country localities where most Filipinos live, spend all their effort analyzing rural poverty rather than rural industry. See *The Philippine Road to NIChood*, W. Scott Thompson and Wilfredo Villacorta, eds. (Manila: De la Salle University and Social Weather Stations, 1996), or two more recent publications with similar titles: *The Philippine Economy: Alternatives for the 21st Century*, Dante B. Canlas and Shigeaki Fujisaki, eds. (Diliman: University of the Philippines Press, 2001), and *The Philippine Economy: Development, Policies, and Challenges*, Arsenio Balisacan and Hal Hill, eds. (Manila: Ateneo De Manila University Press, 2003).

[34]See, for example, Prince of Songkla University, *Farming Systems Research and Development in Thailand* (Haad Yai: Thai-French Farming Systems Research Project, 1988), 5 ff., which argues that a "systems" approach can combine these two.

that confirmed their traditional patrons in local power and prevented independent entrepreneurship.

FAMILY-LIKE SMEs

Small and medium firms, rather than large ones, initiated the economic booms in Taiwan, China, and Thailand — although Thai documentation of this fact is less than in the earlier cases. A relative lack of small and medium enterprises in the Philippines brought lackluster economic performance there for a long time. The development of small manufacturing in these countries went through several stages: a phase in which small factories with fewer than 20 workers displaced household manufacturing, a second stage in which those factories grew quickly, and a later phase in which medium-scale production tended to displace small-scale plants at least in those commodity lines, and economic growth continued at a slower pace.[35]

Very small firms, in the first stage, seldom exported directly. Cumulatively they might influence national politics if the system were electoral (in Taiwan or Thailand), because together they hired a great many workers who were also voters. They often formed patronage networks and small political machines, not just profit-making firms. In systems where the political economy was either monitored by Leninist cadres (as in China) or by well-established local gentry leaders (as in the Philippines), small firms had to deal with those local powerholders to run their businesses for the domestic market. But they had, and needed, no major influence over national policy.

Early household businesses often subcontract with larger companies that export. More important, some of them grow, becoming politically more important. Their emergence can surprise older elites, most of whom very actively dislike entrepreneurial *nouveaux riches*. Yet SMEs have been the most important wellsprings of growth

---

[35]Otte Estler, *Der Beitrag kleiner und mittlerer Unternehmen zum Entwicklungsprozess Thailands* (The Contribution of SMEs to Thailand's Development) (Hamburg: Institut für Asienkunde, 1998), 194.

in several Asian "dragons."[36] Larger corporations produce more data, but convenience of documentation does not correlate with economic performance.

Many small entrepreneurs begin by accumulating capital in retail trade. In Asia, this often meant rice trading and milling. Then they typically went into more diversified or wholesale commerce. After their assets expand further, they used the profits to set up factories.[37] Functional flexibility has been an essential ingredient of SMEs' economic success. The kind of flexibility in which they have excelled has not relied much on their own searches for foreign markets or new technologies. Foreign partners or Overseas Chinese living in North America or Europe (or more experienced Hong Kong or Taiwan marketers) have been important in these roles. Nor has the kind of flexibility most prominent in East Asia depended heavily on their own new research and development. Innovation has come largely from overseas sources or from people educated on other continents. (This contrasts with the 'permanent technological innovation' and 'craft-based flexibility' described by Piore and Sabel for European SMEs that manufacture garments, purses, and luxury goods.) Instead, Asian SMEs tend to sell directly or indirectly to the Wal-Marts of the world. They are market-responsive in their immediate contexts because they can pay low wages and charge low prices. Their employees are seldom unionized and have minimal or no pension perks. Such firms attract workers who make even less in fields than in factories.

---

[36]SMEs have also been extremely important for maintaining economic vibrancy in developed economies. Extensive data show that American laws and habits encourage the formation of small businesses better than do the laws and habits of highly developed economies in Europe. This difference has tended to make U.S. unemployment lower and long-term growth somewhat faster. See *Are Small Firms Important? Their Role and Impact*, Zoltan J. Acs, ed. (Boston/Dordrecht: Kluwer Academic, 1999).

[37]SMEs are defined variously by different governments and surveyors. So the only practical gambit for a book like this one about comparative politics is to note the substance of their conclusions about smaller and larger firms, but without any pretense that the term SME has been standardized. Further information is in Susan Greenhalgh, "De-Orientalizing the Chinese Family Firm," *American Ethnologist* 21:4 (1994), 757.

SMEs not only absorb a great deal of labor; small factories are also important for developing the skills of ex-peasants who are taking their first industrial jobs. When such employees have scant formal education, as is usually the case, the SMEs are crucial schools in the styles of modern accurate work, accomplished to time schedules.[38] Large firms hire employees who are already better-educated than those in SMEs. The small firms thus contribute more to a nation's "social capital" accumulation. Ambitious and talented SME employees set up their own companies and become their own bosses, further strengthening market competition. SMEs can proliferate nimbly. Their workers in one place can move to another, bringing technology, know-how, and business connections. They do this when urban wages rise and managers of capital seek cheaper labor elsewhere, or when an experienced employee in an SME resigns to start a competitor firm.

Small firms are not spread evenly over the geographies of any of the four places studied in this book. As a study of Taiwan shows, they prosper best in diversified settings that have high population densities, including areas that were recently rural.[39] Because the high traditional yield of rice raised the value of paddy land, the economic and demographic border between urban and rural places in East Asia has not been as sharp as in the West.[40]

SMEs contribute to exports. The statistics that governments can gather often understate this, especially for countries like Thailand, where large combines have not yet established international brands, because major exporting companies outsource processes to small

---

[38]See Otte Estler, *Der Beitrag kleiner und mittlerer Unternehmen*, 196, and for a comparative overview, Alex Inkeles and David Smith, *Becoming Modern: Individual Change in Six Developing Countries*, (London: Heinemann, 1974).

[39]Liu Li-Wei, *The Growth and Transformation of Small and Medium Enterprises in Taiwan: Reassessment and Analysis from a Spatial Perspective* (Ph.D. Dissertation, Cornell University, January 2000), 125.

[40]On the "green city," see Lynn White, "Shanghai-Suburb Relations, 1949–1966," in *Shanghai: Revolution and Development in an Asian Metropolis*, Christopher Howe, ed. (Cambridge: Cambridge University Press, 1981), 241–68.

firms. The relative value added by SMEs to exports is difficult to survey, because small factories generally compete in tighter markets than do large firms — and they hide their production from tax collectors far more efficiently. In China, it is estimated that 40 to 60 percent of the value of all exports come directly from SMEs. This is a large amount, although even the Chinese government is unsure of its extent.

In Taiwan similarly, 56 percent of exports in 2000 still came directly from SMEs (and in the island's economy, exports made up nearly half of total GDP). Thai data are less complete, but just one-tenth of exports were recorded as coming directly from SMEs — although in the mid-1990s, three-tenths of the total Thai GDP left the country.[41] According to the best available estimates, Thai SMEs contribute about 50 or 60 percent of the country's total product, and also roughly half of Thailand's exports. They employ 60 or 70 percent of industrial workers.[42] Comparable data for the Philippines have not been collected or found, but the importance of primary-sector crop and mineral exports (largely from Mindanao plantations and mines) would make such figures difficult to compare anyway. Philippine SMEs' proportional contributions to exports were much smaller than in Taiwan, East China, or Thailand.

EXPLAINING CAUSES OF LOCAL DYNAMISM

Entrepreneurship was the basis of economic booms, whenever they occurred. Whence did this risk-taking come? It happened largely in firms that were run by ethnic Chinese families. Modern researchers have found clannish solidarity in many Chinese businesses. They also find a widespread personal norm that one should be one's own

---

[41]Charles Harvie and Boon-Chye Lee, "East Asian SMEs: Contemporary Issues and Developments," in *The Role of SMEs in National Economies in East Asia*, Harvie and Lee, eds. (Cheltenham: Edward Elgar, 2002), 9.

[42]These estimates are by Frederic Deyo, reported in Peter Brimble, David Oldfield, and Manusavee Monsakul, "Policies for SME Recovery in Thailand," in *The Role of SMEs in National Economies in East Asia*, 205, quoted from Deyo.

"boss."[43] Families are ideally solid, and underlings are supposed to follow the lineage head. Families are enduring collective actors in politics, national as well as local. They have readily identifiable names and permanence. They are like bureaucracies in this sense: action based on family loyalty is relatively predictable. They thus enjoy the political strengths of reliability that Max Weber attributed to modern bureaucracies, although family predictability is not based on legal-rational norms, and Weber could not see its use in markets when he wrote.[44]

Susan Greenhalgh treats the "Chinese family firm" as a politically constructed patriarchy. She argues that, "The Confucian thesis is a form of Orientalist economics that arose in the context of, and in turn supported, a very conservative politics. By simultaneously valorizing Chinese 'collectivism' and obfuscating gender, ethnic, and other inequalities [it] lent support to a new, flexible form of capitalist accumulation that is based on exploitation of gender and other social inequalities."[45] This view accords with the proposition that a Confucian culture can provide a ready environment for economic construction. Nasty, unstately, violent aspects of "Asian values" do not gainsay their productivity.

Some writers claim that a clan's support for "indolent" members discourages individualism, thereby reducing efficiency.[46] The cases for and against the economic value of Chinese familism have risen or fallen, respectively, along with the economies dominated by Chinese businesses. This chart-watching might seem too unintellectual a means to decide the question about the importance of norms that Chinese families tend to propagate. Yet no other data could offer more comprehensive evidence on it. Weber never claimed that

---

[43]See Shieh Gwo-shyong, *"Boss" Island: The Subcontracting Network and Microentrepreneurship in Taiwan's Development* (New York: Lang, 1992), and also *The Economic Organization of East Asian Capitalism*, Marco Orrù, Nicole Woolsey Biggart, and Gary Hamilton, eds. (Thousand Oaks: Sage, 1997).

[44]See Reinhard Bendix, *Max Weber: An Intellectual Portrait* (New York: Doubleday, 1960).

[45]Susan Greenhalgh, "De-Orientalizing the Chinese Family Firm," 746.

[46]Mario Rutten, *Rural Capitalists in Asia: A Comparative Analysis of India, Indonesia, and Malaysia* (New York: RoutledgeCurzon, 2003), 28.

ascetic Protestantism was the sole cause of modern economic success in the West, but only that it had an "elective affinity" with this modern result.[47] Many data in the following chapters demonstrate that firms started by ethnic Chinese families or family-like collectives had a similar affinity with economic success.

Linda Grove shows that traditional habits (these could be called cultural factors) in rural Chinese enterprises have persisted for many decades. Such customs of saving, organizing, and marketing go far to explain the dynamism of small firms in the recent booms of both Taiwan and China.[48] This family-business culture describes underlying endemic causes. Only spark factors are needed, in addition, to explain why the cultural organizations of this form got (or in the Philippines did not get) the autonomy to ignite the booms at particular times.[49]

---

[47]"Elective affinity" has become, because of Reinhard Bendix's scholarship, the standard but loose translation of the word Weber used, *Wahlverwandschaft*. This began as a term in chemistry, referring to substances that have a tendency for combination. Goethe chose it as the title of a novel that is broadly about the usual (but not sure) attraction of men and women for each other. "Elective affinity" refers not to causality but to a likelihood of connection between different factors (acids and bases, men and women, religious beliefs and business motives, or any different parts of a cultural complex that tend to go together — especially when they portend change). Weber's epistemology is more subtle and more substantive than that of most social scientists. In contemporary terms, it is "postanalytic" rather than "analytic" — except that he wrote earlier.

[48]See Linda Grove, *A Chinese Economic Revolution*.

[49]Students of China or of other specific places are more aware than are abstract "analytic" epistemologists of the need to consider both endemic and spark causes of events. For example, to account for the 1949 change in China, Bianco and many others stress underlying social factors, while Johnson pioneered an account of the additional causes needed to explain timing. Other Chinese events, e.g. violence after 1965 or rural industrialization after 1971, require similarly multiple approaches (and an awareness of randomness in real processes, such as Esherick notes). The search for general laws in social science, supposed to be applicable without respect to geography or history, has hindered rather than helped the development of better epistemology. See Lucian Bianco, *The Origins of the Chinese Revolution, 1915–1949* (Stanford: Stanford University Press, 1971), Chalmers A. Johnson, *Peasant Nationalism and Communist Power: The Emergence of Revolutionary China, 1937–1945* (Stanford: Stanford University Press, 1962), and Joseph Esherick, "Ten Theses on the Chinese Revolution," *Modern China* 21:1 (1995), 45–75.

Thai entrepreneurs are also mostly Thai-Chinese. The government owns the national airlines, the oil company, Siam Cement, and the Krung Thai Bank. But Sino-Thais own the Bangkok Bank (which is the richest financial institution by far), the Saha conglomerate (largely in textiles), and the Charoen Pokphang agrobusiness, as well as the Hongkong/Bangkok Karnchanapas conglomerate corporation in trading, real estate, and construction — and more important, a myriad smaller firms of the type from which these emerged.

Non-Chinese families in the Philippines, by contrast, control many of the large companies there. The Ayala family's holding company developed the Makati district of downtown Manila and controls the Bank of the Philippine Islands as well as a major life insurance company. The San Miguel corporation, founded by the Sorianos, makes and sells far more than beer. The Lopez clan controls a bank and a power company. The Concepcion family runs Republic Flour Mills and related industries. The Aboitiz are in transport and trade, and the Villanuevas are in engineering. The Elizaldes, Aranetas, de Leons, and Montelibanos are among the Filipino families that have made fortunes in sugar refining.[50] Some Chinese Filipinos are now involved in these enterprises, but the portion is lower than in other Southeast Asian countries partly for political reasons (offered in later chapters). Takeovers by Chinese Filipinos of firms established by families that make more claim to Philippine nativism have sometimes been highly conflictual, as when the Cojuancos (the Co syllable in *pinyin* romanization is the surname Xu) fought the Sorianos for control of San Miguel.[51] Relatively few and large companies have been founded

---

[50]Some of these families are partly of Chinese ancestry, and some of the sugar wealth (including that of the Cojuangcos) was made by families that included Chinese. This relies on Yoshihara Kunio, *The Nation and Economic Growth: The Philippines and Thailand* (Kuala Lumpur: Oxford University Press, 1994), 20–22.

[51]This is the largest combine in the country. See the excellent (anonymous) Wikipedia entry on the history of the San Miguel Corporation.

on that archipelago, and laws have been passed to hinder Chinese from setting up firms.

Any culture has incompatible elements from which valid but opposite conclusions may be drawn. It is circumspect to take a practical view of truth.[52] Usefulness trumps falsification as a virtue of any proposition, and eliminating errors is important only when it does more to aid than hinder long-term usefulness.[53] Newton admitted he could not explain gravity, but he had the wit to link an apple's fall with a planet's orbit. It is possible to distinguish the "'big question' of where norms and interests originate" from the "'little' questions of how they actually affect public and political life."[54] "Little" questions may be more practical and more researchable than "big" ones and may thus tell more truth. Neat or complete accounts are often less good than useful explanations. Chinese business success in Southeast Asia is robust enough to withstand any epistemology.

NONSTATE LEADERS FOR CREATIVITY OR STABILITY?

There are two kinds of economic leaders: "specular" entrepreneurs who innovate and bring new talent into an elite, and "rentier" leaders who most value the consolidation and integrity of their own group. "Specular" entrepreneurs are the economic equivalent of political

---

[52]Toward a "postanalytic" epistemology (and ethics), see pragmatists such as William James, *Essays in Radical Empiricism* (Lincoln: University of Nebraska Presss, 2003 [1912]), or James, *The Meaning of Truth: A Sequel to 'Pragmatism'* (Amherst, NY: Prometheus Books, 1997 [1909]), or Rorty in Richard Rorty and Pascal Engel, *What's the Use of Truth?* (New York: Columbia University Press, 2007).

[53]"Error elimination" is as close to truth as Karl Popper allows, but his epistemology is too thin to explain why propositions, errors, or tests would be advanced in the first place. See Karl Popper, *The Logic of Scientific Discovery* (London: Routledge, 1959).

[54]David Leheny, *Think Global, Fear Local: Sex, Violence, and Anxiety in Contemporary Japan* (Ithaca: Cornell University Press, 2006), 14.

"foxes," and economic "rentiers" are like political "lions."[55]
Chinese or any other people can be either entrepreneurial or rentier.
In Taiwan's and China's Leninist parties, there have been conserva-
tive rentier lions aplenty. But when the KMT after c. 1947 and the
CCP after c. 1969 lost their ability to prevent local "specular"
SMEs to be founded, and when Sino-Thais met scant resistance
establishing firms, the results were booms. In the Philippines, ren-
tiers remained dominant.

An economic boom raises the local influence of autonomous
managers, no matter whether they control private or collective property. They circulate into elites, as they have done conspicuously in
Taiwan, East China, and Thailand. If a country's habits are electoral
during such a boom, as Taiwan's and Thailand's were, the power of
these managers over 'higher' administrative levels of the state
increases more quickly. But electoral procedures alone do not raise
the representativeness of government, as the Philippine case makes
clear; more mature industrialization is needed for that. Nor is
allowance of markets alone, or of private as distinguished from socialized property, enough to increase the portion of the people whom
elections may empower.

Pluralizations of politics can be explained more directly by booms
than by regime types or property arrangements. In a period of quick
economic and social development, autonomous actors create new
wealth. Expanding SMEs need, for this purpose, connections with

---

[55]The lion-or-fox (conservative-or-reformer) distinction originated in Machiavelli's
political rhetoric, and it was adapted by Pareto for his theory of the circulation of
elites, including business leaders. Vilfredo Pareto, *The Rise and Fall of the Elites: An
Application of Theoretical Sociology* (New York: Arno Press, 1979; orig. 1901), 6–9,
also associates the specular/fox tendency with a dominant "residue" (a relatively
invariant sentiment or habit) of "combination" (a 'tendency to invent or embark on
adventure'). The rentier/lion type is linked to the dominant residue of "preserva-
tion" (a 'tendency to consolidate and make secure'). This is mainly a matter of elite
socialization. Pareto's words, and his reactionary politics, have distracted attention
from a theory can be used to add structure to idea of "interest groups" in David B.
Truman, *The Governmental Process: Political Interests and Public Opinion*, 2nd ed.
(New York: Knopf, 1971 [1st ed., 1951]).

police and tax regulators. So they spend some of their money for new local power. SMEs differ in the extent to which they are involved in networks with other firms. A small independent shop that supplies a reliable auto part to a car assembly corporation in Taiwan is not the same as a small *sari-sari* general store in the Philippines, even though both might be classified as "SMEs." Quick growth of industry and commerce has been a crucial factor for pluralization, but this process is not the same as substantive democratization. Commercial-industrialization nonetheless usually precedes stable structures of government that serve the people in many sizes of collectivity.

Businesses politick, either secretly or openly, if they want to influence politics. Their registered existence as institutions may be enough to ensure some private power, but this can be greatly strengthened if they organize together. Small businesses and large international corporations also politick, but the mechanisms through which small firms exert local influence are subject to even less public monitoring. Cumulatively, they do more to change the climate of decisions than to determine particular policies. Their power is considerable, even though it is more endemic than specific. As Richard Doner notes, the best approach to development "recognizes the utility of combining political support for local firms with pressure on them to conform to market forces."[56] Actually, they often conform on their own initiatives if doing so brings profit advantages over rival (including government) firms. In other words, states can be developmentalist, but so can local firms. Policy is not a monopoly of large power networks only.

Latin Americanists such as Peter Evans have pointed out that international capitalists, state dirigiste capitalists, and nonstate local capitalists can all shape development.[57] These same categories of leaders also affected Taiwan, China, Thailand, and the Philippines.

---

[56]Richard F. Doner, "Limits of State Strength: Toward an Institutionalist View of Economic Development," *World Politics* 44 (April 1992), 401.

[57]Fernando Cardoso and Enzo Faletto, *Dependency and Development in Latin America* (Berkeley: University of California Press, 1979), and Peter Evans, *Dependent Development: The Alliance of Multinational, State, and Local Capital in Brazil* (Princeton: Princeton University Press, 1979).

The crucial question, especially for political rather than economic evolution, is which of these types made the most self-sustaining decisions that led to booms and increases in their own legitimacy. A general answer, at least for Taiwan, China, and Thailand during their booms, is that local nonstate decision makers maintained themselves best.

Decentralized politics has an "elective affinity" with flexible production.[58] Economists have debated whether central state guidance aids allocative static efficiency within and between firms, but few would claim that government control increases the Schumpeterian "dynamic efficiency" of entrepreneurs.[59] Some business people are politically disadvantaged and restricted, by bureaucracies, from access to inputs and markets they could use to provide goods and jobs. They may be able to grow quickly only by illegal means. "Some forms of corruption may actually be market-rational attempts to circumvent or break down these disadvantages."[60] Corrupt rent-seeking reduces market efficiency, but it may also increase chances for the risk-taking "dynamic efficiency" that can overwhelm the costs of lowered market-rational allocative efficiency.

This interaction is mostly missed by the neoclassical "convergence" interpretation of development, which regards the process as marketization. And to a lesser extent, it is also missed by the "experimentalist" school, which for example regards China's "model" as an adaptation of profit incentives to the state's insistence for harmonious stability.[61] A "heterarchy" of property and management arrangements

---

[58]Richard Doner and Eric Hershberg, "Flexible Production and Political Decentralization in the Developing World: Elective Affinities in the Pursuit of Competitiveness," *Studies in Comparative International Development* 34:1 (Spring 1999), 74.

[59]See Cui Zhiyuan, "Epilogue: A Schumpeterian Perspective and Beyond," in *China: A Reformable Socialism*, Gan Yang and Cui Zhiyuan, eds. (New York: Oxford University Press, 1995), 145–68.

[60]Pasuk Phongpaichit, Sungsidh Piriyarangsan, and Nualnoi Theerat, *Guns, Girls, Gambling, and Ganja: Thailand's Illegal Economy and Public Policy* (Chiangmai: Silkworm, 1998), 2. Mushtaq Khan is an economist who has made this Schumpeterian argument.

[61]See Woo Wing Thye, "The Real Reasons for China's Growth," *The China Journal* 41 (January 199), 115–37, and other sources to which Woo refers.

encourages diverse organizing principles that are most likely to strike a balance between short-term adaptation and long-term adaptability.[62]

Business that is entrepreneurial to the point of corruption can in some cases be defended on grounds that it is Schumpeterian. It may disserve that business's market competitors or the government's tax collectors, while simultaneously serving a larger public's interest in commodities and jobs. If so, it is corrupt from the viewpoint of some, but clean from the viewpoint of others. No use of the word "corrupt" is possible without implying two identifiable and different groups.[63] This is not a blanket warrant for corruption, but it puts that concept in perspective. Every gift by a parent to a child, every airplane flight that pollutes the atmosphere, or every official act for welfare could be claimed as corrupt from the viewpoint of a group that did not take the action. Boom times amplify the difficulty of defining clean politics.

For their size, SMEs often require high bribes in order to begin operations. Their licenses and other legal permissions require expenses that are relatively large as portions of their revenues. Not only do they hire more voters per unit of capital, they also need to spend more for bureaucratic connections. Some economists imagine that SMEs have low market-entry costs, compared with the barriers to startup of larger firms; but a study of Thailand suggests exactly the opposite.[64] These investments tend to pay off, if they are made.

Peter Evans argues that, "As local economic groups grow and gain economic stature [money], the tutelage of the developmental state is less appreciated.... The increasing power and wider options of local

---

[62]See David Stark, *Heterarchy: Asset Ambiguity, Organizational Innovation, and the Postsocialist Firm* (Ithaca: Cornell School of Industrial and Labor Relations Working Paper 96–21, 1996).

[63]See Lynn White, "Changing Concepts of Corruption in Communist China: Early 1950s vs. Early 1980s" in *Changes and Continuities in Chinese Communism*, Yu-ming Shaw, ed. (Boulder: Westview Press, 1988), 316–53, and the works by Benjamin Nelson and Max Weber to which this refers.

[64]Otte Estler, *Der Beitrag kleiner und mittlerer Unternehmen*, 195.

capital weaken business support for sustaining a Weberian bureaucracy and increase the likelihood that connectedness will degenerate into capture [of state agencies].... Some counterweight is needed to keep public-private networks oriented toward collective goods rather than particularistic rent seeking."[65] Democratic elections do not provide that counterweight, and they can become means for seeking new rents when they can be bought.

As capitalists "embed" themselves in the state, they often weaken it either by buying elected politicians in democracies, or else by buying bureaucrats directly under any kind of regime. This is sometimes true of big capitalists who serve export markets, and it is true of small domestic capitalists who also effectively erode state-bureaucratic power. But the entrepreneurs do this slowly. At first, they may support the idea of elections so that (if they or their representatives win) they have access to official titles, allowing them to deal on a more equal basis with state bureaucrats. Their intentions, to the extent motives can be determined, are less democratic than profit-maximizing. Goals such as fairness to all people, reduction of violence in dispute resolution, or respect for individuals are seldom their priorities. The long-term unintended effect of these entrepreneurs' success, however, is to broaden political participation beyond the set of civilian and military bureaucrats who traditionally ran the state.

Greedy capitalists may therefore over the long run be democrats in effect but not by design. In the economy, they provide new kinds of jobs; in the polity, they provide new infrastructure. A question is why new types of local political leaders are recruited in most countries as they develop, whereas in others (e.g., the Philippines) the types of local elites change slowly. One reason, applicable in Thailand, Taiwan, and East China is that any entrepreneurs who provide new jobs may have so much local public acceptance that rival local elites cannot ostracize them. Rural voters may be swayed not solely by money, but also by other traits in candidates (to the extent these can

---

[65]Peter B. Evans, "State Structures, Government-Business Relations, and Economic Transformation," in *Business and the State in Developing Countries*, Sylvia Maxfield and Ben Ross Schneider, eds. (Ithaca: Cornell University Press, 1997), 66–67.

be separated from wealth) that recent ex-peasants deem admirable.[66] This still does not ensure that leaders, once chosen, take actions to the long-term benefit of the electorate.

Bureaucracies develop more slowly than other parts of their political systems, and this is particularly true of mandarin bureaucracies. In Taiwan, where many parts of the government have changed radically since the 1950s, the ministries have changed less. In China, the Cultural Revolution swept over offices and closed them down for while, but the longstanding tradition of appointing bureaucrats on the basis of academic credentials was later restored. The main post-traditional change in the current PRC is only that education for rule is now technocratic, and officials are largely engineers.

In Thailand, the late-1980s bureaucracy was still "largely unre-constructed," essentially similar to that of the 1950s.[67] Sarit Dhanarajata (or Thanarat), who was Thailand's military premier for the half decade 1958–63, established free-market norms that have prevailed since then. Bangkok bureaucrats had to get along with Sino-Thai capitalists, who likewise profited from links to officials. Although Thailand had a nascent state sector, Sarit reigned over a mixed coalition of generals, bureaucrats associated with the court, and Sino-Thai merchants. He allowed provincial entrepreneurs (e.g. in the Northeast, with which he identified strongly) to found industries that the state did not control.

This implicit compact was like the one between mainlanders and Taiwanese that the KMT organized in its own political interest from the 1950s onward. It was also like the patterns that emerged in China after the depredations of the Great Leap Forward and the Cultural

---

[66]Daniel Arghiros argues this way in *Democracy, Development, and Decentralisation in Provincial Thailand* (London: Curzon, 2001), 274; but the logic is even more cogent in a more fragmented country, as shown by Benedict J. Tria Kerkvliet in "Contested Meanings of Elections in the Philippines," in *The Politics of Elections in Southeast Asia*, R.H. Taylor, ed. (Washington: Woodrow Wilson Center, 1996).

[67]Andrew Turton, "Local Powers and Rural Differentiation," in *Agrarian Transformations*, 72.

Revolution separated local from national institutions.[68] None of these cleavages were institutionally consolidated at their first emergences. In each case, they provided some local balance to central power. State predations on local industrialization and on the creation of local wealth were kept at bay, and local economies flourished.

In the Philippines, however, the civilian bureaucracy has always been weak politically. Marcos's attempt to technocratize it was a centralizing effort, but that venture did not last because his technocrats also charged high informal rents. The state remained fragmented, and Marcos as a central warlord could not hold his ground against the cumulative powers of many local warlords, who handily reasserted themselves after his demise.[69] A more solid future Philippine development may emerge from changes of the links between national and local leaders, or of those between soldiers and business people, if they become willing to lift recent impediments to entrepreneurship.

Most economic politics, which can transform weak states, is outside state control. When local leaders have policies of their own to develop local wealth and power, they do so. When they lack enough autonomy to do this or lack the political need to do so (as in the Philippines), development stalls. Their decisions are not much affected by whether the national regime type is authoritarian or democratic. But developmental results are greatly affected by the two-way "embeddedness" of local and central networks, with each "penetrating" the other sufficiently to influence it but not sufficiently to stymie it.

COMPARISONS WITH ALTERNATIVE VIEWS

This interpretation has both similarities and differences with claims by previous writers. Comparison requires referring to several of them

---

[68]See Yang Dali, *Calamity and Reform in China* (Stanford: Stanford University Press, 1996), and Lynn White, *Unstately Power: Local Causes of China's Economic Reforms* (Armonk, NY: M.E. Sharpe, 1998).

[69]Marcos's situation was like Chiang Kai-shek's on the Chinese mainland before 1949. The title "president" is, in such situations, more grandiose than meaningful.

who have contributed major analyses to what political scientists generously call "the literature." Some have modeled state-society relations in terms of "corporatism," which has usually been *defined* as necessarily a top-down, state-organizes-society regime type. Analysts as sensitive as Ruth and David Collier, for example, look at corporatism in terms of actions initiated by the government. For them, it involves "(1) state structuring of groups that produces a system of *officially sanctioned*, non-competitive, compulsory interest associations, (2) *state subsidy* of these groups, and (3) *state-imposed* constraints on demand making, leadership, and internal governance."[70]

Jean Oi in her early works also had a mostly top-down view of "communist" corporatism, although this view altered as China changed. Corporatism can actually be initiated by local cadres, not necessarily by central authorities. It can be called "local state corporatism," in Oi's phrase, to the extent that its controllers are cadres rather than entrepreneurs.[71] Yet the word "corporatism" has more classically been used to describe a national regime type. If corporatism is really local, can it be called "state"?

Philippe Schmitter puts the matter in perspective of other regime types. While describing "corporatist," "syndicalist," "pluralist," and "monist" systems along several dimensions, he leaves open the question of whether the corporatist type is generated at state initiative, or instead at the behest of more local power networks.[72] In practice, small networks affect the state no less than vice-versa. Jürgen Habermas, too, sees modernization as a double process. The state

---

[70]Ruth Berins Collier and David Collier, "Inducements vs. Constraints: Disaggregating 'Corporatism,'" *American Political Science Review* 73 (1979), 968; italics in original. This definition has been widely quoted, for example by Shelley Rigger, "Mobilizational Authoritarianism and Political Opposition in Taiwan," *Political Oppositions in Industrializing Asia*, Garry Rodan, ed. (London: Routledge, 1996), 302.

[71]Jean C. Oi, *Rural China Takes Off: Institutional Foundations of Economic Reform* (Berkeley: University of California Press, 1999), 12.

[72]See Philippe C. Schmitter, "Still the Century of Corporatism?", *Review of Politics* 1 (January 1974), 98.

increasingly affects unofficial networks, while society increasingly penetrates the state.[73]

Peter Evans advocates "an extra effort to delve into the ideologically unpopular sequence in which the structure of the state helps the character of business in such a way as to enhance possibilities for transformation" and increased productivity. But he confesses that "starting with the structure of the business community may be equally fruitful" and finds that "corporate coherence plus dense ties" between the state and business "lies at the structural heart of economically successful 'developmental states'."[74] They are not just bureaucratic states; they are also politically networked societies. Evans calls this combination "embedded autonomy," when a Weberian bureaucracy is in bed with a well-organized community of businesses. There is empirical evidence from many places that this spurs economic development.

Andrew Turton argues from Thai data "that it is not possible to consider local powers without some attempt, however provisional, to characterize the nature of the state, and indeed such a characterization would be incomplete without the local focus."[75] Turton wants to treat the Thai state in "post-structuralist" and "neo-Gramscian" terms, referring both to classes and status groups. He says the Thai "ruling power bloc" changed during the boom from military dominance into dominance mainly by a "fractionalized bourgeoisie." This transition affected both central and local regimes together. Various leaders only sometimes acted together as a unified ruling bloc.

The normal question about business participation in politics is: have entrepreneurs influenced policy at the national level? Yet this suggests an overly narrow view of politics, as something that takes place only in public space. If "politics" is present in any application of power, as it is, then much or most of politics takes place (for better or

---

[73]Jürgen Habermas, *The Structural Transformation of the Public Sphere: An Inquiry into a Category of Bourgeois Society* (Cambridge: Polity Press, 1989).

[74]Peter B. Evans, "State Structures, Government-Business Relations, and Economic Transformation," 64–65.

[75]Andrew Turton, "Local Powers and Rural Differentiation," 74.

for worse) in private. Documentation is usually scanty, but there is enough circumstantial and direct evidence that political scientists can have hope of covering the majority of their proper subject.

LOCAL PATH DEPENDENCE AND BRINGING ALL POLITICS "BACK IN"

State and nonstate power networks seldom openly conflict with each other, but they shape each other. One way of thinking about their relationship is to distinguish "formal" state politics from "informal" politics. The system of the government is often considered more "formal," but in fact it is just more official. In China and many other countries, it is only somewhat less personalistic than local nonstate power networks. Informal politics may grow on the "trellis" of formal structures.[76] In many cases, though, the more solid trellis is increasingly nongovernmental.

Nonstate policies have been crucial for promoting development in Taiwan, East China, and Thailand. In the Philippines, they have mostly discouraged growth. In all four places, local policies largely, though not wholly, trumped policies coming from the capitals. SMEs and other local institutions such as families have typical policies that are not just reactions to state edicts. Many phenomena in East Asia elude understanding until this is recognized.

By no means are state agents the only powerholders with whom business owners (as well as regional gangsters and mob-affiliated political canvassers) make liaisons. They also link up with each other. The coherent state, even if it behaves as a single actor, is just one of the interlocutors for other networks in either a fair or coercive "civil" polity. Most small and large political institutions in ordinary times change slowly, especially as regards their strength. Colonial governments, if strong, often remain so after independence. If they were

---

[76] Joseph Fewsmith, "Formal Structures, Informal Politics, and Political Change in China," in *Informal Politics in East Asia*, Lowell Dittmer, Fukui Haruhiro, and Peter Lee, eds. (New York: Cambridge University Press), 142, and references there to work by Lowell Dittmer.

weak, they tend to remain weak. Atul Kohli has studied this phenome-non in a variety of states.[77] Structures that were established during colonial periods in countries as different as South Korea, India, Brazil, or Nigeria last for many years thereafter. This current book applies the same principle of "path dependence" (a.k.a. history) to smaller collec-tivities too. Nonstate power networks affect and are affected by growth.[78] Like governments, these networks aid or hinder economic growth with an effectiveness that is surprisingly constant over time, even if revolutions or wars or dictatorships interrupt them.[79]

The focus of this approach is not on any direct comparison of state and nonstate power, because that is not a zero-sum relation.[80] The main issue is not even whether "the state," a lanky institution of many administrative levels, is strong or weak. Nor is the issue the strength or weakness of "civil society." The focus here is simply on showing that booms create more pluralized forms of politics both inside the state and outside it. Booms, which are not just economic, make the sum of power and reasons for conflict grow in many socio-political organizations.

---

[77] Atul Kohli, *State-Directed Development*, 8 and *passim*.

[78] This emphasis on nonstate, local institutions is the current book's only comple-ment to Kohli's account, whose thesis that the "purposive" aim of industrialization is somewhat more likely to arise in centralized regimes such as South Korea under Park or Brazil during Estado Novo or the military dictatorship than in civically active democracies such as India — and growth is far less likely in patrimonial states, espe-cially fragmented ones such as Nigeria. Among other authors with somewhat parallel theses, such as Amsden in *The Rise of the Rest*, development is mainly defined in terms of the growth of well-documented large firms; so SMEs are naturally neg-lected. It is possible to see the importance, in some late-developing economies, of SMEs without claiming that free market policies create growth separate from the national and local politics behind them.

[79] The most obvious examples in modern history are the post-war economic perform-ances of Japan and Germany. Much that was industrial in those countries was bombed. The war impoverished many there down to "third world" levels, but they restored modern economies in a passion of "path dependence."

[80] Many have argued this. See, for example, Alfred Stepan, "State Power and the Strength of Civil Society in the Southern Cone of Latin America," in Peter B. Evans, *et al.*, eds., *Bringing the State Back In* (Cambridge: Cambridge University Press, 1985), 317–43.

Modernization is a process in which local people reinvent their links to the state. Localities are important in redefining larger political environments during socioeconomic change. Political links are more difficult to quantify reliably than are many other aspects of change, as elites at many sizes of collectivity make decisions on how to resolve differences among themselves. These disputes are resolved by violence or by referring matters to dictators or monarchs who may be seen as legitimate, or perhaps by involving non-elites. Booms are a locally and nationally chosen context in which elites redefine the kinds of links among themselves, or between themselves and new local leaders.

"Bringing the state back" into discussions of development is an important aim, but *bringing local politics outside the state back in* is at least as important. In practice, calls to "bring the state back in" are American. Throughout East Asia, and much of the rest of the world too, it has scarcely occurred to most thinkers that the state might be "out," even when it has actually been so.

GROUP IDENTITIES IN BOOM TIMES

The nationality of entrepreneurs has been officially unproblematic, but politically a matter of some concern, in all four of this book's cases. Taiwanese and mainlander business people have long been conscious of a distinction between these "ethnic" groups. During the period of the fastest growth on Taiwan, they knew that the government favored large industries in which the seven-eighths Taiwanese majority had somewhat less stake than in small firms — although by their sheer numbers, native islanders were prominent in both large and small enterprises.

In south Jiangsu and especially south Zhejiang, the emperor was far away in Beijing, speaking a different language rather than a Shanghainese tongue. Although these Wu-"dialect" speakers were loyal Chinese, their own "Jiangnan" regional self-esteem matches that of the famously proud citizens of the northern capital. Because of high tax rates that Shanghai and southern Jiangsu (Sunan) had long endured, these Yangzi delta entrepreneurs and officials have long known that they were not the same as the Shandong and north Jiangsu cadres appointed to monitor them after 1949. The latter did not speak a Wu language natively, although their Third Field Army "liberated" East China and had high political and military prestige. Many non-Jiangnan cadres remained in high local Sunan and Zhejiang posts for three decades after 1949.[81]

In Thailand, despite exceptionally tolerant traditions of national assimilation, Thais who were Sino-Thai recognized their difference, which was paralleled by a difference of average wealth. Doner and Ramsay describe Thailand as having "a commercial class whose economic position made it critical to the Thai elite, but whose ethnic minority status made it politically subservient."[82] This was the traditional situation. The boom changed it. In Thailand as in Taiwan, a subethnic division kept bureaucrats and businessmen wary of each other for many years — until the boom gave businesses the upper hand and eventually the politics of the division decreased. In Thailand, the king and generals still retained monitoring authority into the new millennium.

In the Philippines, with subethnic divisions aplenty, localism was even stronger. Many localities had a single dominant family; so control of access to markets was very political, albeit not national. Regional identifications have been extremely important in the Philippines. Before independence, the Spanish and then American authorities provided this archipelago of separated islands with nothing like the sense of unity or institutions of unity that were bequeathed by Chinese emperors, Japanese colonialists and Chiang Kai-shek, or Thai kings. Nationwide election to the Philippine Senate was originally proposed as a device to reverse strong local traditions in regions such

---

[81]Tensions between Sunan (south Jiangsu, including Shanghai) and Subei (north Jiangsu) or Shandong groups are documented in Emily Honig, *Creating Chinese Ethnicity: Subei People in Shanghai, 1850–1980* (New Haven: Yale University Press, 1992).

[82]Richard F. Doner and Ansil Ramsay, "Competitive Clientelism and Economic Governance: The Case of Thailand," in *Business and the State in Developing Countries*, Sylvia Maxfield and Ben Ross Schneider, eds., (Ithaca: Cornell University Press, 1997), 241.

as Ilocos, Pampanga, Bikol, Cebu, and elsewhere. But the plurality rule for senatorial election has meant that this centralizing effort, like others, has failed. The small Chinese mestizo minority among entrepreneurs also remained distinctive. Their wealth may have aided their assimilation, but Philippine laws did not.

GROWTH HAPPENS WHEN LEADERS OF THE EFFECTIVE SIZES OF COLLECTIVITY WANT IT

A tenet of neoclassical economic theory is that sustained booms occur mainly because of increased efficiency, and this is supposed to require free markets, so that no competing firm can use coercion to determine its relative profits. In practice, however, increases of allocative efficiency in East Asia have arguably been less important than increases of entrepreneurship. Oligopolists, monopolists, and dictatorial local tycoons (often licensed by officials who have been bribed to prevent free market competition) have been prominent in the fastest periods of growth. As the Philippines show, a structure that allows profit-seeking habits alone does not sustain an economic boom. Bribes by themselves do not spur growth any more surely than free markets do.

Risk-taking entrepreneurs are the political agents of booms. High per-capita income is a cultural trait that correlates with the previous establishment of entrepreneurial institutions. Rising or peaking wealth-per-person correlates with the founding of such institutions, especially local SMEs. Booms have been particularly intense in some time periods, but the places where they occurred often prospered relatively well at earlier and later times, too. Data from those places are not restricted to the eras of fastest economic growth alone. Undynamic "presentist" explanations that try to capture all causal factors at a single moment of time fail to show processes. A movie is needed, not just a photo. Comparative historical analysis seeks trends over time, true stories rather than posited statements.[83]

---

[83]Compare Dietrich Rueschemeyer, Evelyne Huber Stephens, and John D. Stephens, *Capitalist Development and Democracy* (Chicago: University of Chicago Press, 1992), 7, although the aim there is to explain democracy.

The growth rate of any economy may depend as much on its current level of GDP per capita as on the political factors this book discusses. That does not make politics irrelevant. Growth rates depend both on local political autonomies and on current levels of income, as much as on the factors that economists normally use to calculate production functions (i.e., the amounts and costs of capital or labor, or 'technology' that is usually folded into an error term). As the exceptional economist Yoshihara Kunio argues, and as many other scholars of development would not, "an economy is strongly influenced by what an economy has inherited from the past.... our choice is affected by the institutions we encounter and the culture under which we have grown up. It is about time to realize that the national economy is not driven by an ahistorical, amoral people."[84]

When this author asked several neoclassical (mathematical) economists to describe the relationship between per-capita income and its change, they all immediately began to cite sources on a different question: "whether poor countries or regions tend to grow faster than rich ones."[85] Authors such as Barro or Mankiw (refining previous work by Solow) have mainly inquired whether growth rates in wealthy countries tend to "converge" at higher incomes per capita. Solow related growth to increasing output per worker (rather than just to capital, as the Harrod-Domar model had done); and this rise of labor productivity was thought to depend on technology, which should in theory be globally available.

Practically all the economists' articles start with beautifully consistent equations premised on diminishing marginal returns to capital as more money becomes available or labor productivity rises. Empirical data are used to test assumptions more than because they are inherently suggestive. (A aphorism about this approach is, 'Never believe

---

[84]Yoshihara Kunio, *Asia per Capita: Why National Incomes Differ in East Asia* (London: Curzon Press, 2000), vi.

[85]The quotation is from Robert J. Barro, and Xavier Sala-i-Martin, "Convergence," *Journal of Political Economy* 100:2 (1992), 223; see also Gregory Mankiw, David Romer, and David Weil, "A Contribution to the Empirics of Economic Growth," *Quarterly Journal of Economics* (May 1992), 407–37.

the facts until they are proven by theory.') But it is difficult to find a linear relationship between per-capita income and its rate of growth, especially among poor countries. Also, labor productivity is subject to many factors that are hard to measure. This is true even after data are tweaked by adjustments that can be made by including other standard kinds of economic numbers. So this question, about the link between GDP/cap and growth rate, has been shortchanged by mathematical economists.

Trouble arises mainly because the facts are disorderly with respect to usual assumptions. Only "conditional convergence" of decreasing growth can be shown, on a logged per-capita income axis, for relatively high GDP/cap countries. If convergence of growth rates among rich countries is the original question (as it became for these analysts mainly because they started by wanting to find correlations), it applies only to wealthy economies. Other "conditions" such as investment rates and population growth adjust the data so that they can any kind of regular line somewhat less distantly. A "technology" X-factor (including as administrative 'techniques' all the state and nonstate politics this book considers, as well as everything else that cannot be easily expressed in standard quantitative measures) is really an error term in these equations, although many economists deny it is random because in principle it should have knowable generators.

So this neoclassical approach is to write a "production function" in which time figures mainly as a period for gathering data. Processes of sociopolitical change have not been seriously included. Capital and labor supplies are very important in these models, as surely they are in real economies, but the causes of long-term changes in these statistics are not considered within the model's equations, which remain inapplicable abstractions until more is known about the changes. So development economists are honest to label their most usual framework an "exogenous growth model." It provides guidance about what is likely to happen under specific quantitative assumptions (which often cannot be made except over short time periods and uncertainly) about savings rates, depreciation, population growth, and the mysterious technology-management-politics X factor. These are exogenous to the model. The equations themselves offer no clues about these values, why they differ between economies, or how they change.

Entrepreneurship, which Joseph Schumpeter emphasized, is totally obfuscated in the "X-factor" term. It is taken as a matter about which disciplined thinking would difficult, because it does not adapt itself easily to quantification and to the limited kinds of mathematics that economists normally use. Mainstream neoclassical economics might be useful for rich societies, but it is historically limited. It was conceived after the European and American periods of fastest growth and Depression, and it is dubious as an adequate economics of contemporary development. It scarcely covers the long periods of unlimited supplies of labor at near-subsistence wages, which Arthur Lewis's classical (not neoclassical) macrotheory showed to be important in economies where modern technology allows major capitalist accumulation.

When these temporary opportunities to exploit labor are included, the question changes and becomes more relevant to development: it is not about convergence of growth rates among rich economies alone, but instead about growth differences in all political economies. Many writers have observed that both the poorest and the richest nations tend, in general, to grow more slowly than countries at low-middle levels of wealth. This relation between wealth and growth is broadly curvilinear — but especially variant at low levels of wealth. An ordinary correlation cannot catch it. A more fundamental problem is that the deductive search for general laws, normal though it has become in modern orthodox social science, reflects a basic misunderstanding of the meaning of truth, which comes originally from observation and induction.[86] Data, if not pre-digested, reveal at least as much as proofs of "laws" at probability.

---

[86]Richard Rorty attempts to combine insights from James and Dewey, and apparently the later writings of Wittgenstein, in Rorty and Pascual Engel, *What's the Use of Truth?* His view is radical, but general knowledge is not the only kind. It certainly is not the only useful or meaningful kind. Max Weber and Giovanni Sartori are cited to parallel effect elsewhere in this book.

Charles Jones offers a scatter diagram that relates GDP growth rates, 1960–90, to 1960 GDP per worker for many countries.[87] The general shape of the curve is suggestive, despite the impressive scatter. It rises sharply, with many nations off the curve, until roughly a US$7000 wealth level is reached (by that measure). Then for richer countries, it decreases less sharply and with less variance. China or Thailand (with India just slightly behind them) are now near or approaching a medial "soft spot" in which many countries tend to grow most quickly. Taiwan, now mainly a "first world" economy, is now clearly lower (growing less fast) and to the right (richer) on the scattergram. The Philippines is lower, but to the left since it is poorer, although the archipelago is most unlikely to stay there forever. The islands' nonstate political constraints on growth will predictably and politically erode, as this nation approaches the medium-low-income soft spot at which many other economies have expanded most quickly.[88]

There is nothing automatic about movement along this very diffuse curve, however. The reasons for the overall shape are not entirely clear (although Lewis and Schumpeter suggest them). State policies and especially nonstate local policies cause many countries, especially poor ones, to grow either faster or more slowly than their current wealth per person would predict. International trade and crises also vary national rates over time. To see this, readers are urged to visit an interactive website, http://www.gapminder.org/world,

---

[87]Charles I. Jones, *Introduction to Economic Growth* (New York: W.W. Norton, 2002), 60, Fig. 3.8. An interesting aspect of this diagram is that the wealth axis is not logged. It might be hard to write an equation to cover the data even approximately; the shape is much like an apex, or a tilted sharp parabola, and variance off the curve is great for poor countries especially (although some middle-rich ones are also below the curve). The dates chosen, especially the 1960 starting date, and the fact that the horizontal is a measure of wealth at that time only, sharply affects the results — for example, Japan and S. Korea are on a finial off the top of the apex, and they would be located differently if different timings to calculate product or different starting and ending dates had been selected.

[88]Especially if more of the remittances by Overseas Filipino Workers went into commercial and industrial investment rather than consumption, that economy could grow more quickly. See the Philippine chapters for details.

selecting countries of interest and choosing GDP-per-capita growth on the vertical axis. Whatever provable reasons or theoretical premises underlie the pattern in data about past growth, economies tend to boom most at middle levels of wealth. This should, for example, encourage Taiwanese to be more content with their recently lowered economic performance. It could also encourage Filipinos to press for realization of the advantages into which their country may come, as it enters the low-middle level of wealth at which many other countries have prospered.

No such change is apolitical. Economies can boom and then stall. Historians are well aware (just to take one example) that Uruguay or Argentina once developed quickly but then lost momentum — for reasons that available theories scarcely begin to approach. Why? Why has China boomed for so long, while Thailand boomed and recovered at a lower rate? Why has Philippine take off been late? What made India's economy soar near the turn of the millennium, rather than earlier, or in the future?[89] The answers to these economic questions are partly political, but many economists have an ideology in the sense that professional interests cause them to advocate ideas whose narrowness they must sense.[90] The economists may later return to studying economies, rather than just economics.

ELECTIONS AS ECONOMIC FACTORS AND RESULTS

Are elections always democratic? The conditions under which voting constrains governments to serve the substantive interests of many citizens are more dependent on the power of private monied networks than many liberals admit. The traditional democratic logic seems easy: hold an election to ask voters which candidates they prefer, then put their choices in charge of government. This logic works passably,

---

[89]This question is partially answered in Ye Min, *Embedded State: Foreigners, Diasporas, and the Economic Transitions of China and India* (Ph.D. Dissertation, Politics Department, Princeton University, 2007).

[90]The classic on politically useful lapses of conscience is Karl Mannheim, *Ideology and Utopia: An Introduction to the Sociology of Knowledge* (London: Routledge, 1936).

though not perfectly, in modern societies where the preferences of many voters have been normalized by their statuses or occupations. But elections become dubiously democratic, over time hindering rather than advancing most people's interests, in polities where differences between the types of local networks that socialize people's preferences are indistinct or where most such networks are patronist. Elections do not assure any social policy differences between rival leaders' communities. Voting that legitimates a system to disallow policy choice would be hard to describe as democratic without evidence that the government helps most people anyway. In some cases, elections can serve anti-democratic ends.

Contemporary political scientists tend to reduce all politics to mechanisms of interest aggregation. They write as if all mediation of preferences occurs in public institutions such as states and parastatals (mostly parties). By simplifying their concepts of people's interests to generic notions of happiness that are not specified in ways that vary among normative cultures and work situations, they cannot explain democratic deficits. Socialization of interests, not just aggregation of interests, will receive more attention before we have an adequate political science of democracy.

Butler, Penniman, and Ranney nonetheless claim that, "the critical difference between democratic and non-democratic regimes is to be found in whether or not they hold elections, and, if they do, what kind."[91] This is a disputable account of democracy, unless it be understood as tautological and true by definition. Philippine experiences suggest that electoral procedures alone do not guarantee government for the people. The International Foundation for Election Systems, receives USAID and other donations to encourage democratic procedures worldwide. American elected politicians do not want to consider the undemocratic role of money in politics, because they spend so much time raising campaign funds. Minority interest groups (medical, pro-Likud, anti-Castro, pro-gun) spend lavishly to maintain policies

---

[91]David Butler, Howard Penniman, and Austin Ranney, "Introduction," in *Democracy at the Polls*, Butler, Penniman, and Ranney, eds., (Washington: American Enterprise Institute, 1981), 1.

that arguably hurt the U.S. majority's interest — but the majority mobilizes less cash.[92] Dwight Eisenhower warned against policy distortions because of underpublicized power in the "military-industrial complex."[93] Democrats in the West tend to equate liberalism with the electoral habit, rather than with separations of legitimate power between institutions for mutual monitoring, both state and nonstate.

Democrats in East Asia stress voting too. Some on Taiwan think unification with the mainland may become acceptable when China holds free elections; they neglect the chance that direct universal-franchise PRC elections could empower a patriotic demagogue (like Hitler, winner of Germany's 1933 election), whose top priority could become an attack on Taiwan.[94] In Thailand, soldiers in a junta have equated elections with the modernity of the Thai state, despite their disgust with corruption after the elections Thaksin bought. Filipinos

---

[92]See Jacob S. Hacker and Paul Pierson, *Off Center: The Republican Revolution and the Erosion of American Democracy* (New Haven: Yale University Press, 2005), as well as many documented treatments of the other issues mentioned.

[93]This term was famously used by President/General Eisenhower in his 1961 "Farewell Address to the Nation." Extensive evidence shows that more recent Republican and Democratic administrations have continued to be part of the "military-industrial complex" that has monetary reasons to be both unrepresentative and undemocratic. Contemporary Leninists develop similar "complexes" in their countries too.

[94]Chinese democrats, including many in Hong Kong who are frustrated with their local constitution, do not see the anti-liberal potential of direct PRC elections. Their rich "special administrative region" has separate powers (at least in the judiciary and press) so that HK elections would pose no such danger — unless they were taken by mainlanders as a sign that China as a whole could use the same procedure before the local Party branch monopoly of all appointments in each jurisdiction were curtailed. For more, see Lynn T. White III, "America at the Taiwan Strait: Five Scenarios," *Asian Perspective*, 31:4 (2007). Also see reports on the advocacy of more direct PRC elections by senior PLA officers who also would like to maintain the current structure, through which the Army could start a war with civilian support only from one person (e.g., Hu Jintao, who has no military background): "influential thinker Lieutenant General Liu Yazhou... has publicly called for political reform in China, a move that would be dangerous for most senior Chinese officials" but might make the military more influential in foreign policy. David Lague, "One of Beijing's Mysteries: Who is Really in Charge?" *International Herald Tribune*, June 23–24, 2007, 4.

turn out in high portions to vote for leaders who do little for them, making a fiesta more surely than a government.

The presumed modern function of voting is to legitimate leaders for temporary fixed periods. As Weber suggested, normative legitimacy and situational force is the combination that creates power. But liberal political scientists have often defined power in a different way: it is evidenced when a follower is influenced by a leader to do something that the follower would not otherwise do.[95] This view of power is unrealistic, because it is just individualist. Weber more carefully defined "power" in a way that takes account both of its collective and individual aspects. He said power is "the chance of a man or of a number of men to realize their own will in a communal action even against the resistance of others who are participating in the action."[96]

This may be applied to the factor of power, i.e., legitimacy, that elections are supposed to convey. People vote not just as individuals but in terms of networks that are meaningful to them. Many kinds of connections can affect people's incentives to vote (or not to vote). Relatively well-educated networks in rich polities tend to be structured in a politically horizontal fashion, with basic equality between many local decision makers. Networks in less developed countries and less well-educated networks tend to be more communalist, with hierarchical structures.

Vote-buying in democracies takes many forms, some of which are direct, especially in low per-capita income countries. Others involve advertising to support ideologies that dissuade voters from casting ballots that would benefit themselves. Ballots can be bought in traditional societies not usually because electors who would have cast their votes otherwise can effectively be punished, nor because they consider the trade to be an ordinary economic exchange, but because the acceptance of money inspires a moral need to reciprocate.[97]

---

[95]Robert A. Dahl, *Modern Political Analysis* (Englewood Cliffs: Prentice-Hall, 1963).
[96]See *From Max Weber: Essays in Sociology*, H.H. Gerth and C. Wright Mills, eds. (New York: Oxford University Press, 1958), 180.
[97]For more, see Daniel Arghiros, *Democracy, Development, and Decentralisation*, 262–63.

Warm gifts are not like cold cash. Traditional help in politics implies a long-term link, not limited to a single commodity transaction. But modern vote-buying becomes a cash nexus bargain; after money is transferred and a ballot is cast, neither side has an obvious continuing obligation. The voting booth, a technology that allows secret balloting, separates elections from social relationships. The secret ballot (like 'blind' justice and other hopes of modern politics) seems unnatural to many traditionalists — whose leaders in various countries have been able to organize resistance to ballot reform.[98]

Elections or appointments provide the possibility of increasing local prestige through "becoming a mandarin" (*zuoguan* in either Taiwan or China). When a Filipino construction engineer was asked why he wanted to go into politics, he answered, "Because I cannot buy the title of Honorable (*Kagalanggalang*) in a supermarket."[99] He could and did buy it in an election. Nonstate institutions, including feasts, commercial clubs, temples, churches, lineage coalitions, and other customary associations provide vehicles for expressions of political hierarchy and fellowship. Tertiary-educated intellectuals, in either China or the West, tend to assume that the main interests of local leaders of a democracy must be the same as their own, i.e., to shape or join the state. But few local politicians in Asia or elsewhere are ardent devotees of public policy. They mainly care how many people like them.

Village elections in China increase both "clan trust and clan suspicions; they temporarily moderate conflict within clans and intensify conflict between clans."[100] Village voters tend to cast ballots for

---

[98] Alain Garrigou draws on Foucault to make this point, according to Frederic Charles Schaffer, "Disciplinary Reactions: Alienation and the Reform of Vote Buying in the Philippines," paper for the American Political Science Association Annual Meeting, 2002, 2–3. Schaffer also provides examples from South Africa of resistance to ID cards as proof of eligibility to vote.

[99] Kimura Masataka, *Elections and Politics, Philippine Style: A Case in Lipa* (Manila: De La Salle University Press, 1997), 91.

[100] Melanie Manion, "Democracy, Community, Trust: The Impact of Elections in Rural China," *Comparative Political Studies* 39:3 (April 2006), 306, quoting Chinese sociologist Xiao Tangbiao.

candidates in their lineages. Among Filipino election winners, there is much local fluidity, and this randomness often appears in contests between leaders of segments in local two-faction patterns. Similar dualism has been found on Taiwan.[101]

Hinge leaders at various sizes of collectivity hold their networks together. These canvassers are the mechanics of local politics. In early modern systems, they have various names, and as a type they are more important for most citizens than are national leaders with more famous titles. Local Filipino barangay chiefs or *liders* are substantially identical to Thai *huakhanaen* canvassers, as well as to Taiwanese *tiau-a-ka* who similarly organize local voting blocs. In China, which still lacks elections to offices that allocate any substantial resources, mobilization roles are nonetheless often performed by township heads, *xiangzhang*, or by economic entrepreneurs, *qiyezhe*, who have now replaced Maoist "responsible cadres" (*youzeren ganbu*) as crucial hinge leaders in the Chinese system. Pierre Landry shows the means by which that polity coheres together despite its pluralization. Each local leader, at any administrative level, can be promoted only by approval of a level high enough to assert authority yet low enough o monitor the loyalty of the relevant personnel. This is a scalar approach to governance in a huge nested system.[102] Recurring references, in each of these polities, to the local importance of hinge leaders show that any of these states would without them have no hope of linkage with most of the people.

BOOMS AND GREED IN LOCAL POLITICS

"Civil" society in patronist contexts, such as are still frequent especially in rural parts of the three poorer countries under study, is often violently uncivil. Patrons have many sanctions against clients who displease them. They can deny loans that farmers or others need. They

---

[101] Joseph Bosco, "Taiwan Factions: *Guanxi*, Patronage, and the State in Local Politics," in *The Other Taiwan: 1945 to the Present*, Murray Rubinstein, ed. (Armonk: Sharpe, 1994), 114–44.

[102] Pierre-François Landry, *Decentralized Authoritarianism in China: The Communist Party's Control of Local Elites in the Post-Mao Era* (New York: Cambridge University Press, 2008).

can offer loans only at exorbitant rates of interest — with documents that do not distinguish principal from interest repayments, so that evidence of illegality is hard to show. Landlords often can deny water or tractors, or can make sure that agricultural inputs are sold to unruly retainers at special high prices. They can often forbid the use of estate roads, vegetable plots, or places to gather bamboo or firewood. A local boss may also try to harm physically the family members of a farmer he dislikes, perhaps using connections with institutions such as clinics, brokers, government offices, secret societies, the national army, or hired goons. A landlord can also, according to Fegan,

> arrange in his capacity as a politician or through allies for the harassment of a tenant... harass, burn haystacks, run off or release or impound livestock, chop down trees, destroy fences, lavatories, and animal pens, run a tractor through crops, put a road through fields, etc.... take out fake mortgages so that the tenant has no clear landowner to deal with.... owners [use] the law itself as a weapon.... The purpose of most of this intimidation is to persuade the tenant to go to the owner and personally beg [*humingî* is the Tagalog word] a negotiated lease rent, rather than the legally calculated one. The landowner is then in the powerful favorable bargaining position of one who is granting a favor.[103]

When small cities and towns grow, they link modern technologies and markets with subsistence wage labor in places that previously lacked factories or large stores. This all happens in democracies and non-democracies.[104] When elections are held and bought, business people naturally expect value for money. Risk-taking in enterprises matches risk-taking in politics. Elections are often excellent investments or purchases of operating capital, but bribes can be offered even in countries where no important officials are broadly elected.

Booms provide the money for this. A political scientist of Thailand writes that, "the benefits of democratic decentralization at the

---

[103]Fegan, "Accumulation on the Basis of an Unprofitable Crop," 118–19.

[104]Examples in a non-democratic context are provided by Fei Xiaotong, *Fei Xiaotong lun xiao chengzhen jianshe* (Fei Xiaotong on the Construction of Small Cities and Towns) (Beijing: Qunyan Chuban She, 2000).

community and provincial levels tend to be captured by local capitalists."[105] The theorist Pierre Bourdieu explores ways to convert different forms of social capital (wealth, power, and prestige) into each other. These resources may be financial (money), physical (e.g., equipment or land), human (training that increases productivity), cultural (training in valued styles), or social (trust from others that comes from being part of a network). Within any culture and context, individuals make these conversions as profitably as they can, increasing the stores of capital to help them take the actions that most interest them.[106] Since businesses typically have money, they spend financial capital for other kinds that usually help them, in later transactions acquire yet more money. Politics depends on social capital and trust. These assets are also affected in practice by resources that causes others to comply out of fear, which can be called coercive capital. With time lags and conversion costs, money can buy political reputation.

A boom of wealth sometimes creates a positive interest in elections among middle-high income people, especially if authoritarians whom they previously supported fail to maintain their status. Purchasable elections are very good news for the rich. Liberal separations of power do not guarantee government in the public interest if judges, reporters, and other state and nonstate actors may also be up for sale. The most democratic solution in boom times is to have multiple restraints, especially on businesses as nonstate power networks. Unsurprisingly, they resist such controls. As a group of writers has argued, "democracy requires governments that are not only accountable to their citizens but also subject to restraint and oversight by other public agencies. In addition to being restrained from below, the state must subject itself to multiple forms of *self*-restraint."[107]

Constructing politics to benefit majorities on a long-term basis requires simultaneous solutions to many problems. Some issues arise

---

[105]Daniel Arghiros, *Democracy, Development, and Decentralisation*, 5 and 7.
[106]Pierre Bourdieu, *The Logic of Practice* (Cambridge: Cambridge University Press, 1992).
[107]*The Self-Restraining State: Power and Accountability in New Democracies*, Andreas Schedler, Larry Diamond, and Marc F. Plattner, eds. (Boulder: Lynne Rienner, 1999), introduction by the editors, 1.

because people easily make mistakes about ways to realize their own happiness. It is presumptuous of any theorist to be overconfident in telling citizens what to do. Majority rule, legitimated by elections, can be a crucial and useful constraint on modern leaders. But elections are most effective when the legitimacy they confer is moderated by other constraints that are functional (judicial independence, academic freedom, and especially safety for journalists). By those means, well-informed specialist leaders as well as popular leaders are put in charge.

Political scientists generally argue that elections strengthen legitimate order only if they are introduced *after* conflict has already been normalized among different elites. Mass participation is deemed safe for liberalism only if it is preceded by legitimate elite contest. The relationship is not just one of time sequence, however. Elections are constraints on government that can interact most effectively with other constraints, which are based in non-resolvable but potentially peaceable social interests in nonstate power networks. Checks on abuse of power are outside the state, not just in it. The reason why democrats, including this author, like elections is not just that competition for votes makes exciting struggles to watch from a distance that is usually safe. More important, elections can eventually remove bad governors, unless the tyrants can use elections to legitimate repression without being checked by other socially recognized institutions first. If elections are compared with other reins on abuses of power, such as judiciaries or opposition legislators or reporters who can publicize government corruptions, mass voting is a relatively slow constraint. Even if elections are instituted after other constitutional separations of power, they seldom fix systemic problems quickly.

Good government has the consent of the governed, but majority support is not the only basis for popular rule. Economic wealth, especially in boom times, gives rich minorities funds to promote public laws that protect private exploitation. Booms often finance ideologies that keep the majority of voters from imagining their own democratic effectiveness. The separation-of-powers emphasis in Madison's *Federalist 51* can be combined with much that the past century has taught about nonstate economic power and violent patriotic demagoguery. Both electoral and functional legitimacies, at many sizes of political network, are the modern formula for justice. The four places studied in this book are, in their own time, slowly developing such legitimacies.

METHODS

Concern for methodology, which has overshadowed attention to substance in many contemporary social sciences, has led to somewhat less inaccurate treatments of Western places than of Asian locales. But 61 percent of this world's people live in Asia. China and India alone approach half of us all. For too long, studies of Asian places (though not of the U.S.) have been deemed mere "country studies." But Taiwan-watching, China-watching, Thailand-watching, or Philippines-watching is a theoretical enterprise. Current theories, especially the most systematic ones in economics, have patently failed to predict what has happened in these countries. The problem is not just that mainstream social science has been too deductive and insufficiently inductive. Instead, the problem is that the inductions have come from too few places. Until social scientists realize that various kinds of Asians differ in crucial ways from different kinds of Westerners and from each other even when the Asians wear suits and neckties, truly comparative politics will not yet exist.

On the first page of *The Social Origins of Dictatorship and Democracy*, Barrington Moore says that the germ of his interest was his belief that "adequate theoretical comprehension of political systems had to come to terms with Asian institutions and history."[108] Yet *theoretical* movement toward understanding Asia has been at least snail-like, perhaps even regressive, in the decades since he wrote, because the methods required to dig up new empirical data that can challenge faulty old theories have become unfaddish in political

---

[108]Barrington Moore, Jr., *Social Origins of Dictatorship and Democracy: Lord and Peasant in the Making of the Modern World* (Boston: Beacon, 1966), xi.

science. It is unfashionable to define methods professionally in terms of eras or geography, at least foreign geography.[109]

That is now the most common mistake in thinking about methods. If the only boon of this book were that it treats Asia, this could be noted as a contribution, because mainstream views of social science especially in the United States have tended to militate against thinking seriously about other places, especially countries that have unfamiliar customs and languages. An important and rightly famous book about *Capitalist Development And Democracy* scarcely mentions East Asia (using just one-third of a page, among 300 pages, to say that in the early 1990s the working class in S. Korea seemed stronger than that in Taiwan).[110] Asian languages have scared away too many comparativists, to the serious detriment of comparative theories. Latin American or African countries, whose politics are documented in European languages, have received more theoretical attention. The upside of this professional lacuna is that many questions about political development remain open. Comparisons of China and Southeast Asia could in the future yield rich fruits.

Southeast Asianists (Benedict Anderson, Clifford Geertz, James Scott, William Skinner, and others) have been able to make major

---

[109]This author once asked Ben Bernanke, then Chair of Economics at Princeton, why his large department contained no active professor who knew the languages of either the fastest-growing or the second-largest economies on the planet at that time (i.e., Chinese or Japanese). The explanation was, "We teach the general principles of economics." Bernanke was a faithful representative; it is unlikely that any voting member of his department would have disagreed. Such responses would come also from most Americanists and many others in political science, and also from most other social scientists (even some anthropologists, although their epistemological faith contrasts with that of the economists). Asia is particularly shortchanged by these professional ideologies, in part because some of its languages are hard to learn and students are supposed to concentrate on learning other methods. A related fad concerns time rather than space: the notion that the insignificance of historical eras can be shown by applying contemporary methods of "narrative" analysis to any time. The implication (which an intellectual historian can easily disprove) is that these methods are timeless.

[110]A seminal book on the role of workers in democratization (whose ideas have aided this author's thinking) is Dietrich Rueschemeyer, *et al.*, *Capitalist Development and Democracy*, n.b. the top of page 294. Barbados, however, receives much attention.

theoretical contributions to social science, even though the number of scholars studying this region is relatively small. Southeast Asia is not more homogeneous than any other part of the world, but too few researchers who write about other continents have paid attention to the states and markets there. Many or all who have done so betray their obvious attraction to the particularities of the Southeast Asian places they study.[111]

We need to get over the notion that all interesting knowledge is general knowledge. Often the most interesting knowledge is local, and general knowledge (even if true) is of dubious use, hard to prove, or both. The usual passion in contemporary social science is to search for correlations that can be described as linear and that apply everywhere. Yet "off the line" cases are just as important for understanding (either practical or theoretical, although there is in principle no difference between these types). The Philippines, for example, are included in this book because they illustrate what Lijphart calls a "deviant" case "to uncover relevant additional variables that were not considered previously, or to refine the (operational) definitions of some or all of the variables. In this way, deviant case studies can have great theoretical value."[112] Actually, no place need be called deviant, albeit some are unusual. A country is not inherently a case. A place becomes a case only to the extent that a question asked about it imposes that restrictive frame.

This book's method is to compare the political origins of growth and the results of quick growth on local politics in four places. If other researchers find similarities or differences between the processes in these places at these times, on one hand, and contexts further afield (for example in Latin America or Africa), that will be interesting, but also they may attempt more generalization than is needed. Max Weber wrote that,

> The most general laws, because they are most devoid of content, are also the least valuable. The more comprehensive the validity — or scope — of

---

[111]See various views in *Southeast Asia in Political Science: Theory, Region, and Qualitative Analysis*, Erik Martínez Kuhonta, Dan Slater, and Tuong Vu, eds. (Stanford: Stanford University Press, 2008).

[112]Arend Lijphart, "Comparative Politics and the Comparative Method," *American Political Science Review* 65:3 (September 1971), 692.

a term, the more it leads away from the richness of reality, since in order to include the common elements of the largest number of phenomena, it must necessarily be as abstract as possible and hence devoid of content.[113]

Weber allowed studies of socialization, but the individualist economist Friedrich Hayek made a similar point in his Nobel acceptance speech: "I confess I prefer true but imperfect knowledge, even if it leaves much indetermined and unpredictable, to a pretence of exact knowledge that is likely to be false."[114] Composing a mosaic about Taiwan, East China, Thailand, and the Philippines, centered on the ways politics affects and is affected by booms, provides a basis for conjectures (but not proofs) in more general political science.

The main such suggestions here are that industrial-commerical booms create new local power networks outside formal political institutions such as governments and parties, and that neither the origins nor the results of economic performance can be understood without looking at the political power of those local networks. This kind of statement can be read only as a generalization from the evidence presented here. If other scholars wish to treat such evidence as "cases" rather than places, suggesting "laws" useful for understanding other places, that is of interest only insofar as they can make similar inductions from new evidence — which may turn out to be different.

A standard question in contemporary social science is about "case selection." Why does this book consider the four places it does, rather than others? A preliminary response might be that all four places grow rice; some arguments here pay attention to the agrarian origins of industrialization as a political process. But a more important answer is: this book is not about cases. It attributes economic booms

---

[113]Quoted by the editors in *Alexis de Tocqueville on Democracy, Revolution, and Society*, John Stone and Stephen Mennell, eds. (Chicago: University of Chicago Press, 1980), 27.

[114]Friedrich August von Hayek, "The Pretence of Knowledge," at http://nobelprize.org/nobel_prizes/economics/.

(and the Philippines' non-boom) to local political leaderships especially in SMEs, and it finds similar patterns in the political effects of money. It makes no claim that such patterns prevail everywhere. In the Far East, for example, the causes of booms in Japan and South Korea were somewhat different than those in Taiwan, East China, and Thailand — and evidence from these four is also somewhat multiform. If other "laws" govern other places, that does not gainsay what has happened in these four, which are important enough to compare and contrast as regards their own traits.

"Comparative analysis is no substitute for detailed investigation of specific cases," as Barrington Moore wrote.[115] Exceptional cases are as interesting as normal ones.[116] The design of this book may be deemed inadequate by some analysts who know that four cases would be insufficient to prove any generalization about causal links between economic booms and changes of local politics, or vice-versa. Complaints may also be raised about selection bias. But they would be based on a misunderstanding of the purpose of this project, which is to compare evidence of elective affinities rather than causations in a variety of countries. The aim here is to explore linkages between growth and changes of structures in four East Asian locations, not to prove a general law that the relationships seen there might obtain worldwide. A larger number of cases would have diluted the investigation of the specific mechanisms in these four. Nauru, Russia, and Switzerland could have been added. This

---

[115]Barrington Moore, Jr., *Social Origins of Dictatorship and Democracy*, xiv.

[116]Compare Evan S. Lieberman, "Nested Analysis as a Mixed-Method Strategy for Comparative Research," *American Political Science Review* 99:3 (August 2005), 435–52. But Lieberman is also exceptionally interested in "off the line" cases (e.g., in Africa, where Uganda or South Africa have had better or worse records controlling HIV/AIDS than comparisons would have predicted, involving factors that led to such control in larger numbers of nations), because the study of unusual cases is particularly useful. See references in notes above and below to various kinds of pragmatists (James, Dewey, Rorty) and their good ideas about truth as used. They see truth as meaningless separate from its discovery in action.

would have increased the statistical N. It would not have improved the meaning.[117]

This book treats its four places not as four data points but as platforms where complex processes involving comparable aspects occur over time. So the N, if needed, is actually much larger than four. That apology would be true but would also miss the more important fact that these are not four cases of any general principle. Studying one of them, or a single aspect of one of them, would be legitimate. They are interesting for themselves, irrespective of any generalities they may or may not exemplify. Even "laws" have jurisdictions and limits of applicability. Correlations do not establish causation anyway. Only process tracing can begin to get at causal mechanisms. A political scientist of Thailand, attending a conference long ago at which his paper about the kingdom was presented alongside others about other Southeast Asian nations, became frustrated by his colleagues' comments. In an offhand moment he blurted out, "What's wrong with this damn country? You can't compare it to anything!"

That kind of objection is always partly true — and is no ultimate objection to studying or comparing places. The good tradition of trying to "see things together" has been honored by social scientists in attempts to model candidate laws of behavior. Most humanists have honored it in a different way, when they try to look at things widely in order to reach understandings that can lead to practical judgement or

---

[117]Overwrought fears about selection bias have caused statistical authors to frame research that compares arguable incomparables, whenever the latter seem to produce enough tentatively reliable numbers that can be crunched. But see *Rethinking Social Inquiry: Diverse Tools, Shared Standards*, Henry E. Brady and David Collier, eds. (Lanham: Rowman and Littlefield, 2004), e.g., chap. 12 by Collier, Brady, and Jason Seawright about "Critiques, Responses, and Trade-Offs: Drawing Together the Debate." These barely begin to free studies of politics from the false premise that all truth is general. Some researchers in fact lump the Nauruan, Russian, and Swiss polities together with others. Correlations are often deemed the golden key to social truth. That is a possible path, providing some views; but it is not the road taken here.

overall wisdom about the situations they study.[118] The aim here is not final truth but better understanding. Because that is the goal, there should be no need to apologize for circumspect or eclectic method. The only need is to restate the value of looking around, because many professionals have developed interests in arguments against it.

An overemphasis on deductive approaches to the understanding of political change has fostered analytic clarity, but it has reduced the reach of understanding that the opposite logical procedure (synthesis) can achieve. Too much stress on deduction and insufficient use of induction has prevented political science from treating many relations of actual politics. Searching among facts even before they have been "proven by theories" is a legitimate way to think. Hobbes's love of the clear definitions and proofs of geometry has inspired many of his followers to see only some aspects of government as people really practice it. Economists are so overdependent on deduction, some have the humor to admit that narrowness — and others have the pride to call it professional.[119]

Students of politics should become more willing to try the usefulness of categories that do not start in concepts that they understand clearly because they have constructed them in their own heads but, instead, start in minimally structured observations of political behavior. The flaws of the orthodox analytic approach are especially obvious in studies of quasi-democratic polities. Perhaps it is natural that American analysts in particular, who may want to identify as democrats and liberals, have let their hopes affect their ideas prematurely. Too few of their researches find common faults in liberal systems.

---

[118]See Louis O. Mink, "The Autonomy of Historical Understanding," *History and Theory* 5 (1965), 24–47.

[119]See Albert Hirschman, "The Search for Paradigms as a Hindrance to Understanding," in *A Bias for Hope*, Hirschman, ed. (New Haven: Yale University Press, 1971), 342–60, and Paul Krugman, "The Rise and Fall of Development Economics," from *Rethinking the Development Experience: Essays Provoked by the Work of Albert O. Hirschman*, Lloyd Rodwin and Donald A Schön, eds. (Washington: Brookings Institution, 1994), 39–58.

Less constrained logics and rhetorics of presentation are required to bring these to light — but doing would better serve serious democratic norms. The solely-analytic-never-synthetic bias hides useful science, *scientia*, in the sense of useful knowledge. It would be wise for most liberals at this point to fasten their seat belts. Not all of this ride through Taiwan, East China, Thailand, and the Philippines will be bumpy, but democrats can expect potholes.

2

Political Roots of Taiwan's Boom

Taiwan is the most liberal sizeable place in East Asia. Its boom showed a combination of fast income growth and equalization that is extremely rare in economic history, and small enterprises were the agents of this performance.

Japan ruled Taiwan until the end of World War II, and important infrastructure for later development predated Japan's defeat. Taiwan had been ceded to Japan in 1895, when China lost the Sino-Japanese War. At the "retrocession" in 1945, Nationalist troops under Chiang Kai-shek accepted the surrender of Japanese troops in Taiwan on behalf of the Allies. Chiang's Kuomintang (KMT) still controlled much of the mainland then, and KMT leaders did not yet have an inkling of the importance Taiwan would assume in their future. A distinctly second-rate leadership was dispatched to the newly acquired island. It was headed by a governor named Ch'en Yi, whom the KMT later executed for corruption.[1] The gross ineptitude of Chinese Nationalist rule on Taiwan in the first years after 1945 is now universally recognized.

---

[1] George H. Kerr, *Formosa Betrayed* (Boston: Houghton Mifflin, 1965); and Douglas Mendel, *The Politics of Formosan Nationalism* (Berkeley: University of California Press, 1970). This KMT Governor Ch'en Yi is no kin of the communist general Chen Yi, whose army at about the same time took Shanghai.

Japanese occupation for half a century had inadvertently fostered Chinese patriotism among the Taiwanese. They speak a Chinese language because their ancestors came from the mainland. Governor Ch'en Yi and his military police managed to dissipate most of their pro-Chinese sentiments in a single year. A climax was reached on February 28, 1947, when agents of the KMT government's Tobacco and Wine Monopoly Bureau arrested an old woman in a Taipei park for selling cigarettes illegally. When she objected to their seizure of her wares and money, one of them knocked her down. A crowd formed. Police fired into it, killing at least one person. Taiwanese resentment had grown steadily over previous months against the administrators whom Chiang Kai-shek had sent to Taiwan while he was still fighting a civil war on the mainland. This spark in the park set off a blaze.

On the next day, much larger crowds protested at the governor's office. Soldiers shot into the crowd and killed several people. KMT police, who had prepared lists of suspected dissidents, rounded up everyone whom they did not like. During March, scattered further violence included assassinations of local Taiwanese leaders. Estimates of government murders in 1947, including the permanent disappearances of scions of traditional leading lineages on the island, range from 10,000 to 20,000.[2] Confrontations quickly spread throughout Taiwan between two ethnic (or 'subethnic') groups. Taiwanese and mainlanders are both ethnic Hans, as are 92 percent of the people in China. But distrust between the overwhelming Taiwanese majority on the island and the armed mainlander minority created a sharp political need, after the KMT's loss of the mainland, for the government to make compromises.

Chiang's regime therefore promoted economic opportunities for the Taiwanese. These could allay the political effects of its early conflicts with them. By 1949, more circumspect KMT leaders arrived on the island, and their economic policies aimed at instilling loyalty among Taiwanese. The KMT retreated to the island with a million

---

[2]Gerald A. McBeath, *Wealth and Freedom: Taiwan's New Political Economy* (Aldershot: Ashgate, 1998), 25.

and a half state employees, both bureaucrats and soldiers, practically all mainlanders.[3] The acknowledged ancestors of about 74 percent of the islanders are Minnan. They came from Fujian province, just across the Taiwan Strait, mostly in the nineteenth century. "Taiwanese," spoken by three-quarters of the islanders and sometimes called "Hoklo," is also the language of southern Fujian. These people are not called mainlanders on Taiwan only because their families arrived before 1945, the end of the Japanese period during which immigration was slight.

Hakkas are another native Taiwanese part of the population, amounting to more than ten percent of the island's total. They speak their own Chinese "dialect" language that is mutually unintelligible with either Taiwanese or Mandarin. Hakka clan temples are somewhat different from Minnan shrines. Because Hakkas generally came to the island later, they usually held land that was less productive. This became important in the KMT's later sequencing of land reforms, which in many locales benefitted Hakkas early. For them and for Minnan people, the land reforms were linked to KMT industrial policies that had the aim of pacifying Taiwanese after the late-1940s conflict.

Mainlanders became a subethnicity on the island, comprising less than 14 percent of Taiwan's population after their post-1945 arrivals and before their extensive intermarriages with Taiwanese. In polite Mandarin, the mainlanders are called "people from outside provinces" (*waisheng ren*); in more colloquial Taiwanese they are still sometimes pejoratively called names such as "mountain men" (*a-bua*, or in Mandarin *ashan*).[4] When Chiang Kai-shek's army came to the island, a high proportion of the ordinary soldiers were bachelors, many of whom later had Taiwanese wives. Their offspring were classified as mainlanders, but time and the gradual Taiwanization of politics gave people incentives to change this identification.

---

[3]Cheng Tun-jen, "Taiwan in Democratic Transition," in *Driven by Growth: Political Change in the Asia-Pacific Region*, James Morley, ed. (Armonk: M.E. Sharpe, 1993), 197.

[4]Arthur Jay Lerman, *Political, Traditional, and Modern Economic Groups, and the Taiwan Provincial Assembly* (Ph.D. dissertation, Politics Department, Princeton University, 1972).

Minnan, Hakka, and mainlander people, who are all Hans, are not quite the island's whole population. Just two percent of the islanders are non-Han Austronesians, originally speaking languages distantly related to those of the Philippines and many other places.[5]

THE POLITICAL INDUSTRIALIZATION OF TAIWAN'S RURAL ELITE

Taiwan, like the parts of East China discussed in this book's later chapters, had strong entrepreneurial traditions. Taiwanese business foundings, notably by the island's most distinguished collaborators with Japan, began long before 1945.[6] Japanese colonialism eroded Taiwan's rentier class, because the imperial government in early reforms had confiscated much land for itself. Taiwanese lineage heads had been avid founders of sugar mills, trading houses, trust companies, banks, and cement firms in the first half of the island's Japanese era. Many industrial holdings of prominent Taiwanese were taken over, however, by the colonial government during the 1930s. These were inherited by Chiang Kai-shek's state in 1945, when sugar refining was still the most important industry in Taiwan.[7] The KMT's politically necessary land reform finished off Taiwan's landlords as a political force, although it gradually converted that

---

[5]Interviews with linguists indicate a consensus that there are at least four groups of Austronesian languages, of which all but one are (or were) spoken solely on Taiwan. These Formosan languages include Ami, Atayal, Bunun, and Paiwan. The fourth or other group, Malayo-Polynesian, includes practically all the Philippine, Indonesian, and Malaysian languages (and Yami on Orchid Island off Taiwan), and it also ranges from Hawaiian, Maori in New Zealand, and the original tongue of Rapa Nui (Easter Island, now in Chile) to Malagasy on Madagascar. The place where a language family has early roots is generally the location where linguistic variance within the group is greatest. For Austronesian languages, that place is Taiwan.

[6]Thomas B. Gold, "Colonial Origins of Taiwanese Capitalism," in *Contending Approaches to the Political Economy of Taiwan*, Edwin A. Winckler and Susan Greenhalgh, eds. (Armonk: Sharpe, 1988), 101–20.

[7]Gerald A. McBeath, *Wealth and Freedom*, 30.

group into petty capitalists. A few of them later became very large capitalists.

Sun Yat-sen, founder of the KMT, had been strongly influenced by Henry George's ideas on rent income. One of Sun's slogans called for "land to the tiller." By April 1949, the KMT regime enacted "Regulations Governing the Lease of Private Farmlands in Taiwan Province." These rules stipulated that no rents could exceed three-eighths of the main crop on any plot. This law was supposed to be implemented by "rent campaign committees" at the province, county/city, and township/district/village levels in Taiwan. But because tenants were less than 15 percent of the membership of the committees in 1949, not a great deal happened at first.[8]

By the early 1950s, KMT leaders (largely from landlord families themselves) were keenly aware that the Chinese communists had used reform to gain political support. The land reform in Taiwan had a similar aim albeit with a different, less violent and more incentive style. (Actually, the kinds of communist land reform in Northern wheat areas and Southern rice areas of the mainland PRC differed from each other in political terms more than is widely known.[9]) The KMT by 1950 had learned sharp lessons on the importance of politics in rural networks outside the state. Its policies, on the island, finally took that experience into account.

The chief planner of the island's land reform and sometime Governor of Taiwan, Chen Cheng, admitted that the mainland's old land tenure system "had provided the Communist agitators with an opportunity to infiltrate into the villages. It was one of the main

---

[8]Elizabeth Green, *Land Reform in China* (B.A. thesis, Princeton University, East Asian Studies Department, 1977); and for comparisons, see Hung-chao Tai, "The Political Process of Land Reform," in *The Political Economy of Development*, Norman T. Uphoff and Warren F. Ilchman, eds. (Berkeley: University of California Press), 295–303.

[9]See Benedict Stavis, "China and the Comparative Analysis of Land Reform," and Edwin Moise, "Comment," *Modern China* 4:1 (January 1978), 63–90. North China had more violent land reforms, because the plots were traditionally small and split between multiple lineages in most villages. Raising land to give away for political support was easier for communists in the South.

reasons why the Chinese mainland fell into communist hands."[10]
This KMT official conceived Taiwan's land reform as a prophylactic
against communist infiltrators to the island. His fears of that time may
now seem overblown, but they provided powerful new political arguments for serious reform within Taiwan's mainlander elite. Chen
could urge thoroughgoing land reform without referring to the
mainlanders' minority status or their need for more islanders' support
after the killings of Taiwanese in 1947.

By 1951, land redistribution in Taiwan became far more thoroughgoing than land reforms have usually become in most
countries.[11] A fresh law reinforced the 1949 one. It was now required
that all enforceable leases be written, and they had to be valid for at
least six years. Changes in the international environment (especially
the Korean War) also opened a stream of American agricultural aid.
A joint ROC-US committee took the lead in establishing farmers'
associations in Taiwan that were similar to groups that the American
occupation had earlier established in Japan. These proved to be far
more effective than the previous rent committees in implementing
rules that had been decreed.

Then, under a "Land-to-the-Tiller Act of 1953," all tenanted
holdings over 8.4 acres of medium-grade paddy (or the equivalent by
output in other grades) were purchased by the government for sale to
tenants at the same price. Farmlands that were owned collectively
by temples and clans were redistributed in the same way. The price
for these plots was fixed at 2.5 times the average annual value of the
main crop.[12]

Previous landowners during Taiwan's reform were paid seven-
tenths in government bonds (bearing 4 percent annual interest) *and*

---

[10]Hsiao Hsin-huang, *Government Agricultural Strategies in Taiwan and South
Korea: A Macrosociological Assessment* (Taipei: Institute of Ethnology, Academia
Sinica, 1981), 105.

[11]See John Montgomery, Tai Hung-chao, Bernard Gallin, and Tsutomu Ouchi in
The Political Economy of Development, Norman Uphoff and Warren Ilchman, eds.
(Berkeley: University of California Press, 1972), 449–59.

[12]Gary L. Olson, *U.S. Foreign Policy and the Third World Peasant* (New York:
Praeger, 1974), 6.

the other three-tenths in industrial stocks. The Nationalist government had industrial shares that it could distribute to former landowners, because it had confiscated factories formerly owned by the Japanese colonial regime. So agrarian land reform reshaped Taiwanese industry too. This was the hook that lifted a rural policy into modern urban industry and commerce. It allowed the KMT to give traditionally prestigious Taiwanese families political leadership in nonstate enterprises, delaying their ambitions for political leadership in government.

LAND AND LOCALIZATION

The KMT's interests after the 1947 ethnic clashes made Taiwan's land reform different from that of other East Asian countries such as South Korea or the Philippines (or mainland China). The Korean generals and Ferdinand Marcos tried to control their reform processes in more detail, more centrally, because they had less political need to gratify a majority population that had an easy-to-organize ethnic potential for dissidence. For many years thereafter, Taiwan and South Korea had many similarities: both were strong authoritarian regimes, both were in danger of military attack from obvious enemies, both had been Japanese colonies, and both depended on rice production for food. Nonetheless, as one analyst says, there are "no analogues in Taiwan to the [later] Tongil green revolution campaign in Korea."[13] Taiwan had a "flexible," less centralized policy for agriculture. Government support was important, but the island's farmers made most of the decisions. Local leaders were in charge.

Farmers' Associations, because they were Taiwanese and the government was still largely mainlander, had a great deal of local power. They combined former Taiwanese peasants with former Taiwanese landlords. The government agency that helped them most was the Joint Committee on Rural Reconstruction, two of whose five members were American technocrats. This structure was not perfectly

---

[13]Larry L. Burmeister, *Research, Realpolitik, and Development in Korea: The State and the Green Revolution* (Boulder: Westview, 1988), 153.

coordinated, but it tended to make well-informed decisions because it sought diverse kinds of policy information. The result for rural output and wealth was an excellent performance — even better than had been predicted, except by a few who counted the political structure as an economic factor. Taiwan's agricultural growth in the ten years after land reform was nearly five percent per year, compounding. This is an exceptionally high rate, over a whole decade and sizeable place, for agriculture anywhere.

The industrial results of land reform were far more important. The decentralized policy created rural wealth that became the basis for new domestic commercial and industrial markets. The most immediate need of the island's government was to find political support among the non-mainlander majority. Over 99 percent of all agriculturalists (either tenants or landlords) were Taiwanese. Land reform would have been politically more difficult and less fruitful for the KMT government, if its connections to wealthy Taiwanese had been closer. The subethnic separation, spurred dramatically by the tragedies of 1947, was prerequisite to implementation of the 1953 reform. But this coin has another side that has frequently been overlooked: land reform would have been economically less fruitful, and politically less effective for the KMT's hard task of garnering some political legitimacy among Taiwanese, if the mainlander government had been able to interfere more effectively in local rural networks.

Separation works both ways. Usual official rhetoric about "high" and "low" "levels" of government obscure the fact that power (in any objective, behavioral sense) is often exercised upward in administrative systems, not just downward. It is seldom in the interest of local leaders to advertise the respects in which they trump central leaders, but they often do so. Local bosses can usually hide their acts, just as central government leaders can often succeed in screening from public scrutiny the actions they wish to keep secret.

Taiwanese farmers who remained on the land benefitted when they could find leaders for the local agricultural associations. This was due in part to the increasingly urban and decreasingly rural interests of formerly rich farmers and landlords. Many villages in Taiwan during the 1950s became "virtually leaderless."[14] Village mayoralties were elective, but many of the ambitious, active, and wealthy members of rural Taiwanese communities had by that time left to live in cities, sometimes frittering away the capital they had received in compensation for their land, but sometimes investing it. The remaining, traditional village heads did not command much local respect. These years also saw broad changes in the structure of lineage relations as political networks.

Agriculture and animal husbandry were not ended by the advent of industry. As the next chapter about East China also shows, green revolution, rural industrialization, and local changes of political networks are one and the same process. Agriculture in Taiwan became better financed, and it used more inanimate power. In Hsinhsing, Changhua County, industrialization meant the end of water buffaloes. It meant that few families still kept pigs and chickens (although earlier, practically every village household had its own swine and poultry). Gradually the main hog-raising household in this village became a specialized enterprise, raising a large herd as a business venture. Duck farming became the modernized speciality of another village household. Rice and vegetables were grown for markets by still other specialized households. The advent of chemical fertilizers meant that compost pits (which had been scattered all over the village before industrialization) slowly disappeared.

Peasant culture changed but was not extinguished by the move of most workers out of fields. The initial effect of economic modernity was to finance traditions better than before. In Hsinhsing, for example, industrialization did not eliminate the Earth God Temple; on the contrary, that shrine was greatly enlarged and profusely decorated. The new entrepreneurs of this village also built a gaudy new temple to Dashigong, a locally revered divinity, complete with colored plastic dragon roof finials pointing up to the sky. No religion stirs more open enthusiasm than the syncretic beliefs of old-style south Chinese farmers. The new temples showed traditional peasant culture with

---

[14]Bernard Gallin, "Land Reform in Taiwan: Its Effect on Rural Social Organization and Leadership," *Human Organization* 22 (Summer 1963), 109–12.

untraditional vengeance. They could be financed best after agriculture supplied no more than a tenth of the villagers' income.[15]

Such changes were inseparable from later developments that were based on institutions established during the land reform. For example, farmers' associations gradually encouraged land consolidation, to change irregularly shaped fields into rectangles with straight sides. This allowed easier tilling by machines. Herbicides became common, along with chemical fertilizers and tube wells that were run by gasoline or electric power. Rural machine shops to repair these implements trained ex-peasants as workers in rural factories. Short-stalk, high-yield rice was also introduced in Taiwan later, but most of these other changes preceded it.

The financial credit required by the new agronomy did not raise the long-term indebtedness of farmers in Taiwan (as it did in the Philippines), because they rather than traditional landlords made the production decisions. The size of the farming workforce plummeted. The output from fields, however, did not fall for many years. Factories, flats, and stores slowly took land that had earlier been paddies. Many of Taiwan's patterns are similar to those that appeared also on the Chinese mainland. But the process appeared later there than on Taiwan. The communists were more confident of their control of a popular majority — and less conscious of technological potentials in the rural economy (despite their Marxism). Their political needs were less monotonic and did not become evident until the early 1970s, as the next chapter shows.

The overall economic results in Taiwan were spectacular, because it is easier to make industry grow more quickly than agriculture. The land reform was a crucial basis for creating an extremely prosperous economic sector of small factories. Taiwan's landlords got less compensation during the land reform than they would have received if an ordinary market for their acreage had existed. But the industrial stocks they received as compensation encouraged some of Taiwan's

---

[15]Rita S. Gallin and Bernard Gallin, "Hsin Hsing Village, Taiwan: From Farm to Factory," in *Chinese Landscapes: The Village as Place*, Ronald G. Knapp, ed. (Honolulu: University of Hawaii Press, 1992), 281–87; and for a picture of the resplendent Dashigong Temple of 1989, 290–92.

leading rural families to go into business instead. New resources and occupational structures created new local power. The rural elite — i.e., most of the leaders of most of the islanders — were industrialized and urbanized by this land reform.

POLITICAL MODELS OF DEVELOPMENT: THE TAIWAN VARIANT

A conventional view of East Asian economic development is that the state leads it. Chalmers Johnson's book about the Japanese Ministry of International Trade and Industry, and its predecessor institutions back to the 1920s, shows the applicability of a state-dirigiste explanation for the rise of Asia's first major modern economy.[16] A strength of that book is its historical analysis of specific institutional developments in a specific country over time. Because nations' trajectories differ, however, lessons from one place are difficult to transfer elsewhere. Taiwan, China, Thailand, and the Philippines (as well as other big Asian countries such as India and South Korea) each has its own institutions that are "path dependent" on the evolution of its own norms and situations over time.[17]

The Republic of China, as its government moved to Taiwan in 1950, retained a strongly presidential system. Chiang Kai-shek was not an emperor, but (like Mao, Deng, and their successors) he had a coterie of close advisors, including some with business pretensions or experience. So a "presidential residence faction," including figures such as Hsü Po-yuan and Yu Kuo-hua (two former governors of the ROC's central bank) were influential in economic decisions. The Chiangs used them to check bureaucratic ministries.[18]

---

[16]Chalmers A. Johnson, *MITI and the Japanese Miracle: The Growth of Industrial Policy, 1925–1975* (Stanford: Stanford University Press, 1982).

[17]Ye Min, *Embedded State: Foreigners, Diasporas, and the Economic Transitions of China and India* (Ph.D. Dissertation, Politics Department, Princeton University, 2007).

[18]Wu Yongping, "Rethinking the Taiwanese Developmental State," *China Quarterly* 183 (2004), 94–96; and Wu Yongping, *A Political Explanation of Economic Growth: State Survival, Bureaucratic Politics, and Private Enterprises in the Making of Taiwan's Economy, 1950–1985* (Cambridge: Harvard University Press, 2005).

Taiwan had a surfeit of economic agencies, and an alphabet soup of the usual kind was used to give them names. Readers may be able to decipher acronyms such as the MOF or MOEA without help, and there is no need here to dwell on the IDC, EDB, CUSA, CIECD, EPD, or BPD. Such agencies rose or fell in power, among the Taipei bureaucracies, depending on the links their heads had with the Chiangs. Economic experts trained in the U.S. were important in rural policy and in arranging aid from America during early years, but they were incompletely trusted for many other purposes in Chiang Kai-shek's presidential office. The effective structure was political, rather than rational in a Weberian sense.

This Taiwan pattern differed somewhat from Japan's dirigisme that was established under different conditions. The Taiwan prototype was more like the structure for economic choices on the mainland during the height of Deng's prestige, when he discussed major economic decisions with friends such as the economic magnate Chen Yun, often during their games of bridge. The central government's economic decision structure in Taiwan (or in China) during boom times was by no means the main generator of growth anyway.

Leaders of small and medium enterprises had that role. The main political impetus for industrial reform was unlike Japan's earlier, because it more clearly came from the power of local leaders. In order to satisfy Taiwan's majority, to optimize use of limited personnel, and to divert Taiwan's domestic bosses from government into business, the ROC regime had an interest in allowing industrialization in rural places that it could not monitor well.

During the island's early development of more diverse factories from 1956 to 1966, the growth rate of manufacturing was 7.2 percent in rural areas — but just 5.3 percent in urban areas. Places classified as rural provided almost half (46 percent) of all new manufacturing jobs.[19] These places only later became urbanized. As late as 1971, half

---

[19]Ian A. Skoggard, *The Indigenous Dynamic in Taiwan's Post-War Development: The Religious and Historical Roots of Entrepreneurship* (Armonk: Sharpe, 1996), 53.

of Taiwan's industrial and commercial firms, and 55 percent of the factories, were located in rural areas.[20]

Mainlanders under Chiang dominated Taiwan's government during the 1950s and 1960s. Officials from the Jiangnan area south of the Yangzi River near its mouth were especially important. (This area is south Jiangsu and Zhejiang, 'East China' as defined in the next chapter; Chiang himself was from Fenghua, Zhejiang.) As late as 1970, nearly three-fifths of the members of the most powerful political body on the island, the KMT's Central Standing Committee, came from three mainland provinces: Zhejiang, Jiangsu including Shanghai, and Hunan.[21]

These ROC officials wished to control but could not fully monitor local Taiwanese elites. More than in Japan or South Korea, the regime lacked close links to most private capital. Several researchers of developmental states have noticed this difference and have been surprised by it. Robert Wade "concludes that Taiwan meets Johnson's developmental state criterion of bureaucratic autonomy, but not the requirement of public-private cooperation." Peter Evans admits that Taiwan's "relative absence of links to private capital might seem to threaten the ability of the autonomous state to secure full information and count on the private sector for effective implementation."[22] Evans finds that, "Relations between the KMT state and private (mainly Taiwanese) entrepreneurs are distant, compared to the tight 'Korea Inc.' ties that bind the state and the *chaebol* together in Korea. The Taiwanese state unquestionably operates with a less dense set of public-private network ties than the Korean or Japanese versions of the developmental state."[23] The state and private sector were connected, but just loosely because the former was largely

---

[20]Rita S. Gallin and Bernard Gallin, "Hsin Hsing Village, Taiwan," 279.

[21]J. Bruce Jacobs, "Recent Leadership and Political Trends in Taiwan," *China Quarterly* 45 (January–March 1971), 138.

[22]These are quoted in Karl Fields, "Strong States and Business Organization in Korea and Taiwan," in *Business and the State in Developing Countries*, Sylvia Maxfield and Ben Ross Schneider, eds. (Ithaca: Cornell University Press, 1997), 123–24.

[23]Peter Evans, *Embedded Autonomy: States and Industrial Transformation* (Princeton: Princeton University Press, 1995), 56.

mainlander and the latter was almost entirely Taiwanese. Locals can be developmental, too.

Comparisons with Thailand's traditionally less pushy state, and with mainland China's much larger and even less monitorable political economy, show further aspects of the politics behind Taiwan's growth that earlier analogies to Japan or Korea missed. East Asian "tigers" are not all identical.

RESOURCE SHORTAGE ALSO SHAPED THE POLITICS OF INDUSTRIAL DEVELOPMENT

Taiwan's scant natural endowment — a resource shortage that is the opposite of a "resource curse" — means that economic change more immediately becomes political. Human labor is the prime production factor.[24] Growth in Taiwan is based on people and not much else. Soil on the island's western plains can grow rice, but the island's ground has practically nothing of value to mine from it. Economic geographer Roger Selya puts the matter bluntly: "Taiwan lacks any semblance of a mineral base."[25] One of the island's most important natural resources is marble. That rock is useful, but it is not in any country the foundation of a comprehensive modern economy. Small reserves of copper, coal, sulfur, and asbestos have been found, but the amounts are economically insignificant.

Energy sources are particularly scanty. The coal is available mainly in "thin, inaccessible seams." Hydroelectricity from the watershed of Taiwan's high mountains was tapped long ago by the Japanese, but the energy obtainable from water is small. Prospecting off the coast has not produced any notable amounts of oil. The important supplies of energy for Taiwan are foreign, especially Saudi Arabian. The ROC government has built several nuclear plants for electricity.[26]

---

[24]For statistics proving that "the resource curse" is not just an anecdote, see Michael L. Ross, "Does Oil Hinder Democracy?" *World Politics* 53 (April 2001), 325–61.

[25]Roger M. Selya, *The Industrialization of Taiwan: Some Geographic Considerations* (Jerusalem: Jerusalem Academic Press, 1974), 24.

[26]*Ibid.*, 66 and *passim*.

The island's main resource is its Taiwanese workforce. Chiang Kai-shek's authoritarian government, like its authoritarian Japanese predecessor, provided relatively good education for workers but did not allow effective unionization to raise wages as fast as productivity. The main method of industrialization was to organize people into units where they labored well at low cost. Foreign raw materials were shipped in when local ones were lacking. On this basis, capital has been attracted, both from abroad and from the growing domestic agricultural and commercial-industrial sectors.

To raise output, this gambit proved immensely successful. Building on a good infrastructure of roads, rail lines, ports, and electric grids first established under the Japanese, an industrial economy was started in the 1950s that could effectively absorb considerable amounts of American aid. Over US$4 billion of economic and military help came to Taiwan between 1949 and 1964. Just one-third of this was economic, but most of that arrived in the form of outright grants. The economic assistance amounted only to about US$10 per islander per year, but it averaged over 6 percent of the annual domestic product.[27] Economists have estimated that the island's actual 1964 net domestic product was 54 percent higher than it would have been without this help.[28]

Taiwan's economic planners in the 1950s had supported "import-substitution industrialization." (As the next chapter shows, the 1970s start of East China's boom was also mainly based on domestic markets, not on the export trade that came later.) By the early 1960s in Taiwan, with the end of American economic aid and the Kennedy administration's political distance from Chiang, ROC economists stressed the creation of "special economic zones" and promoted exports. This required Taiwan's allowance of imports — especially of raw materials because of the resource shortage.

---

[27]Richard S. Page, *Aiding Development: The Case of Taiwan, 1949-65* (Ph.D. dissertation, Politics Department, Princeton University, 1967), 177–78.

[28]See *Economic Development in Taiwan*, Kowie Chang, ed. (Taipei: Cheng Chung Book Co., 1968), 112; and the table in *Taiwan Statistical Data Book* (Taipei: ROC Statistical Bureau, 1976), 31.

EXPORT PROMOTION THEN SHAPES
THE POLITICS OF SME DEVELOPMENT

The profitability of these policies led to a proliferation of small and medium enterprises (SMEs). Many of these subcontracted for larger Taiwan exporters, if they did not export directly. But government financiers were reluctant to give these small firms monetary credit. Because all of Taiwan's banks were controlled by the state, the island's SMEs got capital mainly from each other: through traditional rotating-loan arrangements, underground banks, and lending clubs.[29]

The state did not "embed" itself in these firms; so they did not "embed" themselves in it. The relationship was relatively confrontational in comparison with most state-business links in developing countries. Susan Greenhalgh says it was "an outright struggle, in which the state has attempted to encourage mergers ... while family enterprises have sought to retain their independence by refusing to merge, employing illegal means to maintain profits (going underground, evading taxes, using loans to speculate in the real estate market) and moving transactions through informal channels to avoid government scrutiny."[30] State bureaucrats knew about these small firms but did little or nothing to help them because they could not control them. That encouraged the companies to engage in politics that were as informal as their economics.

During the decade before the oil-price rise of 1973, Taiwan enjoyed annual industrial growth averaging over 18 percent, with inflation for wholesale products running at only 1.7 percent. This was a truly extraordinary economic performance by any comparative standard, even at the medium-low-income "take-off" stage of industrial

---

[29] See Jane Kaufman Winn and Tang-Chi Yeh, "Relational Practices and the Marginalization of Law: Informal Financial Practices of Small Businesses in Taiwan," *Law and Society Review* 28:2 (1994), 193–232.

[30] Susan Greenhalgh, "Families and Networks in Taiwan's Economic Development," in *Contending Approaches to the Political Economy of Taiwan*, Edwin A. Winckler and Susan Greenhalgh, eds. (Armonk: Sharpe, 1988), 242, quoted also in the next source, to which this reference is owed.

development when (as China has more recently found) it is possible for economies to turn in spectacular records.[31]

Import substitution policies had been of limited use in Taiwan, because the island's domestic market was difficult to expand in many products suitable for assembly lines. Taiwan's economy was capitalist partly to engage the ideology of the Americans who protected it and imported from it. Politically, some liberalization allowed good economic careers for ambitious Taiwanese. Leaders of the subethnic majority could earlier have been more dangerous for the regime, if they had gone into politics instead. But Taiwan did not have a pure market economy. The government tried to guide capital accumulation by controlling credit and tariffs, and it had some success encouraging cartels to handle exports such as "textiles, canned mushrooms and asparagus, rubber, steel, paper products, and cement."[32] The dynamic sectors that produced many smaller commodities were separate from the state.

Taiwan's government helped exporters whose support it could co-opt by giving them credit, tax holidays, tariff reductions for equipment and inputs that could be re-exported, and wage-bill savings because martial law prevented unions. Strikes were banned. In Taiwan the rate of wage increases was lower, during the long boom, than in its main competitors South Korea, Hong Kong, and Singapore. Investment in education gave the island some research and development capabilities. A kind of cosmopolitanism emerged from the

---

[31]The classic comparative study of this phenomenon has a subtitle showing the strong influence of Josef Stalin on economic thinking: Walt W. Rostow, "The Take-Off into Self-Sustained Growth: A Non-Communist Manifesto," *Economic Journal* 66 (March 1956), 25–48. Amartya Sen and many other economists have noted the bell-shaped general relation between growth rates and per-capita incomes.

[32]Alice H. Amsden, "The State and Taiwan's Economic Development," in *Bringing the State Back In*, Peter Evans, *et al.*, eds. (Cambridge: Cambridge University Press, 1985), 90; see also 94–96. Amsden's later book, *The Rise of the Rest: Challenges to the West from Late-Industrializing Economies* (New York: Oxford University Press, 2001), contains further information from Taiwan, as well as some from China and Thailand, but it emphasizes heavy or state-led sectors and pays scant attention to sectors in which smaller nonstate firms predominated, although the latter grew more quickly.

island-state's precarious security situation, and this connected Taiwan with the major democracies to which its exports went. External security concerns and internal control of unions combined to make export promotion profitable. Taiwan's industrial structure, involving large government-associated companies that outsourced to many independent SMEs, emerged in this context of external and internal security arrangements.

Foreign ownership in Taiwan's economy was notable, but much of the island's participation in trade was initiated by domestic companies or domestic partners. Since the mid-1960s, industrial free ports called "Export Processing Zones" (EPZs) were established near several Taiwan cities, particularly Kaohsiung and Taichung. In these places, Taiwanese earned foreign exchange by exporting the value of their labor. (China adopted similar policies about two decades later, when 'Special Economic Zones' were established, to create the same syndrome on the mainland.) Industrial raw materials came from abroad, because the island lacked them, but they could be imported duty-free to the "EPZ" walled areas. Taiwanese workers made the products, which were directly exported. These operations were very profitable and increased the islanders' possibilities for employment.

Soon, however, most of Taiwan's exports were not produced in the special processing zones but were manufactured under similar legal arrangements whereby factories received tax and duty concessions for selling abroad. Small local firms, outside the EPZs, increasingly made semi-finished products for factories within the EPZ walls. The island's quick industrial growth in the 1960s and 1970s was also attributable to domestic sectors such as residential construction. Bricks, cement, and other products that are physically heavy for their value played important roles in Taiwan's (and China's and Thailand's) boom. An exclusive emphasis on exports would miss this fact.

Local rather than foreign capital was crucial in Taiwan's construction, textile, plastic, and food processing industries, as well as in services and parts manufactures for exports. Some firms were financed by multinational corporations, especially in electronics. Except for oil refineries and infrastructure, the state's capital was decreasingly important. Textiles were prominent among the industries that flourished early without much government help.

Taiwan's total real annual GNP growth rate throughout the 1960s was a very high 9.4 percent. It declined just a bit in the 1970s, to 8.6 percent. Taiwan's annual real GDP growth rate was 11 percent in 1965–73, and 8.1 percent in 1973–84.

The annual growth of exports in the 1960s was 23 percent; and in the 1970s, 31 percent. Industrial output grew in the 1970s at 16 percent per year.[33]

In 1973–74, a war in the Middle East hiked oil prices, causing a general recession of international trade. Taiwan's production and employment suffered. Real per-capita output declined during 1974 for the first time in most of the population's memory. Unemployment soared (by Taiwan standards) from 1 percent to nearly 3 percent of the workforce. The island's 1974 balance of payments was more than US$1 billion in the red. The long-term trend toward greater income equality among households on the island was temporarily reversed after 1973. But all of these indices recovered sharply by 1976, when global trade revived. Taiwan's rate of industrial growth rose to approach but not equal its previous high levels after the oil slump. (A later comparison with Thailand's more severe 1997 downturn will show some subsequent recovery too, but with comparable political angst.)

It is normal for economies to have slower growth as they approach high "first world" levels of per-capita income, after most of their people have moved from fields into factory or office jobs. In the mid-1960s, agriculture still employed 47 percent of the Taiwanese workforce; but by 1980, this portion was just 20 percent.[34] By 1976, industry accounted for 38 percent of Taiwan's GDP, with only 14 percent from agriculture, 12 percent in commerce, and fully 36 percent in

---

[33]Cheng Tun-jen, "Taiwan in Democratic Transition," in *Driven by Growth: Political Change in the Asia-Pacific Region*, James Morley, ed. (Armonk: M.E. Sharpe, 1993), 199.

[34]Thomas B. Gold, "Entrepreneurs, Multinationals, and the State," in *Contending Approaches to the Political Economy of Taiwan*, Edwin A. Winckler and Susan Greenhalgh, eds. (Armonk: Sharpe, 1988), 180.

other sectors including transport, services, and construction.[35] Much of the manufacturing sector was geared to exports, but Taiwan's domestic economy also boomed. The halcyon growth reduced farmers' importance in Taiwan's political economy, and it raised the relative importance of entrepreneurs.

"ETHNIC" COOPERATION DURING TAIWAN'S BOOM

In the mid-1970s, about one-third (33) of Taiwan's 106 largest business combines (*jituan*) were centered on a textile firm. Many companies had emerged by accumulating shares in the formerly Japanese corporations that had been distributed to landlords during Taiwan's land reform. Just four enterprises (Taiwan Cement, Taiwan Pulp and Paper, Taiwan Industry and Mining, and the Taiwan Agricultural and Forestry Company) accounted for most of the initial distribution.[36] Some ex-landowner recipients sold their shares, putting the capital into firms they could control. After the period of most striking development, by the mid-1970s, more Taiwanese than mainlanders headed large ROC corporations. Far more Taiwanese headed the small- and medium-sized firms that were still the main drivers of the island's economy. Mainlanders were overrepresented, relative to their part of the island's population, mainly in nonindustrial fields: 34 percent in "public administration and professionals," 22 percent in "transportation," and 82 percent in "the military, police, and national security."[37] But the private sector was, like the population, overwhelmingly Taiwanese.[38] The boom was in the economy, not in the central government.

---

[35]Hsiao Hsin-huang, *Government Agricultural Strategies in Taiwan and South Korea: A Macrosociological Assessment* (Taipei: Institute of Ethnology, Academia Sinica, 1981), 58.

[36]Thomas B. Gold, "Entrepreneurs, Multinationals, and the State," 185, also 188–91.

[37]Wei Yung, "The Modernization Process in Taiwan: An Allocative Analysis," *Asian Survey* 16 (March 1976), 262.

[38]See Lindy Li Mark, "Disjunct Growth and Small Industries in Taiwan," paper at the panel on Small Enterprises in China, Association for Asian Studies Annual Meeting, Toronto, 1976.

From 1964 to 1987, at least one quarter of all business credit "within the financial system" of Taiwan came from the curb market.[39] Informal financing for the island's private enterprises was estimated above 35 percent. If commercial paper and loans from nonregistered institutions were included, the portion of informal credit over these decades would be even higher. Chiang Kai-shek's state gave practically no loans to small Taiwanese businesses.

Among tillers, the object of official policy was to make them dependent on the regime, especially during local elections that the American protectors liked to see. Government-controlled banks supplied two-thirds of all credit to farmers. Much of this money was returned to the party-state, however, because it was spent for fertilizers whose manufacture was a KMT monopoly. The price of a fertilizer like ammonium sulfate was about 40 percent higher in Taiwan than on the global market. Most of the farmers paid in rice, rather than money. State purchase prices for rice were so low that the government's implicit revenue from this rigged grain market exceeded its total intake from all income taxes until 1963.[40] Partly because traditional taxes were often in rice, and partly because farmers and their main crop were far easier to monitor than were manufacturing or commercial businesses, Taiwanese who left fields to start SMEs were able to separate themselves from KMT government control.

As Wu Yongping explains, "The real lacuna in the statist account of Taiwan's industrial success is the outstanding performance of small and medium industries."[41] He writes that in Taiwan, "big businesses are upstream suppliers of intermediate goods and services, responding to demands generated by manufacturing networks of small- and

---

[39]Officially the portion was 25.28 percent, but such exactitude is surely wrong, because at least some "curb" financing was unregistered. Culture matters even though Samuel Huntington says so, and the scientistic penchant for hundredths of percents is particularly strong in works from the Confucian culture area. Shea Jia-Dong and Ya-Hwei Yang, "Taiwan's Financial System and the Allocation of Investment Funds," in *The Role of the State in Taiwan's Development*, Joel D. Aberbach, *et al.*, eds. (Armonk: Sharpe, 1994), 202.
[40]Alice H. Amsden, "The State and Taiwan's Economic Development," 86.
[41]Wu Yongping, "Rethinking the Taiwanese Developmental State," 97.

medium-sized firms that, in turn, respond to the demands of buyers external to the producing networks .... Taiwan's large enterprises are not organizing nodes in commodity chains."[42]

Taiwan's Leninist party, the KMT, was like that on the authoritarian mainland, but it was unlike the regimes in Thailand or the Philippines. It required that all business associations belong at least nominally to either of two institutions that the KMT tried to monitor: the National Federation of Industry, or else the National Federation of Commerce. The general secretaries of these two federations, from their foundings at least through the early 1990s, were always concurrently members of the KMT Central Standing Committee.[43] This theoretically tight organization did not mean, however, that all of Taiwan's businesses were branches of the party-state. The island's firms were subject to the ancient East Asian official love of registrations (*dengji*), which was apparently the federations' main role.

A traditional slogan, emphasizing the prestige of the state and the lowliness of commerce, held that "officials supervise and merchants manage" (*guandu shangban*). Taipei bureaucrats, however, could not comprehensively monitor the most profitable sector, the SMEs. The federations did not lobby the government to do anything that was not in the regime's inherent interest. Their main functions were symbolic. Once registration was done, the government's majestic authority had been recognized. Business continued. Money was made. Most Taiwanese kept out of noneconomic national power systems, partly because they could lead in more profitable local power systems.

A few big capitalists (Taiwanese as well as mainlanders) were chosen with approval from presidents Chiang Kai-shek and later Chiang Ching-kuo to join the island's most power conclave, the Central Standing Committee of the KMT. The state was particularly close to their firms, but it was distant from the multitude of SME leaders.[44] Doner and Hershberg refer to the "'small kingdom' mentality of

---

[42]*Ibid.*, 98.
[43]Karl Fields, "Strong States and Business Organization in Korea and Taiwan," 144.
[44]Wu Yongping, "Rethinking the Taiwanese Developmental State," 109.

Taiwan's lower-tech SMEs" and call these firms "molecular."[45] Micro-science analogies are common in discourse about such structures. (Donnithorne later called them 'cellular' in China.[46]) One reason why the KMT maintained its autonomy from private businesses was that it did not need them financially. The KMT was (and still is) exceptionally rich. It enjoyed "financial independence on a scale unheard of in any other representative democracy."[47]

The government *was* a major business, at least until the less wealthy Democratic Progressive Party (DPP) took the presidency. Each year, as late as the early 1990s, the KMT's companies paid it dividends of 400 billion Taiwan dollars. If vote-buying had remained easy on Taiwan as the electorate became better-educated, the KMT would never have lost. Its wealth made it, unlike most parties elsewhere, independent of business donations.[48]

Taiwan's boom slowly affected this situation, reducing the regime's economic clout. Government companies accounted for 57 percent of Taiwan's industrial production in 1952, but only 19 percent in 1975 (by which time, in real terms, the amount was 20 times greater).[49] Taiwan's state-owned enterprises, disproportionately run by mainlanders for some years, were mostly in upstream production. Large private enterprises owned by Taiwanese sold to the island's domestic market, and the party-state could co-opt these

---

[45]Richard Doner and Eric Hershberg, "Flexible Production and Political Decentralization in the Developing World: Elective Affinities in the Pursuit of Competitiveness," *Studies in Comparative International Development* 34:1 (Spring 1999), 57.

[46]Audrey Donnithorne, "Comment: Centralization and Decentralization in China's Fiscal Management," *China Quarterly* 66 (June 1976), 328–39.

[47]Chu Yun-han, "The Realignment of Business-Government Relations and Regime Transition in Taiwan," in *Business and Government in Industrializing Asia*, Andrew MacIntyre, ed. (Ithaca: Cornell University Press, 1994), 132.

[48]The originally Western concept "party" deserves more careful analysis in political science. This word is used for sharply variant institutions. That insight, as applied to China in particular, is reportedly the topic of the next major book by Prof. Zheng Yongnian.

[49]Alice H. Amsden, "The State and Taiwan's Economic Development," 92.

relatively few Taiwanese tycoons, who were recruited into the KMT. These did not threaten the regime. But SMEs, being far more numerous, were harder to oversee. Although "the rise of the SMEs in export markets was not the intent of the state," small firms soon supplied the needs of many diverse buyers.[50] This created new bases for local politics in Taiwan.

SMALL FIRMS AS TAIWAN'S DYNAMO

As Taiwan's boom developed in its fastest decades, the 1960s and 1970s, SMEs added larger rather than smaller portions of the island's total value added. SMEs' dominance of production increased over time. By 1971, of the island's total manufacturing workers, the portion in factories with more than 500 employees was down to 36 percent. By 1986, however, that portion in these large factories was halved, to just 18 percent. This change occurred even as the total number of Taiwan's manufacturing workers more than doubled, from 1.2 to 2.7 million.

Similarly, if this same phenomenon is measured in terms of the distribution of factories rather than of workers, in 1971 only 0.8 percent of factories on Taiwan had more than 500 workers; but by 1986, the portion was halved to a miniscule 0.4 percent.[51] This was not an economy that large firms dominated.

The trend in the Philippines was the opposite. On that nearby archipelago, as later chapters show, more than half of all manufacturing workers were in factories having more than 200 employees.[52] Only one-fifth were in small plants with ten or fewer employees.

---

[50]Wu Yongping, "Rethinking the Taiwanese Developmental State," 110 and *passim*.

[51]Taiwan reported 44,000 factories in 1971, up to 119,000 in 1986. Hsiung Ping-Chun, *Living Rooms as Factories: Class, Gender, and the Satellite Factory System in Taiwan* (Philadelphia: Temple University Press, 1996), 30.

[52]These are 1983 figures in Gustav Ranis, Frances Stewart, and Edna Angeles-Reyes, *Linkages in Developing Economies: A Philippine Study* (San Francisco: ICS Press, 1990), 37.

The portion of workers in middle-sized Taiwan plants (20 to 99 workers) rose considerably, 1971–86, from 20 to 37 percent.[53] This employment structure was important both economically and politically. More medium-sized plants meant more powerful autonomous bosses late in the boom. Because workers in such firms can get quasi-managerial assignments, it also meant more breeding grounds for new entrepreneurs.

The burgeoning SME sector in Taiwan was better linked to the rural industrial and agrarian workforce than, for example, in the Philippines. When small- and mid-size Taiwan firms grew in number, they easily employed many who had been peasants. This pattern continued into later decades, even as the portion of laborers in Taiwan's agriculture shrank.

Small firms began the boom in Taiwan's economy, but they certainly did not disappear in later decades as growth slowed and the economy branched into more diversified production. Nearly 900,000 SMEs were on the government register in the mid-1990s, and this group hired an average of 40 or 50 workers, with their capital typically coming from the members of a single family.[54] As much as four-fifths of all Taiwan's employees now work for SMEs, which account at least for half of Taiwan's aggregate value of exports.

NONSTATE AND STATE CONNECTIONS BETWEEN SMEs

Small and medium businesses in Taiwan are the main contributors to exports and domestic markets alike. They are the most frequent employers on the island. They earn most of the foreign exchange. But as Cheng and Haggard write, "partly because of the social distance that separated the ruling party from the private sector,

---

[53]Shieh Gwo-shyong, *"Boss" Island: The Subcontracting Network and Microentrepreneurship in Taiwan's Development* (New York: Lang, 1992), 35–39. Shieh notes that the survey of enterprises, as distinct from that of employees, "underestimates the workers hired by the smaller units of production, especially those units that do not register with the state" (p. 39).

[54]Gerald A. McBeath, *Wealth and Freedom*, 13.

the regime largely avoided the strategy of politically organizing business .... Small- and medium-sized businesses have maintained their independence from the KMT regime."[55]

They set up their own larger organizations. No firms can prosper separate from business networks, but nonstate (not just government) actors are crucial in these. A group of economists notes that in Taiwan, "small family firms could not survive by themselves. They existed within a network of subcontracting relationships woven between the different sizes of firms. Medium- to large-scale firms played the central role in this net. They got the orders from foreign buyers and contracted these jobs down through the pyramid."[56] Not all demand for products was foreign, however, and it would be equally true to say that large firms in these networks could not have survived without small ones. The latter often worked for multiple big companies, to avoid dependence on just one. SME bosses were careful to retain their operational freedoms.

Large-volume orders spurred horizontal links between SMEs, which cooperated to fill them on time. "The successful central firm needs to be able to get orders continuously, however. As long as there were enough orders to ensure the profits of subcontractors, subcontractors were willing to do their best — that is, to work overtime, to learn new techniques, to improve quality, and to meet urgent deadlines of the parent [or central/expanding SME] company."[57] Loose conglomerates of this kind could also cooperate in purchasing materials for their members. They disseminated information about the traits of products that markets demanded, and they provided legal and other professional services to members. Business success required nonstate and nonpublic political organization.

---

[55]Cheng Tun-jen and Stephan Haggard, "Regime Transformation in Taiwan: Theoretical and Comparative Perspectives," in *Political Change in Taiwan*, Cheng Tun-jen and Stephan Haggard, eds. (Boulder: Lynne Rienner, 1992), 9.

[56]*Industrialization and the State: The Changing Role of the Taiwan Government in the Economy, 1945–1998*, Li-min Hsueh, Chen-kuo Hsu, and Dwight H. Perkins, eds. (Cambridge: Harvard Institute for International Development, 2001), 93.

[57]*Ibid.*, 94–95.

Some industrial groups or "relationship enterprises" (*guanxi qiye*) slowly developed into large, loose corporations that achieved incipient name recognition in both international and Taiwan domestic markets. Formosa Plastics, Tatung, and Evergreen "did not start out large ... nor were close ties to government investment programs the critical ingredient in their success .... These large business groups were simply the most successful of the leading medium-scale enterprises."[58] Most of them developed from family firms or from networks of such firms that could help each other.

Tainanbang Spinners, for example, had its origins in the Hou family's clothing store in Tainan as early as the 1920s. Members of a local Wu lineage were employed in that store too, later departing to found their own company while retaining friendly links to the Hou family.[59] The KMT, after its disastrous political performance in the late 1940s, badly needed political allies in south Taiwan. So its local cadres were happy to cooperate with a Wu family kinsman, who expanded various loosely connected firms that had been founded by both the Hou and Wu clans. By the late 1960s, this conglomerate moved into food processing, becoming the President Enterprises, a collection of 27 separate firms run by various members of related lineages. This became the largest food company in Taiwan, although its legal and managerial structure remained flexible.

Taiwan's "relationship enterprises" have been built with less government guidance than Japan's *zaibatsu* or Korea's *chaebol*. Some, such as Tainan Spinning/President Enterprises described above, have origins among Taiwanese going back into the Japanese period, while others such as the Formosa Plastics Group began in the 1950s. Formosa Plastics began when a Taiwanese lumber store owner named Wang Yung-ch'ing helped a construction company founder named Chao P'ing-chen, who was a mainlander. Chao began ordering lumber from Wang. Chao was a native of Jiangsu, with good government

---

[58] *Ibid.*, 97.
[59] Research by Numazaki Ichiro, "The Tainanbang: The Rise and Growth of a Banana-bunch Shaped Business Group in Taiwan," *The Developing Economies* 31:4 (1993), 485–510, is reported in *ibid.*, 98–99.

connections, and he helped Wang become Taiwan's "plastics king." This aid came initially from an independent mainlander entrepreneur, rather than as an initiative of the government.

The Chientai Cement Company illustrates yet another pattern of networking, in which Taiwan's party-state was involved in ownership. Li Ch'ung-lien was a member of the KMT's Finance Committee and a "good friend" of Chen Ch'ing-hsiao, the father of Ch'en You-hao, an entrepreneur. The KMT reached out to the Ch'ens, father and son, apparently because of their ability to make a profit in a firm named Tuntex. This cement company became a joint enterprise of the KMT and Tuntex.[60]

An entrepreneur's connections and reputation are the sociopolitical capital most necessary for such a start-up. Most SMEs, unlike the firms described above that became large, had no close connection with the state. In Taiwan, even as late as the 1990s, one-third of all enterprises still obtained their founding loans from friends or kin. Another quarter obtained funds from rotating credit cooperatives.[61] A similar pattern will be described during East China's boom.[62]

FAMILY HEAD AUTONOMY AS AN EXISTENTIAL ECONOMIC MOTIVE

Sociologist Shieh Gwo-shyong, in his book *Boss Island*, explores the motives of Taiwanese entrepreneurs, whose nonstate subcontracting networks among myriad small firms spurred the island's grassroots growth. Governments, which are often internally divided on policies, sometimes offer incentives for nonstate industrialization to begin. But if researchers look at official policies alone, they miss most of the

---

[60]Numazaki Ichiro, "The Role of Personal Networks in the Making of Taiwan's *Guanxiqiye* (Related Enterprises)," in *Asian Business Networks*, Gary G. Hamilton, ed. (Berlin: de Gruyter, 1996), 71–86.

[61]Gilles Guiheux, "Enterprises, Entrepreneurs, and Social Networks in Taiwan," in *Politics in China: Moving Frontiers*, Françoise Mengin and Jean-Louis Rocca, eds. (New York: Palgrave Macmillan, 2002), 193.

[62]See Kellee S. Tsai, *Back-Alley Banking: Private Entrepreneurs in China* (Ithaca: Cornell University Press, 2002).

ways in which industrial bosses and workers reproduce themselves. Analysts can bring the most relevant agents, the leaders of small collectivities, 'back into' theories of this change. The picture of what happened is incomplete until these actors are included. Shieh writes that, "the subcontracting network, which is prevalent in Taiwan ... has created conditions under which consent [for the whole system] among workers is manufactured as they seize the opportunities generated by the subcontracting system to become their own 'bosses.'"[63]

A 2004 poll of Taiwanese who used the internet (not a random sample, but an interesting one) suggested that more than seven-tenths of the respondents "were considering starting their own businesses." With less than US$50,000 of capital, many of them thought, they would be able at least to start a franchise and make money. This would let them obtain "self-fulfillment."[64]

When a researcher, in the course of fieldwork, helped a driver pick up products that had been subcontracted for manufacture in homes, the driver spontaneously asked him, "Are you going to open another workshop?"[65] A popular assumption was that everybody naturally wanted to be his or her own boss. The phrase "black hands" (*heishou*) in Taiwan was complimentary; it meant manual employees who worked hard and got grease on their fingers: "Black hands become their own bosses."

The will to be one's own boss (*laoban*) could not be distinguished from a desire to get out of agriculture and into the modern labor market. As Ian Skoggard writes, "rural families responded to the great demand for industrial labor by sending their sons and daughters to factories in cities like Taipei and Kaohsiung. Some years later, the younger generation would come back, knowledgeable about

---

[63]Looking briefly at Korea, Shieh does not see the same pattern there as he finds in Taiwan. Specifically South Chinese entrepreneurial traditions (not 'Confucian families' more generally) may well be responsible for what he finds, and for what has occurred also in Sino-Thai enterprises, for example. Cf. Shieh Gwo-shyong, *"Boss" Island*, 14 and 20.

[64]Anon., "Poll: 70 Percent Want to Start Own Businesses to Pursue Fortune, Self-Fulfillment," *Taiwan Update* 5:5, May 10, 2004, 9.

[65]Shieh Gwo-shyong, *"Boss" Island*, 175.

manufacturing processes and with business contracts, and use their families' savings to set up their own factories." Anthropologist Skoggard even finds resonances between the routines of assembly line production and the rituals of the Yiguan Dao religion that flourishes among Taiwanese.[66] However applicable this particular interpretation may be, ideas of multiplicity and prosperity (many sons, many oranges on a lunar new year tree, many official awards, many coins) are commonly seen virtues in the syncretic Chinese rural religion. They are at least consistent with the excesses of modernity.

The most relevant units socializing such norms were families, not just businesses. A father or boss typically used economic resources to back up his decisions about what wives would do, what children would study, whom offspring would marry, and where they would live. Many SMEs on Taiwan (as on the mainland) are petty tyrannies. "As chief property owner, chief breadwinner, chief boss in the family business, and chief of the family, a father had many sanctions with which to enforce his will. Recalcitrant family members could find their salaries cut or their jobs eliminated."[67] Entrepreneurs of course have different personalities, but politics within families has often

---

[66]Ian A. Skoggard, *The Indigenous Dynamic in Taiwan's Postwar Development*, 133, and on 156 he claims that, "Yiguan Dao is the East's answer to the Protestant ethic: the absolute transcedentality of both Dao and the Puritan God, by default, confers on all things a singularity, authenticity, and equivalency." This is hard to prove, but some Chinese "little traditions" (to use Redfield's classic phrase) have echoes with modern means of time and work management. See also a classic on the social psychology by which peasants become workers: Alex Inkeles and David Smith, *Becoming Modern: Individual Change in Six Developing Countries* (London: Heinemann, 1974). In order to assert a relationship between elements of culture and styles of behavior, it is not necessary to assert that any culture is internally consistent, but only that actors understand some of their activities as supported by at least some of the "symbols" compatible with their identity. Practically no economists or political scientists admit this, because they have careerist reasons not to read the epistemology presented by anthropologists. That phenomenon, based on an ideology in Mannheim's sense, is explicable in terms of a syndrome of academic politics that has no intellectual status whatsoever.

[67]Susan Greenhalgh, "De-Orientalizing the Chinese Family Firm," *American Ethnologist* 21:4 (1994), 758.

been structured by patriarchs' control of wealth. The units that organized Taiwan's prosperity are hierarchal, and they take one of the several forms to which Chinese have been traditionally prone. Any culture that has been useful to many people in varying situations over centuries must provide inconsistent choices, even though none of them is formless or random. Predictable forms in Chinese corporate structure have been found in organizations with many kinds of functions.[68]

Evidence from three different Taiwanese villages (Hsinhsing, K'unshen, and Tingts'un) shows that sharp differences between the economic bases of villages do not lessen the mutual aid that is expected between brothers in a family. These three villages had, respectively, paddy rice, fishing, and mixed-crop/sugarcane economies. They were on different parts of the island. Yet all three "subscribed to the Confucian ideal of the extended family ... and have the same desire to imitate the elite style of life ... that the Chinese gentry have." These norms remained, even though the villagers no longer lived in extended families as their sources of livelihood became more diverse.[69] Booms finance such norms, even as the new resources come from stores or factories.

This is not to say that family organizations that were modally important in Taiwan's (or China's) economy never changed. Lineages (*zu*) in Taiwan, not just in the communist mainland, became less important economically and residentially after rural industry arrived. Many villagers spent increasing amounts of time away from their ancestral homes, in factories, schools, or the dormitories attached to them. Acquaintances made in those places diluted traditional

---

[68]Steven Sangren, "Traditional Chinese Corporations: Beyond Kinship," *Journal of Asian Studies* 43:3 (1984), 391–415.

[69]Chen Chung-min, *Upper Camp: A Study of a Chinese Mixed Cropping Village in Taiwan* (Taipei: Institute of Ethnology, Academia Sinica, 1977), 194. This study of Tingts'un (Upper Camp) also cites Bernard Gallin, *Hsin Hsing, Taiwan: A Chinese Village in Change* (Berkeley: University of California Press, 1966); and Norma Diamond, *K'un Shen: A Taiwan Village* (New York: Holt, Rinehart, and Winston, 1969). For the best "read" about Taiwan, see Margery Wolf, *The House of Lim* (New York: Appleton, Century, Crofts, 1968).

commitments to lineages. When many workers or youths could come home, for example in evenings or on Sundays, the center of life was increasingly the nuclear family, not the lineage hall.[70]

In a suggestive survey of ten small Taiwan companies where interviews could be made, the male family head was also head of the firm (*laoban*). Sons were usually part of the firm too, and wives in about half of the cases. The number of family members in these small businesses was higher than in larger ones, which were surveyed separately.[71]

Economic advantages have been found especially for stem and joint rather than nuclear families. A family company's leadership is easy to structure unambiguously, with a patriarch or matriarch at the top and department heads or foremen in younger generations. Where the incentives to be one's own boss (*dang laoban*) are especially strong, as in Taiwan or southern Zhejiang, family members are less likely to split from one another on economic grounds alone. Secrecy and trust are easier to maintain, if the organization is a family. A group can take risks more easily than an individual. It can involve many members and spread the dangers of loss widely. More members can gather more information about markets, technologies, and competitors. If a firm grows and diversifies, responsibility for its parts can be distributed among kin. Especially where economies of scale are not crucial, or where the strength of collective commitment affects profits, family firms do well.[72]

Standard economists are taught to reject cultural arguments. A good example is an econometric study of Taiwan savings, which says curtly that,

> We interpret a great number of small- and medium-sized (SMEs) to be caused in Taiwan by the low amount of fixed capital needed for setting up low-tech industries. By the World Bank's definition of an SME, where the

---

[70]Rita S. Gallin and Bernard Gallin, "Hsin Hsing Village, Taiwan," 291–92.

[71]Susan Greenhalgh, "De-Orientalizing," 753.

[72]See Susan Greenhalgh, "Families and Networks in Taiwan's Economic Development," in *Contending Approaches to the Political Economy of Taiwan*, Edwin A. Winckler and Susan Greenhalgh, eds. (Armonk: Sharpe, 1988), 231–36.

number of employees is fewer than 100, SMEs account for more than 98 percent of Taiwan's enterprises in the 1961–85 period. We ignore the possibility that the great number of SMEs reflects a unique desire by Taiwanese to be their own bosses as far as possible.[73]

These intellectuals argue, explicitly above, for ignorance of an interpretation they suggest as possibly valid. Most economists see no problem with research procedures that give priority to premises over observations. The difficulty is that their premises may be wrong. Such analytic blinders come from a professional ideology that any serious social scientist should examine as a social phenomenon deserving of explanation; they do not come from the research issue at hand.[74]

FAST GROWTH WITH INCOME LEVELLING: A RESULT OF SME-STATE SEPARATION

Small Taiwanese firms flourished luxuriantly, and they readily absorbed and trained new workers. The government in South Korea, by contrast, ran a different kind of developmental state. It arranged low-cost loans for groups of firms (*chaebol*) when they could establish brandname exports. This policy of easy loans encouraged capital- rather than labor-intensive industries. But in Taiwan, firms got no easy credit, so they were averse to substituting machines for people unless the machines were sure to raise profits.[75]

---

[73]Woo Wing Thye and Liang-Yn Liu, "Taiwan's Persistent Trade Surpluses: The Role of Underdeveloped Financial Markets," in *The Role of the State in Taiwan's Development*, Joel D. Aberbach, *et al.*, eds. (Armonk: Sharpe, 1994), 99–100.

[74]About ideologies, see Karl Mannheim, *Ideology and Utopia: An Introduction to the Sociology of Knowledge* (London: Routledge, 1936). This is the classic study of ways in which thinkers handily hide from themselves parts of what they know, because of immediate (e.g., careerist) benefits of doing so. A major and sometimes useful social science, neoclassical economics, too often has become such an ideology. Particular economists are not so blameworthy; but collectively, most of them are. Socialized "normal science" (to use T. Kuhn's phrase) restricts the expansion of knowledge, which is authentic science.

[75]For this detail, see Leo Paul Dana, *Entrepreneurship in Pacific Asia: Past, Present, and Future* (Singapore: World Scientific, 1999), 157.

Therefore Taiwan's growth, unlike that of most other booming economies, was accompanied by improving distributions of income. Expansion went with equity. The island's Gini coefficients rose, showing more equality, even as per-capita income also did. Taiwan thus violated the "Kuznets" pattern, found in most developing economies: a correlation of fast growth with increasing income stratification.[76] The island had, in this regard, a much better-than-typical development.

The prominence of family SMEs without much government support was the key to Taiwan's improving equalization of assets. States are not the only power systems that can raise or lower welfare. In practice, the KMT's insouciance, letting markets set interest rates, gave small firms more access to credit. Also, Taiwan's government supported general education and infrastructure, and on many parts of the island these external economies attracted investment with no need to subsidize interest.

Small and medium enterprises were important in Taiwan's boom, but they are also important in all "first world" economies. SMEs are not a transitional phenomenon. They are crucial, especially for job creation (and for links between jobs and votes), in most rich economies too. In the OECD countries, SMEs contribute 40 to 80 percent of employment and 30 to 70 percent of GDP (depending largely on how the term 'SME' is defined).[77] Historians and other social scientists tend to write mainly about famous moguls and large companies. Economists tend to downplay firm size as an analytic category (as most of them downplay country size too). Yet SMEs contribute mightily to growth, especially during periods when economies begin booming but also after they become "developed" and expand more slowly.

Shops, like factories, add to economic productivity, and commercial profits are often ploughed into industries. A group of econometricians

---

[76]Simon Kuznets, "Economic Growth and Income Inequality," *American Economic Review* 45:1 (1955), 1–28.

[77]Liu Li-Wei, *The Growth and Transformation of Small and Medium Enterprises in Taiwan: Reassessment and Analysis from a Spatial Perspective* (Ph.D. Dissertation, Cornell University, January 2000), 6.

estimated that capital accumulation accounted for only about 20 percent of Taiwan's GDP growth between 1960 and 1990, but the prosperity came "thanks to an appreciable growth in the rate of domestic savings and a relatively efficient allocation of the savings towards investment." These particular economists also noticed that "cultural traits, a willingness to sacrifice for future generations" may have been a cause of the boom. They criticized "government intervention in the financial sphere," which "reduced the efficiency of the allocation of available savings, imposing on them criteria other than optimal return."

Aside from increased capitalization, they estimated that another 20 percent of Taiwan's boom came from "an increase in the total quantity of labor, mainly due to demographic trends." At least 40 percent came from improvements of total factor productivity, the "X-factor" whose explanations vary and often refer vaguely to improved technology and management, including local and national politics.[78] This was an empirically induced list of proximate factors for Taiwan's economic performance. The heavy weight of "total factor productivity" in this estimate suggests that much of the origin of Taiwan's boom is beyond the reach of mathematical economic theory, although it is refreshing to see some empirical economists trying to note the exogenous sociopolitical factors that determine rates of saving, investment, work, and risk.[79]

Economists have also been able to show that Taiwan's SMEs were more efficient than larger firms, e.g., in textiles, wood, metals, metal products, and some other manufactures. Larger companies had economies of scale only in chemicals. For firms with fewer than 100 employees, in many sectors the total factor productivity of these SMEs was at least as high as that of large firms.[80]

---

[78]Sébastien Dessus, Jia-Dong Shea, and Mau-Shan Shi, *Chinese Taipei: The Origins of the Economic "Miracle"* (Paris: OECD, 1995), 9–10.

[79]*Ibid.* For a comparison, see also Qian Yingyi, "How Reform Worked in China," in *In Search of Prosperity: Narratives on Economic Growth*, Dani Rodrik, ed. (Princeton: Princeton University Press, 2003), 297–333.

[80]See Susan Greenhalgh, "Families and Networks," 229.

Krugman has argued that a long-term weakness of growth among Asian "tigers" is a lack of attention to basic research and development.[81] Although a few large firms in Taiwan's computer industry, such as Acer, could afford much R&D, small firms generally did not. Yet 85 percent of Taiwan's computer firms were SMEs, and "their flexibility and capability gave the industry most of its dynamism, as they can adjust production quickly to changes in market trends."[82]

So Taiwan's SMEs were extremely aggressive in market research if not product research. Some analysts called them "guerrilla capitalists."[83] The SMEs were more important in Taiwan's export promotion than in that of either South Korea or Japan. Small Taiwan firms succeeded because of their Schumpeterian zest in finding new markets and sales methods, not because they had loans from the state or banks, or because they did new technical research except in merchandising. They did what they needed to do, and they certainly made money. Taiwan's SMEs inherited a spirit of commercial piracy that might be traced back to Zheng Chenggong (Koxinga). They were strong political bosses in local nonstate environments, whenever that was possible and profitable. They dealt with state elites sometimes and avoided them when necessary. Their loyalty was not to national collectives, although their success strengthened public institutions and bases for eventual further growth.

LOYALTY TO PROSPERITY

When the price of labor rose in Taiwan as the island's boom slowed, SMEs flocked across the Strait into the People's Republic. The ROC government had policies directing them to invest in Southeast Asia

---

[81]Krugman, Paul, "The Myth of Asia's Miracle: A Cautionary Fable," http://web. mit.edu/krugman/www/myth.html, seen March 20, 2007.

[82]Gerald A. McBeath, *Wealth and Freedom*, 125.

[83]Danny K.K. Lam and Ian Lee, "Guerrilla Capitalism and the Limits of Statist Theory," in *The Evolving Pacific Basin in the Global Political Economy: Domestic and International Linkages*, Cal Clark and Steven Chan, eds. (Boulder: Rienner, 1992), 107–24.

and non-Chinese countries.[84] They exploited mainland and other labor far more egregiously than companies from other countries did.[85] They exported most of the products to U.S. markets.

As profit potentials for Taiwan increased on the China mainland, small firms were the pioneers to make links with local cadres there, before large Taiwan companies were politically brave enough to do so. Seven-tenths of all registered corporations in Taiwan (the vast majority of which are SMEs) now have mainland investments. When large companies put capital in the PRC, their Taiwan subcontractors often moved with them, but most of the early cross-Strait investments came from Taiwan SMEs on their own very unofficial initiatives.

The Taipei government under the DPP was wary of this trend, which drained capital, talent, and technology from the island to environs that Taiwan's officials could not monitor. The communist government in Beijing is less wary but has mixed interests; capital from the "lost province" is welcomed, but local cadres in many mainland places give Taiwan SME investors sweet business deals that break rules for external investors that Beijing tries to set. The United States, whose markets take most of the products, becomes leery of the rising trade deficits with China that Taiwan capital finances — although some Americans realize this extremely profitable triangular relation may help avoid a Sino-American war over the island. American unionists avidly protest labor conditions in Taiwan-owned mainland factories — and they do so on good evidence, although American consumers just as avidly buy the products at low prices. Taiwan SME entrepreneurs deal with all governments only insofar as is needed to make money. A small Taiwanese factory managed to place three million plastic toys of *Tyrranosaurus Rex* in American retail outlets

---

[84]For more, see Lynn White, "Taiwan's External Relations: Identity vs. Security," in *The International Relations of Northeast Asia*, Samuel S. Kim, ed. (Lanham: Rowman & Littlefield, 2002), 301–30.

[85]Anita Chan, "Boot Camp at the Shoe Factory; Where Taiwanese Bosses Drill Chinese Workers to Make Sneakers for American Joggers," *Washington Post*, November 3, 1996, C1.

just a week before *Jurassic Park* opened.[86] These fierce little predators can symbolize the style of organization that made and hawked them.

The prowess of Taiwan's SMEs, as contrasted with the less fabulous performance of the island's large companies, is nowhere clearer than in the automobile industry. Unlike Japan or Korea, whose brand names (such as Toyota, Nissan, Honda, or Hyundai) are world famous, the largest Taiwan manufacturer (Yueloong) has scarcely been known off the island. By 1988, foreign companies had captured three-tenths of Taiwan's own car market. But auto parts, produced by small firms, have been a completely different story. In that field, Taiwan was then a net exporter of US$1.2 billion per year, which was roughly as valuable as exporting 220,000 completed small cars. In that year, Taiwan actually imported half as many (113,000) autos.[87] So if parts exports are included in the industry as a whole, Taiwan was a net exporter of autos — solely because of its SMEs.

The island's firms were small because Taiwan's transition from an agricultural to an industrial-commercial society had been shaped by KMT political needs after 1947 to involve as many islanders as possible in local business rather than government power networks. The boom was the economic result. Its most important local effect (money politics) is the topic of Chapter 6. The next two chapters show only somewhat similar but comparable origins in the rural land and autonomy politics of East China and Thailand that spurred booms there. Chapter 5 explores the local land and autonomy politics of the Philippines that have, thus far, brought a different result. Now please take a trip across the Taiwan Strait.

---

[86]Gerald A. McBeath, *Wealth and Freedom*, 146, fn. 13.

[87]Yueloong, Taiwan's first auto maker, was started by a mainlander from Shanghai, who later reached technology and ownership agreements with Nissan. Such pacts both helped and constrained several Taiwan car makers. The 29 percent foreign capture of Taiwan's own finished car market in 1988 was a particularly dismal showing because the island's tariff's on car imports remained high. See Chu Yun-han, "The State and the Development of the Automobile Industry in South Korea and Taiwan," in *The Role of the State in Taiwan's Development*, Joel D. Aberbach, *et al.*, eds. (Armonk: Sharpe, 1994), 126.

3

Political Roots of East China's Boom

Economic growth in China by the turn of the millennium became a wonder of the world. No academic had predicted it would be so fast. This flourishing was uneven; it began in rich rural and suburban parts of China's south and east. The political factors for it had more similarities with Taiwan's earlier growth than usual distinctions between communist and capitalist systems would suggest.

Both polities were authoritarian, albeit decreasingly so, during their eras of fastest boom. Small- and medium-sized enterprises, rather than state corporations, led the growth on both the island and the mainland. Traditionally rich areas benefitted far more than poor ones, and outlying villages were drained of young leaders. Land and agrarian arrangements, especially as new agricultural technologies became available and required machine shops, provided autonomy for the founders of rural industries on the mainland, as they had earlier on the island. In both places, peasants left fields to enter factories or commercial firms, and job creation was a crucial basis of local non-state politics. Those who remained in fields became more specialized farmers. Both regimes enjoyed widely accepted centralist ideologies, even though most behavior was outside central purview. New enterprises strengthened the government's tax bases over the long term — but they grew in part by violating official rules and evading taxes in the short run.

Deng Xiaoping was the cadre who could most easily admit in public the limited relevance of the central state to China's rural boom. He aided the boom by condoning rather than guiding it. Deng was honest when, in 1987, he met a group of Yugoslav visitors and confessed amazement at the rapid development of China's rural industries:

> Generally speaking, our rural reforms have proceeded very fast, and farmers have been enthusiastic. *What took us by surprise completely was the development of township and village industries....* This was not the achievement of our central government. Every year, township and village industries achieved 20 percent growth.... This was not something I had thought about. Nor had the other comrades. This surprised us.[1]

Deng reached for an ancient phrase to describe his astonishment: *yijun tujing* ('a strange army suddenly appeared from nowhere').

Impressive as the 20 percent annual growth that Deng specified would have been, the actual expansion of China's rural factories was quicker. In 1975, three years before reforms officially began, the output of these industries grew 33 percent. In 1976, it grew another 44 percent. Over the later decade from 1978 to 1987, the average annual growth of Chinese rural-industrial output was lower: 26 percent.[2] (Thereafter, the 1988–92 average annual growth was 32 percent.) The real "reform" of 1978 was a hesitant official confession of what had been transpiring for several years already. The rural-industrial aspect of China's behavioral "reforms" began at least six years before the official

---

[1] *Renmin ribao* (People's Daily) [hereafter *RMRB*], June 13, 1987. Emphasis added.
[2] See Dong Fureng, *Industrialization and China's Rural Modernization* (London: Macmillan, 1992), 3. By the mid-1990s, more than half of all Chinese industrial output was nonstate, largely in areas that had been classed as "rural" in the mid-1970s. Percentages throughout this book are rounded from the sources. In the 1978–87 decade, the annual output growth rate by value for private rural enterprises was 60 percent; but the vast majority of rural factories are technically collectives, acting in many respects like private firms. A calculation on the basis of other sources gives a 1978–87 rural industry output value growth of 29 percent annually, but an accounting change in 1985 is one factor that generates this slightly higher figure.

tentative announcements of many policy "reforms" in 1978.[3] Top leaders had been aware of the quick rural industrialization outside their direct control. Some of them favored it, but they knew they did not initiate or control it.

Unlike Chiang Kai-shek's government in Taiwan much earlier, Deng's regime faced less pressing needs to mollify a majority population. Many on the mainland, especially urban intellectuals, bore sharp resentments at their injuries during the Cultural Revolution. But these people also knew that Deng himself had suffered personally from that movement. They were easier to monitor than were China's rural bosses, whose clients had mainly suffered because of the 1959–61 famine. The most important rural leaders who faced new political needs because of agrarian changes in the 1970s were not central; they were many, powerful cumulatively, and in the countryside. Whether they should be called "state" cadres (as they labeled themselves) or "nonstate" leaders (as a more accurate behavioral description would label them), they were surely local.

GREEN REVOLUTION, GRAIN TAXES, AND POLITICAL OPPORTUNITIES FOR RURAL LEADERS

Rice plants can be engineered to convert greater portions of the sun's energy, which they or their roots capture chemically, into the calories of edible grain rather than into stems that cannot be eaten by humans. Modern short-stalk, high-yield rice requires precise control

---

[3]Figures to 1986 were calculated from *Zhongguo tongji nianjian, 1987* (China Statistical Yearbook, 1987), ed. State Statistical Bureau (Beijing: Zhongguo Tongji Chuban She, 1987); and thereafter from *ibid.*, 1993 edition. An accounting change that occurred approximately in 1985, not reported in most published tables, finally treated the industrial output of low-level agricultural units as nonagricultural; so the growth rates of rural industry before 1985 may be understated. Boundary changes between nominally "rural" and "urban" areas were also frequent in this era; so statistics about them should not be read as extremely precise. These changes often brought productive suburban factories into the non-rural category, however, so Deng Xiaoping's astonishment was not misplaced.

of water levels in paddies. It generally uses inorganic fertilizers, but these can also burn the stems and roots unless irrigation levels are closely adjusted to the plants' height on both wet and dry days. So canals, tube wells and pumps to raise underground water, pesticides, walking tractors, rice-transplanting machines, inorganic fertilizers, and the new seeds (for short-stemmed varieties that respond to these other inputs) can supply more calories per unit of land. Especially because the new agronomy often allows fields to be used for three crops per year, rather than two as in earlier times, it also means more grain taxes for the state.[4]

Green revolution in China was a trigger of rural industrial growth, because it was one of the factors that increased rural leaders' entrepreneurial autonomy. New rice technology was a primary origin of China's industrial reforms. Green revolution in other East Asian places had different effects, although it was in each region important for determining the political economy's course.[5] A second major cause of the new local autonomy what that Communist Party control over rural cadres had sharply decreased because of the policy disasters during and after the Great Leap Forward.[6] A third factor was the Cultural

---

[4]One of the three crops was usually not rice, but a fertilizer crop that raised a paddy's productivity in grain-growing seasons, or perhaps an edible legume or yam. Some areas of sandy soil mainly grew cotton rather than grain. (Chuansha [River Sand] County, now called Pudong just east of central Shanghai, is such an area in East China.) The new agronomy was most useful in carbon-rich rather than silicon-rich soils, such as most of southern Jiangsu, a.k.a. Sunan.

[5]In Taiwan, the new seeds generally postdated other rural reforms that the previous chapter describes. The situations in Thailand and the Philippines were different in yet other ways. Thai farmers resisted using new seeds because of good markets for their traditional varieties, but Sino-Thai rural leaders nonetheless already had the autonomy to create rural industries because the Thai state bureaucrats had never tried to control rural areas so tightly as Chinese ones did; their identity and motives were different. In the Philippines, Marcos's pressure on farmers to adopt "miracle" rice put farmers further into debt, strengthening traditional patron-client ties, rather than creating a new basis for autonomous local entrepreneurship. For more on these differences — and on the crucial similarity, which is that autonomous firms were founded in places that later boomed — read the relevant chapters.

[6]This is the main argument of Yang Dali, *Calamity and Reform in China* (Stanford: Stanford University Press, 1996 [orig. Ph.D. dissertation, Politics Department, Princeton University, 1993]).

Revolution, which decimated urban offices that in other periods had tried to monitor rural industries. These Great Leap and Cultural Revolution erosions of control over rural entrepreneurship, combined with the output opportunities provided by new green technology — and the lure to bureaucrats of greater rice taxes through triple cropping that required machines — to give "production brigade" and "team" leaders more leeway to run rural factories.

The political interests of these leaders' local networks, rather than any interest of the central state (except the passion for more grain tax) was the origin of China's reform boom. The new situation, already by the early 1970s, allowed more jobs to be created in parts of the East China landscape that had high traditional population pressure (e.g., near Suzhou) or a scarcity of fertile land (e.g., hilly areas of southern Zhejiang). It nurtured rural industrialization. Green revolution agronomy required less labor in fields, but factories could absorb these workers for greater profit. In rural and suburban "Sunan" (southern Jiangsu including Shanghai), the new agronomy could produce more rice for food and taxes, if the necessary factors were applied to paddies.

This syndrome did not start uniformly everywhere in the country. The present book uses the term "East China" in an unofficial way, referring to areas that speak Wu (the Shanghainese language and related dialects) in Sunan and Zhejiang.[7] The term "reforms" is also used unofficially in this book, referring to the behavioral syndrome of entrepreneurship that created the economic boom. More usual but

---

[7]In official PRC texts, the phrase "East China" means a very large area over several other provinces (Shandong, Anhui, Jiangxi, Fujian, even Taiwan, in addition to Shanghai, Jiangsu, and Zhejiang), but this book refers to a smaller "East China." Another term, "Jiangnan," means "south of the [Yangzi] river." Usage differs on whether Wenzhou is included in "Jiangnan." Like a few places speaking Wu dialects that are north of the Yangzi, such as Nantong, Wenzhou is in the "East China" area on which this book concentrates. "Wu-dialect region" would be the most exact phrase here, but only linguists would ordinarily use it. There is a common term for the center of the Sunan subregion, "Suxichang," combining Suzhou, Wuxi, and Changzhou, an area of traditionally high agricultural productivity and high pressure of population on land.

less useful definitions refer only to part of this syndrome (central policies formulated in Beijing) without inclusion of local policies and their later effects on central policies. So the word "policy" is also employed in a nonstandard but behaviorally accurate way here, to include the intentions of nonstate and local leaders, whether these policies are expressed in public or just revealed in actions.

Reforms began differently in two different parts of the area this book calls East China. On one hand is the flatland of south Jiangsu and Shanghai (a city with provincial status), Suzhou, Changzhou, Wuxi, and in north Zhejiang the string of major cities from Hangzhou to Ningbo. On the other is southern Zhejiang, centered on Wenzhou but also including booming cities such as Taizhou and Yueqing near the coast, and Lishui inland. In the first, flatter area, especially Sunan, reforms started in a collectivist manner during the early 1970s. But in southern Zhejiang, reforms took off later, especially in the 1980s and 1990s, and they were from the start more privatistic and capitalistic. So "East China" is at least two "cases" in this book, because of the greater ability of restricted elites to manipulate politics in Sunan, as compared to southern Zhejiang.[8]

In traditionally very rich parts of East China, such as the green suburbs around Shanghai, rural development was quick even in the late 1960s. It began on fields, not in factories. Only 17 percent of the cultivated land in Shanghai's rural counties was tilled by machine in 1965; but by 1972, the portion was already 65 percent. By 1974, it soared to 89 percent. The number of transplanting machines in this region tripled between 1965 and 1974.[9] The amount of grain rose, while the number of full-time farmers plummeted.

The green revolution, which the state had fostered mainly for taxes, increased the political needs of rural leaders: how were ex-peasants to make livings, if they no longer farmed? And why should

---

[8]Zhang Jianjun, "State Power, Elite Relations, and the Politics of Privatization in China's Rural Industry: Different Approaches in Two Regions [Wuxi and Wenzhou]," *Asian Survey* 48:2 (March–April 2008), 215–38.

[9]See *Chûgoku no toshika to nôson kensetsu* (Chinese Urbanization and Rural Construction), Kojima Reeitsu, ed. (Tokyo: Ryûkei Shosha, 1978), 293–94 and 299.

the remaining tillers put effort into raising a third crop, when state extraction from their product rose similarly, and the work required to grow that much rose even faster? These problems never had to become fully public. Local governments — formally part of the state, but in fact acting separately — solved them by starting stores and factories in which many ex-peasants got jobs. Those who remained on the land used more machines and served as overseers of immigrants from poorer areas. Non-local people increasingly took the harder jobs in paddies.

The new agriculture was more productive per unit of land; but it pushed (it did not just free) labor from field work. Mechanization aided triple cropping and raised the annual harvest; but new technology also required more work per unit of yield from more specialized tillers. It grew grain, whose transport and sale the state could monitor and tax with relative ease. Even with larger total harvests, many farmers wanted to leave fields and get better compensation for easier work in stores or factories. Local peasant leaders, who increasingly separated from central offices after the post-Great Leap famine and later Cultural Revolution, hired ex-peasants as workers. They established factories larger than the machine shops needed to repair farm equipment, and commercial firms not just to buy new seeds, metal equipment, and fertilizers, but also to engage in other trade.

THE ECONOMIC RESULTS OF MORE LOCAL AUTONOMY

At Tangqiao Commune, near Suzhou, many Great Leap brigade-run industries had been closed in 1962 during the post-Leap economic depression, but they resumed their operations about 1970. The local growth rate of gross industrial output value from 1971 to 1977 at this enterprising Sunan place was a scorching 150 percent annually over those half dozen years (slightly faster than the later 1978–85 yearly average growth there).[10] This commune did not follow the then-current

---

[10]Calculated from data in Xu Yuanming and Ye Ding, *Tangqiao gongye hua zhi lu* (The Way to Industrialization in Tangqiao) (Shanghai: Shanghai Shehui Kexue Yuan Chuban She, 1987), 10–13 and 61.

Maoist state policy of "taking grain as the key link" (*yi liang wei gang*). Local Tangqiao authorities could pick and choose among various directives that came "down" to them from agencies that were officially higher. Some of these condoned industrialization, while others discouraged it. In any case, activities in rural places could often be hidden from urban cadres who might disapprove, so long as senior figures in the locality had a consensus. What local leaders did, they did not necessarily say in public. What they said, they did not necessarily do. Such habits can persist for a long time and are actually normal in power systems. Memories of the post-Leap depression, administrative effects of the Cultural Revolution, and mechanized triple cropping made them unusually prevalent in early-1970s Sunan.

More typical places on the Shanghai delta also had very quick industrial growth. At Tangjiacun, Fengxian County, Shanghai, the portion of gross output from industry in 1970 was still only 7 percent; but by 1971, 11 percent; then in 1972, 22 percent; in 1973, 44 percent; and in 1974, 59 percent.[11] This change before 1978 was not ostensibly a political reform, but its implications for wealth distribution later made it so. It was unarticulated behavior, flying below the radar of state politics as imagined by most intellectuals and politicians. There was no false consciousness about it; there was surely an awareness among local leaders of their clients' interests in silence. The open "transcript" of normative reasons for their actions could be hierarchal, statist, and nonconfrontational, while the concrete effects of what they did countered the state's long-term interests and so were hidden.[12]

As China's most famous social scientist Fei Xiaotong later noted in print, such factories in the early 1970s were secret: "These enterprises, established by local cadres, were illegal [*sic*] at that time. They were 'underground'." Actually, the North China Agricultural Conference and

---

[11]Calculated from Ishida Hiroshi, *Chûgoku nôson keizai no kiso kôzô: Shanhai kinkô nôson no kôgyôka to kindaika no ayumi* (Rural China in Transition: Experiences of Rural Shanghai toward Industrialization and Modernization) (Kyôto: Kôyô Shobô, 1991), 149, where the interpretation in the text is not made.

[12]This partially reverses situations described in James C. Scott, *Domination and the Arts of Resistance: Hidden Transcripts* (New Haven: Yale University Press, 1990).

relative moderates in Beijing during the 1970s condoned locally owned rural cooperative industries, but Cultural Revolution radicals simultaneously passed regulations against them. Fei goes on to explain that, "Farmers did not mind what the nature of ownership was. The only thing they did mind was to keep up their livelihood.... Capital came from collective accumulation; communes used a portion of their funds to develop [industrial] production after the distribution of wages.... This was the only way for peasants to make their living at that time."[13]

Some household enterprises in China were "merely resuming activities that were interrupted at the Great Leap Forward," as Bruun writes.[14] Many other small firms also had pre-reform experience in various businesses. Fully 29 percent of village enterprises in a much later (1997) survey at Kunshan, Sunan, had already been established by 1978 or earlier. The portion founded during early reforms, 1979–83, was smaller, at 18 percent. About one-third (35 percent) were begun between 1984 to October 1988, and the remaining 18 percent were later.[15]

These rural factories processed raw materials that had once gone to urban state plants. The prices of factors rose. Government enterprises eventually had either to pay higher prices for inputs or else cut production. Ex-peasants (still officially classed as agriculturalists) made it impossible for the socialist state to run its businesses as usual.

Shanghai's leading politician in the mid-1970s, Zhang Chunqiao, a radical in the "Gang of Four," railed against "sprouts of capitalism (*zibenzhuyi de mengya*) in the countryside." Zhang knew exactly what he was talking about, as anybody who looks at rich parts of the Chinese countryside can now see. His analysis was perceptive, whatever

---

[13]Fei Xiaotong and Luo Yanxian, *Xiangzhen jingji bijiao moshi* (Comparative Model of the Village and Town Economy) (Chongqing: Chongqing Chuban She, 1988), 5–9.

[14]Ole Bruun, *Business and Bureaucracy in a Chinese City: An Ethnography of Private Business Households in Contemporary China* (Berkeley: Institute of East Asian Studies, University of California, Berkeley, 1993), 239, deals with a rich inland place, but his observation is equally true of East China.

[15]Andrew M. Marton, *China's Spatial Economic Development: Restless Landscapes in the Lower Yangzi Delta* (New York: Routledge, 2000), 166.

one may think of his policy that rural industrialization should be repressed. As a Marxist, he understood that the technological syndrome of triple-cropping and rural industrialization would have political implications. This mechanization, together with the state's desire for more grain tax, led to allowances for rural industrialization. This foreboded the end of China's socialist planning, because factories that the state controlled could no longer get the inputs they needed on the budgets they had. Rural factories bid up factor prices and sold products more cheaply than state factories could.

Other leaders in Sunan had opposite policies. Xu Jiatun, an administrator in Jiangsu's capital Nanjing during the early 1970s, later expressed pride in the province's progress: "I tell you, we took a different road from the rest of the country. [The official slogan held that] 'The planned economy is crucial, and the market economy is a supplement.' We had openly to support this, but in fact we had gone beyond it."[16]

Many other central and provincial leaders unambiguously resisted rural industrialization. After the Jiangsu Party committee ordered lower branches to "oppose capitalist tendencies more energetically" in 1975, peasants reacted by slaughtering team- and brigade-owned livestock and by diverting water to their own plots. In Jiangsu's Nanchang County and Zhejiang's Shaoxing County, there was "widespread sabotage."[17] Xu observes that markets overtook plans early in Sunan. He and his reformist colleagues had few effective helpers in the early 1970s, however, after the Cultural Revolution had cowed so many. They mainly blinked at the change, which radicals among them wanted to stanch. The transformation was led; it was not spontaneous or automatic. But the local elites who led it were "low" only in a nominal bureaucratic sense. They were higher in behavioral

---

[16]Xu Jiatun in *Shijie ribao* (World Daily), May 6, 1993. Xu later became a top PRC administrator in Hong Kong, but after June 4, 1989, he exiled himself to a Buddhist monastery in California, whence he made this statement.

[17]Jiangxi Provincial Broadcasting Station, November 25, 1975, and Zhejiang Provincial Broadcasting Station, November 16, 1975; in Jürgen Domes, *Socialism in the Chinese Countryside: Rural Societal Policies in the People's Republic of China, 1949–1979*, trans. Margritta Wendling (London: C. Hurst, 1980), 90.

power (i.e., in their long-term cumulative ability to make others do what those others would not separately have done) than were officially "higher" radicals whose policies their own policies trumped.

As this syndrome spread throughout the 1970s, the main means for the government to gather information about rural factories was to license and tax them. The new rural contracting to households (*baochan daohu*) spread quickly despite resistance. Contracts enabled families to resume economic decision making, and they led to increases of productivity.[18] After a specialized agricultural family paid its taxes in grain, cadres had no interest to keep farmers from engaging in industrial or commercial work. Local leaders could and did profit from such opportunities.[19] So rural industrialization took off during the 1970s in several rich parts of China, and then by the early 1980s more widely.[20] All of the most salient aspects of China's "reforms" — economic boom, decentralization, inflation of prices for industrial factors, corruption to obtain inputs, massive migrations, the end of most planning, and government deficits — came from locally led processes that neither the government nor anyone else initiated in public.

---

[18]See more on the 1970s in *Rural Small-Scale Industry in the People's Republic of China*, Dwight Perkins, ed. (Berkeley: University of California Press, 1977); and Carl Riskin, "Small Industry and the Chinese Model of Development," *China Quarterly* 73 (March 1977), 145–73.

[19]Some conservative state officials in high provincial offices, as well as hardline local socialists who are now called "leftists" even though they were conservatives for socialism, resisted the shift of labor from farming. High-level reformers, holding power temporarily as late as 1984–85, announced a "second stage of rural reform" to counter them. Output data from the areas studied here suggest, however, that many rural leaders were happy to allow and tax cooperative factories on a local basis.

[20]Anthropological work by Yan Yunxiang and Yang Minchuan shows, for North China and Sichuan villages respectively, that reform there came later and was more focussed on farming than in the Shanghai delta locations reported above. Rural reform in China was spatially uneven — and this is further evidence that concrete local situations, not ideal policy pronouncements from intellectuals who run the central state, were the crucial causes of what happened. See Yang, "Reshaping Peasant Culture and Community: Rural Industrialization in a Chinese Village," *Modern China* 20 (April 1994), 157–79, and Yan, "The Impact of Rural Reform on Economic and Social Stratification in a Chinese Village," *Australian Journal of Chinese Affairs* 27 (January 1992), 1–24.

Rural industry's gross value of output in Jiangsu over the decade and a half from 1981 to 1997 then grew at an astounding rate: more than 29 percent annually. Such an explosion, sustained over such a long time, is very rare in any sizeable economy. This province's contribution to China's overall record in that period was major. Agricultural growth there was 7.6 percent per year, which is also extremely high for farming. The whole province's growth rate (including urban industrial output) was 20.6 percent annually during rural Jiangsu's boom — and it was much higher in Sunan than in the poorer north Jiangsu counties.[21] These figures suggest that Sunan's boom at its peak was even faster than Taiwan's in that island's halcyon era. The later boom in southern Zhejiang was similar, although the income distribution effects there may have been more like Taiwan's because of the greater prominence of openly private SMEs in Zhejiang. All of these regional booms were outstanding in terms of any normal economic comparisons with other places.

NONSTATE COMPETITION WITH THE STATE

According to the government, rural companies are "enterprises organized by the commune [now the township, or *xiang*] or the brigade [now the village, or *cun*], or else by an individual or several individual commune members."[22] Village enterprises are economically as important as the larger but fewer township firms that tend to have stronger connections to local cadres. World Bank economists Lin Qingsong and William Byrd define rural industries as "all nonagricultural activities in rural areas and small towns other than those on state farms."[23] Many such firms are in commerce or transport services, rather than manufacturing. Their market activities are in practice not confined to local settings. State and nonstate companies have tended to compete

---

[21]Andrew M. Marton, *China's Spatial Economic Development*, 7.

[22]*Zhongguo xiangzhen qiye bao* (Chinese Rural Enterprise News) [hereafter *Zhongguo xiangzhen*], March 23, 1984.

[23]*China's Rural Industry: Structure, Development, and Reform*, Lin Qingsong and William Byrd, eds. (New York: Oxford University Press for the World Bank, 1990), 3.

with each other, even when their managers have been politically savvy enough to avoid emphasizing such competition.

The state's response to this challenge from the boondocks was at first largely exhortation: mandates forbade rural industries from competing with urban state factories. The official guiding principle for rural industry was phrased in a slogan, the "three locals" (*san jiu di*): getting inputs locally, processing them locally, and selling the products locally. This would have tied rural enterprises to their particular areas, discouraging profits from specialization, from economies of scale, and from expansion into larger markets. As a 1979 (but substantively pre-reform) central government decree intoned:

> Commune and brigade enterprises should adhere to socialism and actively produce what society needs, but mainly they should serve agricultural production and serve the people while helping big [state] industries and exports. At the same time, they should organize their production with local resources and energy supplies. Do not produce without local resources. Do not make products that are already oversupplied. Do not compete with advanced big industries for raw materials and energy. Do not destroy the state's resources.[24]

This was a moralizing plaint, not an effective order. In practice, many rural factories used inputs that came from a distance, made whatever products they found profitable, and sold to anyone who paid well. Central leaders wanted to keep the effects of rural factories away from urban state industry, but they lacked the means to enforce this.

It was easiest to establish new enterprises in rural areas. So it is unsurprising that leaders of communes' production brigades and agrarian production teams ran most new firms, at first under collective or even formal state ownership. This happened both before and after the Maoist communes were disbanded. Small businesses were set up by a great variety of people: by youths who had been sent "up to the mountains and down to the countryside" during the 1968 purge of Red Guards, by ex-convicts who had been imprisoned for political or other crimes, by pensioners who had to retire at early ages (55 for women, 60 for men) before their personal energies were

---

[24] *RMRB* editorial, September 10, 1979.

exhausted, and by workers or cadres in state firms who were paid less than they could earn in new-sector jobs.

The founders of firms were a strikingly varied group. Fully two-thirds of the 12 million licensed "individual entrepreneurs," i.e., single-person companies, by 1986 were women.[25] Some ran very small businesses, hawking tea-eggs and the like, but collectively they were important. Female entrepreneurs were at first more adept than men at finding market niches that, using scant capital, they could fill — and that socialist planners had simply ignored.[26] A higher portion of the new "individual" factories were run by men, but women organizers were also more important in these than in the state sector.

Rural industries came to dominate consumer markets. By 1990, more than 70 percent of all clothes production, and two-thirds of garments exports, were from rural enterprises.[27] By 1991, the *reported* portions of value from rural factories in selected product lines were as follows: bricks, 78 percent; silk, 45 percent; paper, 38 percent; silk products, 32 percent; coal, 28 percent; cement, 28 percent — and these reports may well be underestimates.[28]

Rural factories also dominated many wholesale markets. Using connections and money, rural purchasing agents established extensive contacts with state factories. The pre-revolutionary practices of giving small red envelopes containing money (*xiaohongbao*) and kick backs (*huikou*) had massive revivals. These practices were not necessarily seen as corrupt if they allowed a factory to stay in business so that its workers would not become unemployed. Rural salespeople could act swiftly, and they worked hard. One of their reported mottoes was that they should "endure many hardships, cross thousands of

---

[25]Willy Kraus, *Private Business in China: Revival between Ideology and Pragmatism*, tr. Erich Holz (Honolulu: University of Hawaii Press, 1991), 61–62.

[26]This idea comes partly from the author's past conversations with Professor Kate Xiao Zhou.

[27]Lu Xueyi and Li Peilin, *Zhongguo shehui fazhan baogao* (Report on China's Social Development) (Shenyang: Liaoning Renmin Chubanshe, 1991), 140.

[28]Officially gathered figures are likely to underreport rural production in which the state had contrary interests. Reports of production are reports of tax bases. *Zhongguo nongcun tongji nianjian, 1992*, 162–63.

miles, speak various dialects, and use all means" (*qianxin wanku, qianshan wanshui, qianyan wanyu, qianfang baiji*).

Since the new rural managers had previously enjoyed only limited contacts with urban industries, they often had to hire city people to make connections for them. When they lacked much education, the rural founders sought urban help to improve their technologies and expand their markets. So they hired "suburban managers" to aid them.

Profitable Sunan SMEs often hired expert consultants who were still employees of larger state companies in big cities. Some were called "Sunday engineers" or "weekend engineers" (*xingqiri gongchengshi, zhoumo gongchengshi*).[29] These people, who often became as wealthy as the factory founders whom they helped, were politically important not just because of their incomes but also because of the greater wealth that they guided in fast-growth, low-tax areas.[30]

A stratum of administrator-profiteers (*guandao*) emerged, specializing in the transfer of resources from state enterprises to rural industries. Through these profiteers (avidly described as such by socialist planners), rural industries were able to buy raw materials at not much more than the state-subsidized prices. China's new "middle classes" include these rural leaders and urban fixers as well as other groups. They tend to be more enterprising than the mid-level bureaucrats who ran state industries before the people's republic gave up socialism in all but a few heavy, telecoms, and banking industries. Many executives of the new firms were able to prosper best in peripheral areas, rather than in central cities where regulations on taxes, labor, and the environment were somewhat better enforced.

The new profits and statuses available to new capitalists were naturally opposed by communists. But such inducements were so attractive,

---

[29]Andrew M. Marton, *China's Spatial Economic Development*, 118, and Lynn White, *Unstately Power: Local Causes of China's Economic Reforms* (Armonk, NY: M.E. Sharpe, 1998), chap. 1.4.

[30]See David S.G. Goodman, "The New Middle Class," in *The Paradox of China's Post-Mao Reforms*, Merle Goldman and Roderick MacFarquhar, eds. (Cambridge: Harvard University Press, 1999), 254.

they spread like a contagion from rich and experimentalist jurisdictions into formerly poor or conservative localities.[31]

URBAN RESULTS OF RURAL CHANGE: UNINTENDED DUAL PRICING AND LESS PLANNING

Physical inputs were often harder for rural companies to arrange than were technical helpers. Sometimes the conflicts over scarce resources were large-scale and interprovincial, extending far beyond East China. For example, when reform markets demanded more rice, Hunan farmers were eager to sell at higher prices in provinces where the boom came earlier. So Hunan socialist planners, still hoping to control the local grain price, induced their provincial police to set up roadblocks, trying physically to stem the flow of rice out of the province. On one occasion, they arrested 200 non-Hunanese buyers and seized vast quantities of illegally sold rice. Large amounts got through anyway, "secretly" according to one report, because Hunan farmers set up what they called "Ho Chi Minh Trails" to sneak rice across the province border.[32] Many further examples involved industrial inputs rather than grain.

The state's monopolistic goals were defeated by avowedly loyalist organizations of ex-peasants. Rural managers could bypass central mandates because they could pay higher prices for raw materials. Their taxes to non-local offices were low — or if raised, could be evaded with the support of local cadres. This was especially true for light industries, which received most factors from the countryside. Fully 70 percent by value of such inputs in 1991 came from rural areas.[33] Under the

---

[31]See Mary Elizabeth Gallagher, *Contagious Capitalism: Globalization and the Politics of Labor in China* (Princeton: Princeton University Press, 2005 [orig. Ph.D. dissertation, Politics Department, Princeton University, 2001]).

[32]Su Ya and Jia Lusheng, *Sheilai chengbao? Zhongguo jingji xianzhuang toushi* (Who is Going to Contract? An Analysis of China's Economic Situation) (Guangzhou: Huacheng Chuban She, 1990), 321.

[33]*Zhongguo nongcun tongji nianjian, 1992* (Yearbook of Chinese Rural Statistics, 1992), ed. Rural Data Group of the State Statistics Bureau (Beijing: Zhongguo Tongji Chubanshe, 1992), 35.

reforms, leaders of farmers could increasingly sell to the highest bidders. So the best quality wool, silk cocoons, and tobacco leaves usually went to rural industries. Country entrepreneurs had big advantages because, with more local knowledge, they could often arrange more reliable and lucrative links to suppliers. The managers of urban state factories for decades had been accustomed to waiting until high-level procurement offices got their materials and capital for them. Their administrative-political habits meant that they became undersupplied.

As Lin Yimin argues, China's post-Mao economy prospers not just because economic markets grew, but also because a "political market" diverts formerly public money to relatively efficient private managers.[34] Rural industry's development contrasts with the stagnancy of Chinese state companies. Jan Svejnar and Josephine Woo write that, "TVPs [township and rural plants] have been able to thrive in a variety of environments. In contrast to state enterprises, TVPs are characterized by great flexibility, harder budget constraints, costs of capital that are more reflective of scarcity, and much heavier reliance on worker incentives." State policy has sometimes opposed their quick expansion, but "their ability to maintain growth under the restrictive macroeconomic policies of the mid-1980s [and after 1989] attests to their viability and superior performance."[35]

Other economists argue that public enterprises have been more efficient. It is probably unwise to generalize about this, in part because public, private, quasi-private, and other firms concentrated in different sectors. Also, efficiency for profits is a matter of finding markets as well as producing goods. Rural industries surged against urban state factories, driving them either to greater efficiency or to financial ruin. Profits per yuan of fixed assets in nonstate country industries were reported 58 percent greater than in state industries (.19 yuan in 1985, as compared to .12 yuan for the state plants). Output production per yuan of fixed assets was 118 percent greater (2.07 yuan, as

---

[34]Lin Yi-min, *Between Politics and Markets: Firms, Competition, and Institutional Change in Post-Mao China* (Cambridge: Cambridge University Press, 2001).

[35]Jan Svejnar and Josephine Woo, "Development Patterns in Four Counties," in *China's Rural Industry,* Lin and Byrd, eds., 83–84.

compared to just .95 yuan in state plants).[36] None of this required any political expression or intent. It nonetheless had long-term implications for the issue of who follows whom, because it meant that local power networks received more of China's money, and central networks received less.

CENTRAL DEBATES AND LOCAL ACTION

Especially after Mao's death, but also to some extent before then, debates raged in the central government between economic reformers and conservatives. By the 1980s, Chen Yun (originally from rural Qingpu, then in Jiangsu but now in Shanghai) was on most issues a conservative, disagreeing with reformers Deng Xiaoping, Hu Yaobang, and Zhao Ziyang albeit in ways that did not destabilize the Party.[37] These stratospheric debates, important though they were for expressions of national policy, affected Chinese public documents more than they affected local economic behavior or the redistribution of power that it brought.

In an attempt to guarantee planned deliveries, the state by 1984 in effect legalized a black market. It let nationalized factories sell items at 20 percent above the state-fixed prices — but only after those firms claimed to have fulfilled their production quotas. The marked-up rate was called the "state-guided price" (*guojia zhidao jia*), as distinct from

---

[36]Calculated from raw figures in *Zhongguo gongye jingji tongji ziliao, 1986* (Statistical Materials on China's Industrial Economy, 1986) (Beijing: Zhongguo Tongji Chubanshe, 1987), 98 and 211. These data almost surely underreport the difference, because the published figures apparently omit industries licensed by villages (*cun*, as distinct from larger *xiang* or *zhen*) that make about half of rural factories' output. Other figures in the source suggest that light industrial profits per yuan of fixed assets were equal (.19 yuan) for both rural and state plants — but this may understate one or both, and heavy industries in the state sector surely lower the profits there. A larger portion of state factory profits are, in any case, remitted to higher administrative budgets from the places where they are earned.

[37]Joseph Fewsmith, "Formal Structures, Informal Politics, and Political Change in China," in *Informal Politics in East Asia*, Lowell Dittmer, Fukui Haruhiro, and Peter Lee, eds. (New York: Cambridge University Press), 154.

the "plan price" (*jihua jia*). China's top leaders could not change the unplanned new structure, in which state factories got money from selling rather than processing inputs. They lost product markets in the long term. Official policies accommodating that situation were reactive. They were made incrementally, not in practice by the state but in accord with the policies of the leaders of coteries of ex-peasants and their procurement agents. These two-price policies were at first unintended, though they have been praised as wise by economists (including Western economists) who more usually say that any commodity, at a single time in a single place, on an efficient market has one rather than two prices.

The urban side effects of this situation were unintended by the top leadership. As Deng Xiaoping said with his usual frankness: "The success of rural reforms gave us confidence. So we decided to apply the rural experience to urban economic system reforms."[38] By 1985, the state had to recognize that price controls on nonquota products were no longer enforceable, so formal recognition of the multiple-price norm spread.[39] This divided production into two parts: one portion that was supposed to be sent to the state at a fixed price, with the remainder sold to anyone at market prices. Leakage between the two markets became a deluge. In 1985 alone, rural industries spent so much money buying raw materials and energy from state enterprises, these nationalized companies gained at least 10.7 billion yuan as profit from purely speculative exchanges.[40] This was certainly an underreport of the actual profits from reselling inputs.

---

[38]Deng Xiaoping, "*Gaige de buzi yao jia kuai*" (To Speed up Reforms), in *Shierda yilai zhongyao wenjian xuanbian* (Selected Important Documents since the Twelfth Plenum), 1444.

[39]Miao Zhuang, "*Zhidu bianqian zhong de gaige zhanlüe xuanze wenti*" (The Problem of Choosing Reform Strategies for System Change), *Jingji yanjiu* (Economic Research) 10 (October 1992), 72–79.

[40]This is on the brave premise that these trades are fully reported. Wang Shiyuan, Li Xiuyi, and Yang Shijiu, *Zhongguo gaige daquan* (Encyclopedia of China's Reforms) (Dalian, Liaoning: Dalian Renmin Chubanshe, 1992), 30, reports the profit; a percentage of total government revenue was calculated using a denominator from *Zhongguo tongji nianjian, 1993*, 215, but it only suggests that the speculation profits were sharply underreported.

State clothing and cigarette factories, in particular, ran short of wool and tobacco. The Shanghai Cigarette Factory, China's oldest and one of the largest, briefly had no leaves to roll.[41] The government issued a document on May 4, 1981, ordering the closure of many rural enterprises that produced cigarettes, textiles, and salt.[42] Stately decrees could not reverse the reforms for long, however. Price hikes for cotton, tobacco, and salt continued because local power networks could pay for them. Cigarettes are an industry from which, despite the devastating health hazards, the Chinese state has sometimes gathered about 8 percent of its total revenues.[43] In September, 1987, the State Council (the Cabinet) decreed:

> Since the procurement of tobacco began this year, many tobacco-producing areas independently raised prices.... This has affected the normal procedure of state purchases. If this situation continues, it will make the state suffer a great economic loss and will also affect the production of cigarettes. This must be stopped.[44]

Rural enterprises often won against state factories in "wars" for raw materials, colloquially known as the "tobacco war," the "wool war," and so forth.

---

[41]Wu Jilian, "*Guomin jingji de kunjing he chulu*" (Difficulties and Solutions in the Civil Economy), *Jingji shehui tizhi bijiao* (Comparative Economic and Social Systems), 6 (June 1990), 6.

[42]*RMRB*, May 4, 1981.

[43]This 8 percent is a medium-low estimate; in some years, the figure has exceeded 9 percent. Raw data on tobacco revenues, from which the calculation can be made, are in *Zhongguo qinggong ye nianjian, 1992* (China Light Industry Yearbook, 1992), ed. Research Center on Light Industry (Beijing: Zhongguo Qinggong Ye Nianjian Chuban She, 1992), 254; fiscal revenues are in *Zhongguo tongji nianjian, 1993*, 215.

[44]Guowuyuan Nongcun Fazhan Yanjiu Zhongxin Bangongshi (Rural Development Research Center of the State Council), "*Guowuyuan bangongting guanyu zhizhi jia-jia qianggou he tiji shougou yanye de tongzhi*" (State Council Ban on Price Rises, Snap Purchases, and Raised Grading of Tobacco), September 1, 1987, in *Nongcun zhengce wenjian xuan, 1985–89* (Selected Documents on Agricultural Policy, 1985–89) (Beijing: Zhongyang Dangxiao Chubanshe, 1987), 344.

UNENFORCEABLE CONTRACTS REPLACE UNENFORCEABLE PLANS

Raw materials prices before the 1980s were generally low and stable, even when there were shortages. The reforms made them higher and volatile. The portion by value of *all* Shanghai factory inputs to be allocated by plan plummeted, from about 70 percent to about 20 percent in the mid-1980s crisis — not because planners wished this, but because they could not enforce deliveries of goods.[45]

The number of products from Shanghai state factories under mandatory production quotas thus had to be allowed to drop in the mid-1980s, from 150 in 1984 to only 37 in 1987.[46] During the same period, the number of products for which Shanghai agencies required mandatory sales to each other also went down, from 53 to 23. The number of raw materials that were distributed on a mandatory basis under city plans likewise decreased, from 19 to 13. Even then, not all the mandated deliveries were fulfilled.

"Developing the commodity economy without commodities is a major vexation for many enterprises in Shanghai," as a sardonic pair of local journalists observed.[47] A mid-1980s survey showed that, for 55 percent of a comprehensive range of products, state factories could no longer process the decreasingly available, increasingly expensive inputs without losing money.[48]

"Contracts replace plans" became a mid-1980s slogan. But contracts at this time were no more enforceable than plans. If a rural unit failed to deliver to an urban factory a contracted amount of raw materials at the contracted price, the factory could sue. But if even if it won a decision in the urban court, the judge there was not

---

[45]The exact time period was not specified. *Jiefang ribao* (Liberation Daily) [hereafter *JFRB*], May 15, 1988.

[46]*Shanghai jingji nianjian, 1988* (Shanghai Economic Yearbook, 1988), Xiao Jun, *et al.*, eds., (Shanghai: Shanghai Renmin Chuban She, 1988), 90.

[47]*Foreign Broadcast Information Service*, November 26, 1986, 3, reporting radio of November 20.

[48]*Shanghai jingji* (Shanghai Economy), January 1985, 5.

appointed by the same CCP personnel department as were judges and police in the rural jurisdiction — which might or might not enforce the decision.

Of all economic litigations filed in Shanghai courts during October 1988, more than half were judicially classed "unresolvable" as soon as three months later.[49] The main immediate reasons for the unresolvable cases lay in enterprises that claimed to have closed, or managers who had absconded (*xialuo buming*), or pressures in favor of manager-defendants who had friends in high places. Judges, who had scant help and much work as contracts replaced plans, lacked time to spend on trials when they guessed the plaintiffs had meritorious cases but when they also guessed their decisions would remain unenforced. They often dismissed these cases on non-legal grounds, during that transitional period of mid-boom inflation, in order to concentrate on legal work that might have some result.

Rural efforts to obtain coal, steel, other metals, and timber usually required dealings with government suppliers. Since state enterprises could often still get these relatively cheaply, state-sector managers could still make huge profits trading them despite laws against this practice. So for example, the Shanghai market price of coal in 1988 was 220 percent of the "fixed" state price; for electricity, 176 percent; for steel, 160 percent; for aluminium, 250 percent; and for timber, over 550 percent.[50] Some materials were still delivered to state enterprises. So rural industries bought inputs from state factories at high, non-plan prices. Such trade violated laws but helped the state economically. It became crucial for keeping state-owned enterprises (SOEs) afloat financially and for paying their workers' wages.

Many rural industrialists, despite their regard for government ideals of hierarchy, quite consciously competed with rival state firms — to make sales, not to undermine the regime. A mid-1980s survey of

---

[49] *Huadong xinxi bao* (East China News), January 28, 1989.

[50] Calculated from raw figures in Hu Heli, "1988 nian woguo zujin jiazhi de gusuan" (The Estimation of Chinese Rent-Seeking in 1988), *Jingji shehui tizhi bijiao* 5 (1989), 10–15.

5600 rural enterprises shows the managers were keenly aware of the state enterprises in their fields. Fully 48 percent responded they were in "competition" with state factories that produced the same products, and only 19 percent indicated they were in a mixed state of "cooperation and competition."[51]

The main long-term loser in this game was the central state. It lost money and authority because of local cadres' illegal transactions, and it failed to stop the process by which rural industries stymied economic planning. Marketization in China was not any leader's bright idea; it was the political result of covert conflicts over resources that central leaders lost to local ones. But the state profited from the syndrome in a major way: the government had a new source of popular legitimacy in the high rate of economic growth.

MOTIVES AND PROPERTY RIGHTS OF THE RURAL INDUSTRIALISTS

A survey of two localities (one was Changshu on the Shanghai delta) suggested that about half of all licensed small firms in the mid-1980s had been founded by people who had previously been forced out of similar activities during collectivization, many years earlier. Many of the founders of China's boom firms were not really new industrialists. They had been required to cease (or at least cease reporting) activities to which they readily returned, as soon as they could. Not all of these enterprises were legally registered. The German scholar Willy Kraus, who has sought relevant statistics heroically, confesses that for the 1980s, even beyond the data he found, "a non-licensed individual economy existed which was just as large as the licensed."[52]

---

[51]The remaining 34 percent were in a mode of "cooperation and subordination" to similar state plants; and presumably these were from private or collective "dependent firms," licensed by a state plant in the same field. See *Nongmin ribao* (Farmer's Daily) [hereafter *NMRB*], September 8, 1988.

[52]Willy Kraus, *Private Business in China*, 63.

Industrialization is what gave rural patrons the wherewithal to attract new clients by offering them jobs, making them followers.[53] Traditionally in China, merchants (*shang*) were disdained by orthodox Confucians who ran the state. Marxism did nothing to raise the prestige of entrepreneurs. Some of the factory founders in the 1970s and 1980s were from backgrounds of Cultural Revolution violence and clear criminality. Other entrepreneurs or early reformers were "sent down youths" (*xiafang qingnian*) who returned, legally or otherwise, to their native cities. Still others were unemployed or even ex-convicts.[54] Rural industrialization financed new kinds of relationships for some of these people. Not only has the total number of China's new entrepreneurs been severely underreported, their backgrounds and the legal property statuses of their firms have often been obfuscated.

Units that collect money in China are divided into two broad types: enterprises (*qiye*) make profits, but service units (*shiye*) such as schools, hospitals, and some hotels and theaters operate under a different set of laws. Enterprises are further divided according to ownership types. The private economy was officially supposed to be a mere complement to the state-owned economy. Chinese communist cadres and Western social scientists alike have squandered many words on these kinds of property, although actual behavior in the boom did not always correlate with these categories. The names on signs in front of offices could sometimes be changed, and they did not faithfully reflect differences behind the doors.

"Private" or "individual" firms had difficulties running under either of those labels. They could distance themselves from the opprobrium of being "capitalist" by persuading cadres to register them as "cooperative," "rural," or "neighborhood" companies. Some succeeded in listing themselves nominally as state-owned firms, although managers

---

[53]A similar pattern was evident in the rich Chengdu basin. See Gregory A. Ruf, "Collective Enterprise and Property Rights in a Sichuan Village: The Rise and Decline of Managerial Corporatism," in *Property Rights and Economic Reform in China*, Jean C. Oi, ed. (Stanford: Stanford University Press, 1999), 37.

[54]See Margaret M. Pearson, *China's New Business Elite: The Political Consequences of Economic Reform* (Berkeley: University of California Press, 1997), 8.

in very many cases treated all assets as if these were privately owned by their patronist networks. Seemly registrations could raise official extraction from firms, but middling-seemly local registrations might allow minimal monitoring and higher retained profits. Fuzzy property rights with quasi-socialist labels were often most useful to managers. The "red cloak of invisibility" was sold so frequently, for firms of various sizes, normal market rates were established in localities for this protection.[55]

De facto private businesses were tacitly resumed as reforms began in the early 1970s, but they were hardly a new phenomenon in China. Before 1949, cities and towns registered 7.24 million private merchants, craftsmen, and industrialists, and 30 to 40 million more ran private businesses in the countryside. After the "transition to socialism" of 1956, only 160,000 small-scale firms remained. Economic policies to revive China's economy after the post-Great Leap depression brought the number to about 1 million by 1965.[56] The Cultural Revolution invalidated many registrations and disabled the offices charged with gathering accurate statistics — but by no means did all the companies close just for those reasons.

In 1984, the very first year when individual-owned enterprises could be officially reported in China, their purported number already exceeded those of all township, village, or jointly owned firms. These private companies had existed earlier in very large numbers, and the political sensitivity of private ownership labels made the mid-1980s statistics almost surely still incomplete. These firms wanted no publicity. A 1988 report found 115,000 "single-person businesses" in China, employing almost 2 million workers. There was an approximately equal number (110,000) of *de facto* private companies that employed at least another 1.7 million. About half of these were legally termed "collective," and slightly more than half were disguised as "cooperative or semi-rural" firms.[57] This 1988 report suggested that a very

---

[55]Willy Kraus, *Private Business in China*, 97.

[56]*Ibid.*, 58–59.

[57]Division of 115,000 by 2,000,000 suggests that the "single-person firms" actually hired an average of over 17 people (this would have been an excess, by a factor of two, over the legal limit if the companies had officially registered as private). For the basic numbers, see *ibid.*, 96.

large number of further businesses were in fact private, making a total as high as 300,000. Even this may well be an underestimate. By 1990, the individually owned enterprises were about five times as numerous as all the other categories combined. The total output of "private" firms, to the extent it may have been reported in 1990, was about the same as that of either "township" or "village" firms, supposedly owned by those local governments.[58] In later years, the "private" portion soared further.

The Chinese state has so many administrative levels, local leaders could try to link up with whichever of them brought most benefits. Local factories during the 1970s often used capital that local governments diverted or reallocated from more centrally controlled firms. Published budgets from that period do not necessarily cover all the resources that went into local plants.[59] Clearly the fastest growing sector in many suburban and rural areas was light-industrial, and the management of this sector was increasingly local.

THE EFFECTS OF PROPERTY LABELS ON CREDIT

"People's credit" (*minjian xinyong*) had long been used in rural China, especially in loan associations organized by peasants. Wenzhou's Cangnan County saw the PRC's first opening of a private bank (*qianzhuang*) in November 1984. Nonstate banks had been common throughout China before 1949, and state banks in the mid-1980s tried intently to squelch their re-emergence.[60] Just as strong or weak state institutions show much path dependence, so do modal nonstate local institutions.[61] A large portion of the capital for small

---

[58] Jean C. Oi, *Rural China Takes Off: Institutional Foundations of Economic Reform* (Berkeley: University of California Press, 1999), 63–65.

[59] Compare Susan H. Whiting, *Power and Wealth in Rural China: The Political Economy of Institutional Change* (New York: Cambridge University Press, 2001), 52.

[60] Kristen D. Parris, "Local Initiative and Local Reform: The Wenzhou Model of Reform," *China Quarterly* 134 (June 1993), 248.

[61] On path dependence in states, including colonial ones, see Atul Kohli, *State-Directed Development: Political Power and Industrialization in the Global Periphery* (Cambridge: Cambridge University Press, 2004).

enterprises came outside official credit channels.[62] Many of these flows were unreported. Interest rates were lower for state loans — when state banks loaned at all to nonstate firms. As late as the 1990s, according to Liu Xinwu,

> Banks did not base their loans on economic considerations but on political ones. Even though private enterprises usually had a higher repayment rate than state-owned enterprises, banks would not loan money to the former. The reason was that, should a private enterprise fail to pay back, the loan officer would be personally responsible for the loss; but if a state enterprise defaulted, the officer could just write a report, saying that the enterprise could not be liquidated, nor could the workers be laid off, and the person could get off the hook.... Some private entrepreneurs did manage to get loans by bribing bank officers....[63]

One way of raising money, if an entrepreneur had a good reputation, was to ask friends for informal loans on personal credit. These were generally at interest rates slightly higher than those offered by state banks for savings accounts. This method frequently worked, and almost all such loans were repaid.

In Kunshan, Sunan, where SMEs and joint firms dominated the economy, total fixed asset investment rose about forty-fold between 1980 and 1998. Individual households provided more than half of the (recorded) local deposits that were the source of this capital.[64] Local savings — not state banks, not local state handouts — mainly financed rural and suburban industries. Fluctuation over time of the residential portion of savings reported by banks suggests that rotating

---

[62]See Kellee S. Tsai, *Back-Alley Banking: Private Entrepreneurs in China* (Ithaca: Cornell University Press, 2002).

[63]Liu Xinwu, *Jumping into the Sea: From Academics to Entrepreneurs in South China* (Lanham: Rowman and Littlefield, 2001), 98.

[64]Local capital exceeded 50 percent in all but one of the nine years for which statistics were available. The portion of local savings from households fluctuated oddly, and it is probably not an accident that the single year in which the recorded portion was less than half (at 46 percent) was 1992, when central efforts at macroeconomic control created many incentives to hide money. See the raw data in Andrew M. Marton, *China's Spatial Economic Development: Restless Landscapes in the Lower Yangzi Delta* (New York: Routledge, 2000), 162.

loan arrangements and nonstate credit agencies provided money informally when the official system would not. The state banks enjoyed economic advantages, but nonstate institutions readily stepped in to meet any profitable demand for credit that was not officially approved.

Informal loans were often unregistered, and this situation produced odd statistics. For example, the World Bank tried to measure the 1999 ratio of private sector loans to total deposits in 78 countries. It ranked China in the lowest fifteen among them (barely ahead of Haiti, Rwanda, Niger, or Sudan).[65] China's high growth rate at this time, and the clear importance of private SMEs in producing that result, might have suggested to these econometricians (apparently more interested in reporting official numbers than in mere institutional country studies) that capital for all that private economic activity must have been coming from somewhere. Chinese bank deposits were undoubtedly high in 1999, but loans to the private sector were also underreported, probably by a large margin.

China's state banking system supports SOEs that lose money. Many private firms, which are mostly smaller but are cumulatively very important for growth, do not need or use the state banks for raising capital. In the 1990s, Beijing established better macroeconomic controls over inflation, but its success in collecting accurate statistics from these SMEs remained incomplete.

THE EFFECT OF PROPERTY LABELS ON PERMISSIONS, TECHNOLOGY, AND PROFITS

Especially in Sunan, where foreign and Overseas Chinese connections could readily be made because of Shanghai's prominence as China's leading economic center, rural and suburban power networks often benefitted by establishing links with state cadres who granted them permissions and licenses. For example, Sunan localities avidly established "development zones" (*kaifaqu*). The city of Kunshan by 1997

---

[65]Reported in Pei Minxin, *China's Trapped Transition: The Limits of Developmental Autocracy* (Cambridge: Harvard University Press, 2006), 116.

had twenty-eight specialized development zones, variously designated as "technological," "touristic," "economic," or other.[66] All these zones could legally try to attract capital, technology, and partners from larger cities or from abroad.

A failing of much East Asian development, according to Krugman and others, is a lack of new research.[67] This is true, but two-thirds of Sunan village enterprises had economic or technical cooperation agreements with larger firms or research institutions.[68] These seldom provided very high-tech help, but exploiting workers and marketing products were the technical skills in which the boom networks excelled. With labor available at such low prices, they really did not need scientific or engineering help at the Einstein or Edison levels, in order to make a profit. These firms obtained enough technology to expand quickly in their environment at that time.

During the period of fastest economic boom, while profits from the capitalist sector remain high because the supply of labor willing to work at near-subsistence wages has not yet dried up, the kinds of technology that firms can use to maximize profits are seldom high-tech by global standards. Krugman's complaint about a weakness of East Asian development applies to just one of the four cases studied here (Taiwan, where wages approach 'First World' levels). The other three have the technology that they can use for the nonce.

The central state was uninvolved in most of the international or domestic linkages that East China SMEs made. Even when disputes with foreign countries arose, local business federations often took the lead in upholding their own interests, with or without the help of any level of the PRC government. The Party-state's support has in many cases been rhetorical, not financial. For example, the European Union restricted imports of Zhejiang cigarette lighters on charges about

---

[66]Andrew M. Marton, *China's Spatial Economic Development*, 152–54.

[67]Paul Krugman, "The Myth of Asia's Miracle: A Cautionary Fable," http://web.mit.edu/krugman/www/myth.html, seen March 20, 2007.

[68]Charles Harvie, "China's SMEs: Their Evolution and Future Prospects in an Evolving Market Economy," in *The Role of SMEs in National Economies in East Asia*, Charles Harvie and Boon-Chye Lee, eds. (Cheltenham: Edward Elgar, 2002), 67.

safety and dumping. So the Wenzhou Tobacco Implements Trade Association (Yanju Hangye Xiehui) hired its own Spanish lawyers to fight this non-tariff barrier. The Wenzhou entrepreneurs won in a European court, but they used no Chinese government funds to do so.[69]

Links abroad or across PRC jurisdictions have helped units lift themselves in the official hierarchy, making permissions easier to obtain when needed. But crucial bases for economic success have also remained local. More than 80 percent of the total capital in rural-industrial firms at Kunshan came from local Kunshan investors.[70] Technical help and useful connections came from people in nearby Shanghai — but just 13 percent of the capital was from the big city. (Foreign partners contributed even less, 5 percent; and investors from elsewhere in China, a mere 1 percent.) In a large sample of local firms in Kunshan's jurisdiction, four fifths were town-level partnerships, and the rest were all at the village level. Many of these enterprises received some initial investment from local governments, but the links with both nonstate and local state managers were more important for profitability. When an enterprise found a niche in which to sell products at a price higher than cost, capital could be regenerated from its own operations and the successes of related local firms.

Local state capital often merely symbolized official links to the enterprises and thus aided business respectability. Connections were for trade. Jean Oi argues that, "Village, township and county-level governments comprise the local corporate state directly responsible for the dramatic growth of rural enterprises in China."[71] Cadres certainly say so. Rhetorical conventions in China attribute to the state (usually Beijing) a great deal that happens. Leadership is always relevant, but

---

[69] Joseph Fewsmith, "Chambers of Commerce in Wenzhou Show Potential, Limits of 'Civil Society' in China," Zhejiang University Conference on "The Development of the Non-State Sector, Local Governance, and Sustainable Development in China," June 24–25, 2006, vol. 1, 85–86.

[70] This is based on a survey of local firms, and it is particularly striking because these were all companies that a foreigner was allowed to study; see Andrew M. Marton, *China's Spatial Economic Development*, 161.

[71] Jean C. Oi, "The Role of the Local State in China's Transitional Economy," *China Quarterly* 144 (December 1995), 1138.

actually it comes at many sizes of collectivity and not just in state units. At some places, local cadres helped the dramatic growth; in others, they hindered it. A net effect of the strength of the "local state" is difficult to generalize partly because that phrase already implies a tension. In most places that prospered, several types of factors, including many that are unrelated to the intended effects of current state policies, were responsible for the dramatic growth of China's rural enterprises.

Successful businesses in China tended to have different labels in different periods. Commune companies became owned by townships (*xiang*) but later were often privatized. Brigade firms became village or small private enterprises. Then many became formally collective "village" or "township" enterprises (*cunban qiye* or *xiangban qiye*), or else "private enterprises" (*siying qiye*) or "individual households" (*geti hu*). Various "joint" (*heying*) forms were amalgams of these or involved "foreign" participation, usually from Hong Kong or Taiwan.

The exact category into which a small firm fell was of great interest to communist theoreticians — and of relevance to entrepreneurs or employees only insofar as it affected money and livelihoods. Often a manager found an umbrella agency that could have purely formalistic ownership or supervisory rights over his or her "dependent firm" (*guahu*).[72] These official umbrella agencies, which might be state enterprises, collectives, schools, or research institutions, were sarcastically called "mothers-in-law" (*popo*). That had also been the informal pejorative name of socialist corporate offices that had tried to coordinate (and technically owned) whole sectors of smaller businesses in Mao's time. Most of these "collective" enterprises actually had strong individual bosses or small local committees controlling everything. They hardly differed in behavior from non-collective firms, whose two types (larger 'private' or smaller 'individual') were distinguished mainly by reported size.

---

[72]For more about *guahu*, see Kate Xiao Zhou and Lynn T. White III, "Quiet Politics and Rural Enterprise in Reform China," *The Journal of the Developing Areas* 29 (July 1995), 461–90.

Karl Marx himself had calculated that an owner who hired seven or fewer employees would not generate enough surplus value to be free from the need to work with them. So Chinese law for many years specified that an individual or "household" could hire that number, without needing to change its status to become a "private enterprise" — and thus without suffering the officially legitimated discriminations that were then designed by law to disparage private entrepreneurs. Article 5 of China's constitution in the mid-1970s provided, however: "The state may allow non-agricultural individual laborers to engage in individual labor involving no exploitation of others, within the limits permitted by law, and under unified arrangement by neighborhood organizations in cities and towns, or by production teams in rural people's communes."[73]

Regulations of 1981 still limited the "individual economy," allowing private entrepreneurs to hire no more than eight workers. Private firms simply violated this rule. Many local cadres winked at their legal transgressions. Also, many larger firms formally registered as "collectives" but were in fact "fake collectives" (*jia jiti*). "Red hat" (*hongmao*) companies were privately run and funded; only their registrations of convenience were in the collective or state-owned economy. Behaviorally, they were petty tyrannies of a vintage exploitative and efficient capitalist kind. Other enterprises found partners abroad, in Hong Kong, or in different provinces. They thus donned "foreign hats" (*yangmao*) or become "fake joint" ventures (*jia hezi*).[74]

Practice varied at different places in East China, depending on local leaders' styles.[75] For many kinds of firms, legal labels could be

---

[73]Quoted in Kristen D. Parris, *Local Society and the State: The Wenzhou Model and the Making of Private Sector Policy in China* (Ph.D. Dissertation, Political Science, Indiana University, 1991), 105.

[74]Kristen D. Parris, "The Rise of Private Business Interests," in *The Paradox of China's Post-Mao Reforms*, Merle Goldman and Roderick MacFarquhar, eds. (Cambridge: Harvard University Press, 1999), 265–69; see also Kate Xiao Zhou and Lynn White, "Quiet Politics and Rural Enterprise in Reform China," 461–90.

[75]Practice also differed between provinces. Most of the north China remained conservative for a relatively long time, whereas parts of the south (notably in the Pearl River Delta) imitated Hong Kong styles. Some scholar should write a book contrasting relatively reform-prone Sichuan with relatively conservative Hubei. Particular provincial leaders were almost surely important, but so were traditions and situations that go far back in time. There is no source note to put here yet, but there should be.

found and changed blithely if entrepreneurs got on well with local officials. For example, when a "provincial office without explanation decided to convert a firm with three private owners into a share cooperative (*gufen hezuo*) company," nobody in the partnership saw any need even to bother finding out what this meant: "Operationally, the company experienced no change as a result of the new category on its license."[76]

Local cadres and nonstate entrepreneurs became types of leaders who were increasingly difficult to disentangle from each other. Many managers established greater autonomy in running their firms. Two farmers in a Fujian village, for example, invested 140,000 yuan in a carton factory. Everyone knew that the factory completely belonged to these two, but the plant carried the name of a "collective" so as to pay low taxes and obtain low-interest loans. After sending a 5000 yuan "management fee" to the village head, as well as another 1000 yuan to the township government, the two ex-peasant executives were left totally alone to run their business.[77]

When private entrepreneurs could not legally transfer ownership of collective or state companies to themselves, they might "lease" such companies. Often this was a transition stage, leading to their later outright acquisition of formerly public property. Precedents for leasing were first established on rural land that "specialist agricultural households" rented. Extension of the same principle to industrial collective or state property was a short step. If the rent was sufficiently low or informal, and if the company bosses who became lessors maintained the dictatorial style that is usual in either socialist or capitalist Chinese enterprises, leasing became hard to distinguish from ownership.

When small and medium enterprises in Shanghai, especially its rural suburbs, were leased out, their economic performance improved. Profits rose on average by 55 percent. Taxes paid to the

---

[76]Liu Xinwu, *Jumping into the Sea*, 3.

[77]Guowuyuan Yanjiushi Geti Siying Jingji Diaochazu (State Council Investigation Team on the Individual and Private Economy), *Zhongguo de geti he siying jingji* (China's Individual and Private Economy) [hereafter *Zhongguo de geti*] (Beijing: Gaige Chubanshe, 1990), 102.

government rose by 24 percent. Bonuses to workers and managers rose 130 percent.[78] Quasi-property, in the form of leasing, affected financial success but not management structure.

Profits could also rise when the joint connection with a different entity was almost purely symbolic. When a Hong Kong company put "cash only" — and enough of that just to buy a "small" percentage — into a Shanghai machinery firm, none of the local managers was changed. The "form and functions of the Party organization were left unaltered." The CCP secretary continued to make some management decisions, especially on personnel. The firm's tax rate on profits was not reduced. Although a consultant's survey showed that 200 of the 900 employees should be fired to improve the plant's efficiency, just two workers were let go. The Hong Kong partners were not represented at the plant on any permanent basis; they visited once a year, just to ask questions, check the accounts, and take their small share of profits.

Yet according to the local Party newspaper, this almost purely formalistic "joint" ownership meant that "superior-subordinate relations between the company and the government were weakened, inspections and appraisals were reduced, and the organizational setup was determined independently." Purchases no longer had to be approved by higher levels. Wage bonuses were no longer taxed through the company, but through individual income taxes. Nonstate partners meant that the government no longer guaranteed the company's materials or its markets — but the firm could now seek both upstream purchases and downstream sales on its own. It could bargain freely on the prices for these. Outside capital was far less important than the firm's ability to generate its own new capital from profits (partly by keeping wages low). The symbolic value of being a joint enterprise lessened "ownership by the state" and strengthened local managers at the expense of supervisory cadres, even when nothing else changed.[79] Old managers raised new profits, if they had new autonomy.

---

[78]Willy Kraus, *Private Business in China*, 109–10.
[79]Cf. *JFRB*, December 2, 1991, trans. in *Inside Mainland China* 14:2 (February 1992), 55–59.

The pre-tax profitability of township and village enterprises in China declined, as market competition grew between 1978 and 1994. TVE profits were said to have plummeted from 40 to 15 percent on average — and the after-tax profitability of TVEs reportedly dropped from 32 to 9 percent. These figures may reflect under-reporting to evade taxes. They may mean that more profits were transferred to more local entities. They certainly meant more competition among these SMEs. In any case, small firms' earnings were much higher than were the yields in more official, larger companies. Among state-owned industrial enterprises, pre- and after-tax profit rates always averaged less. They declined further (from 24 to 10 percent before taxes, and from 16 to a very low 2.8 percent after taxes) between 1978 and 1994.[80]

Entrepreneurs' reputations among local people were often important factors for business profits. So local officials' consent was sought for activities within their jurisdictions. During early reforms, China's private entrepreneurs kept "a low profile, such that they cannot be recognized on the street. They report that they conceal their personal assets and their companies' profit figures out of fear of being known as rich."[81] Workers hired from outside could be treated more callously. Later chapters consider similar situations in Thailand and the Philippines, where this issue centered on the Chinese ethnicity of entrepreneurs, rather than on ideologically dubious property types.

When cadres approved of an enterprise that sprang up, perhaps because the manager bribed them, they could call it "spontaneous" (*zifa*) and good. When they disapproved, it could be castigated as "black" (*hei*), so that it had to go "underground" (*dixia*). Local officials often extracted graft from managers who wanted ideological face, despite the illegality of doing so.[82]

Even socialists saw that independent enterprises could provide jobs and reduce unemployment. So CCP cadres allowed acceptable

---

[80]Charles Harvie, "China's SMEs," 63.

[81]See Margaret M. Pearson, *China's New Business Elite*, 98–99.

[82]Kristen D. Parris, "Local Initiative and Local Reform," 247.

entrepreneurs to be labeled "collective," "individual," and later "private," while giving them practically no credit through official banks. (They were as stingy toward SMEs as their counterparts in Taiwan's Leninist party had been.) These cadres until the mid-1980s also could sometimes use the police to force nonstate companies to pay higher prices for inputs than state firms had to pay.[83] This behavior declined after the relevant state companies had been fatally weakened by the rise of prices for their inputs.

When Chinese households' ownership categories were reclassified, their reported sources of nonagricultural income shifted. In 1978 at the official start of reforms throughout the country, 66 percent of rural nonagricultural income came from "collectives," with another 27 percent from "household firms." By 1985, however, the officially collective portion was already down to 8 percent (from two-thirds just seven years earlier) — and "household" businesses supplied 81 percent.[84] Rural people thus depended very heavily, by the mid-1980s, on "household"-run stores and factories that were in fact private companies.

Formally "private" firms' share of the gross value of all industrial output was officially reported low as late as 1990, but a great deal of China's industrial product came from "dependent firms" and collectives that petty bosses ran in their own interests. The Statistics Bureau's estimate of registered private enterprises was only a fraction of the full number of privatistic, family-based firms.[85] By 1992, China's "nonstate" sector produced more than its "state" sector.[86] The portion depended on the shifting definitions

---

[83]Reginald Yin-wang Kwok, "Urbanization Under Economic Reform," in *Urbanizing China*, Gregory Eliyu Guldin, ed. (Westport: Greenwood Press, 1992), 75.

[84]In 1978, 7 percent of nonagricultural income came from "other sources" such as joint firms; and in 1985, 11 percent. Lu Ding, *Entrepreneurship in Suppressed Markets: Private-Sector Experience in China* (New York: Garland, 1994), 119.

[85]Guo Zhenying, Lu Jian, Song Ning, and Zhang Tai, "China's Changing Ownership Structure," *Social Sciences in China* 2 (Spring, 1993), 185. The Ministry of Agriculture's yearbooks suffer less underreporting of the size of China's private sector than do other official sources.

[86]Liu Xinwu, *Jumping into the Sea*, 1.

of these terms as well as on the exuberant exploitation of labor by China's entrepreneurs.

Property rights result from behavior more than they cause it.[87] In most of the Yangzi delta, especially in rich places like the cities of Wuxi or Songjiang, large collective enterprises flourished in Mao's time. Local cadres and entrepreneurs during reforms had scant incentive to switch their firms to become "private" property, so long as they could continue to make money for themselves and their clients under collective ownership. In a place like Wenzhou, however, where collective enterprises had been less salient for geographical reasons, local cadres and entrepreneurs supported the institution of private property as soon as their boom took off (i.e., later than in Sunan).[88] National norms about property, as expounded from Beijing, were at no time applied uniformly over the whole nation. They were referents for much rhetoric. They mainly caused trends in fashions of naming. They condoned the repainting of signs hung in front of many 1980s collective firms, to relabel them as private in the next decade and new millennium.

Rational action theorists have used much effort to link work incentives in post-Mao China to changes of property rights. But the rural Party, even after decollectivization, has generally turned over to peasants only use rights to land, not the more important ultimate property right to sell land. Farmers just get long-term leases, not ownership. This is China's current version of land marketization. The growth of a diversified rural labor market has correlated with the rise of a land-rental market better than either correlates with changes of formal property rights.[89] New factories and stores, not policy changes about property, are the reforms that transformed rural China.

---

[87]Many studies allow only one direction of effect: from property rights to behavior. That approach, used by some China economists in both the "convergence" and "experimental" schools, may be analytically neat but is realistically narrow. For a different view, crisply expressed, see Woo Wing Thye, "The Real Reasons for China's Growth," *The China Journal* 41 (January 1999), 115–37.

[88]See Susan H. Whiting, *Power and Wealth in Rural China*, 22, as well as Kate Xiao Zhou and Lynn T. White III, "Quiet Politics and Rural Enterprise in Reform China," 461–90.

[89]James Kai-sing Kung, "The Role of Property Rights in China's Rural Reforms and Development," in *China's Developmental Miracle: Origins, Transformations, and Challenges*, Alvin So, ed. (Armonk: M.E. Sharpe, 2001), 58–78.

THE MID-BOOM FLOW OF THE *GUAHU* TIDE

Dependent enterprises use the official licenses of larger or more statist organizations — nationalized firms, bureaucratic offices, or units of the Army — to engage in economic activities. They are "households" (*hu*) that "hang" (*gua*) from companies that have better or earlier political legitimacy.

The "dependent firm" form of property became very common among East China private enterprises. A survey in Wenzhou, where it was most usual, showed that 62 percent of actually private firms were "dependent" in the 1980s. In some areas, the portion was up to 90 percent.[90] At Wenzhou during the early 1990s, out of 12,000 *de facto* private businesses, only 40 were registered as private. The rest were *guahu*.[91] In Changle, Fujian, 80 percent of all rural industries were *guahu* at this time.[92]

Dependent firms come in three types: single households or individuals (*danhu*), two or more allied households (very loosely called *lianghu*); and joint stockholders' dependent companies (*gufen guahu*). While the owners of the first two types actually manage the businesses, in joint-stock firms the owners are not executives. All these *guahu* companies hang on others mainly for nominal purposes that nonetheless also raise autonomy and affect profits. The concrete help they obtain from their formally supervising agencies is local, not central, and it is compensated with payments.

Guahu use state firms or collectives for "three substitutions and three borrowings" (*sandai sanjie*): issuing receipts, keeping books, and paying taxes; sending letters of introduction, writing contracts,

---

[90]Kristen D. Parris, "Local Initiative and Local Reform," 245–46.

[91]Liu Jixing, "*Woguo feigong youzhi qiye ji qunti jiben xianzhuang*" (Nonstate Entrepreneurs and Their Basic Conditions), *Shehuixue yanjiu* (Sociological Research) 6 (June 1992), 13–20.

[92]*Zhongguo de geti he siying jingji* (China's Individual and Private Economy) (Beijing: Gaige Chubanshe, 1990), "Temporary Income Tax Regulations for Urban and Rural Private Businesses in the PRC (Jan. 7, 1986)," 7.

and opening bank accounts.[93] The legitimating agency in effect rents out its good political name. In exchange, it receives a small percentage of profits from the dependent firm, reportedly varying from 8 percent to 15 percent in Zhejiang, or only 1 percent to 5 percent in more conservative Hubei.[94] *Guahu* do not pay the high remittances for which any state firm with a profit is liable. The supervening enterprise does not supervise. It merely cuts red tape for an essentially private business by using its own official chops when these are needed.

State bank loans to private firms have been legally and administratively limited, but fewer credit restrictions apply to *guahu*. In Shuqian, Jiangsu, village collectives and their dependent firms did not need the county-level bank's approval for any loan of less than 5000 yuan; but a "private" business needed high approvals for any credit above 1000 yuan.[95] Interest rates also differed, depending on the borrower. From some banks, annual interest reached 18 percent for private lending.[96] But *guahu* could get the bank privileges of collectives. Issuing a certified receipt, a *guahu* company could call on its supervening firm to seal the paperwork. *Guahu* gave rural firms the ability to write cheques, which they were otherwise denied. "Nondependent" entrepreneurs had to pay for their transactions by carrying huge amounts of paper cash. Some had to hire police for "special

---

[93]Zhang Jinjiang, "*Shixi 'jiti' mingyi xia de siren qiye*" (A Preliminary Analysis of Private Enterprises that Call Themselves 'Collective'), *Chongqing shehui kexue* (Chongqing Social Sciences) 1 (January 1988), 60–64.

[94]Wang Xiaoqiang, Bai Nanshen, Liu Chang, Song Lina, and Zhao Xiaodong, "*Nongcun shangpin shengchan fazhan de xin dongxiang*" (New Trends in Developing the Production of Rural Commodities), *Nongcun jingji shehui* (Rural Chinese Economy and Society), Vol. 3 (Beijing: Zhishi Chuban She, 1985), 69–93; but the data in Hubei are from Kate Xiao Zhou's investigations near Wuhan and in Jinshan, Hubei, 1984 and 1985.

[95]Nongyebu Jingji Zhengce Yanjiu Zhongxin (Economic Policy Research Center of the Ministry of Agriculture), *Zhongguo nongcun: Zhengce yanjiu beiwanglu* (Rural China: Policy Research Backgrounder), (Beijing: Nongye Chubanshe, 1988), 375.

[96]Guowuyuan Yanjiushi Geti Siying Jingji Diaochazu (State Council Investigation Team on the Individual and Private Economy), *Zhongguo de geti he siying jingji* (China's Individual and Private Economy) (Beijing: Gaige Chubanshe, 1990), 17.

protection" while transporting these fortunes. Also, private firms' products were not allowed into some trade exhibitions, but *guahu* could display their wares under the name of the ideologically more presentable supervening firm.[97]

When by 1979 Wenzhou peasants openly re-adopted the tradition of family farming, an office-supply factory that had been losing money in the nearby village of Jingxin was the pioneer dependent firm. At first, local leaders divided the factory into four shops and carried out a policy of "five coordinations and ten autonomies" (*wutong shizi*). The five coordinations involved having the same formal titles for leaders in the supervening firm and the dependent factories, the same factory name, the same bank account — and the same low tax rate (7 percent). The ten autonomies may be summarized as voluntary cooperation, independent work contracts, separate decisions on technology, autonomous production, self-finance, separate machinery, independent production quotas, and separate responsibility for losses or profits. As soon as this reform was adopted, profits soared on both sides. Over time, as more complex specialized contracts increased in agriculture, the terms of these early industrial arrangements were also subject to loosening. Private families or lineages were contracted to take over small factories fully, even if these still bore the names of socialist companies.[98]

Problems can easily arise, however, when a firm becomes dependent under a supervising "mother-in-law." If the *guahu* entrepreneurs are former employees of the sponsoring collective or state agency, as is often the case, their new status as contractors gives them more autonomy — but their former bosses may resent the loss of authority over them. If the dependent firm makes money, as is usually the case, envy (the 'red eye disease,' *hongyan bing*) brings disputes about how to divide the profits. Disagreements about finances, or harassing audits based on personal animosities that such "mother-in-law"/"daughter-in-law" arrangements

---

[97]Ba Xian Xianwei Yanjiushi (Research Office of the Ba County Party Committee), "*Jia jiti xingcheng yuanyin zoushi chutan*" (The Causes for the Rise of Fake Collectives), *Nongcun jingji* (Rural Economics) 2 (February 1993), 13–14.
[98]*NMRB*, September 23, 1987.

often breed, give dependent firms' entrepreneurs frequent trouble. As a report on one such case put it, "In a state-owned enterprise, if one lost money, things would be fine; but the more money one made [in a *guahu*], the more difficult it became to justify oneself."[99]

Dependency is a statist ideal, but local leaders benefit from this norm even more. Dependency is also a capitalist practice, if workers can be made so psychologically subservient that the capitalist can pay lower wages than otherwise would be needed. As an organizational form, dependency allows practical autonomy to the leaders of small groups, while also allowing symbolic "face" to leaders of larger groups.

Guahu status can, if the supervening agency is urban, lead to legal transfers of "dependent" employees' household registrations from boondocks to cities. Entrepreneurs and some workers may thus acquire urban registrations (*hukou*) and other privileges. *Guahu* managers can in some cases become official cadres, and their family members also get urban registrations.

Dependency can also create conflicts among different sizes of collectivity. Village cadres may try to accommodate officials who are above them in the state hierarchy, but relations between bureaucratic levels are often turbulent. Reporting on various parts of China, Guldin found that, "Village cadres were full of complaints about being short-changed at the county level, while the county cadres had equally loud complaints about the pigheadedness of countryside (*xiang* and village level) cadres.... the village cadres were also not reticent about saying unkind things about *xiang* or [higher] cadres, as well."[100]

A town enterprise in Dianshanhu, Kunshan, Jiangsu, for example, imported raw materials to make scents that flavor cigarettes. These came largely from Henan, whose large state tobacco companies had earlier bought up most of these chemical essences.[101] Such actions

---

[99]Both of the conditions suggested here apply to an infrared alarm factory that is studied in Liu Xinwu, *Jumping into the Sea*, 68–69 and 74.

[100]Gregory Guldin, *What's a Peasant to Do? Village Becoming Town in Southern China* (Boulder: Westview, 2001), 91–92.

[101]Andrew M. Marton, *China's Spatial Economic Development*, 145.

could raise tensions between both administrative levels and geographic jurisdictions. Local and provincial firms could co-operate in ways that violated norms of the Chinese bureaucratic hierarchy. The premise of a market economy is that local managers are autonomous. The premise of Leninist discipline is that nobody local is autonomous. *Guahu* legitimation meant that the number of separate local decisionmakers soared.

Also, "local" is a word with more meanings in China than elsewhere. The PRC bureaucracy tries to organize many different sizes of collectivity into levels. The administrative word "levels" implies that smaller units never trump larger ones in behavioral politics. This is not the case. China's administrative structure near the turn of the millennium included 34 province-level jurisdictions (often called 'local' although every Chinese province has many millions of citizens), 332 prefectures[102] plus 265 prefectural cities, 2053 counties and 393 county-level cities, 658 cities at other levels, and 808 urban districts under cities. Other units also exist, including street and residence committees in cities. Each of these "localities," especially the smaller ones that were in fact more local, could engender entrepreneurs in any of the increased types of property management types that reforms allowed.

ZHEJIANG AS CHINA'S MOST CAPITALIST PROVINCE

Zhejiang's population is about 45 million. The GDP growth of that whole province from 1995 to 2005 was reported over 13 percent

---

[102]Prefectures, ever since they were established by the KMT in the 1930s to oversee counties, have been branches of provincial governments (*sheng paichu jiguan*). Prefectures are relatively unimportant despite, or perhaps because of, their large size. They have no people's congresses; they are even more purely administrative than other official jurisdictions. They have relatively small staffs. During the reform boom, prefectures have supervised only the poorer half of China's counties. The richer half of all counties are now supposed to be accountable to city governments. See Zhong Yang, "Dissecting Chinese County Governmental Authorities," Zhejiang University Conference on "The Development of the Non-State Sector, Local Governance, and Sustainable Development in China," June 24–25, 2006, vol. 1, 501–02.

per year, compounding. By the end of this time, Zhejiang had the highest per-capita disposable income among all China's provinces (not counting Taiwan). This was also true for citizens in either "rural" or "urban" locations.[103] Zhejiang had enjoyed the highest disposable income among "rural" people over the previous decade, 1985–95, too. Many rural Zhejiang people had for a long time found nonfarm work, especially in slack agricultural seasons. They had been laboring in factories at places still classified by government decree as non-urban.

The companies that hired them were overwhelmingly SMEs, which distributed income somewhat more evenly, among local bosses but also among their hirelings, than large firms did. As the previous chapter on Taiwan notes, such SMEs allow fast growth, strengthening local managers but also spreading the wealth more equally than do other structures that bring growth. Zhejiang capitalism involved a great deal of exploitation, but many of the exploiters had middling amounts of wealth.

More than seven-tenths of Zhejiang's total product by 2005 came from private firms, the highest portion in any PRC province-level unit. This may be an underestimate, because managers can evade taxes if they do not report all their production. There were regional differences within the province. Northern flat areas of Zhejiang, around Hangzhou Bay, had begun major rural industrialization about two decades earlier, in the 1970s (like the flatlands of Sunan with which they share many traits).[104]

A Hangzhou primary school during the Cultural Revolution established a small stationery factory to give students work experience. Zong Qinhou, one of the teachers, by the mid-1980s realized that soft drinks would be more profitable than paper. After market research to find a zippy name for his firm, he dubbed it the Wahaha Corporation.

---

[103]Interviews in Ningbo and Wenzhou, June 19 and 21, 2006. The province-level cities (Shanghai, Beijing, Tianjin, and Chongqing) are not counted in this estimate.

[104]On the particularly turbulent Cultural Revolution in this province, see Keith Forster, *Rebellion and Factionalism in a Chinese Province: Zhejiang 1966–1976* (Armonk: M. E. Sharpe, 1990). On some of the sequel, see Forster, *Zhejiang Province in Reform* (Sydney: Wild Peony, 1998).

The drink was sold in a distinctively shaped bottle. By the 1990s, the assets of this enterprise were over 400,000,000 yuan, employing several thousand workers. The Hangzhou Education Department technically owned the firm. Zong was praised as a "model worker," although in fact he was the founder-manager, and he made large sums in bonuses.[105]

Rural places in Zhejiang have bred entrepreneurs in many periods, irrespective of the policies of supposedly higher authorities then. In locations where a lineage with a single surname comprised practically all the population, that main clan could easily become the strongest political solidarity (unless its sublineages started feuding with each other). The external state could not seriously compete with it, especially if the location was somewhat isolated.

Local lineage networks could reach mutual accommodations with the state bureaucracy. For example, the Fu lineage of Tengtou Village, in Fenghua County, runs the Aiyimei Garment Co. It now makes several kinds of clothes, including high-end cashmere sweaters. As early as the 1960s, after the famine that followed the Great Leap Forward, the leaders of Fu sublineages in Tengtou (Fu is the surname of 95 percent of the people whose households are registered there) cooperated to move from agriculture into industry. Their capital came entirely from their own operations. Triple cropping in this northern Zhejiang area began at about the same time, in 1965. Payment of the increased grain tax from three crops gave the Fu leaders increased leeway in their business operations.

In later years, large profits from international sales of their sweaters and other garments became very profitable. The Aiyimei lineage enterprise became so successful on international markets that the larger state needed to do little but give it awards. Boom money let the local village polity, in which practically all government and Party officials are named Fu, house all the original villagers' families in sumptuous condominiums. These were only 760 people total — but

---

[105]David S.G. Goodman, "The People's Republic of China: The Party-State, Capitalist Revolution, and New Entrepreneurs," in *Culture and Privilege in Capitalist Asia*, Michael Pinches, ed. (New York: Routledge, 1999), 236.

by 2006, they hired 6,500 outsiders (mostly from Zhejiang) in their factories.[106]

GEOGRAPHICAL ISOLATION AND MARKET AUTONOMY IN SOUTH ZHEJIANG

Southern Zhejiang later became an even more clearly capitalist part of China. Wenzhou private businesses have more flexibility than Chinese private firms elsewhere. They use it to raise capital, lower taxes, recruit committed workers at low wages, and acquire easy access to local government permissions of many kinds. They have these advantages not because they are private, but instead because they are in Wenzhou.

These institutions for quick but late development grew out of Wenzhou's geography. Mountains long isolated this city from the rest of China. Only 5 percent of Wenzhou's population understood Mandarin in 1955, according to one report.[107] Wenzhou was the last sizeable city on the China coast to be linked to China's general railroad network — the first train did not come there until 1998.

"Crossing the river and feeling the stones" has been an experimentalist motto in several parts of China, and experiments were relatively easy to justify in Wenzhou because of its isolation from most of the planned state economy (especially heavy industries). This city, unlike Shanghai for example, had never been a source of major taxes to support powerful ministries. Wenzhou entrepreneurs and cadres recruited by them were therefore free not just to talk about experiments, but actually to try them. Similar entrepreneurs in other parts

---

[106]Interviews and visit in Tengtou Village, June 19, 2006. Most of the imported workers were Zhejiang girls not surnamed Fu. So village men from this wealthy lineage often chose brides among them. But an interviewee noted that if a Fu family had two daughters (which was frequent when the first child had been a daughter), at least one of them almost always had to marry outside the town.

[107]Wenzhou dialect is distinctive; only Wenzhou people can generally speak it or follow it with fluency. Alan P.L. Liu, "The Politics of Corruption in the People's Republic of China," *American Political Science Review* 77 (1983), 614.

of China can seldom get service from such compliant Party cadres. They took full advantage of this autonomy.

Some provincial places prosper because small firms can grow without much regulation, while others remain boondocks. A "boomdock" kind of locality proliferated in suburbs around Wenzhou.[108] Jiaotou, a small town in nearby Yongjia County, became able in the 1980s to supply one-fourth of all buttons sold in China. As this populous country exchanged its "Mao suits" for a more colorful variety of garments, there was a large new market for buttons. Socialist planners gave no evidence of ever having thought about the profitability of buttons. So three hundred Jiaotou household factories quickly organized to produce this small good. Many other Wenzhou firms aimed for and obtained national markets in a wide variety of commodities that the state system had simply ignored despite profit potentials.[109] To ensure sales, "About 100,000 Wenzhou people are scattered over the whole country. They form an information circuit, a business network."[110] One hundred thousand rural purchasing agents were employed by Wenzhou to scour the whole country and globe, by 1984, delivering and buying goods.[111] These salespeople soon diversified into all kinds of commodities, even grain whose trade had once been a state monopoly.

EXAMPLES OF LEADERSHIP IN BUSINESS

Zhejiang entrepreneurs (like Taiwan ones discussed in the previous chapter) have specific histories whose ups and downs often bear scant

---

[108]Scholars should attempt comparisons among places, and among countries, concerning the effects of geographical isolation on starting growth or continuing poverty. These would be complicated, however, because governments publish statistics variously in different kinds of jurisdiction and because firms in areas where tax receipts have been unimportant have reasons to under-report new economic success.

[109]See Liu Yaling, "Reform From Below: The Private Economy and Local Politics in the Rural Industrialization of Wenzhou", *China Quarterly* 130 (June 1990), 293–316.

[110]Fei Xiaotong and Luo Yanxian, *Xiangzhen jingji bijiao moshi*, 5–9.

[111]Fei Xiaotong, "*Xiao shangpin, da shichang*" (Small Commodities, Big Market), in *Fei Xiaotong xuanji* (Selected Works of Fei Xiaotong) (Tianjin: Tianjin Renmin Chubanshe, 1988), 364–83.

relation to the inflection times of national policies. This can best be shown by looking at several of them. A surprising number of south Zhejiang businessmen began as shoe cobblers. Some firms such as the Kangnai Co. stayed in cobbling but then modernized. This company now specializes in high-priced shoes for export. By the new millennium, Kangnai used 45 marketing offices in China and over 100 retailers in thirty countries abroad. This Zhejiang company had outlets and subsidiaries in Britain, Spain, and France that sold shoes at an average price of US$60. Another entrepreneur who began as a cobbler is Nan Cunhui, now CEO of the Chint Corporation in Taizhou City. His firm's 2005 sales of electrical equipment were worth US$1.5 billion, mostly sold within China. It also made electrical machines for the Chinese army.[112]

Another extremely successful businessman who began as a cobbler is Qiu Jibao, now head of the Feiyue Sewing Machine Company of Yueqing City. Qiu was born into an officially labeled poor-peasant family. His parents could not send him to school. Leaving Zhejiang as a teenager, he travelled around north China from 1977 to 1979, doing odd jobs as a shoe repairman. Then returning to Zhejiang, he wanted to set up a factory that would make machines to sew shoes. So by 1986, he used his savings (a few hundred yuan) and a private loan of 300 yuan to start a sewing machine factory. In 1988, he went to Guangzhou, trying to enter the well-known Trade Fair so that he could show his sample sewing machines to foreign buyers. He was refused admission; so he illegally jumped the fence into the Fair, was arrested, fined, and briefly held by the Guangzhou police.

Qiu then went to Shenzhen, the checkpoint into Hong Kong. He could not cross the border but persuaded a resident of the British colony to sell him a Hong Kong telephone book. Qiu called and wrote letters to sewing machine stores there, and this effort led to some

---

[112]Interview with Mr. Nan at the Chint factory, June 20, 2006. It is interesting that half of the Chint company's sales personnel are from Wenzhou, although nine-tenths of their electrical engineers originally hail from outside of Zhejiang. It is definitely not a state secret that Chint makes electrical equipment for China's military; but understandably, foreigners are told no further details about this. This part of the sales is a source of pride for the company.

sales. One of the buyers suggested that Latin America might provide a market for Qiu's machines — and this idea proved to be the basis for very profitable exports across the Pacific. It eventually brought some attention in Beijing, when the Peruvian vice-president, in the capital on a visit to China, asked to see the plant from which so many of Peru's sewing machines were coming.

Qiu was admitted to the Party in 1987. From 1989 to 1994, his Feiyue company in Yueqing sold over US$10 million worth of sewing machines abroad. Later expansion came in Europe, America, Asia, and Africa. By 2005, half of Feiyue's output was exported, although many of the machines were still sold under non-Chinese brand names. Feiyue bought part of an Italian sewing machine company and thus became a multinational. When Qiu was asked about his responsibility to China, he answered that it was indistinguishable from his responsibility to the whole world.

Lu Guanqiu, an older man than the founders of the companies mentioned above, began in another lowly occupation: bicycle and farm implement repairs. He was born in 1945 as the son of a farmer in Xiaoshan, north Zhejiang. In 1969, Lu put 4000 yuan of his own money (the local production team added just 120 yuan) into capital for a company to repair agricultural machines. He had seven employees. Already by 1972, Lu applied to join the Party — but for a dozen years thereafter, he was not accepted as a member because radicals took him to be a private entrepreneur (which in practice he surely was, albeit nominally as head of a collective). His Wanxiang Corporation in the late 1970s began to produce automobile parts, but its financial credit for expansion seldom came from banks unless matching funds or more were raised from private sources. His strong personal link with a particular local Party secretary named Zhu Bingshang kept him going, but Lu could not join the Party until 1984.[113]

Already in the next year, he was named an "excellent Party cadre," and by 1987 he was elected to a local CCP executive post. Wanxiang by the new millennium had its own venture capital company, a holding company, and many other branches (including a large American

---

[113]This information is from a conference with Mr. Lu on June 19, 2006.

headquarters outside Chicago, selling car parts to U.S. automakers). It became a highly diversified multinational corporation, with sales over US$4 billion and 40,000 employees worldwide (31000 in China) in 2005. Lu Guanqiu, whose personal fortune was then estimated at US$600 million, chaired the Wanxiang Corporation board, and he explained that his company aimed for "rolling development" (*guendong fazhan*), finding new markets and technologies in many fields. Wanxiang is a classic "gigantistic" Chinese organization, expanding freely into new fields as opportunities become available. Lu Guanqiu has turned over the CEO post to his son, Lu Weiding.

The Sharmoon Garment Company was founded in the mid-1980s by two brothers named Chen, then living on an island at the mouth of the Ou River. At first, they had in Wenzhou just eight machines to tailor men's suits. They sent samples abroad and gathered information about the international market. By 2003, the company was converted into a joint venture with the Italian firm Ermenegildo Zenga, and the prices of its products soared. The Italians provided a very fancy brand name, and Zhejiang Chinese sewed the suits. Li Yanhui, now heading the Sharmoon-Zenga combine in Wenzhou, said that no part of the Chinese government had any role in his business decisions. The officials "just give awards for high levels of export".[114]

Zhejiang foreign exports by 2005 exceeded US$100 billion, although foreign direct investment into the province was then only US$7.7 billion. The capital for all this enterprise came not from the state and not from abroad, but from local companies' profits. Wenzhou by 2005 made 60 percent of the world's sunglasses and 80 percent of the world's cigarette lighters. The largest firm in these sectors, Zhejiang "Tiger" Lighter Company, had been founded in the 1990s by Zhou Dahu (*hu* means tiger) using capital of 5000 yuan that his wife received for resigning another job. Already by 2000, President Jiang Zemin visited Tiger Lighter, and he was followed by Premier Wen Jiabao in 2004. By that time, the company had a staff of just 1000 workers, who came mostly from inland China.

---

[114]Interview with Mr. Li, June 21, 2006.

Yang Jun, a cadre of the government bureau that "supervises" (*jianguan*) Wenzhou private enterprises, affirmed that the ideal model in that city was "private." This was theorized as an effort to maximize "primitive accumulation." Yang contrasted Wenzhou with his own native Jiangsu, saying that, "Zhejiang people have advanced ideas and a strong sense of innovation." Freedom for them is now seen as good official policy.

This freedom has begun to extend to individuals' decisions about where to live. Five million Zhejiang people (about a tenth of the registered population) were by 2006 working outside the province. They did not generally take jobs involving hard or agricultural labor, as migrants from poorer provinces did. Many made or supplemented their incomes by trading. By 2006, household (*hukou*) registration was simply unenforced in some Zhejiang jurisdictions. Officials in Wenzhou and Hangzhou mooted the possibility that Zhejiang cities might abolish residence registration, which is an ancient symbol of East Asian states' control of citizens since traditional times.

Migration into Zhejiang is also distinctive among Chinese provinces. Many low-wage immigrants reportedly prefer Zhejiang to Guangdong not because earnings in Zhejiang are higher (apparently they are not), but because the lifestyle and extent of exploitation in Guangdong are more severe (especially in factories owned by Taiwanese or Hong Kong tycoons).[115] Companies in China tend to hire, for similar jobs, people who are co-provincials. Capitalist exploitation of labor was at least as intense in Zhejiang as elsewhere, but stronger nonstate norms there boded the possibility of some incipient unionization and more modern freedoms.

Ten percent of all China's registered trademarks originated in Zhejiang by 2005, although the province then reported (or underreported) only seven percent of China's GDP and had just 3.5 percent of the country's population. More important, 23 of China's 50 "most

---

[115]This statement from an interview in Zhejiang matches information gathered from Guangdong by many, e.g., Anita Chan, "Boot Camp at the Shoe Factory; Where Taiwanese Bosses Drill Chinese Workers to Make Sneakers for American Joggers," *Washington Post*, November 3, 1996, C1.

competitive" brands, designated as such by national officials, were based in Zhejiang.

UNDER-REPORTING AND FAKE PRODUCTS IN THE BOOM

Production data are published in China, but their inaccuracy (high or low) varies according to place. Zhejiang may well have under-reported its total output in recent years because its SMEs would have had to pay more taxes if they could have been more precisely monitored. Coastal Zhejiang by 2006 resembled contemporary Taiwan, although the reported output per capita was smaller in Zhejiang.[116] A comparison with Taiwan, where small firms showed the same respect for local tax policies, may be relevant. KMT legislator Chao Shao-kong in the 1980s reported that the Taipei government confidentially estimated that family businesses in Taiwan, underreporting income to evade taxes, actually added 25 or 30 percent above the officially announced GDP figure. A foreign economist guessed the amount was higher: 30 to 40 percent.[117] Tax evasion is certainly not unique to either Taiwan or Zhejiang (or Asia), but it is probably highest in periods of boom anywhere. Over-reporting by cadres is very probable in other parts of China, but where money grows most quickly under-reporting may practically be a factor of production.

Unbridled capitalism can hurt long-term profits, however, because pressure for quick money encourages counterfeits, unreliable credit, and shoddy goods. Wenzhou products were particularly subject to these difficulties. In 1987, "angry citizens in Hangzhou, the capital of Zhejiang province, piled up and burned 5000 pairs of Wenzhou-made shoes."[118] By the following year, private and collective firms, not just

---

[116]The Zhejiang sections of this book rely on the author's observations during a summer trip to that province in 2006. He is extremely thankful to Prof. Zheng Yongnian, and to Mr. Gong Wei and Ms. Catheling Qing, for arranging that journey.
[117]Hill Gates, "Small Fortunes: Class and Society in Taiwan," in *Taiwan: Beyond the Economic Miracle*, Dennis Simon and Y.M. Kao, eds. (Armonk: Sharpe, 1992), 180.
[118]Joseph Fewsmith, "Chambers of Commerce in Wenzhou," 82.

state ones, were recruited into the Association of Industry and Commerce, whose leaders were diverse. They included government, collective, and many private members. The group's main purpose was to reduce problems of product quality. This chamber was not the sole business federation in Wenzhou. Many firms belonged to multiple trade associations, not just in Wenzhou but throughout China and abroad.

Official rhetoric on government-business links remains patronist, even in Zhejiang. Formal discourse still echoes the motto of late dynastic times: "officials supervise while merchants manage." The reality has changed faster than ways of talking about it. The wealth of the new entrepreneurs has been both supervised and managed by themselves.

EXISTENTIAL ENTREPRENEURSHIP AND NETWORK NODES IN THE BOOM

What political and other factors allowed business people to found the factories and stores that created East China's boom? Many reasons relate to inherited infrastructures and unintended conditions (such as soil fertility and canals in some parts of Sunan and Zhejiang). Other reasons are collective and normative, especially in strong regional traditions of commerce. Yet other incentives to entrepreneurship were more individual and shorter-term. It is best to look at all these types, and at the politics they structure, to see which are most important.

Scholars have differed, when explaining what drives farmers to start factories. Barry Naughton argues that the reduction of barriers to market entry ended the official monopoly over industry.[119] But new enterprises also weakened the power of the state, so this reduction came also from local power networks. David Zweig argues that the government at large has therefore tried to constrain the growth of

---

[119]Barry Naughton, "Implications of the State Monopoly over Industry and Its Relaxation," *Modern China* 18 (January 1992), 14–41.

rural industries, despite their quick development.[120] Louis Putterman notes that the state has at least tried to "suppress encroachments on its product monopolies" from nonstate suppliers.[121] Only a few publications have looked specifically at the impact of rural industry on the erosion of China's earlier structure of economic governance.

The major motive of many entrepreneurs was the freedom that the market allowed to heads of economic units. The same phenomenon has been shown in the previous chapter for Taiwan. In Wenzhou, one of every 23 adults by 2005 was a "boss" (*laoban*) of his or her own firm. Some entrepreneurs became so resentful of real or imagined slights by officials, appointed as their bosses in Mao's time, they were eager to "jump into the sea" and start their own firms. They took the risk that later financial failure might force them to do menial labor. Some other managers, however, were risk-averse, especially if they were older or responsible for families. They could stay with their safe status and continue to eat "the emperor's grain" (*huangliang*) in state-sector jobs.

As the main entrepreneur in one small firm explained, "all his life, he had been hair attached to the skin of the state, but now he had the opportunity to get his own skin, and he wanted to become his own master."[122] Impulses of officials to control business people (unless these roles were united) countered entrepreneurs' impulses to freedom. These are the poles between which many scholars have analyzed the rationales of actors in China's boom.

Motives of control versus freedom can structure a discussion of leaders' incentives at the "grassroots," but they explain less about networks or regions. Many new companies in China have hived off from

---

[120]Mixed evidence on the results of these state efforts is presented in David Zweig, "Rural Industry: Constraining the Leading Growth Sector in China's Economy," in Joint Economic Committee, *China's Economic Dilemmas in the 1990s: The Problems of Reforms, Modernization and Interdependence* (Washington, DC: Government Printing Office, 1991), 418–36.

[121]Louis Putterman, "Institutional Boundaries, Structural Change, and Economic Reform in China," *Modern China* 18 (January 1992), 3–13.

[122]Liu Xinwu, *Jumping into the Sea*, 143.

other firms. When entrepreneurs found an independent company, some of their previous co-workers often come along with them. Other employees can usually be hired as the private or *guahu* entrepreneurs see fit. It is common for younger kin and spouses' relatives to join a new firm's work force. Turnover in small companies tends to be much higher than in state businesses or large cooperatives. Enterprises that make specialized products employ sales people in many cities, and by no means do all of them come from the locale of the factory.[123] In China's rough-and-tumble market economy, however, swindling and contract violations are so common that employees who handle money need to trust each other. So companies from Wenzhou, for example, send trusted kin all over China.

Money mixed with both individual and family motives. Local economic leaders, many of whom emerged during the boom from the ranks of ordinary workers, often had material incentives to take jobs in less controlled sectors. Before reforms, the average wages of collective workers had been less than those of employees in state-owned enterprises. By 1984, however, the average wages in private and nonstate sectors were already equal to (although more variant than) wages in the state sector. For more than half a decade after the mid-1980s, average wages in collectives decreased. Many prosperous collectives joined the "other" or private categories. Private sector wages rose much faster than did the salaries of people who remained state employees.[124]

Evidence from a 2002 household income survey suggests that Chinese inequality may, after rising over the next dozen years, by then have begun to decrease. It is not entirely clear whether China as a whole has already reached an inflection at the top of the "Kuznets curve" (which posits a relation between per-capita income levels and inequality). Stratification had increased in the 1990s. But more rural factories, even in some poorer parts of the countryside, caused a spread of labor that was paid wages above the agricultural rates.

---

[123]*Ibid.*, 131 ff.

[124]Lu Ding, *Entrepreneurship in Suppressed Markets: Private-Sector Experience in China* (New York: Garland, 1994), 140–41.

These SMEs were a factor for equalization (as in Taiwan earlier) that may have begun to countervail factors for more differentiated incomes.[125] In the parts of East China where SMEs drove the boom, the general PRC problem of increasing income inequality was at least reduced.

A few ex-peasants became entrepreneurs, even though most new businessmen did not come straight from field work. Farmers migrate and take factory jobs at least in hopes of raising capital so that they can later form their own businesses. In that process, they gain "social capital" and skills of kinds that farmers who till the soil generally lack.[126] Women may have been more able to use such skills than men, on the mainland as earlier on Taiwan.[127]

Most early entrepreneurs reportedly felt that their interests were "constrained by the Chinese state and their material means exploited by the bureaucracy."[128] A 1997 survey of PRC private entrepreneurs indicated that two-fifths (40.1 percent) cited "realizing one's own worth" as the main reason they left the state system; and an additional 7 percent said similarly that they were "unable to use their expertise at their former units." Another two-fifths admitted they mainly had a desire for "increasing income."[129]

Materialistic and idealistic symbols alike pervade Chinese discussions of local leadership during the boom. Sarcasm is as prominent as solemnity in discourses on this topic. An official slogan is that cadres, including those in business, should undergo "four changes" (*sihua*). Promotions are supposed to go to those who are better educated,

---

[125]Carl Riskin, "Has China Reached the Top of the Kuznets Curve?" in *Paying for Progress: Public Finance, Human Welfare, and Inequality in China*, Vivienne Shue and Christine Wong, eds. (Abingdon: Routledge, 2006), chap. 2.

[126]Ma Zhongdong, "Social-Capital Mobilization and Income Returns to Entrepreneurship: The Case of Return Migration in Rural China," *Environment and Planning* 34 (2002), 1763–84.

[127]See Margery Wolf, "Chinese Women: Old Skills in a New Context," in *Woman, Culture, and Society*, Rosaldo, Michelle Z. and Louise Lamphere, eds. (Stanford: Stanford University Press, 1974), 157–72.

[128]Ole Bruun, *Business and Bureaucracy in a Chinese City*, 3.

[129]Liu Xinwu, *Jumping into the Sea*, 146.

younger, more professionalized, and more revolutionary. (The Chinese phrases for these four changes respectively are *zhishihua*, *qingnianhua*, *zhiyehua*, and the incongruous *geminghua*, which now refers not to revolution but to conservative loyalty.) Thus sardonic jokes about cadres also come in fours: four of them are needed to play *majiang*, their new cars have four wheels, their ballroom dancing requires four steps in a square, their homes have as many as four rooms, their banquet tables have four sides. This is the jaundiced interpretation of the official call for "four-ized cadres" (*sihua ganbu*).[130]

Many undoubtedly went into business mainly for the money. But motives of wealth and freedom are inseparable. Those with educations had strong interests in workplace independence. Many hoped, as they said in interviews, to apply technical innovations that fascinated them.[131] The sea was seen as a free environment, as well as a rich one. Expansion, as much as profit, was the new entrepreneurial work ethic. Susan Whiting points out that local rural leaders try to maximize their industrial output regardless of any central mandates, which often priorize other goals such as political stability or tax collection.[132] The founders of new enterprises, and at least some of the cadres who later expropriated public enterprises as their own private property, were producers not just consumers.

A mid-1990s survey found that the most successful private bosses in China averaged more than eleven hours each day on the job. They worked hard. They have changed China's education system by using their money for tuitions at better schools for their children. They have led the consumption boom and, for better or worse, they have set styles that encourage many other Chinese to consume similarly.[133]

---

[130]Gregory Guldin, *What's a Peasant to Do?*, 100, provides the more interesting unofficial version.

[131]See summaries of several entrepreneurs' biographies in Liu Xinwu, *Jumping into the Sea*, 38.

[132]Susan H. Whiting, *Power and Wealth in Rural China*.

[133]See Kristen D. Parris, "The Rise of Private Business Interests," 280–81.

Money speaks to power, just as votes do (albeit still weakly in China), and occasionally as truth does. The individual and collective motives of East China's entrepreneurs were shaped by a cult of expansion that also appears elsewhere on the mainland, in Taiwan, and with somewhat different styles in Southeast Asia.

Chapter

4

Political Roots of Thailand's Boom

Thailand had the world's quickest economic expansion between 1984 and 1994, slightly surpassing that of China. The origins of this performance differ in fascinating ways from the roots of booms elsewhere.

The monsoon in Thailand makes for particularly heavy shifts between agricultural and industrial labor. Only 15 percent of Thai fields need to be irrigated at all, because of rains that are concentrated annually in four months. This situation differs somewhat from those of the other three places this book explores. Two related contextual differences also affect the bases of Thai development: malaria kept the traditional population low, but the rice these people grew had an export market that was lucrative. The taste of Thai rice has such a good reputation in Asia that the country's overall development has been affected — although many hands must work in fields during short busy seasons.[1] The other side of this coin is that a great deal of labor is free for employment in factories and trades during

---

[1] Nipon Poapongsakorn, "Rural Industrialization: Problems and Prospects," in *Thailand's Industrialization and its Consequences*, Medhi Krongkaew, ed. (New York: St. Martin's, 1995), 131; see also Chalongphob Sussangkarn, *The Thai Labour Market: A Study of Seasonality and Segmentation* (Bangkok: Thai Development Research Institute, 1987).

the long agricultural slack seasons. Modern development has roots, not just causes.

The origins of Thailand's boom, as of the booms in Taiwan and East China, are largely rural, but the mechanisms in each place are distinctive. Many corollaries follow from the monsoon labor market and from Thailand's population density, which malaria kept down until recent decades. Farmers have wanted to live close to both their agricultural and slack-season jobs. So small factories have been dispersed deep into the countryside, where government monitors still cannot easily tax or register them. For many years, and to some extent at present, many small Thai enterprises have simply been unrecorded.

Thai rural firms find it difficult to use all their capital during the third of the year when workers are valuable on fields instead, because Thai rice usually brings good prices. Thai farmers have not been very eager to move to larger settlements, because their economic benefit from such migration has often been marginal. Extensive tracts of jungle lasted in Thailand until fairly recent times, and farmers often could legally claim such land as homesteads, but only if they actually lived on it. Less fertilizer was needed for traditional Thai agriculture, in part because (relative to other Asian rice countries) arable for paddy expanded onto fairly flat land whose fertility had not yet been exhausted by previous use. Farmers had relatively less incentive to plant high-yield rice seeds that require petrochemicals, because land cleared from forests remains fecund for several years after it is first put under crops. The expansibility of Thai peripheral land relative to population, even though the availability of new tracts has slowed in recent decades, creates contrasts with the other places studied in this book.

By the same token, a relatively slow growth of second-tier cities in Thailand accompanied the start of industrialization. They grew fast later, after the 1970s, but at first not as fast as Bangkok did. The nation's population size, historically low relative to land, was also held in check by the government's notably effective family planning policies. (On this score, the next chapter shows a sharp contrast with the Philippines.) In Thailand, compared to other developing countries, the price of labor has nonetheless remained quite low, albeit above subsistence, relatively late into industrialization.[2] Dominance of politics first by conservative military governments and then by the Sino-Thai founders of labor-intensive firms has slowed unionization.

Thailand is not incomparable to the other rice polities under study here, but (as the next subsection about centralism and autonomy exemplifies) these particularly unusual Thai traits throw light on links that otherwise would not be so obvious in the other countries. Social scientists who want always to begin with models that are unspecific to place are likely to miss both those lessons and the interactions of these distinctive Thai contextual and sociopolitical factors: high-end rice agriculture, the bequest of malaria to ecology in a country that could have population control, the mixture of monarchy with frontier norms of individual freedom, and Thailand's ability to assimilate ethnically heterogeneous entrepreneurs.

A STATE SO IDEALLY CENTRALIST, IT ALLOWS PERIPHERAL FREEDOMS

Thai kings traditionally granted their court officials land. Nobles collected rents, some of which were forwarded to the king; so they were tax farmers. Local peasants owed corvée labor to the nobles, who were supposed to maintain public works and irrigation. Rights to rents and corvée help could not surely be bequeathed under the old *sakdina* system that ranked all Thais. The old polity distinguished several strata: aristocrats (*nai*), commoners (*phrai*) who owed their aristocratic lords three to six months of labor each year or else taxes in kind, and bondsmen (*that*) who owed all of their labor to the nobles.[3] The aristocrats extracted rice from this system, and some of them intermarried with South Chinese lineages that settled in towns to mill rice and start networks for trade. Only the court bureaucracy

---

[2]Thailand has stretched, but not repealed, the dynamics shown in W. Arthur Lewis, "Economic Development with Unlimited Supplies of Labour," *The Manchester School of Economic and Social Studies* (1954), 139–91.
[3]Kevin Hewison, *Bankers and Bureaucrats*, 34.

could give peerages to top officials, and these were usually not inherited at the same rank within families. Even more easily than in traditional China, local leading families in Thailand rose and fell. Elite mobility was fairly high. Leading Chinese immigrants could also participate as heads of their own communities.[4]

Land ownership was not heavily concentrated, even in the Chao Phraya central basin villages. In two typical towns, just one-fifth of the titled land was held by the five largest family groups together. This relatively low level of land concentration had not substantially risen since the middle of the previous century, the earliest time for which usable statistics were found.

The rate of Thai land concentration was reduced by the tradition of equal-share inheritance.[5] The recent boom counterveiled the importance of this old norm. Land concentration is a greater burden on the poor when nearby industries do not provide alternative jobs.

---

[4]See G. William Skinner, "Change and Persistence in Chinese Culture Overseas: A Comparison of Thailand and Java," in *Change and Persistence in Thai Society: Essays in Honor of Lauriston Sharp,* Skinner, ed. (Ithaca: Cornell University Press, 1975); Skinner, "Overseas Chinese Leadership: Paradigm for a Paradox," in *Leadership and Authority: A Symposium,* Gehan Wijeyewardene, ed. (Singapore: University of Malaya Press, 1968), 191–203; and Skinner, "Chinese Assimilation and Thai Politics," *Journal of Asian Studies* 16 (February 1957), 237–50, reprinted in *Southeast Asia: The Politics of National Integration,* John T. McAlister, ed. (New York: Random House, 1973), as well as Lucian Pye, *Asian Power and Politics: The Cultural Dimensions of Authority* (Cambridge: Harvard University Press, 1985), 62–63. Because Sino-Thai entrepreneurs enter this book's argument soon, it is worth noting that the Confucian tradition of venerating ancestors was relatively absent from Thailand (outside urban Chinatowns). Most Southeast Asians fear rather than revere the dead. In popular Daoism, though not in the anti-superstitious forms of Confucianism, Chinese also fear some ghosts. Another Thai-Chinese difference is that nuclear families, rather than large lineages, were the main social units in Thailand. But minorities adapt. (Just as linguists have found that originally different languages in close proximity adopt structural traits from each other, Sino-Thai entrepreneurs could maximize their benefits by partly copying habits and structures typical of the majority Thais among whom they prospered.)

[5]Laurence D. Stifel, "Patterns of Land Ownership in Central Thailand During the Twentieth Century," *Journal of the Siam Society* 64:1 (January 1976), 266, and for the previous paragraph, 252. More land, however, is ordinarily given to the child who provides eldercare for the landowning parents before they pass away.

When wages in factories are better, more workers leave fields for more extended periods. A mid-1970s United Nations report shows that less than one quarter of the Thai land on which rice might have been grown was, even so late, actually under cultivation.[6]

Because Thai agriculture was fragmented and run by small farmers, the country had no state-linked oligarchy that monopolized free rural markets. As in China, the state was connected to legal ownership more than with management or money. It was always majestic but usually absentee. A 1969 survey of four central provinces (Nakorn Nayok, Ayutthaya, Praphumphani, and Chacheongsao) shows that the old Thai ruling class still owned more than half of the absentee landholdings: 27 percent owned by nobles, 14 percent by ministries, and 10 percent by the Crown Property Bureau representing the royal family. The portions in these surveyed central provinces were high, and old noble families also nominally and existentially owned (but did not manage) land in more remote provinces. During the next few decades, as industrialization started, this pattern changed. Capitalists, large and small, bought more land. Among tillers, landlessness rose. Commercial crops took more of the fields.

Thailand's population in the three decades before 1970 expanded to 17 million from a low base of 12 million.[7] The boom, providing more anti-malarial drugs and new jobs in previously non-industrial provinces, increased the rate of population growth. By 1987, the total was 53 million; and by 2005, 65 million. This demographic change was also spurred by the expansion of paddy to feed more people. These changes were linked, because paddy expansion destroyed forest environments that breed the *Anopheles* kind of mosquito that bears malaria.

During the brief 1973–76 democratic period, Thai intellectuals' hoped for land reform, but these expectations were dashed in the 1976 coup. Then the Kriangsak Chomanan and Prem Tinsulanonda

---

[6]This report by Bindbandha Vasuvat is noted in Laurence D. Stifel, "Patterns of Land Ownership," 267.

[7]Pasuk Phongpaichit and Chris Baker, *Thailand: Economy and Politics* (Kuala Lumpur: Oxford University Press, 1995), 187–88.

governments (1977–88) avoided pressing a reform agenda so as not to worry landowners.[8] But because commercial-industrial profits in small firms owned largely by Thais who had Chinese grandfathers could be used to buy land, typical owners of land slowly changed anyway: mainly, they became more often Sino-Thai. Thailand has lacked a thoroughgoing land reform because the various kinds of central elites in the capital saw no political benefit from such a reform. One analyst wrote that "agrarian reform would have threatened a large number of rural landowners and absentee landlords, large numbers of whom were businessmen, high-ranking military and bureaucratic elites, noble families, and the royal family itself."[9] This lack of a land reform (and, as detailed below, the lack of a green revolution) did not prevent Thailand from booming — because exactly the same bureaucratic reticence against leading land or seed reforms extended to many other non-security fields too. This also meant freedom for entrepreneurs, even Sino-Thais, to establish SMEs all over the country.

When rice farmers need credit, perhaps to finance new agronomy or perhaps after disasters such as typhoons, they may mortgage land. By no means are all mortgages foreclosed (with the cultivators losing their land) if the farmers can make a profit and recover from their losses. But Thai farmers' chances of recovery were greater than those in nearby countries, notably the Philippines, for several reasons that deserve expanded explanations because they show important national differences of local politics.

Thai mortgage creditors tended to be local Sino-Thais, from a minority that was unlike the farmers. Few creditors lived at much distance from the mortgaged land. Few in Thailand ran lending businesses only; they were usually in rural trade too, but they seldom

---

[8]Kevin Hewison, *Bankers and Bureaucrats: Capital and the Role of the State in Thailand*, Monograph 34 (New Haven: Yale University, Southeast Asia Center, 1989), 135.

[9]Quoted in Walden Bello, Shea Cunningham, and Li Kheng Poh, *A Siamese Tragedy: Development and Disintegration in Modern Thailand* (Bangkok: White Lotus, 1998), 149; the authors' footnote withholds the source, however, perhaps because of the mention of the royal family.

managed large plantation estates that could buy the mortgaged land if the farmer could not pay back the loan. As Laurence Stifel writes, "While a large fraction of the mortgagees in Thailand were Chinese, they were more likely to reside in or near the village, and their culture did not clash brutally with the indigenous culture." Absentee landownership in Thai villages was traditional but gradually reduced, to levels between 10 and 20 percent only. "In contrast to other countries of Southeast Asia [including the Philippines], Thailand does not have an urban rentier class. Most absentee landlords have other occupations, and the villagers frequently say that they are more lenient, extract lower rents, and demand fewer extra services than the resident landlords."[10]

Thailand enjoyed an expandable land supply and high international prices for its main brand-name export, Thai rice, so for several decades this country was "an agricultural superpower."[11] Farming accounted for about half of Thailand's GDP at midcentury. Fields at that time still employed 88 percent of Thai labor. The quality of the product sustained this syndrome, rather than the efficiency of its production if measured by tonnage. Thai yields per hectare, even during the 1970s and 1980s, were among the world's lowest (one-third of yields in Japan or Korea, for instance). Thai traditional rice, though, is aromatic, sticky, and favored especially in Asian markets.

Thailand still had plenty of arable land. Thai farmers could grow rice profitably because their product brought high prices. Thai rice productivity per land unit was low, but the farmers seldom found themselves in unrepayable debt, as Philippine farmers often did. Tillers in Thailand were less constrained by state and nonstate hierarchies

---

[10]LW added the bracketed phrase. Stifel notes that during the Great Depression, Thai cultivators lost far less land than Burmese rice farmers did — but his comparison could as easily have been with the Philippines and the time period could have been later. He defines "absentee" owners as those who live in different districts than the village where the land is located. See Laurence D. Stifel, "Patterns of Land Ownership," 258–60.

[11]The term is from Walden Bello *et al.*, *A Siamese Tragedy*, 134.

when making their own local decisions about which seeds to plant, how and when to cultivate, and where to sell.

Most decided against planting high-yield varieties. They did not obtain this independence due to a government's early need for a majority subethnicity's political support (as in Taiwan), nor because the government found in short-stalk rice a way to take more grain tax (as in China), nor because they were coerced (as in Marcos's Philippines). Thais could make profits in markets because of pre-existing laxity of state control. This applied to farmers and business entrepreneurs alike. Political autonomy to use current technologies was the most useful factor the people in any of these countries needed, to start a boom. In different countries, they got this freedom in different ways.

The Thai comparison, because it shows an environment in which business and state networks were loosely integrated with each other, clarifies what was essential about the origins of Taiwan's boom. It also underlines what was important in Sunan and north Zhejiang, and later in south Zhejiang, where the "path-dependent" history of state policies and local counter-policies, plus new technologies, led to rural industrialization. Entrepreneurial prowess among Sino-Thai managers, combined with Bangkok's benign neglect of industry as of agriculture, allowed the founders of small Thai firms to create an economic boom because despite centralist rhetoric they had autonomy in local Thai politics.

In Thailand as in Taiwan and China, the political needs and opportunities of the least constrained networks provided a situation in which new local enterprises could thrive. As later chapters show for the Philippines, constraints by traditional landed oligarchs have thus far prevented a similar boom there. The structure of power and the self-identities of effective leaders are the factors that create or forbid entrepreneurial risk-taking. This is true of all four unique places under study here, despite their sharp institutional and historical differences.

THAI REASONS FOR KEEPING CLASSIC LONG-STALK RICE

Why did Thailand have practically no green revolution?[12] The most common answer to this question is that Thais themselves are exceptionally finicky about the taste of rice, and the high-yield varieties are deemed insipid. Modern varieties of rice might have been exported — at low prices, and with a loss of the national brand-name distinction — but the domestic Thai market was limited. High-yield varieties were on less than 5% of Thai paddy land in 1976. East China and the Philippines showed a contrasting pattern, with different agrarian effects on rural industrialization.

The performance over time of new seeds is not easy to predict, and a Korean comparison suggests that indolent bureaucrats in Bangkok may have inadvertently given local farmers more help than Marcos's enthusiastic bureaucrats in Manila did.[13] Another specific reason may be that the new seeds require a great deal of nitrogen, of which urea fertilizer is the most efficient source. Bureaucrats gave the Thai Central Chemical Company (affiliated with Bangkok Bank) a near monopoly of fertilizer production, but this company built a plant

---

[12]Andrew Turton, describing the pre-1985 period, writes that, "Thailand has scarcely undergone even a modest Green Revolution." Turton, "Thailand: Agrarian Bases of State Power," in *Agrarian Transformations: Local Processes and the State in Southeast Asia*, Gillian Hart *et al.*, eds. (Berkeley: University of California Press, 1989), 56, and 54ff.

[13]The new seeds are difficult to test fully before they are planted extensively and for a long time, as South Korea's sad experience with the "Tongil" high-yield variety shows. Tongil was enormously successful at first. The state encouraged farmers to use it on an increase from 10 to 85 percent of S. Korea's rice acreage between 1973 and 1978, with total output increasing from 3.98 to 5.78 metric tons of rice over that time. But then an unexpected plant disease, a blast, decimated the Tongil harvest. The traditional japonica variety was less affected, and the government eased its previous pressure on farmers. See Larry L. Burmeister, *Research, Realpolitik, and Development in Korea: The State and the Green Revolution* (Boulder: Westview, 1988), 60–64.

to supply a less efficient fertilizer, ammonium phosphate, instead. The bureaucrats protected this investment by slapping an import duty on urea.[14] Farmers thus had even less incentive to plant the new seeds, because they could not easily get the best kind of chemical support.

Bangkok's policies toward farming have "bordered on the schizo-phrenic."[15] The state achieved extremely odd results by imposing an export tax on rice. This was the most reliable earner of foreign exchange, and the basis for more employment than any other com-modity. Ammar Siamwalla and his colleagues (Scott Christensen and Pakorn Vichyanond) write more cogently about officialdom than do most economists who are interested in quantities: "The strength of the country's comparative advantage in agriculture was such that no amount of mismanagement by the government was sufficient to kill its competitiveness in world markets."[16]

VILLAGES, MACHINES, AND OFFICIAL NEGLECT

The export tax kept rice in Thailand. It thus depressed the local price, lowering Thai farmers' incomes relative to the incomes of urban groups. This policy might have led to political instability in rural areas, because it exported real wealth from rural to urban areas. Thai mafias (to be discussed later) put a lid on that danger, but the rice export tax also encouraged rural industrialization.

Thai farmers who adopted new seeds lost wealth. Anan Ganjanapan has written that, "as poor peasants were forced to buy fertilizer on credit, they received less for their money; with small amounts of fertilizer, poor peasants could not get returns high enough to cover the actual cost of their labor.... Tenants receive less return for their labor in intensive commercial production than they did when they worked to grow mainly for subsistence. Most of their

---

[14]Walden Bello *et al.*, *A Siamese Tragedy*, 137.

[15]Scott R. Christensen, Ammar Siamwalla, and Pakorn Vichyanond, "Institutional and Political Bases of Growth-Inducing Policies in Thailand," in *Thailand's Boom and Bust: Collected Papers*, Ammar Siamwalla *et al.*, eds. (Bangkok: Thailand Development Research Institute Foundation, 1997), 40.

[16]*Ibid.*

surplus labor is now captured by landlords through high rents."[17] This is a pattern that the Philippines will also show. But Filipino farmers, because of legal restraints on enterprise, had fewer factories into which they could move for alternative work.

Thai farmers decide by themselves what crops to plant. The state has financed credit cooperatives for them, but Thai bureaucrats have not mandated the use of high-yield/high-input rice varieties. Increased revenues from Thai agriculture, at least before the 1980s in the "golden age" of agrarian growth, came from the increasing availability of malaria-free paddy land that road expansion fostered.[18] Another spur to higher yields was more triple cropping. By 1980–81, in an area near Chiang Mai, 40 percent of all irrigated land was triple-cropped; but a decade earlier, practically none of this land had been used so intensively.[19] The timing of this change was connected with credit availability, because triple-cropping, whether with new seeds or not, requires more fertilizer and dependable water so that the chemicals do not burn plant roots.

By the 1980s, despite this slight increase of prosperity for most agriculturalists, the income sources of the poorest Thai farmers came under threat, and poverty among them increased. Legal titles to land that they had occupied were often uncertain, partly because crown land traditions mixed with a dearth of rural bureaucrats and an orthodoxy (associated in primary school texts with King Ramkhamhaeng, r. 1277–1317) that the king is magnanimous to farmers. Squatters on land planted traditional crops, though by no means just paddy rice since much of "their" land was hilly. Lenders gained authority in this situation of semi-legality. Not to put too fine a point on it, the creditors had access to many instruments of violence.[20] These bosses were

---

[17]Quoted in Walden Bello *et al.*, *A Siamese Tragedy*, 141–2, from the Ph.D. thesis of Anan Ganjanapan at Cornell University, 1984.

[18]Ammar Siamwalla, "The Thai Economy: Fifty Years of Expansion," in *Thailand's Boom and Bust*, 1–20.

[19]Anan Ganjanapan, "Control of Labor in a Thai Village," in *Agrarian Transformations: Local Processes and the State in Southeast Asia*, Gillian Hart *et al.*, eds. (Berkeley: University of California Press, 1989), 107.

[20]Gershon Feder *et al.*, *Land Rights and Farm Productivity in Thailand* (Baltimore: Johns Hopkins University Press, 1988).

often Sino-Thais, and they made local alliances with Thai police and army officers.

Rural prosperity rose, because of profits from sectors such as trucking, machine repair, brick making, house construction, and local banking. Mechanization allowed further expansions of irrigation but also forced labor off fields. The amount of land per agricultural worker increased. Many farmers switched to non-rice crops. The reduction of malaria in upland regions allowed an expansion of arable fields for varied crops such as cassava and pineapples. Roads also aided marketing for these products and for more lowland paddy. The malaria-carrying kind of mosquito does not readily breed in rice paddies; the original environment for *Anopheles* larvae is jungle plants and pools. Deforestation, with land flattening to create paddies, decreases the ecology of this particular species.[21]

New lands were opened for fields that absorbed an increasing portion of all Thai labor. Upland production grew, but this change was not based in a new agronomy. Moerman, studying a northern Thai village when tractors first became available there, stresses the role of peasants' choice: "The tractor, to Western eyes a dramatic innovation in itself and significant as a cause of productivity, was to the [Tai] Lue apparently little more than a larger axe for clearing land and a stronger carabao for tilling it.... When ... the tractor was no longer worth its cost in cash, yields, and autonomy, it was no longer used."[22]

Labor-saving devices such as tractors have been employed more extensively in recent decades, as has more inorganic fertilizer. But the rice crop in 1985–86 was 20 m. tons; and a decade later in 1995–96, it

---

[21]An increase of the ratio of humans to mosquitos, e.g., in cities, also decreases the transmission rate of malaria. This mechanism operates through the species' population biology. Urbanization and deforestation are modern trends that reduce malaria, irrespective of their other effects.

[22]Michael Moerman, *Agricultural Change and Peasant Choice in a Thai Village* (Berkeley: University of California Press, 1968), 185–86. The bracketed term Tai is a standard word for many Thai-related ethnolinguistic groups, such as Lao (in Thailand and Laos), Shan (in Burma), Dai or Zhuang (in China), Lue (in Thailand), and others. Related ethnic groups are important among the peoples of Thailand.

had scarcely risen, to 22 m. tons. Turton reports that, by weight, Thai rice "productivity is one of the lowest in the world, as is the adoption of modern technology in rice production." He shows that the whole agricultural sector "has been massively neglected by [Bangkok] governments, at least in the positive sense of subsidies, supports, and reforms directly aimed equitably to benefit producers."[23]

To the extent that agricultural employment can be distinguished from manufacturing employment, traditional fieldworkers before the boom were far more than half of all Thai workers; but by the late 1980s, they were one-third or less.[24] The portion decreased further in later years, not just because of migrations but because of rural industries.

IMPORT SUBSTITUTION, COMPETITIVE LABOR CONTROL FOR EXPORTS, AND GROWTH OUTSIDE BANGKOK

Thailand's boom was preceded by three decades of import substitution industrialization (ISI). General Sarit Dhanarajata's Revolutionary Council from the late 1940s encouraged Thai capitalists, rather than bureaus of the state, to establish industries. At first, these were largely in Bangkok. They were designed to reduce the nation's dependence on imports. The numbers of Thai capitalists and wage workers rose, as did the country's whole population. Most of this early industrial expansion from mid-century through the 1960s was in small firms founded by Sino-Thai entrepreneurs.

By the late 1960s, because of official fears that the Thai Communist Party's insurgency would spread to cities and because Thai workers were learning how to run strikes, the diet passed a Settlement of Labor Disputes Act. Workers were allowed to bargain collectively, although their associations were not recognized as unions and were prohibited from involvement in national politics.

---

[23]Turton, Andrew, "Thailand: Agrarian Bases," 53.
[24]Partly based on Kevin Hewison, "Of Regimes, State, and Pluralities: Thai Politics Enters the 1990s," in *Southeast Asia in the 1990s: Authoritarianism, Democracy, and Capitalism*, Kevin Hewison, Richard Robison, Garry Rodan, eds. (St. Leonards, NSW: Allen & Unwin, 1993), 168.

After a major expansion of Bangkok worker activism during the early 1970s, another Labor Relations Act somewhat expanded the rights of wage earners in 1975.

Thailand's export-promotion boom from the end of the 1970s reversed this policy. Patriotic demands for Thailand's international competitiveness became arguments for fewer concessions and less pay to workers. Agroindustry fit easily with export-led growth because of internationally famous Thai rice. Other foods, such as canned fish and frozen chicken, were also increasingly exported. In developing these fields, and even when signing cooperation agreements with multinational firms such as Japanese auto makers, Sino-Thai capitalists often managed to avoid close dependency on external corporations. Because rural factories were near paddies where wages were close to subsistence levels anyway, an increasing portion of the industrial economy rose in provinces outside Bangkok.[25]

Bangkok's per-capita annual real growth rate by the early 1970s was just 1 percent. But this growth was much higher — 6 percent — in Thailand's six provinces that had the next highest per-capita income. It was 4 percent in the next group of seven provinces by income, and it was 2 percent in the 34 poorest provinces. As in China and Taiwan, rich rural places (not the richest urban place) started the boom. Immigration to Bangkok continued, but the capital's growth did not match that of mid-sized towns. The highest growth began outside the primate city, in secondary cities.

The wealthiest provinces were not all suburbs of the capital, in this bureaucratic monarchy that has centralized ideals. The average distance from Bangkok of the main cities of the other per-capita-richest provinces was greater than for the next-richest group of provinces.[26]

A 1990 survey of an industrializing rural area showed that only about one-twentieth of households owned local businesses

---

[25]Andrew Brown, *Labour, Politics, and the State in Industrializing Thailand* (New York: RoutledgeCurzon, 2004).

[26]E.R. Lim *et al.*, *Thailand: Toward a Development Strategy of Full Participation* (Washington: World Bank, 1980), 26.

(e.g., brickyards or stores) or large tracts of land for which they hired labor. Another full quarter of households owned some land and agricultural machines, with a bit of capital to lend or use for fertilizer-intensive cash crops. A fifth owned a lesser amount of land and had to borrow seasonal capital. About half had no land, and half of these worked on a piece-rate basis in factories.[27] As the boom continued, the portion of households in the emerging rural lower-middle income groups rose.

The provinces of Chiang Mai in the North and Nakhon Ratchasima in the Isan (Northeast Thailand) enjoyed particularly fast growth, exporting products abroad and parts to factories in Bangkok, as well as making local sales. Many of the employees were "able to work in the city while maintaining residence in their villages."[28] Location in Thai places distant from Bangkok slowed the issuance of factory permits, petitions for various licenses, passport applications to support foreign sales, customs clearances, and other government services. But the trade-offs for these inconveniences were more important: lower taxes and fewer regulations because of reduced government monitoring. Entrepreneurs grumbled about policy biases against provincial factories, but these biases correlated with valuable independence for rural industrialists.

Thailand had double-digit growth per capita in each year between 1976 and 1981. Then the rate slowed for the next four or five years, returning to higher rates thereafter for the main boom decade.[29] Large firms were reported as important producers early in this period, but the fastest overall growth came later, when exports soared and smaller firms predominated. Part of the apparent differences between these two stages of boom, however, was the somewhat more complete reporting from medium-size companies in the later period. From 1978 to 1984, total sales of large companies were still registered

---

[27]Daniel Arghiros, *Democracy, Development, and Decentralisation in Provincial Thailand* (London: Curzon, 2001), 53–54.

[28]Nipon Poapongsakorn, "Rural Industrialization," 135; also 136.

[29]Peter G. Warr and Bhanupong Nidhiprabha, *Thailand's Macroeconomic Miracle: Stable Adjustment and Sustained Growth* (Washington: World Bank, 1996), 63.

as growing faster than GNP.[30] As the export-led boom took off, however, Thailand's pattern more closely resembled that on Taiwan, in
which small subsidiary firms, scattered over increasing areas of the
country, became sources for materials and services.

The 1980s witnessed a second acceleration of Thailand's take-off,
in which the provincial SMEs' role was more fully revealed. In
Ayutthaya Province, near Bangkok to the north, the value of agricultural production decreased slightly between 1989 and 1997 — but
the value of industrial production soared fifteen fold. By the mid-
1990s, more "farm" households received more income from nonfarm activities than from agriculture.[31]

DEVELOPMENT IN A NON-DEVELOPMENTAL STATE

Danny Unger suggests that the long-term "important story in Thailand
is the willingness and ability of Thai *state* officials ... to encourage
private investment. Officials asserted only minimal control over the
allocation of that investment; they left the Chinese, with the help of
foreign capital, to transform Thailand's economy."[32] These officials,
including generals, sometimes intervened in the economy to help
their friends; but they came in many kinds, and (until Thaksin's network briefly organized a more efficient elected kleptocracy after the
turn of the millennium) their efforts were not coordinated on a
national basis. Thai domestic markets remained competitive. A virtue
of the "Premocracy" coalition in the 1980s had been that it "sat back
and let things happen.... No overall strategy guided public sector initiatives." Anand has said that Thailand was "laissez-faire by accident."[33]
The boom was guided by markets, not state plans.

---

[30]Suehiro Akira, "Capitalist Development in Postwar Thailand: Commercial Bankers,
Industrial Elite, and Agribusiness Groups," in *Southeast Asian Capitalists*, Ruth
McVey, ed. (Ithaca: Southeast Asia Program, Cornell University, 1992), 37.

[31]Daniel Arghiros, *Democracy, Development, and Decentralisation*, 46, quoting
Ayutthaya Province official reports and research by Jacques Amyot.

[32]Danny Unger, *Building Social Capital in Thailand: Fibers, Finance, and Infrastructure*
(Cambridge: Cambridge University Press, 1998), 1, and 2 for the next quotation.

[33]Quoted in Danny Unger, *Building Social Capital*, 125.

Thailand's economy coped with two global oil-price hikes in the early and late 1970s, unexpected interest rate rises in the early 1980s, and potential disruptions caused by the 1987–90 global growth in exports of labor-intensive manufactures. Households and firms prevented these shocks from dampening Thailand's overall performance. A group of economists writes that "the more important stabilizing force than the behavior of the government or the Bank of Thailand has been the behavior of the household sector, in particular, the responsiveness of household savings to changes in income." They suggest that "automatic stabilization can always be described as the outcome of policy."[34] If so, the direct agents (the policymakers in this case) are outside the state. The savers were largely Sino-Thai household heads who invested their money well. Thailand during its boom generally followed conservative, standard, neoliberal economic policies. The government avoided deficits and discouraged inflation, but Thailand has been no developmental state.[35]

The Thai tiger was unlike the Japanese one that Chalmers Johnson described in his book on *MITI*. Unger shows that,

> The state in Thailand lacked a politically insulated yet powerful bureaucratic elite, a clearly articulated development strategy, a full range of discretionary policy tools, and the information that would be necessary to make effective use of such tools.... Thailand's success rested not only on stable macroeconomic policies but on an absence of effective sectoral policies [as well as] the specific assets of the Chinese, their social networks that enabled them to overcome market failures, and the absence of key effective market institutions.[36]

This country had no effective economic strategy as it posted its best economic performance. Unger also believes that Thailand's lack of planning might become a long-term drag on the economy. This may

---

[34]Peter G. Warr and Bhanupong Nidhiprabha, *Thailand's Macroeconomic Miracle*, 231–32.

[35]Richard F. Doner, and Anek Laothamatas, "Thailand: Political and Economic Gradualism," in *Voting for Reform: Political Liberalization, Democracy, and Economic Adjustment*, Stephan Haggard and Steven B. Webb, eds. (Oxford: Oxford University Press, 1994), 411–52.

[36]Danny Unger, *Building Social Capital*, 81–82.

later prove true, but it did not slow the boom until 1997 at least, and growth rates in the new millennium have been respectable. Before the boom, local companies, among which only the larger firms received some help from foreign (especially Overseas Chinese) capital, made the economy boom. Bureaucrats naturally omit to admit that they lacked a strategy. Even an expectantly liberal institution such as the World Bank can seldom say that a government, with which it must deal, has no plan. Some disjuncture between the state and businesses apparently encouraged early industrial development. Mutual penetration or embeddedness generally came later.

Research on Thai politics prior to the boom, however, relied heavily on a statist version of modernization theory. David Wilson's *Politics in Thailand* (1962) and Fred Riggs's *Thailand: The Modernization of a Bureaucratic Polity* (1966) emphasized the extent to which official institutions stabilized the Thai polity. They did not emphasize the extent to which special groups could serve their own interests. Nonstate actors, especially in the economy, seemed reasonable to neglect at that time. Their influence was growing, but without fanfare, and certainly without challenging the established order in any open way. Riggs described Sino-Thais as "pariah entrepreneurs," marginal men with useful economic functions that were unpolitical.[37] It would be less cogent to say that the social science of that time was wrong than to say simply that Thailand later changed.

During the boom, organized businesses ended the traditional "bureaucratic polity" by breaking the pre-1980s monopoly of mandarins and generals over economic policy.[38] Not only did the state's relation to other politically effective networks change. The types of those networks and their relations with each other also altered. But no paradigm for understanding is eternal — and the 1997 ended the main economic boom, if not the political structures it had

---

[37]David A. Wilson, *Politics in Thailand* (Ithaca: Cornell University Press, 1962), and Fred W. Riggs, *Thailand: The Modernization of a Bureaucratic Polity* (Honolulu: East-West Center Press, 1966).

[38]Anek Laothamatas, *Business Associations and the New Political Economy of Thailand: From Bureaucratic Polity to Liberal Corporatism* (Singapore: Institute of Southeast Asian Studies, 1992).

constructed in Thailand.[39] This book's treatment of Thailand does not stop in 1997, because the politics remained even after economic performance became somewhat less good.

THE BOOM'S HIGH TIDE

Thailand's annual real GDP growth from 1985 to 1995 was 9.4 percent (or 7.8 percent on a per-capita basis). Manufactured exports had the biggest expansion, rising annually by 28 percent. Manufacturing employment went up 8 percent per year.[40] Other "dragons" or "tigers" such as Taiwan and Singapore had more intent policies to promote manufactured exports. Unlike Thailand, they passed laws to encourage investment and new technology in industries that shipped out goods, and they adjusted tariffs and taxes to favor exporters. With so many SMEs run by culturally Chinese family heads, they did well too. The usual emphasis on state guidance policy explains less of what happened in these places, including Thailand, than does the similarity of SMEs run by ethnic Chinese bosses in them all. If cultural factors were more admissible in economic analysis, economics could account for more than it currently does.

Small-city traders and factory heads, who are mostly descended from Chinese "pillow and mat" founders of retail rural stores, prospered in this environment.[41] By the 1980s, the most successful of these were already expanding Thailand's industrial capacity quickly. That change in Thailand was unexpected, however. Wage employment in the central plains of Thailand as late as 1980 was still almost all agricultural. The central part of the country had, at that time, surprisingly few cities.

Bangkok for years had satisfied the urban "*Stadtluft macht frei*" hopes of modern Thais. No other place in the central plains had more

---

[39]This book was written prior to the availability of Pasuk Phongpaichit and Chris Baker, *Thai Capital after the 1997 Crisis* (Chiangmai: Silkworm Books, 2008).

[40]Pasuk Phongpaichit and Chris Baker, *Thailand's Boom!* (North Sydney: Allen and Unwin, 1996), 3.

[41]"Pillow and mat" capitalism is a revealing phrase developed by the authors of *ibid*.

than 150,000 residents. Aside from raising and processing food, the most obvious wage activities were in town markets, "selling fried bananas, weaving mats, making bricks, making and selling sweets, running beauty parlors, acting as midwives, giving massages, telling fortunes, and repairing simple implements."[42] This situation changed sharply in the 1980s. Most visitors to the quaint poverty of Thailand's central plains in the 1970s would have envisioned the coming boom no more clearly than most visitors to East China at the same time would have done. Any evidence of the looming change would have been scarce and impressionistic.[43] In north and south Thailand, a few cities were larger; but there too, the boom was unexpected.

By the 1990s, quick economic expansion transformed Thai suburban and rich rural places even more drastically. Arghiros reports of his research site north of Bangkok that, "When I revisited the community..., I was disoriented for several hours. A major highway cut straight through.... When I left Ban Thung in 1990, there were no enterprises making bricks. But in 1995, the industry had taken root in the subdistrict, in the form of six thriving brickyards."[44]

Thailand benefitted specifically from Taiwan's earlier industrialization, which (with other rich Asian places) created a better market for Thai rice — and then Taiwanese financed some Thai industry directly. Industrial jobs on the island had raised Taiwan labor costs for paddy farming. As agriculture there slowed, rice traders especially diversified to Thailand. They brought marketing networks and capital. By the 1980s, several notable Taiwan-Thailand joint ventures were established

---

[42]Clyde Michael Douglass, *The Political Economy of Regional Integration: The Central Plains of Thailand, 1855–1980* (Ph.D. Dissertation, Political Science, UCLA, 1982); or C. M. Douglass, *Regional Integration on the Capitalist Periphery: The Central Plains of Thailand, 1855–1980* (The Hague: Institute of Social Studies, 1984), 158 and quotation on 163.

[43]The author recalls that in 1967 on Jen-ai Road in Taipei (where he was then a Chinese language student), he and his wife saw a solitary man in an illegal shack factory, holding an acetylene torch, welding boilers — at the very wee hour of 1:00 a.m. on a Monday. A datum of this kind proves nothing. It is inadmissible social science. It gave a sense that Taiwan's economy was in good hands.

[44]Daniel Arghiros, *Democracy, Development, and Decentralisation*, 43.

in the Isan and Chiang Mai regions.[45] As Taiwan wages rose, and as the government in Taipei was eager to move money almost anywhere except the other side of the Strait, some Taiwan firms switched to manufacturing in Thailand.

Other multinationals also came to Thailand, and they inspired domestic Thai-Chinese entrepreneurs to shift from rural commerce to export manufacturing. As Pasuk and Baker say, "The foreign inflows had such a large impact on the Thai economy *because of the response of domestic business.* If foreign firms found Thailand a competitive platform for export production, why should Thai firms not take advantage too?"[46] Sino-Thai SMEs did exactly this. Manufactures, as a portion of Thai exports, were just 1 percent in 1960, 19 percent in 1975, 32 percent in 1980, up to 78 percent by 1992.[47] And exports were increasingly important in boosting Thailand's average real GDP growth rate from 1987 to 1995 at a rate greater than 10 percent per year.

Savings were 36 percent of Thailand's GDP in 1990–95 (and this ratio remained surprisingly high even during the worst financial crisis years, 1997–99). In 1990–96, Thailand had the highest investment rate in Asia (41 percent of GDP — even higher than the savings rate because of international investments). For comparison, in the island of Taiwan's richer economy from 1990 to 1995, savings ranged between 26 and 28 percent. In China, if the reported data are accurate, savings were 41 percent of GDP in 1990–95 and in each later

---

[45]Yoshihara Kunio, *The Nation and Economic Growth: The Philippines and Thailand* (Kuala Lumpur: Oxford University Press, 1994), 19.

[46]Pasuk Phongpaichit and Chris Baker, *Thailand's Boom!*, 53 (emphasis in original).

[47]This situation can also be described in terms of the declining portion of non-manufactures. In 1970, primary commodities comprised more than nine-tenths of Thailand's exports. These were minerals and foods, especially rice. By 1992, this portion plummeted to one-third. In 1970, only 8 percent of exports were manufactures; but by 1992, manufactures were up to 67 percent; see Richard F. Doner and Ansil Ramsay, "Competitive Clientelism and Economic Governance: The Case of Thailand," in *Business and the State in Developing Countries*, Sylvia Maxfield and Ben Ross Schneider, eds. (Ithaca: Cornell University Press, 1997), 239. See also Andrew Brown, *Labour, Politics, and the State*, 92, based on research by Falkus.

year until 1999, when the portion dropped (or the accuracy of reporting rose) to make the ratio 39 percent. The Philippines tell a totally different story: the 1990–96 savings rate was 15 percent, dropping to 14 in 1997 and 13 in 1998, before rising a bit to 15 percent in 1999.[48]

Thailand's GDP growth rate was 9.2 percent annually in 1990–95 and 5.9 percent in 1996. The Asian financial crisis made it negative, down to –1.8 percent in 1997, then –10.4 percent in 1998, but already back up to a positive 4.2 percent in 1999. Comparable figures for the Philippines were: 1990–95, 3.3 percent annually; 1996, 5.8; 1997, 5.2; 1998, –0.5; 1999, 3.2 percent. For Taiwan: 1990–95, 6.4 percent annually; then 5.7 in 1996; 1997 up to 6.8; 1998, 4.7; 1999, 5.5. For all of China, it is unclear whether the overall data were somewhat inflated, but the 1990–95 annual GDP growth was claimed to be 10.6 percent annually. Thailand's average annual performance in the first half decade of the new millennium neared 5 percent. The financial crisis hurt Thailand badly, but its earlier boom had created path-dependent institutions of entrepreneurship. Thai GDP real growth in the new millennium good but below boom levels: in the 2002–04 triennium, respectively 5.3, 7.1, and 6.3 percent. A tsunami and a coup slowed it only somewhat in the next two years.

IDEAL CENTRALISM AND "DEMOCRATIC" DECENTRALIZATION

The Thai state has more than two million bureaucrats. Bangkok at least nominally used to dominate the provinces (*changwat*) in which nine-tenths of Thailand's people live. In practice, the structure of domination has long been jointed and lanky, although in theory it is centralist. The traditional Hindu "hill of power" image of an idealized Southeast Asian polity applies to Thai norms, if seldom to behavior.[49]

---

[48]Charles Harvie, "The Asian Financial and Economic Crisis and its Impact on Regional SMEs," in *Globalisation and SMEs in East Asia*, Charles Harvie and Boon-Chye Lee, eds. (Cheltenham: Edward Elgar, 2002), 14, and for the next paragraph, 12.
[49]This striking myth is described by Robert F. Heine-Geldern, *Concepts of State and Kingship in Southeast Asia* (Ithaca: Southeast Asia Program, Cornell University, 1956).

Thailand is in some senses at least as centralized as any other country studied in this book. Thai government ideology gives the king, at the center, a cosmic role. This was the notional form of Hindu and Buddhist kingdoms in Southeast Asia for centuries. Among disparate pre-Thai ('Tai') tribes that were long ruled by chiefs, the Sukothai monarchs first effectively propagated this vision of legitimate rule. The Chakri dynasts, who have ruled since 1782, made the most of it. Recent politics bear only a distant resemblance to this idealized view of rule, which nonetheless retains currency among Thais, allows the king to balance soldiers and businessmen (as he did notably in 1992 and 2006), and serves reformers who want to centralize. A corollary of the mindset behind this, however, is that anything happening out-side Bangkok is presumed to be relatively unimportant. Ambitious entrepreneurs outside the capital can and do fly under the radar of the state.

The state in Thailand is relatively strong, at least in comparison with that in the Philippines. Thai macroeconomic control agencies, for instance, have preserved their independence from politicians. They have been unlike many other parts of the Thai bureaucracy in this respect. In the Philippines, by contrast, parts of the weak civil services have been open to plunder for decades.[50] Doner and Ramsay cite an example of this contrast: "Marcos cronies in the textile indus-try used political connections to inflate assets of allied commercial banks and, in one major case, fled the country and triggered a major banking crisis after defaulting on some US$85 million in debt."[51] The Bangkok Bank acted differently, when it financed change in Thailand's textile industry, but Thai centralization in practice is more sporadic. Banks' or governments' interventions are seldom perma-nent. Local leaders have some degrees of freedom.

"Internal colonization" brought Bangkok bureaucrats into provinces and districts. The Ministry of the Interior runs not just the

---

[50]Paul D. Hutchcroft, *Booty Capitalism: The Politics of Banking in the Philippines* (Quezon City: Ateneo de Manila University Press, 1998).

[51]Richard F. Doner and Ansil Ramsay, "Competitive Clientelism and Economic Governance), 274, relying in part on work by Kuo Cheng-Tian.

police, but also the civil administrations of all provinces as well as the Community Development Department. This traditionally centralist system was strengthened during the 1970s, when Bangkok faced a communist insurgency. Wars and failing foreign economies on Thailand's long borders with Burma, Laos, and Cambodia also brought floods of refugees. These events spurred development of the country's periphery and temporarily centralized authority in some places, but the officials ebbed back to Bangkok when they could. Money, during the boom, created a greater variety of local powers to which the Bangkok bureaucracy must relate. New roads made connections with the state, but they also connected nonstate networks with each other.

Democratic decentralization, in which local officials were elected rather than appointed, has been generally opposed by the Ministry of the Interior. Business politicians from the provinces, notably premier Chuan Leekpai during his brief reform government in the early 1990s, nonetheless passed laws mandating elections in localities where the only previous civilian officials had been Interior Ministry bureaucrats. Decentralization was a central project of elected politicians who (like Chuan) had made money in the provinces. A major link between early capitalism and early democratization is that elections then become easier to buy.

New "local state" institutions were established, parallel to the old bureaucracy. Elected councils by the mid-1990s became the local governments. These were called Subdistrict Administrative Organizations (SAOs), charged to "develop the subdistrict economically, socially, and culturally." As Arghiros wrote, "Vote-buying is a pervasive and effective canvassing tool in contemporary Thailand, and there are already indications that control over SAOs is passing to wealthy, vote-buying candidates.... Seats on an SAO enable members to contract out the construction projects that the organization commissions to their or their associates' businesses." This expands democracy in an otherwise bureaucratic system — but it certainly does not soon expand rule by most of the citizens. "Little of what the SAO does is a result of consultation with villagers, and residents of the poorest neighborhoods remain entirely voiceless."[52]

REGIONAL ASPECTS OF THAI POLITICS, BEFORE AND DURING THE BOOM

Regionalism, not just appointive or elective procedures for choosing officials, affected the types of links between government and citizens in Thailand. Much attention has been devoted to the Malay-Muslim south of Thailand because of armed insurgents there, but Thai (or Tai) disunity was also important in the distant history of Siamese politics. There are currently two Tai states, Thailand and Laos.[53] Within Thailand, the largest distinctive region is the large Isan basin, bordered by the Mekong River on the north and east, and by a low range of hills on the south. When elections constitute Thailand's national government, Isan is crucial because it has one-third of the voters.

Isan contains an even larger portion of all Thai farmers. The most common household language in Thailand is not the standard Bangkok dialect of Thai, the official language of government and schools. Instead, it is Lao, which has more speakers in Thailand's Isan than in Laos (where it is official). Isan soil was originally the sandy bottom of an ancient sea. Salt glistens in road cuts there. This land is poor, and the size of farms is larger than Thailand's average.[54] As late as 1990 in the Northeast, 28 percent of the people lived

---

[52]Daniel Arghiros, "Political Reform and Civil Society at the Local Level: Thailand's Local Government Reforms," in *Reforming Thai Politics*, Duncan McCargo, ed. (Singapore: Institute of Southeast Asian Studies, 2002), 233 and 225–30.

[53]On the term "Tai," see fn. 21. David Wyatt, *A Short History of Thailand* (New Haven: Yale University Press, 1984), outlines how Tai *muang* chiefdoms and then larger kingdoms such as Lanna, Chiang Mai, and Sukhotai appeared in the present-day Siamese areas that had earlier largely been ruled by Mons and Khmers.

[54]Ronald Hill, *Southeast Asia: People, Land, and Economy* (Crows Nest, NSW, Allen and Unwin, 2002), 172.

below the official poverty line, whereas in Bangkok the rate was only 4 percent.[55]

Thailand's free allowance of country-to-city migration means that urban poverty rates can exceed those of rural areas. Freedom of movement has allowed many children of farmers, who might have led the countryside politically if they had stayed, go into cities instead. The Isan, and to a lesser extent south Thailand whose subregions have great variations of wealth, contains more poor people than the North around Chiang Mai, or especially the central plain or Bangkok regions.

A 1976 survey showed that 46 percent of rural households in the Isan (and 33 percent of urban households there) were below a nationally defined poverty line. The rural and urban portions in the South were 31 and 32 percent. In the North, the rural and urban portions of people under the poverty line were lower, both at 24 percent. In Central Thailand, the rural rate was 13 percent, and in cities a higher 21 percent, with a 12 percent rate in Bangkok.[56] These data on poverty do not mean, however, that the Isan and Southern economies were stagnant. On the contrary, relatively rich parts of these generally poor areas attracted capital in part because wages were low. The Northeast and South have large populations and sharp income inequalities. Also, money could buy votes there; local patronist hierarchies were strong. As the boom developed, the rural poor, and through elections the governments, were effectively bought by entrepreneurs, in these areas distant from the Bangkok bureaucracy.

The boom also caused individual Thais to migrate among regions at an unprecedented rate searching for better jobs. Agriculture's share of Thai GDP dropped from 33 to 11 percent during the three decades before 1995, and higher factory wages attracted labor from paddies.

---

[55]Suchit Bunbongkarn, *State of the Nation: Thailand* (Singapore: Institute of Southeast Asian Studies, 1996), 17.

[56]The urban poverty rate in the South may have been higher than the rural rate because of rich rice lands there. Chai-anan Samudavanija and Sukhumband Paribatra, "Thailand: Liberalization without Democracy," in *Driven by Growth: Political Change in the Asia-Pacific Region*, James Morley, ed. (Armonk: M. E. Sharpe, 1993), 126.

More than two-fifths of Thai villages by 1994 were reportedly affected by "severe" emigration. The main problem was not a lack of infrastructure in rural areas. It was claimed that, "over 90 percent of villages have electricity and good access to roads, 93 percent of the population is literate, and 100 percent of subdistricts throughout Thailand have health centers."[57] The political system, through the army during anti-communist times and for electoral reasons later, delivered investments in physical and human infrastructure. But there was still great regional disparity — and great rural poverty in areas such as the Northeast.

SINO-THAI SMALL AND MEDIUM ENTERPRISES

Thai growth has been mostly industrial, and it was first based on small-scale, often family-owned firms employing fewer than ten workers.[58] Thailand has an industrial census, but a distinguished Thai economist reported in an informal interview that its figures are highly unreliable. Definitions of "small- and medium-sized enterprises" (SMEs) in surveys differ considerably. Still, they do not diverge so radically among the countries of concern here as to prevent rough comparisons.

All but five percent of SMEs on a global basis, as defined in most surveys internationally, have fewer than 100 employees — but they provide the jobs of most wage earners. For example, by 1996–97 Taiwan SMEs employed nearly eight-tenths of all workers. They hired seven-tenths of the manufacturing workforce in China. In the proportionally smaller Philippine industrial workforce, they employed a lower fraction

---

[57]Brian Corbitt, "T-BIRD Rural Development Projects in Northeast Thailand," in *Development Dilemmas in the Mekong Region*, Bob Stensholt, ed. (Clayton: Monash Asia Institute, 1996), 37.

[58]Sungsidh Phiriyarangsan and Kanchada Poonpanich, "Labor Institutions in an Export-oriented Country: A Case Study of Thailand," in *Workers, Institutions, and Economic Growth in Asia*, G. Rodgers, ed. (Geneva: International Institute of Labour Studies, 1994), 211–253, quoted in Andrew Brown, *Labour, Politics, and the State in Industrializing Thailand* (New York: RoutledgeCurzon, 2004), 8.

(about two-thirds).[59] Data about Thai SMEs suggest that the registration requirements there are considerably more lax than in the three other countries. Several different Thai government departments register SMEs — and classify them variously. There has been no comprehensive reporting system, although this lack of official attention and red tape may make start-ups easier and might help the Thai economy to grow.

The largest bank (the Bangkok Bank, a private institution) has been cited alongside government agencies as a source of authoritative data about Thai SMEs.[60] Bangkok ministries often lack information. Unofficial sample surveys nonetheless suggest the increasing importance of SMEs. It is crystal clear that more small firms existed than were recorded.[61]

Before the boom, in 1963, two-thirds of manufacturing workers in the Bangkok-Thonburi area were already surveyed to be in firms of ten or fewer people. By 1973, more than three-quarters of firms even in this most industrialized area reportedly had ten employees or fewer.[62] The provincial portions outside the metropole of Thailand were higher, and areas south and west of the capital sprouted many new SMEs in the 1980s especially.

---

[59]See Charles Harvie and Boon-Chye Lee, "East Asian SMEs," 3–6, for figures suggesting these approximate portions and for details about the problems of comparison between surveys that use different definitions. An April 2003 attempt to obtain more information from a source this book had used, http://www.acgtetsme.org, still offered mid-1990s figures. The Thai surveys covered only "industrial" workers in a much looser registration regime — although economists, ever eager to tabulate any numbers, seem to have neglected the importance of these differences.

[60]Peter Brimble, David Oldfield, and Manusavee Monsakul, "Policies for SME Recovery in Thailand," in *The Role of SMEs in National Economies in East Asia*, 205.

[61]Economist Chris Hall in 1995 reported that Thailand had just 1.7 SMEs per 1000 people. Taiwan had twenty-two times as many, 37.1 SMEs per 1000 population. This extreme degree of reported difference is unlikely to be accurate. Most Thai SMEs are undocumented. Comparable figures were not found for the Philippines, but the effects there and in Jiangnan (where dubious data can also be found) show differences in registration coverage, and they cast great doubt on such numbers. See Charles Harvie and Boon-Chye Lee, "East Asian SMEs," 8.

[62]Unfortunately, these two surveys did not report the same statistic. Andrew Brown, *Labour, Politics, and the State*, 74, based on research by Sungsidh.

Officially collected statistics, which even by boom times did not include firms with fewer than eight employees, suggest that many Thai rural factories sprang up around Bangkok in the 1970s. In later years, however, industrialization was more evenly distributed in many parts of Thailand. By 1987–91, the growth of the number of industrial firms in provinces around Bangkok (12 percent annually) was reported as scarcely higher than the SME growth in a much larger "outer ring" (11 percent annually, although Kanchanaburi grew at 18 percent, and Angthong grew at 29 percent per year). In the whole North, the average was 12 percent; in Isan, 13 percent; and in the South, 10 percent.[63] Reporting was also probably more complete near the capital.

This provincial prosperity is striking because the central government in those years did practically nothing to finance it directly. Army engineers had built roads and other infrastructure, but the state put little of its money into provincial production or trade. The same pattern appeared among Taiwanese SMEs and in Chinese nonstate (collective, private, or individual) firms. In 1987, Thailand's Board of Investment put just ten percent of its funds in the North, Isan, and South combined. By 1991, this portion had risen only to 30 percent, although a great majority of Thais hail from those regions, which generally prospered.[64]

Many of the production lines involving the greatest growth of profits such as textiles, garments, gem polishing, jewelry, leather products, and furniture were labor-intensive. These goods were produced by small and medium industries employing fifty workers or fewer, as were the endemic machine repair shops and brickyards. This variety of companies sold to local and foreign markets alike. Perhaps surprisingly, a greater

---

[63]Nipon Poapongsakorn, "Rural Industrialization," 118, which unfortunately provides only numbers of registered firms in "selected" provinces, rather than the value of their output. This page does, however, report whole-region data that contradict a thesis of the essay, which is that growth outside Bangkok has been slow. The percentages have been rounded from hundredths-of-percents in the original; this exactitude is very dubious, if only because unregistered firms (apparently including all with fewer than eight employees) were not counted.

[64]Nipon Poapongsakorn, "Rural Industrialization," 120.

part of registered SMEs' products went abroad than of large firms' manufactures. "Small and medium firms," employing 50 workers or fewer, were by the late 1970s, selling 27 percent of their output value abroad — as compared with just 15 percent abroad for Thai firms that had 200 workers or more.[65] The export portion of small firms' output rose further in later years, and rural SMEs also processed semi-finished products for larger combines.

The Thai bureaucracy's stance toward all companies (aside from political contracting, a topic for a later chapter) has been benign neglect. As Parichart writes, "By and large, small- and medium-scale entrepreneurs have had to be self-reliant, having been relatively neglected by state authorities. However, as they have done reasonably well for themselves, especially when compared with farmers and workers, this neglect by the state has been, if not acceptable to both parties, at least not a major cause of conflict."[66] The Chinese Daoist philosopher Lao Zi is rumored to have said, "Governing a large state is like cooking a small fish. It should not be overdone." The Thai government, more than any recent Chinese regime, has taken such advice and has used a very light touch in economic policy.

ENTREPRENEURSHIP, INDIVIDUALISM, SKILLS, AND NETWORKS

The incentives of entrepreneurs to be their own bosses has been strong in Thailand (as in Taiwan and East China). Love of freedom may be more documentably traditional in Thailand than elsewhere in East Asia. Norms of loose interpersonal relations have been common

---

[65]Actually, these export figures for small firms are too low, because the Thai Ministry of Industry did not try to register any firms employing seven or fewer workers; their output was not monitored or counted. The overall export portion of Thailand's manufactures was 14 percent in 1975, 20 percent in 1980, and higher later. Robert J. Muscat, *Thailand's 1992 Elections: Economic Growth and Political Change* (New York: Asia Society, 1992), 160 and 309.

[66]Parichart Chotiya, "The Changing Role of Provincial Business in the Thai Political Economy," in *Political Change in Thailand: Democracy and Participation*, Kevin Hewison, ed. (London: Routledge, 1997), 256–57.

among Thais. Anthropologists John Embree and Herbert Phillips found this pattern in villages and families.[67] The practical degrees of freedom for Thai entrepreneurs and politicians have also been wide. A pioneering economist of Thailand, Thomas Silcock, once claimed that Thailand was a country of "liberalism by default."[68]

If so, this was default by the state but not by entrepreneurs. The combined assets of domestic Thai firms were five times those of foreign and joint enterprises, even in the mid-1990s after a decade of stupendous growth.[69] Many of these assets were in domestic corporations with interlocking directorates and shareholding. But an increasing and under-reported portion was in middle-sized and smaller firms.

Rural industrialization became an official slogan after Thailand's boom was already well underway. From the Bangkok government's viewpoint, rural factories were both nonstate and peripheral. The Thai Business Initiative for Rural Development nonetheless became a nationwide project of the Population and Community Development Association. This largest non-governmental organization in Bangkok received money from international and Thai companies. Its aim was "to transfer business skills to rural settings, to allow villagers to generate income, to enable villages to remain intact."[70] More important, Thailand's tariffs on machinery imports were reduced in 1990 from 20 percent down to 5 percent. This helped provincial entrepreneurs buy equipment and expand their businesses.[71]

Large firms both networked and competed with smaller Thai companies. The relation of SMEs to larger firms has always been complex.

---

[67]See John F. Embree, "Thailand: A Loosely Structured Social System," *American Anthropologist* 52:2 (1950), 191–93, and Herbert Phillips, *Thai Peasant Personality: The Patterning of Interpersonal Behavior in the Village of Bang Chan* (Berkeley: University of California Press, 1965).

[68]Silcock and Anand are quoted in Alasdair Bowie and Danny Unger, *The Politics of Open Economies: Indonesia, Malaysia, the Philippines, and Thailand* (New York: Cambridge University Press, 1997), 155.

[69]See Kevin Hewison, *Bankers and Bureaucrats*.

[70]Brian Corbitt, "T-BIRD Rural Development," 36.

[71]Leo Paul Dana, *Entrepreneurship in Pacific Asia: Past, Present and Future* (Singapore: World Scientific, 1999), 174.

In Thailand's boom (as in Taiwan's or China's), SMEs were the "major competitors" of "a majority of firms in the formal sector," according to an analysis by German economists.[72] Much of Thai economic development has been "bank-based," and the banks are mostly owned by Chinese Thais.[73] They are parts of the formal sector but not (except for a few) parts of the state. Banks invested mostly in urban commerce, rather than any kind of rural activity. The main money lenders to new factory entrepreneurs and farmers were Sino-Thais, who were linked only loosely to the system of mainly private banks.

For the period near the start of Thailand's quick industrialization, Hewison has distinguished four types of capitalism among large firms in Thailand: agrarian, commercial, industrial, and banking capitalisms. The banks were dominant in the large-firm economy, especially the Sophonpanich-Bangkok Bank group, Tejapaibal, Ratanarak, Lamsam, and the Crown Property Bureau.[74] Some industrial, commercial, and food-processing firms were associated with these banks through common shareholding; a few industrial firms were separate. As in other countries that had booms, banks were important coordinators of major companies. But they had little direct connection with the small firms that financed themselves, hired most workers, and later captured most electoral politics.

In the late 1980s, Thai banks also faced liquidity problems. The chair of Asia Trust Bank, Wallop Tarnvanichkul (a.k.a. "Johnny Ma"), was accused of embezzlement and absconded. Siam City Bank almost collapsed. Even the state-owned Krung Thai Bank had many bad loans. In these cases, the government stepped in, guaranteed deposits, and kept the system afloat.[75] It could afford to do so because of the boom. Official oversight of banks was nonetheless very incomplete,

---

[72]Otte Estler, *Der Beitrag kleiner und mittlerer Unternehmen zum Entwicklungsprozess Thailands* (The Contribution of SMEs to Thailand's Development) (Hamburg: Institut für Asienkunde, 1998), 195.

[73]I thank Chai-anan Samudavanija for his advice on this and many other ideas concerning Thailand.

[74]Kevin Hewison, *Bankers and Bureaucrats*, 204–05.

[75]See James Clad, *Behind the Myth: Business, Money, and Power in Southeast Asia* (London: Hyman, 1989), 104–07.

as the financial crisis later showed. Banks apparently played a greater role in Thai development than in Taiwan or probably in East China, but most of these banks were run by nonstate conglomerates. For credit, the SMEs generated most of their own capital.

Of Thailand's top 100 companies in the late 1970s, more than four-fifths were private. These Thai corporations' total assets were reportedly five times greater than those of the 29 largest foreign-owned companies in the country. In banks and other financial services, Thai capital was 92 percent. Thai corporations also invested abroad: in other ASEAN countries, China, and America.[76]

For new technology, Thailand has less research and development than have Taiwan or Shanghai. A "High-Tech Industrial Zone" near Ayutthaya outside Bangkok hosts some R&D, but its role has apparently not been great. Although SMEs do practically no research and development work, they help to expand the range of local technologies through diffusion, spreading skills to the new industrial labor force.[77] Market research by Sino-Thais, often cooperating with Chinese abroad, was more important to the actual situation of Thailand's economy during its boom than was new scientific research. Sino-Thai entrepreneurs showed by their actions that they were substantially patriotic Thai economic nationalists. During the boom, and even during the 1997 crisis, very few Thai businesses (large or small) were bought out by international corporations — even after the crisis when they would have been inexpensive if they had been available for foreigners to purchase.[78]

The two main global influences on Thailand's boom have been the availability of export markets and schooling in skills. Thai urban families have valued education, and the boom has financed far more education than in pre-boom years. Only 2 percent of university-age

---

[76]These firms include Bumble Bee, a U.S. canned tuna company. Anek Laothamatas, "From Clientelism to Partnership: Business Government Relations in Thailand," in *Business and Government in Industrializing Asia*, Andrew MacIntyre, ed. (Ithaca: Cornell University Press, 1994), 202.

[77]Otte Estler, *Der Beitrag kleiner und mittlerer Unternehmen*, 195.

[78]Anek Laothamatas, *Business Associations and the New Political Economy*, 77.

Thais attended colleges in 1965, but by 1985 the portion was up to 20 percent, and it rose quickly thereafter. But they have wanted human and social studies more than science and technology. In this respect, the Thai contrast with East China (and to a lesser extent Taiwan) is very sharp. Relatively few studied science or engineering: only 10 percent of the students by 1987, much lower than in most East Asian countries.[79] This boded badly for technological development. The penchant for humanistic and normative education was surprisingly strong in Thailand. Cultural factors, as they affect both government choices in allocating budgets for education and individual choices by students, are needed to explain this preference for social sciences and arts. In the mid-1990s, Thailand had 3 scientists or engineers for each million workers, while Taiwan had 54. This is a Thai choice on which economists should not frown, if they really believe that individuals' preferences cannot be examined.

THE THAI IDENTITY OF SINO-THAI ENTREPRENEURS

Risk-taking and hard work by autonomous Sino-Thai entrepreneurs is the factor that spurred a boom in the context of scant state guidance and limited Thai social capital. Market competition does not arise spontaneously; markets often grow out of rivalries between patrons, not just because of cost-benefit calculations by traders, with the state providing basic order. Local leaders in Thailand often kept wealth in their localities, rather than sending it to Bangkok or abroad, in order to finance the retention of their clients. If they did not, their followers might be recruited by local rivals. "Competitive clientelism" was crucial force in the opening of Thai markets.[80]

The most obvious fact about Thai small business patrons is ethnic. Most (but not all) entrepreneurs during the boom were paternally

---

[79]For the data, James Clad, *Behind the Myth*, 118–19.

[80]Richard F. Doner and Ansil Ramsay, "Competitive Clientelism and Economic Governance: The Case of Thailand," in *Business and the State in Developing Countries*, Sylvia Maxfield and Ben Ross Schneider, eds. (Ithaca: Cornell University Press, 1997), 239, and also 269.

Chinese Thais. Of Thailand's thirty largest corporations, all but two in the early 1990s were owned by Sino-Thais.[81] A salient trait of the environment in which they operated was its idealized, but not realized, hierarchalism. Unger reports that, "Chinese blood is common in Thais at all ranks of society, including the royal family. Zheng Zhao, who paved the way for the founding of the [current] Chakri dynasty, had a Chinese father and a Thai mother."[82] Perhaps for this reason, King Chulalongkorn is reported to have said of the Chinese, "I regard them not as foreigners but as component parts of the kingdom."[83]

Members of the *sakdina* class that traditionally extracted land rents were courted by less prestigious but increasingly wealthy Sino-Thai entrepreneurs for more than a century before the boom.[84] The modern Thai bourgeoisie, especially those who lived "up-country" (anywhere except Bangkok), emerged from a melding of these two groups, sometimes through marriages of rich Sino-Thai grooms to noble *sakdina* Thai brides.

G. William Skinner has shown how Chinese boys in Thailand could traditionally, at age 18, simply decide to become Thais. They could choose bowl haircuts (rather than queues), responsibility to Thai law (rather than to Chinese judges for most legal cases), and corvée (rather than the higher taxes that were levied on Chinese).[85] They also were free to become temporary monks, as practically all Thai teenage boys did. The vast majority of Chinese in Thailand thus became Sino-Thais. Even if they married Thai women, they remained

---

[81]The two exceptions were the army's Krung Thai Bank and the Crown Property Bureau that is managed by agents of the king. Jamie Mackie, "Changing Patterns of Chinese Big Business in Southeast Asia," in *Southeast Asian Capitalists*, Ruth McVey, ed. (Ithaca: Southeast Asia Program, Cornell University, 1992), 174.

[82]Danny Unger, *Building Social Capital*, 48. Zheng Zhao, reportedly a Hakka, preceded the first Chakri king, Rama I, who took over the state and by most reports was also partly of Chinese ancestry.

[83]Yoshihara Kunio, *The Nation and Economic Growth*, 17.

[84]See Kevin Hewison, *Power and Politics in Thailand* (Manila and Wollongong: Journal of Contemporary Asia Publishers, 1989), 32–33.

[85]G. William Skinner, "Change and Persistence in Chinese Culture Overseas: A Comparison of Thailand and Java."

legally Chinese and could serve as heads of Chinese constituencies for the royal court. They often gave money to charities, learned the language of their adopted land, and were accepted as citizens (more fully in Thailand than in the Muslim or Spanish-Catholic countries of Southeast Asia). Bangkok's policies in the 19th century gave Chinese methods of becoming Thai — and levied higher taxes on their family firms if they decided to identify just as Chinese.[86]

Nineteenth and twentieth century migration from China into Thai cities came in waves. The last big surge was in the 1920s. After 1949 for many years, Thailand had practically no Chinese immigrants. So by the time of the boom, virtually all Sino-Thais had "reached the crucial third generation."[87] They could be proud of their Chinese paternal ancestry, but they also had definitely become Thais.

Even before Thailand's involvement in Western markets, which was originally spurred by the Bowring Treaty with Britain, local Chinese merchants began to create a Thai industrial economy.[88] This trend was not limited to big traders, although the economist Krirkkiat Phipatseritham has listed ten large financial and sixty non-bank business groups that were started by Chinese Thais. These include the origins of most of current Thailand's biggest private companies.

Sino-Thai business groups were "gigantistic," often combining many different lines of production and commerce. They usually started with a small bank or a factory in rice milling or textile weaving, but they readily branched into new types of industry and commerce.

---

[86]See G. William Skinner, "Overseas Chinese Leadership," and Skinner, "Chinese Assimilation and Thai Politics."

[87]Pasuk Phongpaichit and Chris Baker, *Thaksin: The Business of Politics in Thailand* (Chiang Mai: Silkworm Books, 2004), 10–12.

[88]Bowring was British, but Chinese merchants had been in Ayutthaya long before then. They organized trade in their lineage-company ships through Chinese ports as far as Nagasaki (where these were called *tôsen*, or Tang [south Chinese] ships). See articles by Yoneo Ishii from various early 1970s issues of *Tônan Ajia kenkyû* (Southeast Asia Research), whose English the present author, then at the Center for Southeast Asian Studies, Kyoto University, helped to check. See also Krirkkiat Phipatseritham and Yoshihara Kunio, *Business Groups in Thailand* (Singapore: Institute of Southeast Asian Studies, 1983), 3.

This pattern is also common in China.[89] It does not excel at high-tech R&D, but it reflects a constant Schumperterian search for new ways to make money. At that type of research, which requires much "human intelligence" and networking, few kinds of organizations do better than Chinese family businesses.

Lamay in the 1920s wrote that, "The rice grower has always remained Siamese. But the rice dealer is Chinese. So are the rice-miller and all his coolies. So is the boat-builder ... the pawn broker, the tailor, the bookmaker, the dyer of cloth, the furniture maker, the iron-smith, the market gardener, the fish dealer, the old tin can collector, and the hawker."[90] Jennifer Cushman's work on the Khaws, a Sino-Thai tin mining lineage that became very rich during the nineteenth century, shows that they were Thais whose Chinese identification helped both their status in the political bureaucracy and their economic connections.[91] They made money, but they also served Thailand specifically by resisting British encroachments from Malaya up the southern peninsula. Many middle- and lower-class Chinese families in Thailand found it useful not to forget their ancestry, even while loyally building their new country and developing all the skills needed to be Thai. Lower-income businesspeople retained their "Chineseness" more than did the wealthiest Sino-Thais.

PERIODS OF DISCRIMINATION

Anti-Chinese sentiment has certainly not been absent in Thailand, although Thais (unlike Filipinos, Malaysians, Indonesians, and even Singapore Muslims long ago) have never held major riots against Chinese. Periods of discrimination in Thailand have correlated with past peaks of Chinese nationalism. There have been three periods of

---

[89]Franz Schurmann, *Ideology and Organization in Communist China* (Berkeley: University of California Press, 1966).

[90]Quoted in Eliezer B. Ayal, "The Role of the Chinese Minorities in the Economic Development of Southeast Asian Countries," in *Elites, Minorities, and Economic Growth*, Elise S. Brezis and Peter Temin, eds. (Amsterdam: Elsevier, 1999), 152.

[91]Jennifer Cushman, *Family and State: The Formation of a Sino-Thai Mining Dynasty, 1797–1932* (Singapore: Oxford University Press, 1992).

such anti-Chinese movements. The first, under King Vajiravudh, lasted from 1913 to 1925 and was largely inspired by the Thai monarch's doubts about Sino-Thais' loyalty after the 1911 Republican Revolution. During Sun Yat-sen's campaign against the Manchu monarchy, King Vajiravudh wrote newspaper articles about Chinese as the "Jews of the East." As king, he disapproved the movement against Qing dynasts (which as south Chinese many Sino-Thais approved). The Thai "revolution" of 1932, creating a constitutional monarchy, later dissipated this problem.[92]

A second anti-Chinese movement emerged after 1938 in Thailand under General/Premier Phibul Songkhram. The Japanese army during World War II occupied the countries across Thai borders in all directions. It would certainly have occupied Thailand too if the Bangkok government had not collaborated. Yet ethnic Chinese at this time were running major guerrilla operations against the Japanese globally (e.g., in China and Malaya). Bangkok placed restrictions on Chinese schools and on the range of commercial fields that Sino-Thais could enter. Practically all of the banks that had been founded by Chinese in Thailand were dissolved in an act that one analyst, Muscat, has called "ethnocentric dirigisme." As Skinner wrote, "no-one knew when his particular trade might be reserved for Thai nationals,... when the lease of his shop might be challenged, or when his business might be inspected by revenue officials or raided by the police."[93] Comparable economic discriminations, but in peacetime, emerged later in the Philippines, as other chapters detail.

A third period of lesser discrimination came after the war. In 1948, the rightist General Phibul with American help came back to the premiership that he had held from 1938 to 1944. He raised taxes on Chinese — who were nonetheless confident enough to demonstrate

---

[92]Thai ethnicity is a complex object, sometimes strengthened by distinctions with "others," as stressed in Maurizio Peleggi, *Thailand: The Worldly Kingdom* (London: Reaktion, 2007), e.g., 198–205; 214, the last page of the book, refers to "the centrality of ethnicity in the construction of Thainess." At other times, though, Thais have been very assimilative — while many quasi-Thais (such as Shans in Burma or Laos in Laos) have not been of much concern to the central Thai elite.

[93]G. William Skinner, "Chinese Assimilation and Thai Politics," 394.

in Bangkok against these measures. Phibul arrested a few tycoons on suspicion of being crypto-communists. He further restricted the curricula of Chinese schools, and this speeded Sino-Thai assimilation.[94]

The association of China with communism was so strong in Thailand during the 1950s that if police arrested a Chinese for any reason, they could call him a communist. Then money could be extracted, or he could be deported. As a Thai newspaper wrote, "It is the easiest thing in the world to bleed Chinese in our country.... Merely preferring a charge of being communist or having communist tendencies is more than sufficient for members of the police to obtain huge sums of money from them."[95] But as Supang Chantavanich claims, "dual identity is accepted as long as the Chinese prove their allegiance to Thailand and express their nationalist ideology by supporting [the official Thai allegiance to] nation, religion, and king."[96]

None of these hard patches, however, prevented the massive assimilation of Chinese to Thai citizenship and to widespread, albeit incomplete, social acceptance by non-Chinese Thais during General/ Premier Sarit's period after 1958. A sense of cohesion among Sino-Thai business people had been strengthened because of past Thai official discrimination against them. But by then they were also Thais, not mainly Chinese.

Under later Thai governments especially, these businessmen found they could expand their operations if they paid patrons in the Thai Army. When Chinese men found Thai wives, the *jus soli* rule automatically gave their families' offspring Thai citizenship if they wished it — as almost all of them did. (The Philippines uses a *jus sanguinis*

---

[94]Yoshihara Kunio, *The Nation and Economic Growth*, 32–35.

[95]Quoted in Yoshihara Kunio, *The Nation and Economic Growth*, 189, and also in Anek Laothamatas, "From Clientelism to Partnership," 198, and yet earlier in G. William Skinner, *Leadership and Power in the Chinese Community of Thailand* (Ithaca: Cornell University Press, 1958), 303–04, from the paper *Sathiraphab*, August 31, 1955 — presuming an etymology of a quotation is of interest.

[96]Supang Chantavanich, "From Siamese-Chinese to Chinese-Thai: Political Conditions and Identity Shifts among the Chinese in Thailand," in *Ethnic Chinese as Southeast Asians*, Leo Suryadinata, ed. (Singapore: Institute for Southeast Asian Studies, 1997), 232–66.

law, so that birth in the country does not entitle the child to citizenship.) Restrictions in an Alien Business Law did not crimp the style of Sino-Thai entrepreneurs, since they were not counted as aliens.

During some periods, notably in the 1950s, the Thai government established special programs to assist non-Chinese Thai entrepreneurs. These plans generally resulted in state industries, however, rather than private firms. The Thai version of help to "sons of the land" (*bumiputra* is the term used for native groups in Malaysia and Indonesia) was arguably less necessary than in the Muslim countries, because Sino-Thais had become more assimilated even than "Paranakan" Sino-Malays or Indonesian Chinese from old families. Nativist projects existed in Thailand, but they involved a small portion of national investment. They became so diluted that, during Phibul's time, his administration encouraged Thais to set up as barbers or rickshaw pullers — not the kinds of enterprise that can expand easily.[97]

The number of ethnic Chinese in Thailand is impossible to measure accurately because of extensive assimilation (for them, as well as for non-Malay Thai Muslims, Thai Sindhis, and others). A good guess is that Sino-Thais at the turn of the millennium numbered about eight million, or one-seventh of Thailand's population, controlling four-fifths of the market capital.[98]

SINO-THAI FIRMS' FOUNDINGS AND CONSTANT MARKET SEARCHES

Large Sino-Thai companies that started as agribusinesses became famous, and they deserve some attention here because (like the Taiwan and East China specific firms described in earlier chapters), their origins show the ways in which multi-trade companies began as specialized SMEs. C.P. (Charoen Pokphand), the biggest group in

---

[97]The author is thankful to Chai-anan Samudavanija for help.

[98]A slight majority of this group are Chaozhou/Teochiu, and practically all the others are either Fujianese/Hokkien, Hakka, or Cantonese. Leo Paul Dana, *Entrepreneurship in Pacific Asia: Past, Present and Future* (Singapore: World Scientific, 1999), 180.

Thailand, was founded by two brothers from the Teochiu (Chaozhou) area of eastern Guangdong. They exported pigs and other foods to China, largely in exchange for imported fertilizers and manufactures. Their feed mill, together with sales of the resulting chickens and eggs, became the center of their business — but they soon branched out into jute bags, carpets, paints, and then other industrial products.[99]

The Hong Yiah Seng agribusiness was co-founded by the Leopairatana clan head, Leo Keng Hui and the Taepitsawong family leader, Tae Kim Hong. Large Sino-Thai firms such as this were sometimes cooperative projects of two or three different families. They also set up joint ventures with foreign firms, when the latter could bring new technologies. They had major incentives to spread risks in an environment where the Chinese executives knew that, although mostly assimilated as Thais, they remained an ethnic minority. Hong Yiah Seng diversified from trading into milling and rice exports, which became its central business. By the 1980s, this group was also in insurance, finance, manufacturing, and petrochemicals.

Laem Thong is a combine founded by a man who used his Thai name Yongsak Kanathanavanich, at first finding profits in land speculation and rice exports, then branching into food processing.[100] Such firms also became involved in banking, real estate, and construction, although they seldom closed the agribusinesses with which they started.

The largest retail chain in Thailand for many decades has been owned by the Chirathivats. This is a Hainanese family that opened Bangkok shops in the 1920s and then department stores in the 1960s. Many other Sino-Thai clans started small stores with similar hopes of expansion. They expanded into industrial pursuits of all kinds: textiles and zippers and buttons, food processing, chemicals and cosmetics, air conditioners, rubber, tires, auto parts and then vehicle assembly, insurance, advertising, real estate, hotels, newspapers and other media, and (locally and very commonly) brickmaking.[101]

---

[99]Krirkkiat Phipatseritham and Yoshihara Kunio, *Business Groups in Thailand*, 4.
[100]*Ibid.*, 5–6.
[101]Kevin Hewison, *Bankers and Bureaucrats*, 155 and 160–61.

These entrepreneurs showed "dynamic efficiency," often beginning in one field and branching into others.[102] They moved easily from selling to making and vice-versa. They sometimes found niches for profit in trades where potential markets had been neglected, even if distant from the fields in which they started. It is easy to identify the largest Sino-Thai firms — but they by no means control the whole economy because of myriad small Sino-Thai and other Thai entrepreneurs.

COERCION AND CAPITAL IN RURAL FIRMS

Modal local structures are important along with national institutions in determining the development of any political economy. The Thai state floats above a rural society that has been ordered by more local powers that are practically, though not ideally, separate from it. *Sakdina* aristocratic tax farmers have long since given way to local strongmen. Some of these, much less noble, are called *nakleng*, local leaders supposed to have "manly bearing and courage, readiness to fight in single combat or in a riot, fidelity to friends, deep loyalty and respect towards feudal lords and parents."[103] A village *nakleng* kept other similar braves out of his own area and would generally not steal from fellow villagers, although he might lead raids on other towns and arrange to return stolen goods in exchange for a reward. *Nakleng* developed all kinds of relations with police. A young *nakleng* leader might later become a village headman — and if he were also a wealthy Sino-Thai, he would be called by the Teochiu word *sia*, which suggests tycoon status.

---

[102]On a related Asian application of the difference between neoclassical "static" efficiency and Schumpeterian "dynamic efficiency," see Cui Zhiyuan, "Getting the Prices and Property Rights Wrong? The Chinese Reform in the Schumpeterian Perspective and Beyond," in *China: A Reformable Socialism*, Gan Yang and Cui Zhiyuan, eds. (New York: Oxford University Press, 1995), 145–68.

[103]David B. Johnston, "Bandit, *Nakleng*, and Peasant in Rural Thai Society," *Contributions to Asian Studies* 15 (1980), 91, quoted in James Ockey, "*Chaopho*: Capital Accumulation and Social Welfare in Thailand," *Crossroads* 8 (1993), 50.

When, in 1971, the movie "The Godfather" was released in Thailand, it strongly echoed these traditions and had great popularity. The film's Thai name, *Jaopho*, became standard for this kind of leader. Local Thai ideals of fighting prowess were combined with norms from Chinese secret societies and family ritual to reinforce an image of *jaopho* as local leaders.

As the boom began, Turton found in Thai villages "a small capitalist class, though such a position does not fully or unambiguously define their social location and identity." Many villagers often identified with one "person, certainly family — larger landowners, commodity dealers, shopkeepers, village officials, some teachers, rice millers, money lenders, owners of small-scale transport and machinery, large-scale employers of wage labor, etc."[104] The boom increased the power of people who could link local, national, and sometimes even international networks of politics.

As these fixers transformed their local polities, they cumulatively changed the national political economy too. The first signs of this change were not in formal public politics. They were often in styles of consumption, because of the "large sums spent (mainly outside the village economy) on houses, vehicles, and (largely imported) consumer 'durables' of every kind,... on travel, and on social events such as weddings, domestic ceremonies, feasts, drinking parties, and gambling."[105] Many such activities were collective and confirmed local dependencies. Bribes for officials and purchases of votes were only the most obviously "political" instances of this new consumption, although that is a topic mainly for a later chapter.

Christensen and Siamwalla write that firms selling farm products are strongest "where the agro-commercial firm is part of a conglomerate which includes firms in the more politically strategic sectors."[106] These sectors are SMEs that have political links and that benefit from public contracts. Construction is a major source of wealth for town

---

[104]Andrew Turton, "Local Powers and Rural Differentiation," 82.

[105]*Ibid.*, 83.

[106]Scott R. Christensen and Ammar Siamwalla, *Beyond Patronage: Tasks for the Thai State* (Bangkok: Thailand Development Research Institute Foundation, 1993), 31.

entrepreneurs, for example, as are transport, liquor distilling, and distributorships for commodities as varied as cigarettes, trucks, motorcycles, and lottery tickets. Such firms are associated with or run by *jaopho*, who protect and provide for their clients — while also extracting from them and scaring them. They are, for many Thais, the main source of welfare. The coercive part of this picture is inseparable from the economic part, although both are separated from the state hierarchy.

Large firms aided the Thai boom, but small firms are of greater interest to local politicians because they hire more worker-voters. Brickyards, quarries, builders, and other local companies provide the bases for most political organizing. Large companies and exporters can use favorable government policies as surely as domestic marketers can — but public finances for local infrastructure sway more votes. Small companies collectively have at least as great an impact on political development as do large corporations or foreign-owned companies. Large corporations' impact on political evolution is more indirect than is the impact of SMEs and the domestic sector.[107]

"Formal business associations representing larger entrepreneurs at higher levels have tended not to involve themselves actively in electoral politics — preferring instead to depend on their economic weight to enable them to deal directly with bureaucrats," as Arghiros writes.[108] Before the 2006 coup, for example, most large Thai corporations were more silent than other Thai urban institutions about the problems they saw accumulating; only when they sensed that corruptions could be bad for the economy did they begin to react. The managers of big firms mainly wanted stable politics. The Thai state, including its military branch, could not control the country's many scattered entrepreneurs, any more than they could control it. The

---

[107]This issue is general, and it is a subtheme in each chapter of this book. In general, exports almost surely affect economic development more than they affect political development. Their role in both has been better researched than has the role of domestic markets partly because international trade generates customs statistics. But data availability alone does not make social truth. It only provides footnotes.

[108]Daniel Arghiros, *Democracy, Development, and Decentralisation*, 226, relying also on Anek.

polity, as Turton explains, "has a momentum of its own and in large part serves its own somewhat hybrid, parasitic, 'secondary complex of predatory interests,' which constitutes much of the nonbourgeois elements of the power bloc and its local supports, appropriating wealth in often noncapitalistic and sometimes coercive and illegal ways."[109] This predatory-coercive description of Thai politics would apply also in East China and the Philippines, and to a lesser extent earlier in Taiwan. The accumulation of capital and power go together, both locally and nationally.

GEOGRAPHICAL CULTURES OF "CIVIL" AND BUSINESS SOCIETY

Liberal social scientists, especially Americans, have been quick to find Thais atypical of the "Orient," because of a Thai reputation for loving freedom. Long ago, Girling argued that an "aloofness of Thai villagers from collective activities" creates "a virtual absence of permanent associations in most Thai villages [so that it is] difficult for the poorer peasants to organize effective opposition to the power of the rural elite, backed by province officials."[110] The boom changed this situation somewhat by creating new networks. Social scientists have described Thais as individualist, at least in comparison with other East Asians; but the boom linked them in new ways.

Unger argues that Thailand earlier had "low levels of social capital" and that "Thais traditionally were not joiners; they were not embedded in networks of enduring social groups pursuing shared goals. In this respect, Thais differed from the Chinese immigrants."[111] After chiding "Thailand's less than formidable institutional assets," he finds that a lack of social capital explains "the economy's principal weaknesses while also accounting in considerable part for its successes

---

[109]Andrew Turton, "Local Powers and Rural Differentiation," 73–74, partly quoting E. Thompson.

[110]John Girling, *Thailand: Society and Politics* (Ithaca: Cornell University Press, 1981), 174.

[111]Danny Unger, *Building Social Capital*, 21–23.

over the last forty years."[112] Institutional disintegration promotes some kinds of development, just as institutional integration promotes other kinds of development. Sino-Thais, partly because of their minority status, were before the boom the nation's specialists for economic flexibility, while Thais traditionally ran the government bureaucracy.

After going through noncultural attempts to explain why Chinese dominate Thai businesses, economist Yoshihara Kunio asks, "How can all this be explained except by resorting to cultural explanations? Isn't it possible that Chinese and Thais have different preferences for leisure? Nothing is really wrong with a strong preference for leisure. It is a matter of life style. But it does not go well with productivity."[113]

Not all of Thailand's entrepreneurs are Sino-Thais, and bureaucrats as well as others are now in middle-income status or class groups. Thailand's boom nonetheless depended on organization first by Sino-Thais, in a context of free but relatively quiescent, predominantly Thai labor. A mid-1990s estimate of the size of this middle class, including all ethnicities, held that it had "doubled since 1970 and now comprises about one-fifth of the employed population; this is not far short of the urban working population."[114]

The ethnic aspect of Thailand's development is clear, and just as interesting is the geographical aspect. There has been a rise of business people outside Bangkok in suburban and provincial cities during the boom. Some non-Chinese "Thais from rural backgrounds have moved into middlemen roles traditionally occupied by Sino-Thais and Chinese," but both Thais and Sino-Thais in this status group were increasingly outside the capital.[115] The portion of "rural provincial" people in the "upper income" brackets rose between 1987 and 1995 from 12 to 20 percent. Those in "urban provincial" places with "upper" incomes rose from 18 to 22 percent. In Bangkok, the increase

---

[112]Quoted in *ibid.*, 183, in the book's concluding paragraph.

[113]Yoshihara Kunio, *Asia per Capita: Why National Incomes Differ in East Asia* (London: Curzon Press, 2000), 37.

[114]John Girling, *Interpreting Development: Capitalism, Democracy, and the Middle Class in Thailand* (Ithaca: Cornell Southeast Asian Studies, 1996), 43.

[115]Daniel Arghiros, *Democracy, Development, and Decentralisation*, 45.

was just from 16 to 18 percent.[116] A broadly defined well-to-do group, in other words, was richer in the provinces (especially provincial cities) than in the capital.

Nonstate "political space" is often said to be the "sphere" of "civil society." But it would be more specific to talk about actors in their contexts, of which the government is just a part. Hewison claims that, "The breadth of political space and the definition of whether this is 'legitimate' depend on the acceptance or sanction of the state apparatus."[117] But state recognition of political space does not create it. Many actors and networks are engaged in that process.

Industrial and commercial leaders become crucial in modern civil politics. This change has ethnic, functional-occupational, and geographical aspects. Doner and Ramsay write that, "the business community, dominated by ethnic Chinese (Sino-Thais), who make up ten percent of the population, has been politically weak for most of the country's history."[118] This weakness applies more to power in the state, however, than to local organizations. After the boom began, Sino-Thai businessmen were strong both locally and nationally. They have used their rich heritage of civil institutions to get more power within the state. They lead mills and stores, banks, temples, schools, lineages, *tongxiang hui* (associations of people whose paternal ancestors came from the same place in China), church groups, and mafias, and they maintain formal links to the Thai state — which they increasingly use elections to commandeer.

Somchai contrasts two kinds of civil society: an "elite" variety that pursues reform in a top-down manner, and a mass society that raises the power of "ordinary people."[119] Thai intellectuals and monks developed

---

[116]Parichart Chotiya, "The Changing Role of Provincial Business," 253. This report comes from surveyors of the Deemar Media Index, who tried to hold their categories constant.

[117]Kevin Hewison, "Political Oppositions and Regime Change in Thailand," in *Political Oppositions in Industrializing Asia*, Garry Rodan, ed. (London: Routledge, 1996), 74.

[118]Richard F. Doner and Ansil Ramsay, "Competitive Clientelism and Economic Governance," 238.

[119]Somchai Phatharathananunth, "Civil Society and Democratization in Thailand: A Critique of Elite Democracy," in *Reforming Thai Politics*, Duncan McCargo, ed. (Copenhagen: Nordic Institute of Asian Studies, 2002), 125–42.

many nonstate civil organizations with royal patronage. There is a Thai communitarian tradition that has both religious and secular roots and tends to be leftist. Pridi Phanomyong was its foremost modern exponent: as early as 1933 he advocated a state plan for Thailand and declared private enterprise to be "wasteful." His advocacy on behalf of the poor owed at least as much to Buddha as to Marx. Pridi founded Thammasat University partly to propagate a social *thamma* (*dharma*). A later rector there, Puey Ungpakorn, inspired so many students that he had to exile himself from Thailand during the 1976 *coup d'état*. His plane was shot at, as it took off from the Bangkok airport runway. Pridi's and Puey's combination of planning and hope for the poor still inspires current Thai NGOs.[120] This kind of campaign has been more active in propagating norms than in establishing organizations, however; it exemplifies "movement democracy."

Worker politics and ecological movements have been prominent. Environmental issues have been salient in Thailand because they unite activist farmers' interests in preserving forests, and slowing the growth of plantations, with activist students' and Buddhist monks' interests in nature. International and domestic NGOs concerned with saving ecologies provide support for such movements, which are opposed by many generals and business people but recur as politically important because the boom causes ecological damage.

Forests still covered 53 percent of Thailand in 1950. Under military rule by the 1970s, that portion was sharply reduced, and by 1998 it was just 25 percent.[121] Rebels could hide among trees; so from the late 1950s through the 1970s, the Army was given full jurisdiction in forest areas where communist guerrillas flourished. Roads were built, so that instead of "forests encircling cities," as the rebels planned, "cities encircled forests."[122] To repair such damages at least a bit, the

---

[120]See John Girling, *Interpreting Development*, 62–63.

[121]Ronald Hill, *Southeast Asia*, 117.

[122]Http://138.25.138.94/signposts/articles/Thailand/poverty_and_hunger/354. html, 1992 article by Chai-anan Samujavanija and Kusuma Santwongse. At this and other points in the text, the anti-progressive activities in Thailand of the American government might be cited. Domestic Thai conservatives remained crucial in determining political outcomes.

king in 1987 presided over a "Greening of the Northeast" (*Isan khiaw*) project, which was mostly run by soldiers.

Businessmen join bureaucrats and generals in profits from logging old-growth forests, selling off the wood, and then replanting as much of the land as they can claim with commercial crops of fast-growing trees, especially eucalyptus.[123] Farmers protest deforestation and dam-building, but they have scant power to prevent these predations. Logging concessions used to be granted by the government, although many loggers have operated without benefit of any laws. Even before the turn of the millennium, Bangkok authorities ceased giving the licenses, but that did not stop the logging.

In 1988, a Buddhist monk named Phra Prachak led a group of about 40 nuns and monks into the Dong Yai forest in the Isan, urging villagers to preserve the forest. By 1992, he was arrested and imprisoned, then released for lack of having committed a crime, then arrested again in 1994 on the same charge. Loggers really do not like ecological monks.

The NGO movement has grown in Thailand's pluralist booming society, especially after threats to the regime (including the monarchy) were defeated in the 1970s and 1980s. The Communist Party of Thailand, however, had always been implicitly divided between Thais and Sino-Thais. The wars between Kampuchea and Vietnam, and then between China and Vietnam, hastened the Thai Communist Party's breakup, because the adversaries in those nearby wars were all socialist states with different sympathizers in Thailand. That created an atmosphere in which Thai soldiers, bureaucrats, and monarchists had less excuse to repress NGOs, even those with leftist policies.

The government continued building more dams in Northeast Thailand than most of the people there wanted. On the Mun River in southern Isan, for example, rice farmers and fishers were hurt by these projects. Some of their elected MPs urged more attention to their needs, including the breaking of some dams that had been

---

[123]See Chai-Anan Samudavanija, "Economic Development and Democracy," in *Thailand's Industrialization and its Consequences*, Medhi Krongkaew, ed. (New York: St. Martin's, 1995), 248.

recently built. Puey Ungpakorn's Thai Rural Reconstruction Movement and organizations interested in "social Buddhism" revived. Interest groups took their place alongside the traditionally administrative government.[124] Civil society flourished — but its most influential parts still remained in business, and they were rightist.

LABOR-CAPITAL FEUDS AND POLITICAL MODERNIZATION

Much research has been done on the politics of the Thai working class in large factories.[125] Laborers in SMEs have received less attention, partly because the Bangkok bureaucracy collects few data about them. A small minority of manufacturing workers are unionized. Few consider themselves part of a self-conscious working class. The main reason is not that Thailand lacks industries; instead, it is that early industrialization has provided wealth for new business patrons who can sustain client networks.

Most Thai urban industrial workers, who before the boom were Sino-Thais, experienced intimate "interpersonal relations between employer and worker ... since the boss and workers are approximate social equals in a small shop, this pattern does not stimulate working-class solidarity or working-class political activity."[126] Some writers,

---

[124]See also Scott R. Christensen and Ammar Siamwalla, *Beyond Patronage*, 2.

[125]Research in English on the Thai working class is mostly by Australians. Work by Kevin Hewison, Andrew Brown, and others is summarized in Andrew Brown, *Labour, Politics, and the State.*

[126]David A. Wilson, *Politics in Thailand*, 43–44, quoted also by Andrew Brown, *Labour, Politics, and the State*, 5. Australians such as Brown and his teacher Hewison have pioneered studies of the (slow!) growth of proletarian consciousness in Thailand on the basis of Thai language sources. Wilson, writing early, came from the U.S. which is a more populous country than Australia but has recently produced less good work on Thailand. Australia's own political history has sensitized its scholars to pay particular attention to hopes for the growth of political power among Thai (and Filipino and other) workers, perhaps at the expense of neglecting the development of small- and medium-enterprises. In SMEs, workers are more easily repressed as their production has risen quickly and has affected politics in diverse ways.

such as Narong, attribute Thai workers' quiescence to the legacy of traditional *sakdina* ideology, which "produces superior-subordinate relationships between the ruling elite and the common people, between employers and employees.... This restrains the development of working class consciousness...."[127] But in practice, much evidence shows that this tradition has been renegotiated as businessmen have become the mode among patrons.

Thai laws banned rural trade unions in the mid-1970s after the Peasants' Federation of Thailand, mostly composed of poor farmers, was likened by the government to the communist insurgency.[128] But agricultural cooperatives called "farmers' groups" (*klum kasetakorn*) have been important for decades. They were usually led by local people who saw themselves as having responsibilities both to the government and to poor peasants. Most of these co-ops were credit unions, with only a latent possibility of becoming trade unions.[129]

Thai industrial labor enjoyed practically no government protection until the mid-1970s, when an increase in strikes brought a bit of regulation. Toward labor, as toward capital, the Bangkok government has been far from heavy-handed in comparison with the regimes in Taiwan or China during the booms at those places. Chatichai Choonhavan's government in the late 1980s began to intervene lightly in labor markets. Chatichai increased the official minimum wage, hiked the lowest legal working age from 12 to 13 (still very low), and raised from negligible to merely risible the number of Labor Department inspectors.[130] He renamed the Department of Labor a ministry. Passing state laws did not ensure their enforcement, but these were first steps. A two-tier policy was implicit in Bangkok: just a bit of social security for the relatively few medium-compensation workers in important or easily organized industries, and none for the others. The 1989 Social Security Act codified arrangements for

---

[127]See Andrew Brown, *Labour, Politics, and the State*, 11–12; a quote to Narong is on 11.

[128]Andrew Turton, "Thailand: Agrarian Bases," 66.

[129]Andrew Turton, "Local Powers and Rural Differentiation," 92.

[130]Andrew Brown, *Labour, Politics, and the State*, 107 and other sources cited there.

pensions, health, maternity, and insurance that had been developed previously by "tripartite" business-labor-government committees in various industries.[131] This system left out most workers. For many years, though, Thailand had no major labor riots.

Although urban labor has generally been allowed to organize in Thailand since the late 1980s, unions are weak in this business-dominated polity. Contrary to the ideologies of many capitalists, this allowance did not prevent quick Thai development in the 1990s. Chatichai's son, Kraisak Choonhavan, became that premier's particular liaison to unionists. While prime minister, Chatichai presided over the 1989 and 1990 May Day celebrations in Bangkok. Even state employees were allowed to unionize. The result was fewer strikes, rather than more of them.[132]

The main specific labor issue in Thailand has been occupational safety. This briefly became a center of Thai attention in 1993 because of a fire at the Kader Toy Factory, which was owned by a Chinese consortium, including Thai and Hong Kong and Taiwan investors. Workers had been locked in a building, supposedly "to prevent the petty thieving of raw materials," and 188 of them were killed, of whom 159 were women.[133] This factory was a large, export-oriented one in which workers were disconnected from politics in the hometowns whence they had come. Legislation was passed in hopes of preventing the recurrence of such tragedies, but women workers in such factories had little chance of organizing for long-term support of occupational safety or any other benefit. Catastrophes like this fire, which have occurred also in China and other countries, lead to regulations whose enforcement may remain incomplete until the subsistence-wage labor supply dries up and businesses see that the value of workers has risen.

---

[131]Pasuk Phongpaichit and Chris Baker, *Thailand's Boom!*, 102.

[132]Kevin Hewison, "Of Regimes, State, and Pluralities: Thai Politics Enters the 1990s," in *Southeast Asia in the 1990s: Authoritarianism, Democracy, and Capitalism*, Kevin Hewison, Richard Robison, Garry Rodan, eds. (St. Leonards, NSW: Allen & Unwin, 1993), 173–74.

[133]Andrew Brown, *Labour, Politics, and the State*, 116.

The Thai ability to tolerate political influence in large new groups, even workers, that are separate from the old elite has a precedent in the allowance of economic organization by Sino-Thai entrepreneurs. Its tentative application to unions did not end tensions between capital and labor. Wages remained low in an economy that still had many rice farmers. Nonetheless, the generally uncontroversial and politically ineffectual unionization in Thailand has benefitted capitalists and the state they control. Thai unions have done less for workers than in the labor histories of most countries, but Thailand is not yet rich. Further research is needed to explain the relative calmness of Thai workers.

MEDIA AND BUSINESS FEDERATIONS

Public reports of social problems come to the attention of intellectuals, but only sometimes do they reach ordinary citizens. There is a tradition of free speech in Thailand (the only exceptions are insults to the monarchy, advocacy of a communist system, or publication that is seen to threaten national security). But radio stations and newspapers are licensed; and most are owned by tycoons, the military, or the government.[134]

Thailand has relatively weak norms against official repression of media. One reason is public distaste for potential *lèse-majesté* toward the king.[135] Libel suits have readily been brought by officials too. Approvals of press or broadcasting licenses for nonstate media have been politically sensitive. Nonetheless, freedom of expression on many subjects is considerable, and it clearly expanded during Thailand's boom. When Premier Chavalit established a media monitoring unit within the government, members of the press met and

---

[134]Clark D. Neher, "Democratization in Thailand," *Asian Affairs* 21:4 (Winter 1995), 203.

[135]The monarchy's reputation has had historical low points, for example shortly after World War II when King Bhumibol's predecessor died under mysterious circumstances. But Gen. Sarit in the 1950s and 1960s (like Queen Victoria's advisors in 19th century Britain) led a very successful effort to raise the monarchy's prestige. The king's own behavior in later decades has confirmed this status, which is high in the views of practically all Thais.

resolved to ignore advice from this quasi-censorship agency. They set up their own nonstate organization, run by journalists, to audit the accuracy of their reporting.

By far the most important civil power networks in Thai society are businesses, although the word "civil" compliments them too generally. Merchants organized associations in Thailand, as bourgeois have done in other countries. In 1979, Thailand had just four provincial chambers of commerce — but by 1987, seventy-two chambers were operating outside Bangkok.[136]

Thai provincial economic leaders have contacts with each other in business federations, Chinese same-place societies, political parties, alumni clubs, and many other networks that facilitate political decisions — even though they are outside the state apparatus. Local leaders also depend on contacts with Bangkok bankers, who are not part of the government bureaucracy but are important in the Thai political economy. Entrepreneurs need linkages to power-holders, but by no means are all such connections with officials, and not all of those are with the central state.

Thailand's provincial businesses raise much of their capital from friends in business associations, such as Rotary or Lion's clubs, rather than from banks or stock exchanges. As Parichart writes, "most provincial businesses still maintain two account books, one for government [tax or regulatory] officials and a second set for the internal use of the business. To list on the exchange, such practices would have to cease, and the advice and services of investment banking experts, usually highly paid, would be required."[137]

Many experts have written on this topic in Thailand, and a surprising amount of consensus can be found among them. Anek in the early 1990s studied Thai provincial trade groups and found that "most chambers had founders who were from pre-existing trade associations

---

[136]Anek Laothamatas, "Business and Politics in Thailand: New Patterns of Influence," *Asian Survey* 28:4 (1996), 455–59.

[137]Parichart Chotiya, "The Changing Role of Provincial Business," 260–61.

or informal business groups, which had been formed as social clubs or forums to mobilize needed credit for their members."[138] He finds contrasts between Thai business associations and those in Northeast Asia:

> If the power equation between government and business has been tilted clearly in favour of the former in the Northeast Asian NICs [newly industrializing countries], in Thailand it has been a much more equal partnership ... Closely related to this is another crucial difference between Thailand and the Northeast Asian NICs: corruption and patron-client links between officials and business people are pervasive in Thailand.[139]

Callahan claims that "business mob" politics "is for personal enrichment rather than for structural or ideological change."[140] Thai entrepreneurs were in business largely for the money, and they used or coerced low-wage labor when they could. They pluralized the Thai polity, but their eventual effects on it will be beyond their short-term, non-collective intentions.

Girling suggests that the rise of "money politics" is a "deviant" form of capitalism that undermines democracy, and he looks forward to an increase of "civil society." He also lists other "contradictions" to frame his analysis of Thailand's development during the boom. These include tensions with older bureaucratic and military elites, as businessmen gain more power.[141] The only problem with this account is arguably that the pattern is usual, not deviant.

Business people do not necessarily prefer to go through government offices to address their needs. "Provincial chambers of commerce have not confined themselves to working with the government alone. They have provided numerous services to the general public and to

---

[138]Anek had been very successful at student politics (before declining into the abstractions of political science). See Anek Laothamatas, *Business Associations*, 58–59.
[139]Anek Laothamatas, "From Clientelism to Partnership," 207–08.
[140]William A. Callahan, *Imagining Democracy: Reading "The Events of May" [1992] in Thailand* (Singapore: Institute of Southeast Asian Studies, 1998), 95.
[141]John Girling, *Interpreting Development*, 17.

their members as well."[142] They often organize trade fairs, with government agencies participating in a secondary role. Thai businesses approach the state through many channels — some of which are illegal, and many of which are simply unofficial.

Finally, as Anek writes, "The East Asian statist model presupposes that the government is both enlightened in setting economic policies and efficient in their implementation. On the other hand, it views societal actors as short-sighted, self-serving, and obstructive to the making of good policies. Their exclusion from public policymaking is therefore said to be justifiable." Anek proposes that Thailand has a "liberal corporatism" that "neither idolizes the government nor belittles business in terms of policymaking. Strategy or policy formation is not a monopoly of the 'smart' government. Indeed ... the government can be as 'smart' or 'stupid' as business."[143] Officials, not just businessmen, can see the downside of red tape and bureaucratic corruption.

Thai businesses have made a great deal of policy, some in public and some in private. Money politics is common in all democracies despite its undemocratic aspects. Thailand's experiences show that it should be studied by liberals more critically than heretofore. Practitioners of money politics derail the hope that government will serve people regardless of wealth — but also, outside the public sphere, they provide jobs, and they are as surely a part of civil society as are the protestors against their corruption. To the extent that businesses undermine military rule in Thailand, rather than providing reasons for coups, their long-term effect may have been toward more substantive democracy than they themselves directly provide, especially in localities.

---

[142]Anek Laothamatas, *Business Associations and the New Political Economy*, 64; see also 69ff.

[143]Anek Laothamatas, *Business Associations and the New Political Economy*, 168.

Chapter

5

Political Roots of Philippine Stasis

It is impossible to write this book's chapters on the Philippines without noting that country's sometime political and economic defaults. But any implication that these maladies are permanent would be unjustified historically. In the Philippines during the 1950s, there was an era of rising GDP/capita that later stalled. As late as 1959, the Philippines still had a higher per-capita income than Taiwan. This is no longer the case. It is natural to ask why. That issue is, among Filipinos and foreigners alike, the main Philippine question.

Problems in the Philippine political economy will not necessarily last forever. Growth performance in the new millennium has been presentable, although population increase has made GDP/capita performance less good. Yet why have problems lasted such a long time? One explanation cites a cultural cause: the Spanish ideal of a landed gentleman, who is definitely not an entrepreneur. This is an existential self-image that remains documentable among local Philippine elites. Being a local hidalgo is a matter of existential chosen identity, as much as being one's own boss in an SME is.

In Spanish times, practically all of Philippine society was split in two: locally and officially recognized *principalia* hidalgos, who called themselves "don" and owned land, and ordinary peasants (*timawa*) who did not, and who owed labor and personal service to the former. This was a dichotomy, not a spectrum. As Norman Owen writes,[1]

> Outside the narrowly economic sphere, the *principalia* also exercised the kind of predominance that tends to reinforce the theory that they descended from datus.... When the [political, not social] revolution came, the Spanish rulers turned the government of Albay [province] over to the principales, who ran it confidently for nearly a year and a half before the Americans came; *principales* officered the army that resisted the Americans for years, while other *principales*, who had surrendered earlier, ran the local government for the Americans.

They still run Philippine local governments, and through democratic elections they collectively run the national government too. They seldom start economic enterprises, because that differs from the style of their ancestors.

Adam Smith wrote that, "It is not economic motivation that prompts men to work, but status, esteem, moral mettle, qualities which would allow him to be a man of worth and dignity."[2] Nonetheless, it is now a tradition among most economists and political scientists to reject, before research, any proposal that culturally constructed factors such as notions of status, esteem, or dignity can be causal. "Cultural" causes are actually included in substantive socialized "preferences," although the orthodox grammar of individualist

---

[1]Norman G. Owen, *The Bikol Blend: Bikolanos and their History* (Quezon City: New Day Publishers, 1999), 131. The author has learned from conversations with Owen, and from his *Prosperity without Progress: Manila Hemp and Material Life in the Colonial Philippines* (Berkeley: University of California Press, 1983). The Bikol peninsula of southeast Luzon was the first sizeable area subjugated by Spain under Miguel López de Legazpi (who like other notable conquistadors and friars in the archipelago was Basque). Bikol, a.k.a. Kabikolan, has been even more deeply affected than other areas by these Spanish traditions. The five Bikol provinces are certainly not the Philippines' poorest, but their "human development" indices are below average for Luzon; see *Philippine Human Development Report, 2000* ([Manila]: Human Development Network and United Nations Development Programme, 2000), 93.
[2]Cited from another source in Alastair Iain Johnston, *Social States: China in International Institutions, 1980–2000* (Princeton: Princeton University Press, 2008), 84.

social science now tends to deny this. GDP growth has undergone bumpy cycles and prolonged stagnation in many countries, and theories have left more of it unexplained than social scientists care to emphasize. In some nations (Uruguay and Argentina are well-known examples, and the Philippines is another) growth has slowed or stopped after hesitant "take-offs."[3]

Growth occurs only if effective dominant elites want it. That is the most consistent finding from the data in this book. It occurs if local leaders or national leaders, whichever are stronger, see its short-term concomitants (jobs for clients, tax revenues, or the recruitment of new kinds of elite members) as increasing their own power. Otherwise, they prevent it.

For many decades in the Philippines, local landholding leaders have been generally unwilling either to start industrial enterprises of their own or to let others found them. Their control over the population has been sufficiently effective to enforce this will in most places. Their modern torpor is a problem for substantive Philippine democratization, not just for economic growth. The effectiveness of this industrialization-preventing and social democratization-preventing local elite control may later break down — and some evidence presented below suggests this may have started. But for the most part, Philippine stasis has been actively led by local notables. Their positions would be threatened if they allowed too many new commercial or industrial people into "their" regions.

---

[3]Circumspect economic historians such as Douglass North do not deny the possibility of welfare progress but emphasize the extent to which it has been delayed for reasons they do not claim fully to understand. Recent economists studying Latin America show the extent to which governments (contrary to official publicity) have prevented growth in many countries. These economists do not pay much attention to nongovernmental networks, but their work is instructive. See Harold L. Cole, Lee E. Ohanian, Alvaro Riascos, and James A. Schmitz Jr., "Latin America in the Rearview Mirror," *Federal Reserve Bank of Minneapolis Quarterly Review*, September 2006, summarized in *Wilson Quarterly* 31:1 (Winter 2007), 88–89. Nobelist Douglass North made a presentation that included the caveats mentioned above, at the University of Macau, February 2, 2007. The term "take-off" was popularized by Walter W. Rostow, "The Take-Off into Self-Sustained Growth," *Economic Journal* 66 (March 1956), 25–48.

The only reason to study a country's problems is to develop ways to solve them. Just as it is likely that China's or Thailand's growth rates will not remain at boom levels for many more decades (and that Taiwan's wealthy economy may continue to grow at diminished 'First World' rates), it is also likely that the Philippines' recent stagnation is not permanent. Still, the longevity of the Philippine stasis presents a deeper problem for economic liberals, and especially for political liberals, than they have yet wanted to face.

THE POLITICAL PUZZLE IN PHILIPPINE PLACES

Philippine political performance poses a particularly poignant problem for any democrat. Most liberals guess that elections should produce governments that serve the people. They suppose that long-term habituation to electoral contest, when combined with public norms of free speech and constitutional separations of power, should over time promote fairness and progress among the voters. When these proce- dures are used over extended periods, occasionally altering incum- bents to official power, the result is supposed to be a government that responds to the needs of many. But most of Philippine history over the last century provides counterevidence to these hopes for electoral democracy. Something is missing from liberal theory. What?

The answer is local pluralization outside the state, such as industry and commerce promote. Democratic theory's stress on state and open structures, as distinct from nonstate and private structures especially in enterprises, has created a political science that takes insufficient account of behavioral power beyond governments. Money and coercion, not just public parties, administrations, and citizens' attitudes of trust or dis- trust in them, are inevitable parts of the contemporary story.[4]

---

[4]This point is meant to complement, not refute, the understanding brought from attitude surveys that use more quantitative data, as in the beautifully unified chapters of *How East Asians View Democracy*, Yun-han Chu, Larry Diamond, Andrew J. Nathan, and Doh Chull Shin, ed. (New York: Columbia University Press, 2008). See also Ronald Inglehart, *Modernizations and Post-Modernizations: Culture, Economics, and Politics in 43 Countries* (Princeton: Princeton University Press, 1997). But state and nonstate structures are important, not just beliefs.

Preferences are certainly mentioned in liberal theory, but they are conceived as public and static (and in need of 'veiling' when private, as John Rawls imagines).[5] The state, aided by other formal political institutions such as parties, is seen as the mediator or aggregator of nonstate interests. But in practice, nonstate networks of journalists, clerics, academics, and especially business people often referee state and each others' powers instead. They only sometimes do so in any kind of public interest.

Industrialization is often left out of accounts of democratization except insofar as it creates classes or status groups, which turn out in many historical cases to be more pro-authoritarian and less democratic than liberals hoped. Until local and covert powers are brought back into a more critical political science of development, this discipline will remain in danger of being an ideology (an identifiably American one, although that is not the intent of its advocates). The answer to the Philippine puzzle lies outside Manila's weak state and fickle parties. It lies in the archipelago's modal nonstate power networks, which are strong but seldom entrepreneurial.

The aim of this book is not to join the many sermonizers about Philippine non-performance. As Pinches says, "In a region of Tigers and Dragons, the Philippines has almost universally been portrayed as the exceptional failure, and has had to endure the label 'sick man of Asia' as well as the condescending advice of regional leaders like Lee Kwan Yew."[6] Instead, the aim here is to find structural reasons for past Philippine problems, so that the future can be made brighter than the present. The Philippines will later pull out of its long stupor.

LOCAL POLITICS FOR ECONOMIC INVOLUTION

In Spanish and then American times, as Hawes writes, the "regnant model of development alleged that the Philippines' comparative

---

[5]See John Rawls, *A Theory of Justice* (Cambridge: Harvard University Press, 1971).

[6]Michael Pinches, "Entrepreneurship, Consumption, Ethnicity, and National Identity in the Making of the Philippines' New Rich," in *Culture and Privilege in Capitalist Asia*, M. Pinches, ed. (New York: Routledge, 1999), 275.

advantage was in the export of minerals and tropical agricultural products, and such industrialization as there was remained limited to the processing of agricultural goods."[7] Beginning early in the nineteenth century, and especially in the American period, exports grew for sugar (e.g., from Pampanga and Negros), tobacco (e.g., from Cagayan), and coconuts. Paddy fields were displaced, as were areas that had previously been used for slash-and-burn swidden agriculture (*kaingin*). Many parts of the Philippines, and the archipelago as a whole, became rice-importing.

An exception was Nueva Ecija in central Luzon, a populous landlocked province that grew half of Manila's rice and was the largest provincial supplier of that staple in the 1930s.[8] Industry in all regions, though, mainly dealt with products from the land. Foreign and "alien" (Chinese-Filipino) firms were in some periods legally banned from many commercial and industrial sectors. But few local Filipino entrepreneurs started businesses.

The Philippines nonetheless once had a temporary moderate boom, largely in processing industries. Philippine GNP grew at 7.7 percent annually in the first half of the 1950s, with manufacturing (which included much processing of agricultural products) growing at 12 percent. This was a high rate, greatly helped by U.S. grants at a time when the Manila government was fighting a communist rebellion that was especially strong in poor parts of central Luzon, including most of Nueva Ecija and adjacent provinces.

During the second half of the 1950s, however, the growth rate fell to 4.9 percent annually (and for manufactures and processed goods, to 7.7 percent). The modern sector was heavily dependent on extraction from forests, mines, and plantations. Employment in this sector grew slowly, because the processing enterprises tended to use heavy machinery rather than people. Labor-saving technology meant fewer

---

[7]Gary Hawes, "Marcos, His Cronies, and the Philippines' Failure to Develop," in *Southeast Asian Capitalists*, Ruth McVey, ed. (Ithaca: Southeast Asia Program, Cornell University, 1992), 148.

[8]For more, see Willem Wolters, *Politics, Patronage, and Class Conflict in Central Luzon* (The Hague: Institute of Social Studies, 1983), 23–25.

modern workers. When this situation was combined with patriotic policies of import-substitution, restrictions on Chinese in business, and Roman Catholic laws that assured a high birth rate, the result was no boom of income per capita.[9]

Philippine independence from the U.S. had been just marginally political, because it was not economic. The Americans had agreed to send economic aid in exchange for Philippine guarantees to fix the dollar-peso exchange rate and allow imports from the U.S. As Hutchcroft explains, "Only three years after independence [i.e., by 1949], the Philippine state nearly collapsed. Rehabilitation was plundered by the oligarchy to pay for duty-free imports of consumer durables, and the government lacked the means to stem the hemorrhage of foreign exchange." America was mainly interested in supporting the Philippine army against the communist Hukbalahap movement, and crucial economic decisions continued to be taken in Washington, not Manila. This dependency spurred the protectionist patriotic reaction that followed.

The nation's trade balance suffered, as manufactured U.S. imports exceeded Philippine exports. So by 1949, the government in Manila became enthusiastically nationalistic. The state, then under more severe threat from communists than at any time before or since, needed as much nativist legitimacy as it could then muster. So Manila government, for its own political reasons but with American understanding because of the communists, set high tariff barriers, created its own foreign exchange controls, further restricted Chinese entrepreneurship, and used "ISI" policies for import-substituting industries.

Regional families, which had for many decades accumulated land, generally remained dominant in their own areas. They were (and are) no less powerful for being local and decentralized rather than national. They sometimes developed processing industries that used inputs whose supplies they could control. But they were less willing

---

[9]George L. Hicks and Geoffrey McNicoll, *Trade and Growth in the Philippines: An Open Dual Economy* (Ithaca: Cornell University Press, 1971), as reviewed by Martin E. Abel in *Journal of Asian Studies* 32:2 (Spring 1973), 384–86.

either to let new entrepreneurs come into their traditional turfs or to establish plants by themselves in those places. As these local policies combined with the national ISI policies (which were better publicized but no more important), processing industries surged briefly in the early 1950s from a low base — but then did not last. This moderate growth was below the levels seen in other East Asian countries. It endured for about half a decade only. It used machinery and was less important in populous rice-growing areas (most of Luzon) than on islands that grew hemp or sugarcane.

This was a labor-saving change, however, and it distributed new wealth to relatively few Filipinos. It did not create firms hungry enough to diversify "gigantistically" into new industrial and commercial lines, after the available inputs from plantations and mines were exhausted. It thus contrasted with the market-searching growth described in previous chapters. So this temporary Philippine quasi-boom was involutionary and was not sustained. Local power networks were strong enough to prevent its expansion, which at most places they did not perceive to be in their interests.

Leading families in Philippine places had little need to find new wealth to maintain their networks.[10] The inflow of American aid did not mean reform in Philippine politics; it meant reconfirmation of existing local politics. Elites outside the state, who had for decades supported themselves less by production than by rent collection, as Hutchcroft writes, were "loath to make the transition to independence" if that meant changes in their traditional structures of politics.[11]

---

[10]For comparison, see Richard F. Doner and Ansil Ramsay, "Competitive Clientelism and Economic Governance: The Case of Thailand," in *Business and the State in Developing Countries*, Sylvia Maxfield and Ben Ross Schneider, eds. (Ithaca: Cornell University Press, 1997), 274–76.

[11]Paul D. Hutchcroft, "Booty Capitalism: Business-Government Relations in the Philippines," in *Business and Government in Industrializing Asia*, Andrew MacIntyre, ed. (Ithaca: Cornell University Press, 1994), 226 and 231. To support this interpretation, Hutchcroft also refers to earlier work by Benedict Anderson, F.H. Golay, and Gary Hawes.

The Taiwanese and Thai booms also benefitted from U.S. money that arrived largely to defeat communists. But in Thailand, more of these funds provided infrastructure such as roads that helped new industries, which were run by socially marginal (sometimes 'pariah'[12]) Sino-Thai managers, not mostly by established landed families that were less powerful in rural Thailand when the boom began. The generals running the bureaucratic structure in Bangkok discouraged Chinese Thais from expatriating most of their profits, but the new entrepreneurs were allowed to start firms. In both Thailand and Taiwan, new business elites first got new profits and then bought political sway, converting one form of social capital (money) into others (coercive and then state power). The slower Philippine growth did less to decrease the power of old elites and circulate influence to new ones.

Two loose national coalitions of local interests dominated Philippine politics from the 1950s. The "sugar bloc" was supported by sales of sugar to the U.S. under post-colonial free entry arrangements (especially after Cuban sugar supplies were cut). In exchange for this, the sugar bloc wanted maximal free entry of American manufactures to the Philippines. Import substituting industrialists, by contrast, wanted patriotic protection of Philippine products. To this end, they favored tariffs, an overvalued peso, and rice imports that lowered food prices and were thus an implicit subsidy to the wages they paid.[13] An economic problem with such politics was that neither the sugar exporters nor the industrial protectionists had much interest in exploring new markets or new technologies to create new sectors. These were not Schumpeterians, but they dominated the Philippine economy and created a political basis for its long-term stagnancy.

The period of maximum nationalistic import-substitution, the dozen years after 1949, was not an era in which all foreign capital was

---

[12]"Pariah" is Fred Riggs's predicate for Sino-Thai entrepreneurs who just a few decades later, after the boom, led the government in Bangkok.

[13]Note the contrast between these policies and Thailand's rice export tax, described in the previous chapter. Brian Fegan, "The Philippines: Agrarian Stagnation Under a Decaying Regime," in *Agrarian Transformations: Local Processes and the State in Southeast Asia*, Gillian Hart, *et al.*, eds. (Berkeley: University of California Press, 1989), 129.

excluded. Some American money came into agricultural exporting companies. Little went into trade or other industries. In these years, when the ratio of external capital to all capital was high, foreigners contributed one-twelfth of all investment in the archipelago. Filipinos who had money tended to spend it on consumption of foreign goods. External linkages, at this time and later, did little to raise exports except those based on processing outputs from mines or plantations. Foreigners made economic alliances with essentially feudal leaders more than with industrialists. Filipino landed capitalists had more ties to foreign firms than did non-landed or local Chinese entrepreneurs.[14]

President Carlos Garcia (1957–61) set a "Filipino First" policy as the lodestone of his administration.[15] Chinese, who could not easily get Philippine citizenship even if they had been born in the country, had legal trouble founding small companies. So SME growth in the Philippines (unlike this book's three other sites) has been much slower than the growth of large firms. In 1956–62, when Philippine growth was declining but was still higher than in later periods, small firms' value added *fell* 5.4 percent per year (compounded), while larger companies' value added rose 10.0 percent per year.[16] The contrast with other East Asian economies could not be more stark.

The World Bank nonetheless in 1957 hopefully proclaimed that, "the basic economic position of the Philippines is favourable... it has

---

[14]Temario C. Rivera, *Landlords and Capitalists: Class, Family, and State in Philippine Manufacturing* (Quezon City: University of the Philippines Center for Integrative and Development Studies, 1994), 86–87 and 94.

[15]See Wikipedia on Garcia, the only Philippine president who identified with the Visayan island of Bohol. His predecessor presidents Aguinaldo, Quezon, Osmeña, and probably others had at least some Chinese ancestry.

[16]Small firms were, in this survey, those with 5 to 19 workers, and the larger ones had more than twenty. In the same period, the small firms' value added *per worker* (at constant prices) was higher (3.3 percent per year) than in larger firms (2.5 percent) — but their employment was down 2.2 percent. For the data only, see *Entrepreneurship and Small Enterprises Development: The Philippine Experience*, Arnulfo F. Itao and Myrna R. Co, eds. (Quezon City: University of the Philippines Institute for Small Scale Industries, 1979), 15.

achieved a position in the Far East second only to Japan, both in respect to its level of literacy and to per capita production capacity."[17] When economists make estimates that ignore sociopolitical factors — including "cultural" factors with careful use of that term — they can, as this estimate shows, go very badly astray.

Growth of Philippine real GDP in the 1960s was 5 percent annually (before any adjustment for the quick rise of population). Then throughout the three decades after 1975, to 2005, the Philippine real GDP grew only 3.5 percent annually. Per-capita income grew hardly at all, because the annual population increase was 2 percent.[18] The Philippines enjoyed a brief economic upturn in the 1986–90 period after Marcos fell, and then again after an early-1990s recession. Yet even in the year during this period when growth was highest, in 1996, it was only 6 percent.[19] The 1997 Asian financial crisis then struck. In the first six years of the new millennium, Philippine GDP growth varied around 4 or 5 percent only.[20] Because the demographic increase continued unabated, the per-capita growth was just 2 or 3 percent. As many Filipinos who had relatively good educations realized, this performance was not up to East Asian market economy standards.

Booms in particular Philippine localities have occurred — but they also have been transitory. An example is in a southern Tagalog area, Laguna Province, which from the 1980s produced a packaged dessert called *nata de coco* for export to Japan. Mythology and advertising convinced many Japanese that this coconut confection could guarantee a clear skin without blemishes, and it tastes good.

---

[17]Michael Pinches, "Entrepreneurship, Consumption, Ethnicity, and National Identity in the Making of the Philippines' New Rich," in *Culture and Privilege in Capitalist Asia*, M. Pinches, ed. (New York: Routledge, 1999), 105, quoted from the World Bank.
[18]Anon., "Democracy as Showbiz," *Economist*, July 1, 2004, http://www.economist.com/printerfriendly.cfm?story_ID=2876966, seen January 21, 2007.
[19]Edgard Rodriguez and Albert Berry, "SMEs and the New Economy: Philippine Manufacturing in the 1990s," in *The Role of SMEs in National Economies in East Asia*, Charles Harvie and Boon-Chye Lee, eds. (Cheltenham: Edward Elgar, 2002), 139.
[20]The author thanks John Wong, senior economist at the East Asian Institute of the National University of Singapore, for several of these estimates.

So Japanese women paid for *nata de coco* in immense quantities. Laguna households and small factories made excellent profits for some years, even though the packaging (later canning) and quality of their product were uneven. Then their businesses were ruined by the mid-1990s, when Taiwanese investors started buying Laguna coconuts directly and producing *nata de coco* of more reliable quality.[21] If the local entrepreneurs had more impulse, earlier, to diversify their activities and to move up the value chain by manufacturing a more consistent product, their prosperity would have continued.

Household food production for the domestic market is widespread in the Philippines, but it is seldom profitable. Manufacturing is also surprisingly uncommon, except for traditional handicrafts that make scant money. Metal processing, except for transport equipment repair, is notable for its absence. Some interviewees report that obtaining metal supplies is difficult in the rural Philippines. Iron and steel have been far more available in Taiwan or Jiangnan, and local factories in those Chinese places use metals extensively. In China, the presence of heavy industries helps small and medium-sized ones by providing some inputs. Very local firms there, even households, can then do more kinds of profitable subcontracting. A combination of firm sizes is needed for sustained economic takeoffs, but major Filipino capitalists seldom went into heavy industries such as iron making. Lack of mineral supply cannot explain this. Taiwan had no more ores in the ground than Luzon had. (The basic geology of these two adjacent islands is comparable: subduction of the same plate caused uplifts and old volcanoes that rendered fertile soils for rice, but not much else of mineral interest.) The difference came from local political decisions to use, or not to use, all profitable opportunities and to import what was needed for that purpose.

Thai-Philippine comparisons also show other differences. In the decade after 1987, the per-capita consumption of electricity in Thailand rose by 145 percent — but just by 19 percent in the Philippines. Thailand in 1995 was using 3.3 times as much energy of

---

[21]Interview report from Alex Magno.

all sorts as was the Philippines.[22] Thailand's economic growth was faster than that of the Philippines not only in the decade after 1985, but also in every five-year-or-longer period before that, as far back as the mid-1950s. From 1950 to 1960, Thailand's GDP annual growth at constant prices was only 6.3 percent, while the Philippines' was 6.1 percent. But from 1960 to 1965, the Thai rate rose to 7.24 percent, and the Philippine rate was 5.21. In 1965–70, the rates were 9.14 in Thailand and 5.09 in the Philippines. In 1970–75, they were respectively 6.27 and 6.03; and in 1975–80, they were 7.55 and 6.27 (unless Marcos's bureaucrats overreported). From 1980 to 1985, the Thai economy grew at 5.1 percent annually, whereas the Philippine rate was negative, at –0.5 percent.[23] Although the fastest Thai boom time, later, was important in connecting the local and central politics of that country, the basis for this restructuring began earlier than the mid-1980s. The Philippines has suffered "late, late industrialization."[24] To a large extent, the reason is that its elites have prevented the rise of new autonomous entrepreneurs. This acceleration of the archipelago's relative shortfall shows what happened in Thailand, but even more clearly it shows what did not happen in the Philippines: the emergence of local industrial politics.

FLASHBACK ON EARLY DEMOCRACY THAT CONCENTRATED LOCAL NONSTATE POWER

These economic problems continued over time partly because of the evident legitimacy that democratic elections gave to decentralized

---

[22]Calculated from Ronald Hill, *Southeast Asia: People, Land, and Economy* (Crows Nest, NSW: Allen and Unwin, 2002), 188, on kilowatt hours per person and 190 on total primary energy consumption in kilocalories. Chapter 2 provides parallel data on electricity consumption for Shanghai's green suburbs in early industrialization.

[23]Jamie Mackie, and Bernardo Villegas, "The Philippines: Still an Exceptional Case?" in *Driven by Growth: Political Change in the Asia-Pacific Region*, James Morley, ed. (Armonk: M.E. Sharpe, 1993), 116.

[24]The phrase is that of Paul D. Hutchcroft, who complains eloquently about his favorite country in "Booty Capitalism," 223.

elites. This is the main part of the Philippine conundrum for ideological democrats like the present author. First origins of the problem lie far back in time. Americans, like Spaniards before them, needed a friendly native oligarchy to help administer their colony. William Howard Taft as Governor-General of the Philippines, before he became Secretary of War and then President, had a "policy of attraction" to coopt Filipino elites. An early anti-sedition law made advocacy of Philippine independence a capital crime. But democratic elite *ilustrados* who were willing to go along with the colonial regime were warmly welcomed. Taft cultivated these as early as 1900, especially when they joined a pro-American *Partido Federal*, even as pro-independence guerrillas were still fighting the U.S. Army in the bush.[25]

Land controlled by Catholic religious orders under the Spanish was appropriated by the U.S. administration. This land became a major resource with which to recruit elite Philippine families. As Lara and Morales write, "the rural elite accepted colonization as a means of dealing with peasant unrest, since it opened up land for later appropriation, reproducing unjust property relations."[26]

The Americans' colonial regime ran municipal elections in the Philippines as early as 1901. Provincial governors were elected by 1902. Representatives to an archipelago-wide Philippine Assembly won competitive elections by 1907. In 1916, this had become a bicameral legislature, and political parties developed further in the 1920s. Voting was regular and competitive, turnouts were high, and the parties were multiple. By 1935, Manuel Quezon was directly elected as the first President of the Commonwealth of the Philippines.[27]

---

[25]Based on Paul D. Hutchcroft and Joel Rocamora, "Strong Demands and Weak Institutions: Addressing the Democratic Deficit in the Philippines" (essay provided by courtesy of Dr. Rocamora); see also Michael Cullinane, *Ilustrado Politics: Filipino Elite Responses to American Rule, 1898–1908* (Manila: Ateneo de Manila Press, 2004).

[26]Francisco Lara, Jr. and Horacio Morales, Jr., "The Peasant Movement and the Challenge of Democratization in the Philippines," in *The Challenge of Rural Democratization: Perspectives from Latin America and the Philippines*, Jonathan Fox, ed. (London: Frank Cass, 1990), 145.

[27]John T. Sidel, *Capital, Coercion, and Crime: Bossism in the Philippines* (Honolulu: University of Hawaii Press, 1999), 16.

Democratically chosen officials at the relevant levels controlled the appointments of bureaucrats and police throughout this time, as well as after World War II for decades.

How, after all this experience, was the democracy so feeble that in 1972 Marcos could cancel it for fourteen years? (The other interruption, by the Japanese in 1942–45, was much shorter.) Some analysts of the Philippines still treat this country as a new democracy, the first Asian one in the "third wave," counting from Marcos's demise in 1986. This approach is not just inaccurate Philippine history. It takes the relatively brief Japanese and late-Marcos periods as all of the twentieth century. This interpretation is also very problematic political science, because it fails to ask what went wrong with the usual notion that populations normalize democracy when they become accustomed to it. Competitive elections have voted candidates into power for a hundred years in most Philippine localities.

The Philippines is currently one of the world's ten largest democracies. With nearly 100 million citizens it is now the twelfth most populous nation on earth. This country can count a great deal of democracy: there is one elected politician for each 1,400 voters — far more elective officials per capita than most liberal states have. Before votes, the local campaigns touch practically everyone. Anderson writes that, "this very expensive and malignant system... was designed to secure cacique hegemony and was not in any way the expression of new political power accruing to the rather small urban bourgeoisie.... The enormous costs (in money and violence) of cacique democracy led to ever-greater pillaging of the state...."[28] Participation and contestation can both be very extensive, without much delivery of substantive democracy to the people.

When poor respondents in Manila were asked to associate a Tagalog word with the cognate *demokrasya*, the overwhelming response was *kalayaan*, which means "independence" or "freedom."

---

[28]Benedict Anderson, "Elections and Participation," in *The Politics of Elections in Southeast Asia*, R.H. Taylor, ed. (Washington: Woodrow Wilson Center, 1996), 24. The data on elected officials per voter come from the mid-1980s. The etymology and meaning of *cacique* are discussed later.

That is what they expect of democracy. There is considerable evidence that poor people want rulers who are benign — and on that condition, they are willing to overlook faults of corruption, dubious morals, violent biographies, even reputed stupidity. Schaffer finds that Filipino poor people want a "class politics of dignity," in which rulers may be rich but must be respectful of all.

Upper-class reformers deride such "traditional politics" as "*trapo*" (an abbreviation that also means 'dirty rag' in Tagalog). These children of the Enlightenment call for cleanliness, transparency, and intelligent policy.[29] The contemporary reforming *ilustrados*, however, are a tiny portion of all Filipinos. To get at the interests of most of the people, it is necessary to look locally and in rural areas.

THE POLITICS OF RICE AS AN UNPROFITABLE CROP

North and central Luzon is mostly rice country, in contrast to many of the Visayas and most of Mindanao (and the southern Bikol peninsula of Luzon) where corn for food and sugar or coconut for export take somewhat more of the cropped area.[30] This book takes most of its examples from Luzon, whose traditional rice economy better resembles the Chinese, Taiwanese, and Thai research sites of interest, even though other grain crops are not wholly different from rice agronomy.

Different crops foster different forms of economic relations — and partially different local politics. Sugar, for example, is mostly grown in plantations (although there are also some small cane farms). It is cut by workers who are hired seasonally by patron-jobbers. Sugar refining is generally local; the crystals or juice are far less heavy than equivalent cut cane. Tobacco, principally grown by small farmers, creates

---

[29]Frederic Charles Schaffer, "Disciplinary Reactions: Alienation and the Reform of Vote Buying in the Philippines," paper for the American Political Science Association Annual Meeting, 2002, esp. 22, also 15–16.
[30]See an excellent map in *View from the Paddy: Empirical Studies of Philippine Rice Farming and Tenancy*, Frank Lynch, ed., *Philippine Sociological Review*, 20:1–2 (January/April 1972), 228–29.

another pattern: the growers are dispersed, but they sell to a monopoly that is often linked to the state. Coconuts mainly grow on plantations, selling to various intermediaries. Paddy cultivation, the main topic here, requires small-farm attention combined with commercial intermediaries to provide credit, to sell fertilizer, and to mill the rice.

Fegan shows that, "rice production under the terms of trade and natural risks prevailing in the Philippines in the [1980s] has been unprofitable. Mobile capital has sought other investments." State subsidies for credit, together with state support for the prices of fertilizer and fuel, created a situation in which "capitalist entrepreneurs stay out of farming, finding niches upstream and downstream of the farm."[31] This mix of technology and policy kept the poor impoverished and the rich wealthy. It also maintained patronist controls over a large (and politically conservative) majority of sharecropper-voters.

The "green revolution" for high-yield rice was initiated by the Rockefeller Foundation and supported by the U.S. government and by Robert McNamara after his move from running the Vietnam War to the World Bank. Perhaps neither he nor the agricultural scientists realized that, because short-stalk rice requires peasants to go into debt but drowns easily in typhoon years, it makes tillers more dependent on creditors over time. Writers such as Ernest Feder, in his book on *Perverse Development* in the Philippines, show that the green revolution helped only "a minority of Asian rice producers." Even if ordinary farmers could increase their productivity with new agronomy (as Feder confirms they can),

> There is nothing to prevent the large producer to increase his yields too, and in fact he is likely to do so. He has better access to inputs. He can also buy inputs cheaper. And the small producer is handicapped in the rice market and most likely receives a lower price for the same product than the commercial producer. If the small producer is a tenant, any increase in yield (income) would be siphoned off by his landlord. Even if prices go down, the large producer can put up reserves and buy more land and equipment.

---

[31]Brian Fegan, "The Philippines: Agrarian Stagnation," 176.

The small producer cannot. So in the end, the small producer *cannot* be better off.[32]

The new short-stalk-rice seeds require greater inputs of fertilizer and water (from tube wells or canals) as well as other machines. So the new agronomy requires farmers to take out bigger loans per crop. Green revolution promotes the use of irrigated land, and it benefits regions that have high water tables if they can prevent floods. The new seeds may well increase both the geographical and social unevenness of incomes. Green revolution tends over time to raise the portion of grain going to feed animals for protein (rather than to buyers of grain for human calorie consumption). It favors farmers who can buy combine harvesters and other machines that leverage labor, and it tends to increase land ownership concentration. High-yield seeds are not neutral with respect to farm size. Their social effects may not always match the description laid out above — and they raise output in most areas — but these are the most usual consequences.

Tenants pay a percentage of whatever they reap, in either a good or a bad year. Leaseholders pay a set amount, calculated on the basis of average yields from previous years. If the harvest comes in well, lessees can make better incomes than tenants. But in a lean year, especially if they grow new rice, both kinds of tillers can find themselves deep in debt.

Ecological conditions, definable by altitude, also affect this situation. Low-lying land may be rich, fertile, flat, and good for paddies — but bottom land is also subject to floods. Farmers there may have difficulty controlling the water level, and short-stalk rice is relatively subject to drowning. Fertilizers, which the new high-yield varieties require, are easily washed away. Even traditional seeds do reasonably well in only three out of five years on average.[33] So tenants in such areas resist becoming lessees. The new agronomy does not assure

---

[32]Ernest Feder, *Perverse Development* (Quezon City: Federation for Nationalist Studies, 1983), 24 (emphasis in original), see also 20.

[33]Brian Fegan, "Between the Lord and the Law: Tenants' Dilemmas," in *View from the Paddy: Empirical Studies of Philippine Rice Farming and Tenancy*, Frank Lynch, ed., *Philippine Sociological Review*, 20:1–2 (January/April 1972), 114.

good results for them, and they are very loath to bear the downside risks in bad years. Lowland farmers, however, are also often in a good position to supplement their rice incomes with shrimp, fish, bamboo, or vegetables. Patronage systems in such areas are somewhat weaker than in the higher-altitude ecologies.

Higher flat areas that are further from rivers, often using pump irrigation, have many of the opposite characteristics. Rice from the International Rice Research Institute (IRRI) at Los Baños on Luzon does well in these places. Especially there, "the transfer to leasehold is attractive, in the abstract, to most farmers."[34] Deforestation has nonetheless raised the portion of such land that is subject to flooding — and Luzon (unlike Mindanao) is in the middle of a fierce typhoon belt. Luzon often has heavy rains even when the centers of these huge storms do not strike the island directly. Average rice yields per hectare have risen in non-riverine areas of Luzon during recent decades, but the ties that bind farmers to their rural patron-creditors have also become stronger there.

A third kind of ecology occurs at still higher altitudes, where the land is steep rather than flat, and generally less fertile than at lower elevations. Crops are largely rain-fed. Some new rice varieties, such as one called IR-5, have done well in highland environments even if the plants become rather dry. Farmers there tend to be poorer and more scattered than at lower altitudes, but they are often willing to use new seeds and sign up for lease arrangements, even when their landlords do not like such changes.

Global institutions strongly favored high-yield varieties of rice, which were largely developed at IRRI. But even World Bank President McNamara admitted that, "In Asia... the cost of fertilizer and pesticides required to make optimum use of the new high-yielding varieties of wheat and rice ranges from 20 to 80 dollars per hectare. But the small farmer there is spending only 6 dollars per hectare, because that is all he can finance."[35]

---

[34]Fegan, *op. cit.*, 115.
[35]Robert McNamara to the World Bank Board of Directors, meeting in Nairobi in 1973, quoted in Feder, *Perverse Development*, 104.

REFORMS, INDEBTEDNESS, AND NON-MANAGER KLEPTOCRATS

Ferdinand Marcos's "Masagana-99 Scheme" mandated that participating farmers use the new seed varieties. Americans who had financed the rice research were naturally pleased. Some imagined that the program would create for Marcos a populist constituency, but its more important political corollary was at the elite level. Considerable land was in the hands of big owners who opposed Marcos. He used the program to expropriate, on a selective basis, rivals who were his enemies. Marcos apparently overestimated the extent of land concentration in the rice-growing areas, and his reforms were resisted and sabotaged by large owners. He nonetheless provided credit for the necessary inputs, and he put very strong government incentives behind the push for "miracle" rice.

By 1973 in a Bulacan province village not far from Manila, the new hybrid varieties covered "all but a tiny fraction" of agricultural land in the monsoon season.[36] The portions of harvest that were paid for rent dropped, but the costs for fertilizers and machines rose — as did indebtedness. Patrons became less likely to farm land themselves. Their children emigrated for education and jobs to larger towns. The livelihoods of relatively rich rural families improved. Landless households saw not much change. New land was brought under the plow, as population and total yield both rose. "No villager has bought land from farm profits," however.[37] The net profitability of rice agriculture declined.

Land reforms in the Philippines thus switched many small farmers from a sharecropping to a lease system without giving them new job opportunities. With sharecropping, a landlord usually pays for farm expenses except labor. A farmer with a contract lease, however, only gets land and is responsible for all non-land inputs. This entitles the contract farmer to keep a larger portion of the crop than

---

[36]Relying partly on work by David Wurfel, see Brian Fegan, "The Philippines: Agrarian Stagnation," 133, and also Fegan's article cited immediately below.

[37]Brian Fegan, "Accumulation on the Basis of an Unprofitable Crop," in *Agrarian Transformations*, 160–62.

a sharecropper — but it also entails input expenses that rise sharply if high-yield seeds are planted. The Green Revolution commercialized traditional agriculture, but as a peasant said, "Rice farming these days is akin to gambling."[38] Occasionally it gave bumper crops, but often it meant that the farmers lost their shirts.

High-yield rice is even more sensitive to proper supplies of water than to proper supplies of fertilizer. Typhoons are an even greater danger to short-stalk rice than to traditional kinds; and when there is drought, the petrochemical fertilizers used with it burn the roots. So major or total losses are a risk with the new rice in unlucky years.

The Philippines is estimated to forfeit up to 2 percent of its GDP, as an annual average, to natural disasters — especially tropical storms.[39] Taiwan also suffers floods, earthquakes, and typhoons that are almost as terrible as those in Luzon or the Visayas. The difference is not just that Taiwan's economy has developed more resources to combat these catastrophes when they strike, or that its land reform preceded American enthusiasm for technical miracles in Asia, but instead that the ethnic politics of agricultural development on Taiwan encouraged (rather than discouraged) a dispersed form of local industrialization. So the economy and people there are not as dependent on chancy agronomy. When their fields fail, they still have their factories.

Careful quantitative research on the costs and payoffs from high-yield rice varieties (planting, fertilizing, transplanting, irrigating, harvesting, and hauling) in central Luzon has shown that, over time, farmers have lost wealth when they plant "miracle" rice. This has happened even though total rice production has risen. "The largest debt incurred by farmers was in the rental arrears to the landlords."

The main beneficiaries of the Green Revolution were landed elites. High-yield rice technology gave them fresh resources they could have used to modernize themselves as industrial elites. Few did so, apparently because they could not conceive themselves running

---

[38]Umehara Hiromitsu, "Green Revolution for Whom?" in *Second View from the Paddy*, Antonio J. Ledesma, *et al.*, eds. (Manila: Institute of Philippine Culture, Ateneo de Manila University, 1983), 38–39.
[39]Ronald Hill, *Southeast Asia*, 285.

factories. Many went into a Philippine kind of private banking, however. Umehara writes that, "no significant conflict between landlords and commercial elites was observed.... Smart landlords... joined the ranks of the commercial elites." The new rice technology gave them new ways to extract financial interest. Rent came from owning local debt, not just from owning local land. Profits from managing factories or stores involved work of kinds that many Philippine elites disdained to do. That, at least, was their "revealed preference," shown in their behavior.

By 1980, three-quarters of all Philippine farms were planted with high-yield varieties of crops; in 1968, the portion had been only one-fifth.[40] Fertilizer consumption more than doubled in the Philippines between 1967 and 1983. The government in Manila granted a monopoly on fertilizer production to a Filipino company. Acreage devoted to food crops rose 37 percent from 1960 to 1980 in the Philippines — but acreage devoted to commercial crops (for exports, non-subsistence consumers, and animal feed) rose 146 percent.[41] Formerly forested areas were plowed as fields after large companies cut down the trees. Irrigated land was expanded for food, but the expansion of acreage for commercial crops was greater. None of these trends gave the Philippines a robust industrial economy.

The Marcos reform made it legally more difficult for rural capitalists to do what few of them now wanted to do anyway, i.e., to go into farming themselves, or even to rent land directly. Profits came not from growing rice or providing agricultural inputs. Instead, money now came from local finance, from interest collected on loans for inputs and from milling and distribution. This kind of commercialization was banking, not trading, and certainly not manufacturing.

---

[40]*Contract Growing: Intensifying TNC [Transnational Corporation] Control in Philippine Agriculture*, Antonio J. Tujan, Jr., ed. (Manila: IBON Foundation, 1998), 17, gives the figures 75 percent and 21 percent for these two years, considering all kinds of crops.

[41]Feder, *Perverse Development*, 163.

RICE REFORM AND POLITICAL PATRONAGE

Philippine patronage networks were strengthened, not weakened, by the kind of agricultural modernization for which Marcos pressed. Local elites who remained rural often went into finance, collecting interest or rent. In seasons when weather was fortunate, profits could be made. But in inclement seasons, farmers — or renters who were normally paid from the crop and had supplied fertilizers — could lose their shirts because of the high costs of inputs for output that might be nil. Tilling land, or even renting land for others to till, became higher-risk than local banking. Typhoons could ruin a harvest, but they could not ruin a debt note.

If loan repayments came directly from the harvest, the creditor had often also rented a thresher and driver, who would take grain just as soon as it was off the field. For example, when a central Luzon rural capitalist named Totoy gave loans (at the standard interest of 10 percent per month), "this proved a bad investment, as he had no collection mechanism until [a trusted relative, his wife's brother Siso in this case] bought a threshing machine.... Totoy lent money for fertilizer on condition that Siso's machine did the threshing."[42]

New threshers also reduced the portion of the harvest going to labor by half (from about one-fifth to one-tenth). They both threshed and winnowed. They also eliminated a need to bundle and haul the sheaves. As Fegan writes, "Whatever might be argued by IRRI about the advantages of shortening turnaround time and the possibility of multiple cropping, in areas of single-crop water supply the thresher caused a large gain to capital but a large loss to labor."[43] The scientists at Los Baños did not restrict themselves to making designer rice. Their engineers also designed an "axial-flow" thresher, which worked well in muddy situations and further fostered the development of rural lending and capital.

---

[42]See Brian Fegan, "Accumulation," 167–68.
[43]See *ibid.*, 175.

Marcos subsidized bank loans and, as Kerkvliet writes,

> Tenants now have to pay all farming expenses, whereas before land reform the landowners paid half... many tenants ended up worse off than they were when planting older varieties.... besides repaying the debts, the borrower volunteers personal services to the patron creditor — cooks and serves at parties the creditor hosts, repairs the creditor's house or car, cleans the creditor's yard, among others. Some borrowers have switched to the creditor's religion.... The borrowers also sell their rice to the creditor, even though other buyers offer higher prices.[44]

After the Marcos government installed a credit scheme in a central Luzon village to finance the new rice agronomy, 20 to 30 landholders had been able to borrow money — but just a few years later, more than half of them had defaulted and were no longer deemed creditworthy. The money they had borrowed for new rice made them poorer.

The rise of inequality can be decried as a problem — but an even greater problem was that the wealthier Filipino local elites did not use their windfall to invest in factories and create a modern economy. What did not happen was as important in the long run as what happened. The green revolution and the rise of commercialized agriculture have probably benefitted the incomes of many rural households, but these changes also created welfare losses for many.

A study of household nutrition in part of the Philippines that had experienced extensive non-rice commercialization concluded that for every two households that benefited by having better nutrition, better schooling, taller children, better housing, and higher incomes, one household lost access to land and income.[45] A Manila foundation found that high-yield varieties "reduced real farm income as much as 52 percent within an eleven-year period from 1970 to 1981" — even

---

[44]Benedict J. Kerkvliet, "Class and Class Relations in a Philippine Village," quoted from an unpublished typescript, 14–5, 23, and 31, in Feder, *Perverse Development*, 93–94.

[45]Based closely on Howarth E. Boudis and Lawrence J. Haddad, *Agricultural Commercialization, Nutrition, and the Rural Poor: A Study of Philippine Farm Households* (Boulder: Lynne Rienner, 1990), 148.

while rice volume rose 72 percent.[46] The costs to farmers grew 51 percent, but the prices they could get fell by 46 percent. The new agronomy increased both production and poverty.

If land fertility dropped locally and farmers could not go to creditors to buy the needed chemicals, they could be pushed off their land by debt collectors. The losing third of the families were generally small landholders. Some gained in terms of economic welfare. Practically none gained, however, in terms of independence from creditor patrons. The green revolution, for rice and other crops too, strengthened patron-client local polities in the Philippines. It was a conservative revolution.

CULTIVATING RICE AS A NON-ECONOMIC ENTERPRISE

The Philippines is a rice importer. This by itself is a sardonic achievement, in view of the islands' ecology. The government in Manila affects the rice price in two ways: by running agencies that buy directly from farmers, and by having the National Food Authority import enough additional rice to assure low prices in cities.[47] The greater growth of Thai industry, as compared to that of the Philippines, did not cause as great a decrease in the portion of labor on fields, because Thai agriculture remained profitable to rural households. Seventy percent of the Philippines' economically active population in 1960 was in agriculture, but this fraction shrank to 40 percent by 2000. About 85 percent of Thailand's economically active population were agriculturalists in 1960, and that portion was still reported over 55 percent in 2000.[48] Even if

---

[46]Evidence that high-yield grains raised production and lowered farmers' incomes. This has been found in the Philippines by many researchers: by Hirohitsu Umehara, by an IRRI team involving Violeta Cardova and Robert Herdt, and by the ACES Foundation of Manila. See Rolando B. Modina and A.R. Ridao, *IRRI Rice: The Miracle that Never Was* (Quezon City: ACES Foundation, 1987), 35.

[47]For comparison, see Robert H. Bates, *States and Markets in Tropical Africa: The Political Basis of Agricultural Policy* (Berkeley: University of California Press, 1981).

[48]Ronald Hill, *Southeast Asia*, 123, based on UN Food and Agriculture Organization figures whose comparability across nations may be doubted.

these statistics come from surveys using somewhat different national categories for gathering data, it is evident that the Thai boom and its associated political changes were not based on farmers' year-round departure from agricultural work.

With high-yield seeds, rice farming could become less profitable in the Philippines; so investors largely go to other sectors, away from rice. Commercial banks reduce their business of lending to small farmers, who in bad-weather years cannot repay. After formal credit institutions pull out, the informal ones last longer because their loans are linked to the local power of creditors, but leaders face the same basic problem. Land becomes less valuable as collateral. The money to be made farming it is negative, paltry, or less than in alternative kinds of business that provide other sorts of collateral.

Where entrepreneurial traditions exist (as they do in other parts of East Asia), money goes into new factories and commercial ventures. But where existential entrepreneurs are absent or few (as in southern or northeast or inland Luzon), capital grows slowly and becomes more urbanized. Capital flows away from the rural poor, making them poorer. For these reasons, patrons often take on the burden of financing their serfs for local-political rather than economic reasons. Traditions bind patrons to clients, not just vice-versa. The green revolution affected patronage by making it more contentious, more indenturing for clients where it remained and at the same time less beneficial to patrons.

Still, "rice is a religion," as Alex Magno writes. Whether or not that crop is profitable, most inland Luzon villagers leave other pursuits and go to the fields during the busy seasons of planting, transplanting, and harvesting.[49] Cynthia Bautista, a University of the Philippines sociologist, has found that in the mid-1990s only 20 percent of the total household income of farm families in central Luzon came on average from rice. The remaining four-fifths (from a low and stagnant

---

[49] Alexander R. Magno teaches in the Political Science Department of the University of the Philippines. He hails from a township family in Nueva Ecija and speaks with authority about that context. The area on which he reports engages in double-rather than triple-cropping.

average) came from other kinds of work: the wife of the family might grow and trade vegetables or other non-staple foods, a husband might drive a tricycle taxi, a daughter might become a nurse, a son might accumulate enough money to buy a truck or jeepney and go into transport. But when it was time to tend the paddies, central Luzon villagers did that job as a communal duty, just as they attended Sunday Mass. If people worked as individuals only for the benefit that work brought to each of them separately, this and most other economic behavior would be inexplicable. But data from Luzon show that rises of rice productivity correlated with declines of rice farmers' incomes.[50]

POLITICAL FAMILIES

These changes, brought by agrarian reform, occur in political contexts that are local. Philippine countryside contexts have a specific modal form that came out of a distinctive history. The barangay is by all accounts the basic unit of Philippine politics, and the archipelago now has nearly 50,000 of them. Another flashback is needed to put the green revolution in perspective of the typical history of the communities in which most Filipinos live.

Barangay originally meant a "boat" in which people came to settle a new place. The canoe was conceived as holding a family, e.g., of early settlers in Luzon who had no raja or sultan (unlike other parts of Southeast Asia) but only the family captain. Political scientist O.D. Corpuz writes that as settlement evolved, "the chief figure was the *datu*, generally a son or other blood relative of the founder." This was "a kinship group," although the kinship was partly fictive.[51]

---

[50] John J. Carroll, S.J., "Growth, Agrarian Reform, and Equity: Two Studies [in Bulacan and Bikol]," in *Second View from the Paddy*, Antonio J. Ledesma, *et al.*, eds. (Manila: Institute of Philippine Culture, Ateneo de Manila University, 1983), 22.

[51] Quoted in Kikuchi Yasushi, *Uncrystallized Philippine Society: A Social Anthropological Analysis* (Quezon City: New Day Publishers, 1991), 9. Another very distant Austronesian-speaking group, the Maoris, also define their tribes as having arrived in separate canoes (from an undefined 'Havaiki' further north in Polynesia). These tribes remain important as owners of very extensive communal lands under New Zealand law and the Treaty of Waitangi.

Every barangay is, according to one Filipino social scientist's account of local traditions, centered on a "house of stone," *bahay na bato*. The town patriarch reigns there, and smaller houses of less durable materials surround his fort. A. de Morga, a 16th century historian, describes Luzon as having "no kings or lords," but "many chiefs were recognized." The Spanish brought in very few soldiers and could maintain some loose control only by dubbing each of these chiefs a *cabeza de barangay*. Local polities were far more important to most folks than the colonial polity; people in the same town still referred to each other as *cabanca* (boat companion).[52] The names of local bosses or "big men" were commonly accompanied with honorific prefixes such as *Gat* or *Apo*. "Men of prowess," including some who claim superhuman abilities, are nothing new in Southeast Asia.[53] Marcos was, to many of his followers, "Apo Ferdinand."

The Spaniards found, in this modal structure of the traditional Philippine polity, a framework for indirect rule. After the voyages of Columbus and Magellan, they had come quickly into a huge empire but lacked enough staff for all of it. Their most distant colony remained populous, in part because previous unrecorded migrations had made its Old World inhabitants relatively immune to the imported diseases that more than decimated Spain's American lands.

Cacique is etymologically an Arawak West Indian word for chief, but it was soon used throughout the Spanish colonies for local potentates such as the barangay heads described above: "a strong and autocratic leader in local and regional politics whose characteristically informal, personalistic, and often arbitrary rule is buttressed

---

[52]The canoe is a widespread Austronesian/Nusatarian symbol of basic community, from Yamis in Taiwan to Maoris in New Zealand at least. The de Morga quotations are from Kikuchi Yasushi, *Uncrystallized Philippine Society*, 8–10.

[53]See a collection of essays on the oddly unifying pre-European-contact history of the whole area, in which the Philippines are solidly included along with Thailand and Java, by O. Willem Wolters, *History, Culture, and Region in Southeast Asian Perspective*, rev. ed. (Ithaca: Southeast Asia Program, Cornell University, 1999). For a treatment at the state level, see the similarly magistral summary by Robert F. Heine-Geldern, *Concepts of State and Kingship in Southeast Asia* (Ithaca: Southeast Asia Program, Cornell University, 1956).

by a core of relatives... and is marked by the diagnostic threat and practice of violence."[54] Caciques are nonstate. They also are invariably coercive. They depend, as Anderson explains, on a "cacical family," which occasionally splits into conflicting factions but is usually held together in rituals of brotherhood, cemented by marriages and godparent links.

There was some flexibility in this colonial structure, especially as Spain lost most of its other territories in the early 19th century. Primary exports allowed landowners in the Philippines to make more money. Late-Enlightenment *ilustrados* reduced the racism that had been important during Spain's earlier ecclesiastical governance of its populous Asian colony. Powerful families emerged in specific parts of the archipelago.

A few of them can be listed, roughly north to south, although some of the strongest had interests in more than one place. Singsons, Crisologs, Barberos, and Paredes were in north Luzon (a mostly Ilocano region where Marcoses were notable only later), Josons and Diazes in Nueva Ecija, Aquinos and Cojuangcos in Tarlac, these and a greater variety of other families in Pampanga, Ayalas and an even greater variety in the Manila area, Montanos in Cavite, Laurels in Batangas, and various Basque and other mixed lineages in conservative Bikol. Then south of Luzon were Roxas on Panay, Romualdezes in Leyte (and in Bulacan on Luzon), Montelibanos on Negros, Osmeñas and Duranos in different parts of populous Cebu, Dimaporos and many others in Mindanao — these families and others like them tried to maintain permanent political rights in their particular patches of the Philippines.[55]

Land concentration by these families was a gradual process from the 18th through the 20th centuries. A land-owning Spanish and mestizo gentry chose members of municipal ruling bodies called *principalia*.

---

[54]Paul Friedrich, "The Legitimacy of a Cacique [in Mexico]," in *Local-Level Politics: Social and Cultural Perspectives*, Marc J. Swartz, ed. (Chicago: Aldine, 1968), 247.

[55]James Clad, *Behind the Myth: Business, Money, and Power in Southeast Asia* (London: Hyman, 1989), 35, and Benedict J. Tria Kerkvliet, "Contested Meanings of Elections in the Philippines," in *The Politics of Elections in Southeast Asia*, R.H. Taylor, ed. (Washington: Woodrow Wilson Center, 1996), 138.

These were state-registered gentlemen. Their economic power grew on the basis of sharecropping. Commercial entrepreneurs, often Chinese-Spanish and Chinese-Filipino, could at that time buy large tracts. Central authorities in Manila, even the weak ones of both the Spanish and American periods, affected local landholding because they sometimes acted against the interests of the church authorities. After the Americans invaded in 1898, huge ecclesiastical estates were put up for sale to local elites. The result was a rise of local gentry power, confirming indirect rule under the new colonial regime — and further weakening the central state in Manila.[56]

Claims by local family bosses in the Philippines sometimes became cosmic (and comic). Sidel writes that, "In Barrio Dungo-an, Danao City, just a 45-minute drive north from Cebu City, lies the Philippines' twentieth-century answer to Borobodur, Pagan, and Angkor Wat: the burial grounds of the late Ramon M. Durano, Sr. (1905–88)." Around his tomb are "busts representing all the popes in the history of Christianity, each facing the late Durano." He had called himself merely "a repentant Sinner" but also admitted that others had called him "Godfather, Warlord, Killer, Boss... Caesar of Cebu, Political Kingpin."[57] Although Durano played a role in national politics, his dominance was local and Cebuano. Ramon Durano is also said to have claimed that all of Jesus's apostles (except Judas) were his distant cousins.[58] Family was very important to Durano.

Patronism was the mode of politics. An analyst of traditions in "Sugarland," Negros, pointed out that Philippine clients were somewhat like slaves. "Men and women are free to leave the *hacienda* to try to find work elsewhere, but for practical purposes, many are owned body and soul by their masters." As a *hacendero* boss put it,

---

[56]Willem Wolters, *Politics, Patronage, and Class Conflict in Central Luzon* (The Hague: Institute of Social Studies, 1983), 15–16.

[57]John T. Sidel, "The Philippines: The Languages of Legitimation," in *Political Legitimacy in Southeast Asia: The Quest for Moral Authority*, Muthiah Alagappa, ed. (Stanford: Stanford University Press, 1995), 136 and 138.

[58]Anon., "Democracy as Showbiz," *Economist*, July 1, 2004, http://www.economist.com/printerfriendly.cfm?story_ID=2876966, seen January 21, 2007.

"In such a system, you control the community, because everybody is dependent on you, and you have a say in everything they do."[59] A politician, describing the history of his locality (Itogon, Benguet, north Luzon) noted the continuing power of gentry. Under a Republic Act of 1900 that the Americans passed, "the first [local] *presidente* was Jose Smith Fianza. Nothing of great significance could be illustrated during this time except the strong paternal powers of the *presidente*. His words were then the law of the town. The constituents were subject to the wish of the local *presidente*. If he said work, the people worked."[60] Soon thereafter, township leaders were formally chosen by election — but nothing in this report, which covers a long period up to 1993, indicates any basic change in the structure of local power.

Nongovernment organizations existed, and they were increasingly linked to a national "Peace and Order Council." Barangays held assemblies that were supposed to listen to grievances, although in practice they listened to speeches by local politicians. When disputes arose, mediators were chosen "to solve cases without going to the higher court" that might decide with less reference to local power. People could present information to their leaders in the Philippines, but as one administrator remarked of the barangays, "I am not sure how many of them have conducted general assemblies...." The Ford Foundation sponsored a meeting in Itagon to improve this situation there, but a speaker noted that "the participation of people in local governance is very minimal.... This is true all over the Philippines.... We Filipinos are very paternalistic."[61]

Students of high-income countries construct their theories as if important political institutions do not include the family.

---

[59]Berlow, Alan, *Dead Season: A Story of Murder and Revenge on the Philippine Island of Negros* (New York: Pantheon, 1996), 81.

[60]Speeches by Filipino local officials in *Assessing People's Participation in Governance: The Case of Itogon Municipality*, Steven Rood, ed. (Baguio: University of the Philippines, College of Baguio, Cordillera Studies Center, 1993), 5–6.

[61]*Assessing People's Participation in Governance*, 17, 19, 28–30.

This unit is seen as merely "social," not political. States, churches, companies, unions, courts, armies: these are variously recognized as crucial agents of politics, but families are not. Even the Adamses, Roosevelts, Tafts, Kennedys, Clintons, and Bushes have not inspired American political scientists (as distinct from journalists or old-school historians) to pay any serious theoretical attention. For many developing countries, notably the Philippines, neglect of the family as a political institution almost totally cripples analysis. The political system there has been aptly described as an "anarchy of families."[62]

Aquinos, Ayalas, Cojuangcos, de Guzmans, Laurels, Macapagals, Osmeñas, Romualdezes, and other families do not retain their power automatically. Aversions to discussing this most solid kind of human institution *as political* is one of the reasons why Philippine data have not influenced general ideas in modern political science. In the future, for the same reason, Philippine political studies can make contributions to comparative theory. In that country, for long periods and many purposes, the state has been weak while clans have been very strong.

They need local constituents. To keep their power, they breed political savvy among their sons and daughters. They need continued access to wealth from land, prebends, industrial or commercial profits, legalized or illegal monopolies, or other reliable sources of rents. Prominent families can decline or disappear politically, when these requirements are not met. The longevity of their strength is greatest when they have more assets and coercive abilities than rivals do, in their specific areas.

---

[62]See Alfred W. McCoy, "An Anarchy of Families: The Historiography of State and Family in the Philippines," in *An Anarchy of Families: State and Family in the Philippines*, Alfred W. McCoy, ed. (Madison: University of Wisconsin Center for Southeast Asian Studies, 1993), 1. As McCoy points out, a few Latin Americanists have also paid attention to the political importance of families there, such as the Pessoas in northeast Brazil or various Mexican clans.

VIOLENCE AS A PILLAR OF NONSTATE POLITICAL LOCALISM

The strength of many magnates is not general but is specifically coercive.[63] When Americans first ran the Philippine state, local bosses were also potent in the U.S. Force, not just landownership, has been at the heart of widespread Filipino "bossism." In 2007, after a north Luzon provincial governor was assassinated, the head of the national police force Oscar Calderon estimated that "politicians" had over ninety "private armies" in Philippine localities. But this problem was not recent; in 1972, the Elections Commission chair Jaime Ferrer said he "knew all about the political warlords" and their private militias. He said at least six were senators, thirty-seven were representatives, and others were provincial governors, mayors, and "relatives of prominent politicians."[64]

Not all the bosses with official titles are high patrons; many are hinges between large and small factions. Not all politicians are bosses of this kind; increasingly, some are professionals or celebrities from previously poor families. Not all landowners are notably coercive. The Osmeñas of Cebu City, for example, have maintained their dynastic rule for decades without obvious private militias or much direct repression. Hegemony and habit, rather than uninstitutionalized force, has been important for integrating some local polities. Many others are held together by forthright sincere violence.

Many landlords in the Philippines are absentee, running profitable firms and participating in the politics of Manila. They need bailiffs and

---

[63]See Alan Berlow, *Dead Season*, and John T. Sidel, *Capital, Coercion, and Crime.* Sidel (e.g., on page 10) emphasized that the state was strong, at least in the Manila suburb that he studied. Many Filipino political institutions at all levels, national as well as local, lacked enough resources and exclusive legitimacy to meet their goals. Coercion, in this context, was the main political resource.

[64]Compare Anon., "Philippine President Orders Disarming of "Private Armies," *Agence France Presse*, January 25, 2007, 5, with Filemon V. Tutay, "Who Me?" Philippines Free Press editorial, February 5, 1972, http://philippinesfreepress. wordpress.com/2007/02/05/who-me-february-5-1972, seen May 12, 2007.

armed henchmen to collect rents in their homelands; so they hire guns or learn how to shoot (this was also a custom among European gentry). Newly rich families such as the de Guzmans developed traditions of personal expertise in marksmanship. As anthropologist Fegan says, a second de Guzman son joined his elder brother as overseer and rent collector on their estates and on those of the older de Leon family. Bienvenido de Guzman was "a tough-guy, a gambler, and a crack shot.... He was shot and killed when bandits tried to rob him of a big win... but he left two of them dead."[65]

The third brother, Kardeng, had an even more varied career: estate guard at one time, peasant union organizer at another, pro-American guerrilla against the Japanese, then host to the General Secretary of the Philippine Communist Party, bandit, then Civil Guard, buffalo thief, and elected politician. He protected some farmers against other landlords. Most particularly, he protected the delivery of de Guzman rents. The fourth brother was a communist intelligence officer and commander — and after that movement declined, he became an armed guard at his family's Manila film studio.

The fifth and youngest brother, Grasing, also known as "the Godfather," eventually took charge of the family's estates in Nueva Ecija. He controlled mayoralties in four towns and delivered votes for the local congressman, the mayor of Cabanatuan City, and the governor. His relations with the local Philippine Constabulary were very close. Advance information from the PC warned him to be absent from his suburban Manila house when it was attacked by three hundred men, some of whom had automatic weapons, because of his personal dispute with a relative of his wife. Although at one point Grasing was charged with multiple homicides, a court found him not guilty. He proudly admitted to an American researcher that he had been skillful enough to bribe judges and prosecutors (and his opponents' lawyers). He mused that he himself might have been a good lawyer. But then he reconsidered:

> No. I could never have survived as a lawyer. I am a man of honor.... I would have to bribe judges, out of responsibility to my client. But judges are venal

---

[65]Brian Fegan, "Entrepreneurs in Votes and Violence: Three Generations of a Peasant Political Family" in *An Anarchy of Families*, 36.

and may sell the case to the other side if it intervenes with a higher bid. Then I would have to kill the judge.... It is well that I used my talents otherwise.[66]

Grasing ran gambling games "out of civic duty," and he claimed that the profits went to supplement the low salaries of hardworking public officials, such as the PC chief and the provincial governor. He was appointed by a PC general as a "special agent" for the police.

Younger generations of the de Guzman clan did not need to engage in so much violence. The power of the family rested on members' reputations as political organizers, able to threaten foes and protect clients, more than on their wealth, or the land they owned, or blood kinship, or the number of their family members. Other lineages owned more land, and the de Guzmans were often able to coopt them on a local basis.

Philippine warlords sometimes ran their own arms factories. The Durano clan of Danao City, for example, manufactured guns into the 1980s at least — and Ramon Durano could replenish his arsenal even after Marcos issued a martial law decree ordering private armies to surrender their weapons.[67]

Political violence has in some periods been liberally administered by the central state as well as by local tyrants, often in coordination with police or army officers. From 1977 through February of 1986 in Marcos's time, 2,500 people were "salvaged," i.e., killed extrajudicially, and another 709 simply "disappeared". After Marcos's demise, through 1991, the monthly rate of disappearances was practically unchanged — 6.45 persons per month under Marcos, as compared to 6.13 under Aquino. The rate of "salvagings" was reduced by about one-third.[68]

---

[66]*Ibid.*, 39.

[67]Alfred W. McCoy, "An Anarchy of Families: The Historiography of State and Family in the Philippines," in *An Anarchy of Families*, 22.

[68]The data are from G. Sidney Silliman, "Human Rights and the Transition to Democracy," in *Patterns of Power and Politics in the Philippines*, James F. Eder and Robert L. Youngblood, eds. (Tempe: Arizona State University Program for Southeast Asian Studies, 1994), 107–09 and 114. Most of the Marcos killings were in the 1983–85 era, after the assassination of Benigno Aquino.

With the "people power revolution" not helping all the people, Corazon Aquino had reasons to try to end this violence. But she was merely president and the state was weak. She took advice from Chief of Staff Gen. Fidel Ramos and Interior Secretary Jaime Ferrer to support armed civilian paramilitaries and vigilantes who were fighting Muslim and communist rebels. If she had not done so, these militias would have continued their operations anyway. Manila has never controlled many of the decentralized and semi-centralized coercive forces, such as landlords' goon squads. It did not control the army units that attempted a serious 1989 coup against Aquino.[69] Change at the top in Manila meant little for state or nonstate coercive agencies that retained habits to which they had become accustomed over decades.

Private companies and landowners often hire private militias to defend their businesses by threatening violence against competitors or unionists. "Active auxiliaries" received up to three-quarters of the revenue of the "Sugar Development Fund" run on Negros by planter elites in the late 1980s. At Lubao, Pampanga, goons paid by landlords evicted tenant farmers who were said to be violating laws against squatters. At Toledo, Cebu, vigilantes were hired by the Atlas Consolidated Mining Development Corporation to stamp out a labor union. There are numerous other examples. Clergy were not exempt if they were seen as leftists. At least ten priests were killed in the half decade after Marcos's demise at the hands of private gunmen hired by landlords, loggers, or businesses.[70]

The Hobbesian or Weberian view that the state has a legitimate monopoly of violence is, on these islands, thus far no more than an interesting proposal. As Wolters writes, "The classic state monopolies known from European history, namely those over violence and taxation, have never been fully developed in the Philippines. This means that in the rural areas private armies have increasingly played a major

---

[69]Much more about coups is in Chapter 9. See Marites Danguian-Vitug, *Kudeta: The Challenge to Philippine Democracy*, Rigoberto Tiglao, ed. (Quezon City: Philippine Center for Investigative Journalism, 1990).
[70]Silliman, "Human Rights," 129–31.

role."[71] Nonstate extraction is very common in the world. Nonstate violence has been exceptionally frequent in the Philippines.

Coercion is crucial, in rural Philippine places, for maintaining the traditional pattern of extraction. When shops sell paddy seed to farmers, they often insist on exclusive rights to buy the resulting grain, which is thus sold quickly in the harvest season when the price the shops pay is lowest.[72] It can be physically unsafe for farmers to delay fulfilling their commitments to sell. Commercialization of crops does not require that large companies own land, if they can enforce "contract growing."[73] Independent growers provide the fields, labor, and supervision, as well as all the agricultural inputs. The mills are assured of contracted deliveries, so farmers are assured of buyers — but usually at a local monopsony price during the least favorable season for sellers. Modernized commercial agriculture does not benefit grassroots producers in part because crop prices can be lowered by coercion.

When local households refused to sell to the Tadi Corporation as many pineapples as the company had expected (because it offered just 1.10 pesos per kilo, while another mill offered 3.30 pesos), Tadi brought a legal suit whose result was inconclusive. So to obtain quicker results, Tadi's security chief, the son of the politician Jose Sison, Jr., organized "private armies," albeit commandeering some government trucks, to confiscate pineapples and bring them to the Tadi plant. According to an independent foundation in Manila, "Special Forces of the Philippine Army have also set up detachments in Banga, Surallah, and T'boli towns to control growers from selling to other buyers."[74] Farmers can sometimes try to "pole-vault" into another market and refuse to sell to the mill that had expected their produce at a low purchase price. This leads to conflicts. When the farmers go up

---

[71]Willem Wolters, *Politics, Patronage, and Class Conflict in Central Luzon,* 4.

[72]See *ibid.,* 52–53.

[73]*Contract Growing: Intensifying TNC [Transnational Corporation] Control in Philippine Agriculture,* Antonio J. Tujan, Jr., ed. (Manila: IBON Foundation, 1998), 125.

[74]*Contract Growing,* 73.

against big landowners, they usually lose. McCoy has noted that provincial politicians

> ... both adopt and abandon the use of private armies. A minor datu such a Ali Dimaporo or an ambitious peasant like Faustino Dy has very little choice but to use violence to establish his political and economic base. After securing wealth and power in a locality through armed force, provincial politicians can begin to barter votes to win both immunity from prosecution and benefices in the form of rents, cheap credit, or licenses. With his position thus legitimized, the family's founder, or his heirs, can enter a mature phase of old wealth and respectable politics.[75]

DYADIC, CONFLICTING, AND FICTIVE FAMILIES

The tradition of family-like politics can promote disunity, not just unity. If a single clan has been politically strong in an area, as is the case in many rural parts of the Philippines, that strength may nonetheless be challenged by rivals. Elections are occasions for such challenges. Mary Hollnsteiner studied a Bulacan place where two networks, each centered on a major family, had competed from the Spanish period onward.[76] Willem Wolters likewise found a long-term bifurcated structure in Barranca, Nueva Ecija, in which by 1971 three factions were evident.[77] Kimura Masataka in Lipa City, Batangas, and Aprodicio Laquian in Metro Manila found factions that fluctuated, changing with every election.[78] A spectrum of network stability/instability is evident in comparing these places.

Carl Landé offered the classic interpretation of Philippine politics before Marcos, stressing that the Nacionalista and Liberal parties had been based on patron-client relations. He documented perennial

---

[75]Alfred W. McCoy, "An Anarchy of Families," 15.

[76]Hollnsteiner, Mary R., *The Dynamics of Power in a Philippine Municipality* (Quezon City: Community Development Research Council, University of the Philippines, 1963), also cited in Kimura, *Elections and Politics*, 257.

[77]Willem Wolters, *Politics, Patronage, and Class Conflict in Central Luzon.*

[78]Kimura Masataka, *Elections and Politics*, 257.

conflicts between two coalitions of such networks in many Philippine localities, each of which was usually dominated by one of the two.[79] As a recent Japanese researcher notes concisely, with this pattern "there is no room for the state to intervene."[80] Landé's thesis has been somewhat eroded, in the decades since it was written, by Marcos's failed attempt to create a stable authoritarian government, by a tendency of patron-client ties to become more specifically political, and by some increase of professionals rather than landholders in the elite. These changes, which relate to the Philippine economy's slow evolution, can nonetheless be overstated. Most observers remain impressed by the resilience of Philippine patronism, especially when it takes dyadic and fictive forms.

The Tagalog term *angkan* is used for kin or quasi-kin groups. When there is a blood relationship holding such groups together, it may be either matri- or patrilineal. Kinship in the Philippines is bifurcated, through both fathers and mothers. Each Filipino in such a family has a great many relatives, although one set of them can easily come into conflict with the other because this bilateral system is non-hierarchic. Elite families also tend to include high numbers of half-brothers and half-sisters, as well as fictive kin. So the permutation of kin becomes very large, without defining any sure order of precedence among the members.

Such a structure differs from the Chinese kinship system, which stresses a hierarchy of brothers in paternal lines. Some analysts believe that Chinese clans foster stronger organizations in business and less conflict in politics than Filipino kin networks do. The mechanisms that create such linkages deserve more research.

Lucian Pye argues that Philippine hierarchies are less stable than those of most other Asian countries. He sees bonds of loyalty to patrons in the islands' political culture as more "dynamic" than in Confucian societies. Institutionalization of informal patterns of politics

---

[79]Landé, Carl H., *Leaders, Factions, and Parties: The Structure of Philippine Politics* (New Haven: Yale University Southeast Asia Monograph Series, 1965).
[80]Kawanaka Takeshi, *Power in a Philippine City* (Chiba: Institute of Developing Economies, 2002), 9.

is therefore harder to achieve. There is patronism aplenty, but no stable hierarchy of patrons.[81]

In Philippine tradition, godparents are nearly as important as blood parents. The Spanish developed *compadrazgo*, a kind of ritual co-parenthood, under which "parents with many offspring developed relationships with several ritual kinsmen, who are considered investments for the future." Individuals sought personal links with others in their generation, on the basis of actual or imagined kinship through either their mothers or fathers. They did so irrespective of class. As anthropologist Kikuchi writes,

> Big landowners, politicians, and high-ranking officials of the government or military establishment generally have several dozens of godchildren. These members of the elite, who are asked to be sponsors, seem willing to fulfill their obligations and economic duties as ritual parents.... In a bilateral kinship group founded on the principle of consanguinity, people expand their personal relationships horizontally within their generation and among ritual kinsmen, toward better socioeconomic security.[82]

Offering to work without pay is a means by which a subordinate may establish fictive kinship. Much labor in the Philippines is not monetized. In San Isidro, Bataan, Mang Dante had worked for much of his life as a driver-bodyguard — without wages — for the family of the local congressman, Payumo. He explained that the elite family "sent some of my children to high school for free, and sometimes they gave me pocket money." Mang Dante received some money as a driver for the family's logging business. His closeness to the congressman's relatives encouraged others to approach him for jobs — which they received, apparently for minimal wages but also to establish links to the dominant local family. His first cousins, Mang Ely and Mang Lando, got jobs on a dump truck and a log truck. These patron-client connections were at once economic, social, and political.

They were not necessarily permanent. Such relationships were forged by individuals, and they could change. Problems arose when

---

[81]Lucian W. Pye, *Asian Power and Politics* (Cambridge: Belknap Press of Harvard University Press, 1985).

[82]Kikuchi Yasushi, *Uncrystallized Philippine Society*, 43–44.

Mang Dante got into a personal conflict with another family that was also connected to Congressman Payumo. So Mang Dante was eventually read out of the congressman's network. He then willingly took up with the Payumos' strongest local rival. The bonds holding Philippine local polities together are personal, flexible, and socio-economic. This kind of integration is not tight, even though the participants at each point in time say it is solid.[83]

Cesar Cala writes that, "the traditional elite maintains their hegemony not only through their much-touted powers of guns, goons, and gold but by ruling through what Gramsci would call the people's common sense."[84] As Steven Lukes and John Gaventa suggest, the strong trump the weak not just in open conflict that can be documented by public behavior. Secondly, they also maintain their dominance not just by creating legal and other constraints on the issues that can come on public agendas and that determine which voices are influential and which are not.[85] But also thirdly, the powerful preserve their position by promoting fatalistic beliefs, so that the powerless are less likely to think their problems can be solved by any social mechanism in this world.[86] No account of influence in the Philippines could cover actual politics there, without attention to ideologies that

---

[83]Myrna J. Alejo, Maria Elena Rivera, and Noel Inocencio Valencia, *[De]scribing Elections: A Study off Elections in the Lifeworld of San Isidro* (Quezon City: Institute for Popular Democracy, 1996), 49–52. A traditional polity that goes even further in this direction is detailed in Fredrik Barth, *Political Leadership Among Swat Pathans* (London: Athlone Press, 1959). Adult males join a "men's house," and they are expected to fight for the head of that house (and be treated as guests there) — until they decide that it would be better to go fight in the rival men's house, as they often do. Barth's book explains a great deal about Afghan/Pashtun politics. In comparison, the modal Philippine structures seem organized.

[84]Cesar Cala, "Publisher's Foreword," in Myrna J. Alejo, *et al.*, *[De]scribing Elections*, xii.

[85]A classic treatment of this mechanism is E.E. Schattschneider, *The Semi-Sovereign People: A Realist's View of Democracy in America*, intro. by David Adamany (Hinsdale, IL: Dreyden Press, 1975).

[86]John Gaventa, *Power and Powerlessness: Quiescence and Rebellion in an Appalachian Valley* (Urbana: University of Illinois Press, 1980), and Steven Lukes, *Power: A Radical View* (London: Macmillan, 1974).

are actively supported to deflect most citizens from attempting any serious influence.

DEBTS OF GRATITUDE

Carlos Romulo, while serving as Marcos's foreign minister, wrote that

> gratitude, or *utang na loob*, is an important key to Filipino behavior. Extrapolated on a national scale, this is an explanation for the notorious relationship between politicians and voters in a system of never-ending reciprocation of favors. The length of a politician's life is measured in terms of the favors, such as jobs or loans of money, he is able to give his supporters. In turn, the latter are obligated according to the code of *utang na loob* to keep the politician in office.... The landlord who has once saved the child of a tenant from illness feels free to exploit the services of the tenant with perfect impunity, since he is protected by a code freely accepted by all within his society. Indeed, he would not even realize that he is exploitative.[87]

Utang means "debt," ordinarily monetary. *Loob* means "inner being" or "inner self." So this kind of debt is lifelong, total, existential. As an observer writes, "such debts are like those owed to one's parents, guilt-laden obligations which both parties understand can never be fully repaid. *Utang na loob* carries an ontological weight that is tied up with the debtor's sense of honor, self-esteem, and basic morality."[88]

The sharecropper (*kasamá*, accenting the last syllable) was the archetypical Filipino client. Any such worker was objectively low in a power network that was vertical; the cropper was dependent on the landlord for livelihood. Yet both the patron and the client were supposed to refer to the other as a companion (*kasáma*, with the stress on the second syllable). Normatively, each owed the other an internal debt of gratitude. Such a link was imagined to include a kind of equality, a horizontal aspect, because creditors and patron-bosses ideally

---

[87]In Romulo's introduction to Beth Day, *The Philippines: Shattered Showcase of Democracy in Asia* (New York: M. Evans, 1974), 9.
[88]Berlow, Alan, *Dead Season*, 82.

owed thanks to their underling workers. But it also included political inequality and an unrepayable money debt.[89]

This ideology bolstered Philippine stratification. It caught both patrons and clients in an ideally comfortable and stable relationship, which was seen as normal and proper, while justifying sharp differences of material wealth and political power. No aspect of this hegemonic power relationship was separate from explicit or implicit coercion. The dearth of resistance to this stratification, symbolized in debts, would be more surprising if such relations had not been present historically in many societies.[90]

These norms also justified sharp stratifications of property. The Philippines apparently has the most polarized land distribution in any populous Asian nation.[91] Four-fifths of land in the archipelago is owned by one-fifth of the population, and seven-tenths of farmers own no land.[92] But this objective measure actually underestimates the extent of local political inequality, the extent of social indebtedness, and the psychological uses to which both patrons and clients put them.

NEW PREBENDS JOIN OLD LAND AS SOURCES OF POWER

Owning territory has long meant political influence in the Philippines. This situation is changing slowly. Dante Simbulan studied 169 "politically dominant" families at the provincial level up to

---

[89] *Utang na loob* is the Tagalog phrase that this author found more of the specialized Filipinists romanizing than any other. See, among others, Willem Wolters, *Politics, Patronage, and Class Conflict in Central Luzon*, 99 and 273.

[90] Historically in the West, to take just one example, the imprisonment of debtors (or their forced exile to colonies such as Australia) was another coercion that bolstered the dependence of clients on their patrons back in the home countries.

[91] Jonathan Fox, "Editor's Introduction," in *The Challenge of Rural Democratization: Perspectives from Latin America and the Philippines*, Jonathan Fox, ed. (London: Frank Cass, 1990), 6.

[92] Francisco Lara, Jr. and Horacio Morales, Jr., "The Peasant Movement and the Challenge of Democratization," 144.

the mid-1960s, and of these only 11 (7 percent) "did not have land as an essential component of their socioeconomic base of power."[93] Nonetheless, some of the Philippine's new professionals come from previously unknown families. Many landowning clans send members to Manila or other cities to establish commercial (or less frequently, industrial) enterprises or real estate projects. Marcos encouraged this trend, which had begun earlier, because it allowed him to help friends and hurt opponents through state licensing of trade.

Some of the major landowning families have diversified their economic activities, although others still mainly collect rent and interest. For example, Tadeco is the Philippines' "number one agri-based company," owned by the Antonio Floirendo family "whose business interests range from fresh fruits to automotive dealerships."[94] Manufactures are generally missing. Other major Filipino conglomerates are also associated with particular families: San Miguel with the Sorianos, Purefoods with the Ayalas who have also developed part of the Makati district in Manila, General Milling with the Uytengsus, Republic Flour Mills with the Concepcions, and Universal Robina with the Gokongwei Group.[95]

Bossism in urban places is often based on prebends, which in some cases are held by leaders without much land. Describing the "new men" in Cavite near Manila, Sidel calls them "political operators whose close links to provincial politicians initially catapulted them into office, and whose control over the local state apparatus — rather than an independent economic base in land ownership — remains a centerpiece of their small-town empires."[96] Their systems depended on institutionalized links with units of the state. These prebends were like rented land.

---

[93]In this survey, the other two components were business and professions. Temario C. Rivera, *Landlords and Capitalists*, 51.

[94]*Contract Growing*, 39.

[95]*Ibid.*, 41. Some of these rich families are Filipino-Chinese; others deny that status.

[96]John T. Sidel, *Capital, Coercion, and Crime*, 39. Sidel does not stress that access to rents from the state is like rents from land.

Connections with government offices can supply wealth as land did — and in a democracy, elections allow government offices to be bought. In Taiwan during the 1960s, such links between officials and local entrepreneurs were often weak. In East China, they have been varied: public when they were essential for business, but hidden if uncovering the corruption would hurt local entrepreneurs. Both of those patterns can be found also in Thailand during its boom. In the Philippines, as compared to these other places, land rents and state appropriations were both important, relative to money generated from commerce and industry. The archipelago had "new men," but they were less often entrepreneurs. They more often had close links to landowners.

Bases for state prebends often started because of connections between harvesting crops and processing food. Marcos set up marketing boards for sugar and coconut. These were controlled by two "cronies," Roberto Benedicto and Eduardo Cojuangco. (The latter was a kinsman of Marcos's rival Corazon Cojuangco Aquino; but in the Philippines, prebends could be as valuable as family ties.) These marketing boards became tools to weaken other regional leaders whom Marcos deemed disloyal.[97]

Some firms were confiscated by the Marcos government and then given to new owners. Companies that had previously belonged to the Lopez family in the Visayas, for instance, were turned over to the Romualdez clan, of whom the president's wife Imelda Marcos was the most prominent member. Another example was her cousin, Herminio Dishini, originally a broker in charge of Marcos's personal assets, who was later given a monopoly on cigarette filters that he parlayed into a combine of fifty firms, including a construction company building a nuclear power plant.[98] Many such enterprises, including those of Herminio Dishini and Roberto Silverio, collapsed even before Marcos fell.

---

[97] Jamie Mackie, and Bernardo Villegas, "The Philippines: Still an Exceptional Case?" 104.

[98] Koike Kenji, "The Reorganization of Zaibatsu Groups under the Marcos and Aquino Regimes," *East Asian Cultural Studies* 28:1–4 (1989), 129.

WEAK STATE AND PREBENDAL CORPORATIONS

Small firms got scant support from either local or national leaders. The state was only interested in big capital. If small capitalists hoped to start factories, they faced barriers from bureaucrats who often served the interests of local families that try to control all economic activity in their regions. From 1974 to 1976, Marcos's Ilocos region received more industrial loans than any other part of the country except Metro Manila.[99]

Importers of manufactured goods were often in the best position begin import-substituting industries for the same products. Centralization of ISI development projects could stymie them, however. Thai and Philippine efforts to develop national automobile industries on the basis of domestic capital in the early 1970s, for example, ended very differently. The Thai government lowered political barriers to startups of domestic firms making auto parts. The Philippine government under Marcos raised obstacles to the entry of Philippine entrepreneurs to this industry, unless they were friends of the president.[100]

Cars require many parts. Manufacturing them takes a mixture of coordination and quality control, on one hand, with competitive outsourcing so that specialized smaller firms making windshields, tires, flywheels, frames, and engines can deliver reliable products at good prices.[101] As Manila's traffic jams make clear, the country has many cars. They are mostly assembled by Filipinos who use imported parts.

---

[99]Loans from the Development Bank of the Philippines and the International Guarantee and Loan Fund (from each of these separately, Ilocos did better than any place except the capital) are tabulated on *Entrepreneurship and Small Enterprises Development*, 60.

[100]This paraphrases the explanation offered by Richard Doner, "Politics and the Growth of Local Capital in Southeast Asia: Auto Industries in the Philippines and Thailand," in *Southeast Asian Capitalists*, Ruth McVey, ed. (Ithaca: Southeast Asia Program, Cornell University, 1992), 191–93.

[101]Eric Thun has written best about the political context of effective auto manufacture, and the present author's ideas are heavily indebted to him. See his *Changing Lanes in China: Foreign Direct Investment, Local Governments, and Auto Sector Development* (New York: Cambridge University Press, 2006).

The main kind of vehicle manufactured in this large country is the jeepney. Scattered plants, e.g., in Laguna and Batangas south of the capital, have put these open busses together for many years — but they have not expanded into automobile production.

Ricardo Silverio was tapped by Marcos to found an auto-exporting industry for the Philippines. The plan was to replicate the Hyundai *chaebol,* but with Philippine characteristics. Islanders whose family shops had some experience painting autos or making parts for them, such as the Yulos, Concepcions, Yutivos, Franciscos, or Del Rosarios, lacked the requisite political links to the president for the establishment of a large national industry; and they were also short of money. Others that had capital, such as the Zobel-Ayala or Soriano clans, might have attempted car manufacture; but their relations with Marcos were sufficiently strained that they demurred to try to make a profit in a Philippine automobile industry. There was no even playing field, but fairness is just one of the market factors. No family could muster the combination of enough investment money, enough managerial skill, and enough presidential support concurrently. Ricardo Silverio tried, and he had Marcos's support as the national car-maker-designate; but he eventually dropped the ball. Silverio courted Toyota, a highly credible foreign partner eager to enter the Philippine auto market. But he diverted or used money so inefficiently that even Marcos's technocrats, with World Bank and IMF support, saw that his company was headed for bankruptcy. He stopped producing in 1984.[102]

Thailand, by contrast, had a larger number of power nodes within the government, and no single politician there was as dominant as Marcos was in the Philippines. Thailand also had more competition between banks, which were needed to underwrite credit arrangements for small-parts manufacturers, if they succeeded so well that their needs for capital rose. Many Thai companies could, and did, try to make auto parts and assemble cars. No single firm was especially favored by the government. Old companies like Phornprapha, Yip

---

[102]This analysis follows Richard Doner, "Politics and the Growth of Local Capital," 161 ff.

In Tsoi, and Boonsung, as well as newer manufacturers such as Lee Issaranukul, Sarasin, and banking groups such as those run by the Phanchart family or the Bangkok Bank, all participated in this market. Some of the operators were inefficient and went bankrupt. Others survived, however. So Thailand acquired a nascent auto industry.

Local business growth is stymied in the Philippines because many lines of trade are state-licensed monopolies. Contracts change when governments do. When Corazon Aquino succeeded Marcos, she cancelled the contract of a kinsman of Imelda Marcos to run the Philippine Port Authority — and gave that monopoly to her own relative in the Cojuangco family.[103] When Aquino took over, some families whose properties Marcos had confiscated were able to regain their assets. Others, such as the Todas who had earlier owned Philippine Airlines or the Jacintos who had owned the National Steel Corporation, had less luck. Their assets remained state property or were divided into shares for sale to the public. Court cases about company ownerships were rife after the national dictator gave way to more local authorities.

Judiciaries in democratic polities are often assumed to stabilize property rights. But courts can easily be swayed by traditional precedents of force and ideology, even in apparently liberal countries. Philippine judges have sometimes been so corruptible that no less an authority than President Joseph Erap Estrada called them "hoodlums in robes." Estrada's archbishop enemy, Jaime Cardinal Sin, preferred religious referents and called them "judicial Judases."[104] The movie star and the cardinal, both politicians in fact, agreed on little else. The problem is that court decisions have often been sold to the highest bidder. This liberal application of the free market meant that contracts became difficult to enforce. The weak legal system also meant that new enterprises received scant protection.

---

[103] James Clad, *Behind the Myth*, 33.

[104] Paul D. Hutchcroft, "Sustaining Economic and Political Reform: The Challenges Ahead," in *The Philippines: New Directions in Domestic Policy and Foreign Relations*, David G. Timberman, ed. (Singapore: Institute for Southeast Asian Studies and New York: Asia Society, 1998), 33.

Industrial wealth in the Philippines is relatively scanty and locally concentrated. As late as the mid-1980s, only 2 percent of the firms produced 85 percent of the industrial value added. The Harvard Institute for International Development found that nearly three-fifths of Filipino industrial workers were in companies with more than 200 employees. Just one fifth of workers was reported in small firms with fewer than 10 employees.[105] The SMEs that local elites founded to lead East Asian booms elsewhere were missing or prevented in the Philippines.

KUDETA CONFIRM THE STATE'S WEAKNESS

Corazon Aquino's arrival to the presidency seemed to bolster civilian legitimacy over soldiers at the top of Philippine politics. At local levels, however, the situation was very different — and localities affected national structures. Strongman Marcos's departure hurt the fortunes of some regional lords, but it allowed a larger number of others to reassert power, including coercive power, in their traditional areas.

The Aquino government's negotiations with both the communist New People's Army and the Moro National Liberation Front soon broke down. Cory Aquino declared "total war" against both these movements in February 1987, assuring her important supporters in the Philippine armed forces and the U.S. government that she was interested in campaigns by the police and army.

This structure of precedence has lasted up to the present. Eva-Lotta Hedman much later wrote hopefully that, "the primacy of civilian political competition, whether through regular elections or the 'people power' interruption of Joseph Estrada's presidency in 2001, has severely circumscribed the influence of the military in Philippine politics and society."[106] Yet it is unclear that "people power" was the

---

[105]Gustav Ranis, Frances Stewart, and Edna Angeles-Reyes, *Linkages in Developing Economies: A Philippine Study* (San Francisco: ICS Press, 1990), 34 and the graph on 35. The reporting on small firms was almost surely incomplete here, as elsewhere.
[106]Eva-Lotta E. Hedman, "The Philippines: Not So Military, Not So Civil," in *Coercion and Governance: The Declining Political Role of the Military in Asia* (Stanford: Stanford University Press, 2001), 165.

effective cause of Estrada's demise, any more than it was of Marcos's demise. Potent generals — and in each of those two turnovers, the defense minister — defected just before those presidents decided to depart the Malacañang Palace.

Kudeta (Tagalog for *coups d'état*, but with the additional meaning that the soldiers may change government policies without actually overthrowing the president) was almost as frequent a topic of discussion in 21st-century Manila as in the late 1980s. Gen./Sen. Gregorio "Gringo" Honasan, a recurrent leader of coups (which all failed but in each case pushed presidential policies to the right), tried another serious *kudeta* against President Arroyo on July 27, 2003. This was not the first or last quasi-coup. There have been so many, including some that are difficult to document, that *kudeta* are arguably more important than elections for determining policies in this democracy.[107]

---

[107]In Manila, such events have occurred frequently in recent decades, and major documented ones include these:

— 1970, the "First Quarter Storms": demonstrations largely by students against corruption were reduced until they were finally stopped by Marcos's 1972 martial law decree, which they were used to justify;
— February 1986, EDSA 1, "People Power": major demos on EDSA Boulevard in Manila, during which Army Chief Ramos and Defense Secretary Enrile switched their support from Marcos to Aquino but delayed a coup until certification of the election results made it unnecessary;
— July 1986, Arturo Tolentino, Marcos's VP, holds a failed coup trying to claim the presidency after Marcos's resignation (but Tolentino was elected to the Senate again in 1992);
— August 1987, Gregorio B. Honasan, commandant of the Army's Special Operations School, attempted to overthrow President Aquino; he was later captured and managed to escape by convincing his guards of the correctness of his cause;
— December 1989, Honasan's second coup attempt against Aquino also failed; the presidential Malacañang Palace was bombed and strafed until rebel airplanes were chased off by U.S. fighters from Clark Air Base; about 100 people died (Honasan was again captured, again escaped, and was eventually amnestied by President Ramos in 1992; by 1996, Honasan campaigned for one of the 24 Philippine Senate seats on the basis of his bravery in *kudeta*; he won this democratic election);
— January 2001, EDSA II (always pronounced as in Spanish, "EDSA Dos") Estrada allowed himself to be evicted from the presidency extraconstitutionally, because he

Revisions of the Philippine penal code in 1989 (after an earlier Honasan attempt against Corazon Aquino) made *kudeta* a crime that was supposed to carry a penalty of forty years in jail. The 2003 event mentioned above was nonetheless the ninth documentable major coup try in the seventeen years after Marcos fell. As soon as Honasan's "Philippine Guardian Brotherhood" plotters failed, their leader went into hiding. Arroyo's spokesman, when asked by reporters whether Honasan would be arrested if he came out into the open, practically gave assurances that the senator-rebel would be forgiven. The law against coups was mostly unenforced. "The Macapagal-Arroyo administration had reached an understanding with the Senate that there should first be a preliminary investigation of the case...."[108]

The military that specializes in these semi-coups is not tightly unified, but some of its officers have close local connections with important families in the areas where they are posted. The Armed Forces of the Philippines (AFP) developed out of the Philippine Constabulary of the American colonial era. Never since independence has it had to bear a

---

knew that otherwise a coup would be launched against him; the Army and police had joined an EDSA demonstration; the Senate had voted, 11–10 (with three senators absent), not to look at evidence relevant to a motion for Estrada's impeachment;

— July 2003, the Oakwood Mutiny of about 300 soldiers and sailors, against President Arroyo withered; they had seized an office block in Makati, Manila; Arroyo in 2004 freed 133 of the 321 soldiers, after their leaders apologized to her; the Navy leader of this mutiny, Antonio F. Trillanes IV, used the mutiny's striking flag and patriotic rhetoric in his later (successful) campaign for a Senate seat;

— February 2006, Arroyo invoked powers under an emergency law, claiming that a coup had been launched against her by 14 junior officers and Brig. Gen. Danilo Lim of the Scout Rangers; Sen./Gen. Honasan again went into hiding after this event, but it is not clear to what extent the coup attempt was real or, instead, was a convenient claim by the president to make arrests; this instance shows that coups, semi-coups, and claimed or rumored *kudeta* can become addictive for governments, not just militaries.

In the May, 2007 democratic elections to the Senate of the Philippines, former *kudeta* leaders Gregorio B. Honasan and Antonio F. Trillanes IV were among the twelve newly elected senators (as were Benigno Aquino III and Joker Arroyo, to mention other people who have prominent family names).

[108] Cf. Inquirer.net (*Philippine Daily Inquirer*, Makati), http://www.inq7.net/nat/2003/aug/05/nat_1-1.htm, seen August 20, 2004.

major task of external defense. Its main national jobs have been on the archipelago against large communist and Muslim rebellions, and for many years the United States has guaranteed the Philippine defense against foreign threats under a mutual security treaty.[109]

The AFP is a weak force, even for domestic missions. The Moro independence movements in Mindanao (a plantation island that is mostly outside the scope of this book) remain strong. The communist rebellion has been weakened in some periods, but the Philippines' continuing poverty still provides it with perennial recruits, for example in parts of Nueva Ecija and Tarlac. The "Maoists" provide practical rationales for rightist elites to use non-state coercion in their traditional areas against any enemies they perceive. Local vigilantes remain important in the Philippines, as in parts of Latin America. Both the radical and rightist elites would lose certain benefits if their mutual tensions ended. So the low-level war is an equilibrium that has endured for many decades.

DECENTRALIZATION AND PATRONISM

Money is the resource that can most easily be decentralized. The Local Government Code of 1991 (Republic Act 7160) mandates that four-tenths of central government revenues must be sent to the local governments. But seven-tenths of this devolved money, since that time, has gone into administrative salaries.[110] This means that most of it finances existing patron-client networks. Local politicians have

---

[109]This holds true for all major threats against the main Philippine islands. A problem arose, however, when China in the late 1990s raised the aptly named "Mischief Reef" further above high-tide level and built a three-storey structure with radars, antennas, a helipad, and a wharf in part of the sea that the Philippines claims. This reef is 135 nautical miles from Palawan and much further from Hainan, but ownership is disputed and has not been adjudicated. The Philippines Armed Forces are not equipped to defend such a place. U.S. State Department officials have called on China and the Philippines to negotiate. The reef was discovered by Henry Spratly in 1791 and was named for a German sailor in his crew, Heribert Mischief; see http://www.425dxn. org/dc3mf/mischief.html, seen August 20, 2004.

[110]Interviews with longstanding experts on the Philippines, August 30 and 31, 2004.

more funds to pay their friends and relatives. The next most important use of the remaining devolved money, after the bulk of it has been devoted to this use, is health services. Agricultural extension and "loans" to farmers (on which the repayment rate is trivial; these become grants, creating moral debts) are smaller items in the devolved budgets.

Even less is spent on infrastructural investments, such as roads that might provide external economies for enterprises. The local authorities are in charge of such disbursements; so continuous roads that link jurisdictions are relatively rare. Municipal bosses may decide to pave the streets in front of friends' homes or businesses, but the distances of macadamized surface are often short and unconnected. The bumpiness of long-distance Philippine routes, even those that were previously paved, has become famous.

The 1991 law led, already by 1992, to a doubling of local government expenditure. This partly reflects the previously low base of such spending. But "the Code's ability to open up the political system at the local level... is a largely unfilled promise."[111] Decentralization simply put more money in the hands of local elites. Recent Philippine theorizers about democracy have stressed decentralization as a central government policy. They hoped that a top-down legitimation of non-state organizations, to which much of this money was supposed to go, would spur more effective popular participation.

Local governments or NGOs are units to which central power (such as it is) may be decentralized. But these tend to be strongly controlled by local elites, mostly with rentier backgrounds. Some urban civic organizations are controlled by intellectuals who are politically to the left of most Filipinos and have trouble sustaining themselves. Also, it is difficult to combine decentralization with the development of a strong central state. The Philippines needs, at all sizes of collectivity, more robust institutions that serve majorities. Democracy as a belief sustains itself very well in this country, even while it has produced few services for ordinary people.

---

[111]Kent Eaton, "Restoration or Transformation: *Trapos* vs. NGOs in the Democratization of the Philippines," *Journal of Asian Studies* 62:2 (May 2003), 487. The law aimed to double local government spending as a portion of GDP.

What percentage of the money that has been devolved to local governments under the 1991 law has been spent to capitalize industries? What part has gone to finance infrastructure that would give them infrastructure to raise profits and create new jobs? The answer to both these questions, according to a very experienced interviewee, is: "Roughly zero."

Other sources of direct or infrastructural investment are likewise few. Outside cities, barangay councils are closely linked to rural cooperatives that are supposed to promote agricultural extension, food trade regulation, and rural credit. Neither the cooperatives nor the barangays, however, generally sponsor local factories. This is surprising, if manufactures would prove profitable, because the compensation of barangay officials is based on the level of prosperity (the "income class") of the region they represent. If they could make their constituents prosper, and if their official salaries were of importance to them, they could raise their own wages by encouraging local enterprises. There is no evidence, however, that such legal incentives are effective, because government salaries are low and because the main interest of these minor rulers is not mundane money; it is their link to prominent local families. The community honor of being an elected official, and in many cases of keeping up family traditions of local prestige, is far more important than any wage the government would pay.

A Filipino social scientist opined that the barangays are "too small" to support factories. If they followed the path of grassroots regimes in the other three countries this book studies and began to found small firms, however, these new stores and factories might grow. The problem is that local Philippine leaders who have enough rank to set up businesses usually decline to do so. They see themselves as gentry, not merchants.

MINORITIES, DISCRIMINATION, AND ENTREPRENEURSHIP IN LARGE FIRMS

A very few famous Philippine families have bred business people for decades, including some industrialists. This began before those who had obviously Chinese ancestry could start factories. For example, the Pampanga region has been relatively prosperous (in comparison with other parts of the Philippines) for a very long time. Pampanga is not Sunan, but it shows some traditions of enterprise. In the 19th century, Kapampangans were known as traders — and many of their firms were run by people who did not have much Chinese or Spanish ancestry, although those mestizo groups were also present in the province.[112] Kapampangans were famous for hard work and attention to details, an "obsessive-compulsive" stereotype.[113] Their factories historically made pots and pans, handicrafts, processed foods, and the best furniture in the islands.

Pampanga has reportedly been seen as a den of political renegades by several Filipino presidents. To take a recent example: "Estrada can't get along with the governor," according to one report; and his experience was not unique.[114] Long ago, the Spaniards used Kapampangans as mercenaries against a Pangasinan kingdom that formed an alliance with warlord-pirates from South China. Pampanga people also set up at least some outposts in distant places and had trading networks. Migrants from Pampanga to Luzon's northeastern province, Cagayan, built and are still important in Tuguegarao City, that province's largest. The Kapampangans have retained considerable autonomy in their own area. They acquired reputations for cosmopolitanism, luxurious living, and an ability to reach a modus vivendi with the Spanish.

The main group with an entrepreneurial reputation, however, was deemed more foreign. Filipino Chinese and Filipino-Chinese mestizos were, during the Spanish period, banned from some professions. They nonetheless prospered from trading rice and other commodities.

---

[112]Chinese mestizos are descended from immigrants who have adopted Philippine Catholicism and languages after intermarriage with Filipinas or Spaniards. Their numbers are difficult to estimate, but Wickberg finds concentrations in Manila, Pampanga, and Bulacan. These are also areas in which general levels of entrepreneurship are relatively high. See Temario C. Rivera, *Landlords and Capitalists*, 63.

[113]This is the impression of Alex Magno, a University of the Philippines Tagalog political scientist from an adjacent province.

[114]Interview with Alex Magno.

Some earned *ilustrado* social status, and their wealth meant that their sons might go to Spain or elsewhere in Europe for higher education. Upon return, perhaps because of a sense of marginal status, even among youths whose mothers were wholly "Indio" non-Chinese, these middle-class mestizos very often joined the anti-Spanish revolutionaries. Their main patriotic network, the Kapitunan, involved blood oaths and took obvious organizational lessons from both Freemasonry and Chinese secret societies.

Filomeno V. Aguilar writes that, "by the 1740s the Chinese mestizos, those masterful opportunists... were numerous enough to form a distinct category within indigenous society and were on their way to supplanting the increasingly inactive, impoverished, and uncharismatic old elite."[115] But for reasons that his choice of words implies, many of them downplayed their Chinese side. Many Filipinos, including some intellectuals, are documentably anti-Chinese.[116]

Snobbish attitudes toward business have been very common in the world. Traditional Chinese bureaucrats, for example, viewed merchants (*shang*) as a low status group. Especially in some parts of the Philippines, Spanish traditions fostered similar views. In Bikol, "landlords don't become entrepreneurs, even if they have surplus money, because they would not see such business as appropriate for Catholics," according to an interviewee.[117] Profits are "a Chinese thing to do" ('*pag-instsik*' is the derogatory phrase). Bicolano gentlemen do not found factories.

Jose Rizal, who is deservedly the most famous Philippine national hero, was martyred by the Spanish before their demise. He was partly Chinese — but he emphatically denied this in public.[118] Emilio

---

[115]Filomeno V. Aguilar, *Clash of Spirits: The History of Power and Sugar Planter Hegemony on a Visayan Island* (Honolulu: University Press of Hawaii, 1998), 78.

[116]Blogs contain great amounts of further contemporary evidence on this, even the officially sponsored http://www.gov.ph./thread.asp?rootID=50380&catID=18&page=9, seen April 25, 2007.

[117]Author's interview in Quezon City. See also Norman G. Owen, *The Bikol Blend*.

[118]Rizal proudly claimed, "I am a pure *Indio* [Filipino]." This must have been a statement of political rather than genealogical identity. Rizal chose to word it without his usual literary clarity. An exhibit at the Bahay Tsinoy, the "Museum of the Chinese in Philippine Life" at Intramuros, displays a family tree showing seven separate

Aguinaldo, who declared the independence of the Republic of the Philippines in 1898 and became its first president, was also a Chinese mestizo. Vicente Lim, the first Filipino to reach the rank of general in the American colonial army (before his death fighting the Japanese), has his portrait on the 1,000 peso note; and other Chinese-Filipino generals have followed. President Corazon Cojuangco Aquino, other politicians at all levels, Tagalog pop singers, a Chief Justice of the Supreme Court, philanthropists, Jaime Cardinal Sin, and many other kinds of Philippine notables have also been partly Chinese. Since the portion of the national population that is Chinese or Chinese-mestizo is small, this group's achievements are outstanding. Their relatively small number, combined with difficulties acquiring Filipino citizenship and legal restrictions against Chinese ownership, has nonetheless meant the Philippine local industries that they have established are limited.

Philippine regional elites, including the mestizos among them, have for decades interacted with a state that their own local power networks dominated. The government has been dependent on them, at least as often as vice-versa, although this is less true in the Manila area than beyond it, where most of the people live.

State policies have never ostensibly discouraged a general growth of wealth. So why have these elites not yet led their country, or at least their local communities, into an economic expansion like the booms of nearby nations? Part of the answer lies in the near-totality of the fragmented elite's control of local power and resources. Many business leaders in the Philippines have not been socially "marginal" in any sense, unlike entrepreneurial groups in many countries. They have also not needed to give much to poorer Filipinos. Their situations did not require them to ignite the engine of growth that can be found in raising wages and domestic demand.

---

pre-grandparents of Rizal who were Chinese (plus two who were Spanish and many who were indeed 'Indio'). When this author saw this chart, the (Chinese-Filipino) museum staff was politic enough to avoid giving it any caption at all; it just showed the names of Rizal's ancestors. See also Teresita Ang See and Go Bon Juan, *The Ethnic Chinese in the Philippine Revolution* (Manila: Kaisa Para Sa Kaunlaran, 1996), 12, which is also politic and avoids details, perhaps thinking that they would offend non-Chinese Filipinos or that Rizal's genealogy is more appealing as a well-known secret.

Despite cleavages among elite Philippine clans, their heads seldom fostered new, upwardly mobile types of entrepreneurs or politicians, such as rose during booms in other countries. Major families often kept or shared power locally, bickering among themselves but without much mobilization of new talent. The Cojuangco family may serve as an example, although it is exceptionally large and wealthy. It was renamed in the late nineteenth century by Chinese businessman Co Guioc Huang, then in Bulacan.[119] The Cojuangcos are now most closely identified with Tarlac, but they have major interests also in Pampanga. Such a family produces many politicians, and in this case it is divided into at least three parts that often have feuds: one now owns the San Miguel brewery, another is largely in television, and the third (Corazon Cojuangco Aquino's) runs enterprises including sugar mills in the part of Tarlac that speaks Kapampangan.

ENTREPRENEURS AS ALIENS

Chinese Filipinos have been estimated at just 1.2 percent of the national population. More than half live in Metro Manila. Informally, they are called *Tsinoy* (or *Tsinong Pinoy*). Chinese people living in the Philippines report they are 70 percent Catholic, 13 percent Protestant, and only 2 percent Buddhist. In 1995, only 13 percent said that they normally spoke any dialect of Chinese (rather than Filipino languages or English) at home. Nonetheless it has been legally difficult for them to assimilate. Over 70 percent of those who acquire citizenship do so by having a Filipino parent, usually a mother who herself is not mestiza and who is already a citizen. There is no age at which a Chinese in the Philippines can simply choose Filipino nationality (as there has been in Thailand). The constitution uses a *jus sanguinis* (law of blood) criterion, so that simply being born in the Philippines does not qualify a person for citizenship, regardless of the number of decades or even centuries a non-citizen family may have

---

[119]Eric Guttierrez, *The Ties that Bind: A Guide on Family, Business, and Other Interests in the 9th House of Representatives* (Pasig City: Philippine Center for Investigative Journalism, 1994), 112; see also 178 and *passim*.

lived there.[120] The *jus soli* (law of the soil) rule, used in the U.S. or Thailand, makes all local-born babies eligible, but *jus sanguinis* makes many locals into legal aliens. Teresita Ang See claims that, "Chinese in the Philippines... can be Ilocanos, Tausugs, Bicolanos, Samals, Manilans, Negrenses, and so forth without discarding the truth that they are of Chinese origin."[121] But they cannot easily become Filipinos. This has economic effects.

The Retail Trade Nationalization Law, first passed in 1954 just before the fastest period of Philippine economic expansion ended, provided that within a decade all new retail businesses should be fully owned by Filipino citizens. This law affected non-Filipinos who qualified for citizenship and were willing positively to renounce other nationalities. It was harmful to the islands' economy, according to many outside observers (not including many economists, however, since few want to pay analytic attention to ethnic bases of entrepreneurship or to periods as long as a decade). Discouraging ownership or co-ownership by Chinese dampened the Philippines' long-term economic performance. This thesis is difficult to prove because the causes of development are many, but the available evidence suggests it strongly. This is an unintended natural test of cultural factors in economic growth.

The Philippine Supreme Court, in *Ichong v. Hernandez* (1957), upheld the Retail Trade Nationalization Law, opining that:

> Freedom and liberty are not real and positive if the people are subject to the economic control and domination of others, especially if not of their own race [*sic*] or country. The removal and eradication of the shackles of foreign economic control and domination is one of the noblest motives that a national legislature may pursue. It is impossible to conceive that legislation that seeks to bring it about can infringe on the constitutional limitation of due process.[122]

---

[120]Teresita Ang See, "The Ethnic Chinese as Filipinos," in *Ethnic Chinese as Southeast Asians*, Leo Suryadinata, ed. (Singapore: Institute for Southeast Asian Studies, 1997), 158–210.

[121]Teresita Ang See, "The Ethnic Chinese as Filipinos," 160.

[122]Yoshihara Kunio, *The Nation and Economic Growth: The Philippines and Thailand* (Kuala Lumpur: Oxford University Press, 1994), 37.

This anti-Chinese legal regime was not unprecedented. As early as 1903, a discriminatory land-ownership law was passed by an early Filipino elected legislature that operated under the Americans (who at that time also had discriminatory laws against Chinese). Naturalization was not impossible for Chinese-Filipinos after 1954, but it was difficult or expensive. A mid-1960s estimate placed the cost for an ordinary middle class Chinese at about US$4,000, two-thirds of which would typically go for bribes and the remainder for lawyers' fees — but rich people had to pay considerably more. There were other barriers too. In any case, only a few hundred Chinese were naturalized per year through the late 1960s. The total prohibition of non-Filipinos in retail trade, combined with the blood-line rule on citizenship, slowed economic expansion in the Philippines.

Marcos, however, issued a presidential decree lowering the financial and language requirements for citizenship. In the 1970s, about 38,000 Chinese heads of households became legal Filipinos. During this decade, the Philippine and Thai GDPs per capita rose at almost identical rates. The latest year in which the Philippine wealth per person was higher than Thailand's was 1982.[123] Together with a collapse of sugar prices (because a high sugar quota in the U.S. market expired with a treaty in 1974), several major non-Chinese Filipino landowning families lost wealth. This raised the relative economic importance of the islands' Chinese.

One of the contrasts between the Philippines and Thailand is that the portion of Chinese in the islands' population is far smaller. By the mid-1970s, Chinese in Thailand were surveyed to be 10 percent of the population (between 4 and 5 million then, although perhaps some Sino-Thais were not counted). In the Philippines, however, the portion was said to be barely over 1 percent in 1950.[124] Chinese assimilation, as well as lying to surveyors, makes both these statistics inexact. A difference between the two countries is nonetheless clear enough.

[123]Derived from Yoshihara Kunio, *The Nation and Economic Growth*, 31 and table on 7; see also 22.

[124]Krirkkiat Phipatseritham and Yoshihara Kunio, *Business Groups in Thailand* (Singapore: Institute of Southeast Asian Studies, 1983), 12.

Sino-Thai families who became important in industry or banking began as traders, often rice merchants. This was also true of Chinese entrepreneurs in the Philippines, but there were simply fewer of them as a portion of the islands' population. Some Filipino or Spanish families without much Chinese ancestry owned very large private companies (although in Thailand, non-Chinese did not).[125] The Ayalas and Elizaldes were originally Spanish; the Puyats, Marcelos, and many others were Spanish-mestizo or Filipino. Many of these did not start their modern enterprises in trading. For example, the Ayalas began in real estate, or the Sorianos, in brewing and mining. Of the largest 250 Philippine manufacturers during the late 1960s, identifiably Chinese families owned one-third. Identifiably Spanish and Filipino families owned approximately another third, and the last third were owned by non-Chinese foreigners.[126]

In the early 1980s when the Philippines' 259 largest firms were surveyed again, Filipino and mestizo companies had a combined sales volume nearly twice as great as that of "Chinese" firms (including those owned by Philippine citizens bearing Chinese names). Chinese had a majority of the firms in sectors such as tobacco, textiles, and half of the food companies. But Chinese owned only about one-tenth of the lumber and chemical companies, or those for non-metallic mineral extraction. The average *reported* assets of the Chinese firms were only a third of those with non-Chinese ownership. Inventory turnover in the Chinese businesses was nonetheless much faster, and working capital was used more efficiently.[127] It is difficult to see how non-cultural factors could account for these differences.

Hicks and Redding, who offer statistics to show the good performance of Chinese businesses in the Philippines, refer archly to

---

[125]Formally, the word "Filipino" once referred to Spanish people born in the islands, while "Indio" was used for non-Spanish natives. Those usages have now been superseded.

[126]Krirkkiat Phipatseritham and Yoshihara Kunio, *Business Groups in Thailand*, 11 and 17.

[127]Interpreted from tables in George L. Hicks and S. Gordon Redding, "Culture and Corporate Performance in the Philippines: The Chinese Puzzle," *Philippine Review of Economics and Business* 19 (1982), 205–06, and 212–13; the later quotation is on 200.

"the still sporadic, and so far unfruitful, flirtation of economics and sociological disciplines handling culture."[128] Yoshihara argues similarly that it is arbitrary for any economist to discount the cultural effects of discrimination on Philippine development, especially because Chinese businesses have propelled development in other Southeast Asian countries.[129]

According to one estimate, Filipino-Chinese have control of less than one-third of the country's 500 top corporations. This is a lower portion than in any other capitalist Southeast Asian country.[130] In Cebu City, some large Chinese enterprises have prospered in furniture and handicraft industries, as well as electronics, while others have gone into real estate and banking.[131] Developments in these and other sectors, including much suburban construction around Manila, have nonetheless failed to create the kind of economic exuberance that has been obvious in Taiwan, East China, or Thailand.

"Social distance" surveys indicate that people of Chinese background are regarded by other Filipinos as "business-minded, good in mathematics, rich, industrious, thrifty... exploiters, abusive employers, shrewd businessmen, and tax evaders... economic animals."[132] Many Filipinos say Chinese control the Philippine national economy, and many political figures stress this view in public. Gen. Jose Almonte, an advisor of President Ramos, said that "Our so-called Taipans... can pay our indebtedness, and that is about US$30 billion. That's a lot of money. Now, it's all right if this was acquired through means acceptable to the national community, but they were not, and we must get

---

[128]George L. Hicks and S. Gordon Redding, "Culture and Corporate Performance," 200.

[129]"In Thailand, the period of Chinese discrimination was short; the level of discrimination was lower [than in the Philippines]; and government intervention was less.... Unlike in the Philippines, [Chinese] did not have to go through a turbulent period in which many businesses declined and some rose for non-business reasons." Yoshihara Kunio, *The Nation and Economic Growth*, 26.

[130]Rigoberto Tiglao, "Gung-ho in Manila," *Far Eastern Economic Review*, February 15, 1990, 68.

[131]Michael Pinches, "Entrepreneurship, Consumption, Ethnicity, and National Identity," 121, and an interview with a Filipino-Chinese businessman from Cebu.

[132]Teresita Ang See, "The Ethnic Chinese as Filipinos," 169.

them to show a greater responsibility to the community.... The problem of insurgency is no longer in the mountains of the Sierra Madres and the Cordillera but in the boardrooms of Binondo and Makati."[133] Hukbalahap communists once thrived in the mountains, but Binondo is Manila's Chinatown.

Many Filipinos regard local Chinese influence in national politics with suspicion. Erap Estrada was roundly criticized for close links to Chinese-Filipinos who were famed for their wealth and for their gambling. "Names like Charlie 'Atong' Ang, Jaime Dichaves, Lucio Tan, Lucio Co, George Go, Dante Tan, Raymond Ang, William Gatchalian, became 'household names' during [Estrada's] impeachment trial."[134]

Many cities have two chambers of commerce, one that is often called the "Philippine Chamber of Commerce and Industry" and the other called the "Philippine-Chinese Chamber of Commerce." Entrepreneurs who identify as exclusively Filipino participate only in the former. In large cities, businesspeople whose ancestors include Spaniards (few of whom still speak Spanish in their homes, although they are proud of their backgrounds and tend to be patriotically protectionist) form their own "Makati" chambers, similarly.

Philippine media frequently present hopes of economic success in Chinese terms. The word "*taipan*" often appears, as do expectations of the islands' future "dragonhood." Wealthy Filipino-Chinese have often provided financial backing for electoral campaigns, and some have themselves run for high offices. Alfredo Lim's last name did not prevent him from being elected Mayor of Manila. Lim was as credible as most candidates for the presidency in 1998. Jose Yap, Corazon Aquino's uncle, was elected to Congress from Tarlac. There is nonetheless some anti-Chinese political movement in the Philippines and it apparently hurts electoral candidates somewhat. Lim's campaign for the nation's highest office was hampered by allegations that he was

---

[133]*Ibid.*, 172.

[134]Dirk J. Barreveld, *Erap Ousted: People Power versus Chinese Conspiracy?.... How the Philippine Nation almost became a victim of a Chinese Conspiracy to Turn the Country into a Gambling and Entertainment Paradise, With a Blueprint for Survival* (Mandaue City, Cebu: Arcilla Travel Guides, 2001), 358.

disqualified by the constitutional requirement that any president must be a natural-born Filipino. Several different birth certificates for Lim, which contained various information about his nationality and birthday, became subjects of public debate. In the context of normal Philippine electoral campaigns, in which scandal, rumors, and mudslinging are widespread, this attack on Lim was unexceptional. Candidates tend to revile each other on any available basis, regardless of falsity or truth. This occurs in other electoral democracies too, although political scientists have not yet paid it much theoretical attention.

FEW SMES

When Philippine SME owners, a small group relative to the large national population, were surveyed on the reasons for their difficulties in obtaining loans, the top two responses were "too many paper requirements" and "red tape."[135] According to researchers at the Philippine Institute for Development Studies (an independent government-sponsored think tank), Filipino bureaucrats discriminate against small entrepreneurs.[136] A survey of Philippine SMEs in the 1975–77 period nonetheless found that "small industries in the regions have fared much better than those in Metro Manila." Specifically, small provincial firms grew in employment by 28 percent, whereas those in Manila grew 16 percent.[137] So Philippine SMEs fared best when they were provincial (as in other East Asian countries) — but they were relatively few. They grew, but their growth has not yet sparked a boom.

---

[135] *Entrepreneurship and Small Enterprises Development*, 71.

[136] For evident reasons, the two sources of this opinion cannot be identified here.

[137] The difference of the annual growth rates of sales (25 percent in the provinces, 20 percent in Manila) was less impressive — but in either case much faster than the growth of larger firms. *Entrepreneurship and Small Enterprises Development*, quotation 118, figures 136 and 138. Although Myrna R. Co, an editor of this tome, has an evidently Chinese surname (as other authors may also have), the word "Chinese" apparently appears nowhere in the 154 pages of the book, despite its subject. Even democracies can show self-censorship through political correctness.

Small and medium Philippine enterprises that responded to a World Bank survey in 1998 had an average of 67 workers. They were medium rather than small in size. More than half of these firms (compared to just one-fifth of larger Philippine companies) were "foreign-owned," partly by Chinese. Three-quarters of them (compared to just one-third of the large companies that responded) were exporters.[138] This pattern among the islands' medium-sized firms arose partly because of an increase, during the 1990s, of many in information technology. They employed relatively few, well-educated technicians who could handle English. (The most famous of these experts launched the 'I love you' computer virus on the worldwide web.) Such SMEs were definitely not small *sari-sari* stores, and they were also not factories with unskilled employees. They were urban for the most part. They provided services, including some exports, rather than manufactures. Above all for purposes here, their usual non-involvement with sizeable populations meant that they had scant effect on Philippine local politics.

The government has published a "Magna Carta" for small industries in the Philippines, nominally encouraging them.[139] Not a great deal of activity has followed this declaration, however. Some money went to private companies that sell houses and lots. A former Speaker of the House of Representatives, Manny Villar, is a real estate developer representing Las Piñas, just south of the expanding Manila urban zone. He owns large land companies.[140] The Housing Development Council, a branch of government, is supposed to aid such projects. Social security accounts can be used to make down payments on houses and land. Villar has a local enterprise, and he has been in a superb position to assure that the state favors it. It is not, however, in manufacturing, and it does not sell a good or service that can easily be expanded to other places.

---

[138]Edgard Rodriguez and Albert Berry, "SMEs and the New Economy: Philippine Manufacturing in the 1990s," in *The Role of SMEs in National Economies*, 139.

[139]See http://www.dti.gov.ph/bsmbd, official website of the Department of Trade and Industry of the Philippines.

[140]Interview material. See also Eric Guttierrez, *The Ties that Bind*, 282, for an analysis of the assets of Manuel Bamba Villar, Jr., as of the early 1990s, before he became Speaker.

Credit is allocated in rural areas on a very personalistic basis. The Philippine government appropriates money that is supposed to go to farmers, but the main effect is to finance traders. It is reportedly easier for people with Chinese surnames to get credit than for other Filipinos, because official and unofficial lenders know that any default would be a shame to the Chinese lineage, which would therefore repay the loan even if the borrower could not do so. Unpayable existential "debts of gratitude," *utang na loob*, may be useful for normalizing identities in Philippine-Malay culture, since they provide comforts to both patron and client. When Chinese make loans, however, they really want their money back.

Bank lending, gambling, rackets, and remittances from Overseas Filipino Workers are all common ways of accumulating capital in the rural Philippines. The proceeds from such operations often go first to consumption, however. Houses and electric appliances are early purchases among many who get some funds. The Filipino savings rate is far lower than in other East Asian countries. Economists' ideology makes them hope for a convincing non-cultural explanation of this long-term important economic phenomenon, but thus far none has appeared.

Godparenthood is a prime basis for the distribution of Philippine loans, government benefits, and jobs. This custom of extended fictive kinship, *compadrazgo*, is as important in economic relations as in political links. An ideally permanent kind of hierarchal relationship, called *suki* in Tagalog, is established between sellers and customers who rely on each other regularly.[141] Markets are partly between actors who see themselves in vertical rather than horizontal networks.[142]

---

[141]See Hung M. Chu, Evan Leach, and Russell Manuel, "Cultural Effect and Strategic Decision among Filipino Entrepreneurs," http://www.icsb.org/pbs/98icsb/j010. htm, website of the International Council for Small Business.

[142]Suppliers and demanders operate, in economic theory, independently on an equal or horizontal basis. Yet in practice, some exchanges of goods are vertical (even when money flows in the other direction). Scholars such as Prof. Kate Xiao Zhou, a former student of this author, have gathered information to show that women, at least in some societies such as rural Hunan, often specialize in horizontal markets, leaving men more often to deal in the mixed markets that have both horizontal and vertical aspects. Research on this latter kind should become more serious among economists.

Compadrazgo as a cultural form does not, at least yet, correlate with risk-taking productive entrepreneurship.

In Thailand, businesses get capital from banks, more than from government grants. In the Philippines, however, direct political allocations are important, especially in poor rural areas. Also, the Thai macroeconomic control system is more insulated from politics than is the Philippine central bank. Filipino landholding is more concentrated, while most of Thailand is owned by numerous unwealthy landholders. In the islands, land rents provide locally important families with a higher proportion of their income than in Thailand where the local rich get more of their money from industry. Winning elections in the Philippines has added to the political autonomy of local notables there (as in Thailand) — but this legitimacy is not balanced by the separate kind of authority that arises in Thailand from traditions of the royal court and its military and civilian bureaucrats. These many disparate factors together mean that, in most localities, Philippine patronage networks are more stable than Thai ones.

Since local Filipino elites do not take many risks to establish local firms, the country has relatively few businesses for its population. After the 1997 financial crisis, the registered number of SMEs in the Philippines rose slightly. Bureaucrats, however, retained a perennial distrust of small firms. This was the view of various Philippine social scientists, expressed in interviews, no matter whether they had radical or liberal policy perspectives. Enterprise startups receive support only when major patrons in their areas want them. Many such leaders were democratically elected, but that did not make them devotees of free markets.

At least one-third of all startups in Philippine manufacturing fail to survive for two years. Somewhat higher company longevities are usual in other countries.[143] As the economists Rodriguez and Berry concluded in 2002, "The Philippines has shown slow growth for decades.... By the mid-1990s, Philippine SMEs appeared to have recovered from a long period of decline, but their performance by

---

[143]Edgard Rodriguez and Albert Berry, "SMEs and the New Economy: Philippine Manufacturing in the 1990s," in *The Role of SMEs in National Economies in East Asia*, 145.

itself does not seem to have been vigorous enough to boost the Philippine economy after the 1997–98 crisis."[144] The SME sector has been the main chance, for igniting growth in East Asia; but it has been politically repressed in the Philippines.

SPATIAL ASPECTS OF STAGNANT DEVELOPMENT: MIGRATIONS AND OFWs

Filipino migrations have been atypical in comparison with movement in and from other developing countries. Country-to-city flows have affected a lower portion of all migrants than elsewhere. There have been migrants to Manila and Cebu City, but there would have been far more urban immigration if entrepreneurs in cities had offered more jobs.

Two other forms of migration, however, have been exceptionally prominent in the Philippines: first, a large and very distinctive diaspora of laborers has gone abroad, especially to jobs in services rather industries. Overseas Filipino Workers (OFWs in official parlance) send large amounts of money back to their homes. After their first contracts end, they often buy a house. They can obtain more capital by signing second or later contracts for work abroad, but they seldom start small factories upon returning home.

About one-fifth of the archipelago's workers (nearly 10 percent of the country's whole population) are abroad. The Overseas Filipino Workers labor in many fields ranging from construction and household help to professions such as medicine and nursing. They leave their country temporarily, going to places and to kinds of jobs in which (as for all migrations) others have preceded them. No other sizeable nation has nearly so large a portion of its work force abroad.

One reason why Filipinos are able to emigrate with relative ease is the continued currency of English in their own country, although Tagalog has become the main language of primary and secondary education. Many OFWs have tertiary degrees, although much (not all) of the foreign work even of this group is menial. Holders of engineering

---

[144] *Ibid.*, 153.

degrees, for example, can make higher incomes abroad as housekeepers, ironing clothes, than they can in Manila as engineers or architects, because too few industries have been founded back home. The rate of OFWs' return to the islands for retirement is high. Interviewees sometimes opine, correctly or not, that many Filipinos who might have set up factories go abroad instead.

A second and less well-known migration has been "out to the rural frontiers of the archipelago... a movement of remarkably large numbers of Filipinos... toward new land, new islands, and new crops. The development of the frontier and the emergence of an export economy together present a more complicated and integrated pattern of change than one in which the city is seen as the center of modernity and the countryside as the center of tradition."[145] This pattern has developed slowly. As with the *transmigrasi* program in Indonesia (largely taking Javans to Papua, Kalimantan, Sulawesi, and Sumatra), part of successive Philippine governments' motive has been to move more Christian Filipinos to Mindanao as a counterweight to the centuries-old Muslim rebellions on that island.

There are some loose parallels in Thailand, although migrations into former forests there has been linked to an expansion of paddy rather than of other export crops whose distribution is more centralized, as in the Philippines. Internal movements of Filipino labor, as compared to Thai or Taiwanese or Chinese labor, have been greater to places that lack factories. Business and industry is the part of all social politics that is still missing from the history of this would-be democracy.

LOCAL POWERS AND TECHNOCRATS VS. NEW BUSINESSES OR UNIONS

Large areas of the archipelago, even in recent years, have almost completely lacked factories. The foremost student of central Luzon, publishing in the 1980s, reported broadly that, "During the past decades

---

[145]David Joel Steinberg, *The Philippines: A Singular and Plural Place*, third edition (Boulder: Westview, 1994), 41, especially citing work by John A. Larkin.

not one factory, large or small, has been established in Nueva Ecija."[146] This was barely an overstatement. Logging and a few cottage handicrafts, making rattan or wood products, were the extent of all manufacturing there. No city was really large, and towns lacked factories.

Modern worker or welfare politics has thus far had no sustainable basis in the Philippines, because there has been scant industry. Except in big cities, there is scant commercial business too. A few labor unions began to organize during the American colonial period. The Commonwealth government tried to suppress them in the mid-1930s, because of concerns about the growing influence of radicals in the *Partido Komunista ng Pilipinas* and their alleged links to Stalin's Comintern. The Japanese occupation easily banned all unions. Soon after the war ended, landlords' fears that the Hukbalahap communist peasants might make connections with workers led to almost as many restrictions.[147] When the government was repressive, unions became more militant and clandestine, but many of the leaders were dissident bourgeois, not proletarians. Despite periods in the mid-1950s, 1970s, and the early Corazon Aquino years when workers could organize, the Philippine labor movement has been very weak.

The main factor preventing industrial action in the Philippines has been a lack of industries. In an economy where beer brewing is a notable part of the manufacturing sector, there are not many workers to unionize. Democratic parties cannot arise from this mainly preindustrial context to normalize the usual modern pattern of left-right politics. Workers' and entrepreneurs' interests still have unsure bases in local power networks, so national politics is still organized almost entirely by short-term enthusiasms for particular personalities. Policies are practically irrelevant.

Capitalists in many countries are legitimated by the wealth they can bring and the jobs they provide. But Filipinos who have spare

---

[146]Willem Wolters, *Politics, Patronage, and Class Conflict in Central Luzon*, 35.

[147]Jane Hutchison, "Class and State Power in the Philippines," in *Southeast Asia in the 1990s: Authoritarianism, Democracy, and Capitalism*, Kevin Hewison, Richard Robison, Garry Rodan, eds. (St. Leonards, NSW: Allen & Unwin, 1993), 202–09.

money generally do not put it where it regenerates itself. Ichimura Shinichi found that more capital was needed, per increment of output, over several decades in the Philippines than in Thailand, by a ratio of 4.0 to 3.5. This relative inefficiency increased over time in the Philippines. An index of the Philippine lag of competence in using capital was two-fifths higher in 1974–83 than it had been in 1965–73.[148] Some money went into this economy, but it reproduced itself slowly.

Most economists and political scientists write as if all the policies that are needed to make economies prosper come from national states. But if quick growth is the aim, evidence from the Philippines suggests that technocrats alone cannot provide it. The Philippines under Marcos had a stronger state than previously. It had support from the IMF and World Bank, foreign aid from the U.S., some investment, and plenty of standard advice from economists — yet these factors, separately or together, did not create a boom.

Taiwan, Jiangnan, and Thailand all had much local (not just state) support for their transitions from import substitution to export promotion. Most especially, each of these places had local (not sure central) support for SME development. Parochial power networks of small businesses helped rather than stymied these East Asian economic drives. In the Philippines, however, the bourgeois who ran the relatively weak import-substituting industries also ran the weak state. The point is not just that they could selectively veto export promotions and low tariffs for manufactures. The point is their political reason for doing so: a rise of new local entrepreneurs, becoming wealthy from both foreign and domestic sales, would have reduced the powers of traditional elites in places where their families wanted continued domination of permanent clients.

---

[148]Partly calculated from data in Ichimura Shinichi, "The Pattern and Prospects of Asian Economic Development," in *The Challenge of Asian Developing Countries: Issues and Analyses*, Ichimura Shinichi, ed. (Tokyo: Asian Productivity Organization, 1988), 48 and 19–21, also cited in Alasdair Bowie and Danny Unger, *The Politics of Open Economies: Indonesia, Malaysia, the Philippines, and Thailand* (New York: Cambridge University Press, 1997), 99.

Regular, competitive democratic Philippine elections pitted, against each other, leaders who generally had an interest in keeping the export-promotion issue off the national agenda. These leaders often made patriotic appeals against aliens, both foreign and domestic. Their policies raised their strength in local polities and weakened their nation as a whole. Democracy legitimated the continuing political commitment not just to import substitution in the Philippines but also to slow domestic industrialization. Elites remained stable, but the usual East Asian route to wealth was precluded for most Filipinos, who remained poor. Would-be liberals have not paid enough attention to the role of elections in legitimating this syndrome.

Peter Evans suggests that a state's effectiveness in promoting development depends on two traits that are opposites: "a Weberian bureaucratic insulation" and "intense immersion in the surrounding social structure."[149] The Philippine state for decades has been so thoroughly immersed in surrounding social structures, it has not been autonomous from them. One might say that Philippine power is at the "bottom" of that polity, except that power is by its own definition at the top. The most influential authorities in the Philippines have been local but not pro-development. They seldom founded factories, and they successfully prevented local rivals from doing so. As Chapters 1 and 9 suggest, however, this situation will not last forever.

---

[149]Peter B. Evans, "Predatory, Developmental, and Other Apparatuses: A Comparative Political Economy Perspective on the Third World State," *Sociological Forum* 4: 4 (1989), 561.

6

Political Results of Taiwan's Boom

Taiwan's land reform of the 1950s became an informal business school for the previously agrarian Taiwanese elite. It sanctioned this elite to act locally, though not yet in high government offices. The reform also distributed private land from about 106,000 previous renting families to 220,000 tiller households. Both the ex-rentier and farmer groups were 100 percent Taiwanese, not mainlander.

Surveys show that half (48 percent) of the original landlords and fully three-quarters (75 percent) of the original tillers "became more enthusiastic about politics after land reform."[1] One-quarter (24 percent) of the ex-landlords eventually became canvassers in local elections either for the ruling KMT Nationalists or else for independent (*'wudang wupai'*) oppositions that merged much later into the DPP (Democratic Progressive Party). The portions of sons of the previous landlord group who acquired college degrees rose from 5 percent in 1953 to 32 percent by 1978. New land and industrial laws gave ambitious Taiwanese opportunities in local power networks that did not, at first, threaten mainlander control of the state. Quite the

---

[1] Some of those who had rented some land that the reform removed from their ownership (with compensation in stocks and bonds) nonetheless also tilled other plots. On the survey, see J. J. Chu, "Taiwan: A Fragmented 'Middle' Class in the Making," in *Culture and Privilege in Capitalist Asia*, Michael Pinches, ed. (New York: Routledge, 1999), 211, for the quotation and numbers in the next sentence.

contrary, these land and industry laws legitimated the KMT regime by channelling the leadership skills of Taiwanese into economic power networks.

New political interests rose, in rich and suburban rural areas. In parts of the island where industrial-commercial change did not occur, however, politics became so quiescent that even the traditional lineage leaderships were weakened. Bruce Jacobs, observing Mazu township in the period of Taiwan's fastest growth, found two overlapping but distinct polities. The "bureaucratic political system" included local offices of the KMT and state, including schools and police. A "community political system" engaged only Mazu leaders and was "considerably more autonomous."[2] The KMT party-state wanted to coopt local leaders everywhere. But on Taiwan, more than on the mainland where modern changes eroded residence controls very slowly, poor rural places lost leaders. Why should ambitious people stay in Erh-shui (a town where two streams meet), when they could move to Taipei or Kaohsiung?

Village elections in parts of Taiwan during the 1960s were, according to anthropologist Bernard Gallin, highly noncompetitive. They were quiet to the point of being anti-conflictual. Elections at that time were just new vehicles for old politics. In a village with four major lineages (*zu*), their coalition

> to arrange elections was a rather welcome means to check potentially competitive or conflict situations. This desire for consensus and the elimination of competition was very evident on the village, *xiang* [township], and even *xian* [county] levels.... Even in the less important elections of village *lin* [neighborhood] heads, this desire was evident. Although a vote took place, the election of *lin* heads in the village was purely by consensus. The members of any *lin* discussed and decided the matter in advance.[3]

---

[2] J. Bruce Jacobs, *Local Politics in a Rural Chinese Cultural Setting: A Field Study of Mazu Township, Taiwan* (Canberra: Contemporary China Centre, ANU, 1980), 13.
[3] Wade–Giles romanizations in the original are changed here to pinyin. Bernard Gallin, "Political Factionalism and its Impact on Chinese Village Social Organization in Taiwan," in *Local-Level Politics: Social and Cultural Perspectives*, Marc J. Swartz, ed. (Chicago: Aldine, 1968), 385. A somewhat similar and humorous description of a village election in Gansu during the early 1950s is in Chen Yuan-tsung, *Dragon's Village: A Novel of Revolutionary China* (New York: Pantheon, 1980).

In these environments, more than in modernized parts of the island, the authoritarian KMT had little opposition but also few committed cadres. The Party sponsored many kinds of grass-roots organizations, including credit cooperatives, temple maintenance committees, fishers' associations, and farmers' associations (*xinyong hezuo she, simiao guanli weiyuanhui, yuhui,* and *nonghui*). KMT "civilian service stations" (*minzhong fuwu zhan*) have existed in most villages and townships (*zhen* and *xiang*), although they were seldom established in immediate neighborhoods. Much later, the DPP, lacking the many institutions that Taiwan's older Leninist party had created, for a while after its founding declared that elections at the village and township levels should be abolished — a proposal to which the KMT naturally did not agree.

A two-part analysis of Taiwan politics, as either mainly "central" or "local" during the boom, however, would not do justice to the geographical and economic variety of places on the island. Centrally monitored and benignly neglected locations are both easy to find on Taiwan (or the mainland). Cadres' rhetoric and or statist organization charts described ideals that were often unrealized.

The authoritarian Kuomintang kept *nomenklatura* lists of posts whose incumbents required Party approval. This was a proper Leninist party. In Chiang Kai-shek's time, some high positions were in practice unavailable to Taiwanese. In particular, local SME interests were not represented in the central government. Chiang Ching-kuo began to reach out to larger Taiwanese businesses as early as the late 1950s, when his father was still alive. He acted indirectly through provincial assembly leader Hsieh Tung-min, who later became governor and vice-president. This process accelerated after the 1973 elections and the generalissimo's 1975 death. The KMT had previously chosen many of its local Taiwanese candidates from upward-mobile lineage factions. Another of Chiang Ching-kuo's advisors, Li Huan, co-opted into the KMT many new entrepreneurs of corporations. But links to the myriad SMEs remained far more tenuous than to large firms.[4]

---

[4]Edwin A. Winckler, "Elite Political Struggle, 1945–1985," in *Contending Approaches to the Political Economy of Taiwan*, Edwin A. Winckler and Susan Greenhalgh, eds. (Armonk: Sharpe, 1988), 168–69.

KMT membership increased more than four fold in the quarter century after 1950. By the mid-1970s, four-fifths of Party members were Taiwanese, although most of the highest officials were still mainlander. Taiwanese who were deemed potential dissidents were often co-opted.[5] A prominent example was Kao Yu-shu (Henry Kao), repeatedly elected Mayor of Taipei before 1967, when he was widely considered to be independent of the KMT. Chiang Ching-kuo later felt it was safe to appoint him to the same post, which ceased to be elective when Taipei City was raised to province status.

Some Taiwanese had for decades been favorably inclined toward the KMT. A few leaders among them had been educated in mainland China during the Japanese occupation, and these Taiwanese were important for building sociopolitical bridges between the two subethnic groups. Mainlanders (post-1945 immigrants) from southern Fujian did the same thing in the other direction.

In a 1972 Cabinet reshuffle, Chiang Ching-kuo gave slightly more than one-quarter of the portfolios (including the Ministry of the Interior) to Taiwanese politicians. Chiang's 1970s reconciliation campaign may have been more effective among Minnan Taiwanese than among Hakka ones, although Lee Teng-hui was a Hakka and many of the earliest beneficiaries of the 1950s land reform had been Hakka rather than Minnan.[6] Chiang Ching-kuo was able to adopt a more populist style of politicking than his father had ever wanted to use.

The main opposition in Taiwan, even before the liberalization of 1986, was centered on the "question of provincial registration" (*shengji wenti*). Chiang Ching-kuo, inheriting the mantle of KMT leadership and the presidency of a country that was approaching nine-tenths Taiwanese, wanted simply to deny that this problem of provincial identity existed. At one point, he declared "I am a

---

[5]Not all the anti-KMT dissidents were Taiwanese. On intellectuals, see, Mab Huang, *Intellectual Ferment for Political Reforms in Taiwan, 1971–1973* (Ann Arbor: University of Michigan Papers in Chinese Studies, 1976).
[6]See table 3 in *Taiwan's Future*, Yung-Hwan Jo, ed. (Tempe: Arizona State University Center for Asian Studies, 1974).

Taiwanese" — and in practical terms, he hastened the process of Taiwanization (even though none of his own ancestors were born on the island).[7] Chiang promoted Taiwanese to high offices, including Hsieh Tung-min, Lin Yang-kang, and Lee Teng-hui.

The first DPP platform, written in 1986 while that party was still technically illegal, called for "self-determination" by the "people of Taiwan," which it defined as those whose "identity" (*rentong*) was Taiwanese and also those who "cared for" (*guanxin*) the island. The DPP thus tried to suggest that mainlanders were welcome in its party, while KMT members were an ethnic group.[8]

The KMT contained diverse factions under the Chiangs, but the president's control of appointments was thorough. Chiang Ching-kuo saw that change was inevitable, if only because of the subethnic proportions together with the electoral habit that pleased the American protector. But also, business power in Taiwan's government became more important as tensions rose among top KMT leaders.

Surveys show no evidence that the late authoritarian regime lacked legitimacy.[9] The democratization that followed is hard to explain, as has sometimes been attempted, solely by either the subethnic Taiwanese-mainlander difference or by Chiang Ching-kuo's personal decisions, even if these were factors in a process that had multiple concurrent causes. The rise of business politics in both the KMT and DPP was a contextual factor that shaped the democratic transition. The island's political agenda was, in effect, corporatized by the boom. The DPP emphasized ethnic labels, even though many voters were also interested in their economic situations; and the KMT de-emphasized such labels, because it stood no chance of winning

---

[7]The Chiang family home was originally Fenghua, Zhejiang. Chiang Ching-kuo's wife, Faina Vakhreva, was born in Belarus.

[8]Chang Mau-kuei, "Toward an Understanding of the Sheng-chi Wen-ti in Taiwan," in *Ethnicity in Taiwan*, C. Chen *et al.*, eds. (Taipei: Institute of Ethnology, Academia Sinica, 1994), 95–96.

[9]This is shown by David Dahua Yang, "The Bases of Political Legitimacy in Late Authoritarian Taiwan," in *Legitimacy: Ambiguities of Political Success or Failure in East and Southeast Asia*, Lynn White, ed. (Singapore: World Scientific Press, 2005), 67–112.

elections without support from Taiwanese. Above all, no serious political group could be anti-business, because enterprises were rich and had created Taiwan's boom.

After the Chiangs' deaths, a partly mainlander group that was called the "New KMT Alliance" (*Xin Guomindang lianxian*) came into tension with an all-Taiwanese group within the KMT called the "Wisdom Coalition" (*Jisi hui*). By the early 1990s, this Taiwanese KMT group had become the "mainstream" under President Lee Teng-hui. But the "New KMT Alliance" joined with Lee's rival, ex-Jiangsu mainlander Premier Hau Pei-tsun, until Hau lost power. The Alliance by 1993 split from the KMT, becoming the "New Party" (*Xin dang*).[10] Hau had been a military general, and he became the last major traditional KMT politician.

Chiang Ching-kuo had chosen Lee Teng-hui as his Taiwanese successor — although even Lee remarked, decades later, that Chiang did not know exactly what he was doing. As vice-president, Lee upon Chiang's death had succeeded constitutionally to the presidency. Lee's "mainstream" (*zhuliu*) faction, barely forming at that time, lacked support from important military, police, and bureaucratic interests, whose standard bearer was Premier Hau. So Lee broadened Taiwan's politics by bringing more Taiwanese business leaders into high KMT councils. They balanced the mainlander group who had stayed in the KMT. This arrangement allowed Lee to prevail politically.[11] These business interests were Taiwanese, but they were also nonstate, and this fact moderated later KMT-DPP politics. External policies changed somewhat during Lee's era, but both major parties were pro-business.

---

[10]Cheng Tun-jen and Chou Tein-cheng, "Informal Politics in Taiwan," in *Informal Politics in East Asia*, Lowell Dittmer, Fukui Haruhiro, and Peter Lee, eds. (New York: Cambridge University Press), 49. See also Lynn White, "The Political Effects of Resource Allocations in Taiwan and Mainland China," *The Journal of the Developing Areas* 15 (October 1980), 43–66.

[11]See Chu Yun-han, "The Realignment of Business-Government Relations and Regime Transition in Taiwan," in *Business and Government in Industrializing Asia*, Andrew MacIntyre, ed. (Ithaca: Cornell University Press, 1994), 126–27.

TAIWAN'S ARMY AND THE DEMOCRATIC CHANGE

Coercive agencies tend to like authoritarian regimes and often found them. Transitions to democracy, when they occur, are often subject to the consent of generals or ex-generals. As chapters concerning Thailand and the Philippines show, military officers (like elected leaders) are prone to corruptions. They can determine state policies even when they do not directly seize government power. In China, army and police leaders are supposed at all levels to be under Party guidance, but in localities where they are posted, these officers are also crucial power-holders within the Party. This is a topic for Taiwan too, at least until the early 1990s, although it has been little explored there. The Republic of China Constitution provides "no person in active military service shall concurrently hold a civil office" and that "no political party and no individual shall make use of the armed forces as an instrument in the struggle for political power."[12] These were idealistic provisions. Generalissimo Chiang Kai-shek needed no coup, because he already owned the government.

Lee Teng-hui was the choreographer of a shift of Taiwan's military from KMT party control to government control. That was a change from command by former heads of the army and security apparatus (Chiang Kai-shek and Chiang Ching-kuo, then Hau Pei-tsun) to control by civilian politicians whose associates were largely traders. ROC general Sun Chin-ming wrote that, "after Lee Teng-hui took over the presidency, many of his words and policies began to create doubts among ROC loyalists. [But] with the help of Gen. Chiang Chung-ling, President Lee was able to recruit top brass followers and establish connections in the military."[13]

---

[12]Lo Chih-cheng, "Taiwan: The Remaining Challenges," in *Coercion and Governance: The Declining Political Role of the Military in Asia* (Stanford: Stanford University Press, 2001), 143.

[13]Sun Chin-ming (Gen.), "Taiwan: Toward a Higher Degree of Military Professionalism," in *Military Professionalism in Asia: Conceptual and Empirical Perspectives*, Muthiah Alagappa, ed. (Honolulu: East-West Center, 2001), 69. Gen. Chiang Chung-ling was apparently not a kinsman of Chiang Kai-shek, but he was accused by President Chen Shui-bian (without published evidence) of plotting a coup d'état after Chen's election.

The easiest way to describe this transition is in terms of the slow political estrangement of Hau from Lee. This drama was long-drawn-out, involving many actors and unexpected changes of plot. Martial law ended in 1987, although before that many of Taiwan's ministers, provincial governors, and diplomats had military backgrounds. When President Chiang Ching-kuo died on January 13, 1988, Lee Teng-hui succeeded him, and Lee had an advantage in being the first president from the island's overwhelming majority, which is Taiwanese. After more than four decades of rule by mainlanders, this fact gave Lee predictable popularity.

Chief of Staff Hau Pei-tsun and other mainlanders could appreciate that. With Lee's support, Hau reshuffled 35 high-ranking officers in May 1988. Sixty percent of these could be identified as a "Hau faction." Some of Lee's late-1980s policies on Taiwan did not meet Hau's approval, but the two got along well enough because Lee supported Hau's pet project of developing an Indigenous Defense Fighter aircraft (IDF). The U.S. had refused to sell FX planes to the island, and Hau persisted despite technical problems in early tests of the Taiwan-made jet. Lee balanced diplomacy that Hau's mainlanders distrusted, on one hand, with the appointment of Hau to be Defense Minister — and then in May 1990 (against strong DPP opposition) to be Prime Minister.

While ex-General Hau Pei-tsun was Premier, despite a rise of elected DPP representatives, he said plainly in the Legislative Yuan that, "The army will not protect Taiwan independence."[14] This was, for a short while, an issue on which a coup might have been launched; but with Lee Teng-hui in the presidency, it did not happen. In 1991, however, Lee used his presidential prerogative to appoint Admiral Liu Ho-chien as Chief of Staff. Liu's policies favored naval and air power. Much of the army brass, including Hau, were displeased, although Lee's stock rose in the Navy and Air Force.

The dissolution of the Taiwan Garrison Command in 1992 meant that the three armed services were separated from the police. By this time, Hau Pei-tsun was the only remaining soldier on the KMT's

---

[14]Lo Chih-cheng, "Taiwan: The Remaining Challenges," 144; also 150–55.

central Standing Committee. When the IDF project was completed, Lee urged Hau to resign from the premiership, which Hau did in 1993. The old officers in Taiwan were defeated politically. By the 1990s at least, they knew their mainlander group was too small on the island to attempt a sustainable coup against Lee's Taiwanization policies.

A crucial event in the taming of Taiwan's military was the December 1992 Legislative Yuan election, which reduced the influence of ex-General Hau. The legislature set up an Intelligence Committee, one of whose functions was to monitor the armed forces. Various industrialists funded private think tanks that offered views of defense policy.[15] These agencies and a legislative committee later investigated lax training, the effectiveness of jet fighters, anti-ballistic missile systems, and other matters that had previously been only under party and army purview. They showed that professionalism in the army had declined, and they reported probable "illegal kickbacks from arms dealers."[16] But after Lee civilianized control of Taiwan's armed forces, debates about the military on the island became typical of those in modern democracies elsewhere.

Lee Teng-hui's victory against factional rivals, not just mainlander Hau Pei-tsun but also Lin Yang-kang who might have become the first Taiwanese president instead of Lee, led to a split within the ruling party. KMT "mainstream" leader Lee Teng-hui was increasingly seen by many as a vehemently self-confident leader surrounding himself with servants who would implement rather than refine his policies. Lee turned out to be a skilled factional infighter, and his peasant-like persona on the stump made him an extremely effective campaigner for votes. Few academics (even agricultural economists like Lee, able to mix well with ex-peasants) could garner so many votes in elections. Some who disliked Lee nonetheless remained in the KMT for a long time, because it was still a strong and wealthy institution.

---

[15]Tien Hung-mao and Cheng Tun-jen, "Crafting Democratic Institutions in Taiwan," *The China Journal* 37 (June 1997), 11.

[16]Sun Chin-ming (Gen.), "Taiwan: Toward a Higher Degree of Military Professionalism," in *Military Professionalism in Asia: Conceptual and Empirical Perspectives*, Muthiah Alagappa, ed. (Honolulu: East-West Center, 2001), 65.

The recruitment of capable leaders into the DPP pushed Lee's KMT into a more gradualist or long-term-autonomist policy on unification with China. Lee's policies were sensitive to many Taiwanese voters' ambivalence about national identity. This apparent moderation, along with the enormous advantage of the long-time ruling party in campaign finances and local organizations, led to a big KMT win in the December 1991 National Assembly elections. This allowed his mainstream KMT to cooperate in the early 1990s with the DPP factions who wanted practical independence but were also mindful (as DPP radicals were not) of Taiwan's security. In mid-1990, the KMT and DPP called a National Affairs Conference. Although intellectuals from the more radical wing of the DPP proposed writing a new constitution for the government, the conference majority reached a consensus on amendments: to retire superannuated mainlanders from posts they had held since the 1940s, to use proportional representation for some Legislative Yuan seats, to restore rights that were still restricted after the lifting of martial law, and to elect the ROC president directly.[17]

Whether the island should be considered Chinese or Taiwanese has influenced writings on practically all social issues, including analyses of the political effects of new local business managers. Many mainlander families fostered personal democratic values but nonetheless supported the authoritarian KMT government. Many Taiwanese in the middle class were also avid democrats; they knew that Taiwanese were more than seven-eighths of the voters, enough to win any election. They also knew that business and security interests must in the long run affect their politics, even though these non-ethnic issues were chancier as political platforms for gaining votes.

LINKS AND GAPS BETWEEN STATE AND BUSINESS POLITICAL NETWORKS

Heads of large Taiwan companies have often been on the KMT Central Standing Committee. These include Koo Chen-fu of the

---

[17]See Tien Hung-mao and Cheng Tun-jen, "Crafting Democratic Institutions," 5.

Hexin Corporation, Kao Ching-yen of the Tongyi Corporation, Wang Yu-tseng of China Rebar, and Chen Tien-mao of a Kaohsiung family that runs several companies including Taiwan Coca-Cola.[18] These large companies, rather than the economically more dynamic SMEs, could be recruited as political supporters by presidents Chiang Ching-kuo and Lee Teng-hui. Many of the elite tycoons were Taiwanese, yet their interest in business prosperity was at least as great as their interest in Taiwanese pride. Island patriotism after the boom nonetheless inspired many voters in the new democracy.

The Taiwanese-mainlander and capital-labor cleavages might have been politically cross-cutting, but the subethnic difference tended to dominate public rhetoric on Taiwan. Local business networks' corporate policies, especially as regards relations with mainland companies, often tensed against more mercantilist government policies to protect the island. Potential bases for right-left (capital-labor) politics were created by Taiwan's industrialization, but they were not expressed in those terms early.

Factories and urbanization on Taiwan brought some social disorientation among ex-farmers, and less-well-off people became discontent. Taiwanese ex-landlords who did not go into industry or commerce after the land reform suffered a sharp decline in status. Government officials, who were still disproportionately mainlander, included some sinecures.[19] The political system, in which the KMT and the opposition proto-parties alike were linked to businesses early, provided scant recourse for these discontents. The Taiwan state followed Chinese traditions by regulating commerce, and it did so in the interests of itself rather than of the social groups that were disadvantaged by economic change.

---

[18]Françoise Mengin, "Taiwanese Politics and the Chinese Market: Business's Part in the Formation of a State, or the Border as a Stake of Negotiations," in *Politics in China: Moving Frontiers*, Françoise Mengin and Jean-Louis Rocca, eds. (New York: Palgrave Macmillan, 2002), 244.

[19]*Taiwan shehui li de fenxi* (An Analysis of Social Forces in Taiwan), Chang Ching-han, ed. (Taipei: Tahsüeh Tsungk'an, 1971), and Allan B. Cole, "The Political Roles of Taiwanese Entrepreneurs," *Asian Survey 7* (September 1967), 645–54.

The government did not stay out of the economy, even though Taiwan's businesses developed beyond official control. This created local political conflicts that some citizens thought the government handled unfairly. For example, any truck in Taiwan was licensed to operate only within a specific local jurisdiction, whose name had to be painted in big characters on the back of the truck — and just four companies were allowed to haul goods between these zones.[20]

Conflicts over banking regulation were also a problem. As Gerald McBeath writes, "Small firms needed to find capital, but they had scant collateral. The interest rates that they paid often reached 300 percent." When Taiwan's banking laws were finally loosened in 1989, after tensions between Taiwanese and mainlanders were beginning to surface within the KMT, small and medium-sized banks were still cut out by a clause in a "deregulation" law (which actually increased regulation despite its name) that required any bank to have assets over US$370 million. The opportunities for Taiwanese-mainlander and government-entrepreneur conflicts were manifold, in such a quickly growing economy. They became worse after the growth slowed.

Bosses of most SMEs tended to support oppositionists rather than KMT candidates. The vast majority of contestants for the Legislative Yuan, county magistrate posts, or other offices have support from business groups. Associations of large businesses, however, "face competition from SMEs, which in increasing numbers seek political support independently and decline to enroll in associations."[21] Small firms can easily claim an inability to afford the fees. The separation between large and small businesses was not identical with that between the KMT and DPP, or with that between mainlanders and Taiwanese, but it was important in electoral organization.

The dominance of SMEs in Taiwan's economy continued for decades after the halcyon 1960s, because small firms still provided

---

[20]Roger M. Selya, *The Industrialization of Taiwan: Some Geographic Considerations* (Jerusalem: Jerusalem Academic Press, 1974), 37.
[21]Gerald A. McBeath, *Wealth and Freedom: Taiwan's New Political Economy* (Aldershot: Ashgate, 1998), 141, quotation on 143; see also 164.

most of the flexibility that responded to quick-changing demands, both foreign and domestic, and thus increasing portions of the money for politics. SMEs were "the engine ... of the whole Taiwan economy by virtue of their backward-linkage to upstream SOEs and intermediate large enterprises.... The SMEs' share of the value of exports was over 60 percent from 1981 to 1985." The SMEs' portion of Taiwan's total production value did not decline after the island's economy recovered from the 1973 oil crisis. Actually, the SME portion rose a bit (from 46 percent in 1976 to 48 percent in 1984).[22] SMEs' nimbleness remained the secret of Taiwan's economic success. It was also the key to China's boom, although on the mainland it was kept even more secret. Local managers did best when they avoided *lèse-majesté* to the state.

ELECTIONS, FACTIONS, AND THE BUSINESS OF POLITICS

By the late 1950s and 1960s, when full-throttle industrialization was beginning on the island, Gallin noted that,

> a new kind of people had begun to compete with gentry-type leaders for office. They became known as 'Black Society' people — an epithet used to describe local rascals and people seeking power, position, and their own economic advantage without particular regard for the traditional moral or normative rules for political behavior.... *These men realized that... open elections made participation by almost anyone possible and that those elected to public office, especially on the higher levels, could easily use their elected positions to derive economic advantages* .... they used any and all means to win. Buying votes became a common practice.... But some Black Society people, having gained real power through such expedient means, strive for and actually achieve prestige and respectability.[23]

The advent of elections and "black societies" (*hei shehui*) sometimes pitted lineages against each other, even if they had formerly

---

[22]Wu Yongping, "Rethinking the Taiwanese Developmental State," *China Quarterly* 183 (2004), 98.

[23]Bernard Gallin, "Political Factionalism and its Impact on Chinese Village Social Organization in Taiwan," in *Local-Level Politics: Social and Cultural Perspectives*, Marc J. Swartz, ed. (Chicago: Aldine, 1968), 386; see also 392–94. Italics added.

cooperated. Members of different sublineages (*fang*) often voted for different candidates. Elections became new form of clan ritual. Voting was a way to avow loyalty to an ancestral group, a new way to pay moral obligations and affirm one's humanity (*renqing*). The scope of these early politics was very local.

By the mid-1970s, mainlanders at the center of the KMT had a second epiphany that they needed more Taiwanese political support. This reinforced the first KMT epiphany to this effect after 1947. Foremost in this leadership was the new president, Chiang Ching-kuo. Nixon's trip to China understandably raised KMT concerns about the regime's future. So Chiang Ching-kuo by the mid-1970s shifted his economic promotion policies to become more universalist and less selective among firms. Choosing large corporate "flying geese," as Japanese planners had done, became politically less beneficial to the state. It had become evident that the economy's dynamo was small Taiwanese enterprises, which in any case hired more voters. Non-KMT independent politicians got sympathy and money from some of these SMEs. The KMT reacted, trying to boost its political base.

Monetary policies and financial market regulations became more cross-the-board after this second epiphany. As economist Wu Yongping writes, "The consequences for the SMEs were highly significant: immunity from competition from the state-owned enterprises and large enterprises without the loss of the inputs of [their] intermediate products, and a marketplace that facilitated societal goods."[24] State enterprises, in heavy and energy industries particularly, continued to invest in economic projects from which returns were predictably low but reliably long-term. The state built infrastructure. SMEs continued to use their flexibility to find products and markets that drove the island's economy forward. They could do this especially in sectors that had relatively low capital requirements, such as computers and international commerce.

The boom gave these entrepreneurs satisfaction under an authoritarian government they generally supported. "For almost three

---

[24]Wu Yongping, "Rethinking the Taiwanese Developmental State," 110–11.

decades, the KMT faced an unorganized and weak political opposition, consisting primarily of defiant local factions which harbored no national political ambitions," as Chu Yun-han writes.[25] Dissidence varied by locality. Yilan County, on Taiwan's northeast coast, had since the 1950s a particularly high frequency of non-KMT (*dangwai*) politicians. A series of such county magistrates, including Chen Ting-lan and You Hsi-kun, made this county an opposition stronghold. Taichung County is another place where the DPP and its antecedents had early successes, in part because the structure of local factions there was particularly complicated. A few factional leaders crossed party lines (from the KMT to the DPP), although this had been rare elsewhere in Taiwan. Usually the opposition candidates relied not on support from local factions, but on presentable images, policy proposals, and appeals to Taiwan identity. The KMT still retained support from many in both suburban and rural areas, and in much of north Taiwan.

Prior to the mid-1980s, the authoritarian KMT could often link itself separately to rival factions within an electoral district. Each of these factions would field a KMT candidate. The party was able to judge the number of voters who would cast ballots for the candidates, because it knew the factions' sizes. Under the electoral laws it passed, the party could maximize the number of its nominees who would win. Taiwan had a system that gave each voter a single ballot but elected multiple representatives from each district. By 1986, when Chiang Ching-kuo found that it was necessary to legalize opposition parties, an advantage for the nascent DPP was that new factional networks began to form among Taiwanese in many places. The KMT, to maximize its number of winners after this change, had to withdraw party support from some KMT incumbents who led smaller factions or lacked money and prestige to make the number of their voters grow.[26] The KMT tried to dissuade some of its own sitting members from running for re-election. This was politically painful for the ruling party — especially when they ran anyway as independents. This took away votes from authorized KMT candidates, who then

---

[25]Chu Yun-han, "The Realignment of Business-Government Relations," 116.
[26]Wu Hui-lin and Chou Tein-chen, "Small and Medium Enterprises," 15–30.

might not have sufficient pluralities to win under the multiple-representatives-per-district system.

The authoritarian KMT often counted on support from two different, potentially rival, coalitions of local factions in many specific places (for example in Taichung, Chiayi, Changhua, and Yunlin [Touliu] counties). So in districts that had two seats, for example, it was often possible to run two KMT candidates, one from each coalition — and both might win. In single-seat elections, KMT candidates sometimes alternated between factional coalitions in different years.

As a canvasser in a Taiwan election said, "Only by knowing everything about ourselves and everything about the enemy can we win every battle. From pulling [discouraging] votes and encouraging votes to checking up on votes. Who's helping us in every ward? Every neighborhood? Did they get money? Did those who got money vote? This is the work we have to do."[27]

The KMT coopted local politicians who, for their own largely economic reasons, would cooperate with the ruling party. Such notables established local factions (*difang paixi*) that organized voting blocs along classic patronage lines in townships, villages, wards, and neighborhoods (*xiang*, *cun*, *li*, and *lin*, respectively). They created "corporatist organizations (farmers', women's, and irrigation associations, etc.), and societies (religious, business, and community leaders)." Shelley Rigger reports that these local bosses (*tiau-a-ka* in Taiwanese, or *zhuang zai jiao* in Mandarin) canvassed support for their factions' chosen candidates. *Zhuang* means pillar and *jiao* means foot; these bosses were, from any candidate's viewpoint, the bases of Taiwan politics.[28] The factions provided political help and social status, as well as business licenses, government contracts, and jobs in the bureaucracy. Later chapters of this book highlight the importance of very similar local vote-canvassers in Thailand, called *huakhanaen*, and in the Philippines where this type of local canvasser, *lider* in Tagalog, is just as common.

---

[27]Shelley Rigger, *Politics in Taiwan: Voting for Democracy* (New York: Routledge, 1999), 143.

[28]The author thanks Shelley Rigger for an e-mail about this.

Conflict at this local level was not essentially between national parties, but between factions whose local heads could choose to join parties. As one of Rigger's KMT interviewees in Tainan reported, "The most important thing, as far as factions are concerned, is to defeat your enemy. And the enemy is the other faction, not the DPP."[29] Local competition between the businesses that were often associated with factions also encouraged political rhetoric about the Taiwanese-mainlander issue that could displace other rhetorics. A capitalist-worker, right-left cleavage would have fostered a discourse that businesses do not like — because workers have more votes than capitalists in democracies, and a proletarian platform is seen to threaten higher taxes and lower profits. Emphasizing existential national identities is a pro-business agenda. Locally, this practice financed factions. Over the whole island, it gave the DPP, which needed a platform against its far richer rival, to remain a business party.

Political participation thus expanded from private economic into public governmental power networks. As sociologist Chang Mau-kuei wrote at that time, "Taiwan's authoritarianism, severely criticized as it is,... does allow extensive and elaborate participation at both the local level since 1950 ... and at the congressional level (though to a partial degree only) since 1972 when Taiwan's legitimation problem became more obvious."[30] Tamed opposition outside the KMT had channeled business complaints against the authoritarian government for a long time without threatening regime stability. Early ethnic Taiwanese complaints had been violently repressed. This kind of regime could not last forever, however, particularly since the island's external American protector was a democracy that had needed to establish relations with China.

Only in the 1990s did KMT hegemony collapse, and by that time the boom had made both major parties pro-business. In many of

---

[29]Shelley Rigger, "Mobilizational Authoritarianism and Political Opposition in Taiwan," *Political Oppositions in Industrializing Asia*, Garry Rodan, ed. (London: Routledge, 1996), 304–05.

[30]Chang Mau-Kuei, "Middle Class and Social and Political Movements in Taiwan," in *Discovery of the Middle Classes in East Asia*, Michael Hsiao Hsin-huang, ed. (Taipei: Ethnology Institute, Academia Sinica, 1994), 161–62.

Taiwan's 21 counties, KMT faction leaders threatened to support other parties, usually the DPP. Some places (for example, Yilan County) were long since effectively lost to the KMT; the DPP controlled them. Taipei County was a special case, because of its great variety of companies, migrants, and residents. Politics was more fluid in such places. Kaohsiung had three major groups (colorfully named the white, red, and black factions) rather than the usual two. A common denominator was that, after the boom and in part because of it, single-party rule frayed.

As KMT resources declined because the party lost patronage that the headships of counties in particular brought, the DPP stood a better chance of winning at the national level. The percentage of votes for either party has fluctuated erratically in national and municipal elections. Opposition candidates got only 10 percent of the vote in 1980; but by the municipal elections of 1997, they and the DPP received more votes than did the KMT.[31] The issues that the DPP (and Lee Teng-hui's mainstream KMT) presented to the electorate increasingly focussed on the China-Taiwan issue — but the effects of industrialization on local politics were also important in changing Taiwan's political structure, because the boom gave more money to more actors.

For many years, the KMT had coasted along with a policy of benign neglect toward small entrepreneurs. But SMEs increasingly needed land-use variances, credit, and other kinds of help. The Party could "purchase their compliance through pork barrel schemes and kickbacks to the grassroots political networks, to which most of these entrepreneurs belonged."[32] Entrepreneurs did not enter the political system as a group. But as individuals they could pay *tiau-a-ka* canvassers, the local hinge leaders, and receive benefits in exchange. They could get better roads to their buildings, contracts, and other perquisites doled out mostly on a retail basis.

---

[31]One reason for this delay was that the KMT changed many of its policies during the 1990s under Lee Teng-hui. Shelley Rigger, *Politics in Taiwan: Voting for Democracy*, 28.
[32]Shelley Rigger, *From Opposition to Power: Taiwan's Democratic Progressive Party* (Boulder: Rienner, 2001), 40.

The boom nonetheless increased Taiwan's propensity to have an eventual capital-labor cleavage. Political preference formation is a multi-layered phenomenon. The subethnic cleavage could be used by business elites in Taiwan's democracy to trump the socioeconomic one.[33] Other issues whose development inevitably related to these included the rate of democratization and problems of ecological cleanliness, legal crime, and dirty corruption. Few political developments are determined monocausally.

LOYALTIES AND ISSUES IN TAIWAN'S POLITICS: A MODERNIZING BALANCE

Not all politics are matters of preference aggregation (although many political scientists conjecture otherwise). Some political phenomena take this form, however, even when formal elections are not held. The now-classic Michigan model of voting behavior suggests that the variables determining an elector's ballot choice may be treated as if they were made sequentially in time, through a "funnel of causality" that has three stages.[34] In the first instance, socioeconomic and demographic variables (such as ethnicity, class, type of occupational status, sex, age) predispose a voter — but these categories become activated only insofar as the elector identifies with them. So a second stage of decision is cognitive, relating these general categories to particular situations (e.g., where does a voter who is by general category an ethnic Taiwanese stand on the more specific issue of independence from China, which has security aspects?). A third stage of decision involves the voter's evaluation of the political choices actually presented (the charisma or dubiousness of particular candidates or particular parties). This model can be understood as a general approach to preference formation.

---

[33]For a comparison, see E. E. Schattschneider, *The Semi-Sovereign People: A Realist's View of Democracy in America*, intro. by David Adamany (Hinsdale: Dreyden Press, 1975).

[34]See Angus Campbell, Philip Converse, Warren Miller, and Donald Stokes, *The American Voter* (New York: Wiley, 1960).

Future expectations of candidates' effectiveness are demonstrably important to Taiwan voters. A careful study of voters' evaluations of the prospective and retrospective performance of candidates in the 1996 presidential election showed that ballots were less determined by the ways in which economic, domestic crime, or external security situations had been handled in the past than by anticipations about the ways leaders might in the future handle the economy, the crime wave, and the mainland.[35]

Voter pragmatism was one result of Taiwan's boom. Quick expansion created economic networks that only partly related to the subethnic cleavage on Taiwan. The boom made individuals more circumspect, less surely tied to political patrons. For example, government employees had usually supported the KMT, regardless of their ethnicity. But J.J. Chu shows that white-collar employees on Taiwan in the 1990s no longer automatically gave "unrestricted loyalty ... to any party unless the elected parliamentarian members of that party strived to deliver welfare goods." This accounts for some electoral victories of "opposition and ex-KMT independent candidates who creatively campaigned for welfare policies, and the appalling defeat of those who aggressively pushed such ideological issues as unification with China or Taiwanese independence."[36]

It is sufficient to describe Taiwan political mobilization in two categories: canvassing based on "factions," when voters cast their ballots according to their connections with particular local leaders, and canvassing based on "ideology," which long meant different parties' positions on the Taiwan independence or Chinese safety issue. Economic policy issues, which frame important ideologies in most countries, are less contentious because businesses provide the funds for both parties — to fight each other mainly on other issues. Class-based politics has been of secondary importance. After the early 1980s, there was a sharp increase in organized social movements and social protests on

---

[35] John Fuh-sheng Hsieh, Dean Lacy, and Emerson M.S. Niou, "Retrospective and Prospective Voting in a One-Party-Dominant Democracy: Taiwan's 1996 Presidential Election" (Durham: Duke Working Papers in Taiwan Studies, 1997).

[36] J.J. Chu, "Taiwan: A Fragmented 'Middle' Class," 216.

Taiwan. A score of issue areas were involved.[37] But only gradually have some of them become noticeable. Ideological mobilization works best in large rather than small electoral districts, among urban rather than rural voters, and in elections for executive rather than legislative offices. But factional mobilization is more effective in local districts and among less modernized voters.[38] The ideological sources of Taiwan politics have received more attention than the factional ones, but they are not demonstrably more important for the behavior of most voters.

A long-term historical view of this situation is revealing. Pluralization and a rise of "civil society" groups, including notable Buddhist leagues, has been financed by Taiwan's industrialization. Some of these are apolitical; others forge links with local factions just as parties do. The number of registered civic associations in Taiwan in 1952 was recorded at 2,560, but by 1989 it had risen to 13,400.[39] These figures count large organizations. The Taiwan Human Rights Association, the Association for Taiwan Farmers' Rights, and the Autonomous Workers' Federation were registered and were linked to the anti-KMT opposition. Even more important was the rise of business clubs, including many local branches of international ones such as Lions, Kiwanis, and Rotary.

Overly sharp distinctions between rising wealth, rising Taiwanese nationalism, and rising political participation would be misplaced. Bernard Yack and Liah Greenfeld show that nationalistic envy and resentment of other countries were crucial bases of sociopolitical development during periods of growth in the first democracies. In Britain's early stages of expanding political participation, tensions with Spain, and then France and Holland, consolidated the British

---

[37]See Hsiao Hsin-Huang, "The Rise of Social Movements and Civil Protests," in *Political Change in Taiwan*, Tun-jen Cheng and Stephan Haggard, eds. (Boulder: Lynne Rienner, 1992), 57–72.

[38]See Joseph Bosco, "Factions versus Ideology: Mobilization Strategy in Taiwan's Elections," *China Quarterly* 137 (March 1994), 28–62.

[39]Tien Hung-mao, "Taiwan's Evolution Toward Democracy: A Historical Perspective," in *Taiwan: Beyond the Economic Miracle*, Dennis Simon and Y.M Kao, eds. (Armonk: Sharpe, 1992), 12.

national community. Patriotic resentment and envy of Europe played a parallel role in the early U.S. To the extent that democracy has national characteristics, it has been spurred everywhere by rivalries with other regimes.[40] Modern patriotism and wealth are created and led, not natural, and they have correlated histories. That is certainly the case on Taiwan, where the obvious rival is nearby on the Chinese mainland.

FORMAL DEMOCRATIZATION ON TAIWAN: SPARK AND LONG-TERM FACTORS

The rise of liberalism was also spurred by immediate, nonstructural causes. New money was an important factor spurring Taiwan's democratization, but concurrent short-term spark factors for the authoritarian elite's allowance of democracy were also crucial. A catalyst that spurred the KMT to lift martial law and legalize the DPP opposition was an October 15, 1984, assassination in Daly City, California, of Henry Liu, a dissident Chinese-American journalist from Taiwan. This shooting was contracted by the "Bamboo Gang," apparently the largest crime syndicate on the island. By mid-January 1985, however, the Government Information Office in Taipei admitted that the orders had come from the Intelligence Bureau of the Ministry of National Defence. Even the Reagan administration, fairly sympathetic to Taiwan, took very sharp umbrage at this killing by a foreign government of an American citizen on U.S. soil. Some members of Congress, as is their wont, went ballistic. The House Foreign Affairs Committee

---

[40]See Bernard Yack, "Reconciling Liberalism and Nationalism," *Political Theory* (February 1995), 166–82, and Bernard Yack, "The Myth of the Civic Nation," *Critical Review* 10:2 (Spring 1996), 193–211, and Liah Greenfeld, *Nationalism: Five Roads to Modernity* (Cambridge: Harvard University Press, 1992). These analyses by political philosopher Yack and political-intellectual historian Greenfeld are different but related. The literature on this topic is huge, and it could be related to that by international relations scholars who explore the documentable fact that states which newly institute elections tend to be bellicose. (This does not contradict the documentable fact that well-established liberal states do not attack each other.) There is no space or need here to cite all the authors in relevant debates.

held a hearing to find whether the assassination indicated "any consistent pattern of active intimidation and harassment against individuals in the U.S."[41]

This event came at approximately the same time as a large financial scandal in Taiwan's biggest savings and loan association, Cathay Investments. Former KMT premier Yu Kuo-hua was implicated. Taiwanese resentment at the imprisonment of leaders of the Kaohsiung Incident half a decade earlier also remained strong. Faced with all these political predicaments, President Chiang Ching-kuo gradually approved a thaw. By September 1986, oppositionists announced the formation of the Democratic Progressive Party, even though that act was still formally illegal. No serious move was taken against them. The DPP won more than a quarter of the votes that December in Legislative Yuan elections. By July 15, 1987, martial law ended after nearly four decades of decreasing enforcement. Taiwan's growth of wealth, and the rise of business networks that accompanied it, was the context of the island's political opening. Short-term spark factors were important too, as they are in all politics.

ECONOMIC AND POLITICAL GROWTH

Cheng Tun-jen's early analysis of Taiwan's democratization, made before the "identity issue" dominated public discussion, suggested that the democratic trend derived from quick economic growth. Entrepreneurs became political and were joined by "social-science trained intellectuals with professional skills and legal expertise ... socially connected to small and medium businesses." Cheng found evidence that, "the middle-class intellectuals who fueled the democratic movement were connected to leaders of small and medium businesses via various social ties based on school, regional, and workplace affiliations. Such businesses, especially those in the export sector, offered political funds and a fall-back career to leaders of the political opposition. In many cases, the latter even had successful

---

[41]Parris H. Chang, "The Changing Nature of Taiwan's Politics" in *Taiwan: Beyond the Economic Miracle*, Dennis Simon and Y.M Kao, eds. (Armonk: Sharpe, 1992), 28–29.

business careers in the export sector."[42] This describes opposition leaders, but it also could apply to many Taiwanese business people who later helped the "mainstream" KMT. These were the elites who organized larger groups of local leaders. Most were professionals, industrialists or merchants, although a few religious leaders also affected Taiwan politics.[43]

Money for parties and factions increasingly came from small family firms that identified strongly with Taiwan. Already by the end of the 1970s, there were nine Taiwanese capitalists for every mainlander capitalist. This slightly exceeded the Taiwanese portion of the island's whole population — which is unsurprising because of the greater portion of mainlanders still in government, military, and teaching jobs. By that time, even "among capitalists at the highest level, the hundred largest business groups, mainlander advantages are fading."[44] The total capital of Taiwanese-run firms was twice that of mainlander-run and state or KMT companies. The Taiwanese enterprises' total net profits were more than twice as much as in mainlander-managed firms, and this differential expanded in later years. Of course, not all this money went to opposition parties (or to the KMT, which also increasingly had many Taiwanese in its top leadership). If money has "ethnicity," most of it on the island was Taiwanese in increasing amounts.

Politics as a business that the boom financed was inseparable from the subethnic issue. This was most evident in the ruling party.

---

[42]Cheng Tun-jen, "Democratizing the Quasi-Leninist Regime in Taiwan," *World Politics* 41:4 (July 1989), 474 and 483–84.

[43]The most famous Buddhist (representing a majority religion on the island) is a nun, the abbess Tzu Chi. Her convent is in the east-coast city of Hualien, from which she runs an extensive network of religious and service agencies that cover Taiwan and extend abroad. Her organization also has international branches (including one in Hong Kong, although not in mainland China). Tzu Chi tries to be politically neutral between the KMT and DPP. A leading Buddhist monk, Hsing Yun, has some KMT connections. The author is grateful for ideas from Richard C. Madsen, presented in a November 2006 talk in the Sociology Department of Hong Kong University.

[44]Marshall Johnson, "Classification, Power, and Markets: Waning of the Ethnic Division of Labor on Taiwan," in *Taiwan: Beyond the Economic Miracle*, Dennis Simon and Y.M. Kao, eds. (Armonk: Sharpe, 1992), 81; see also 82–83.

The KMT in the transition decade, 1987–96, was at least two parties calling itself one. This division was not just along the subethnic cleavage; it was largely between those who had been appointed to their posts (or to KMT candidacies in safe districts) and those who ran against real opposition (especially in places where Taiwanese SMEs also supported the DPP). The latter group, increasing over time, were not in sinecure jobs. They had to politick constantly to keep their posts. As Shelley Rigger reports,

> Many SMEs enjoyed close ties with local factions, which supplied their friends with valuable benefits. Local governments awarded juicy public works contracts to friendly construction companies and assigned such local monopolies as inner-city bus routes to their political supporters.... disgruntled business people became an important (if surreptitious) source of financial support for the opposition.[45]

The government could sanction businesses that officials did not like, e.g., by threatening tax audits. On the other hand, entrepreneurs could also serve officials' interests. These networks related to each other. They had to deal with each other. The structure was corporatist, but it would be wrong to say that either business or government was always on top. They were "embedded" in each other horizontally, not having solely vertical relations.[46]

The *nouveaux riches* were not coopted wholly by the KMT, nor by the opposition. The DPP also had support from scattered unionists and environmentalists. KMT ideologues sometimes tried to depict their opposition as leftist, and DPP rejection of a few policies that could arguably be described as pro-business, such as the development of nuclear power plants, gave some plausibility to this charge. But many businesses supported the DPP even though its legitimacy could not rest (as the KMT's largely did) on past stewardship of an

---

[45]Shelley Rigger, "Mobilizational Authoritarianism and Political Opposition," 308–09.
[46]This text's use of the word "embedded," which has now become a frequent term among social scientists, purposely violates the original geological analogy that Karl Polanyi made, after becoming entranced with sociopolitical analogues to coal seam beds in north England. His rock beds were mostly horizontal, but upturned vertical beds also exist. Political links between those would be more equal (horizontal).

economic boom. The DPP had difficulty formulating a coherent platform of economic policies. But both parties had varied constituencies. The DPP emphasized identity. The KMT despite its wealth tried to emphasize efficiency (and when caught out for ineptitudes, this was embarrassing). Neither major party called mainly on either side of the left-right cleavage that informs most democracies. Their stances were moderated by economic interests and affected by a security issue that cross-cuts this usual divide: the need for credible policy toward the big and fearsome mainland.

SOCIOPOLITICAL CLASSES IN TAIWAN

Leaders of the early democratic coalition in Taiwan were middle class, but most members and voters were not. The anti-authoritarians were an amalgam of former landlords (including some families that had squandered or lost their capital after land reform), small shopkeepers, and a few unionized workers.[47] Urbanization and economic wealth created "more ready ears among an increasingly articulate, self-assured, and economically secure electorate," to which both KMT and opposition candidates appealed.[48] Taiwan's early land and industrial reforms had been the bases for enrichment of a large group of middle-class Taiwanese entrepreneurs. Until the early 1980s, however, these people were kept out of governmental power. By that time, their money and the KMT's international problems created a circulation of new people from local economic elites into the island's political elite.[49]

---

[47] Jürgen Domes, "Political Differentiation in Taiwan: Group Formation within the Ruling Party and the Opposition, 1979–1980" *Asian Survey* 21:10 (October 1981), 1016.

[48] Hu Fu and Chu-yun Han, "Electoral Competition and Political Democratization," in *Political Change in Taiwan*, Cheng Tun-jen and Stephan Haggard, eds. (Boulder: Lynne Rienner, 1992), 180.

[49] Samatha Ravich, "Taiwan: The Bringing In of New Elites," in *Marketization and Democracy: East Asian Experiences*, Samantha Ravich, ed. (Cambridge: Cambridge University Press, 2000), 95–136.

Recent research by David Yang has shown that DPP strategist Chang Chun-hsiung persuaded his party, whose money resources after its founding were a tiny fraction of the KMT's, that it should try to mobilize voters on the clearly majoritarian Taiwanese issue. This, as he successfully argued, would be the most effective political gambit against KMT candidates. It was a less risky proxy, instead of mobilizing them according to class interests.[50]

Many SME owners identified with their workers (among whom some of them had recently labored), proud of the dirt under their fingernails and proud to call themselves "black hands" (*heishou*). These new members of the middle class, having become their own bosses in SMEs, had themselves chewed betel nuts. They were from the same Taiwanese social groups as many of their employees. They generally regarded the KMT (although some were also co-opted by that richer party) as too slick and cosmopolitan, not mainly too Chinese.

Of course, the DPP also had lawyers and other professionals as its central leaders. These not only wore business suits, they usually served business interests. But Taiwan's democratization involved more participation by workers as such than the usual ethnic explanations of it suggest.[51] The DPP eschewed "class struggle," even though this was its natural issue, in view of KMT abilities to coopt many large business owners. Proletarianism was anathema on the island. It sounded communist. That was not the most effective way for the DPP to make appeals. Both rival parties needed Taiwanese support because that ethnic group is the vast majority of voters. Also, Taiwanese local traditions still valued hardscrabble pioneering by

---

[50]David D. Yang, "Classing Ethnicity: Class, Ethnicity, and the Mass Politics of Taiwan's Democratization" (MS provided by courtesy of the author, a doctoral student in Politics at Princeton, 2007). An earlier essay cites careful surveys proving high KMT legitimacy just before democratization; David D. Yang, "The Bases of Political Legitimacy in Late Authoritarian Taiwan," 67–112.

[51]Labor-capital issues are found to be crucial for other successful democratizations in Dietrich Rueschmeyer, Evelyn Stephens, and John Stephens, *Capitalist Development and Democracy* (Chicago: University of Chicago Press, 1992).

individuals, not welfare.[52] The DPP, to win power, had to get backing against its very strong rival by appealing to its core constituency, which the boom created among workers and SME owners who were tired of KMT imposts. But it had to do so on grounds that were politically presentable, and these grounds were Taiwanese.

The KMT could decreasingly use its Leninist appointments to keep small businesses at bay politically. Their prosperity changed the political landscape first in localities and then in the whole polity. The boom made social and political mobility in Taiwan high (perhaps higher than in any other Asian country).[53] Quick development encouraged consumerism and middle-status groups, but there are now so many *nouveaux riches* that income-based class categories are scarcely relevant. People move up and down sharply between income levels within a generation. Since the idea of "class" usually implies some stability between generations, it is hard to use in Taiwan (or the mainland now). The boom raised mobility, eroding classes and status groups. Both types became less stable. Middle-income coteries had less collective consciousness because individuals in them were so busy creating and consuming new wealth.

A "new middle class" of salaried administrator-professionals and their helpers in the mid-1980s comprised about half (in one survey,

---

[52]These traditions almost surely have origins in local clan warfare and mutual discriminations, e.g., against boat people, in Fujian, and then in the taming of Taiwan's jungles and ethnic cleansing of Austronesians after Zheng Chenggong's (Koxinga's) expulsion of the Dutch. The most articulate modern presentations of these hardscrabble ethics come from anti-welfare discourses in Singapore, whose main Chinese population is from South Fujian as is Taiwan's. See Chua Beng-Huat, *Communitarian Ideology and Democracy in Singapore* (London: Routledge, 1995), and especially see Chua's sociological classic on the arrangements for enforcing such values, *Political Legitimacy and Housing: Stakeholding in Singapore* (London: Routledge, 1997). Pasuk Phongpaichit and Chris Baker write similarly about "pillow and mat capitalism" among Sino-Thais, albeit they mostly came from other localities in South China.

[53]Taiwan-South Korean comparisons are fascinating. The Koreans had much more unionization, but the quasi-ethnic Kyongsang-Cholla division afflicted S. Korea and may have affected overall mobility. Fordham University professor José Alemán, a former student of the author, is using Korean sources to write about such issues comparatively in Korea and Chile.

53 percent) of Taiwan's bourgeois. Roughly one-third were state bureaucrats. The remaining fifth were independent professionals. Together this "new middle class" was about one-tenth of the island's labor force. The "old middle class" of self-employed managers and sales and service workers were practically all of the remaining half (43 percent) of the bourgeoisie.[54] Politically, however, they were less surely tied to the government, to which they raised demands for their businesses.

BOOMS AND ETHNIC PRIDE

The boom pluralized Taiwan, but it also inspired pride in the image of a unified island community. The rise of Taiwanese patriotism cannot be separated from rising pride in the boom. Situational success has affected normative identity on the island, making practically everyone who lives there proud to be Taiwanese or, if that claim is too obviously false, at least "new Taiwanese." (Later, on the mainland, the boom there also made cockiness about national identity soar. This happens in all countries that experience quick growth, e.g., the USA in the late 19th century, and it almost surely abets national decisions to get into avoidable wars.)

Circumspect scholars do not rely solely on either "primordial" norms or contextual "rationality" in attempts to explain political identifications.[55] The ethnic category relevant to any instance of behavior

---

[54]Based on work by Sheu Jia-You, see Chang Mau-Kuei, "Middle Class and Social and Political Movements," 132–33; see also Hsiao's table, in *Discovery of the Middle Classes in East Asia*, Michael Hsiao Hsin-huang, ed. (Taipei: Ethnology Institute, Academia Sinica, 1994), 10.

[55]David Laitin, in his early work on Nigeria, showed links between the normative and contextual generators of ethnicity. But now Laitin stresses that it is useful to find a clear single marker of ethnic identity. Language is the easiest of these (a researcher can readily tell, for example, whether a conversation is in Estonian or in Russian). Better prediction will come from considering, together with the short-term contextual data that interest rational actionists such as Laitin, longer-term normative data about the types of choices actors are likely to imagine. This requires research about intentions and customs, not just about unintended situations. For these ideas, I am in debt to Eric McGlinchey, "David Laitin and Ethnicity: The Value of Rediscovering One's Old Identity," paper in a 1997 seminar at Princeton University.

is the one actually chosen by the actor in that instance, not in any other situation. The difficulty with stressing a single criterion of ethnicity is that, in practice, everyone has multiple potential identities.[56] These options need not be consistent with each other. Accurate predictions about what people or groups will do in one situation may not come from observing what they do in other situations.

Class can also be a quasi-ethnic category. Regional study of Southeast Asia could clarify this among political scientists, whose concepts are not yet adaptable globally.[57] On Taiwan, either subethnic or class structure is relevant mainly at the whole-island size of collectivity. In local politics, where factional issues are crucial, neighbors tend anyway to be of the same subethnicity and/or of the same class. Many Taiwan neighborhoods contain no mainlanders. In a few other places (such as sections of Taipei or 'military villages' near bases) mainlanders are the majority. In either of these contexts, people may care about the ethnic issue in central politics, but it is irrelevant locally if everybody is the same. Political parties then seek local hinge leaders who can deliver blocs of support.

Non-"ethnic" questions of structural change in Taiwan politics have received less sustained attention than has the mainlander-Taiwanese cleavage. Questions of pluralization along social dimensions other than those affecting KMT-DPP conflict have been deemed less important. But at least two other topics also concern practically everybody on the island: how get along securely with China, and how to make Taiwan's new democracy function with more obvious mutual tolerance among politicians. The democratic question, not just the China question, resonates strongly in the middle class that the boom created.

Taiwan has more political scientists per capita than any other country on earth. The island's most sophisticated political surveyor,

---

[56]See Crawford Young, *The Politics of Cultural Pluralism* (Madison: University of Wisconsin Press, 1976).

[57]See Wang Gungwu, "The Study of Chinese Identities in Southeast Asia," in Jennifer Cushman and Wang Gungwu, ed., *The Changing Identities of Chinese in Southeast Asia* (Hong Kong: Hong Kong University Press, 1988), 17. Wang shows the difficulty of distinguishing class from ethnicity in many Southeast Asian contexts.

Wu Nai-Teh, found that the middle class was "the sector most inclined towards democratic values ... There is a high correlation between political ideology, i.e., democratic ideas, and electoral support among general voters. The more democratic a voter's attitude is, the more likely he is to support the [then-] oppositional DPP."[58]

A 1986 survey differentiated five "classes" (farmers, workers, state employees, the middle class, and capitalists) and explored the odds they favored either the KMT or DPP in the elections that year. The two groups most connected to business were the most anti-government. Voters in the "middle class" by a considerable margin (1.69 to 1) favored the DPP over the KMT. Voters in the wealthier "capitalist" group tended to flip in the same direction (by odds of 1.28 to 1). Workers split more evenly, while farmers and especially state employees tended to be pro-KMT.[59] This strengthening of the democratic opposition in Taiwan came not from the subethnic cleavage, but from wealth and demands that the boom had created.

EXTERNAL AND INTERNAL ISSUES FOR DEMOCRATIC DEBATE

Dankwart Rustow and other comparativists have stressed the importance of establishing a national arena for politics before any choice of government type is likely to be stable.[60] A democratic principle, for example, is that an alternation of elites must be possible. But if there

---

[58]Nai-Teh Wu and Chia-Long Lin, "Democratic Consensus and Social Cleavage: The Role of the Middle Class in Political Liberalization in Taiwan," in *Discovery of the Middle Classes in East Asia*, 214.

[59]By "ethnicity," mainlanders had 1.69 to 1 odds of favoring the KMT, and the majority "Minnan" Taiwanese had odds of 1.31 to 1 of doing the same thing in this first competitive election (which the KMT won) — but the Hakka minority was pro-DPP by a surprisingly heavy rate of 2.22 to 1. The chance that a farmer was at this time pro-KMT was 1.46 to 1; the land reform was apparently not forgotten. Workers were by a slight margin (1.19 to 1) pro-DPP. Computed from a large sample by Hu Fu and Chu-yun Han, "Electoral Competition and Political Democratization," 191.

[60]See Dankwart Rustow, "Transitions to Democracy: Toward a Dynamic Model," *Comparative Politics* 2:3 (April 1970), 337–63.

is no fundamental agreement on the territory or institutions in which they are alternating, the political actors mount a shaky stage. In Taiwan, rival politicians struggle for support in democratic elections partly because the American foreign protector prefers for this state form. This factor, and in recent years the interest of some Taiwanese in China's economic success, also affects the problem of defining the island polity.

Concern about the mainland threat sharply intensified in Taiwan after the 1979 U.S. derecognition of the ROC.[61] This angst soon centered on speculations about the time period when the PRC might predictably have a military advantage over Taiwan.[62] Nonetheless, many local island businesses were undaunted. Following the Schumpeterian principle of seeking new profit opportunities even if risky, they developed economic interests across the Strait. Large corporations, however, were hesitant. The first major Taiwanese investments on the mainland, in the 1980s, were by SMEs. Not before the mid-1990s did big Taiwan firms put much money into China.[63] Taiwan's SMEs began to invest (on a recorded basis) in plants across the Strait in 1986, just as the island's authoritarian period was ending. Big firms in Taiwan paid more attention both to security-minded bureaucrats in Taipei and to post-1989 conservatives in Beijing; so their large mainland investments were after 1992.[64]

By the mid-1990s, more than 70 percent of registered companies in Taiwan (i.e., those with a capitalization over NT$2 billion) had mainland investments. These several thousand companies, whose heads are mostly Taiwanese, had tended to support the KMT under

---

[61]One analysis is *Guofang baipishu* (National Defense White Paper), Taiwan Research Foundation National Defense Research Small Group, ed. (Taipei: Taiwan Yanjiu Jijinhui, 1992).

[62]Some analysts argued that the cross-Strait military balance might tip in approximately the year 2010. See Ch'ü Ming, *2010 nian liangan tongyi: Zhonggong maixiang haiquan shidai* (Unification of the Two Shores in 2010: The Era When Chinese Communism Leaps to Sea Power) (Taipei: Jiuyi, 1995).

[63]Richard C. Bush, *Untying the Knot: Making Peace in the Taiwan Strait* (Washington: Brookings Institution Press, 2005), 28–29.

[64]Françoise Mengin, "Taiwanese Politics and the Chinese Market," 237.

Chiang Ching-kuo, then the KMT mainstream headed by Lee Teng-hui, and later a variety of parties.

The Kuomintang, running large profit-making companies of its own, is the richest political party in the world. KMT corporations were originally not allowed to invest in the mainland, but a DPP legislator in 1997 said that at least one of them operated a joint venture with a mainland company based in Hong Kong.[65] He also estimated that the KMT had assets of NT$10 billion in the mid-1990s, whereas the DPP had just NT$150 million. Nationalism in each of Taiwan's major parties has been spurred by a combination of fears and business interests.

The DPP was and is divided sharply between its various leaders, who disagree factionally about personnel decisions and (even in public) about long-term policies on how to handle the "China problem." Partly for this reason, the DPP has adopted internal rules that require its legislators to vote together. They face a choice between stiff fines or expulsion for casting votes against the DPP line on any legislation. Almost as soon as it was started, the DPP was divided into groups that became the New Tide (*Xinchao*) and Formosa (*Meilidao*) factions. The New Tide group wanted the DPP to take a clearer stand in favor of Taiwan independence and to have a new constitution for the island. The Formosa faction was more satisfied with presumptively permanent autonomy and was willing to join with "mainstream" KMT politicians to amend the island's constitution to protect that autonomy, which is effective independence but retains name "China."

Kang Ning-hsiang, a co-founder of the DPP, became alienated from it because he was thought to be too soft against unification with China. He was a member of the Formosa faction, deemed by others in the DPP to have carried moderation too far. DPP politicians at some times in the past have called anybody who favors lifting cross-Strait exchange bans a "CCP fellow traveller" (*Zhonggong tonglu ren*) or a "hasty unificationist" (*jitong pai*).[66] Chen Shui-bian began as a member

---

[65]Interview, Taipei, August 8, 1997.

[66]Chu Yun-han, "The Politics of Taiwan's Mainland Policy," paper for a conference at the Centre of Asian Studies, University of Hong Kong, February 1996, 29.

of the pro-independence Righteous United Front (*zhengyi lianxian*) faction of the DPP. As Mayor of Taipei and then DPP nominee for president, however, Chen tended to avoid talking about the unification issue. In office, he tried so hard to guard against future chances of agreement with China, ignoring long-term security and U.S. warnings about it, that in 2008 the electorate gave both the Legislative Yuan and the presidency to the KMT.

Businesses, including those that trade across the Strait, have nonetheless been crucial to DPP success. The "Welfare" (*Fuliguo*) faction of the DPP lived up to its name by raising issues of social security, care for the elderly, medical services, and similar welfare issues.[67] But this DPP group was less powerful within the party than were others, notably the "New Tide" and "Formosa" factions. DPP mayors and magistrates tried to show that they could manage administrations as efficiently as the KMT, and this businesslike performance helped to earn them votes. DPP politicians left Taiwan's pro-market policies and ideology fully intact.

LABOR POLITICS ON TAIWAN

Shortly after the ban on forming new political parties was legally lifted in 1988, a Labor Party (*Laodong dang*) was registered — and soon sank with scarcely a trace.[68] It came into existence along with other small new political groups in the 1980s, and its program attracted some attention among intellectuals but little among voters.[69] The Labor Party was weak to the point of invisibility. A few of its members even claimed closeness to socialist market-regulatory ideas, and they mentioned the relevant communist policies. But this was an extremely odd position for a would-be party on Taiwan,

---

[67]See Wang Tso-jung, *Fuliguo bushi meng: Jingji gongping yu guoji jingji* (A Welfare State Isn't a Dream: Economic Equality and International Economics) (Taipei: Shibao, 1996).

[68]Shelley Rigger, *Politics in Taiwan: Voting for Democracy*, 129.

[69]See Wang Yi-hsiang, *Bu liuxue de shehui geming: Wo weishenma yao changzhu Gongdang* (Bloodless Social Revolution: Why I support the Labor Party) (Taipei: Jiubo, 1989).

because the CCP as an institution (as distinct from China as a nation) has practically no popularity on the island. Also, the CCP on the mainland was in fact doing little for workers there. Taiwanese investors know well that China is a place for capitalists to exploit labor maximally for profit.

Low wages and cases of labor repression on the island were nonetheless issues on which the very free press reported. The political ineffectiveness of the Taiwan Workers' Party stemmed from the same source that caused its ideological extremism: most Taiwan leaders were interested in mobilizing support on the basis of other issues, especially market prosperity, ethnic identity, and island security. These could displace, in public discourse, serious attention to the betterment of workers.

Democratization in Taiwan involves pressure from businesses to keep tax rates low, but also from civil interests to pay for some welfare. Socioeconomic issues and well-being compete with identity issues for political attention. Natural and medical disasters periodically affect politics. Earthquakes are a recurrent example. Taiwan would never have risen above the waves except for a subduction zone between two geological plates; so the island is prone to severe earthquakes. Any government inefficiency in responding to earthquakes or typhoon flooding becomes a hardy perennial issue for whichever party is in opposition. The SARS epidemic created problems that are politically similar.

The boom sullied Taiwan's ecology. Resentment against environmental pollution has correlated with local nationalism in Taiwan (as in Brittany, Scotland, and elsewhere). Nuclear plant construction, especially by the state-owned Taiwan Power Company, has been a lightning rod for protests. Conservationist movements in Taiwan have been based on love of the land, its birds and mangroves, mountains and forests.[70] These provide occasions to attack officially supported construction projects, which have also been supported by businesses.

---

[70]Hsiao Hsin-huang, L. Milbrath, and R. Weller, "Antecedents of an Environmental Movement in Taiwan," in *Capitalism, Nature, Socialism* 6:3 (September 1995), 91–104.

Especially after winning legislative or executive power, however, the DPP has more effectively supported businessmen than environmentalists.

The DPP has done well only when the KMT and other "Blue" parties split into factions under rival leaders, dividing voters who do not mind being Taiwanese Chinese. Chen Shui-bian's 1994 mayoral and 2000 presidential victories both depended on this phenomenon — which during that period balanced the KMT's very great financial strength.[71] As late as 1997, the DPP had about 100,000 members; but the KMT had twenty times as many. To finance itself, the DPP enforced a system of party dues; the KMT did not need such rules. When the KMT-allied parties hold together, they win many elections, as they did in 2008.

Business-state tensions on Taiwan are tempered by concurrent interests in which entrepreneurs join officials. Neither of these groups generally favors high spending on social welfare. Neither likes trade union politics. Neither is very environmentalist. Businesses and government on Taiwan have both been conservative. The rise of a left-right cleavage has been delayed on the island by the Taiwanese-mainlander cleavage instead — to the clear advantage of all employers on the island.[72] This concurrence of interest between businesses and

---

[71]The 2000 example, in which the DPP's Chen Shui-bian won the presidency with less than two-fifths of the vote, emerged because the PFP's James Soong Chu-yu and the KMT's Lien Chan split the "Blue" vote. In the 1994 Taipei mayoral election won by Chen Shui-bian, he also received just a plurality of the votes. Chen had a majority in just one of Taipei's six electoral districts — District Four, which was also a place where the New Party candidate (Huang Ta-chou) did better than the KMT candidate (Chao Shao-kang). In District One, the only other place where the NP got more votes than the KMT in this election, the DPP almost won a majority (49.6 percent). See Liang Shih-wu, "*Yijiujiusi nian Taibei shizhang xuanju zhi yuce*" ("Predictions on the 1994 Taipei Mayoral Election"), *Xuanju yanjiu* (Electoral Research), 1:2 (November 1994), 118.

[72]This political logic was first broached in E.E. Schattschneider, *The Semi-Sovereign People*, which shows the ways in which (during America's fastest boom) questions of injustice to workers and southern Blacks were displaced by issues of economic development of interest to businesses. Just two Democrats won the presidency between the Civil War and the Depression, and both were closer to business than to labor. The logic may apply to politics during any boom. A particularly striking example is in "communist" China, which is still Leninist but not (currently) proletarian. Sociopolitical "harmony," "primitive accumulation," and patriotic pride are the main rhetorics there.

bureaucracies has smoothed political transitions: from mainlanders to Taiwanese within the KMT, and then from the KMT to the DPP and back in the presidency. All the politicians lean toward business, even when they were leaning hard against each other.

THE CORRUPTION ISSUE: LINKS AND ORIGINS IN DEMOCRATIC CONFLICT

When the state was mainlander-run, its leaders claimed that too much official connection with Taiwanese businesses might lead to corruption. New wealth anywhere tends to create "black gold politics" (a common term in Taiwan, *heijin zhengzhi*). So Chiang Ching-kuo once issued "Ten Commandments" that required all government employees to report to the Bureau of Personnel any major social engagements with private business people. Officials were particularly discouraged from accepting invitations for dinners at expensive restaurants.[73]

A problem with this policy was the deep involvement of the KMT party-state in Taiwan's economy. Government- and Party-owned enterprises in Taiwan could no longer, during the transition to democracy, prevent private firms from competing with them. Yet in a polity like Taiwan's, which developed effective separations of power, this mixture of politics and business bred scandal.

A legislator "virtually single-handedly blocked an investment plan of state-owned China Steel to move into a specialized steel market." That company was also prevented from entering a joint venture abroad, because "Taiwan's small private steel firms objected to their state-run competitor tapping public funds to gain strength overseas. In the light of developments of this sort, many state-owned enterprises have learned to 'bribe' lawmakers to protect their budgets and operational autonomy by awarding them sweet business deals."[74]

---

[73]Karl Fields, "Strong States and Business Organization in Korea and Taiwan," in *Business and the State in Developing Countries* Sylvia Maxfield and Ben Ross Schneider, eds. (Ithaca: Cornell University Press, 1997), 143.

[74]Chu Yun-han, "The Realignment of Business-Government Relations and Regime Transition in Taiwan," 129–30.

Businesses in Taiwan (as in East China and Thailand) could "buy out" local factions that win political posts. The office holders could then corruptly favor these firms for government contracts.[75]

Taiwan candidates have personal support organizations (*houyuan hui*, a term that uses the same characters as for such networks in Japan, *koenkai*).[76] In these, the main activists are the local election canvassers. Vote buying in Taiwan began, during the 1950s and 1960s, with presents that were small tokens such as hand towels, cigarettes, or fruits. As the economy boomed, however, money in traditional red gift envelopes became more common. The practice was seen as morally wrong, and it remained illegal. But Taiwan's electoral system, which usually gave each voter just a single ballot in a district that returned more than one representative, meant that most nominees were elected with pluralities. So candidates paid even for votes they were unsure would be cast for them. Some voters spoke of "getting rich off elections" (*fa xuanju cai*), although in fact the amounts of money given to any ordinary citizen was not large.[77]

Presidential elections were less affected by vote-buying than were legislative elections. Vote-buying, inefficient in all races because of its illegality and the secret ballot, brought such uncertain returns for presidential candidates that they seldom bothered to buy votes. Opprobrium from doing so would weaken their broader campaigns. Vote-buying was in any case mainly a phenomenon of the late authoritarian period, when the presidency was not decided by popular election. Both the presidents Chiang and president Lee, however, cared who won in local races.

Unofficial factions were at the heart of local politics, especially in rural areas. Jacobs explains that, "Factions developed primarily as an organizational structure suited for competing in elections at a time when land reform had undercut the basis of prestige, and elections offered new opportunities for regaining this prestige."[78] Whether

---

[75]Shelley Rigger, *Politics in Taiwan: Voting for Democracy*, 102.

[76]See also Nathaniel Thayer, *How the Conservatives Rule Japan* (Princeton: Princeton University Press, 1969).

[77]This relies extensively on Shelley Rigger, *From Opposition to Power*, 183 and *passim*.

[78]J. Bruce Jacobs, *Local Politics in a Rural Chinese Cultural Setting*, 82.

factions were based in lineages or not, they relied on conflicts, notably in elections. Also, factions at one administrative level tended to generate factions at others. A rural informant put this in particularly formal analytic terms:

> If our opponents support a candidate for county office, we cannot support him because the *guanxi* [personal relationship] between the candidate and our opponents will be closer than the *guanxi* between the candidate and ourselves. In the future, our opponents will be better able to rely on him; and should he need help, he would go to our opponents, not to us. People would say that we have no candidate to support and, thus, no influence. Of course, we would also have no face.[79]

Money inevitably related to such prestige, and the boom supplied much more money.

Vote-buying was illegal in Taiwan, but it was seldom reported. Even when reported, it was rarely investigated. Each vote cost about NT$300 to 500 in Taiwan's 1989 election, "enough to buy a dinner for two in an inexpensive sit-down restaurant."[80] But the amounts can be figured per candidate, rather than per voter. In 1990, in a race for a mere township mayoralty, the two factions together spent US$307,000. In the 1991 National Assembly elections, candidates generally needed to hand out between US$1.2 and 2 million each. Muckraking reporters found that some nominees spent up to US$20 million.[81]

In Taiwan, a political candidate with a large supply of cash could show "strong feet" (*zhuang jiao*) by throwing banquets. "Interminable feasts" (*liushui xi*) were offered to voters, at which the politician and his boosters gave speeches. By no means did all the people who came to eat at these feasts end up voting for their hosts. The purpose of such events was sometimes electoral only for show; they were a way of asserting social prestige.

A government office, won in an election, might serve the same purpose. It was not merely useful for determining state policy.

---

[79]Quoted in *ibid.*, 83.

[80]The price was similar in the 1992 and 1998 elections. See Shelley Rigger, *Politics in Taiwan: Voting for Democracy*, 96.

[81]Gerald A. McBeath, *Wealth and Freedom: Taiwan's New Political Economy*, 67.

Sometimes official institutions of island-wide politics (including parties) co-opted institutions of more local and social power. But at other times, an official election was mainly an occasion to have a local potlatch. This aim was often foremost in the minds of faction leaders during Taiwan elections before the turn of the millennium. Leaders could care as much about their general prestige as about whether they ended up winning. The second of these questions was a reason for the first. Feasts "showed strength" to supporters, no matter what happened thereafter.

Secret ballots meant that candidates might be gambling huge amounts when they gave money to electors or paid for banquets. A survey of canvassers in Taiwan's 1989 elections concluded that, "most campaign activists and election observers thought that a candidate could expect to receive only two votes for every ten 'purchased.' Obviously, buying votes is an expensive way to get a small number of votes."[82] The nominees (or their business donors) paid the money nonetheless, at least in these competitive elections of the past century. The number of candidates on each ballot could be large in multi-seat districts, and the boom let them finance a new form of conspicuous consumption: bids for state offices.

Sometimes the money was also serious investment. This was political risk-taking, and it was not just consistent with the economic boldness that typified Taiwan SMEs, it was actually venture capital. In Taiwan, as Chu Yun-han writes,

> the broadening scope of electoral competition and the rising importance of the legislature provided the business elite with ample new opportunities for influence-buying. The results have been highly disturbing. Politicians linked to criminal groups infest representative bodies at the county and township levels. The Legislative Yuan is an arena of horse-trading among state officials, party officials, and lawmakers acting as proxies for local factions and businesses.[83]

---

[82]Shelley Rigger, *Politics in Taiwan: Voting for Democracy*, 143.

[83]Chu Yun-han, "Taiwan's Unique Challenges," in *Democracy in East Asia*, Larry Diamond and Eric Plattner, eds. (Baltimore: Johns Hopkins University Press, 1998), 141.

The KMT, as Taiwan's very rich ruling party, was for many years especially vulnerable to criticisms of corruption. By the mid-1990s, it was evident that KMT vote buying had been rampant in county council elections. The government appointed a commissioner to reduce corruption, Ma Ying-jeou, but he could indict only a few of the offenders. There were too many cases to examine, too many of the guilty were locally powerful, and too many were crucial in local KMT organizations. The mainland's Leninist party later faced a similar trade-off between the needs to retain personnel and to paint a public image of cleanliness.

TAIWAN'S VOTING SYSTEM AND FEISTY POLITICS

Under Taiwan's multi-incumbent electoral district system, which the KMT had established, benefits came to parties that could maintain internal discipline. Any party had an interest in fielding exactly the number of nominees for which it would have sufficient support that each would win. If it fielded more or fewer, or if one of its popular candidates drained too many votes from another nominee on the same ticket, the party would end up with fewer elected representatives. If independent candidates without party approval ran, taking votes away from the approved ones, then other parties also might win more seats.

A party with money, like the KMT, could pay pollsters to assess its support better than an impoverished party could — and it could get out its vote more precisely. When a party was divided into factions, as all Taiwan parties were, this system nearly forced the factions to cooperate. (The Liberal Democratic Party of Japan, which is also rich and factionalized, instituted the same system for the same reasons. Taiwan's election law was somewhat changed in 2004, well after the DPP took the executive branch, but the single-vote/multi-member-district system has prevailed during most of the period examined here.)

This system encourages an odd combination of party discipline with personalistic politics.[84] The local links or charisma of candidates matter more than policy stances, and often more than party affiliation.

---

[84]See Nathaniel Thayer, *How the Conservatives Rule Japan*.

The use of multiple-incumbent districts also tends to recruit local leaders relatively quickly into state offices. Personal reputations for honesty and political cleanliness can become crucial in parts of a district in which a candidate may have relatively few kin or connections. Reputations for benevolence or favoritism are important among closer constituents. Reputations for decisiveness, patriotism, and even willingness to use spectacular words or violence can also bring votes. Since only a plurality is needed to win, almost any kind of clear image may be enough to secure a seat.

Teamwork between government incumbents, or between members of the same party from the same district, is discouraged by this voting system. Fellow candidates from a single place, especially if they are co-partisans and share similar policy stances, have under this system solid electoral reasons to distrust each other. Party factions at the island-wide level therefore seldom include legislators from the same district; instead, when representatives need allies, they seek peers from distant places.

Two kinds of electoral neighborhoods in Taiwan were of particular interest to the KMT through the mid-1990s at least. In the first, the residents were usually Taiwanese (Minnan and Hakka). The buying of votes (*maipiao*) occurred mostly in these classic sites for machine politics, where KMT local organizations were strong for decades. A second kind of KMT neighborhood, less important because less common, was "military villages" (*junzhuang*), where the KMT could generally count on "iron votes" (*tiepiao*). These were geographically concentrated. Until the advent of the mainlander-oriented New Party, and later the People First Party, they were very safe constituencies for KMT candidates. The ruling party reacted to the NP and PFP threat in such areas by somewhat raising the quota of soldiers on candidate lists — changing the previous principle that had made various groups (businesspeople, workers, bureaucrats) have quotas of candidates according to their proportions of votes. Also important in retaining this KMT vote were moves to renovate housing near the military bases.

These tactics certainly did not guarantee electoral success all over the island, however. The DPP, seeing its KMT and NP and PFP rivals at each other's throats in such areas and calculating the effects of the multi-incumbent district system carefully, might send particularly strong candidates to such places in hopes of picking up a sufficient plurality to take a seat.[85]

The KMT gave most of the banquets (at least through the late 1990s) simply because it had most of the political money. But DPP candidates nonetheless did very well in elections. When they were poor, they were not expected by voters to throw feasts. Instead, their forte was their platform (anti-corruption, pro-Taiwan) and in some cases the personal reputations of DPP candidates.

The DPP has often been able to recruit attractive people to run for office. Chen Tang-cheng, for example, was in the United States and entered the Legislative Yuan as a DPP member through a proportional representation system as a representative of Overseas Chinese voters. Seeing the success of the industrial zone that had been established in Hsinchu (which accounts for more than ten percent of Taiwan's exports), he pushed for a similar zone in his native Tainan. This led to a major DPP political career for him in that city.

Personal extremism, such as TV broadcasts made evident during bloody fist fights on the floor of the Legislative Yuan, was also clearly encouraged by this electoral system. If candidates appeal to a sufficient number of voters, they can be elected even if their behavior is also disdained by most. So Taiwan's Legislative Yuan after the 1992 election became a very lively place. Some members, especially DPP politicians who had been repressed, jailed, or exiled by the KMT in earlier years, physically attacked their fellow lawmakers. Their constituencies included a sufficient number of voters who honored personal feistiness. Reporters avidly cover such violence when it draws blood from other legislators and makes headlines. Verbal combat also became far sharper than it had been in the Legislative Yuan before the mid-1980s.

Accusations of thievery had dogged the KMT throughout the decades of mainlander rule. A popular Taiwanese term for Chiang

---

[85]Interviews with Chang Ying-hua and Gunter Schubert aided the author here.

Kai-shek's friends was "the old crooks."[86] Mass resentment of parasitism had been common against ethnically distinctive elites. In Europe and China alike, it often preceded uprisings in towns especially.[87] Close relations between the KMT and businesses were often seen as corrupt in Taiwan. Without them, and without direct KMT ownership of some profit-making firms, it would have been difficult for Lee Teng-hui's mainstream to pension off aged mainlanders who had staffed Chiang Kai-shek's party and army. They could be compensated with advisory positions in KMT corporations.

The amounts of money available to the two main parties continued to differ sharply, but the uses of money became subtler as the electorate's general level of education rose and as journalists' critiques of corruption had a cumulative effect. In the 1994 Legislative Yuan elections, the KMT was able to spend NT$5 billion, while the DPP had just one-hundredth as much, NT$50 million. The KMT at that time could use its money in many ways. During the month before an election, for example, major local supporters of the party were asked to invite numbers of their followers for full Chinese feasts with eight or ten courses. Fifty, sixty, or more than a hundred people might attend these affairs, at which candidates give speeches. Although donations to the party were certainly not discouraged at these times, the main purpose was to solidify support for the KMT and for its local faction leaders. The KMT and DPP both relied on "restaurant meetings" (*canting hui*) of supporters, sometimes at breakfasts rather than dinners. But the KMT had more funds to pay for these.

Just before an election, local canvassers directly bought votes (*maipiao*). They knocked on doors, made pitches for their candidates, and did not necessarily need to use traditional red envelopes (*hong-bao*) to cover the cash that they delivered to householders. Several thousand New Taiwan dollars per vote was the going rate for many

---

[86]Tien Hung-mao and Cheng Tun-jen, "Crafting Democratic Institutions," 4.

[87]Frederic Wakeman, Jr., *Strangers at the Gate: Social Disorder in South China, 1839–1861* (Berkeley: University of California Press, 1966), 77.

Legislative Yuan races in the mid-1990s.[88] It was estimated that vote buying was only 40 to 50 percent effective in Taiwan constituencies where it was attempted, but that did not deter the KMT, which had a great deal of money. Citizenship was, for these few years, like owning stock in the state; people were paid dividends. Then they did what they liked with the proceeds. There was no way for canvassers to be sure that people who promised to vote for their candidates actually did so, and clearly many did not.

The DPP fared increasingly well, even while the KMT had more grass-roots organization and more money. The importance of money in Taiwan politics decreased as the boom slowly wound down. A sophisticated statistical analysis of the factors that led to success for candidates in mid-1990s city mayor and county magistrate elections tends to support the conclusion that "individual traits" (*geren tezhi*) of the candidates contributed importantly to their wins or losses. Party affiliation or current office, for instance, were less accurate predictors of success than level of education, age, gender, and length of residence in the district.[89] Care in handling the identity issue was still crucial for island-wide candidates wishing to win the presidency, but local nominees had to face a broader range of issues.

MATURATION IN TAIWAN'S DEMOCRATIC POLITICS

Taiwan has eventually reached per-capita levels of income at which no place grows very quickly. GDP growth rates were often less than 5 percent, far slower than in the earlier halcyon days of the 1960s and late 1970s. The retreat of the island's boom has been accompanied by a transparency of political tensions that is distinctly modern. As Taiwan's economy slowed noticeably in the 1990s, the SMEs that

---

[88]About 35 to 40 New Taiwan dollars then equalled US$1, but of course votes in different places had different costs.

[89]Ho Chin-ming, "*Houxuanren shengxuan yinsu fenxi moxing chushen*" ("A Preliminary Model Analysis of the Factors Allowing Candidates to Win Elections: Case Study of the Eleventh Election for Mayors and Magistrates"), *Xuanju yanjiu* (Electoral Research), 1:1 (May 1994), 111–46.

had been the powerhouse of the boom also somewhat declined. Greater equality of household wealth, which was one of Taiwan's most remarkable achievements during the boom, ceased to improve as the economy slowed. There was "increasing social inequality resulting from a sharp escalation in land and stock prices that benefitted asset owners but brought higher costs of living to those on fixed incomes."[90] Growth with equity was replaced by less growth with less equity.

Laws favoring conglomerates also reduced the salience of SMEs. At the same time, however, the DPP made electoral inroads against the KMT in campaigns that excoriated the KMT's wealth and money politics. Public sensitivity about corruption rose in Taiwan's industrialized political economy.

Interviews in Taiwan as late as 2000 showed that some voters still linked the KMT with organized crime, gangs, money politics. Although vote-buying was by then rare in Taiwan's urban areas, it was still reported in rural places, where a vote might cost as much as NT$5,000 (US$170). The 2000 presidential election reportedly cost the KMT much more than the DPP or PFP spent — but Chen Shui-bian and James Soong got 39 and 37 percent of the vote respectively, while the KMT's Lien Chan got just 23 percent.[91] The KMT, after losing the presidency in 2000, wanted to remake its image to become a strictly "clean party." It passed rules that a KMT member, if convicted, would also be automatically expelled from the party. No member was supposed to receive a gift worth more than NT$3000.

Chen Shui-bian and his family were plagued by corruption charges in 2006–07, and his opponents rose in fierce reaction, holding huge demonstrations demanding his recall from office. President Chen could not prevent the arrest of his son-in-law on insider trading charges, nor could he stop the press from repeated accusations against his wife for influence peddling. Chen's friend and DPP legislator Ye Yi-chin said that, "The President has been frustrated, thinking

---

[90]Gerald A. McBeath, *Wealth and Freedom*, 71.
[91]Lin Gang, "Taiwan's Power Reconfiguration and its Impact on Cross-Strait Relations," *Journal of Chinese Political Science* 6:1 (Spring 2000), 27.

it was unfair for the opposition and some media to pick on him over the use of the state [pension] fund, because what he did was no different from what previous Kuomintang leaders had done in the past."[92] That, however, was precisely the problem.

Evidence that anti-corruption politics could trump identity politics in Taiwan came when ex-DPP chair Shih Ming-teh put on red clothes to lead street demonstrations demanding Chen's resignation after a prosecutor made clear that only Chen's presidential immunity protected him (while in office) from corruption charges. As Shih claimed, "The DPP can't say, 'Since the KMT did it [money politics], why can't I?' That's why the people took power from the KMT. If we don't make Chen resign, people will say, 'He could do it, so why can't I?' Then we will never have clean politics." At least in the new millennium, Shih put anti-corruption ahead of Taiwanese identity as an issue. This was striking from a Taiwanese leader who had spent 25 years in KMT jails during the authoritarian period.

Money corruption vied with "identity" as the main issue in Taiwan politics. Governance was increasingly viewed as a business, whose efficiency could be rated. Winning DPP candidate Chen Shui-bian had previously enjoyed a major issue in KMT gaffes during the previous half-decade delay in opening a rapid transit line, a "44 billion [New Taiwan] dollar joke."[93] The DPP also did well running as a clean party in elections for county magistracies, whose public funds for patronage

---

[92]Lawrence Chung, "Chen Set for Red Face Tomorrow," *South China Morning Post*, October 9, 2006, A-7.

[93]This line runs from central Taipei to suburban Mucha. Cost overruns, engineering problems, and difficulties with the main foreign contractor (a French company) allowed Chen to excoriate the KMT's inefficiency. Italian tiles in the station were seen as unnecessary (one of Taiwan's very few natural resources is marble), trains often would not line up with platforms for safe entry and exit, the ride was bumpy, and the ashtrays were exorbitantly expensive. This issue was certainly not the sole one in such Chen's crucial election as Taipei mayor, but Chen's use of it to discredit KMT claims of management ability helped produce the most startling DPP victory to that date. This author is grateful for interview information from Dr. Joseph Jauhsieh Wu.

rose when the province government was downgraded.[94] Local notables who had earlier delivered their followers' votes to the KMT
could switch easily to the DPP. But Chen found that the Taiwan
identity issue could not easily restore his reputation when he too was
accused of monetary corruption.

Ma Ying-jeou has been popular on Taiwan for having fought
crime and corruption. As Minister of Justice in 1996–97, Ma led
"Operation Chih Ping," which arrested about 100 gangsters, including some politicians. Ma Ying-jeou accelerated "the process of liqui-
dating the party's property" and downsizing the KMT's staff from
3800 in 1996 to less than 900 in 2006.[95] This "Mr. Clean"
announced at the beginning of June 1998 that he would run against
Chen Shui-bian for Mayor of Taipei. Chen lost re-election in that
year, although he then ran for the presidency in 2000 and won. The
New Party's candidate for Mayor, Wang Chien-shien, who stood
scant chance of winning, said about Ma's announcement that "his
candidacy is a personal misfortune [for me] but a great fortune for
the nation."[96] Ma's reputation for integrity did not stymie his 2008
presidential campaign even after he was brought into a court on relatively minor misreporting charges, and then he won the presidency.

SEPARATIONS OF POWER IN TAIWAN'S GOVERNMENT, MEDIA, AND PUBLIC

The central KMT apparatus eventually lost control of many of its local
faction leaders. They put up their own candidates in local elections if

---

[94] James Soong Chu-yu, the KMT ex-Governor of Taiwan whose jurisdiction the
KMT mainstream faction nearly abolished, was a formidable campaigner on Taiwan
despite the fact that he was born on the mainland. Factionalization caused the KMT
to lose the 2000 presidential election. Lien Chan, the ex-Premier, was nominated by
the KMT; but Soong opposed Lien, splitting the "Blue" vote; so Chen Shui-bian
won the presidency.

[95] Su Chi, "Taiwan's Security: A KMT Perspective," US-Taiwan Business Council,
Denver, September 11, 2006, http://www.taiwansecurity.org/News/2006/Su-
110906.htm, seen November 15, 2006.

[96] *South China Morning Post*, Hong Kong, June 7, 1998, 6.

they did not agree with the choices that the ex-Leninist KMT made. For example Kau Yü-jen, ex-Speaker of the Provincial Assembly, was a KMT legislator; but he had his own faction independent of the party. Kau had been on the KMT Central Committee. When the party supported a candidate in an election for which Kau's candidate also ran, Kau simply resigned from the party.

Media access was one of the KMT's major resources into the mid-1990s, and to some extent beyond that time. A statistical comparison of voting behavior with media use showed that KMT supporters read their official party papers more regularly than did voters for other parties. Also, they more regularly read print media that could be classified as "mainstream." The island has three main TV networks, which are commonly called Taishi, Zhongshi, and Huashi. The latter two have more programs in Mandarin and are politically "mainstream." KMT voters look at them with greater frequency than do DPP voters.[97]

The DPP established a television station in Kaohsiung, the "Whole People Station" (*Quanmin dianshi tai*), to promote a greater sense of Taiwan identity and provide programs in the local language. It had considerable public influence and received support from advertising by companies such as the Yimei Food Corporation, which sells ingredients for Taiwanese cuisine. By the late 1990s, however, the level of such support was reportedly declining.

There is a strong public sense, bolstered by reports in Taiwan media, that the island's politics must be clean. But reports of mainland corruptions and injustices are equally common in Taiwan. A thick 1997 book detailed the egregious scandals of Beijing Mayor Chen Xitong.[98] On the mainland, TV footage of Legislative Yuan fighting

---

[97]Weng Shieu-chi and Sun Hsiu-hui, "*Xuanmin de moujie shiyong xingwei ji qi zhengzhi zhishi zhengdang bianhao yu toupiao xingwei zhi jian de guanlian*" ("The Relations between Media Use, Party Preferences, and Voting Behavior [in Taiwan's 1993 elections]"), *Xuanju yanjiu* (Electoral Research), 1:2 (November 1994), esp. 18–19.

[98]Chen Fang, *Tiannü: Shizhang yaoan* (The Wrath of God: A Mayor's Severe Crime [English trans. on orig. paperback cover, which is also marked *dalu jinshu*, "prohibited book on the mainland"]) (Taipei: Yuanjing, 1997).

in Taipei was shown widely, to suggest that democracy was dangerous. Each side advertised the dark aspects of the other's politics.

Taiwan's major newspapers developed identifiable positions on the unification issue. The most important centrist paper has been the long-established *Zhongyang ribao* (Central Daily), party organ of the KMT. The largest-circulation major daily, however, is the *Ziyou shibao* (Freedom Times), which has a largely Taiwanese readership. The *Taiwan shibao* (Taiwan Times) tends to be pro-independence, although some Taiwan nationalists raise questions about its consistency when the publisher's brother makes large investments in mainland China. The *Taiwan ribao* (Taiwan Daily) and *Minzhong ribao* (Commons [its official translation]) are other pro-autonomy papers. The other end of that spectrum is represented by the *Zhongguo shibao* (China Times), which like the English-language *China Post* is basically opposed to Taiwan independence and close to the New Party. A similar position, which is unfairly classified by some Taiwanese as indistinguishable from Beijing's, is held by the *Lianhe bao* (United News).[99] When analyzing the three other countries discussed in this book, there will be somewhat less to say about media, especially in the case of the Chinese mainland that has a far more constrained press.

Presidential elections in Taiwan differ from local elections because of issues and also because of resources. Exercising Taiwanese identity by voting in local elections for candidates who support Taiwan independence is safer than implementing the same sentiment by voting for an independence advocate for president.[100] The China issue and the corruption issue alternate with each other, and with

---

[99]This information is mainly from interviews. Many evening and tabloid "small papers" (*xiaobao*) also graced Taiwan's newsstands, but intellectual interviewees in Taiwan did not assign them any more importance than do those in the mainland, when speaking about the popular dailies.

[100]President Chen Shui-bian spoke more moderately about island autonomy than had the 1996 DPP presidential candidate Peng Min-ming, who got only two-thirds of the votes that had gone to his party in preceding local elections. Apparently because Peng was at that time considered reckless in statements that could provoke the mainland.

issues of personality, as the boom has wound down.[101] Neither major party could afford to be completely monotonic on these topics.

After Chen Shui-bian's extremely narrow victory in the 2004 presidential election (which he might have lost without a sympathy vote after an assassination attempt that many Chinese considered fake), and especially after his wife was charged with corruption, the anti-graft campaign against Chen was organized by both Blues and Greens. The prosecutor who indicted Chen was a "deep Green." A widely respected former head of Taiwan's Academia Sinica, to whom Chen in 2000 probably owed his first presidential margin of victory, also suggested in public that Chen might consider resigning.[102]

Feisty legislators of all Taiwan parties now uncover more information relevant to government policy than was public in earlier decades. The KMT bureaucracy for years hid data that could undermine what the executive branch wanted to do. The Legislative Yuan now has specialized committees that conduct public hearings at which

---

[101]Ethnic politics on Taiwan was complicated not just by corruption scandals, but also by unexpected issues such as the island's overproduction of fruit. From May to November, 2006, the price of bananas on Taiwan dropped from US$2 per kilo to 80 cents or less. Most farmers support the DPP — but they care more about bananas than about any parties. They are numerous and vocal on the island. So DPP Prime Minister Su Tseng-chang urged his cabinet ministers personally to consume more fruit, creating a slogan: "Love Taiwan, Eat Bananas." The pan-Blues could be no less pro-banana, insisting the DPP executive should, during the price crisis, allow direct shipping of these fruits to China. The CCP, also wanting to woo Taiwan farmers, quickly ordered thirty tons of bananas (although mainland farmers may have had a different view that they could less easily express). This matter might seem a joke to those distant from it, but politicians took it seriously. Taiwan's democracy means that no issue of importance to any sizeable group is ignored unless there are organized countervailing interests for ignoring it. See Tsai Ping-I, "Taipei: Yes, We Have no Bananas," Asia Times Online, November 5, 2006, http://www.atimes.com/atimes/china/HJ-28AB01.html, seen November 8, 2006.

[102]A sign of Beijing's rising sophistication in managing its Taiwan links was its relative silence during the fierce street protests against Chen Shui-bian. A cadre of the PRC's Taiwan Affairs Office said, "We have clearly stated that [the corruption/resignation issues] should be resolved by Taiwan people." See Ralph Jennings, "China Quiet on Taiwan Protests to Avoid Backlash," Reuters, September 28, 2006, http://www.taiwansecurity.org/Reu/2006/Reuters-280906.htm, seen November 14, 2006.

bureaucrats evade questions only as well as they can, as in many other democracies.

When elections give more power to local elites, private companies that bankroll candidates benefit. The other side of this coin is the reportedly "pernicious effect" of elections, especially the role of money in campaigns. Smear tactics become common. Electoral expenses on a per-capita basis rise until laws are passed aiming to limit them. In Taiwan, such costs were on a per-capita basis among the highest in the world. Radical kinds of political advocacy come from candidates trying to gain attention.[103] Single-nontransferrable voting creates intense competition among campaigners, exacerbating all these problems. But money from booms is convertible to power in authoritarian systems, too.

The increasingly liberal transparency of Taiwan's government institutions, which increased as the boom slowed, allowed the press to help develop more information-rich decisionmaking processes for the island. The variety of facts in public rose. For example in 2006, a presidential assistant was indicted for accepting US$222,000 from a businessman to bribe judges in an embezzlement trial. When this came to light, another presidential assistant visited the prosecutor's office, reportedly asking it to alert the Judicial Yuan if any of the judges had been involved in this corruption case. The main fact about such incidents is that they are discussed in public on Taiwan.[104]

As James Madison wrote in *Federalist 51*, "you must first enable the government to control the governed; and in the next place oblige it to control itself. A dependence on the people is, no doubt, the primary control on the government; but experience has taught mankind the necessity of auxiliary precautions."[105] Separation of

---

[103]See Tien Hung-mao and Cheng Tun-jen, "Crafting Democratic Institutions in Taiwan," 14.

[104]Rich Chang, "Judicial Yuan Denies Interfering in Taipei Prosecutor's Probe," *Taipei Times*, July 20, 2006, 3.

[105]James Madison, *The Federalist No. 51*, http://www.constitution.org/fed/federa51. htm, seen December 2, 2006.

powers is his recommendation, and it requires that the parts of the government be generated independently from each other. Madison envisaged three parts: legislative, executive, and judicial. The constitution on Taiwan, a document imported by Chiang Kai-shek from the mainland (although he suspended it in favor of martial law), listed these three and two others, one to give civil service tests, and one to investigate all other parts of the government with the aim of keeping them uncorrupt.

These two, added to the Montesquieu-Madison trio, have clear Chinese characteristics. The Examination Yuan (Kaoshi Yuan) does not give tests in Confucian classics, as Chinese emperors' examiners once did, but it tries to assure that people staffing the state bureaucracy are smart enough. The Control Yuan (Jiancha Yuan) has ombudsman-like investigative powers. It could become more important if, as some of its leaders advocate, it were given more power to sue the miscreants it uncovers. Thus far, it can only refer cases to the Ministry of Justice, which is part of the executive under the premier and president, whose friends are thus more difficult to investigate.[106]

Taiwanese now give much evidence of their contented pleasure with liberalism despite its messiness. They are embarrassed by scandals of corruption (e.g., when public funds bought from Tiffany a diamond ring for the president's wife, provoking mass demonstrations). As political scientist Emile Sheng put it, "In ten years, when we look back, this could be a turning point for Taiwan's democracy to become mature. Right now, it is a disgrace and quite humiliating. But once we get past this, I think Taiwan's politics will get a lot cleaner." A People's First Party (PFP, 'Blue') legislator, aware of the "Green" background of the prosecutor, said, "This is

---

[106]The Control Yuan can bring charges against officials and can refer cases to the Ministry of Justice (which is in the Executive Yuan under the presidential party). For a general treatment, see Andreas Schedler, "Conceptualizing Accountability," in *The Self-Restraining State: Power and Accountability in New Democracies*, Andreas Schedler, Larry Diamond, and Marc F. Plattner, eds. (Boulder: Lynne Rienner, 1999), 16, based on work by Larry Diamond.

very hard evidence that at last we have a fair and independent-minded judicial branch. The principle of separation of power has taken root in Taiwan."[107]

This political system, not mainly because of its elections but because of its institutions that can legitimately generate diverse information for the public, has become better adapted to the plural problems of a rich society than (thus far) have the systems in East China, Thailand, or the Philippines. Taiwan's boom has ended. The polity it leaves behind is modern.

---

[107] Jim Yardley, "Chaos in Taiwan Cloaks Political Maturation: Democracy Tested by Chen Scandal," *International Herald Tribune*, November 24, 2006, 1 and 4.

7

Political Results of East China's Boom

In China, the relation between economic boom and civic change is harder to assess comprehensively than in the other places this book compares. The reasons lie in China's continuing authoritarianism, which is strengthened in relatively modern parts, such as East China, by political influences from the leaders of poorer parts. Political change in rich areas such as Sunan or Zhejiang has been moderated by integration with inland provinces that develop more slowly. Also, both official and unofficial discourse in China remains heavily statist. Talk of nonstate power or central weakness brings more danger and less profit in the PRC than in Taiwan, Thailand, or the Philippines. That does not prevent changes, however.

Deng Xiaoping told people to get rich.[1] This allowance recognized the capabilities of mid-level leaders who make money. Electoral democracy in China is still very local, but candidates for village elections in rich areas such as coastal Zhejiang immediately began to use their new economic resources to establish networks and canvas for

---

[1]Deng was like a less inspiring American politician, Calvin Coolidge, who said that America's business was business. A classic U.S. critique of this phenomenon is Sinclair Lewis, *Babbit* (New York: Harcourt Brace, 1922).

votes. Their issues, even in speeches campaigning for very weak posts, likewise tended to be economic.[2]

Growth strengthens the nation, but money politics also threatens corruption. Public concepts of corruption in China during the early 1950s were tightening, but during reforms they have loosened.[3] Corruption is nonetheless the most important political problem in China today, as public opinion polls regularly report.[4] "Black money" during China's early reforms came partly from allocations of government budgets.[5] Officials could buy commodities at low state prices and then re-sell at higher market prices. The central Beijing authorities (and organizations such as the World Bank that necessarily dealt with them) were so eager to paper over their inability to control commodity prices, they advertised that two-track pricing was a brilliant idea. It was, instead, a reflection of the fact that the state still had enough power to control trade in some places but not everywhere. Leakage of low-state-priced commodities into high-priced markets meant that rent seeking became more profitable than entrepreneurship. Dual pricing was a bureaucratic arrangement to hide the *lèse-majesté* that the state could no longer plan the China market. The amounts of money that profiteers could make by shifting goods from lower- to upper-track prices was enormous.

---

[2]Credit is due to suggestions from Prof. Lang Youxing. The author also thanks his friend Prof. Zheng Yongnian for immense help in Zhejiang research. Shelley Rigger and others have found comparable situations on Taiwan.

[3]Lynn T. White, "Changing Concepts of Corruption in Communist China: Early 1950s vs. Early 1980s," in *Changes and Continuities in Chinese Communism*, Yu-ming Shaw, ed. (Boulder: Westview Press, 1988), 316–53.

[4]Corruption is difficult to define and measure exactly, but perceptions of it can be surveyed. Melanie Manion, "Democracy, Community, Trust: The Impact of Elections in Rural China," *Comparative Political Studies* 39:3 (April 2006), 304, reports convincingly that corruption "has ranked at or near the top of every public opinion poll as the most urgent problem confronting the country." Some of these polls are published. Probably the best ones are conducted on a confidential basis, with great regularity and nervousness, by departments of the Chinese Communist Party.

[5]See Sun Yan, *Corruption and Market in Contemporary China since Economic Reform* (Ithaca: Cornell University Press, 2004).

MIGRANT WORKERS AND THE POLITICAL REDEFINITION OF CITIES

New industries have created grey areas in new semi-rural town settlements that used to be green. This mix is clearly visible in all fast-growing parts of China, where town and country were once more distinguishable. Words such as "rural" or "urban" do not suffice to describe this new industrial form of "townization." (It has a name in Indonesia, *kotadesasi*, because rural industries also now add more grey to the green parts of that country too.[6]) In China, officially "rural" people are often engaged in industry. Most theories of urbanization start with the idea that cities sprawl out from existing urban centers.

In areas like Sunan and Zhejiang, however, rural industrialization — not just the outward branching of towns — has been a major pattern of urbanization.[7] Population densities and calorie-producing technologies in China's richest agricultural areas were so advanced, the paddies were, from the viewpoint of land economics, like green factories. Their replacement by grey factories is not a total change. A geographer of the lower Yangzi calls for "transactional" thinking that "relies less on the distinction between rural and urban, focusing instead on the conditions which create interactions and the circumstances within which they exist."[8] Green-grey areas often modernize faster than plain-grey ones, because entrepreneurs there could explore markets more freely. Migrants who return from cities deeply affect rural development.[9]

---

[6]This word combines the Indonesian terms for village and town, and it sometimes appears in a simpler form, *desakota*. See Gregory Guldin, *What's a Peasant to Do? Village becoming Town in Southern China* (Boulder: Westview, 2001), 14.

[7]A related interpretation is in Andrew M. Marton, *China's Spatial Economic Development: Restless Landscapes in the Lower Yangzi Delta* (New York: Routledge, 2000). See also Lynn White, "Shanghai-Suburb Relations," in *Shanghai: Revolution and Development in an Asian Metropolis*, Christopher Howe, ed., (Cambridge: Cambridge University Press, 1980), 240–68.

[8]Andrew M. Marton, *China's Spatial Economic Development*, 29.

[9]Rachel Murphy, *How Migrant Labor is Changing Rural China* (Cambridge: Cambridge University Press, 2002).

China has been the least urbanized of all countries that have a low-to-middling per capita income level.[10] This is irrespective of China's population size. The portion of "rural" workers in China's total labor force was 82 percent in 1965. By 1978, these ruralites declined to 74 percent; and by 1986, to 59 percent. A major reason for the pattern was not migration; it was the increased number of jobs and workers in industries at grey-green places that were incorporated by administrative fiat into towns and cities.

"Leaving the land but not leaving rural areas" (*li tu bu li xiang*) was a slogan. People did not act because of the slogan, but because they could get better pay in factories than in fields. By no means did all of them have to change their places of residence. A large portion of Sunan "rural" people lived in villages but worked in nearby towns, largely commuting by bicycle. This "swinging population" (*baidong renkou*) in 1985 was 28 percent of the size of the total population registered in towns.[11] During the busiest seasons for agriculture, they might not come to their industrial jobs. Were these people urban or rural? Were they farmers or workers? The most accurate answer to both questions is yes.

China's most famous social scientist Fei Xiaotong opined that, "China has neither the financial capability nor the other necessary assets to develop the urban sector quickly. The implementation of the responsibility system in the rural areas has meant the release of much surplus labor power for which the urban areas can in no way provide adequate employment opportunities or living standards. Only migration to the rural towns offers a way out of this dilemma."[12] Migrants,

---

[10]This was true at the start of the 1980s. Later the pattern changed, after urban boundaries were extended to include many rich areas that had previously been classed as rural. China then became a less extreme outlier among nations in respect of its portion of non-"urban" industry. See Chan Kam Wing, "Post-1949 Urbanization Trends and Policies: An Overview," in *Urbanizing China*, Gregory Eliyu Guldin, ed. (Westport: Greenwood Press, 1992), 59.

[11]Ma Rong, "The Development of Small Towns and their Role in the Development of China," in *Urbanizing China*, Gregory Eliyu Guldin, ed. (Westport: Greenwood Press, 1992), 135–138.

[12]Fei Xiaotong, "Foreword," in *Urbanizing China*, Gregory Eliyu Guldin, ed. (Westport: Greenwood Press, 1992), ix.

acting on their own interests and not needing instructions from planners, came both to big cities and smaller towns.

China's migrant workers are young, and many are literate. They have affected politics in PRC towns and cities.[13] The growth of tabloid newspapers printed for them has been fast, and they write letters. An aged south China postman, speaking at the end of the last century although he had been carrying letters since the Japanese era, said his load of local newspapers shot up in the late 1970s and 1980s. He made deliveries to "women working in electronics factories" and exclaimed that, "As for letters, heavens! About 800 daily. So many letters now, because of our migrant workers. Prior to 1978, we'd get about 20 to 30 per day.... this wasn't much more than before Liberation [1949].... Of today's 800 letters, fully 600 or more go to migrant laborers in the factories. Little of it is commercial mail; nearly all personal."[14] Successes of PRC primary education in Mao's time created new kinds of workers, and many went to new places seeking greater opportunities for themselves as individuals.

Data on migration and urbanization in China are assiduously collected (and massaged) by government officials, because the state is explicitly concerned that migrants might organize politically against police controls on their movement.[15] Migration during the reform boom has been massive. China's recent country-to-city shift is the largest migration in world history. A wide variety of numbers (all far over 100 million) has been proposed to estimate its size since the 1970s. Changes of city boundaries and other factors mean that any attempt to understand the published statistics as exact would be misinformed.

---

[13]Erik Johan Mobrand, *Internal Migration and Urban Conflict in Chinese and South Korean Industrialization* (Ph.D. Dissertation, Politics Department, Princeton University, 2006).

[14]Gregory Guldin, *What's a Peasant to Do?*, 118.

[15]This author in mid-2006 happened to be walking along a Beijing street in front of the Supreme People's Court, where a crowd of migrants had gathered to submit petitions for urban *hukou*. They were mad at the government for putting them through this process, and one blurted out to the insufficiently responsive foreign visitor, *"Zhongguo meiyou renquan"* ('China has no human rights!').

The boom, more than any other factor, caused this migration. People who move are supposed to register at local police stations. Many, however, do not.[16] Migrants have both conflicts and synergies with regular urban residents.[17] Citizens in Chinese cities are of several types: Household registrations (*hukou*) are held by long-term residents and legally approved permanent migrants (*qianyi*), whereas the "flowing" (*liudong*) people have temporary permits or lack any official imprimatur to be in the places where they live. During reforms, outlying settlements have been incorporated into cities and towns. Migration statistics in China are therefore hard to compare directly with migration data from other countries. Boundaries have been extended widely by bureaucratic diktat, so that some that some nominal "city people" (*shimin*) can still be found tilling fields. Most of these would rather be in factories, where work is usually better compensated and less hard, or both.

Arthur Lewis showed that capitalists enjoy windfall profits so long as they can sell in markets while the wages they pay unskilled factory workers are held down by a large labor force remaining in near-subsistence-wage farming.[18] John Harris and Michall Todaro took up the spatial aspect of Lewis's insight to construct a model of country-to-city (or at least field-to-factory) migration.[19] These theories apply to development in general, but they best describe particularly fast processes during booms of capital accumulation.

To simplify their presentations, these economists distinguished just two sectors (capitalist and subsistence-agrarian for Lewis, urban

---

[16]See Gregory Guldin, *What's a Peasant to Do?*, 239, for confirmation in another part of China.

[17]Solinger, Dorothy J., *Contesting Citizenship in Urban China: Peasant Migrants, the State, and the Logic of the Market* (Berkeley: University of California Press, 1999).

[18]W. Arthur Lewis, "Economic Development with Unlimited Supplies of Labour," *The Manchester School of Economic and Social Studies* (1954), 139–91.

[19]John Harris and Michall Todaro, "Migration, Unemployment, and Development: A Two-Sector Analysis," *American Economic Review* 60:1 (March 1970), 126–42.

and rural for Harris and Todaro).[20] Most households on the Yangzi Delta, by the mid-1980s, were engaged in both farming and industry. A survey of four villages of Wujiang County, southern Jiangsu, put the percentages of "both worker and peasant" (*yigong yinong*) households between 44 and 70 percent, depending on the local level of industrialization. Many ex-farmers came into towns daily for work, whether or not they were formally registered there. In a large 1984 survey of Sunan towns, more than half (52 percent) of the daytime population were "worker-peasants."[21] Most people actually in towns, by day at least, were not legally registered there. In county seats, which are larger, one-fifth of the daytime population was "worker-peasant."

By the middle 1990s, many in earlier waves of migrants had settled down in urban places. The part of the population laboring at some distance from their supposedly agricultural homes was at least one-quarter of China's work force then (up from one-tenth in 1980 and one-fifth in 1990). This included slightly less than two-fifths of all male workers, and one-sixth of woman workers.[22] The boom made young migrants by far the most dynamic force among China's workers. It made them a sizeable plurality of all Chinese laborers, and a majority in some of the fastest-growing local economies.

A tradition of Chinese bureaucrats, dating from imperial times, has been to dub locations with stately ranks. They can raise the official

---

[20]Distortions of reality created by Harris and Todaro, or especially by Lewis, because of their just-two-sector simplifications are less egregious than those forced by recent political scientists, notably Adam Przeworski, Michael E. Alvarez, José Antonio Cheibub, and Fernando Limongi, *Democracy and Development: Political Institutions and Well-Being in the World, 1950–1990* (Cambridge: Cambridge University Press, 2000). Before crunching their numbers, these analysts presume every state is either a democracy or a dictatorship. No mixed or transitional cases are allowed to confuse the analysts' logic.

[21]Yok-shiu F. Lee, "Rural Transformation and Decentralized Urban Growth in China," in *Urbanizing China*, Gregory Eliyu Guldin, ed. (Westport: Greenwood Press, 1992), 97–98 and 100.

[22]These are rough estimates, based on work by William Parish, Zhexiao Ye, and Li Fang, reported in Gregory Guldin, *What's a Peasant to Do?*, 169.

titles of jurisdictions in hopes of monitoring them better. During the reform period, rich counties were often reclassified as "county-level cities" (*xianji shi*).[23] When this happened, the promoted unit acquired more powers to collect revenues, negotiate for outside investors, demand better transport links, and deal directly with provincial rather than just prefectural cadres. The townships (*xiang*) of a county-level city were eligible for presumptuous elevation to the higher status of "designated town" (*jianzhi zhen*). At the individual level, not all citizens of a county-level city became official urbanites immediately, but more of them had rights to press for this status if they wanted it.

Some places, even extensive ones, nonetheless turned down such honors. The leaders of Longjiang, near Wenzhou, Zhejiang, were offered in the early 1990s a higher rank for their whole county. They politely declined (reportedly with winks of understanding from some officers in the provincial capital, Hangzhou) because they knew that a higher status would have meant more bureaucrats, including tax collectors, looking over their shoulders. Longjiang became a large and very prosperous settlement, and it organized normal educational, medical, welfare, and fire prevention services without its official status being raised.[24] This case was exceptional but revealing — and radically untraditional in the Chinese polity.

County and lower cadres, to the extent that local socialism survived when rural enterprises prospered, were supposed to have powers that they could try to protect. They could decree that specific firms should buy or sell to specific other companies, especially those within the same area.[25] These petty autarkies or "palace economies" were in many cases temporary; they gave the remaining planners in local governments access to political rents, which sporadically decreased during

---

[23]This happened to Kunshan in July 1989. Andrew M. Marton, *China's Spatial Economic Development*, 98.

[24]Interview in February 2007, with a Chinese academic who had done fieldwork in Longjiang.

[25]Andrew M. Marton, *China's Spatial Economic Development*, 117, based on interviews in Kunshan; see also 171.

reforms. By 1997, local enterprises in Kunshan, Jiangsu, got only 15 percent of their inputs locally, while 28 percent of their materials came from nearby Shanghai, 19 percent from the rest of Sunan, fully 31 percent from the rest of China, and the remaining 7 percent from foreign countries. This diversification shows how the free market eroded the power of local economic cadres. It did so more quickly than it eroded their ideologies, however. As Erik Mobrand writes, "industrialization, in an early stage, limits what the state can do."[26]

Government institutions are slow to adapt, and official intentions affect nonstate ones. For example, non-agricultural registration (*feinongye hukou*) is still generally coveted by rural Chinese. Their urban brethren have access to better pay and unionized jobs in state enterprises that sometimes still come with housing, medical plans, pensions, and similar benefits. So cadres established illegal markets in which they "sold" non-agricultural registrations. Police were paid bribes to issue proper papers. Buyers of these documents might then approach urban schools, hospitals, and jobbers in cities.

The decline of the state sector, together with bureaucratic ukases that extended town and city boundaries, creating a glut of new "urban" people, has somewhat altered this situation. Agricultural registrations may imply lease rights to land, originally for tilling but now with less exactly planned purposes. Non-agriculturalists are supposed to need just one kind of real estate: their apartments. Because land in fact has many uses and rural land is less monitored, the early pressure to switch from agricultural to non-agricultural status (*nong zhuan fei*) was in some places reversed.[27] The state's sectoral and spatial categories became less constraining, when people could move more easily among them.

"COMMUNIST" CAPITALISTS: DIFFERENCES BETWEEN SUNAN AND WENZHOU

Among private entrepreneurs in the Party after the turn of the millennium, a mere 6 percent nationwide joined after founding their own

---

[26]Erik Mobrand, *Internal Migration and Urban Conflict*, 192.
[27]Quoted in Gregory Guldin, *What's a Peasant to Do?*, 139–42.

businesses.[28] The other 94 percent of "private" entrepreneurs had been in the CCP earlier. In south Zhejiang, this was less true than in Sunan or nationwide, and the data obscure the extent to which the Party coopted managers of still-"socialist" small firms before they were privatized. Most of these communist capitalists had expropriated, as their own property, the state or collective firms they had earlier managed as independent cadres.

Entrepreneurs in the Party use official networks in their business. Still, according to one, "there is not a real connection between the Party and small and medium enterprises."[29] Sunan elites' secrecy about the privatization process contrasts with the relative transparency of this change in southern Zhejiang.[30] Founders of Wenzhou SMEs, whether in the Party or not when they took the risks of establishing their firms, were not just influenced by the local Party, because they could influence it. The situation in Sunan has involved smaller groups of controlling cadres, despite variation among leaderships within that large area,[31] because Sunan has attracted government attention for decades and centuries on account of its rich tax base.

When a manager heads any company that grows to be very large or hires many workers, the local Party generally co-opts that firm's leader. This happens no matter whether the manager actually founded the firm or acquired control of it through leasing that moved into ownership, or taking loans to buy it. State banks were legally not supposed to loan money for equity purchases, but flows of funds especially in rural China (and in southern Zhejiang more usually than in

---

[28]Pei Minxin, *China's Trapped Transition: The Limits of Developmental Autocracy* (Cambridge: Harvard University Press, 2006), 93.

[29]Interview with a very successful Zhejiang entrepreneur in June 2006.

[30]Zhang Jianjun, "State Power, Elite Relations, and the Politics of Privatization in China's Rural Industry: Different Approaches in Two Regions [Wuxi and Wenzhou]," *Asian Survey* 48:2 (March-April 2008), 215–38.

[31]Variant local leaders' responses to policy incentives (in a rich vegetable, a rich grain, and a poor Sunan brigade) are described by David Zweig, "Peasants, Ideology, and New Incentive Systems: Jiangsu Province, 1978–81," in *Chinese Rural Development: The Great Transformation*, William L. Parish, ed. (Armonk: M.E. Sharpe, 1985), 141–63.

Sunan) are very hard to track. Cadres often had trouble locating collateral with which to guarantee repayment of the loans by which they acquired public property they had previously managed.[32] Many found ways to solve this problem and steal from the public, however.

Business cadres with Party membership were in good positions to expropriate public property if they wished. The means by which they heisted state or collective property to their individual ownership, when they do so, were various. Such procedures were more complex and more difficult to pull off in Sunan than in southern Zhejiang, for example, where more of the now-private firms were really built by their current owners. Even there, however, as late as 2006 only a minority of entrepreneurs who were selected into the Party, or who wished to join it, had actually founded their firms.

Especially in Sunan, there are downsides as well as business advantages for an entrepreneur who is a Party member. As one of them said, such a manager must "carry out the responsibilities of being in the Party." Membership could aid possibilities for expansion, but it also could increase costs. Many cadres and successful businessmen in prosperous areas treat themselves to fancy banquets or to Mercedes cars and drivers. Others are more ascetic, eating rice in their offices and pedaling bikes. Their personalities and the norms of their communities, not just the extent of their new wealth, determines what they do. As Guldin reports, "Many cadres still have not yet lost their revolutionary élan, particularly some of the older ones who still believe in the Party's mission to uphold the laboring classes and defend the Chinese nation."[33] The boom, however, temporarily reduced the portion of honest officials.

Studies of China's business politics have sometimes explicitly excluded the managers of collective township and village enterprises, although these SMEs are crucial to China's boom.[34] The bosses of

---

[32]Interview with a Hong Kong investment banker who had extensive experience in both Sunan and Zhejiang, July 2007.

[33]Gregory Guldin, *What's a Peasant to Do?*, 99.

[34]For example, SME managers running Taiwan- or Hong Kong-invested firms in China have been omitted from some studies on the report that "their status is not high." See Margaret M. Pearson, *China's New Business Elite: The Political Consequences of Economic Reform* (Berkeley: University of California Press, 1997), 9 and 13.

SMEs now have great amounts of money to raise their status. One way to do this is to pay local rather than central taxes. Local governments naturally want to foster firms whose revenues stay in the locality. Administrations in places where agriculture and industry have conflicted, for example over land issues, usually tend to prefer the higher tax base generated by industry. Local cadres, when they decide on zoning in suburban Jiangsu places, favor factories over paddies.[35] The central government in Beijing often stresses the need to keep up rice production instead. Local authorities' desires for more industrial revenues can usually trump agricultural interests, where part-time tillers get much of their incomes from factory work anyway.

In Mao's time, e.g., 1965, reported taxes and government profits from China's state-owned companies were fully 30 percent of those firms' gross output value. This was the state's main source of money. By 1979, the state's extraction from its own industries had gone down to 25 percent of output — then down further to 19 percent in 1985, 15 percent in 1989, and 12 percent by 1990. The boom shrank the state's main previous tax base. All state revenues as a percentage of total national income in 1979 were 33 percent; but by 1990, just 18 percent. In effect, many state-owned enterprises (SOEs) were taxing the central government rather than vice-versa. Government subsidies to state-owned firms were about 32 billion yuan in 1986, and they rose to 50 billion yuan by 1989.[36]

Rural industries increased the relative wealth of local power networks, especially as compared to the wherewithal of the central government. Rural SMEs thus had funds to reduce unemployment and expand the number of their clients by offering jobs. By 1991, rural and private firms employed more than 92 million ex-peasants, and

---

[35]Gregory Veeck, "Suburban Weigang, Jiangsu: A Transformed Village," in *Chinese Landscapes: The Village as Place*, Ronald G. Knapp, ed. (Honolulu: University of Hawaii Press, 1992), 211–20.

[36]The government subvention of SOEs is measured in nominal yuan; the amount of 1989 subsidy in 1986 yuan was 40 billion. Foreign borrowing is included in "all state revenues" and was about 1 or 2 percent in each of these years. See Lu Ding, *Entrepreneurship in Suppressed Markets: Private-Sector Experience in China* (New York: Garland, 1994), 150–55.

this number soared in later years.[37] The state sector by 1991 hired only 18 percent of all workers.[38]

By 1992, at least 40 percent of China's industrial output came from rural plants. The government-managed share of all Chinese output value, counting agriculture and services along with industry, was by 1992 no more than one-quarter — and it continued to drop in the mid-1990s.[39] Profits from state-owned firms sank as a source of revenue for all sizes of jurisdiction, not just the central government.

State taxes (*guoshui*) are mostly imposts on value added. Local taxes (*dishui*) of counties, townships, and towns are quite different: these imposts are based on the profits of local enterprises. The 1994 fiscal reform separated state from local taxes. Value added tends to be fairly stable so long as an enterprise exists and employs workers. But local profits vary. They have generally decreased as market competition has risen. So local governments received, in taxes, a lower portion of local product than they did before the mid-1990s, while the central government got more.[40] Beijing's mid-1990s effort to recentralize revenue collection, after the central extraction from GDP went as low as 3 percent, meant that local governments especially in poor areas ran out of money. This exacerbated regional inequalities, because quickly industrializing rich areas could get funds from

---

[37] *RMRB*, February 19, 1991. These firms came in many forms (collective, private or individual, and joint), as defined later.

[38] *Zhongguo tongji nianjian, 1993* (China Statistical Yearbook, 1993), ed. State Statistical Bureau (Beijing: Zhongguo Tongji Chuban She, 1993), 26, which also reports that by 1992 private sector production had risen to 7%, as compared with 6% in 1990 and 2% in 1985.

[39] The 40% figure, above, may be an underestimate omitting some factories licensed by villages (*cun*) as distinct from townships or towns (*xiang* or *zhen*). But see *Economist*, "When China Wakes," November 28, 1992, 4.

[40] Based on Choi Eun-Kyong, *Building the Tax State in China: Center and Region in the Politics of Welfare Extraction, 1994–2003* (Ph.D. dissertation, Politics Department, Princeton University, 2006), and Zhong Yang, "Dissecting Chinese County Governmental Authorities," Zhejiang University Conference on "The Development of the Non-State Sector, Local Governance, and Sustainable Development in China," June 24–25, 2006, vol. 1, 509–10.

various fees that the center could not fully monitor, whereas poor regions could not.[41]

Yet Beijing's mid-1990s effort to direct more taxes into central coffers was far from a complete success. Eun-Kyong Choi has shown that Jiangsu and Zhejiang were far below the national average in their reported effectiveness collecting the most important industrial tax, the value-added tax, at least in 1997. These rich provinces collected that tax on only 43 and 42 percent, respectively, of the apparent base to which it should legally have been applied. In China as a whole, the VAT revenue was on average higher, at 54 percent.[42]

Local cadres generally prefer that tax revenues stay in localities rather than go to central coffers. Entrepreneurs and local officials in Sunan and Zhejiang evaded central taxes even when impost rates were low. Politicians' status with Party personnel departments continued partly to depend on the delivery of revenues upward. Levies on jurisdictions were partly regularized in contracts, a tax-farming model that was barely modernized until the mid-1990s reform. Cadres before that time could raise their status by agreeing to extra-contractual "contributions" (*gongxian kuan*).

In some areas, high-tax jurisdictions bordered much lower-tax places. In 1991, for example, the gross product of Jiading, in Shanghai, was virtually the same as that of Kunshan, in Jiangsu just across the province border. But Jiading's tax revenues in 1991 were four times

---

[41]Christine Wong, "Can the Retreat from Equality be Reversed? An Assessment of Redistributive Fiscal Policies from Deng Xiaoping to Wen Jiabao," in *Paying for Progress: Public Finance, Human Welfare, and Inequality in China*, Vivienne Shue and Christine Wong, eds. (Abingdon: Routledge, 2006), chap. 1.

[42]In 2000 and 2002, the reported figures suggest a movement in these provinces towards the national average. For fine detail, see Choi Eun-Kyong, *Building the Tax State*, chap. 4. Tycoon-run governments (such as Taiwan or Thailand, or city states like Hong Kong) are often low-tax regimes, so that maximal money goes into capital. See Lynn White, "Future Fortunes vs. Present People in China's Richest Cities," in *Social Policy Reform in Hong Kong and Shanghai: A Tale of Two Cities*, in Linda Wong, Lynn White, and Gui Shixun, eds. (Armonk: M.E. Sharpe, 2004), 239–56.

higher than Kunshan's.[43] So the tax system was not uniform, nor was its enforcement. This was not changed until the mid-1990s, when the 1994 tax reform somewhat improved central monitoring of localities.

Eun-Kyong Choi has also found that China's local governments refund, through their finance bureaus, high portions of the revenue that their tax bureaus collect. Localities compete to attract capital by offering such rebates. The amounts are large, estimated at 20 to 30 percent of all local government collections on average. Choi reports that local tax bureaus also refrain from auditing the firms from which they collect revenues. Their cadres even coach local enterprises on ways to avoid tax audits by national revenue officials.[44] This is the "local state" in action.

Restructuring revenues in the mid-1990s was necessary for Beijing to finance itself, and the resulting system was less uneven than in early reforms. It was less based on *ad hoc* commitments by local cadres to remit agreed amounts to higher administrative coffers in exchange for their own promotions.[45] In general, relations between top cadres, local cadres, and ordinary citizens in China have become less hierarchic during reforms. Specific situations and personalities still shape these links, but officials are generally less fearsome than heretofore. In a rural southern place, a woman reported that some cadres in the past could get away with harassing citizens and simply taking property: "We worried most about *choudou* [being selected for criticism], but now, when the Party secretary visits, we realize he's giving us face and invite him in to drink tea. It's all very polite."[46] In particular, employment is no longer a function of the local state for most people.

The ancient motto, "officials supervise and merchants manage," was challenged by Jiang Zemin's "theory of three represents"

[43]Susan H. Whiting, *Power and Wealth in Rural China: The Political Economy of Institutional Change* (New York: Cambridge University Press, 2001), 94–95.

[44]Choi Eun-Kyong, *Building the Tax State*, 140 and 147.

[45]See Lynn White, *Shanghai Shanghaied? Uneven Taxes in Reform China* (Hong Kong: University of Hong Kong Centre of Asian Studies, 1989).

[46]Gregory Guldin, *What's a Peasant to Do?*, 96.

(*sange daibiao*). Jiang said that the governing communist party should include "advanced productive forces," most of whom are *de facto* capitalists. Officials had become merchants (and merchants had become officials in smaller numbers) long before this rather stilted formulation of their ideal relationship was put forward by the leader of the ex-proletarian dictatorship. On July 1, 2001, when Jiang Zemin made his "Three Represents" speech, CCP personnel departments did not need sharply to change their admission policies. Among all entrepreneurs in the Party for several years after that, less than half of 1 percent had been admitted after the date of Jiang's speech.[47]

Already in 1988, Zhejiang province and many local jurisdictions issued explicit rules allowing cadres to retain their official posts while simultaneously engaging in business. As Willy Kraus notes, "A large number of the private businessmen in Wenzhou are former cadres who remain members of the Communist Party of China." They were not brought into the CCP as private entrepreneurs; they were in it already. Economically, private entrepreneurs did very well for themselves during reforms, whether they were in the Party or not:

> The average annual income of private businessmen [in the mid-1980s] runs to about 30,000–50,000 yuan, with 150,000 yuan at the very top end of the scale. The income of workers is generally about 1,500 yuan, the highest wage of 6,000 yuan being paid to technological specialists. The general ratio of businessman-worker income amounts to 22:1, in a few cases 50:1. The average income of peasants had already reached 500 yuan by the mid-1980s....[48]

Chinese government officials can simultaneously hold commercial jobs, and they usually earn much more from their private moonlighting than from their complementary, prestigious state posts. As Pei writes, "In Nanjing a deputy mayor held the chairmanship of the board of a local industrial park; a district party chief occupied the chairmanship of a real estate development firm; and the head of

---

[47]Pei Minxin, *China's Trapped Transition*, 93.
[48]Willy Kraus, *Private Business in China: Revival between Ideology and Pragmatism*, trans. Erich Holz (Honolulu: University of Hawaii Press, 1991), 101, also 136.

the city's urban development bureau was the chairman of a local real estate investment firm."[49] By 2000 in a rural Shanghai county, 36 of 52 CCP branches had Party first secretaries who were business people.[50]

THE ROLE OF SHARE SALES IN PRIVATIZING PUBLIC PROPERTY

Reforms require resources. A traditional way for companies to raise capital is to sell shares. This happened without much regulation among private firms, and as early as 1984 Shanghai municipality also legitimated such sales for collectives. State firms soon joined this "pioneering activity" of share sales (which was actually pioneering only in contrast to the practices of Mao's time). By 1987, Shanghai firms together had raised a billion yuan from selling equity.[51] State-owned factories and stores needed capital, and therefore a restructuring of ownership, to buy new equipment and to pay for inputs whose prices rural industries had bid up. The stock market was a means for SOEs and collectives to raise capital for survival.

The cadres who ran firms were naturally in charge of reforming them. The terms of such change — the share prices of initial public offerings, qualifications of buyers, dividend amounts, and portions of a state or collective firm that could be sold — were issues that current cadres had the most information to manage and the most opportunity to abuse. Officials and their relatives could thus often lay ownership or quasi-ownership claims, either *de facto* or *de jure*, to former state property.

This was not always easy to arrange, however. Sometimes it involved placing the property in joint enterprises with foreign or

---

[49]Pei Minxin, *China's Trapped Transition: The Limits of Developmental Autocracy* (Cambridge: Harvard University Press, 2006), 154.

[50]Bruce Gilley, "The Yu Zuomin Phenomenon: Entrepreneurs and Politics in Rural China," in *The New Entrepreneurs of Europe and Asia: Patterns of Business Development in Russia, Eastern Europe, and China*, Victoria E. Bonnell and Thomas B. Gold, eds. (Armonk: Sharpe, 2002), 74.

[51]Willy Kraus, *Private Business in China*, 123–24.

Overseas Chinese partners.[52] Sometimes it meant leasing companies at very low rates. Sometimes it involved cooking accounts so that firms could be sold at low prices. Sometimes it required loans from distant jurisdictions where suits against borrowing would be unsuccessful. Sometimes companies were split so that managers acquired the profitable lines of trade, leaving low- or negative-return departments in the state or collective sectors. Such practices were illegal, but local leaders often gladly and greedily consented to them. A survey shows that half of all privatized firms in China became owned by the same bosses who had previously run them as cadres of state or collective companies.[53]

Cadres' degrees of freedom varied locally and among large regions. A study of corruption in China shows that many areas showed a "top-down" pattern, in which high state officials were the initiators of illegal transactions and embezzlements. In other places, including much of East China,[54] a "bottom-up" model applied, because private business interests were the most usual instigators and beneficiaries of corruption, according to a survey of legal cases that had been filed.[55]

Cadres in government administrative offices benefitted from the unexpected exuberance of local markets during the boom. So non-economic officials generally condoned what the professional business cadres did. The new private economy nonetheless placed strains on the budgets of state offices. Government workers increasingly expected higher bonuses. If their local colleagues did not allow the corruptions that greased the market to create new wealth, their

---

[52]Ding Xueliang, "Informal Privatization through Internationalization: The Rise of Nomenklatura in China's Offshore Businesses," *British Journal of Political Science* 30:1 (January 2000), 121–46.

[53]Pei Minxin, *China's Trapped Transition*, 94.

[54]Guangdong during the 1990s was also such a region. Leaders in counties such as Shunde took local initiatives to violate regulations. Central norms were so vague that, in practice, local notables could sell public assets to themselves. Linda Chelan Li, "Prelude to Government Reform in China? The 'Big Sale' in Shunde," *China Information* 18:1 (2004), 29–65.

[55]Sun Yan, *The Transition to the Market and Post-Communist Corruption*, 178.

incomes rose less fast than inflation. Most stayed at their official posts and supported local development, legal or illegal. Some "jumped into the sea" (*xiahai*) of the private economy, either moonlighting or on a full-time basis. The socialist cadres had been as bossy as they later remained. After the privatizations, their links with remaining officials remained largely unchanged. When state-owned enterprises were reformed, the aim of restructuring was purposely confused with the aim of strengthening local government leaders.[56] As Kraus writes, "Cadres have founded production and service firms, using public funds as capital, but often pocketed the ensuing profits themselves."[57]

AGENCIES ARMED FOR PROFITS

Local officials and others thus built "dukedom economies" (*zhuhou jingji*).[58] Local "mafia states," some of which used violence although others made profits in legal operations too, became prominent in many parts of China.[59] Connections of the army and police with businesses were natural in such situations. High levels of the government launched sporadic campaigns against "five don'ts": official agency profits, bribes, drunkenness, gambling, and prostitution. But all five documentably rose during reforms.

Nightclubs and *karaoke* bars catered not just to rich foreign, Taiwanese, and Overseas Chinese businessmen, but very extensively also to mid-level PRC cadres, military or police officers, and "princeling" sons of government and Party officials, including local ones. Especially when discos offered hostesses and discreet bedrooms, the prices were

---

[56]Anthony B.L. Cheung, "Bureaucrats-Enterprise Negotiation in China's Enterprise Reform at the Local Level: Case Studies in Guangzhou," *Journal of Contemporary China* 14:45 (November 2006), 695–720.

[57]Willy Kraus, *Private Business in China*, 129, also citing Barbara Krug, "Korruption in der Volksrepublik China: Ein neues problem?" *Neue Zürcher Zeitung*, May 28, 1988.

[58]The author was first told in detail about "dukedom economies" by his friend Zhong Yang of the University of Tennessee.

[59]Pei Minxin, *China's Trapped Transition*, 161–63.

reportedly high: US$1,000 just for the cover charge at some establishments. The journalist providing the most detailed report on brothels writes that would-be patrons sometimes had to know passwords before they were admitted.[60] As one report had it, "If the PLA is a partner in your brothel, or the PSB [Public Security Bureau] shares the girls from your karaoke bar, who's going to crack down on you?"[61]

The People's Liberation Army, with professional cooperation from Hong Kong's Sun Yee On (*Xin yi an*) Triad, which provided effective unofficial operatives, in 1994 reportedly ran the "Top 10" club and other bars in an area north of central Nanjing Road, Shanghai. This partnership was also said to manage discos ("Casablanca" and "Galaxy") near the intersection of Yan'an and Zhongshan roads.

Particular coercive organizations dominated particular districts. It is possible to draw a map of Shanghai indicating regions of influence by the PSB, the PLA, and various overseas mafias.[62] Taiwan's Bamboo Gang, perhaps because of favoritism to an island of official interest, seems to have needed no PRC institutional partner in its karaoke and massage enterprises along Siping Road.[63] The manager of the "Dedo Club" on Nanjing Road claimed that he did not arrange assignations for men who came to his disco — but he also did not restrain independent female entrepreneurs who might come: "Well, doing P.R. work for herself is okay, but she should not overly harass my customers. Public Security wants this to look like a cultural place,

---

[60]Angelina Malhotra, "Shanghai's Dark Side: Army and Police Officers are Once Again in League with Vice," *Asia, Inc.* 3:2 (February 1994), 32–39; see also the comment from the Thai editor, Sondhi Limthongkul, 4. The author's discussions in Shanghai during the early 1990s suggested the existence of vice rings involving not just family members of high officials, but reportedly also the high officials themselves. He does not know which reports were true, but their frequency was a fact. The following paragraphs, however, rely mainly on the Hong Kong Indian journalist Malhotra, and they repeat some information from Lynn White, *Unstately Power: Local Causes of China's Intellectual, Legal, and Governmental Reforms* (Armonk, NY: M.E. Sharpe, 1999).
[61]Angelina Malhotra, "Shanghai's Dark Side," 35.
[62]The Malhotra article supplies such a map.
[63]The most important was "a blue glass, neon-crowned tower called Shanghai Taiwan City." *Ibid.*, 32.

not a red-light zone." He felt official sponsorship was essential: "You need a good partner to run a club in China, and Public Security is a good partner."[64] This was just as true of less dubious industries in less urban locations, where only the reporting of it was not so detailed.

Gambling can become a psychological addiction, and thus a nearly bottomless source of funds to those who can control it. The mid-1980s saw local approvals of some legal public lotteries. But the government offices that administered lotteries also ran "illegal betting games on the side, from which Party functionaries and state officials — through dummies, of course — often took their cut."[65] An official campaign against gambling dens in Nanshi District, Shanghai, in early 1989 netted a large number of poker house owners, who were sentenced to several years of prison each — not because they had run the dens (which were illegal) but reportedly because they had cheated at cards.[66]

A likely major issue in forthcoming CCP internal politics is the extent to which local Chinese jurisdictions should or should not be allowed to use gambling addictions, including those for lotteries, to raise revenues. Smuggling, similarly, is easy for officials who run customs bureaus, although unofficial agents also engage in it. Taiwan and mainland fishing boats, including those from southern Zhejiang, have engaged in boat-to-boat trade for many decades.[67] These exchanges

---

[64]This manager, whose club was jointly owned by the PSB and by "an anonymous Japanese group" that may have been like the underworld *yakuza* that made similar investments near Huaihai Road, had previously managed a nightclub at a hotel run by the Army. See *ibid.*, 35–36.

[65]One reason for high-level CCP sponsorship of Macau's special status as a center for gambling (under Chief Executive Edmund Ho, as well as Stanley Ho and now also U.S. tycoons Wynn and Adelman) may be a hope that gambling can be thus limited in other parts of China. This expectation would show lack of research into the gambling habit as a psychological addiction. On related issues, see Willy Kraus, *Private Business in China*, 128.

[66]One of the card sharks had cheated to make 2,200 yuan in fifteen rounds of poker, which at that time was a notable sum. *Shanghai fazhi bao* (Shanghai Legal News), January 30, 1989.

[67]Author's interview in Nankang, Taiwan, with the son of a Taiwan fisherman who made such trades very frequently from the 1950s to the 1970s, regularly meeting in the Strait trawlers that came from Fujian and Zhejiang.

were illegal according to both the PRC and ROC governments. That did not prevent them.

Petty tyrannies are now more common in local than national jurisdictions. Yu Zuomin of Daqiuzhuang village, in a rural part of Tianjin in north China, became a widely known entrepreneur-politician. He started community enterprises in steel-rolling and printing that earned big profits. From the 1970s to 1993, he fully controlled his locality, and he was reputed to have made Daqiuzhuang "the richest village in China." Party conservatives rightly saw that the "Yu Zuomin phenomenon," if it spread across the country, would mean the end of centralized government. Actually, many parts of China (including East China) had local despotisms of this kind; but Yu's had become famous. A 1993 murder of a Daqiuzhuang villager, in which Yu may well have been complicit, brought a paramilitary siege of the area by police. Yu was arrested and given a 20-year prison sentence. He died as a jailed convict in 1999, probably of suicide.[68]

Yu Zuomin was by no means the only former commune official to become famous nationally as a local quasi-capitalist dictator, bringing wealth to his clients but taking the "local state" idea much too far from Beijing's viewpoint. Chen Yiner, party secretary of Qiuer village in Zhejiang during the 1980s and early 1990s, expanded his Yinfa Group of metals factories very profitably. Chen was a delegate to the 1992 CCP Central Committee, and he "built a resort in the United States where he sent political allies on vacations in return for their support."[69] He also paid cadres with his companies' stock when they supported his businesses. This mix of politics and profits violated laws. So Chen fled to the U.S. and then to the Philippines, before being extradited back to China for a six-year sentence on bribery charges.

---

[68]Bruce Gilley, *Model Rebels: The Rise and Fall of China's Richest Village* (Berkeley: University of California Press, 2001).

[69]Bruce Gilley, "The Yu Zuomin Phenomenon: Entrepreneurs and Politics in Rural China," in *The New Entrepreneurs of Europe and Asia: Patterns of Business Development in Russia, Eastern Europe, and China*, Victoria E. Bonnell and Thomas B. Gold, eds. (Armonk: Sharpe, 2002), 77.

Other such cases abounded in many parts of China. Pei Anjun enriched Qiancun village, Shanxi, but he ran afoul of laws on grain taxes and land titles. So in 1996, the provincial government purged him and most members of his local Party committee. These famous anecdotal cases obscure that the phenomenon of local economic magnates was very common in many parts of China. Some such leaders became famous only after the egregiousness of their gangsterism and legal violations forced central authorities to arrest them (and sometimes, but not always, other Party cadres who were their local associates). If all such cases had been prosecuted when by law they should have been, the Party would have lost many regional leaders. So wise chiefs built their small empires without attracting too much attention.

Coercion in PRC localities has been more frequent than reporters or scholars have details to document. By no means are all examples of illegal coercion known to central or provincial authorities, although high officials finance secret surveys that give them better data on such problems than they dare publicize. Even the Falungong organization, which China's Party-state has politicized to a greater extent than those adamant Buddhists admit, underestimates the number of death sentences and extrajudicial executions carried out by local Chinese police.[70] Beijing has regulations against beating prisoners to death, but these are sometimes ignored. It has regulations against bribing judges or police, e.g., by families of prisoners to prevent such beatings. A reason for the effectiveness of such bribes is that killing a prisoner prevents further blackmail of the same kind from the same family later. The boom has supplied more money for all these processes. Statists and intellectuals in China want to change such patterns, but they shy away from the separations of power that have tended to solve similar problems in the histories of other countries.

Laws are not enforced where local CCP organization departments appoint all local officials, not just police and prosecutors and judges but also nonstate officials such as journalists who might investigate or protest illegal acts. There are, in theory, no local independent powers

---

[70]This comparison of estimates is based on an interview in China with an officially safe but highly knowledgeable source.

in China. This is a centralist ideal, rather than a practice. The state tries to follow it, but many bosses do not.

Flaws in the Leninist system parallel the corruptions that flow from bought elections (and bought bureaucrats) in many democracies. They will persist until separate functional legitimacies may be normalized for PRC coercive agencies and defense lawyers, lawmakers in bodies that are small enough for serious deliberation, and especially local NGOs and journalists. Until the Chinese state becomes strong enough to make these kinds of local leaders safe from violence, China will have a repressed polity that seems harmonious only to inattentive observers.

The transformation of Party apparatchiks into CCP entrepreneurs has created many problems, but this change has defenders too. Some PRC scholars have dubbed this a new "politics of capable people" (*nengren zhengzhi*). Such leaders are variously called "experts in getting rich" (*zhifu nengshou*), "locomotives" (*huochetou*), or "people who take the lead" (*daitou ren*).[71] They are practically never ideological democrats. In their work style, they are often petty tyrants — although they can be delegitimated if their community projects fail. Their rise, when their principled ruthlessness is matched with famous wealth, provides examples of leadership that delay the development of liberal forbearance in China.[72] When they extract enough from their underlings to support their local rule and pay off official agencies that might try to monitor them, they can remain princes in their small realms for long periods.[73]

---

[71]Bruce Gilley, "The Yu Zuomin Phenomenon," 74.

[72]See Mary E. Gallagher, "Reform and Openness: Why Chinese Economic Reforms Have Delayed Democracy," *World Politics* 54 (April 2002), 338–72.

[73]A beautiful sketch of this kind of "*kapitan*" leader, who prospers by extracting more than the sum that both his local and larger constituencies require to maintain his hinge position, is by the major China-and-Southeast Asia anthropologist G. William Skinner, "Overseas Chinese Leadership: Paradigm for a Paradox," published far too obscurely in Gehan Wijeyewardene, ed., *Leadership and Authority: A Symposium* (Singapore: University of Malaya Press, 1968), 191–203. The same logic, with emphasis on the risks borne by such leaders, is used by his student Helen F. Siu, *Agents and Victims in South China: Accomplices in Rural Revolution* (New Haven: Yale University Press, 1989). For more on hinge leaders, see also Grant Evans, *Lao Peasants Under Socialism* (New Haven: Yale University Pres, 1990). Anthropologists have probed local politics better than many political scientists have done.

BRIBES AND "FACE TAXES"

If China's economic growth in the 1990s neared double digits, the growth of corruption cases was even faster. Either because of more courts or because of more corruption (probably both), the number of corruption cases spurted 12 percent annually, compounded, between 1993 and 1999.[74] A 2002 survey of over 3,500 bankers, managers, farmers, and private entrepreneurs in 29 Chinese cities asked them whether "financial institutions use their power of credit/capital allocation to engage in corrupt transactions." No less than 82 percent of the respondents replied that this practice happened "quite often" or was "prevalent." Firms often pay an extra 5 percent of any loan before receiving it, and another 4 percent to "maintain relations with the bank." Respondents estimated that bank managers raised their own total compensation by about half, and loan officers by a third, because of such practices.[75]

The Transparency International "Bribe Payers Index" is based on surveys of economic "experts" in 15 emerging market countries. They were asked the following question: "In the business sectors with which you are most familiar, please indicate how likely companies from the following [mostly developed] countries are to pay or to offer bribes to win or retain business in this country." Major international bribe payers, such as France, the U.S., and Japan, scored almost halfway down the 10-to-1 (best-to-worst) scale, at 5.5, 5.3, and 5.3 respectively. Taiwan companies were more prone to pay bribes, with a score of 3.8 — and PRC companies yet more so, at 3.5.

The main conclusion from this survey, however, was that domestic companies within these emerging economies far more frequently offered corrupt side-payments. Only their overall score for all 15 countries was reported, at a truly dismal 1.9.[76] Domestic bribery is far more common than international bribery.

---

[74]Pei Minxin, *China's Trapped Transition*, 133.

[75]*Ibid.*, 119–20. The survey also suggests that corruption rates were somewhat lower in East China than in the North or other parts of the country.

[76]Transparency International's website http://www.transparency.org/policy_research/surveys_indices/bpi, seen November 1, 2006.

Local leaders also condoned many other kinds of economic cheating, most of which were not monetized. In the tumult of China's transition to markets, such skirting of norms took numerous forms. In some places, workers and officials could go absent without leave from their state jobs, even if they did not formally resign. They retained their bureaucratic titles and (small) salaries but spent most of their time on private work instead. In the Wenzhou area, some state cadres simply left their offices without formally leaving their posts in order to raise their incomes. Others, who helped local entrepreneurs, imposed fees that were informally called "face taxes" (*mianzi shui*) or "[good] opinion taxes" (*yijian shui*).

Cheating the government or the public could be accomplished in myriad ways: accepting salaries without doing work, taking bribes from those who needed general or specific official help to which they were entitled without payment or at low cost, buying commodities at low planned prices but then selling at high market prices, or straightforward candid embezzlement. Such activities were almost always carried out in the interests of small collectivities, not just for individuals.

The monetary value of these infractions is difficult to measure partly because of their variety. Hu Angang in China (like Pasuk Phongpaichit in Thailand or Sheila Coronel in the Philippines, as the next chapters show) has nonetheless been brave enough to attempt these econometrics of corruption. Hu, one of the CCP's most cited academic advisers, has estimated that in 2001 corruption cost as much as 17 percent of China's GDP. Hu considered bribes, contract prices that were high because of political connections, insider trading, and sincere embezzlements too.[77] Whether his 17 percent estimate is accurate or not, a great deal of anecdotal evidence suggests that corruption has soared in many countries during their periods of fastest economic growth.[78]

---

[77]Quoted in Pei Minxin, *China's Trapped Transition*, 228.

[78]Edward Chen, one of Hong Kong's most distinguished economists, when he was a member of Gov. Christopher Patten's Executive Council, mentioned in public the fact that corruption has historically correlated with growth. Newspapers had a field day, in Hong Kong which is justly proud of its Independent Commission Against Corruption. But Chen's statement of this truth did not prevent his later appointment as President of Lingnan University.

In Deng Xiaoping's time, entrepreneurial "able people" could be subject to officially lenient treatment even in corruption cases. A speech by Deng at the Shanghai Public Prosecutor's office in 1992 precipitated a wave of judicial appeals by "able people" who had been hauled into criminal courts for actions that prosecutors considered corruption. The executives merely considered their actions private risk-taking entrepreneurship.[79] Deng's speech stirred debate about the links and contradictions between corruption and development. It also led to a Law on Administrative Supervision, under which officials as well as business people were subjected to new constraints. It is clear from the experiences of many countries that agencies and laws to reduce corruption are ineffective unless they deal simultaneously with both state and nonstate agents.

Many cadres have been legally dubbed corrupt without being punished, because the CCP needed their talents and their dubious acts could be interpreted in interests of their work units. Fully 82 percent of the Party members who were officially "found to have committed corrupt acts" received no penalty beyond verbal reprimands from 1992 to 1997. Only 18 percent of the CCP members convicted of corruption during this half decade were expelled from the Party.[80]

Comparisons with another Chinese polity, across the Taiwan Strait, suggest that frequent public reports of corruption may forebode a reduction of its amount. In Taiwan's democratic environment, the late 2006 indictment of the wife of President Chen Shui-bian sued against that family's private use of nearly US$500,000 of public money. Half a million dollars may seem a considerable sum — but China mainland (or Thai or Philippine) reported corruption amounts are often very much larger.

The head of the PRC Statistics Bureau, Qiu Xiaohua, reportedly sent his mistress US$6.3 million, not counting what he may have taken for himself, from the Shanghai Pension Fund. Two Bank of China executives were arrested for embezzling US$486 million. Inspectors found US$6 million of gold bars cemented into the walls of the house

---

[79]Sun Yan, *The Transition to the Market and Post-Communist Corruption*, 29.
[80]Pei Minxin, *China's Trapped Transition*, 151.

of a former mayor of Shenyang. Chen Liangyu, Shanghai CCP Secretary, reportedly took "hundreds of millions" from the US$1.6 billion that sleuths from the Party Discipline Committee said had disappeared from the Shanghai retirement fund — and some in China thought they only investigated cadres whom Hu Jintao suspected of disloyalty.[81]

In that largest case, nine top government and company officials were charged as criminals for misappropriating three billion yuan, including former heads of the Shanghai Labor Bureau, the Fuxi Investment Company, the Shanghai Industrial Investment Group, the Shanghai Housing and Land Administration, Baoan District, and the Shanghai Electric Company.[82] A reason for China's silence, as its arch-nemesis Chen Shui-bian in Taiwan was pilloried for corruption, was that public discussion of the huge sums that had disappeared on the mainland could have made clear that the PRC needs even more housecleaning.

As Yang Zhong points out, "subordinates do not dare to speak out against illegal activities of superior officials for fear of retaliation." But this code of silence (the mafia's term is *omertà*) and the presumption of bureaucratic solidarity extend to higher officials, not just lower ones. Because of this norm to hide news, "the Party control system becomes a double-edged sword: it can strengthen the center's control of localities, but at the same time it can also undermine the center's efforts and ability to bring localities in line."[83] As social wealth rises during China's boom, even the state finds some interest in openness.

---

[81]Nobody suggests that Chen Liangyu could himself have stolen as much as US$1.6 billion, although apparently he took some of that. Most of the "missing" money went into Shanghai capital investments for which the pension fund had not been approved. The extent of lax auditing is often as critical as the extent of theft during booms. For more, see Augustine Tan, "China's Strange Silence on Chen's Troubles," *Asia Times*, November 17, 2006 http://www.atimes.com/atimes/China/hk17Ad01. html, seen November 21, 2006.

[82]All nine were expelled from the CCP before their trials, although Chen Liangyu was still being called "comrade" on the publication date of Bill Savadove, "Nine to Face Trial in Shanghai Pensions Scam," *South China Morning Post*, March 7, 2007, 1.

[83]Zhong Yang, "Dissecting Chinese County Governmental Authorities," Zhejiang University Conference on "The Development of the Non-State Sector, Local Governance, and Sustainable Development in China," June 24-25, 2006, vol. 1, 497.

Local leaders gain independence because of norms that limit the distribution of information. These rules were originally established by the state to bring these same local leaders under more central authority.[84] But in practice, they allow local tyrants or small groups of leaders to do whatever they like — without letting higher administrative levels know — so long as they can limit the variety of local opinions and form a consensus among themselves.[85] Leninist organization, though it may seem elegant, often works against itself in the long run. Because appointments are approved in localities under this system, it centralizes to them rather than to "the center" in Beijing.

Joel Hellman shows that new democracies with market systems control corruption better than developing authoritarian systems do.[86] Market authoritarianisms in developing countries, of which China is the prime example, present a mixed case. Chances for changing the incidence of corruption may depend not only on high-level leaders' will to uproot this threat to their legitimacy, but also on rivalries between leaders for local legitimacy. Allowing peaceful disharmony is the key to long-term stability. Boom growth is, for most people, a more important benefit than the accompanying corruption is a cost. A comparative survey of China and India has found that, in China, perceived corruptions did nothing to dampen support for economic reform.[87]

---

[84]The current author made a similar argument about organizational causes of the Cultural Revolution, showing how central norms of scaring local elites with campaigns, putting them under unique bosses, and labelling them for a dozen years after the early 1950s inspired these local elites (especially young members of their families) to use exactly the same norms against the Party-state when a brief lapse of police control in 1967 allowed them to do so. See Lynn White, *Policies of Chaos: The Organizational Causes of Violence in China's Cultural Revolution*, (Princeton: Princeton University Press, 1989).

[85]See Susan L. Shirk, *The Political Logic of Economic Reform in China* (Berkeley: University of California Press, 1993), chap. 9.

[86]Joel Hellman, "Winners Take All: The Politics of Partial Reform in Post-Communist Transitions," *World Politics* 50:2 (1990), 203–34.

[87]Pradeep K. Chhibber and Samuel Eldersveld, "Local Elites and Popular Support for Economic Reform in China and India," *Comparative Political Studies* 33:3 (April 2000), 350–73.

CHINESE MIDDLE-CLASS LIBERALISM?

Local entrepreneurs and politicians such as Yu Zuomin have been bluntly anti-democratic. Yu appointed his own henchmen to county-level posts, and he opined that, "Elections would probably bring into power a bunch of nice old guys, but they would not necessarily produce benefits. Many capable people would never be elected."[88]

Chinese entrepreneurs have flourished under a national regime that is less authoritarian than most of their own local networks. Very few new PRC capitalists have demanded a democratic state.[89] They do not shy away from using non-public influence over people in their business environment. Their rising wealth and social prestige are unlikely, however, to allow them to stay forever separate from local and then broader public politics.

It is possible to argue that reform China has two hierarchies, one for business and one for politics, with only a few leaders having crucial posts in both.[90] For entrepreneurs, accommodation with the state (at least through bribing its cadres) can be helpful; but too much politics hurts profits. Use of any behavioral definition of power would show that power exists in nonstate business networks, not just in official networks.[91]

Not all politics is in the government. Not all politics encourages participation in public. Rich people often prefer to use their money to buy influence, rather than trying to use their voices to obtain it.

---

[88]Bruce Gilley, "The Yu Zuomin Phenomenon," 78.

[89]See Kellee S. Tsai, "Capitalists without a Class: Political Diversity among Private Entrepreneurs in China," http://www.jhu.edu/~polysci/faculty/tsai/capitalists.pdf, posted August 5, 2002, 26 and 28 for quotations.

[90]Ole Bruun, *Business and Bureaucracy in a Chinese City: An Ethnography of Private Business Households in Contemporary China* (Berkeley: Institute of East Asian Studies, University of California, Berkeley, 1993), 13, and 212–23.

[91]Dahl has proposed such a definition: Power is evidenced when a leader induces a follower to do something that the follower does not otherwise do. Nothing about this behavioral definition of power applies solely to states. Nothing about it applies just to deliberations or actions in public. See Robert A. Dahl, *Modern Political Analysis* (Englewood Cliffs: Prentice-Hall, 1963).

If businesses can buy the government directly, why should they need to buy elections? The wholesale price of cadres, already organized in their state agencies, is often less than the cumulative retail price of voters would be.

This is a difference between the political effect of the boom in China and that in democratic Taiwan or Thailand. Westerners, especially Americans, overemphasize the difference between dictatorships and democracies when they study political development. Most politics, as most people experience it, occurs in local nonstate networks. This is as true of "developed" countries as of others. Most of these networks (corporations, schools, churches) are formally dictatorial. Differences of state regime types affect common attitudes, because states can be assiduous propagandists, but they do not affect all behavior. Much of the real change during modern development is a separation of the practical types of power (military, governmental, economic, or social) and an increase in the ways they can be exchanged for each other.

One study of China's private entrepreneurs suggests that they have not "converted their economic position into political influence, or have done so under very limited conditions."[92] Yet political influence can be particularly difficult to detect, when managers are trying to get into an established elite without any popular mobilization that would threaten its current members. This is actually the most usual kind of business politics in any country. Business managers tend to lie low in public. They pay, rather than shout, for what they need. That does not mean they stay out of politics.

Old Bruun found, on the basis of interviews with inland business people, that "When 'democracy' was referred to, it was linked to economic freedom: the freedom to establish and run family a business without infiltration from above and the freedom to manage available profits independently."[93] The recent expansion of wealth in China can change traditions, as growth has done elsewhere in many societies. There is constant interaction between norms and situations.

---

[92]Foreign-sector managers are also covered in Margaret M. Pearson, *China's New Business Elite*, 9.

[93]Ole Bruun, *Business and Bureaucracy*, 3–4.

Culture matters, or at least modal culture does, for the ways in which Chinese family-like groups form local businesses. The cultural modes that are available for forming the Chinese state are nonetheless more varied than may at first be obvious. Samuel Huntington once claimed that, "no scholarly disagreement exists regarding the proposition that traditional Confucianism was either undemocratic or antidemocratic."[94] This is untrue. For example, William T. de Bary has written about *The Liberal Tradition in China*,[95] Vitaly A. Rubin has documented similar themes,[96] and Liu Honghe has published *Confucianism in the Eyes of a Confucian Liberal*.[97] Confucius may have been scarcely more democratic than Madison, but his and Mencius's ideas on "humanity" and "the people" have found many modern uses. Also, Confucianism is not the only Chinese way of thought.[98] Culture matters especially when it provides various, albeit culturally limited, options among which people can choose.

"Democracy" is nominally an ideal of the People's Republic. It is a CCP hope, although its liberal aspects have thus far been seen by each successive leadership as a project for future generations. China has "democratic parties" that are "led by the Communist Party" but are not formally parts of it. One of them, the China Democratic League (*Minmeng*) has more than 100,000 members, who are mostly educated intellectuals. This might become a mass party, recruiting from other groups too, except that CCP disallowance of such expansion is abetted by many Chinese intellectuals' unwillingness to form political coalitions with ordinary citizens, of whom they often opine there are too many.

---

[94]Samuel Huntington, "The Clash of Civilizations?" *Foreign Affairs* 72:3 (Summer 1993), 15.

[95]William T. de Bary, *The Liberal Tradition in China* (Hong Kong: Chinese University Press, 1983).

[96]Vitaly A. Rubin, *Individual and State in Ancient China: Essays on Four Chinese Philosophers*, trans. Steven I. Levine (New York: Columbia University Press, 1976).

[97]New York: Peter Lang, 2001.

[98]See Arthur Waley, *Three Ways of Thought in Ancient China* (London: Allen and Unwin, 1939).

The CCP chooses leaders of the Democratic League and of smaller "parties." In the liberal heydays of 1988–89, two Democratic League conferences rejected the chair the CCP had picked, the sociologist Fei Xiaotong, but this was an unusual event. The "democratic parties" do not yet live up unarguably to either part of their name. They can in any case mobilize only a tiny portion of China's people. They occupy small niches of "civil society space." They resemble professional associations, but the CCP-state is so thoroughly embedded in them that they have, and claim, scant autonomy. Businesses, especially in rural areas, have far more independence, partly because their power networks are not labeled as political. They can be conceived as merely economic.

The All-China Federation of Industry and Commerce (ACFIC) is far larger than any of the parties, and it is also much wealthier. Especially since a May 1993 conference in Taiyuan, the ACFIC has tried to recruit more "private entrepreneurs" and to raise the political legitimacy of money making.[99] Many of its leaders had been managers of collectives or state enterprises before these were relabeled as "private." ACFIC participants are often concurrently open members of the Communist Party (as members of the 'democratic parties' are not, although such parties include secret members of the CCP). By the Sixteenth Communist Party Congress in 2002, many Federation members were "entrepreneurs," in other words, communist capitalists.[100] Yet the ACFIC is as yet only a bit more independent of the CCP state than the democratic parties of intellectuals — not just because business people often need official connections to make profits, but because the influence implicit in their wealth poses a greater potential political danger to the Party. Their financial

---

[99]See Anita Chan, "The Changing Ruling Elite and Political Opposition in China," in *Political Oppositions in Industrializing Asia*, Garry Rodan, ed. (London: Routledge, 1996), 173; also 196.

[100]See Li Cheng and Lynn T. White III, "The Sixteenth Central Committee of the Chinese Communist Party: Emerging Patterns of Power Sharing," in *China's Deep Reform: Domestic Politics in Transition*, L. Dittmer and G. Liu, eds. (Boulder: Rowman and Littlefield, 2006), 81–118.

need to protect this influence also makes them more predictable than intellectuals.

Business associations may in the future become politically more important both at the national and local sizes of collectivity. This will happen if the growing wealth of small capitalists in China buys more political legitimacy. Democratization is not something that occurs only within the state, or only in attitudes (either trusting or feuding) among citizens. Instead, democratization is a process of relating governmental and unstately networks to each other. The relevant non-state entities are not exclusively businesses; perhaps later they may include unions.

All commercial and worker organizations in China are supposed to be Party-controlled. But the booming market has eroded CCP control of profit-making enterprises more than of any other important kind of power network. In the atypically diversified context of southern Zhejiang, more than three-quarters of Wenzhou trade associations claimed that they elected their chairman "in accordance with their own rules of operation" rather than at official behest.[101] They said they structured their boards similarly. It is likely that Party personnel departments were still consulted in this process — Wenzhou is a highly exceptional part of China in such respects — but the purpose of these units during China's boom is increasingly to co-opt business leaders into officially approved organizations, not just to monitor them in Leninist style.

New local economic elites have strong interests in cooperating with the Party-state, but they are distinct from the government and are devoted above all to business. Officialdom now needs them as much as vice-versa. The previous chapter showed that Taiwan's ruling party had only partial success in co-opting SMEs, even though it directly owned many large firms. One observer in the 1980s said that the KMT "ceases to be a party of devoted cadres [and] is evolving

---

[101] Joseph Fewsmith, "Chambers of Commerce in Wenzhou Show Potential, Limits of 'Civil Society' in China," Zhejiang University Conference on "The Development of the Non-State Sector, Local Governance, and Sustainable Development in China," June 24–25, 2006, vol. 1, 87.

into an aggregation of heterogeneous interests, a catch-all party managed by professional party workers."[102] These words could apply just as well to the ruling CCP across the Strait.

When the CCP had to co-opt more leaders because of their local prestige or wealth, rather than because of their commitment to Party goals, it expanded its reach but diluted its discipline. This Leninist party long enjoyed many levers of control, but these have slowly decreased. Its leaders face unavoidable natural policy choices that divide them, during a period when economic boom creates social problems. Business interests do not dominate PRC policy so thoroughly as they do in many booming counties (e.g., Thailand in Thaksin's time), but they are increasingly important in East China localities.

"CIVIL SOCIETY" AND GOVERNMENT DURING THE BOOM

Many nonstate associations are neither explicitly political nor economic. The growth rate of registered civil societies other than enterprises was at least 34 percent annually from a low in 1989 to 2003. Although the post-1989 figures were decreased by CCP fears of dissidence, many non-business civil organizations by the mid-2000s did not register. These associations in some categories suffered from "shortage of funds, low capacity, low efficiency, and bad internal management."[103]

Yet Andrew Marton argues that, "development in China was more a product of Chineseness than of anything else." He guesses "there were latent patterns... built into Chinese socioeconomic and institutional sub-structures, which were emerging as more prominent

---

[102]Cheng Tun-jen, "Taiwan in Democratic Transition," in *Driven by Growth: Political Change in the Asia-Pacific Region*, James Morley, ed. (Armonk: M.E. Sharpe, 1993), 215.

[103]He Zengke, "A Study on the Institutional Barriers on the Development of Civil Society in Current China," Zhejiang University Conference on "The Development of the Non-State Sector, Local Governance, and Sustainable Development in China," June 24–25, 2006, vol. 1, 42.

under the reforms."[104] This culturalist approach can be used to eluci-
date important aspects of China's boom (as other chapters suggest
for Taiwan and Thailand; and the cultural constraints of hidalgos also
throw light on the Philippine non-boom).

In any case, it is very certain that boom prosperity did nothing
to dampen the interest of Chinese people in religious cults. On the
contrary, "religious crime," as defined by the state, was particularly
rife in the most enterprising East China province, Zhejiang.
Detailed records of local Zhejiang public security bureaus have
been surveyed by the Duihua Foundation, and they show the ineffectiveness, over the whole province in both rural and urban areas
and through all the reform years, of official efforts to stamp out
"religious crime."[105]

Business associations were less subject to police repressions than
non-business civil societies. They had more resources to forestall such
controls. But profits, more than politics, are the natural main interests
of firms, whatever their other values. Entrepreneurs were silent on
PRC political reforms for about two decades after 1989, although the
private Stone Group of companies in Beijing had been an important
financial support for the Tiananmen demonstrators.[106] Interviews in
1991 and the mid-1990s indicate, over this relatively short time, a
slight increase of managers' willingness to speak with foreigners

---

[104]Andrew M. Marton, *China's Spatial Economic Development*, 3.

[105]The Duihua Foundation, led by John Kamm who at times has been able to
establish a highly unusual degree of mutual trust with both Chinese and American
police and prosecutors, has produced spectacularly detailed research on state-
defined "religious crimes," i.e., the incidence of rites in any religious organization
disapproved by Beijing. During Zhejiang's quick boom, these prominently include
the Protestant millenarian "Shouters" (*Huhan pai*), the Buddhist Falungong, and
Catholics who are loyal to Rome. Numbers of adherents in each of these cases are
large. See Duihua Foundation, *Political and Religious Crime in Zhejiang Province*,
Occasional Publication # 20 (San Francisco: Duihua Foundation, December
2005).

[106]Scott Kennedy, "The Stone Group: State Client or Market Pathbreaker?" *China
Quarterly* 152 (December 1997), 746–77.

about the possibility that they could influence official policies.[107] They did not often hold much hope of changing top government leaders' ideas directly but could very often circumnavigate policies that inconvenienced them.

Firms regularly violate the labor laws that limit the work week to forty hours unless overtime pay at fixed rates is offered. They disobey laws that prohibit deductions and delays in wage payments, that guarantee one day off per week, and that mandate safe working conditions.[108] Adhering to such regulations in any serious rather than nominal way would raise costs and inhibit the state's goal of development. So long as China's government maintains its practical bias for business rather than labor, entrepreneurs have sure reasons to support the Party.

Outside investors somewhat affect PRC policies. Taiwan's firms in particular have been able to create alliances with local notables to assure low labor costs in communist territory: "In short, the Taiwanese investors' associations had succeeded in uniting with local bureaucrats against the central power, in particular so as to postpone the implementation of the [PRC] labor law," as Françoise Mengin writes.[109]

Workers and entrepreneurs have been crucial for many countries' evolutions after Leninism, but these events have taken two alternative forms. The relatively confrontational post-communist transition of Poland, for instance, contrasts with the more endogenous

---

[107]Presumably Jiang Zemin's later teaching that the Party should represent "advanced productive forces" gave entrepreneurs somewhat greater leverage. Margaret M. Pearson, *China's New Business Elite*, 105.

[108]Zheng Yongnian, "The State, Firms, and Corporate Social Responsibility in China," Zhejiang University Conference on "The Development of the Non-State Sector, Local Governance, and Sustainable Development in China," June 24–25, 2006, vol. 1, 184–99. Foreign multinationals and foundations, which give more to Chinese charities than do PRC firms, may slowly be changing the pattern described in the text.

[109]Françoise Mengin, "Taiwanese Politics and the Chinese Market: Business's Part in the Formation of a State, or the Border as a Stake of Negotiations," in *Politics in China: Moving Frontiers*, Françoise Mengin and Jean-Louis Rocca, eds. (New York: Palgrave Macmillan, 2002), 240.

reformist change in Hungary. Polish Solidarnosc, starting as a trade union, became the core of a movement attracting many kinds of dissidents among Polish intellectuals and masses, growing so large that it overwhelmed the state. The Hungarian Communist Party, however, reformed itself. It concentrated largely on business issues to coopt economic elites who otherwise would have become more dissident. Entrepreneurs and middle managers joined many bureaucrats of the Hungarian party-state to form a "grand coalition" that was led by the communists in an increasingly liberal style.[110] China's evolution might conceivably take a Hungarian course rather than a Polish one.

Change in China is especially driven by rural leaders who have become industrialists. They have great traditional respect for state institutions, and also for the hierarchies of their own lineages, but sometimes they very insistently press their parochial interests against agencies of the state. The high-level head of a district water-and-electricity company in south China complained that his efforts to supply a booming village brought scant thanks: "They aren't satisfied! They keep complaining about things!... They don't have any concept of law or regulations! And the government is afraid of villages like these.... Why are they such a pain in the butt?"[111] They demanded more than before, in order to sustain their boom. They could complain loudly, when their needs were specific and they needed the arthritic state to keep up with them.

China's new entrepreneurs have varied backgrounds, and these affect the ways in which they politick. A few were peasants. Some were employees of offices or state enterprises. The extent of the socioeconomic transformation that they abet is more obvious than the best framework to interpret their politics. Their political action is

---

[110] Janina Frentzel-Zagorska, "Patterns of Transition from a One-Party State to Democracy in Poland and Hungary," in *The Development of Civil Society in Communist Systems*, Robert F. Miller, ed. (Sydney: Allen & Unwin, 1992), 40–64.

[111] This example from Huangpu, Guangdong, may have involved some special "ethnic" tensions, because the villagers were "Tanka" former fishers, whereas apparently the cadre was Punti Cantonese. Gregory Guldin, *What's a Peasant to Do?*, 34.

not all organized, not all clear as to its intentions, and not all visible in public.[112] It may become more organized, clearer, and more public in China later — but perhaps not soon, if CCP technocrats act in ways that maintain their own ability to govern without inhibiting continuance of the boom.[113]

Although many Chinese intellectuals claim that inequalities of wealth are a great danger to the stability of the state,[114] these disparities probably are less important politically than morally.[115] According to one survey, the richest 1.3 percent of Chinese families controlled 32 percent of the country's assets in the early 2000s, while the poorest 44 percent of families controlled just 3 percent of assets.[116] This contrast is largely between localities, not within them. Wealth differences within most places were lower than between places.

A survey of four inland counties showed that factory managers hired, at low wages that were essentially set in paddies, the most productive workers they could find to exploit, rather than employing relatives or people with connections (*guanxi*). Private enterprises gave rural households even more equal opportunity to be bilked than did collectives.[117] But the main determinant of equality or inequality was whether people worked in factories that paid relatively high compensations, in fields that paid less, or in both so that the difference was obvious.

---

[112]See Frances Fox Piven and Richard A. Cloward, *Poor People's Movements* (New York: Vintage, 1979).

[113]Yang Dali, *Remaking the Chinese Leviathan: Market Transition and the Politics of Governance in China* (Stanford: Stanford University Press, 2005).

[114]An extreme case is vividly described in Joseph Fewsmith's review of "Leninger's" *Disan zhi yanjing kan Zhongguo* (Looking at China Through a Third Eye), *Journal of Contemporary China* 7 (Fall 1994), 100–04, which describes China's peasants as a "volcano" that could destroy China.

[115]Albert Hirschman, "Changing Tolerance for Income Inequality in the Course of Economic Development," *World Development* 1:12 (1973), 24–36.

[116]Yao Shuntian, "Privilege and Corruption: The Problem of China's Socialist Market Economy," *American Journal of Economics and Sociology* 61:1 (2002), 292.

[117]James Kai-sing Kung, and Yiu-fai Lee, "So What if there is Income Inequality? The Distributive Consequence of Nonfarm Employment in Rural China," *Economic Development and Culture* Change 50:1 (October 2001), 19–46.

In the long run, SMEs lead the change to more equality. In the short run, they decentralize wealth to local leaders while supporting national authoritarians. A humorous example can illustrate this. When the Beijing government announced in newspapers that it planned to issue personal identification cards throughout the nation, partly to assure better administrative control over individuals, ex-peasant entrepreneurs expressed no human rights objections. This was obviously a state attempt to monitor civil liberties, but Zhejiang's new businessmen in the burgeoning plastics industry did not mind at all. Quite the contrary, rural managers in Jinxing, Zhejiang, immediately sent to the Ministry of Public Security samples of plastic laminated ID cards — proposing to sell one each for more than a billion Chinese citizens.[118]

ELECTIONS

Local elections have received much attention by students of civil society who sometimes imagine that voting confers so much legitimacy that the power of Party secretaries will be soon displaced by that of elected village heads. Survey research shows, however, that three-fifths of township officials believe Party secretaries do have not felt challenged by these elections in recent years. Less than one-eighth of the elected village chiefs responded positively to the suggestion that, "You have more power than the Party secretary," or that "The secretary is more powerful than you are because s/he holds economic power."

In Zhejiang, both Party secretaries and village heads are often given leadership posts in village economic associations, while most of the members are business people. Party leaders were mostly "entrepreneurs," probably because many had kept their roles in the former collectives that they had managed to transfer to their own private ownership. They achieved this no less frequently than did

---

[118]The government also announced plans for rural credit reform, requiring additional cards that the Zhejiang factories also hoped to manufacture. Fei Xiaotong, *Fei Xiaotong xuanji* (Selected Works of Fei Xiaotong) (Tianjin: Tianjin Renmin Chubanshe, 1988), 375.

elected officials.[119] Both CCP and elected leaders increasingly had business interests.

A survey by Oi and Rozelle found that villages led by factory managers were less likely to have contested elections for local committees. They were also had less frequent village assembly meetings.[120] Local elections attract less participation in rich places than in middle-poor ones.[121] Several causes bring this result. Strong local leaders, who gain wealth organizing new enterprises, may not need or want to brook the dissent that elections might express. As wealth increases in a village, people also may have fewer grievances against non-elected leaders. Also, everybody knows that lowly village governments have scant power. To the extent that influential government officials make public decisions for businesses that really constrain enterprises, this often happens above the administrative levels to which most elections are still restricted, so entrepreneurs do not much care who wins.

People's congress delegates, especially in local assemblies, are sometimes called "three hands representatives": they can raise hands to vote for policies they did not make, they can clap their hands for leaders' speeches, and they can shake hands with higher officials.[122] At a meeting attended by veteran soldiers (including Admiral Liu Huaqing and General Zhang Zhen), an "influential elder" reportedly said, "If popular elections were held in China, the Communist Party would win the first and the second polls without difficulty. Starting with the third election the party's grip might slip, and it is conceivable it might lose power by the fourth election."[123]

---

[119]He Baogang, "The Theory and Practice of Chinese Grass-Roots Governance: Five Models," Zhejiang University Conference on "The Development of the Non-State Sector, Local Governance, and Sustainable Development in China," June 24–25, 2006, vol. 1, 70–72, based partly on 1998 surveys and interviews in Wuyun Township, Zhejiang.

[120]Jean C. Oi and Scott Rozelle, "Elections and Power: The Locus of Decision-Making in Chinese Villages," in *Elections and Democracy in Greater China*, Larry Diamond and Ramon Myers, eds. (Oxford: Oxford University Press, 2001), 162.

[121]*Ibid.*

[122]Zhong Yang, "Dissecting Chinese County Governmental Authorities," 499.

[123]*South China Morning Post*, December 21, 1997, 6.

Such predictions, which are often associated with Deng Xiaoping, were too exact. But they showed CCP leaders' concern that their party would lose heaven's mandate. As Chinese, they know this will happen someday. The decline and fall of regimes is a recognized national tradition. Communists only want it to happen later, after utopia comes nearer.

For the nonce, the most obvious way for them to bring new blood into the polity is to co-opt entrepreneurs and encourage CCP economic managers to "jump into the sea." Business people are frequent nominees for elections, because "people think businessmen are cleverer than most folks."[124] Such nominees now seem at least as legitimate as the choosing of bureaucrats, untraditional though business people may be. Candidates to people's congresses (or to political consultative conferences) must still be approved by the locality's Party personnel organization department at the next highest administrative level. Entrepreneurs are usually selected for such posts when they have previously been active in "united front" organizations, especially the Federation of Industry and Commerce or the Democratic National Construction Association. These groups and the Self-Employed Laborers Association are supposed to be the Leninist "bridges" (*qiaoliang*) between the government and enterprises.

Private businesses nonetheless often receive short shrift in public decisions as such. They are often sidelined if they try to gain access through political offices separate from private payments. For example, a noodle stand owner, who was a member of both "bridge" federations and a local people's congress deputy too, was cold-shouldered by city and district officials when a decision was made to force closure of a market in which he was interested. "They just ignored me. I am supposed to be a bridge, but how can I be a bridge when no-one comes to meet me from the other side?"[125]

---

[124]Gregory Guldin, *What's a Peasant to Do?*, 93.

[125]Kristin D. Parris, "The Rise of Private Business Interests," in *The Paradox of China's Post-Mao Reforms*, Merle Goldman and Roderick MacFarquhar, eds. (Cambridge: Harvard University Press, 1999), 280–81; also 274.

This does not mean that local entrepreneurs who provide jobs, bribes, and philanthropy are powerless. It only means that they cannot depend on the formal political structure alone to fulfill their needs. In rich Chinese villages, especially those with large collective enterprises, local leaders have many resources with which to co-opt clients. Party notables in rich villages can ignore directives from the Ministry of Civil Affairs to hold competitive local elections with minimal pre-screening of candidates, for example — so long as the local economy does well, and so long as these leaders have links to businesses that make local prosperity.[126]

Despite their lack of power, elected village chiefs in some Zhejiang places after 2000, "thought to control village 'stamps,' the symbol of village power, by appealing to village laws."[127] Local balloting may well raise political diversity in China from the viewpoint of most citizens more than county or province elections do, because there are more villages than high-level bureaucrats can monitor. Leninist personnel controls remain formally effective over elected chiefs who might reverse policies set by higher officials. But the "low" levels and units are so many, their policies can be autonomous if quiet.

As Yang Zhong reports, after research in Zhejiang, "Due to the limited power of the county people's congress, few people take it or its election seriously."[128] If in future more entrepreneurs are increasingly approved by the CCP for elections, this situation may change. The intermediate result would not be democratic; it would mainly show more influence of business in government. Later, as workers begin to react to the consequent capitalist policies, the opposition of labor and capital that has sustained most democracies might more obviously begin to frame public governance.[129]

---

[126]Wang Xu, *Mutual Empowerment of State and Peasantry: Village Self-Government in Rural China* (Ph.D. dissertation, Princeton University, Politics Department, January 2001), 249.

[127]He Baogang, "The Theory and Practice of Chinese Grass-Roots Governance," 75.

[128]Zhong Yang, "Dissecting Chinese County Governmental Authorities," 501.

[129]See Dietrich Rueschemeyer, Evelyne Huber Stephens, and John D. Stephens, *Capitalist Development and Democracy* (Chicago: University of Chicago Press, 1992).

After the fifth round of Shanghai's rural elections in 1999, an exceptionally high portion of the representatives on village committees (81 percent) were Party members — but only 59 percent of the village committee chairs were re-elected. In the 1996 Jiangsu and 1999 Zhejiang elections, respectively 48 and 51 percent of the members of village committees were Party members; this was somewhat lower than the national averages.[130]

If elections were expanded to the national level before greater separations of power and journalistic reporting became legitimate, there is a danger that nationalist-socialist demagogues might come to power in Beijing.[131] Democratic reversals have been spectacular after liberal periods in Weimar Germany and Taishô Japan during the 1920s, or again during the 1960s in South America's southern cone. Some Chinese intellectuals are aware of this danger, and in 2006 they sponsored a documentary TV series of "The Rises of Great Powers" (*Daguo Jueqi*) that discussed not only the German and Japanese tragedies, but also the relatively smooth domestic historical trajectories of several other countries. Nobody can yet be sure what course China will take in this respect. Many students of comparative politics, such as Robert Dahl and Samuel Huntington, strongly suggest that orderly maintenance of legitimate contest in a political system is crucially important as political participation rises.[132] Elections can return anti-democratic leaders especially if economies do not fare well.

THE POLITICAL BOOM AND CHINA'S FUTURE

Even if China's boom continues, it may still take about a decade to reach the level of wealth after which no liberal regime has been over-

---

[130]Wang Xu, *Mutual Empowerment of State and Peasantry*, 176.

[131]For comparison, see Jack Snyder, *From Voting to Violence: Democratization and Nationalist Conflict* (New York: Norton, 2000).

[132]See Robert A. Dahl, *Polyarchy* (New Haven: Yale University Press, 1971) and Samuel Huntington, *Political Order in Changing Societies* (New Haven: Yale University Press, 1968).

thrown (provided that a liberal government has been previously established by a national elite, as has not happened in China). But a worldwide survey shows that the chance of liberal defeat decreases before that level is reached. In China, the probability in comparative terms is already low.[133] The more important question is whether China's Party will or will not make a decision to try more circulation into local and national leaderships, and to institute serious separations of power at least within the CCP. If it did so, corruption could be monitored downward, debates would raise further the quality of decisions, and the resulting regime would be more stable.

China's reforms are often described by contrasting them with Russia's. The Chinese change is said to be only economic, not political. China's ruling party is understandably comfortable with this description. The PRC economy has grown quickly from a much lower per-capita base, while the Russian one been stagnant except for oil extraction. China's Leninist political system still retains some of its previous strengths. But recent Sino-Russian contrasts have been overdrawn. Pluralization (not yet democratization) in middle-size and small collectivities of China's rich regions has changed local politics in ways that may "trickle up." This transition below the top of the system has taken aback many of China's recent national leaders, whose intellectual-technocratic condescension remains strong. They have budged ideologically and are now in practice pro-capitalist. Their police apparatus remains intact, and no big change in the structure of public decisionmaking has been advertised. But actually, a great deal has happened and continues to happen, because the resource base of local power has changed.

---

[133]Adam Przeworski estimated the regime-safety level for democracies at about $6,000 GDP per-capita purchasing power in 1985 dollars. By the start of the 2000 millennium, this was up to approximately $10,000 because of inflation. China's actual level in 2005 was about half that. But such a level would actually sustain a democracy, *if* Beijing's elite decided to establish one. See Adam Przeworski and Fernando Limongi, "Modernization: Theories and Facts," *World Politics* 49:1 (1997), 155–83; Carles Boix and Susan Stokes, "Endogenous Democratization," *World Politics* 55:4 (2003), 517–49; and the classic essay by Dankwart Rustow, "Transitions to Democracy," *Comparative Politics* 2:3 (1970), 337–63.

Many foreign social scientists of China have likewise been taken aback by rapid changes in PRC property rights, new media, evidence of nascent norms in Party elections, the extent of cooperation between factions at the top of the system, the apparent political quiescence of the army for many years after 1989, and freedom of private speech.[134] But Chinese politics, especially in rich areas, has almost surely altered more (and Russian politics has changed less) than simple contrasts between them would suggest.

"Peaceful evolution" (*heping yanbian*) is a derogatory phrase used by Chinese conservatives for changes they disliked, but many other Chinese favor both peace and evolution. The problem is that educated Chinese tend to have a "worrying mentality" (*youhuan yishi*), inspired since the nineteenth century by attacks on their polity that make them think in a Darwinian way, alleging that China may not "survive." In objective terms, this fear is absurd. China is the most populous nation on the planet; it will survive. Yet that detached analysis of the worry would not be enough to understand it. A more probable cause is that globalization threatens the legitimacy of rule by intellectuals, who once were exam-accredited Confucians and now are degree-accredited technocrats. The danger of peaceful evolution, from the viewpoint of Communist Party conservatives, including most of the engineers who now run China's government, is that it may lead to a more modern concept of legitimacy. Consent of the governed, not just the academically tested, might become a demand made by Chinese of more diverse types. Local entrepreneurs are foremost among these types, but their interests are not yet well represented at high levels of the state.

"Policy" is usually defined as ideas that are openly expressed in public by top officials. But Chinese often qualify this in a sensitive way: "The top has policy; the bottom has counterpolicies" (*shang you zhengce, xia you duice*). Countervailing, ostensibly loyalist policies, when implemented by local leaders below the radar of the state, often erode regime plans even if they practically never result

---

[134]On some of these changes, see Li Cheng and Lynn White, "The Sixteenth Central Committee," 81–118.

in explicit political opposition. These counterpolicies are seldom conceived as confrontational, but their influence cumulates. They do not randomly cancel each other out, because local leaders' opportunities and problems often take parallel forms. The Chinese central state's organizational penetration into local politics, which rose in the 1950s, has at least temporarily ebbed because of the economic boom.[135]

---

[135]A somewhat different view, which nicely covers many unintended effects of rural policies and may accurately describe the state's *long-term* potential strength but conflicts with many recent data (including some found by the same author), is Vivienne Shue, *The Reach of the State: Sketches of the Chinese Body Politic* (Stanford: Stanford University Press, 1988). See also *Bringing the State Back In*, Peter B. Evans, Dietrich Rueschemeyer, and Theda Skocpol, eds. (Cambridge, England: Cambridge University Press, 1985). "Penetration to the village level" in the 1950s is described in Franz Schurmann, *Ideology and Organization in Communist China* (Berkeley: University of California Press, 1966).

Chapter

8

Political Results of Thailand's Boom

Bureaucrats dominated traditional Thai politics. Business people were mainly in the Sino-Thai minority and were imagined as mere trades people, dealers in materials rather than dignified matters of state. The central regime consisted of the king and his assistants. This tradition lasted for some time after the end of absolute monarchy in the (political but not social) "revolution" of 1932. That was a bloodless *coup d'état*, whose leaders launched a democratic constitution.

Between the first Thai national elections of 1933 and the end of World War II, all but 5 of the 174 cabinet members were state bureaucrats. Later, only 5 of 85 Thai ministers were businessmen during the long period between the start of authoritarian capitalism in the late 1950s (after another coup) and yet another in 1973.[1] Under Premier-General Sarit in 1963, all members of the Thai cabinet were bureaucratic or military elites. None were business people. By contrast, in the 1995–96 Banharn cabinet, after the effects of the boom on politics, only 5 ministers were state bureaucrats or military officers — but 43 were business people.

The term "bureaucratic polity," much used in Latin American and other regional studies, was coined by Fred Riggs to describe 1960s

---

[1]Anek Laothamatas, *Business Associations and the New Political Economy of Thailand: From Bureaucratic Polity to Liberal Corporatism* (Singapore: Institute of Southeast Asian Studies, 1992), 3.

Thailand.[2] Military and civil mandarins until the 1970s were "only minimally inconvenienced" by Thailand's democratic institutions.[3] The behavioral constitution included the king, the bureaucrats, elected politicians, and generals. For many decades, if the generals did not like the elected politicians, they just held a coup. Their right to do so was not quite written into the formal constitution, but like the monarchy, the bureaucracy, and the modern nod to an electoral habit, coups became a part of the Thai behavioral constitution.

The boom empowered elected authorities. Bidhya says that, "Thailand is in transition from a bureaucratic to a democratic polity."[4] In practice, the transition thus far has mostly been to a business polity; its relation to democratic rule by all the people is moot at best. The boom changed the profile of Thai politics. As in Taiwan, though not yet in China, this transformation has reached the top of the government.

The Thai king has, for about three decades, been in a position to check egregious corruption by businessmen-politicians when he acts together with generals — or alternatively, to check political violence by the generals when he acts together with the bourgeoisie. He can do that only when injustices by capitalists or by soldiers become extreme and obvious. Political pluralization has been mediated, at least under the present king, by the royals' sometime ability to constrain the effects of modern police power or of mass electoral participation. This royal authority preceded others in Thailand, and (*if* future constitutional monarchs continue King Bhumibol's 1976, 1992, and

---

[2]Fred W. Riggs, *Thailand: The Modernization of a Bureaucratic Polity* (Honolulu: East-West Center Press, 1966).

[3]Pasuk Phongpaichit and Chris Baker, "Power in Transition: Thailand in the 1990s," in *Political Change in Thailand: Democracy and Participation*, Kevin Hewison, ed. (London: Routledge, 1997), 22.

[4]Bidhya Bowornwathana, "Thailand: Bureaucracy Under Coalition Governments," in *Civil Service Systems in Asia*, John Burns and Bidhya Bowornwathana, eds. (Cheltenham: Elgar, 2001), 281 and 286.

2006 performances), it could become crucial to the future smooth development of Thai polyarchy.[5]

Local business power networks, which are now the strongest force in Thailand, have gained some local legitimacy by making more Thais rich, even while exploiting many of them. They act, often corruptly, in their own interests, but they have also created a national boom. The distinctive role of the king and a continuing role of the army provide a constitutional separation of powers that might partly mitigate the usual worst cycle of problems in emerging democracies: the buying of elections, followed by politicians' profits from public contracts that are widely perceived as corrupt, followed by coups under generals who cannot manage the economy, and then elections again.

ETHNIC, GEOGRAPHICAL, AND OCCUPATIONAL CHANGE AMONG POLITICIANS

Before the boom, the modal politician in Thailand was an ethnic Thai general, whose career had mainly been in Bangkok. Because of the boom, at least since the late 1980s, the modal politician is a Sino-Thai businessman, whose main career has been in the provinces. The influx of wealth apparently lessened the implicit public stigma previously borne by Chinese Thais. Kukrit Pramoj, who was prime minister by 1975, openly discussed his Chinese great-grandmother Ampha, who was a consort of Rama II so that Kukrit was also of royal descent. Kukrit was "a living symbol of the Thai aristocracy," although he admitted having Chinese ancestors and performed lineage rituals to honor them.[6] This attitude, and its acceptance by non-Chinese Thais, opened wide a political door for Sino-Thais in later decades.

---

[5]This book is written during the reign of King Bhumibol Adulyadej, Rama IX. On "polyarchy," see Robert A. Dahl, *Polyarchy* (New Haven: Yale University Press, 1971), or for similar basic ideas, Samuel Huntington, *Political Order in Changing Societies* (New Haven: Yale University Press, 1968).

[6]Anek Laothamatas, *Business Associations and the New Political Economy*, 77.

According to one report from the 1990s, "a Bangkok MP was invited to preside at a charity function dedicated to 'the prolongation of Thai culture.' She got up on the stage and sang an old Chinese song."[7] Thailand is not China, but that nation has assimilated and rewarded the economic talents of South Chinese immigrants at least as thoroughly as any other country has done. These entrepreneurs have repaid the welcome by making the nation richer than it previously was.

From 1980 to 1988, premier Prem Tinsulanonda oversaw a transitional period that set Thailand on a path of quick economic growth. Doner and Anek describe "a balance of two major contending forces — the military and the parties — within a semi- or restrained democratic system.... By playing these forces against each other, by using their fear of each other, and by capitalizing on the desire of each force to have him lead the regime, Prem [like later premiers whom the king supported] was able to protect his pro-adjustment cabinet ministers and senior technocrats from the groups hurt by adjustment."[8] Joseph Wright has shown that Pareto's circulation-of-elites paradigm can be used to structure a discussion of this and earlier balances in Thai politics.[9]

Prem survived two unsuccessful coups, over a period that involved several elections and cabinet reshuffles. Prem was a non-Chinese Thai from the far south, born in Songkhla, and he increasingly brought southerners into government. (Sarit, from the Isan, had similarly been accused of regionalism by his rivals.) Prem's successor Chatichai Choonhavan took over during the economic growth of 1988–91. Chatichai, not just because he was a civilian prime minister, became politically vulnerable because of corruption in his cabinet.

---

[7]Pasuk Phongpaichit and Chris Baker, *Thailand's Boom!* (North Sydney: Allen and Unwin, 1996), 136.

[8]Richard F. Doner and Anek Laothamatas, "Thailand: Political and Economic Gradualism," in *Voting for Reform: Political Liberalization, Democracy, and Economic Adjustment*, Stephan Haggard and Steven B. Webb, eds. (Oxford: Oxford University Press, 1994), 427. (The parenthetical within the quotation was added by LW.)

[9]Joseph J. Wright, Jr., *The Balancing Act: A History of Modern Thailand* (Oakland: Pacific Rim Press, 1991).

He fell from the premiership, however, because he refused to follow the dominant military faction's advice about army postings. The premier's right to determine military assignments was the aspect of civilian government that the soldiers found hardest to stomach. So yet another a coup displaced Chatichai. By that time, however, the generals could no longer admit they were anti-democrats. So the junta immediately appointed another civilian government, led by Anand Panyarachun in 1991–92.[10] Two of these former premiers, Prem and Anand, were politically active through 2006 and remained important senior advisors to others in Thai politics.

The first half of Thailand's boom was a period in which Sino-Thais became more frequent as top leaders. After Chatichai, at least one premier, Chavalit Yongchaiyudh, downplayed the Chinese genealogy that he had (as in the Philippines, many including Jose Rizal did). But aside from Chavalit, from Chatichai onward practically all the premiers have been unapologetic about their Chinese backgrounds, and all have had these ancestries. After Prem resigned from the post in 1988, Chatichai, Suchinda, Anand, Chuan, Banharn, Chavalit, Chuan again, then Thaksin (and the post-2006 premiers Samak Sundaravej and Surayud Chulanont) were all Sino-Thais. Of course, politicians' ancestries were not their most important traits, and Thais of many backgrounds acquired power in this documentably tolerant country. But Kukrit's and later Chatichai's succession to the top government post marked a long-term political change linked to the boom, which had been mostly led by Sino-Thai businessmen. This change involved ethnicity, but it also involved a shift of some political weight to provincial areas that had previously been seen as marginal, and above all a shift from bureaucracy to business.

This change applied both to politicians who earned relatively clean reputations and to those who were widely lambasted for corruption. Chuan Leekpai was premier in 1992–95, and then again in 1997–2001 after severe public criticisms of financial depravity in the Banharn and Chavalit governments. Chuan's father had sold

---

[10]Robert J. Muscat, *Thailand's 1992 Elections: Economic Growth and Political Change* (New York: Asia Society, 1992), 2–4.

goods in a south Thai urban market and had worked as a Chinese language teacher. Banharn Silpa-Archa, also Sino-Thai, got a reputation for leading one of Thailand's most corrupt governments. His father was a Chinese immigrant trader at Suphanburi.

The geographical aspects of the change were at least as important as the ethnic aspects. The Thai army, since its origins in the 1880s, has been heavily centralized in Bangkok. As Ockey writes, "In the few cases where facilities have been relocated elsewhere, it was only after significant compensation was paid for the land (and the new facilities were sited near Bangkok). There is no military reason for the excessive number of troops and bases in Bangkok."[11]

The growth of provincial cities, where the military bootprint was less strong than in either Bangkok or the borders, was crucial to Thai development during the boom. New political networks grew in these middling towns, especially in places that the state civilian and military bureaucracies had largely ignored. These new power networks had a frontier style of semi-lawlessness, almost as in a gold rush. Some of the richest political godfathers came from coastal areas where smuggling was convenient, or from places near forests for logging, or from provincial towns that grew quickly because of changes from subsistence to cash agriculture. The boom was fastest in populated peripheries where the exploitation of all resources was relatively unregulated.

THE PARTIAL DECLINE OF THE MILITARY VETO

The military-to-civilian aspect of change during the boom was linked to the ethnic and geographic aspects. This issue goes back to the start of the constitutional monarchy. The rise of business interests in politics stirred (and still stirs) some traditionalist opposition in the Thai army. Generals, or at least some groups of them, saw scant need to circulate elites. After Gen. Phibul in the 1930s and Gen. Sarit in the 1950s, any top militarist who had not yet been the Premier of

---

[11] James Ockey, "Thailand: The Struggle to Redefine Civil-Military Relations," in *Coercion and Governance: The Declining Political Role of the Military in Asia* (Stanford: Stanford University Press, 2001), 208.

Thailand assumed he was the heir apparent to succeed to that post. From Sarit's coup of 1957 through the early period of communist insurgency in 1968, Thailand held no elections. The reintroduction of balloting was part of the effort to quell the insurgency (and militarists in Thailand, like those in Taiwan, knew their American ally had a liking for elections, as did urban intellectuals). But soldiers and bureaucrats remained in charge.

Security, along with enough economic development to foster political stillness, was the soldiers' top priority. Popular rule was not. After the student-led uprising of October 1973, however, many weak political parties emerged to contest elections. As the Americans pulled out of Vietnam and Saigon (and Phnom Penh and Vientiane) fell to communists in the mid-1970s, the military elite in Bangkok became nervous. Thai soldiers shot at protestors on the Thammasat University campus in October 1976. So Gen. Kriangsak and then Gen. Prem ruled, albeit with support from political parties that were willing to cooperate, until 1988.[12]

The military officers knew that the army was gradually losing the legitimacy of its veto in running Thai politics. They had presumed this right since 1932. Some resisted the trend. Gen. Arhit Kamlang-ek in 1983 launched an effort to amend the Thai constitution so as to preserve the army's power through the Senate. He wanted to give senators the authority to censure officials and serve in cabinets. The political parties were able to defeat this effort, albeit narrowly. A equilibrium was preserved because of a continuous implicit standing threat that any government policies unacceptable to the military would lead to a coup. This arrangement was not as normalized as Philippine *kudeta* became, however, only because the threat events were somewhat less frequent in Thailand.

---

[12]This account relies partly on Chai-Anan Samudavanija and Parichart Chotiya, "Beyond Transition in Thailand," in *Democracy in East Asia*, Larry Diamond and Eric Plattner, eds. (Baltimore: Johns Hopkins University Press, 1998), 147–67. The fact that Kriangsak and Prem were both ethnic Thai, not Sino-Thai, is notable; and of course both were generals.

Doner and Anek write that the danger of military coup in the 1980s "was the principal reason why democratic elements supported Prem and his reform measures." The polity was flexible, as regards economic policy, because it was tensioned. "Democratic or authoritarian forces alone would have derailed reform. Their interaction within a restrained democracy facilitated it."[13] Frictions between lions and foxes, rather than victory by either, gave Thailand's political economy some suppleness to accommodate new entrepreneurs while maintaining macropolitical and macroeconomic stability. This equilibrium has lasted for a long time.

Whenever the foxes captured the field, for example when currency speculators ran on the baht in 1997, the Thai system reset itself. On most such occasions it changed enough to restabilize without a new coup. Still, vote buying and contract corruption showed that electoral democracy could stymie substantive democracy, which then the generals (of all people) claimed a right to restore. They prevailed, when the king backed them.

The seemingly modern habit of elections created a kind of politics that many progressive Thai intellectuals nonetheless regarded as dirty, corrupt, and backward. Many who held these views were in the army, whose top officers have received considerable education. The Thai military contains factions, some of which have been relatively liberal and most of which have been conservative. Army leaders have long believed that, with the king, they have a special protective role in Thai politics. Graduates of the Royal Chulachomklao Military Academy in Bangkok possess an old-school-tie coherence that makes them stick together politically, especially in their successive graduating classes.

At least three groups, "Young Turks," "Class 5," and "Democratic Soldiers" became important as rivals of each other. After the 1973 riots, when one period of army rule ended, a group of graduates from the Chulachomklao Royal Military Academy coalesced to refurbish the army's image so that it might resume its influence in Thai politics.

---

[13]Richard F. Doner and Anek Laothamatas, "Thailand: Political and Economic Gradualism," 412.

These Thai Young Turks thought "a general with clean hands" should take charge of the country. Gen. Prem became premier with their support. But he disappointed them because businesses could increasingly link to the premier directly, not through others in the military. So by 1985, the Young Turk group within the army tried to lead a coup against him on behalf of Gen. Arhit Kamlang-ek, although that effort failed. These Thai "Turks" were indeed relatively young. Like practically all who lead coups, they stressed their nativism, patriotism, uncorruptable (perhaps) integrity, and decisive bravery.[14] Then a separate group of mid-level soldiers, Class 5, which had graduated from Chulachomklao earlier, organized to counter the Young Turks, whose actions their seniors likened to insubordination.

More reformist than either of these groups were the Democratic Soldiers, many of whom were attached to the Internal Security Operations Command. They felt the danger of communism in Thailand could not be suppressed unless elections produced national leaders who would represent the poor, not just the rich who could buy votes.[15] They also argued for functional representatives (especially military ones) in parliament. They wanted a corporatist system, like the institutions established by Gen. Suharto in Indonesia. This recurrent constitutional proposal appealed neither to Bangkok intellectuals nor to provincial business people, however, so little came of it.

The new types of Thai military elites circulated because of political problems and opportunities that the boom created. Under Prem and his advisor Chavalit during most of the 1980s, all the various "Turk," "Democratic," and "Class 5" factions of the Thai army made political compromises with civilian ministers. But both the generals

---

[14]Similar *kudeta* makers in the Philippines, such as Honasan of the Army and Trillanes of the Navy, advertise the same brave-and-patriotic political platform. On these Thais, see Chai-Anan Samudavanija, *The Thai Young Turks* (Singapore: Institute of Southeast Asian Studies, 1982), especially the sections about an attempted 1981 coup.

[15]Suchit Bunbongkarn, *State of the Nation: Thailand* (Singapore: Institute of Southeast Asian Studies, 1996), 47–49.

and the bureaucrats still generally distrusted party politicians.[16] Prem was able to reign as premier by maintaining balances among all these groups. The "Premocracy" (1980–88) was based on coalition governments, often involving former supporters of Kukrit, along with conservative Chart Thai and more liberal Democratic party politicians who were largely in businesses.

BUSINESSMEN TAKE POWER

Chatichai got the top job after Gen. Prem's unexpected resignation. He continued similar coalitions in a government that was regarded by many as increasingly corrupt. Chatichai was, like his predecessors, an army general; but Chatichai was in addition a Sino-Thai. He appointed many civilian businessmen to his cabinet after they had won election as MPs. Doing this on such a scale was an innovation that most of the military mandarins disliked. Chatichai expanded the scope of political participation in a way that some generals deemed dangerous. The main problem was that many of the civilians were really corrupt.

Thailand's subdued democracy-with-generals from 1978 to 1992 was crucially supported by economic growth. Such a regime provided sufficient order, so that entrepreneurs could prosper. Men who had Chinese backgrounds could and did, at this time, use their money to win elections. Some also rose to high military officerships. Legitimacy for the regime came from expanding wealth and construction contracts, more than from public propriety.

The political networks that the boom created were loose and local; they were not disciplined national parties. To recruit support from regionalist members of parliament who were elected locally outside the ruling coalition parties, Gen. Prem had introduced an "MP fund" for each representative to use for constituency "development" projects. (The next chapter finds the same kind of allocation for Philippine congress members, who however were less entrepreneurial.) These monies, which were not included in ministerial budgets, often

---

[16] John Girling, *Interpreting Development: Capitalism, Democracy, and the Middle Class in Thailand* (Ithaca: Cornell Southeast Asian Studies, 1996), 23.

went into Thai government contracts involving corrupt rake-offs. They gave local notables a great interest in holding national offices, because they added value to each parliamentary seat. The military-business alliance provided a period of "semi-democratic" government.[17] It reached a further stage in 1989, when Chatichai became premier, because unlike most of his predecessor generals Chatichai was elected rather than appointed to parliament.

Chatichai arranged for a constitutional amendment that increased the power of the lower-house National Assembly at the expense of the Senate, to which Prem had appointed many generals. The army's political power thus decreased; parts of the army thus turned against Chatichai. By February 1991, Gen. Suchinda Kraprayoon had the support of many businessmen as well as bureaucrats to mount yet another coup, on behalf of "Class 5" from the Chulachomklao Academy.[18]

This 1991 *coup d'état* became unsustainable. It was crude, in Thailand's socioeconomic context at that time. Suchinda at first promised not to assume the premiership — but he reneged on that promise the next year, provoking mass protests in Bangkok. Tension between the purist-military and democratic-electoral forms of legitimacy was endemic during the whole boom period. Neither type of government alone could solve Thailand's problems, because the crucial power networks were increasingly in businesses outside both the bureaucratic and military parts of the state. A localist, not centralist, view of Thai politics is needed to understand the main problem (corruption) and the emerging basis of legitimation (wealth). Either military or bureaucratic parts of the government could be bought by coteries of entrepreneurs, especially provincial ones, when elections formed the government. After 1991–92, riots and bloodshed in the capital resulted in a fifteen-year victory of the electoral-business form of government over the military-business form.

---

[17]See Chai-Anan Samudavanija and Parichart Chotiya, "Beyond Transition in Thailand," e.g., 158 and *passim*.

[18]Class 5 was the Class of 1957, who graduated five years after that school adopted a curriculum modeled on that of West Point. By the late 1980s, the most crucial posts in the Thai military were occupied by ex-cadets from Class 5.

Suchinda's 1991 seizure of power was unlike previous coups, because by that time there was no possibility that the army could rule alone without major royal or business support. Martial law lasted just a few weeks. Suchinda was to make way, within a year, for general elections. Press freedoms were unchanged, and political parties were not banned. When the army tried to continue its control after the March 1992 balloting, major riots in Bangkok by May sent the soldiers back to their barracks.

The issue, as Suchinda and other conservative generals saw it, was electoral corruption. Vote-buying has long been criticized by Thai army officers. Corrupt "parliamentary dictatorship" has served as the rationale for coups.[19] As Suchinda Kraprayoon had said proudly in 1990,

> We hope that a military officer has dignity and will not submit himself to politicians. I will not submit myself to politicians .... I am supposed to have breakfast with the Prime Minister [Chatichai] every Wednesday ... but I do not go .... I have dignity .... I cannot go begging for votes .... I cannot lower myself.[20]

Ethnic politics also played a role, since most of the rich Thai politicians who bought votes were Sino-Thais. But the partial delegitimation of coups after the early 1990s strengthened business people such as many in the army had previously disdained.

Generals could nonetheless still encourage promilitary parties that were wealthy enough to buy votes and thus influence the cabinet. Because Thai society had changed during the boom, Suchinda's coup turned out to be a "bridge too far," which the generals could not hold politically because of changes wrought by the boom. That did not mean the army was permanently out of Thai politics, but only that its boots had to tread more lightly.

The middle classes of Bangkok had at first stood aside, accepting Suchinda's 1991 coup against civilian politicians. But the same middle

---

[19]Clark D. Neher, "Democratization in Thailand," *Asian Affairs* 21:4 (Winter 1995), 198.

[20]Quoted in Kevin Hewison, "Of Regimes, States, and Pluralities: Thai Politics Enters the 1990s," in *Southeast Asia in the 1990s: Authoritarianism, Democracy, and Capitalism*, Kevin Hewison, Richard Robison and Garry Rodan, eds. (St. Leonards, NSW: Allen & Unwin, 1993), 163.

classes opposed the military by 1992, because by then many bourgeois thought the army posed an equal threat to economic profits and political stability. The soldiers' greed and incompetence rivaled the greed and incompetence of the elected politicos.[21]

The middle classes eventually favored civilian extractors over army ones. Urbanites wanted less military corruption. Generals wanted more assured military control of appointments and promotions within the army.[22] In the event, Suchinda's troops arrested the demonstrators' leader, Bangkok Governor (and liberalized ex-general) Chamlong Srimuang, shortly after the urban anti-government protests started.[23] Chamlong had built a political coalition called the Confederation of Democracy that consisted largely of civilian businessmen, including many from outside Bangkok. Demonstrators expected that once their leader Chamlong was in prison, the movement would stop (as had occurred when Thammasat student leaders were jailed in the 1986 demonstrations). Six months later, Chamlong himself said, "When I was arrested, I thought that the demonstration was supposed to end. I thought that everyone would go home."[24] He was wrong. Shortly after his arrest, the army declared a curfew — but

---

[21]See Kevin Hewison, "Political Oppositions and Regime Change in Thailand," in *Political Oppositions in Industrializing Asia*, Garry Rodan, ed. (London: Routledge, 1996), which cites similar views of Pasuk and Anek on 85, and of Chai-Anan on 87.

[22]The Thai army reshuffles the assignments of its officers annually; and until the mid-1990s, it was jealous of its autonomy to do this. Even civilian prime ministers, such as Chuan Leekpai in his first term, simply signed the postings that had been decided within the army. But Premier Banharn and his defense minister exercised their legal right to change the list. In 1997, Chuan Leekpai, succeeding ex-Gen. Chavalit as premier, named himself concurrently defense minister. This was highly unusual, since he had never been an army officer. He also took a more active role than previous non-military premiers in vetting military promotion and assignment lists. He might have had a greater effect on appropriations for the military, except for the Thai Army's "secret budget," about which little is publicly known. See Suchit Bunbongkarn, *State of the Nation*, 65.

[23]Chamlong was a "Young Turk," a devout Buddhist, and founder of the Phalang Dharma Party. His father had been an immigrant from Shantou, Guangdong, China.

[24]William A. Callahan, *Imagining Democracy: Reading "The Events of May"* [1992] *in Thailand* (Singapore: Institute of Southeast Asian Studies, 1998), 86.

50,000 citizens put up barricades around Ramkhamhaeng University and established a "commune" that the military could not control.

If a pollster had, at that time, asked these demonstrators for their "account of democracy," the response would surely have been inchoate. What they knew was that they did not like Gen. Suchinda. They wanted that non-elected soldier out of the premiership. Eventually the urbanites got what they wished for — elections — but they might have wished more carefully, because they did not realize the extent to which the majority of voters (who are rural) would elect superpatriots just as corrupt as the generals could be.

The palace intervened to stop the Bangkok street conflicts, in which several people had been killed. Early on the morning of May 20, 1992, Princess Sirindhorn took the initiative (apparently with her father's permission) to go on TV, calling for an end to violence. Sirindhorn is highly admired by many for her care in public activities. Her devotees include Bangkok intellectuals but also Thais in many other walks of life. She is unmarried and will not have children, but she is third in line to the throne (after the crown prince and his son) under a constitution that was changed to allow female succession implicitly because of this princess's clear political abilities.[25] Crown Prince Vajiralongkorn that evening broadcast a similar appeal, which may have been effective among some military officers with whom he is associated (although confirmed rumors about Vajiralongkorn's personal behavior have made many liberals wish King Bhumibol an especially long life). Most striking was the king's own TV broadcast that night, which showed Suchinda and Chamlong crawling together on their hands and knees toward their seated king, who reprimanded them both and told them in public, and in no uncertain terms, to stop the violence.

Chamlong, thus released from arrest, asked his followers to disperse. Suchinda was forced to amnesty all the protesters and support a constitutional amendment requiring that future premiers be elected. Three days later, he resigned. Military influence over high Thai politics had not completely ended. The king's role in moderating the

---

[25]More information is at Wikipedia on Sirindhorn.

Paretan fluctuation between corrupt business and military elites at the top level was confirmed. The king's senior advisor, southern royalist Prem, clearly had a role in arrange the outcome in 1992 (and again in the later crisis of 2006).

Top generals' normal ladder to the premiership was kicked aside when the middle classes demonstrated against coup-makers and the king stepped in to mediate. The special power of the army — its coercive threat on civilian politicians — at that point became unusable without clear royal consent. This was a seismic shift in high Thai politics. The structural change was permanent, and Suchinda's coup would probably have been Thailand's last if the boom had not also combined with democratic electoral procedures to bring yet more corruption in later years.

Civilian and military conservatives did not disappear. Their most important leader in the 1990s, Gen. Chavalit, returned to the premiership for a year after November 1996. But their lock on the pinnacle of political power in Thailand had ended. The boom had created everyday rule by business interests instead.

This did not necessarily mean that merchants dropped their work to run for elections. Some who were elected to political posts were retired businessmen or had other kinds of nonstate jobs. Economic growth nonetheless reduced the portion of serving or retired bureaucrats (or military bureaucrats) in elected positions. It is important to look not just at the premiers and cabinets, but also at long-term changes in the backgrounds of Thai parliamentarians.

The main shift was toward regional business power. Government functionaries had in some earlier eras made up more than half of the Thai House of Representatives. By the 1970s they were still one-fifth of that body — but already after the election of mid-1986, bureaucrats were only 7 percent of the House. The percentage of ministers who were businessmen was higher than two-fifths in practically none of the cabinets from 1963 to 1980; but after the start of the 1980s, the business portion of parliaments and cabinets was practically always more than that.[26] Almost half (46 percent) of the MPs elected in

---

[26]Anek Laothamatas, *Business Associations and the New Political Economy*, 33–34.

March 1992 were business people.[27] Other MPs at that time were
jaopho "godfathers" or their representatives, who supported but did
not actually run businesses. Choosing leaders by election automatically disperses power to provinces. In the first Thai election of the
twenty-first century, the portion of successful MPs with Chinese fore-
bears has been estimated between 60 and 90 percent. These lawmakers
were practically all from business backgrounds.

THE BOOM'S CONFUSION OF
PUBLIC AND PRIVATE INTERESTS

Thailand's prosperity made keeping power through money a safer
bet than trying to keep it through the state or army. The bureaucratic and military patrons of Sino-Thai entrepreneurs increasingly
relied on companies in which they were directors, rather than state
agencies in which they were officials, to assure their own welfare.
This confirmed bureaucrats' interest in private property, and it also
gave them a cosmopolitan interest in allowing profitable joint investments with foreigners.

The trend of giving more shares of industrial property to individual
official patrons paradoxically weakened the earlier norm that government patronage was necessary for economic success. It somewhat
altered the practical identity of the government, making many civilian
and military bureaucrats into businessmen (or at least into people who
wanted to make sure that specific businesses would prosper). It greatly
affected the plans of officials' children. As Doner and Ramsay write,
"The Thai political elite is sprinkled with the offspring of past military
leaders who made wise investments."[28] To remain high in politics, they
had to be business people first and officials or officers second.

---

[27]Surin Maisrikrod and Duncan McCargo, "Electoral Politics: Commercialisation
and Exclusion," in *Political Change in Thailand: Democracy and Participation*,
Kevin Hewison, ed. (London: Routledge, 1997), 141.

[28]Richard F. Doner, and Ansil Ramsay, "Competitive Clientelism and Economic
Governance: The Case of Thailand," in *Business and the State in Developing
Countries*, Sylvia Maxfield and Ben Ross Schneider, eds. (Ithaca: Cornell University
Press, 1997), 263.

Bureaucrats in Thailand are still called "royal servants" (*kharachakan*). A traditional but outdated saying was that, "Ten merchants cannot match one senior *kharachakan*." The modern version, however, is that, "Ten senior *kharachakan* cannot match one merchant."[29] A mid-1990s survey in the large Isan city of Khon Kaen asked who was powerful in that local capital. Not a single government bureaucrat there was considered "politically influential." Respondents nonetheless gave their MP and a local godfather that kudo.[30]

The boom recruited bright young Thais from township schools all over the country into Bangkok universities. They flocked by the early 1990s into economics courses and then into finance companies. Fewer went into the traditional state bureaucracy, where they knew promotions would be much slower. Real estate was, for a while, the fastest way to make a profit, and speculation has financed a "yuppy" lifestyle among these people.

Legal restrictions on civil servants exacerbated the bureaucracy's recruitment problem. "Thai law transforms officials into non-citizens," as Michael Nelson puts it. "That is, unless they quit government service they lose their basic political right even to stand in elections. Understandably, most are not prepared to take this risk. Consequently, the field of politics and political offices is effectively left to businessmen."[31] The administrative government has thus been separated from the effective, behavioral "government" in businesses, which gain power from competitive elections as the "bureaucratic polity" fades into history. This rule was apparently based in hopes that electoral-economic power might not corrupt officials. But it practically excluded the state from politics and led to low government salaries. Thai civil servants "usually take a second job or resort to corruption to make ends meet."[32] Their wages are inadequate to

---

[29]Bidhya Bowornwathana, "Thailand: Bureaucracy Under Coalition Governments," 300.

[30]John Girling, *Interpreting Development*, 80.

[31]Michael H. Nelson, *Central Authority and Local Democratization in Thailand* (Bangkok: White Lotus Press, 1998), 210.

[32]Jon S.T. Quah, "Combating Corruption in South Korea and Thailand," in *The Self-Restraining State: Power and Accountability in New Democracies*, Andreas Schedler, Larry Diamond and Marc F. Plattner, eds. (Boulder: Lynne Rienner, 1999), 252.

keep up with inflation and are lower than private-sector salaries for comparable jobs.

Even before the boom and the electoral habits that it financed, businesses sometimes could "buy" individual bureaucrats. After the boom, and with democratic elections, they could buy whole sections of the government (and by Thaksin's time, the entire bureaucracy). Provincial elites found that the road to official funds ran through ballot boxes. They could institutionalize their claims to parts of ministries' budgets by controlling seats in parliament. A business politics patron in Chonburi explained that,

> People cannot rely on bureaucrats (*kharachakan*), who have only small salaries. But I have much and I can distribute much. Whenever I sit in the local coffee shop (*ran kafae*) people can come and consult me. I am a man of the people already. I am more accessible than bureaucrats. On any matter where the bureaucrats cannot help, I can. And I do it willingly and quickly. It's all very convenient for people .... Most of what I do is about giving employment and improving the local facilities.[33]

The penury of Thai civil servants is a very old story. For centuries they have been paid with stately glory, not state money. From about 1500, when they had no official salaries at all, they collected taxes in the king's name but sent just a small part to his granaries. Chulalongkorn as early as 1873 set up a "Revenue and Audit Office." He began to pay salaries and ordered all taxes sent to the royal treasury. This was done with great hope and some effect. But as late as 1972, a "Board of Inspection and Follow-Up of Government Operations" had to be created. Its five members were shown to be corrupt themselves, after the 1973 change of regime. Many prime ministers since then have appointed boards that were similarly subverted. The 1975 Counter Corruption Committee and its successors have made scant headway against this problem, which burgeoned as the economic boom put more money in provinces that are remote from Bangkok.[34] A standard

---

[33]This Chonburi godfather's words echo a description of the same phenomenon on another continent, in Chinua Achebe, *A Man of the People* (New York: Anchor, 1988 [orig. 1966]). Quoted in Pasuk Phongpaichit and Sungsidh Piriyarangsan, *Corruption and Democracy in Thailand* (Chiang Mai: Silkworm, 1997), 86.

[34]Jon S.T. Quah, "Combating Corruption in South Korea and Thailand," 249.

East Asian centralist method for trying to deal with this difficulty is to separate state satraps from local leaders, so they develop no family-like links to each other. This technique becomes very hard to use, when elections return political bosses whose main aim is precisely to sequester public resources for uses that are decided locally and privately.

The Thai bureaucracy, like the Chinese one, rotates provincial officials in hopes they will not be corrupted by attachments to the localities where they are sent. Bureaucrats also are not supposed to serve in the provinces where they were born. These norms inhibit links between bureaucrats and local notables.[35] They are difficult to enforce uniformly, however, and they have opposite effects from the norm of parliamentary supervision of government, because elected diet members naturally have very strong local interests. Bureaucrats are often transferred between provinces, but local entrepreneurs remain powerful in their own places for many years.

Elections in Thailand, as Arghiros writes, often empower "representatives who are only a little more accountable than non-elected civil servants .... As councils obtain greater influence, there is often a reversal in status between members and bureaucrats. Council members may emerge the superior party. Such a scenario tends to arise where a nascent rural stratum of capitalists exists, but where otherwise there is little by way of 'civil society.'"[36] Popular sovereignty thus becomes franchised to local economic leaders, even as it also constrains unelected state appointees.

EVIDENCE AND MEASURES OF CORRUPTION

In many polities, either authoritarian or democratic, there is a feedback syndrome between wealth, connections, and power: "without

---

[35]Anderson, Benedict, "Murder and Progress in Modern Siam," *New Left Review* 181 (1990), 33–48.

[36]Daniel Arghiros, "Political Reform and Civil Society at the Local Level: Thailand's Local Government Reforms," in *Reforming Thai Politics*, Duncan McCargo, ed. (Singapore: Institute of Southeast Asian Studies, 2002), 224–25. The phrase "local powers" is expanded in Andrew Turton, "Local Powers and Rural Differentiation," in *Agrarian Transformations: Local Processes and the State in Southeast Asia*, Gillian Hart *et al.*, eds. (Berkeley: University of California Press, 1989), 70–97.

money, no network; without network, no power; and without power, no money."[37] Corruption is difficult to measure precisely, but circumstantial evidence shows the times when there is a lot of it. The most thoroughgoing attempt to quantify it in Thailand concludes that fiscal amounts of corruption were somewhat higher during periods of military rule than during parliamentary eras.

The quantities of direct private expropriations before 1990 were, in objective terms, not extremely great even though their illegality meant they were perceived to be so. The estimated leakage because of bureaucratic corruption varied between 5 and 3 percent of government spending in the Sarit, Thanom, Kriangsak, Prem, and Chatichai periods from 1960 to 1990. Rates of additional diversion of public funds into the pockets of politicians were lower than the rates of diversion to bureaucrats and contractors. Total corruption may have averaged as low as 1 percent of GNP in these years, according to careful estimates by scholars who are unlikely to have understated these amounts.[38] It is probable that recent direct thefts of public property in both the democratic Philippines and authoritarian China are higher portions of GDP than they have been in Thailand. In the early 1990s, long before Thaksin became premier, Pasuk and Baker interviewed him about the going rate for kickbacks on contracts. Thaksin's reply was a measure of his openness: "10 percent was normal, but could drop down to 3–5 percent on projects with a large budget."[39]

Allowance for illegal economic activities generates much larger amounts of money. Pasuk and her colleagues estimate that Thailand's illegal economy from 1993 to 1995 generated about one-tenth of all Thai GDP (8 to 13 percent).[40] The illegal subsectors, in order of their

---

[37]David L. Morell, *Power and Parliament in Thailand: The Futile Challenge* (Ph.D. dissertation, Woodrow Wilson School, Princeton University, 1974), 635; quoted also in Richard F. Doner, and Ansil Ramsay, "Competitive Clientelism and Economic Governance," 250.

[38]Pasuk Phongpaichit and Sungsidh Piriyarangsan, *Corruption and Democracy*, 39.

[39]Pasuk Phongpaichit and Chris Baker, *Thaksin: The Business of Politics in Thailand* (Chiang Mai: Silkworm Books, 2004), 42.

[40]Pasuk Phongpaichit, Sungsidh Piriyarangsan, and Nualnoi Theerat, *Guns, Girls, Gambling, and Ganja: Thailand's Illegal Economy and Public Policy* (Chiang Mai: Silkworm, 1998), 7–8.

contribution to "product," were gambling, prostitution, drugs, diesel oil smuggling, labor trafficking, and trading contraband weapons. If illicit logging, endangered species and animal parts trade, other smuggling, and other illegal activities are included, these careful political econometricians think the value may have been twice as much, i.e., one-fifth of GDP.

Of course, any measured portion of this sort must be based on criteria that define what is corrupt and what is not. Socially accepted standards of corruption change over time. In medieval Europe, for example, lending at interest to coreligionists was corrupt usury; but now, paying interest on loans is seen as ethical and necessary for development.[41] Issues of exact definition and measurement are overwhelmed, however, by evidence that the extent of corruption in Thailand during the boom rose quickly. Many local leaders were involved. King Bhumibol himself opined that, "If all corrupt persons were executed, there would not be many people left."[42]

VIOLENCE

The word "politics" (*kanmuang*) has pejorative connotations in Thai — and in many other languages even though professional political scientists and political philosophers tend to ignore this fact. Politics is suspected by many as a realm of public irrationality and violence.

A handgun, as well as a medal, were given by Minister of the Interior Chavalit Yongchayudh to the man he selected as Ayutthaya Province's "outstanding *kamnan* [local official] of the year" in 1995. Returning for a religious ceremony to mark this event at his brickyard, the *kamnan* invited Buddhist monks to bless not just the medal, but also the revolver.[43] He appreciated Chavalit's symbolic gift (a pistol

---

[41]Benjamin N. Nelson, *The Idea of Usury: From Tribal Brotherhood to Universal Otherhood*, No. 3, "History of Ideas" Series (Princeton: Princeton University Press, 1953).

[42]Jon S.T. Quah, "Combating Corruption in South Korea and Thailand," 253.

[43]As an elected *kamnan*, this man (unlike civilian Thais) had a right to bear a gun. This was one of several immunities that his success in the democratic voting gave him. See Daniel Arghiros, *Democracy, Development, and Decentralisation in Provincial Thailand* (London: Curzon, 2001), 118–19 and 128. Chavalit in the next year was elected Premier of Thailand.

made in Brazil), but he deemed it insufficient as a practical weapon. So this *kamnan* continued for normal workaday use instead to wear his semi-automatic.

Local notables, who are theoretically deputies of the government, obtain special rights to own guns. The Thai state makes many kind of links to leading village families, who comprise about 5 to 10 percent of the rural population, by providing gun rights, loans, salaries for teachers and officials, per diem allowances for attending government meetings, agricultural advice, economic information, and unofficial preferred access to the police, courts, hospitals, and schools.[44]

The Thai Ministry of the Interior has sufficient contacts with local leaders who wield guns that "it is sometimes colloquially referred to as the 'ministry of the mafia." A local leader may start out as a ruffian or protection-gang head, before moving into the more mature role of organizational godfather. Then he (seldom she) may even win election to parliament and/or take the chairmanship of a group of companies.[45] Turton's profile of a typical leader of "gun hands" depicts a local type:

> He is a provincial assembly elected representative, owns a transport company, and is involved in sales of agricultural inputs, ... is engaged in construction work .... has various district and subdistrict officials 'in his pocket.' He receives some provincial funds for his 'territory,' from which he may take a percentage before passing it on .... a member of the local branch of Rotary (or Lions, Jaycee, etc.) .... He or his subordinates are likely to have 'gun hands' (*mü pün*) to do their dirty work for them .... He is also chairman of the local Village Scouts and a generous provider of funds for weapons for the local volunteer forces.[46]

The army was an early role model for decisive coercion. During the long period of military dictators in Thailand, the army used violence freely against rural protestors. As Gen. Panlop Pinmanee put it, "In the

---

[44]See Andrew Turton, "Local Powers and Rural Differentiation," 82.

[45]James Ockey, "*Chaopho*: Capital Accumulation and Social Welfare in Thailand," *Crossroads* 8 (1993), 66.

[46]Andrew Turton, "Local Powers and Rural Differentiation," 87, information collated with Andrew Turton, "People of the Same Spirit: Local Matrikin Groups and their Cults," *Mankind* 14 (1984), quoted in Arghiros, 24–25.

past, we had a 'hunting unit.' It was easy. We got a list of Communist leaders, then ... Bang! That's it. Then we went home and rested."[47]

As both urban and rural civilian organizations proliferated during the boom, however, the use of violence in most of Thailand became less military and more subtle. Associations such as the Small-Scale Farmers of the Northeast, the Northern Farmers' Network, the Thai Farmers' Federation, and especially the Assembly of the Poor became active. The army did not like them, but they could mount demonstrations, occasionally flooding into central Bangkok parks. The press reported all this. TV showed it. Farmers' groups could sometimes forge links with urban intellectuals or international NGOs and, less frequently, with urban business federations. Only sometimes did such links lead to military or nonstate violence against them.

An index of Thai democratization, as violence was normalized in the booming provincial political economy, was an increase of gangland assassinations of elected representatives. As Benedict Anderson writes,

> What all these killings suggest is that ... the institution of MP has achieved a solid market value. In other words, not only does being an MP offer substantial opportunities for gains in wealth and power, *but it promises to do so for the duration*. It may thus be worth one's while to murder one's parliamentary competition — something inconceivable in the 1950s and 1960s, when parliament's power and longevity were very cheaply regarded.[48]

Winning an election usually assured the representative access to state funds for projects to help constituents, thus increasing his or her monetary advantage over rivals in the next election. This is actually a pattern in all democracies, and the varied extent to which they control it should become a topic of far more dispassionate research than political scientists have yet accorded it. Passage of laws that effectively end lawmakers' own use of public funds is understandably difficult. The pattern is so common, democratic politicians do not always call it corrupt. They almost never do so when contracts provide public services and the rake-offs are not obvious.

---

[47]Pasuk Phongpaichit and Chris Baker, *Thaksin: The Business of Politics*, 19.

[48]See Benedict Anderson, "Murder and Progress in Modern Siam," 46, quoted also in Arghiros, 18.

Actually, Thailand has suffered remarkably little bloodshed, for a country experiencing frequent coups (and tacit involvement in a world war) since the end of royal absolutism.[49] The Philippines, for example, has suffered more deaths from such causes. Several Thai changes of government have involved rare mortalities, but never in large numbers. The national politics in Thailand has been mainly non-violent, especially in recent decades. But local politics has involved bloodshed and threats of it.

THE ARMY AND POLICE IN CENTRAL POLITICS

The army has tried to build mass organizations of many kinds, both before and during Thailand's boom. To do this, generals increasingly formed alliances with local businesses.[50] Marriages and other connections between the families of entrepreneurs and officers (as well as civilian bureaucrats) have been important for decades.[51] As the economy

---

[49] Thai coups and attempted coups include the following:

— 1971, Field Marshal Thanom Kittikachorn revokes the Constitution and dismisses parliament.
— 1976, After a 1973 student-led ousting of military "tyrants" who had ruled Thailand for more than a decade, a coup installed a rightist government again.
— 1977, Gen. Chalhard Hiranyasiri attempts a coup against fellow officers in the military regime, but it fails.
— 1977, Adm. Sangad Chaloryoo tries again, and this time succeeds in a bloodless coup.
— 1981, Military units try to overthrow Prime Minister (ex-General) Prem Tinsulanoda, but they fail.
— 1985, Another attempt by retired army officers also fails.
— 1991, Gen. Suchinda Kraprayoon deposes Prime Minister Chatichai Choonhavan; but by 1992, after fifty pro-democracy demonstrators in Bangkok were killed by troops, the king forces Suchinda's resignation. This coup, which was expected by many to be Thailand's last, at least delayed the next coup until long after the 1997 fiscal crisis (which would have justified a coup by pre-boom criteria).
— 2006, Premier Thaksin Shinawatra's business-oriented regime becomes so obviously corrupt that the king supports a coup led by Gen. Sonthi Boonyaratglin.

[50] Pasuk Phongpaichit and Chris Baker, *Thailand: Economy and Politics* (Kuala Lumpur: Oxford University Press, 1995), 335.

[51] Kevin Hewison, *Bankers and Bureaucrats: Capital and the Role of the State in Thailand*, Monograph 34 (New Haven: Yale University, Southeast Asia Center, 1989), 210–12.

expanded, it was natural that the business side of these symbiotic linkages became more important; but before the boom, the military side was dominant. For example, Bangkok Bank head Chin Sophon-panich linked up with Police General Phao Sriyanond in the 1950s. This was crucial for the bank's success until Phao's rival, General Sarit Dhanarajata, came to power. Phao fled the country, and Chin likewise retreated for some years to Hong Kong. A relative, Boonchu, was left to tend the bank, and he formed an alliance with rising Gen. Prapass Charusathien, who became Chairman of the Board of the Bangkok Bank.[52] This turned out to be wise, because Prapass became even more important politically after Sarit's death.

The "Bangkok Bank mafia" restored its bureaucratic power as former bank executives took official posts. Mackie says, "growing pluralism in Thai politics has required that businesses establish links with a range of bureaucrats and parties rather than one or two powerful protectors." A single protector became less essential to profits; companies got help from an ever-greater variety of potentates. Mackie then makes an even stronger claim: "Not only is political connection not crucial to business success, but the most 'political' of Thailand's large conglomerates are not the most successful or the most modernized. On the whole, they are those which continue to operate ... in areas which are highly dependent on bureaucratic or political contacts, or which rely on corruption for their success."[53] As in China and the Philippines, political links led firms to profits, but not to long term efficiency.

Sino-Thai entrepreneurs in the provinces cultivated contacts with agencies that had coercive resources, the local police and army district commanders. Even before the boom began, the Thai military became heavily involved in rural development, especially in populous parts of the Northeast where the government feared communist

---

[52]Krirkkiat Phipatseritham and Yoshihara Kunio, *Business Groups in Thailand* (Singapore: Institute of Southeast Asian Studies, 1983), 24.

[53]Jamie Mackie, "Changing Patterns of Chinese Big Business in Southeast Asia," in *Southeast Asian Capitalists*, Ruth McVey, ed. (Ithaca: Southeast Asia Program, Cornell University, 1992), 175.

insurgents. Many civilian Isan godfathers in Northeast Thailand became wealthy and powerful. Civilian bureaucrats had previously run development projects in Thailand, but army engineers now built canals and reservoirs, propagated soil fertilization methods, and made political connections with Northeast business people. Sarit, born in the Isan, had seen the army as the national institution most likely to bring prosperity there.[54]

Some military leaders became "commercial soldiers," gaining control over companies that were run or partly owned by the state. Soldiers established their own firms or received free stock in companies managed mainly by Sino-Thais.[55] State security agencies' control over employment may have seemed reasonable in opposition to communism, but this change extended the range of the military profession broadly.

There was nothing subtle about connections between army officers and Sino-Thai entrepreneurs during the early stages of the boom especially. At the start of the 1970s, *each* of eighty top officers was connected to at least one company, usually serving on the board of directors. Six top civilian politicians at that time had similar connections with between 20 and 50 corporations.[56] The Thai military was tamed by businesses that gave generals shares and directorships in companies. (In Taiwan, General-Premier Hau Pei-tsun lost out to Lee Teng-hui for different, subethnic, reasons. In China, the CCP's military commissars were institutionalized in both the Party and state constitutions; so the political issue there was business involvement not just in the army, but in the whole state. In the Philippines, soldiers repeatedly deemed themselves free to threaten *kudeta* until governments changed policies, and non-land business powers were weaker.) Top Thai generals practically all served concurrently on companies' boards of directors. A *quid pro quo* for their professionalization was their continued compensation by businesses.

---

[54]Erik Martinez Kuhonta, *The Political Foundations for Equitable Development in Malaysia and Thailand* (Ph.D. Dissertation, Politics Department, Princeton University, 2003), 195.

[55]See Chai-Anan Samudavanija, *The Thai Young Turks*, 14–22.

[56]Anek Laothamatas, *Business Associations and the New Political Economy*, 31.

The electoral system confirmed this equilibrium, until corruption became so egregious as to involve the king in reducing it. Sino-Thai business people liked the system, because elections tended to legitimate their status. Generals put up with it and were compensated economically. So long as top political offices were normally up for sale, Thai generals could garner rents while avoiding the risks of management.

LOCAL PATRONISM

The top of any political system, however, is not most of the system. As Daniel Arghiros writes, "It is politics at the village, subdistrict and provincial levels that arouse the most interest in rural dwellers of Thailand."[57] Exploiting clientelistic ties at the better-monitored national level could create scandals, but local patron-client corruptions were rampant. This pattern was normalized by provincial businessmen. Local chambers of commerce, if enough of their members wished to compete for public contracts on an "even playing field," might sometimes call for open bidding on official contracts. The Khorat (Nakorn Ratchasima) chamber did this in 1986, for example. Nonetheless in most localities, clientelism has been "pervasive not only in the operation of business firms, but — most probably — also in the operation of business associations." As Anek writes, there is patronage "between the bureaucracy and extra-bureaucratic organizations, as well as patronage within extra-bureaucratic organizations."[58] Chambers of commerce became especially powerful nonstate networks.

Democratic elections were means by which rural patronist systems legitimated themselves. The measure of success was money. Callahan and McCargo distinguish four kinds of Thai diet candidates: those who are running for the first time, former MPs, former MPs who are wealthy enough to hope for the simultaneous election of

---

[57]Daniel Arghiros, *Political Structures and Strategies: A Study of Electoral Politics in Contemporary Rural Thailand* (Hull: University of Hull Centre for South-East Asian Studies, 1995), 1.
[58]Anek Laothamatas, *Business Associations and the New Political Economy*, 103.

themselves and of allied candidates in the same district, and former MPs with even more money so they can hope to help allied candidates in other districts (and afterward can expect a cabinet ministry).[59] Nominees in any of these categories, but especially in the wealthiest ones, are often backed by "influential figures" (*phu mi itthiphon*) or "godfathers" (*jaopho*), who are mostly Sino-Thai business people who accumulated their assets through both economic enterprise and political licenses that competitive democratic electoral procedures made available.

Thai political patrons have a surprisingly common biography. Usually they are the sons or grandsons of immigrant Chinese who did well in petty trading. They went to regular schools and then joined their family businesses. Their ethnic marginality may be a factor in the entrepreneurship that they show, but profit opportunities from political contracts are concurrently important. Third-generation Chinese in Thailand tend to be somewhat less distinctive from other Thais, and the fourth generation in this category scarcely exists for specific historical reasons.[60]

Sons and grandsons of immigrants were able to establish upcountry businesses, especially trading cash crops and milling rice. The ones who became rich could then shift to trades that required more

---

[59]William A. Callahan and Duncan McCargo, "Vote Buying in Thailand's Northeast: The July 1995 General Election," *Asian Survey* 36:4 (April 1996), 381.

[60]In Thailand any young man coming of age (at least in the nineteenth century) could choose to be Thai: to join the Buddhist *sangha* for a while, to receive a tattoo making him liable for corvée labor under the supervision of royal bureaucrats and Thai village heads, and to wear a normal Thai male bowl-style haircut. Most Chinese, who took Thai wives and after the second generation usually had Thai mothers, chose this self-identification (which was not available in the Muslim countries of Southeast Asia). The alternative choice — to maintain Chinese and *mahayana* religions, to receive a different kind of tattoo indicating payment of a tax in lieu of corvée, to be legally responsible to a Chinese headman, and (before 1911) to wear a Chinese pigtail haircut — was seldom taken by third- or fourth-generation immigrants, who could often be accepted as fully Thai. See G. William Skinner, "Chinese Assimilation and Thai Politics," *Journal of Asian Studies* 16 (February 1957), 237–50, reprinted in *Southeast Asia: The Politics of Natioanl Integration*, John T. McAlister, ed. (New York: Random House, 1973).

government permissions, such as logging or mining, but which also required more capital and offered higher profits. It was necessary, in these businesses, to have good links with the police, the military, and relevant kinds of civilian bureaucrats.

At this point, such entrepreneurs often faced a choice: to emphasize illegal trade, especially in drugs, guns, loan extortion, or prohibited logging — or alternatively, to go into legalized service industries such as construction, real estate, hotels, transport, and distributorships for goods that ranged from liquor to gasoline. In either case, it was useful to have government officials willing to blink at illegalities and to sign permissions when needed. So Sino-Thai entrepreneurs became political donors and patrons for business reasons.[61]

Ordinary Thais know how godfathers get their wealth and power — but this knowledge does not necessarily or immediately reduce the leaders' legitimacy. On the contrary, a godfather's prowess may be admired. Illegalities may be understood as bad, and coercions are resented, although this happens only sometimes. Local bosses' powers can be eroded because as markets expand clients find employment under other protectors. The national police may become more organized. Vote-buying can increase godfathers' prestige, but this is a less sure way to obtain permanent support than traditional bonds of loyalty are. Especially as godfathers or business people or parliamentarians come to live in Bangkok rather than near constituents, their connections with clients become detached.

Money in Thailand tends to win elections — but not always. If candidates do not mix gift money with ostensible concern for their electors, they can lose. As Anek writes, "Voters have rejected incumbents despite their generous vote buying because they subsequently rarely visited the village or helped resolve problems." They prefer to take money from "candidates who are deemed sincere, honest, and helpful."[62] Ballots are cast simultaneously on the bases of pubic

---

[61]Pasuk Phongpaichit and Sungsidh Piriyarangsan, *Corruption and Democracy*, 82ff.

[62]Anek Laothamatas, "Tale of Two Democracies: Conflicting Perceptions of Elections and Democracy in Thailand," in *The Politics of Elections in Southeast Asia*, R.H. Taylor, ed. (Washington: Woodrow Wilson Center, 1996), 207.

reputation and personal pay-off. Willem Wolters distinguishes traditional patron-client links from the different, less intimate kind of patronage that emerges when a politician hands out money for reasons that are "short-term, impersonal, instrumental, and based on a specific transaction."[63] Politicians benefit when they are seen to adhere to norms of permanent reciprocation, such as hold traditional patron-client factions together. Mere gifts to constituents do not automatically establish close ties.

Rural politics is sometimes conceived solely in terms of patronist factions, with the heads of these small networks nested in extended factions of local leaders. But that conception ignores rural politics that occurs on the basis of other kinds of situation or identity. Patrons, for example, almost always have higher incomes than their followers; so class analysis offers a different perspective on their politics. Regional politics in Thailand is an affair of rich businessmen but also others, e.g., Buddhist abbots. Business people's wealth and prestige, and their use of it in rivalries, is both separable from and related to their interest in attracting clients. The aim of patrons is to maximize their followers' number and commitment by creating bonds of debt. Comparable network politics are evident in the Philippines, and the Thai equivalent of the Tagalog phrase *utang na loob* (unrepayable indebtedness to the benevolence of others) is *bunkhun*.[64]

Commonly used phrases or ways of speaking document basic hierarchies. Language tells more about politics than most American political scientists have yet admitted.[65] When a Thai client is indebted to a patron, he or she is said to "stick to good karma" (*tit bun*) in that relationship. But it is an index of Thai individualism that another common phrase is used when someone "doesn't want to stick to *bun* [or *punya*]" (*mai yak tit bun*).[66] Avoiding too much indebtedness is seen as good too.

---

[63]Wolters, O. Willem, *Politics, Patronage, and Class Conflict in Central Luzon* (The Hague: Institute of Social Studies, 1983), 229.

[64]William A. Callahan and Duncan McCargo, "Vote Buying in Thailand's Northeast," 379.

[65]American political science pays too little attention to languages, especially Asian ones. But see Pierre Bourdieu, *Language and Symbolic Power* (Cambridge: Polity Press, 1991).

[66]Thanks for this and other Thai linguistic help go to Dr. Anthony Diller, former head of the Thai Studies Program at the Australian National University.

BOSSES, ELECTIONS, AND VOTE-BUYING

Vote buying is sometimes called "investing" (*longthun*). Such money is capital for the production of further profits from government contracts.[67] In Turton's words, "local economic agents are often 'vote bosses' (*huakhanaen*) at election time. Personal funds of 1 or 2 million baht may be spent on campaigning. There is usually no formal local political party organization ... at once politicizing commercial, administrative and other less formal relations and contributing to the depoliticizing of the majority or at least excluding them in the short term from effective political processes."[68] All these political-economic relations come in a variety of sizes of collectivity. *Huakhanaen* canvassers arrange elections in advance; they woo votes (*ha siang*) in both large and small places.

Organizing jobs is often indistinguishable from marshalling votes. Rural leaders are economic and political at the same time. "Like politicians, employers try to obligate individual workers, households, and sometimes entire temple communities. Employers regularly act as ritual patrons of temple ceremonies at their workers' temples .... Thirty or so residents from Village Three of Ban Thung (the subdistrict's poorest village) formed the dependable core of the workforce of the district's largest brickyard (owned by the *kamnan*, who is the [Brick Manufacturers' Association] vice-chairman)."[69] Coercion, prestige, and money were all factors in local Thai politics. The Chief of Police in Chonburi freely admitted that his staff, although formally part of the national bureaucracy, was a tool of the local godfather: "And it wasn't just the police who were under his control. Other government officials who could benefit his interests all came under his protection."[70]

In localities, and therefore nationally, left-right differences in Thailand have not yet mainly been worker-capitalist differences. They

---

[67]Daniel Arghiros, "Political Reform and Civil Society at the Local Level," 241.
[68]Andrew Turton, "Local Powers and Rural Differentiation," 86.
[69]Daniel Arghiros, *Democracy, Development, and Decentralisation*, 62.
[70]Quoted from the police chief by James Ockey, "*Chaopho*: Capital Accumulation and Social Welfare in Thailand," 69.

have been cleavages over the proper extent of rule by rural business-men and specific groups of them. These disputes were sometimes set-tled by violence. A Chart Thai candidate for provincial election ran his campaign on the slogan "Right Kills Left." As Pasuk and Baker remark, "Against the background of political assassinations at the time, this slogan was not meant to be read too metaphorically."[71]

The *Bangkok Post* reported that sales of bulletproof vests rose ten-fold during a campaign period. Arghiros also reports on earnestly nasty mechanisms of rural and suburban control: "Vote brokers were menacing. Core faction members and vote brokers were armed."[72] Young men "joked" that one candidate had gone off to shoot another, whose corpse they would collect the next morning.

Money was nonetheless usually less expensive than violence as a way to local prestige during the boom's progress. A Thai election canvasser was heard to complain that, "It's a fully fledged democracy; they [voters] want money."[73] As a poor Isan farmer said, "A general election is a time for collecting money. Democracy? I must pay off my debts first, before thinking about it."[74]

Early in the boom, Thai candidates offered banquets, free medi-cines, and film shows to entertain their voters. A 1979 law prohibited these practices, but in the boondocks such laws were difficult to enforce. "Chinese table" parties (*tojin*), with a set cost per seat, became a major form of Thai politicking and socializing in the mid-1980s.[75] Canvassers increasingly diverted political funds from banquets into straightforward vote buying. This is also illegal, of course, but harder to detect. As Suchit says, "Money is usually given to local leaders or canvassers who are responsible for giving the money to the voters and mobilizing them .... Money has become a symbol of generosity and sportsmanship, not only wealth and influence."[76]

---

[71]Pasuk Phongpaichit and Chris Baker, "Power in Transition: Thailand in the 1990s," 31.

[72]Daniel Arghiros, *Democracy, Development, and Decentralisation*, 99; also 211.

[73]*Ibid.*, 39.

[74]Quoted from Kulick and Wilson, in Jon S.T. Quah, "Combating Corruption in South Korea and Thailand," 251.

[75]Daniel Arghiros, *Democracy, Development, and Decentralisation*, 73.

[76]Suchit Bunbongkarn, *State of the Nation*, 83–84.

Local tycoons in locally dominant industries became the main politicians, whether or not they ran for office. "Prosperity is brought to any subdistrict over which a brickyard owner presides," a manufacturers' association speaker claimed. Private entrepreneur-politicians vied among themselves to take credit for projects. Public infrastructure plans, such as government-funded roads, were widely seen as keys to communal wealth. In a Thai place where bricks were an important industry, nearly a quarter of the locally prestigious *kamnan* (subdistrict chiefs) were brickyard owners and members of the Brick Manufacturers' Association. They were rich from the boom, but not because of exports.

Other rural industries' leaders were also well represented among *kamnan*. "There is an implicit notion, among many rural economic elites, that they should acquire the prestige of office once they have wealth. The progression is seen as a natural one. It is worth reiterating that a *kamnan* who wins the position by out-bribing the opposition has no less status and prestige than a *kamnan* who won the basis of popularity alone." These small capitalists are "driven by a combination of material and cultural factors," both money and status.[77]

Before the boom, being a village or subdistrict head in Thailand was more burden than honor. Rewards were few, except for an official title that proved the esteem of both the government and fellow citizens. But the boom made political offices valuable, not just prestigious. They were factors of production. It was often easier to make money by dealing with the Thai bureaucracy than by dealing with other Thai entities. As Arghiros writes, "When fulfilling public sector contracts, businessmen can, in league with bureaucrats, make extraordinary profits from skimming grants — overstating the cost of a project and/or using fewer and cheaper materials — and to an extent rarely possible in the private sector."[78] Contractors can also be assured of payment, since the payor is as creditworthy as the state. So businessmen naturally turn to government, and some of them turn into politicians. An interview with the director of the Thai government's

---

[77]Daniel Arghiros, *Democracy, Development, and Decentralization*, 224; also 83.
[78]*Ibid.*, 24; also 71.

division for decentralizing power estimated that between 80 and 90 percent of provincial councillors also, in their private capacities, had business contracts with the state.

Low-level elected bodies in Thailand have informally been called "contractors' councils." Nonetheless, "Thailand's democracy, warts included, is a vast improvement on all its former bureaucratic regimes."[79] When elected politicians are too egregiously greedy, the free speech norm may give them problems at the next election.

In many localities, the popularity of business people from offering jobs precludes any need to offer money for votes. They (or their candidates) are elected anyway, because of prestige from wealth or because they give local people wages. A survey of 1986 general election voters, asked whether "buying" had occurred in their constituencies. It found "yes" responses of 28 percent in the Northeast, 25 percent in the North, 15 percent on the central plain, and 5 percent in Bangkok and in the South.[80] These attitudinal figures may be behavioral undercounts. They in any case show a strong positive relationship, among Thai areas, between vote buying and relative poverty.

A sample of Bangkok voters was asked in October 1996, "What should the people responsible for the election do?" A full 51 percent replied, "Arrest vote buyers."[81] Thai business associations have been legally banned from financing election campaigns. Their individual members may give money, however. As in many other democracies with such laws, the loopholes are legion and people with money readily use them.

Despite extensive assimilation, Sino-Thai election candidates have sometimes been subject to ethnic slurs (though less frequently than in the Philippines). The father of a Thai candidate referred to the rival nominee as a "cheating Chinese pig thief."[82] This did not prevent the Sino-Thai from acquiring enough votes, and abstentions

---

[79] *Ibid.*, 280.

[80] Anek Laothamatas, "Tale of Two Democracies ... Elections and Democracy," 205.

[81] Professor Sukhum Chaleysub made this result available, and Ms. Nittaya Vairojanavong translated it from Thai for this author.

[82] Daniel Arghiros, *Democracy, Development, and Decentralisation*, 105.

from kin of the Thai nominee, to win the election. Money in booming democracies often trumps macropolitical issues, even those that relate to ethnicity.

When there are votes, they can usually be bought. *Coups d'état* close down this particular market, although they open other opportunities for corruption. During times when elections are seriously competitive, even if many citizens lack much education, vote-buying is like a small nonprogressive tax rebate. It is a small impost paid back to ordinary families by political elites. This pattern will probably not last long in Thailand, as it did not in other democracies where it was common earlier. Booming societies normally have stratified income and asset structures. The reverse tax of vote-buying sustains rather than changes this inequality. Such a minor festival of fiscal Saturnalia undergirds a system that gives much larger pay-offs to businesses.

Thai rural voters also favor candidates who come to visit them personally, give to local temples, attend traditional and family festivals, and promise legislative pork.[83] For example, a Sino-Thai godfather and village head started with rice mills and a rural credit company, then moved on (with the help of government licenses) to a sawmill, a whiskey concession, and a construction company. He also provided loans for business startups by friends, medicine money for ill constituents, donations to schools, and informal judgements in disputes among villagers.[84]

Donations to temples are particularly prestigious. As a Thai abbot said in a sermon, "I really ought not to come canvassing (*ha siang*), but I'm not canvassing. I'm not canvassing, but I want to say that we [at the temple] are in debt to them [benefactor candidates] and so it is necessary that we repay that debt."[85] Sacred approval has its price. A Thai candidate for provincial councillor advertised that he was not a rummaging merchant or capitalist and would not buy votes (although

---

[83]Anek Laothamatas, "Tale of Two Democracies ... Elections and Democracy," 206.
[84]James Ockey, "*Chaopho*: Capital Accumulation and Social Welfare in Thailand," 61.
[85]Daniel Arghiros, *Democracy, Development, and Decentralisation*, 201–02; also 91 and 148.

in fact he did so to a limited extent). These rhetorical positions earned him some local respect — and he lost the election. If he had either paid more or been more consistent, he might have won.

In a 1990 election for *kamnan* of an area where daily wages were about 50 baht per day, normal votes cost 100 baht. Votes cost twice as much in villages where other factors gave each rival candidate a serious chance of winning. If voters' kin or village ties link them to an opposing candidate, bribes might also be offered to induce abstentions. Canvassers for a candidate without strong ties to a village can "buy," or lease for the election day only, the identity cards of voters who for social reasons could not cast ballots for the canvasser's boss. These voters, by abstaining, place peripheral rather than "deep" bets on the contest.[86]

After criticizing vote buying as "not good," a candidate for *kamnan* in 1990 eventually accepted his campaign advisor's view that he had to buy votes. Even in villages where he had kin, he was advised to bribe voters who were not obviously in his camp — because his opposition did so. Voters were intimidated, in a poor village, when canvassers for one candidate tried to "buy" away every ID card, noting the names of those who refused to sell. Then canvassers for the rival approached each house, taking down the names of those who could not show their cards. The implication was clear to all: the winning candidate would use his post to disfavor households that had not met his demand for votes.

Turnout in Thai provincial elections may have been reduced because of these temporary rentals of ID cards by canvassers from voters whose kin or informal networks would not allow them to favor the canvassers' candidates. The 1992 election saw an expansion of the PollWatch organization (which is like the Philippines' ComElec or Namfrel). This NGO planned to send 30,000 volunteers to check on polling stations and thus promote a "less corrupt election."

Chamlong Srimuang, called "Mr. Clean" because of his notably uncorrupt seven-year tenure as Governor of Bangkok, joined Buddhist

---

[86]This is like the types of bets described in Clifford Geertz, "Deep Play: Notes on the Balinese Cockfight," in *The Interpretation of Cultures* (New York: Basic Books, 1973), 412–53.

organizations in campaigns to persuade candidates not to buy votes. A solemn ceremony was held at a temple in Nonthaburi. Candidates attending this rite sipped from a bowl of holy water brought from many Thai temples all over the country. "With a Buddhist monk looking on as witness, [they] demanded divine retribution if they violated their no vote-buying oath."[87] Thirty-four candidates were invited to this ceremony. Seven came.

The leader of the Chart Thai party, who claimed that he never bought votes, was seen during his campaign buying a bowl of noodles from a hawker in his southern Thai constituency. He plumped a bill worth fifty times the price of the noodles on the top of the cart. He did not buy the vendor's vote, but those were very expensive noodles.

Vote-buying has been common in Thailand, and the prices differ. As in Taiwan, votes for local government heads cost more than those for MPs. Province and municipality heads, directly and through their connections with ministers, make more place-specific decisions about the use of public money than do MPs who are not ministers. The 1992 election, in high boom times, saw "brazen vote-buying all across Thailand .... canvassers handing out everything from 500-baht notes to movie tickets to live ducks to lipsticks." In an Isan province, a candidate was said

to have paid tailors to mend clothes for voters, while in central Chachoengsao province, a political party has offered voters free appointments with a dentist .... In a typical case, a party canvasser goes into a village and takes a bet of five baht (or about 20 cents) from a villager, agreeing to pay out 500 baht if the party's candidate wins. The villager is then left with a strong financial incentive to support the party.[88]

For the 1995 balloting, the Thai Farmers Bank Research Center estimated that "up to 17 million baht had been spent on the elections by all candidates." Much of the money went to buy votes, but some also went simply to "buy MPs from other parties."[89]

---

[87]Daniel Arghiros, *Democracy, Development, and Decentralisation*, 93 and 97.

[88]Philip Shenon, "It's Business as Usual in Thailand (Votes for Sale)," *New York Times*, March 18, 1992, A-4.

[89]John Girling, *Interpreting Development*, 82–83; see also 39.

After Banharn Silpa-Archa and his Chart Thai party won the 1995 election and formed a government that many analysts call one of the most corrupt in recent Thai history, King Bhumibol made a speech stressing that politicians should have "legitimacy" (he used that word in English), honesty, ability, justice, and moral integrity. But a heavy majority of Thailand's voters are rural. The local bosses whom they select as MPs pave their roads and often bring them schools and clinics better than the royal bureaucracy does. These godfathers also infect politics with coercion; in effect, they put government up for sale. According to the Thai Farmer's Bank Research Center, the 1996 legislative election campaign cost between 20 and 30 million baht — more than the total value spent in that same year's American presidential campaign.[90]

Just as 1996 was the peak of the Thai boom, it was also one of the high points of corruption. The amounts spent by candidates for investing in the government temporarily decreased in 1997, as did many other factors for profits. An equally important effect was that, although financial incentives to voters increased turnouts, they decreasingly assured that candidates who paid would actually get votes for their money. (This phenomenon also occurred in Taiwan, as chapter 6 shows.) A 1999 campaign in Chiang Mai province sought to propagandize against vote-buying. As Laura Thornton writes, this campaign was followed by "a slight increase ... in the number of participants who believed that it was wrong to sell their votes and not vote for the buyer."[91]

---

[90]It is unclear whether the U.S. political expenditure is fully recorded in this estimate, because hiding campaign money is a common game in many democracies. Thailand is nonetheless a less populous country than America, and it has a very much smaller economy. See Pasuk Phongpaichit and Chris Baker, *Thailand's Boom and Bust* (Chiang Mai: Silkworm Books, 1998), 250.

[91]Laura Thornton, "Combatting Corruption at the Grass Roots: A Thailand Experience, 1999–2000" (Bangkok: National Democratic Institute for International Affairs, 2000), 29, quoted in Schaffer, *op. cit.*, 39. Thornton is a graduate of the Woodrow Wilson School.

PARTICIPATION AND CORRUPTION

Electoral politics made for corruption, but it also made corruption an issue. In traditional Siam, during the era before elections, it had been entirely normal for state bureaucrats to put some of their allocated budgets into their own pockets. Even in more recent times, everyone knew that officials were underpaid, and a nominal rake-off was scarcely seen as corrupt. But if the amount became large, the result was perceived as immoral. "Eating the state" (*kin muang*) was socially disapproved only when the rate of informal extraction was very high. When elections became important in Thailand, especially during the boom that produced far more wealth, rival politicians could accuse each other of corruption. Only then did corruption become a major matter in public debate.

There is no good way to translate the word "corruption" into Thai. The closest phrase is "*choorat bangluang*" ('to defraud the state' or steal from the king). Kulick and Wilson claim that, "unlike Westerners, [Thais] expect their leaders to be corrupt too, and accept the fact as part of life."[92] Not all of them now have this view, however, and the king sometimes moves against systematic thefts.

Electoral victory gives winners power over official spending, so Thai *jaopho* godfathers set up "vote banks" for particular candidates. Pasuk and Sungsidh describe one such godfather, from Chonburi:

> Kamnan Bo [a.k.a. Kamnan Poh, or Somchai Khunpluem] helped candidates through his network of informal influence with *kamnan, phuyaiban* [village heads], businessmen, and local officials who were able to influence voters to attend the poll and vote on behalf of Bo's candidates. He also helped by more extreme methods. In an interview he revealed that he used his influence to vote on behalf of eligible voters who did not turn up at the polling booth. His men would keep going into the polling booth repeatedly, using their own identity cards, and the poll officials were persuaded to cooperate and pretend not to know what was going on. He confessed that

---

[92]Quoted in Jon S.T. Quah, "Combating Corruption in South Korea and Thailand," 253.

the large turnout figures in Chonburi polls may have been the result of his subordinates' over-enthusiasm.[93]

A Thai government department in 2003 ran a questionnaire asking constituents, "What do you think is the vote-getting measure most welcomed by the voters?" Fully 65 percent replied, "offering money and gifts." Only 10 percent referred to "making good public speeches."[94] From a candidate's viewpoint, such high financial demands could only be met by business profits, legal or illegal. One of them said, "Now you go into a village and it's money, money, money. In my first campaign, people would just drink liquor and eat noodles [both provided by canvassers] and they were happy. All villagers want now is money. Being honest, we two [rivals] will spend at least six million."[95]

The boom inflated the price of votes as of all other factors in Thailand. It is estimated that vote-buying cost 300 to 400 million baht in the 1986 general election, then 4 to 5 billion in 1988, up to 10 billion in 1992, up further to 17 billion in 1995, and then 20 to 30 billion in 1996.[96] Banharn's political enemies in Bangkok called him a "walking ATM," because he dispensed cash so generously to his supporters.

Turnouts of Thai voters increased during the boom, from just 44 percent in a 1979 national election, to 62 percent by 1992. Bangkok had the *lowest* turnout of all Thai provinces in all but one of the seven elections held between those years (its average turnout being about 40 percent).[97] This pattern is opposite to that in most democracies, where urban people, as well as educated and rich people, go to the polls most often. The reason for the anomaly is evident, however: Rural

---

[93]Pasuk Phongpaichit and Sungsidh Piriyarangsan, *Corruption and Democracy*, 70–71. In the 1871 Chicago election, citizens were famously urged to "vote early and often." Kamnan Poh would have heartily agreed.

[94]Anek Laothamatas, "Tale of Two Democracies .... Elections and Democracy," 205.

[95]Daniel Arghiros, *Democracy, Development, and Decentralisation*, 195.

[96]Pasuk Phongpaichit, Sungsidh Piriyarangsan, and Nualnoi Theerat, *Guns, Girls, Gambling, and Ganja*, 261–62 and 266.

[97]Suchit Bunbongkarn, "Elections and Democratization in Thailand," in *The Politics of Elections in Southeast Asia*, R.H. Taylor, ed. (Washington: Woodrow Wilson Center, 1996), 192–93.

Thai canvassers paid handsomely for votes, especially among citizens who otherwise might not have bothered to go to the polling stations. They turned out village electors more effectively than canvassers in the big city did. They apparently knew that rural citizens, if given money, would often requite by voting for the candidate who had paid.

Party affiliations of voters are stronger and more stable in Bangkok than in the provinces. Surveys show that Thais who cast ballots also say they engage in conversations about candidates prior to elections, and this may be especially true in the capital, at least among citizens whose ID cards allow them to vote there.[98] But Albritton and Bureekul have evidence that high political participation in Thailand correlates with membership in formal (not informal) organizations. They show that participation in civil society movements is more by older people rather than youths, poorer people rather than the wealthy, and folks in rural areas rather than urbanites.[99]

Each of these empirical findings is counterintuitive, since political protest is usually conceived as youthful, bourgeois, and urban. Yet most participation in Thailand is by people who are mature, from any class, and rural. Vote-buying may account for participation in elections, but various kinds of Thais express themselves politically in various ways, and not just in elections.

Sure votes became increasingly tricky and expensive to buy. Canvassers in Thailand used their funds only at the last minute before balloting (as they did also in Taiwan). During a 1995 Isan election, households in some villages might receive 1000 baht each — but only on the night before the voting. "Decisions on final payments were not made until immediately before the polls."[100] Vote-buying is only the last step of a competently run electoral drive. Formal campaigns last only for a month; but they are preceded by many weeks in

---

[98]Clark D. Neher, "Democratization in Thailand," 200.

[99]Robert B. Albritton and Thawilwadee Bureekul, "The Role of Civil Society in Thai Electoral Politics," paper for the American Political Science Association Annual Meeting, 2002.

[100]William A. Callahan and Duncan McCargo, "Vote Buying in Thailand's Northeast," 386 and *passim*.

which candidates and canvassers are recruited. Campaigning never really ends in Thailand (or other electoral democracies in which money plays an overwhelming role). Cash goes mainly to influence votes at the last minute.

Money is also used in Thailand to compensate people who attend political rallies, to fund ostentatious donations for temples and community groups, and to bribe local officials. When Thailand's PollWatch during one election sent thousands of volunteers into villages searching for cases of balloting fraud, which is illegal, they reported many violations to local police and to border patrol officers. The police, under the Interior Ministry, generally neglected the PollWatch reports and made no arrests.

Thai intellectuals, as well as soldiers who remember their pre-boom prominence in politics, find this democracy defective. Many Westerners, under the pull of elected politicians, have existential or ideological reasons for downplaying the dangers that arise when money can buy the state. A sarcastic phrase, heard in Bangkok, is based on the modern Thai word for capitalism, *thunniyom*. Thus "people power" or "democracy," *prachathipatai*, can be transformed into "capital power" or "capitalocracy," *thunathipatai*. That is what happens when elections let private funds buy votes for politicians who can turn public revenues into private money.

BANGKOK REFORMERS AND MEDIA VS. PROVINCIAL MINISTERS AND MONEY

Thailand has a clear primate city, but the provinces produce far more votes for members of parliament. Provincial and "county" (*muang*) capital cities are in aggregate very important. The population of Bangkok is less than the combined population of the next five largest cities, and it is also about equal to the total in all remaining Thai towns with more than half a million people each.[101] So the capital is prominent, as many writers have emphasized, but the rest of the country

---

[101]Ronald Hill, *Southeast Asia: People, Land, and Economy* (Crows Nest, NSW, Allen and Unwin, 2002), 245.

is at least as important in terms of long-run political and economic development.

Bangkok politics differs from politics in other parts of Thailand. Bangkok elites organized the Chart Thai, Social Action, and Democrat parties in the mid-1970s, but each of these was taken over by provincial business interests a decade later. Chavalit eventually organized the New Aspiration Party in the 1990s, and it made alliances with many provincial MPs.[102] Chamlong, known for his political integrity and devout Buddhism, founded the Palang Dharma party in a bid for the Bangkok governorship in 1985. His opponents had far more money, but Chamlong won in that urban electorate by a landslide. Many middle-class voters in the capital liked his rejection of Thai traditional politics (*trapo* is Tagalog for the same phenomenon). Three years later, his party won 10 of Bangkok's 37 parliamentary seats, and the following year he was re-elected as Bangkok governor. This is just one case of regional success by a party, or at least by a politician.

Thai political parties, like most of the government, generally stayed in Bangkok. They had to go upcountry to deal with rural patrons before elections, but their voters' loyalty was to local *jaopho* patrons, not to parties. As one godfather put it, "We go for friends, and not for the party. This is the way of us countryfolks."[103] The Chart Thai, Chart Pattana, and New Aspiration parties had particular connections with patrons in the Northeast. The Kitsangkom (Social Action) Party was linked to local leaders in the central plains, where Chart Thai candidates also did well. The Democrat Party has been less dependent on rural patrons — and largely for this reason, it was often unsuccessful during the 1990s at mustering votes outside Bangkok.[104] The Thai party system is strongly regionalized, like those in many past democracies (including the United States during its 1865–1929 decades of fastest economic growth, or South Korea with

---

[102]Pasuk Phongpaichit and Chris Baker, "Power in Transition: Thailand in the 1990s," 30–31.

[103]Quoted in Pasuk Phongpaichit and Sungsidh Piriyarangsan, *Corruption and Democracy*, 93.

[104]Suchit Bunbongkarn, *State of the Nation*, 89.

its Kyongsang-Cholla divide during its quickest boom). Premier Banharn, who got few votes in the capital, announced in 1996 with great pride that, "Bangkok is not Thailand."[105] This was politically (not just geographically) very accurate, though the relatively good documentation from Bangkok has somewhat obscured it among political analysts.

Regionalism plays a major and open role in Thai politics. Party leaders who stood for election in the Northeast in 1995, including Chatichai and Chavalit, asked voters to choose an "Isan prime minister."[106] (Before them, the Isan authoritarian Premier-General Sarit, an ethnic Lao, did not really need votes.) The Lao/Isan population is large enough to make this kind of appeal meaningful, but any potential premier should have coalition partners from other regions too. Ethnic or religious appeals, aside from the Palang Dharma Party's use of Buddhist rhetoric and political organizations among Thai Muslims in the South, can seldom be used effectively. Money, not ethnicity, is what swings votes now in Thailand.

Corruption has been the most hardy perennial issue in Thai politics, but reformist Bangkok politicians hoping to win national power on the basis of this issue are outvoted most of the time. Provincial seats are four-fifths of the Thai parliament. No stable government can be formed without very extensive support outside Bangkok. But coalitions organized by personalities rather than policies can be unstable. Parties based mainly outside the capital led the ruling blocs in 1995 and 1996, for example — and both these governments fell because of corruption investigations spearheaded by Bangkok MPs, only to be replaced by other cabinets that were later deemed to be just somewhat less corrupt. Money was increasingly the lubricant of democratic governance. As the quotable Chart Thai leader Banharn once commented, "For a politician, being in opposition is like starving yourself to death."[107]

---

[105]Danny Unger, *Building Social Capital in Thailand: Fibers, Finance, and Infrastructure* (Cambridge: Cambridge University Press, 1998), 39.

[106]Surin Maisrikrod and Duncan McCargo, "Electoral Politics: Commercialisation and Exclusion," 135.

[107]Pasuk Phongpaichit and Chris Baker, "Power in Transition: Thailand in the 1990s," 31.

Thai ministers developed the habit of taking a small percentage of their ministerial budgets for personal use — and many considered this practice entirely normal. Under Banharn, the rake-off reached 7 or 8 percent, a rate that many in Bangkok considered unacceptably high. The Thai parliament in 1998, which had been elected under the previous constitution, contained about fifty full ministers and vice-ministers among almost 400 MPs. Fifty is a large number, in view of the claims on public money that their constituents expected them to make.

The overall size of the Thai budget has usually been set, under norms that are constitutionally mandated, by the National Economic and Social Development Board. This is Thailand's agency to draw up flexible economic plans, at least for the government, and it consults with other technocrats in the Ministry of Finance and the Bureau of the Budget (which is part of the premier's office). So the total size of any Thai budget is mostly fixed by bureaucrats.[108] The House of Representatives is constitutionally empowered only to cut the budget, not to raise it. Increasingly over the years, ministers, deputy ministers, and legislators have influenced appropriations, even though the Thai Diet is on a budgetary diet. These domestic fiscal rules tend to stabilize the baht.

The amount parliament can appropriate receives a ceiling from the bureaucracy — but then cabinet ministers (rather than all parliamentarians) determine the division of this state money. Spending bills for specific projects may not originate in either the upper or lower houses. Parliament just allocates a bloc appropriation to each ministry. The relevant ministers decide specific appropriations.[109] That pattern gives entrepreneurial groups major incentives to cultivate cabinet members in all possible ways.

The aim of every Thai politician is to become a minister, or at least a vice-minister, in an important department. Two ministries, those of

---

[108]Richard F. Doner and Anek Laothamatas, "Thailand: Political and Economic Gradualism," in *Voting for Reform: Political Liberalization, Democracy, and Economic Adjustment*, Stephan Haggard and Steven B. Webb, eds. (Oxford: Oxford University Press, 1994), 438.

[109]Ueda Yoko, *Local Economy and Entrepreneurship in Thailand: A Case Study of Nakhon Ratchasima* (Kyoto: Kyoto University Press, 1995).

Transport and Communication (in charge of contracts for roads and much infrastructure) and Interior (in charge of all Thai police and provincial governments) are "four-party ministries." Chavalit, Banharn, and Chuan negotiated their coalitions by giving at least vice-ministerships in those two ministries to MPs from four parties each. Less lucrative units, such as the ministries of Justice, Foreign Affairs, Labor, and University Affairs are usually just single-party ministries.[110]

Patronist factions are the real "parties" that claim ministerial posts. Perhaps the most famous such group was headed by Sanoh Thienthong, leader of the Wang Nam Yen bloc of about twenty MP's from the Northeast in the 1990s. They supported Banharn (from Suphanburi, in the west of the central plain) as premier. But when Chavalit won the top post, they smoothly switched to him — and then again to Thaksin when the latter became premier. Their real party was to be in cabinet posts that controlled state money. Ruling coalitions came and went. But political fragmentation made Sanoh and his flexible followers, who had just one well-known principle, unlike a political party in a crucial respect: they could not lose.

As quid for the quo of their support in parliament, Sanoh's followers were careful not to demand top ministries such as Interior or Defense. They limited themselves to Transportation, partly because of the importance of road building in the Northeast whence the coalition members came. Construction contract money, rather than high posts for their personnel or any other kind of policy, was their priority. These were politicians with a solid predictable ethic. For whomever was elected premier, they became loyal supporters.

Thai politicians follow "the factional imperative" when organizing governments in Bangkok, but this is nearly irrelevant to the way most of them leave the provinces for parliament in the first place. Parties in Thailand have been little more than alliances of leaders who have their own separate power bases. A prominent Thai academic said that, "The parties are functioning as anti-democratic entities." In his view, Thai parties are no more than "gangs of personalities eager to get money."[111]

---

[110]See the table in Bidhya Bowornwathana, "Thailand: Bureaucracy Under Coalition Governments," 291.

[111]Based on an interview with a Thai political scientist who has been influential in efforts to improve his country's constitution.

Urban politics, however, is somewhat different. Because municipal district councillors in Bangkok control budgets that are heavily influenced by MPs from rural areas, the representatives from urban constituencies cannot easily win elections just by delivering "pork." They are more oriented to policy than to the financing and networking that are keys to success in rural elections. A relatively large portion of voters in the capital have usually identified as Democrats, if they identified with any party.

Party loyalty is more important in the capital than in rural Thailand. Bangkok voters were polled in October 1996, just before an election, concerning the criteria they would use to decide their ballots. More than half (54 percent) replied they would "look at the party." Another 28 percent said they would "look at both the party and the candidate" — while only 17 percent said they would "look at the candidate" alone.[112] It is unclear whether these attitude survey responses reflected the respondents' actual voting behavior, but it is very clear that rural citizens looked at candidates and canvassers first. Bangkok people have been more extensively surveyed, but their interests do not set the national agenda.[113]

In the populous Northeast, elections are candidate-based even though parties like Chavalit's New Aspiration Party, Thaksin's Thai Rak

---

[112]Professor Sukhum Chaleysub made this result available, and Ms. Nittaya Vairojanavong translated it from Thai for this author.

[113]A Dusit poll in Bangkok and its suburbs in October 1996 asked voters which media supplied most of their information about elections. Fully 63 percent said the most important source was TV. A surprisingly high 20 percent said they got most of their electoral information about candidates from organized political rallies. No other source (posters, newspapers, radio, or hand-out pamphlets) were cited by more than 10 percent. The kinds of information that Bangkok voters said they most wanted from different media was not uniform. From newspapers, one-third said they wished to read "true and unbiased" specifics, and this was the most common response regarding the press. From radio, a slightly higher portion said broadcasting stations should urge voters to go and exercise their election rights. From TV, the most common response (also about one-third) indicated the popularity of live interviews with candidates. Another 28 percent said they learned from candidates' televised speeches. Another Dusit poll found nearly the same response rates to the question, "What kind of media is most influential." Thanks are due to Professor Sukhum Chaleysub for the poll results and to Ms. Nittaya Vairojanavong, for translating the questions from Thai.

Thai bloc, and similar conservative coalitions coopted most of the winning candidates. North Thailand around Chiang Mai shows that same pattern, where the Chart Pathana, New Aspiration, Thai Rak Thai, and similarly personalistic parties elect practically all the representatives. The central Chao Phraya plain is divided among various conservative parties, of which the Chart Thai was once most prominent. The South, especially in years when Chuan Leekpai was prominent, has sometimes supported Democrats. (Muslim MPs, representing Malay groups near the southern border, have at various times joined the New Aspiration or Democrat parties, but the situation of this small but much-reported minority raises issues beyond this book's necessary scope. In the next chapter, the Muslims of Mindanao are similarly neglected.)

Local bosses and canvassers in most parts of the country are more important to citizens than are politicians with higher titles. For example, the two MPs representing Ayutthaya Province were both eager in the 1990s to use their influence over state funds to secure support from *kamnan* and subdistrict heads. Neither MP, though they were in different national parties, had any coherent ideology. Their party membership was irrelevant to their electoral successes.[114]

By the same token, high government officials are not always the patrons when they are in clientelistic relations with business people. Which is the patron, and which the client, depends on behavior, not on titles. The superior in a dyadic patronistic link can be either public or private. The Tourist Authority of Thailand, for example, is a government organization; but many of its activities are financed by private funds, so that officials readily become the clients of business people, rather than vice-versa. Their patrons are not ordinary citizens: "some of them are ... former cabinet members, leaders of political parties, friends of the prime minister, and so on."[115] Only sometimes are they formal state officials.

When the Ministry of Commerce had to negotiate with the American government to make sure that Thailand could export rice

---

[114]Daniel Arghiros, *Democracy, Development, and Decentralisation*, 101.
[115]Anek Laothamatas, *Business Associations and the New Political Economy*, 107.

to the U.S., this official agency was by no means the only Thai actor. In these talks, the Ministry bureaucrats relied extensively on leaders of the private Thai Rice Exporters' Association as negotiators. This non-state network had more political influence than the state ministry did. The Association's leaders were courted by top Thai politicians, who wanted the very large blocs of rural ballots they could deliver in districts where many voters are rice farmers. The Association's leaders canvass votes only for politicians who help their businesses. The bureaucrats, ultimately appointed by the politicians, know that businessmen are at the top of this hierarchy.

The Bangkok government does not take on the job of mediating all major business conflicts. For example, the Society of Drug Stores of Thailand, representing ordinary pharmacies all over the country, established a scheme under which medicine manufacturers were forced to give special discounts to Society members as a monopsony, reputedly to finance a school in northern Thailand where the sons and daughters of Society members could study pharmacy. A very large German drug company, Schering, at first refused to grant this discount and sold directly to drug stores outside the Society — whose members then boycotted Schering, cancelling all orders from that company and refusing to pay past Schering bills. The government apparently did not dare take sides. Later Schering relented and gave a formal apology to the Society.[116]

Thai domestic companies could come under similar pressure. When the country's largest spinner, Thai Melon Textiles, needed official permission to install 250,000 more spindles to make yarn for export on which the company would pay low taxes, smaller producers within the Thai Textile Manufacturers' Association objected. Thai Melon was allowed to produce its low-tax yarn only with a delay, after concessions were made to smaller factories. The SMEs were scattered, but they were able to organize.

Scott Christensen and Ammar Siamwalla have noted that, "Thailand is experiencing a rapid shift from an administrative-centered to an interest-centered government, whereby individuals

---

[116]*Ibid.*, 110; and for the next item, see 111.

and groups from various quarters of society have penetrated the State and are increasingly shaping the goods and services it supplies." Somchai Pakapaswiwat writes even more plainly: "Nowadays, political influence is tantamount to business influence."[117]

The media in Thailand provide more varied information than do those in many parts of East Asia, but they serve the business people who own them. Thai media can be linked to political parties, but it is at least as valid to associate them with tycoons. Individuals owning the main Thai dailies, such as *Thai Rath, Siam Rath*, and the *Daily News*, have fairly clear party allegiances. *Siam Rath*, once considered the best newspaper in the country, was bought by a "godfather" who got his start in gambling. It became popular partly because of the political scandals and rumors that it reported. Among television stations, most channels in the late 1990s were still owned by government or military agencies, although the news department of Independent Television (ITV), founded by a syndicate of investors, became proud of its muckraking against police corruption. When media sold stocks and became publicly owned, they were harder for the government to control — until Thaksin bought many media outlets and used them to help get nearly complete control of the civilian government.[118]

Thailand's parties are more fluid than those in many places (e.g., Taiwan), but the urban parties are less fluid and more policy-oriented than those in the Philippines. After a detailed study of the Democrats, the Palang Dharma group, and New Aspiration party, McCargo suggests that, "The frequent emergence of new parties testifies not simply to instability in the political order, but also to a continuing dynamism."[119] Leftist parties of labor or rightist parties of capital are hard to find in Thailand. Parties that promote specific politicians are

---

[117]Both quoted in John Girling, *Interpreting Development*, 45.

[118]On the pre-Thaksin material, see Duncan McCargo, *Politics and the Press in Thailand* (London: Routledge, 2001).

[119]Duncan McCargo, "Thailand's Political Parties, Real, Authentic, and Actual" in *Political Change in Thailand: Democracy and Participation*, Kevin Hewison, ed. (London: Routledge, 1997), 114–15.

easy to identify, although some take positions that identify with Buddhism or reform. Personalistic parties are practically the only kind in the Philippines, but they are less important now in richer Taiwan.

When elected politicians try to reward their supporters with construction contracts or licenses, small businesses tend to prosper. They have less reputation to lose than do big firms. Large corporations prefer to make longer-term plans in a climate of less political caprice, and many are headquartered in Bangkok. The underdevelopment of a system of policy-oriented parties gives big firms few obvious political organizations to support. Corporations have generally liked the predictability that comes from reforms such as those of the Anand regime, e.g., instituting a value-added tax, a Security and Exchange Commission, and some mild environmental laws.[120] But the Security Exchange of Thailand has allowed few companies to be listed (only 94 in 1990), so the influx of capital, like that of FDI, was for a long time limited to large firms that hired a small minority of the labor force — and controlled few votes in elections.[121] This situation will change, and has begun to change, as Thailand develops larger industries.

THE TRADITION OF CONSTITUTIONAL FIXES

The most obvious shift when royal absolutism ended was the establishment of a constitution. This scripture was endowed with some of the previously royal legitimacy that no politician or general could begin to claim. Thailand's constitutions since then have been many: seventeen basic laws between 1932 and 2006. They have evolved gradually. New editions crib long passages from earlier ones. Major institutions such as the monarchy, the bureaucracy, the army, and the

---

[120]See Scott R. Christensen and Ammar Siamwalla, *Beyond Patronage: Tasks for the Thai State* (Bangkok: Thailand Development Research Institute Foundation, 1993), 24–25.

[121]See James Clad, *Behind the Myth: Business, Money, and Power in Southeast Asia* (London: Hyman, 1989), 97.

parliament have fluctuated in power but have not in ideal terms sup-
planted each other permanently. Even when generals seized power, as
they frequently did, they felt the need for a written constitution,
either composing a new one or reviving an old one.

The 1973 shift from military to civilian government and the
army's popular or electoral failures of 1991–92 and 2007 showed a
long-term trend of change that had many ebbs and flows. For the
period emphasized in this book, the Thai constitutions of 1978,
1991, 1997, and 2006 are most important. The 1978 constitution,
in particular, struck a balance between conservative and reformist
forces and tended to stabilize Thai politics. The anti-inflationary
norm that bureaucrats rather than politicians set the overall size of
the state budget, as well as a norm that the king should finalize a
constitution's approval, have been important principles in that and
later constitutions.

Thai parties have long been fragmented or personalistic, and
recent constitutions aimed to make them more unified and policy-
oriented. In the parliamentary elections of the mid-1970s and mid-
1980s, however, no party ever emerged with a majority of seats.
There were always at least three or four major parties, each of which
had more than 10 but less than 30 percent of the seats.[122] These were
joined my many smaller "parties" centered even more obviously on
specific patrons. By the 1990s, the Thai constitution required that
parties had to field as least half as many candidates as the total number of constituencies (one per province, plus three for Bangkok). Its
aim was to make parties less regional and more national. The personalism and parochialism of parties was only slightly reduced by this
rule, however. Coalitions were formed to meet the legal requirement,
but that was not sufficient to hold them together after the voting, as
money had to be divided.

In the Thai 1995 general election, most constituencies were mandated to choose two or three MPs. Especially when districts elected

---

[122]Chai-Anan Samudavanija, "Thailand: A Stable Semidemocracy," in *Politics in Developing Countries: Comparing Experiences with Democracy*, Larry Diamond, Juan Linz and S.M. Lipset, eds., 2nd edition (Boulder: Rienner, 1990), 285; see also 292.

three deputies, candidates from the same party often had to compete with one another. Also, parties had sometimes been legally required to field as many candidates in any district as there were available seats. When the number of parties was large (up to eleven in some areas), they in practice designated their "real" candidates, with other party nominees on the ballot merely as "stunt men" to satisfy the legal requirement. As in Taiwan, this electoral system encouraged vote-buying, because small pluralities could sometimes win seats.[123]

CONSTITUTIONAL EFFECTS OF THE FINANCIAL CRISIS

The financial crisis of 1997 was severe enough to assure a coup under pre-1990s norms. But the army and king in 1997 quietly condoned political reform instead. The crisis became a test of the army's professionalism and ability to remain low-profile in active politics, at least until business corruptions became very egregious among civilian politicians. Coups had been entirely normal responses to lesser catastrophes before 1992. Thailand's soldiers not only stayed in their barracks during the 1997 fiscal crisis; most of them apparently wanted to do so. They came out to stanch Thaksin's political-economic greed nine years later, but only after they had strong backing from the king.[124]

Thailand's constitutional change of September 1997 was designed to strengthen the party system. After a reformed constitution came out of a committee of sages that was chaired by Anand and reputedly approved by the king, one hundred of the parliamentary seats were reserved for parties that achieved five percent or more of the vote across all of Thailand, and the other four hundred seats were elected from single-member districts. So each voter cast two ballots for representatives: one for an MP running in a single-member geographic

---

[123]William A. Callahan and Duncan McCargo, "Vote Buying in Thailand's Northeast," 378.

[124]The army is not a political monolith, and some officers continued to assume major roles in the government. As late as mid-1998, for example, the Army Chief Chetta Thanajaro had apparently not foreclosed the possibility that after retirement he would run for parliament (where his daughter-in-law already sat).

district, and one for a party list of candidates that was (for each of the parties) uniform throughout Thailand. Although 400 MPs were elected from single-member districts, the remaining 100 were chosen from the party lists in accord with the percentage of votes each list received nationally (and in accord with each party's ranking of names on its roster prior to the election). A party naturally put its best-known candidates on its national list.

Party list candidates, under this system, had an additional advantage in obtaining cabinet posts, because when such a candidate was elected but then had to resign from parliament to take a minister-ship under the new arrangement, the highest-ranked non-elected candidate on the same party's list automatically got the parliamentary seat. The other class of candidates, running in districts, could not so blithely resign for the sake of gaining a ministry, because that would threaten the party's control of the legislative seat. If a geographically chosen representative left parliament to become a minister, a bye-election was required — and in this contest, another party's candidate (perhaps the runner-up in the first campaign) could win.

Anand's constitution-writing committee thus tried to give the parties incentives to build strong internal organizations. Their candidates had to agree on a ranking among themselves prior to an election. Parties also were supposed to have big incentives to put forward major candidates of national stature, who could attract support throughout Thailand rather than merely among local voters, and to build strong party organizations in many parts of the country.

Anand's committee also proposed other institutions whose legitimacies were functional, rather than electoral. A Constitutional Court contained fifteen judges, whom the king appointed after approval by the Senate (which was constitutionally mandated to seek advice from academics and experienced statesmen not currently involved in politics). This body included five justices from the Supreme Court, two from the Supreme Administrative Court, five lawyers, and as many as three political scientists. The theory was implicitly Rawlsian: to find sages who could make decisions separate from their immediate interests.

Another 1997 institution was a National Election Commission, whose members could not be in political parties or hold other offices. This group was empowered to invalidate corrupt elections, and it was supposed to complement and strengthen the National Counter-Corruption Commission. Anand's committee did not foresee that a money-based single party (Thaksin's) could begin by working within the constraints these eminently sensible separate powers imposed on it, until that party's electoral mandate became so overwhelming that these institutions could be simply suspended.

The new constitution was also designed to reduce corruption by upgrading the national laws against it. It did not take full account of the design of more local power networks that the boom corrupted, but being "unusually rich" (the legal phrase for 'corrupt') became unconstitutional.[125] Although previous laws had made "unusual richness" illegal, albeit under necessarily complex definitions and court procedures, parliamentarians had been immune from prosecution. Anand's reforms required that anyone assuming a ministry or vice-ministership had to declare all personal assets, as well as all assets of immediate family members. Upon leaving office, the same declaration was required again. Under previous laws, such declarations had been filed with an Anti-Corruption Committee — but in secret. The Committee had usually taken no action on the basis of them. (When Chavalit's ministers later had to file declarations in public after the new constitution took effect, the press had a field day explaining whence their money had come.)

Anand's committee incorporated many provisions that seemed futuristic — such as the requirements that all MPs should have baccalaureates, that corrupt elections could be invalidated by the new monitoring commission, and that a plurality rather than a majority of parliament was sufficient to start investigations of ministers accused of corruption. Wealth was no longer supposed to be enough to qualify office-holders for posts such as provincial governorships or deputy

---

[125]For Chinese comparisons, see Melanie Manion, *Corruption by Design: Building Clean Government in Mainland China and Hong Kong* (Cambridge: Harvard University Press, 2004).

governorships, or for ministries or membership in parliament. This constitution asserted the arguably undemocratic Asian (notably Chinese) norm that officials own a right to rule because of exam-tested knowledge, rather than because they win popular votes.[126] The new requirement nonetheless caused temporary consternation among Thai Chinese entrepreneurs, some of whom wanted high offices but lacked the requisite academic credentials.[127]

Another 1997 clause indicated that a petition by any 50,000 Thai citizens would force a special investigation of charges about corruption in any holder of a state office. A plurality of MPs could do the same, so that the ruling party or coalition was supposed to rule uncorruptly. (Anand's group did not foresee that the party of a populist patriotic demagogue, Thaksin, could win so many seats that the opposition would lack enough votes for corruption probes.) The legal result in 1997 was startling, not so much for what it accomplished immediately but for what it seemed to promise in the future. If the new procedures were to take hold firmly, their advocates thought, they could decisively change the style of Thai politics.

Why was the new constitution passed, even though it ran against the interests of most politicians? Clearly the economic crisis of late 1997 was the crucial factor in causing approval of this fundamental reform. The Thai Cabinet had to vote on the new constitution, approving or disapproving it, at the same session when it had to develop a policy for the financial crash. At this time, the felt need for basic change was intense.

---

[126]For more, see Daniel A. Bell, *East Meets West: Human Rights & Democracy in East Asia* (Princeton: Princeton University Press, 2000).

[127]Politically ambitious people with money soon became adept at solving the problems presented by new rules. For example, many foreign universities would, for tuition fees, provide easy correspondence courses leading to suitably titled degrees. Within Thailand, entrance to elite institutions such as Chulalongkorn and Thammasat universities remained subject to strict tests; but open admission was available at other institutions, such as Ramkhamhaeng University, which by the turn of the millennium reportedly enrolled 300,000 students. "School ties" among politically prominent and wealthy graduates of Ramkhamhaeng became important in Thai politics.

Some politicians may well have thought such institutions were so far removed from Thai political practice that they could never be implemented. MPs called for amendments to weaken many provisions. Premier Chavalit and other conservatives clearly preferred these amendments, but they were finally unable to dilute the document in a direct way. Democratic Bangkok intellectuals tended to think that 1997 had produced "two steps forward." They defended the new document as a whole, realizing that the political management of its adoption had been a rare opportunity, under the very exceptional circumstances of that year. "One step back" might be acceptable, according to some intellectual interviewees, but only to allow time for implementation.

It is surprising in comparative perspective that the 1997 constitution was approved. The reason for its passage were two. First, a very prominent conservative leader (the king) subtly let it be known that he favored the changes Anand's committee had proposed. As a merely constitutional monarch, he did not have standing to speak directly in public about these reforms. But he did not suppress a public rumor that the state of Thai politics in late 1997 was making the king physically sick. A medical doctor, who claimed to be the royal physician, asserted this. (Later investigative reporting revealed that this man was in fact not the king's doctor, but silence from the palace strengthened the constitutional reformers nonetheless.)

The most savvy of the king's children, Princess Sirindhorn, appeared at a meeting several weeks before the parliamentary vote on the new basic law, wearing a green T-shirt printed by a constitutional reformist group. This was not quite a statement from the throne, but many observers took it (and were no doubt intended to take it) as a clear sign that the palace wanted Anand's document to be passed. A crucial factor for this major constitutional reform, which the premier and cabinet disliked, has been partly neglected because it was royal, and kings are not very modern things.

Social scientists tend to see this factor as a cultural relic, outmoded, presumably decorative, even when they are bemused that Thais repeatedly and explicitly treat the monarchy with great seriousness. The army, under these conditions, did not oppose the constitutional change. The royal appeal was spurred in part by the financial crisis, and the crisis situation made many intellectuals hope that political reform could be put on a fast track. So there was pressure on parliamentarians to support the draft constitution, despite the reluctance of the majority who were business politicians. They ended up voting for it.

The creative thinking that went into the 1997 constitution was proceduralist, and the schemes by which politicians undermined it were also extremely creative. Trying to build a stronger and less chaotic central state, Anand's committee unintentionally aided the creation of Thaksin's electorally legitimated centralism. It underestimated the power of new money to circumvent and corrupt legal procedures. As most formal political scientists tend to do, the constitution-writing committee also underestimated the extent to which networks outside the state could shape the government.

The new constitution, along with Chuan Leekpai's resumption of the premiership after Chavalit, nonetheless altered the mood of Thai politics. The financial crisis did not lead to a collapse of public faith in government. Thailand already had a relatively diversified economy, when compared to most others in its region. Even during the crisis period 1997–98, Thailand's GDP was as much as 24 percent of the total of the nine main economies of Southeast Asia (nearly equal to that of Indonesia which had 3.4 times as many people, while the Philippines and Malaysia each had only 14 percent of the regional GDP).[128] Despite the crisis, Thailand was still doing relatively well. Its GDP per person was US$2,200 on a conventional basis, or US$5,840 on a purchasing-power-parity basis. (The corresponding figures for the Philippines, whose temporary downturn because of the financial crisis was less, were only US$1,050 and US$3,540.)[129]

---

[128]In 1998, Thailand had 60.3 million people, and the population was growing fairly slowly (demographers predicted 68.9 million by 2015). The Philippines had 72.9 million (96.7 by 2015). Indonesia had 206.3 million (over 250 million by 2015). Malaysia had just 21.4 million (27.5 million by 2015). See United Nations Development Program, *Human Development Report 2000* (New York: Oxford University Press, 2000), 224–25.

[129]*Ibid.*, 158, gave Thailand and the Philippines almost the same human development index for 1998, but even in this year Thailand's economic component in that index was higher, while the Philippines' educational component was higher. See also Ronald Hill, *Southeast Asia*, 140.

The International Monetary Fund staff, seeking whom to blame for the Asian financial crisis, indicted Asian banks' bad loans, speculation in currency and property, "crony capitalism," authoritarianism, and corruption.[130] The IMF found no fault with itself or the World Bank. Economists who want to deal with governments cannot easily speak about official failings — or even officially unintended lapses. When a crisis came, these neoclassical economists resorted, albeit just temporarily, to political sociology.

By mid-1998, a new labor law was passed to reduce the ill effects of the crisis and of the IMF bailout closures on ordinary workers. It specified rates of severance pay that companies were supposed to pay (even if they were so small as to have just one employee). Young Democrat MPs from Bangkok, although they were not a majority in the parliament, took many cabinet posts. The Thai polity was jolted but not cleansed of all its problems, because most of these were local and outside Bangkok.

Chuan's government took actions at the national level that did not solve the problems of rural leaders. It decided to publish its "letters of intent" to the IMF in Thai (as well as English), to publish economic data weekly, to fire many top cadres of the central bank, and to bring court suits against previous bankers whose malfeasance could be evidenced. But the governor of the Central Bank of Thailand had held his office on the sufferance of the Minister of Finance — and thus at the pleasure of monied politicians. At the same time, the 1997 IMF package for Thailand in effect bailed out financial institutions by cutting back public projects that had benefitted poor people (as well as politicians). "Fiscal discipline" was at the expense of the poor, although the previous lack of fiscal discipline had also benefitted the rich.

The hope that writing a better constitution will result in better politics ignores two factors that this book emphasizes. First, the power network of a whole nation is not, for many citizens, the most important power network; nonstate local structures (families, villages,

---

[130]See Hock-Beng Cheah, "From Miracle to Crisis and Beyond: The Role of Entrepreneurship and SMEs in Asia," in *Globalisation and SMEs in East Asia*, Charles Harvie and Boon-Chye Lee, eds. (Cheltenham: Edward Elgar, 2002), 236.

schools, factories, shops, temples) for many purposes trump state institutions in either behavioral or normative terms. Second, not all power is public and governmental; much influence, especially in periods of booming change, is private and economic. Wise constitutions are much better than uncareful ones. But it would be expecting too much of any document that constitutes a state to solve the all the political problems that emerge from modern nonstate institutions in smaller networks.

THE POPULIST PERSISTENCE OF A PORK POLITICIAN

Chavalit, ousted into opposition by Chuan and by the financial crisis, was quick to criticize the new rulers who had deposed him for hurting ordinary Thais. At a rally in the Isan, he proclaimed that, "The opposition [his New Aspiration Party] is extremely concerned, because it will not be long before ten million poor starve, if the government fails to bring about economic recovery."[131] Chuan tried to respond by raising foreign investment in Thailand and by amending old laws that had restricted alien businesses and foreigners' land-ownership rights. So an "Alliance for National Salvation" associated with Chavalit accused the government of benefitting foreigners at the expense of locals (even though that was what Chavalit had also done before the crisis).

Chuan's Democratic Party fought back with revelations about public scandals during the previous regime. Chuan had support from many in the business community as well as most intellectuals. He could also offer increasing evidence that foreign capital inflows were helping to revive the economy. Many newspapers blamed Chavalit's regime for having allowed banks to extend loans imprudently and for asking taxpayers to foot the bill for bankruptcies.

Because of the 1997 financial crisis, many small Thai enterprises went bankrupt. They could not get loans to meet obligations they

---

[131] *The Nation*, Bangkok, Aug. 11, 1998, quoted in Carlos Manuel Lazatín, *The Challenge of Economic Reform in a Democracy: The Philippines and Thailand in the 1990s* (Princeton University Senior Thesis, Woodrow Wilson School, 1999), 62; see also 61 and 67.

had already undertaken. The turnover among such firms is often high, however, and the entrepreneurs do not always disappear, even if their companies do. By 1998, the Ministry of Industry prepared a "Master Plan" for small and medium firms, partly out of awareness that their founders could readily return to contributing jobs and product to the economy. Legislation for an SME Promotion Bill, and later for an SME Promotion Fund that could syphon public money to local entrepreneurs, found quick support in the Democrat, Chart Pattana, and Thai Rak Thai parties. Such plans were easily approved in the House of Representatives, although the Senate delayed some of them.[132]

After his election to the premiership in 2001, Thaksin Shinawatra adopted a more interventionist economic policy, especially for businesses, than had the previous government. In the earlier era under Chuan, retention of pre-1997 rules had forced many Thai firms to break up or sell interests to foreigners. Thaksin, consistent with his Thai Rak Thai/"Thais love Thais" party name, reversed this trend. His ministers pushed banks to help medium and small enterprises. The government directly bought some local companies' stocks to support their prices. The Thailand Assets Management Company assumed non-performing loans of 700 billion baht (US$17 billion), with the mandate that the debtor companies be rehabilitated rather than liquidated whenever possible. By 2002, Finance Minister Somkid Jatusripitak announced that, "The government aims not to be a savior, but a venture capitalist."

That meant yet more intervention. An economic journalist wrote that Thaksin had a "folksy industrial policy, by which the government guides small and medium sized enterprises up the value-added ladder into better-branded niche products and away from dependence on lower value-added manufacturing."[133] Recovery

---

[132]Peter Brimble, David Oldfield, and Manusavee Monsakul, "Policies for SME Recovery in Thailand," in *The Role of SMEs in National Economies in East Asia*, Charles Harvie and Boon-Chye Lee, eds. (Cheltenham: Edward Elgar, 2002), 206–07 and 217.
[133]Shawn W. Crispin, "Thaksin's New Deal," *Far Eastern Economic Review* (August 1, 2002), 37.

from the financial crisis was an ideal platform for a centralizer like Thaksin, who presented himself to urbanites as a populist — and to rural voters' bosses as the politician who gave them yet more public money.

Centralizing leaders often adopt populist policies so that they can delay the need to accommodate urban elites that want more liberal rule. The mid-nineteenth century French dictator Louis Napoleon restored universal male suffrage, and he wrote to friends in the Prussian government of 1861, advising them to do likewise: "In this system, the conservative rural population can vote down the liberals in the cities."[134] Often such leaders have strong ties to police; Thaksin or Marcos (or Putin or Stalin or Hitler) have followed Louis Napoleon and many other dictators in this respect.

Thailand's experience with Thaksin was certainly not the only political effect of its boom. Still, that leader deserves specific attention here, because he shows much about the structural change that the boom wrought Thai politics. Thaksin's great-grandfather, Seng-sae Khu (a.k.a. Khu Chun-seng), had arrived as a Hakka boy in Thailand shortly before 1870. By 1890, he was a tax farmer for gambling revenues in Chantaburi. His wife was Thai, named Thongdi. She helped him, as a crucial member of this Sino-Thai family that now called itself Shinawatra, to collect gambling profits. Later they moved to Chiang Mai, a city that still had considerable autonomy as the center of north Thailand. Prosperous Sino-Thai families such as the Shinawatras could support many sons. Thaksin's grandfather was the second of Seng-sae Khu's nine offspring, his father was the fourth of twelve siblings. (Thaksin himself is the second among ten.) The family diversified into cloth and silk, and several members attained university degrees, army officerships, and political posts. Thaksin's father, Loet, was elected an MP in 1969 and 1975 — although by the following year's elections, he had lost his fortune and stepped aside to let his brother take the seat in parliament.

---

[134]Quoted in Pranab Bardhan, "Dominant Proprietary Classes and India's Democracy," in *India's Democracy: An Analysis of Changing State-Society Relations*, Atul Kohli, ed. (Princeton: Princeton University Press, 1988), 216.

Thaksin entered the national police academy in 1969 and graduated at the top of his class in 1973. He got a scholarship for an M.A. in criminal justice from Kentucky, returned to take a Bangkok police job and to be married in 1975–76. But he "tangled with his superiors at the police station, who were running protection rackets for illegal businesses in their jurisdiction."[135] So Thaksin took a civil service commission exam for a scholarship to study for a Ph.D. in criminal justice at Sam Houston State University, Texas. His dissertation was based on a survey of students there, seeking to discover whether education in criminal justice improved their view of the rule of law. The finding was that it does so, but very marginally.

Back in Bangkok, Dr. Thaksin Shinawatra was put in charge of police planning. On the side, with varied degrees of business success, he opened a silk shop, a movie distribution company, an apartment building, and a firm that leased IBM computers. After several periods of indebtedness, this last venture succeeded, in part because the Bangkok Municipal Police needed computers. Thaksin's fortune came from telecom contracts, especially those issued by the Chatichai government in 1988–91 for card phones, data networks, and satellites. Links with the Telephone Organization of Thailand, a government agency, were vital to his wealth.

Senator Chirmsak Pinthong, famous for speaking his spicy views in public, in mid-2002 claimed that the state was increasingly dominated by people close to the Shinawatra family. Previous Thai political families, including the Kittikachorns, Thanarats, and Charusathiens, had also wielded great influence in earlier times, but an aim of the Senate was (in Chirmsak's opinion) to be independent of such pressures. He said that half the Senate had become "possessed by the government.... In the past, we had military dictatorship, but now it's a money dictatorship. Keep a close watch on the Shinawatra, Damapong [Thaksin's brother-in-law's] and Wongsawat [Thaksin's sister's] families, which will have the same political control as the

---

[135]These paragraphs rely on Pasuk Phongpaichit and Chris Baker, *Thaksin: The Business of Politics*, 30–45.

Kittikachorn, Thanarat, and Charusathen clans [once had]."[136] This political structure is nearly Philippine, although more of the political money in Thailand came from industrial-commercial profits rather than land rents.

Methamphetamine drugs provided Thaksin with an excuse to justify police ferocity — in practice, against almost anyone he chose in the countryside. By the turn of the millennium, three million Thais (out of 62 million total) were taking 700 million pills annually, and 300,000 were reportedly addicted. The government, dismissing concerns about the rule of law, set out provincial and district target quotas for arrests of traffickers. Officers were offered a bounty per pill they seized. Drug dealers were told, in official announcements, that they had to surrender themselves or risk death in efforts to arrest them.

Gangland-style killings, which had been known in Thailand for many years, quickly soared. The government claimed that godfathers were eliminating potential informers. Some of the murders, however, were committed by masked gunmen — perhaps in official pay — soon after the victims had left interrogations at police stations.[137] Many military and police officers, as well as politicians, were publicly suspected to profit from drug sales. Thaksin's campaign resembled Marcos's early moralism against big landholders whom the elected dictator did not like.

THE PSEUDO-POPULISM OF A NATIONAL *NAKLENG*

By late May 2003, police General Sombat Armornwiwat, in charge of the government's "anti-mafia" division, announced that a secret blacklist was on file, including "139 gunmen, 447 suspected gunmen, 13 underworld figures for whom arrest warrants have been issued, and a further 218 suspected mafia figures."[138] In his very popular war

---

[136]"PM's Clan Taking Over, Senator Says," *The Nation*, Monday, August 12, 2002.

[137]Pasuk Phongpaichit and Chris Baker, "Thailand's Brutal Campaign in the Name of a Drug War," *International Herald Tribune*, May 27, 2003, 7.

[138]Jason Gagliardi, "From Drugs and Bugs to Thugs," *South China Morning Post*, May 25, 2003, 12.

on drugs, Thaksin understood Charles Tilly's principle that, "a king's best source of armed supporters was sometimes the world of outlaws. Robin Hood's conversion to royal archer may be a myth, but the myth records a practice. The distinctions between 'legitimate' and 'illegitimate' users of violence came clear only very slowly."[139]

Thaksin held a special meeting of his cabinet at Pattaya, the headquarters of the most famous godfather, Somchai Khunpluem, a.k.a. Kamnan Poh. His trial for murder of a business rival was just beginning in the Criminal Court. Kamnan Poh was said to control seven Members of Parliament, two of whom were his own sons. Thaksin claimed that his hunt should expand, at this time, beyond drug lords to include also fourteen further categories of "dark influence":

— bid-rigging for government contracts,
— extorting money from motorcycle ('tuktuk') taxis,
— extorting money from factories, shops, and businesses,
— smuggling contraband liquor, petrol, cigarettes, and other goods
— operating gambling dens or illegal bookmaking operations,
— human trafficking,
— prostitution rackets,
— offering false placements for jobs overseas,
— cheating foreign tourists,
— maintaining networks of hit men,
— managing debt collectors who use violent methods,
— trafficking in weaponry,
— encroaching on public land or destroying natural resources, and
— bribing police to wink at offenses on highways and public land.[140]

Social evils of all these kinds were rife in Thailand during Thaksin's rule, but he called them corrupt only when they originated among his rivals rather than in his own coalition.

---

[139] This is a considerably broader form of a point made by Charles Tilly, "War Making and State Making as Organized Crime," in *Bringing the State Back In*, Peter Evans, *et al.*, eds. (Cambridge: Cambridge University Press, 1985), 173.

[140] This useful list of "dark influences," applicable to Thailand but also in other places, is from Jason Gagliardi, "From Drugs and Bugs to Thugs," 12.

This centralizing premier had a social program large enough to match his personal ambition and decisiveness. He became the national *nakleng*. Thaksin was not just another traditional politician without a platform. The Thai Rak Thai (TRT) party by 2005 developed a new kind of policy politics that aimed to attract the rural voting networks. Thaksin opined that, "Democracy is just a tool.... The goal is to give people a good lifestyle, happiness and national progress." He was openly illiberal (not just because his main opposition was labeled the Democrat Party). He touted a popular patriotic program, including basic health care for a standard price of 30 baht, a moratorium on farmers' debt repayments, a one-million baht government fund for villages, and a "one tambon, one product" development scheme — in short, a coherent program that justified sending money to rural networks supporting him.

This majoritarian version of policy politics was so successful in the 2005 election that Thaksin's TRT won all but 123 of the 500 seats in parliament. Because the 1997 constitution provided that 200 members were needed to initiate no confidence motions against ministers, this election legitimated an apparently patriotic demagogue to do anything he wished. The TRT trounced its opposition, so it could govern corruptly — and democratically — without fear of official inquiry.[141] Populist policy politics had put a small elite, headed by Thaksin and based among similar provincial businessmen, in nearly complete control of the government — except for some generals, Prem, and the king who was responsible for Thaksin's resignation a year later and then for the coup against him.

DEMOCRATIC KLEPTOCRACY

Thaksin's family sold to the Singapore government's holding company valuable licenses and concessions in Thai telecommunications

---

[141]Erik Martinez Kuhonta and Alex M. Mutebi, "Thaksin Triumphant: The Implications of One-party Dominance in Thailand," *Asian Affairs* 33:1 (Spring 2006), 40–44; quotations from 42 and 43. The provinces in which the opposition Democrats did best were the Malay-Muslim areas of the far south, Narathiwat, Pattani, and Yala.

that his Shin Corporation had obtained through political influence. Not a single baht of Thai tax was paid on the sale. The "Thais Love Thais" name was put in doubt by such behavior. When the news broke, Thaksin tried to relegitimate himself by calling a snap election in April — and his canvassers spent enough to win it. The king then virtually instructed the judiciary to annul the result and forced Thaksin into a caretaker premiership. So Thaksin planned another election, which he again could almost surely have won, for November. Democratic procedure had become the most reliable support of a corrupt regime.

Thaksin fully realized that he also needed army support. So he cultivated links between the police and Chulachomklao Military Academy officers from Class 10, especially Maj. Gen. Prin Suwanathat. But the Chief of Staff, Gen. Sonthi Boonyaratglin, had taken care to move the commanders who might have followed Maj. Gen. Prin out of Bangkok.[142]

On September 19, 2006, Sonthi led a coup against Thaksin, who was in New York at the time. Sonthi had long been known for his close links to the king, whose dislike of Thaksin had also long been rumored. There is evidence that the palace encouraged the coup before it occurred.[143] Mid-autumn had been a normal time for the Thai prime minister to rotate army commanders; and Thai top elites (surely including Thaksin) realized that any coup would occur before that event. That is what happened.

It is an index of Thai abilities to assimilate the talents of ethnic minorities that Sonthi is Muslim, not Buddhist. One of his policy

---

[142]Peter Alford, "PM Outmaneuvered," *The Weekend Australian*, September 23–24, 2006, 12.

[143]A Thai specialist who is a friend of the author noted that Princess Sirindhorn extended invitations to several Thaksin associates to accompany her to a Thai event in Paris that got them out of the country on the coup day. They could scarcely decline such a royal invitation. The coup planners succeeded in exiling a number of people who would have opposed their action, including Prime Minister Thaksin, and this probably helped them make the coup bloodless. For more, see Andrew Drummond and Peter Alford, "Thailand's Bloodless Coup," *The Australian*, September 21, 2006, 1, and related items on 8, 9, 11, and 12.

differences with Thaksin was that he hoped the army's ability to quell the Pattani movement in Thailand's Muslim south might be aided by talks with the rebels in which Thaksin refused to engage. This hope was hard to realize, even after the coup, because both the Pattanis and the local soldiers kept fighting.

Many foreign democratic leaders issued denunciations of the coup by the king and his generals. But the bloodless takeover was popular at first and in Bangkok, where crowds gathered to give soldiers flowers. Any democrat is bound to regret coups, and such acts certainly do not ensure clean or fair government. But Thailand's documentably corrupt politicians associated with Thaksin could buy any election, and democrats should find ways to regret money politics just as much as coups. Thus far, they have generally failed to do so.

The U.S. State Department announced, "We have made very clear in our statements that we consider the military move... a very sad development for Thai democracy. We are also reviewing our assistance to Thailand in light of the various legal implications for a country in which there has been a military coup to overthrow an elected civilian leadership."[144] Sonthi's golpistas called themselves the "Council for Democratic Reform under Constitutional Monarchy," but this made scant difference to Western elected politicians or their spokespeople.

Thailand's National Counter-Corruption Commission, which had been inactive for sixteen months, resumed its work with a new membership less than a week after the coup. It had a backlog of about 10,000 cases, but the priority was investigation of the sale for 73,000,000,000 baht by Thaksin's family of controlling interest in the Shin Corporation telecoms group to Temasek Holdings of Singapore. The Thai central bank estimated that most of this value (50,000,000,000 baht) went directly to Thaksin's family but was still inside Thailand.[145] It is unclear whether this commission (like the Philippine one trying

---

[144]Quoted in Peter Alford, "US May Deny the Junta Aid Funds," *The Weekend Australian*, September 23–24, 2006, 13.

[145]Peter Alford, "Thailand's Corruption Watchdog Reborn," *The Australian*, September 25, 2006, 1.

to pin crimes of theft on Marcos) would fail to reach anything more than a "not proven" Scottish verdict, because Thaksin had many ways to hide the channels through which money went during the time he was in power.

The generals could not fully maintain all the populist policies that had legitimated Thaksin's government, because their basis was provision of state funds to rural political networks that were locally private. So by the summer of 2007, thousands of protestors rallied in a Bangkok park to hear a video address by Thaksin (broadcast from his London townhouse) calling for a new election, telling the soldiers to go back to their barracks, and denying the legal charges against him. A small business owner at this rally, who had benefitted from one of Thaksin's microcredit programs, told a reporter, "I have come here for democracy and I want Thaksin to come back."[146] The assistant manager of a provincial textile factory, speaking between puffs on his cigarette, praised Thaksin's provision of free health care. His wife had opened a food stall on microcredit. This seemed more important than any thefts Thaksin made on his own behalf.

Soldiers could not by fiat change the monetized structure of the local politics in Thailand that the boom had created. The junta could not easily penetrate this structure without itself becoming corrupt. Elections had not reduced corruption; on the contrary, they had increased opportunities for graft. Democratization is in large part caused by the same factor that causes corruption: the rise of small industrial-commercial interests that control a tide of new money. Growth is accompanied by an increase of rich networks that can buy corrupt links to the state, by electoral or any other means.

MIDDLE-CLASS MODERN POLITICS IN THAILAND'S FUTURE?

Pasuk wrote in 1999 that the "period since the relaxation of military controls in the mid-1980s has seen a rapid explosion of social and

---

[146]Thomas Fuller, "Thousands Gather to Hear Thaksin: Video Address Sends Challenge to Military-Backed Leaders," *International Herald Tribune*, June 16–17, 2007, 3.

political demands that had been bottled up in earlier years." She sees this as

> a time of jolting social change, marked by the dramatic boom-bust cycle of the economy, large-scale migrations of people on a temporary and permanent basis, new patterns of work and consumption, and a much broader dissemination of ideas and information. These changes have provoked fear of a major social reorganization which would threaten long-established interests.... there is strong resistance to any form of democratisation which would give greater [non-purchasable] weight to the rural majority, or to the rapidly growing urban labour force.[147]

Thai workers' attempts to unionize have been partly hindered by the importance of small firms in the country's economic development. They were also arguably hindered by some of the tenets of Theravada Buddhism (e.g., precepts that enjoin quietistic acceptance of one's place in life, rather than strikes, although alternative Buddhist doctrines emphasize norms of justice). The surest way in which capitalists prevented Thai unions was straightforward "violence, threats, intimidation, and the harassment of labour activists."[148] High rates of subcontracting, typical in Thailand as in all Asian "tigers," led to high productivity but scant unionization.

So political reformists' hopes were mostly pinned on the "middle class." Actually, the several different Thai middle classes have a spotty history as regards democracy.[149] Many capitalists at first supported

---

[147]Pasuk Phongpaichit, "Civilizing the State: State, Civil Society, and Politics in Thailand," Wertheim Lecture (Amsterdam: Centre for Asian Studies, 1999), 9–10.

[148]Andrew Brown, *Labour, Politics, and the State in Industrializing Thailand* (New York: RoutledgeCurzon, 2004), 100.

[149]Members of the "middle class" (*khonchanklang*) found more interest in financing and asserting their Thai identity than social-scientific anti-culturalists would perceive. Commercial schools for the teaching of Thai dance (*ram thai*) sprang up in many cities, and "amateurs who practiced in these sites submit themselves to attaining and embodying a 'Thai-ness' and a range of cultural values associated with the nationally sanctioned, classical dance culture of the court... the new middle class emulates the lifestyle of the old elite...." Paritta Chalermpow Koanantakool, "Thai Middle-class Practice and Consumption of Traditional Dance: 'Thai-ness' and High Art," in *Local Cultures and the "New Asia": The State, Culture, and Capitalism ion Southeast Asia*, C.J.W.-L. Wee, ed. (Singapore: Institute for Southeast Asian Studies, 2002), 222.

Suchinda's 1991 coup. But Suchit describes modal views among one of the several middle classes, urban intellectuals: "When the coup broke out in 1991, the democratic mood was too strong to be wiped out."[150]

During the long political boom, elections increased the conflicts between reformists and conservatives. Voting first expanded in a period of "quasi-democracy" under the technocratic premier Prem. Famous watersheds in this process, especially from 1973 to 1992, provided precedents among intellectuals and urban bourgeois families suggesting a possibility of serious "people power." Movement democracy of this sort affected hopes more than it affected institutions. Slow changes in the structures of provincial economic decision making were just as important as the better-reported democratic resurgences in Bangkok. Local tyrants could increasingly buy votes, and they could repress reactions against exploitation of labor. The socioeconomic bases of local authoritarian rule became stronger, and reactions at the national level only sporadically weakened the political bases of local authoritarianism. With a king in Thailand to balance other forces (despite his own natural conservatism), few Thais were killed when these two tendencies clashed. Conservative populists and reformist urbanites alternated in power.

The turbulent politics of the early 1990s merit a final analysis in light of what followed, because they show the shape of Thai politics through the whole boom. In the May 1992 demonstrations, the press dubbed parties like the Democrats that had opposed Suchinda "angels," and those like the Chart Thai "devils." The Democrats were then the largest party. With fellow "angels" the Palang Dharma and New Aspiration parties, they almost had a majority in parliament — but they needed the smaller "devil" Social Action Party to form a government. Chart Thai and Chart Pathana became the opposition — as they probably would not have been, if they had not split conservatives in the election. Some parts of the Thai middle class supported the May 1992 protestors, but large capitalists did not. As Hewison writes, "The ready support of many middle-class people for the demonstrations contrasts starkly with the position of organized

---

[150]Suchit Bunbongkarn, *State of the Nation: Thailand* (Singapore: Institute of Southeast Asian Studies, 1996), 18–19.

capitalists, who were slow in throwing their support behind the demonstrators."[151]

Chai-Anan argues that the democratic movement was "a reunion, a revival of political activism that had less to do with economic well-being than with a common generational orientation." The seeds of democracy had been sown two decades earlier, and by the early 1990s they "came back in full bloom. Many of this generation now hold important positions in both the public and private sectors.... some have since organized informal groups of politically concerned businesspeople.... Thailand will [after this] always have dormant 'troops' of citizens that respond to oppressive regimes."[152]

As it turned out, Thailand actually has several different kinds of troops. The power to set basic political agendas cycles; at the national level it alternates among different kinds of legitimate leaders. According to intellectuals, the most vociferous but often weakest major actors, national policies usually do not represent what local people want; they represent what *jaopho* bosses want. National policies are sometimes set by the civil society elite, sometimes by soldiers, sometimes by the king, and now usually by politicians representing small businesses bosses who supply new jobs to rural citizens.

Thai liberals have hoped that democracy will become natural or inevitable as the country prospers. Thai participation in the global economy demonstrably meshes best with domestic liberalism.[153] But it is easy to jump the gun toward a conclusion that electoral democracy will work well soon in a country whose increasing spread of prosperity is still based on local tyrannies. Politics in Thailand still mostly concerns infrastructural investments and contests for money among lawmakers representing their provincial places. Such investments promote economic development, and eventually perhaps liberalization, but they also tend to damage the environment, force poor people to move their homes, empower owners of capital against

---

[151]Kevin Hewison, "Political Oppositions and Regime Change in Thailand," 84.

[152]Chai-Anan Samudavanija and Parichart Chotiya, "Beyond Transition in Thailand," 164.

[153]Kevin Hewison, "Of Regimes, States, and Pluralities," 182.

workers, and hinder effective unions. They are abetted by bureaucracies that permit scant participation.[154] To reduce the role of money in politics, Thai constitution writers have tried to define the object of politics as different from short-term development — whether or not most Thais yet want to define it that way.

The 2007 constitution, Thailand's eighteenth since 1932, was drafted by a committee of 35 members chosen by the junta. Its aim was to ensure that separate parties would be strong enough to compete with each other, so that no future prime minister could become as omnipotent as Thaksin. To this end, half of the Senate was to be appointed by a committee including judges, the heads of the Election Commission and the National Countercorruption Commission, and the president of the Constitutional Court. The House was to remain elected, but some constituencies would return multiple members, and the prime minister was restricted to two terms.[155]

This design produced a fragmented government, somewhat like those of the mid-1990s, but it could not surely produce institutionalized checks and balances unless parties emerged to represent non-personal interests. The designers mooted, but defeated, a provision that in case of a future political crisis, a special committee consisting of the prime minister, the leader of the opposition, and trusted judges would meet. Making elections combat rather than foster corruption is a very difficult task. They can do so only when wealth is less efficient at buying government than at structuring broader political interests that parties represent.

The Thai top elite shows very slow changes that suggest future developments will bring less corruption. Even during the early 1990s, the House of Representatives became more professional and better-educated. In Chuan Leekpai's first parliament, almost one-third of the members were baccalaureates, 70 had master's degrees, and 19 had doctorates.[156] This certainly did not guarantee their probity, and not

---

[154]See Bruce Missingham, "Local Bureaucrats, Power, and Participation," in *Political Change in Thailand*, Kevin Hewison, ed. (London: Routledge, 1997), 149–162.

[155]Thomas Fuller, "Thai Draft Constitution Ends Senate Elections," *International Herald Tribune*, April 19, 2007, 3.

[156]John Girling, *Interpreting Development*, 84.

all the degrees were from top-notch universities. But this change paralleled others in Taiwan, China, and in this case also the Philippines.[157]

People knew that democracy was modern and that rich countries were liberal. For a long time, with encouragement from the West and especially America, they still defined democracy mainly as elections rather than as separation of legitimate powers in government and among nonstate elites. Classical Thai lacked a word for democracy. When the absolute monarchy ended, a name for this concept was needed. Putting together Sanskrit-Pali roots for "people" and "rule" (demo+cracy), the result was *prachathipatai,* a made-up word. By the time of Thaksin's premiership, intellectuals who wished it could mean more in Thai practice, as well as those who did not much like it, sometimes laughingly made fun of it, calling it *hehathipatai,* "ho-ho-cracy." They did this because elections during the boom temporarily destroyed the government's integrity.

Democracy was originally seen as desirable by many citizens who later came to rue its results. When Bangkok voters were asked, after one boom time election, what they had learned from experiences at the ballot box, two-fifths reported that they now regretted past votes for representatives who turned out to be "wrong or not knowledgeable." Another fifth said they did not get the kind of government they had expected. More than ten percent gave each of the following responses: vote buying was a scandal, candidates did not live up to their promises, and the government was a partial cause of economic disasters.[158] A poll in Bangkok does not represent the whole country, but these respondents suggest they want more than they got from their democracy.

---

[157]Li Cheng and Lynn White, "Elite Transformation and Modern Change in Mainland China and Taiwan," *China Quarterly* 121, March 1990, 1–35, and Li Cheng and Lynn White, "The Sixteenth Central Committee of the Chinese Communist Party: Emerging Patterns of Power Sharing," in *China's Deep Reform: Domestic Politics in Transition,* L. Dittmer and G. Liu, eds. (Boulder: Rowman and Littlefield, 2006), 81–118.

[158]The total of these responses is almost 100 percent. Some of them are unsurprising, since most Thai voters are not in Bangkok, where this particular survey was made. Thanks go to Ms. Nittaya Vairojanavong for translating the Dusit Poll questions from Thai to English for this author.

Elections presented problems even for those who ran or won. In a poll of candidates all over Thailand, one-third (32 percent) said that vote-buying was the greatest hindrance to their being elected. Another 17 percent said that "dirty politics and influence-peddling" was the greatest hindrance, while 10 percent simply admitted they had "not enough money." When the candidates were asked "What do you want to convey to the voters?" the most frequent response (albeit only 21 percent) was clear: "Don't sell your vote! Don't elect those who buy votes!"[159] Candidates, including vote-buyers, had practical problems with the high degree of corruption in Thai elections.

The king admitted in public that he did not know what a democratic constitution should say. On several occasions (1992, 1997, 2006), he called on very experienced Thai statesmen and scholars to figure that out, ordering them to write a democratic constitution that would bring fair results, not bad ones. Councils of sages tackled this problem repeatedly. But in all modern societies, crucial power networks are in businesses. An essential element of democratization is industrialization. Regulation of the new social groups that development conjures is a constitutional need.

In 2007, the junta held a referendum on its new Constitution, which passed despite losing in the populous Northeast and receiving a 40 percent "no" vote nationwide. Then, in election of a new parliament, a reconstituted People's Power Party (Palang Prachachon) of Thaksin supporters won a near-majority of 233 seats, as against 165 for the next largest Democrat Party, even though Thaksin was still in exile and the military had tried "to prevent Palang Prachachon from benefiting from its financial resources."[160]

DEMOCRATIC DELAY

The distinguished Thai political scientist Chai-Anan has for many years been sad about his own prediction that industrial interests

---

[159]This Dusit poll was managed by Professor Sukhum Chaleysub. Thanks also go to Ms. Nittaya Vairojanavong for translating the questions for this author.
[160]James Ockey, "Thailand in 2007," *Asian Survey* 48:1 (January–February 2008), 24.

would defeat farmers' interests in Thailand, and that this would hinder democracy. He predicted that the supposed Western pattern, in which a rising middle class might support democracy, would not apply in Thailand, "because the bourgeoisie is politically weak, especially when it is an ethnic minority; that is why we cannot expect the political trickle-down effects of gradual democratization."[161]

This omen proved true for a time, but it may well have been too pessimistic for the long run in Thailand — and also too rosy as a report of Western experience. The business minority continues to grow in power, and it regularly cooperates with bureaucrats and generals to overlook the interests of rural people who are a majority of Thais. The polity has nonetheless pluralized. That process typified the West too, where plutocrats ruled during past periods of fast growth.

The increase business influence during Thailand's past boom could lead later to wider political participation among underrepresented Thai groups, especially workers. At least the state power of generals and bureaucrats has been joined by a very strong nonstate group: managers. Others will try to follow, and eventually they will have success.

---

[161] Chai-Anan Samudavanija, "Economic Development and Democracy," in *Thailand's Industrialization and its Consequences*, Medhi Krongkaew, ed. (New York: St. Martin's, 1995), 239.

9

Political Results of Philippine Stasis

Philippine civil society, in the sense of local oligarchs, has throughout history wielded more power than the state. Spain named the archipelago for its King Filipe II and set up an unusual form of government in which the main local administrators were ecclesiastical friars. These supplemented a very scanty staff of Spanish bureaucrats in Manila. When the Americans overturned this colonial regime easily, they were drawn outside the capital mainly because of armed resistance, especially in areas such as Mindanao where the Spanish had never exercised much control. In other regions, the friars were largely replaced, as official leaders of local politics, by pre-existing landowning elites who were further politicized in this process.[1]

American political ideology favored limits on state power. This accorded well with trying to run a populous polity that had never been tightly centralized. Governor-General William Howard Taft wanted to turn the Philippines eventually over to leaders who would have a "modern lawyer-politician" style.[2] So the Americans had a small government in Manila. Neither of the Philippines' colonial masters

---

[1]See Paul D. Hutchcroft, "Colonial Masters, National Politicos, and Provincial Lords: Central Authority and Local Autonomy in the American Philippines, 1900–1913," *Journal of Asian Studies* 59:2 (2000), 277–306.

[2]Joel Steinberg, *In Search of Southeast Asia: A Modern History*, J. Steinberg, ed. (Honolulu: University of Hawaii Press, 1987), 277.

did as much to unify power as did contemporary regimes in China or even in Thailand.

The Philippines continues to have a weak state. It does not extract high taxes, and these are from a recorded tax base that leaves out much of the GNP. As late as 1993, 40 percent of the archipelago's economy was estimated to be "informal," unmonitored, and often illegal.[3] Formally, there are social security and residence registration laws, but they have no effect on most people. This state is a bureaucracy in the capital, but in other regions its organs have been deeply penetrated by local oligarchs. When it seemed strongest, under Marcos, its strength came from the temporary success of one patron who kicked others out of influence in the central regime. But that merely forced them back into local networks, where they remained potent. When Marcos fell, they returned to Manila and continued to conflict with each other, as had been their wont for many decades, in ways that prevented state institutions from mediating their disputes. These elites not only have generally avoided diversifying their own younger generations into new types of leaders, e.g., in business and industry, they have actively prevented others in the Philippines from circulating into power.

The Filipino state, feeble as it was under the reluctantly colonial Americans, lost further ground to families after independence. At that time, the army could scarcely hold its own against warlords who had their own militias, such as Muslim quasi-sultans like the Dimaporos of Lanao, or the Duranos and Osmeñas and Cuencos of Cebu, or the Hukbalahap communists of central Luzon.[4] Often the state was just one of multiple armed actors in these places. Filipino families often conflicted with each other — as the Lopezes or Montanos did with

---

[3]Filipe V. Miranda, "Political Economy in a Democratizing Philippines: A People's Perspective," in *Democratization: Philippine Perspectives*, Felipe V. Miranda, ed. (Quezon City: University of the Philippines Press, 1997), 162.

[4]Alfred W. McCoy, "An Anarchy of Families: The Historiography of State and Family in the Philippines," in *An Anarchy of Families: State and Family in the Philippines*, Alfred W. McCoy, ed. (Madison: University of Wisconsin Center for Southeast Asian Studies, 1993), 19 and 22.

the Marcoses during the latter's presidential period. Periodic threats of military coups have weakened the presidency. Transnational interests, especially from the U.S., have intervened often, as have subnational forces ranging from radical rebels to conservative vigilantes.

MARCOS'S CENTRALIZATION ATTEMPT

Ferdinand Marcos, establishing his dictatorship, stressed the question of "What Went Wrong" in the Philippines. Many observers, both local and international, had castigated the nation's poor economic performance in comparison with that in neighboring countries. Social violence was rising by 1970. An American apologist for Marcos found the cause of the problem in politics: "Not only has the legislative arm routinely blocked the executive, but the judiciary also has often exercised a 'passion for pure law' at the expense of desperately needed government progress."[5] So Marcos suspended Congress and brought the courts to heel, "purifying" Philippine law and ruling by presidential decree. This kind of centralization by fiat, however, mainly led to Marcos garnering more rents from the weak economy, leaving less for his rivals. What had gone wrong was a lack of local entrepreneurs willing to allow some circulation of elites in their home places. Tinkering with state structure alone could not solve that problem, which was sited mainly in nonstate power networks.

Marcos was an ostensible near-revolutionary, a seeming populist in comparison with other landowners who were his opponents. He was seen by many citizens at the start of his presidency as a leader strong enough to push the Philippines out of the doldrums by establishing firmer central power. It was obvious to many that the country needed a serious land reform, and Marcos presented himself as a president willing to fight well-established landowning families to achieve that result. He also appeared to support free markets. He hired technocratic

---

[5]Beth Day, *The Philippines: Shattered Showcase of Democracy in Asia* (intro. by Carlos Romulo, Sec. of Foreign Affairs) (New York: M. Evans, 1974), 29, in a chapter entitled "What Went Wrong."

economists and promised the Philippines "new industrializing country" status.[6]

The result, however, was less tiger-like than the hope. Marcos's approach turned out to be mostly traditional. He gave prebends to political friends. This president did not eliminate patronism, he recruited some clients to his own service and tried to repress others. His main innovation was to have more success, albeit just temporarily, than any Philippine president who had preceded him. Marcos tried to centralize the state, but his attempt was so coercive that the contrary reaction after his demise decentralized it again.

Marcos appointed better-educated advisors to ministries than any previous president, but he also promoted "crony capitalists" on the basis of their personal loyalty to himself. Many but not all of his acolytes came from well-established Philippine clans. Marcos seemed to be raising political mobility. His own family had not been extremely prominent in Ilocos Norte, although his father Mariano Marcos had twice lost National Assembly elections to a man named Julio Nulundasan. Ferdinand Marcos in the 1930s was convicted of Nulundasan's murder. From jail, he studied law and persuaded the Supreme Court to acquit him.[7] Much later, when he was president, some of his appointees' lack of traditional social resources made them more dependent on him. He grew into traditional politics (*trapo* in Tagalog) by reorganizing it, more than by resisting it.

Marcos's martial law decree was a centralization. He closed Congress and abolished the previously separate Commission on Appointments of military commanders. Both moves reduced the clout of local lords, giving more power to the national lord. Marcos used "money raided from the national treasury and printed by the mint. His most brazen use of funds to entice blocs of votes was his handing, often personally, of 2000 pesos to nearly every barrio captain in the nation, supposedly for village development but in fact

---

[6]Gary Hawes, "Marcos, His Cronies, and the Philippines' Failure to Develop," in *Southeast Asian Capitalists*, Ruth McVey, ed. (Ithaca: Southeast Asia Program, Cornell University, 1992), 145.

[7]Wikipedia entry for Ferdinand Marcos, seen May 15, 2007.

for votes."[8] He wanted to lead a more unified Philippines. An advisor later said that Marcos thought "he could have a vision for society ... and still loot it."[9]

Changing the military appointment system brought more officers into the presidential camp, but it also put promotions wholly under presidential control. Previously, ambitious young officers had appealed to their friends in Congress or to the Commission when they wanted higher ranks. With these bodies closed, the potential patrons besides Marcos were reduced to very few: Gen. Fabian Ver (holding unprecedentedly high posts for a soldier who had never attended either the Philippine or U.S. military academies) and non-military politicians such as Defense Minister Juan Ponce Enrile or Imelda Marcos. Fewer promotions were made. Retirement pensions for all but the highest officers were minimal.

So a Movement to Reform the Armed Forces grew, mostly on a clandestine basis, among mid-level soldiers. By the 1980s, these officers were disaffected from Marcos — and when the president dismissed Enrile in 1983, the former defense minister became an advisor to this group (which included Gregorio Honasan and other participants in coup attempts that persisted long after Marcos's demise).[10] Enrile survived an anonymous bombing of his car in 1972, and he

---

[8]Benedict J. Tria Kerkvliet, "Contested Meanings of Elections in the Philippines," in *The Politics of Elections in Southeast Asia*, R.H. Taylor, ed. (Washington: Woodrow Wilson Center, 1996), 142.

[9]Quoted, from one of Marcos's advisors during a retrospective interview, in Alasdair Bowie and Danny Unger, *The Politics of Open Economies: Indonesia, Malaysia, the Philippines, and Thailand* (New York: Cambridge University Press, 1997), 128. It should be noted, however, that the government's Sandiganbayan anti-graft court, investigating the reported US$10 billion that Marcos may have misappropriated to himself and his family, failed to find much even after two decades of searching. Either the fiscal looting was less than earlier imagined, or (quite possibly) the paper trail was hidden by experts. See Carlos H. Conde, "Marcos Family Returning to the Limelight in the Philippines," *International Herald Tribune*, July 7–8, 2007, 1.

[10]Eva-Lotta E. Hedman, "The Philippines: Not So Military, Not So Civil," in *Coercion and Governance: The Declining Political Role of the Military in Asia* (Stanford: Stanford University Press, 2001), 172–80.

was concerned for his own safety after the assassination of Benigno Aquino in 1983.

Philippine presidents can strongly affect, but not necessarily determine, the strength of other local patronage networks. After arrogating extraordinary powers to himself under martial law, Marcos intervened actively in provincial politics throughout the archipelago. In Iloilo, he tried to destroy the political family of Eugenio Lopez, Sr., who had started as a local figure but by the early 1970s had used previous presidents' patronage to become the wealthiest man in the republic, head of the Manila Electric Company, a sugar magnate, director of the largest media conglomerate — and an ardent opponent of Ferdinand Marcos. Shortly after declaring martial law, Marcos had Lopez's son imprisoned on capital charges and forced Lopez to give up all major business interests.[11] The Lopez family returned to prominence in Iloilo, however, after Marcos fell.

In northern Cebu, Marcos received support from the Durano patronage network — but he also appointed a non-Duranista as governor to counterbalance their power. After Marcos was defeated nationally, the next president was able to remove a young Durano from the mayoralty of the major north Cebu city, Danao. But even then, "policies allowed the Duranos to retain the coercive mechanisms they had built up over nearly forty years of political dominance."[12] Any president could weaken, but could seldom destroy, local power networks based in families.

Marcos's era saw more circulation of political elites than occurred under his successors, because many of the people whom he promoted were technocrats.[13] Some were "newcomers" in urban business. Their profits depended largely on their connections with Marcos's

---

[11]Alfred W. McCoy, "Rent-Seeking Families and the Philippine State: A History of the Lopez Family," in *An Anarchy of Families*, 429.

[12]Michael Cullinane, "Patron as Client: Warlord Politics and the Duranos of Danao," in *An Anarchy of Families*, 185.

[13]Robin Broad, *Unequal Alliance: The IMF, the World Bank, and the Philippines* (Berkeley: University of California Press, 1988) remains the main work on Marcos's technocracy; this book began as a Ph.D. dissertation in Princeton's Woodrow Wilson School.

own networks.[14] The sequel was a less centralized resurgence of local powers, confirmed by means of democratic elections. A state dictator was replaced, and more local and nonstate dictators reasserted themselves. The transition involved excitement, which is always a major attraction of any electoral struggle.

NONSTATE INSTITUTIONS IN THE CORAZON AQUINO PRESIDENCY

Benigno Aquino, Jr., who had been Marcos's rival for the presidency, was murdered on August 21, 1983, immediately upon his return to the Philippines. (Manila's international airport, the site of this crime, now bears his name.) Marcos mandated the "Agrava Commission" to investigate. The president denied any complicity, but evidence implicated his chief of staff, Fabian Ver, who had to resign. Partly to placate demands from the U.S. where Aquino had been in exile, Marcos in October 1985 called for a "snap presidential election," even though his constitution did not require one, to be held in mid-February 1986.

He apparently thought it would be a snap, but it turned out otherwise. The widow of the martyr, Corazon Aquino, proved to be an unexpectedly strong candidate. The anti-Marcos Roman Catholic primate, Jaime Cardinal Sin, persuaded veteran political heavyweight Jose Laurel, Jr., to run on Aquino's ticket as vice-president. Campaigning in a yellow dress that became her logo, Aquino drew huge crowds at rallies.

She narrowly won the election. Marcos nonetheless attempted to rig the count and claimed victory. Officials tallying the vote walked off in protest (and on live TV) when the government count showed Marcos winning. There was major fraud in this election, so the "people's power revolution" began. Defense Minister Juan Ponce Enrile and Gen. Fidel Ramos on February 22 turned against Marcos, withdrawing to the safety of Camp Aguinaldo on EDSA Boulevard in

---

[14]Koike Kenji, "The Reorganization of *Zaibatsu* Groups under the Marcos and Aquino Regimes," *East Asian Cultural Studies* 28:1–4 (1989), 127–29.

central Manila. Huge demonstrations on that street demanded Marcos's resignation. He ordered tanks to quell the crowd, but nuns and school children were in the front rows. The tank drivers did nothing. This was all televised globally.

Marcos on February 24 had himself sworn in for a new term. At an almost simultaneous ceremony elsewhere in Manila, Corazon Aquino also took the presidential oath. Finally Marcos realized that the army would no longer obey him; so he was persuaded by telephone calls from U.S. diplomats and politicians to board American aircraft, first to Clark Air Base in Pampanga and then to Hawaii, where in 1989 he died.

Corazon Aquino's victory was, by February 25, 1986, the result of an extra-constitutional election backed by a practical coup under Defense Minister Enrile and Chief of Staff Lt. Gen. Fidel Ramos. One month later, on March 25, President Cory Aquino's "Proclamation No. 3" established a new constitution, on which a referendum soon passed. Local elected officials from the Marcos camp were replaced by presidential appointees, mostly politicians who had campaigned in those places for the Aquino-Laurel ticket. Because the Marcos machine had earlier used extensive coercion, because the referendum on the new constitution had passed, and because Aquino had won the presidential balloting despite distortions in the vote count, these municipal changes could be described as democratic. They did not, however, change the modal form of Philippine local politics, in which the constant theme was rivalry among dominant families or lineages.

History has been understandably benign to Benigno Aquino because he was an articulate and brave martyr. When he was a contender against Marcos for the presidency in 1971, an earlier grenade attack had apparently also been an attempt to assassinate him. In this climate, Aquino had said he would impose martial law if he won the top job. Some Filipinos claim that Aquino "was the only man who could beat Marcos at his own game."[15]

---

[15] James Clad, *Behind the Myth: Business, Money, and Power in Southeast Asia* (London: Hyman, 1989), 36.

When his widow became president, however, the cronies changed more obviously than the crony system did. Although some new professionals entered politics after 1986, the Marcos era was at least as good a time for political *parvenus* (who included Marcos himself). Some leaders in all these decades have come from families outside the old gentry, but this change can be overstated. The old clans were sustained by their scions. New leaders, entering power, often fell out of it later because they lacked the stable networks and local bases of the old families.

Soon after she assumed power, President Aquino appointed new officials. An example, about one place, shows much about modal local politics in the Philippines at this time: Aquino wanted Ruben Umali as Mayor of Lipa City, Batangas, not far from Manila — but that post had in the interim been occupied by a man whose earlier election Marcos had illegitimated. Two weeks of local negotiations were required to persuade the outgoing mayor to give up physical possession of his desk in city hall. Crucial in these talks were representatives of the Aquino administration, whose local kin had historically friendly relations with the family of the outgoing mayor. Aquino's man, Umali, promised in his inauguration speech to retain civil service employees — or at least to observe their "performance" before firing them. Appointments went at least temporarily to various factions in Lipa that had best supported the new regime.

The most senior civil servant in this particular locality chose to resign and was replaced by a supporter of the new mayor. Vacant civil service positions, like previous elective offices, were filled by political appointments. Many of the posts were openly advertised but then filled in closed political meetings of Umali's advisors. The Civil Service Commission had to approve new employees. "Umali exerted efforts to facilitate the approval." Some from the old regime simply "switched their loyalty to the new mayor," and this was accepted.[16] The crucial post of City Engineer, in charge of contracting to build roads, went to a relative of Mayor Umali.

---

[16]Kimura Masataka, *Elections and Politics, Philippine Style: A Case in Lipa* (Manila: De La Salle University Press, 1997), 164–65, and further pages to 168.

Barangay captains, who by law are supposed to stand for elections on a nonpartisan basis, flocked to Umali's office, asking to join his UNIDO party. The new mayor was increasingly asked to stand as godfather at baptisms and weddings. He presided at the Lipa City Fiesta in January and at Foundation Day in August. At the latter event, he crowned Miss Lipa Charity and was the official host at an all-night ball. For this, the city's elite dressed up, began with Spanish colonial *regodon* dances, and then moved to pop music. Philippine politics is colorful, partly because it is so contentious. But all the politically important policies are about personnel only.

Creation of a strong state was an aim, despite their differences, of both Ferdinand Marcos and Benigno Aquino. It is also an aim of most Philippine social thinkers. Temario Rivera's conclusion for his country is that, "Short of a successful social revolution ignited by worsening social conflict, only a strong, autonomous state could break the continuing power of the traditional agrarian elites and negotiate more favorable trade and investment terms with transnational actors."[17] More broadly, Rivera and many other analysts call for "constructing a growth coalition" that would involve the state but also local and international institutions.

Democracy has not yet centralized police powers or tax collection in the Philippines, even though such change would serve the people. Social revolution might do that, but such experiences usually become bloody. The circulation of elite types, especially of entrepreneurs founding factories, is slower in the Philippines than it has been Taiwan, East China, or Thailand. In a context of decentralized landowner tyrannies, it is difficult to find ways to preserve order while allowing both risk-taking entrepreneurs and worker organizers to flourish.

---

[17]Temario C. Rivera, *Landlords and Capitalists: Class, Family, and State in Philippine Manufacturing* (Quezon City: University of the Philippines Center for Integrative and Development Studies, 1994), 129.

RESTORING DISINTEGRATION:
MILITARY AND STRUCTURAL CAUSES

Early in her presidency, Aquino suggested that she would hold negotiations with the leftist National Democratic Front as well as Muslim autonomists in Mindanao. She appointed reformist ministers such as Jose Diokno, Joker Arroyo, and Augusto Sanchez. Several were lawyers who had defended political prisoners tortured by soldiers under Marcos. The Philippine army and the Reagan administration, however, opposed these reformers, and so did Juan Ponce Enrile. He resigned as Defense Minister because of his connivance with a "God Save the Queen" semi-coup against Aquino in November 1986. His departure balanced the firing of reformist Labor Minister Sanchez.

Kudeta became frequent even though the generals did not replace incumbent presidents outright. The golpistas never pressed their military advantage actually to take the Malacañang palace from Corazon Aquino (or from later presidents including Gloria Arroyo). In most cases, they merely threatened to do so until they got assurances that reformers would be sacked from the cabinet. After receiving such guarantees, the coup-makers went back to their barracks. The soldiers did not need actually to seize the government, if they determined what it did.

Peasants from some parts of the Philippines had been in the broad coalition that opposed Marcos in 1986. After Aquino assumed the presidency, a rally of peasants was held at Mendiola Bridge in Manila, where agrarian reformers had previously conflicted with Marcos's troops. After several days of camping out and negotiating with Aquino's advisers for better land policies, they marched toward Malacañang. Police and marines opened fire, killing 13 and injuring hundreds.[18] The communist agrarian guerrilla organization immediately withdrew from

---

[18]Francisco Lara, Jr. and Horacio Morales, Jr., "The Peasant Movement and the Challenge of Democratization in the Philippines," in *The Challenge of Rural Democratization: Perspectives from Latin America and the Philippines*, Jonathan Fox, ed. (London: Frank Cass, 1990), 143.

peace talks with the Aquino government and soon thereafter ended its ceasefire. The power of traditional landlords in the Philippines was too great for Aquino to resist while keeping her job.

In the spring of 1987, Aquino made a speech at the Philippines Military Academy, saying that she had "unsheathed the sword of war" against the communists and Moro Liberation Front. She abolished the Presidential Committee on Human Rights that had been investigating abuses (by soldiers) during Marcos's time.[19]

Officers launched nine *kudeta* attempts against Cory Aquino, of which two led by Col. Gregorio Honasan in 1987 and 1989 nearly toppled her.[20] In December 1989, air force rebels strafed the Malacañang palace. From Clark Air Base, the United States sent Phantom jets on "persuasion flights" over Manila to disperse them.[21] Aquino was lucky to survive these attacks, although her military and social policies moved to the right after each such event. The president often had to fulfill specific demands of the *kudeta*-makers, most of whom then returned to their barracks without any punishment. "Gringo" Honasan, famous for his role in launching coups, was a decade later a senator. No effectively injurious shame was heaped upon him for having attempted the praetorian, anti-democratic mode of political succession. He was like a Thai *nakleng*, but with high army rank. His boldness, combined with rhetorical patriotism, made him a charismatic candidate.

The effective use of rental and prebendal money to determine election winners, combined with a lack of major profits from industrial-commerical entrepreneurship in the Philippines, meant that most post-Marcos politicians remained heavily dependent on landowners and the military. Local army and police support helped to maintain rural elites' economic activities, including businesses such as illegal

---

[19] Joel Rocamora, "Lost Opportunities, Deepening Crisis: The Philippines under Cory Aquino," in *Low Intensity Democracy: Political Power in the New World Order*, Barry Gills, Joel Rocamora and Richard Wilson, eds. (Boulder: Pluto Press, 1993), 198–201.
[20] See fn. 106 in chapter 5, and also Alfred W. McCoy, *Closer than Brothers: Manhood at the Philippine Military Academy* (New Haven: Yale University Press, 1999), 259.
[21] Eva-Lotta E. Hedman, "The Philippines: Not So Military, Not So Civil," 182.

logging. Especially in places where continuing counterinsurgencies brought troops, civilian politicians needed army help to sustain either the coercive or financial bases of their electoral victories.[22]

In 1992 when Gen. Fidel Ramos became president, the frequency of coup attempts decreased. As a former soldier, Ramos was able to head off sporadic pressure on policies from the army (when his own policies sometimes differed from those of recent comrades-in-arms). Ramos was therefore able to act more independently than any other Philippine president since Marcos. The earlier pattern soon returned, however, when Ramos left office. Joseph Erap Estrada, with his former career in movies rather than in barracks, was less adept at many governance tasks than Ramos had been — but Estrada lost the top job for a more specific reason: Defense Minister Orlando Mercado and Chief of Staff Gen. Angelo Reyes joined an anti-Estrada EDSA Boulevard rally that is now called "EDSA 2," recalling the earlier rally that toppled Marcos.[23] Gloria Macapagal Arroyo's ascent to the presidency looked constitutional, because she was vice-president. Her father Diosdado Macapagal had been president in the early 1960s, before losing a re-election bid to Marcos. The military, with support from others, pushed Estrada out of the top office unwillingly; he had been duly elected, and he did not offer to resign. Several later *kudeta* semi-coups, at least one of which again involved Honasan, were launched against Arroyo too. The structure of Philippine central power was unchanged, and it is unstable.

Even though the Philippine army is relatively weak, either in relation to other forces within that country or in comparison to the armies of other countries, the central bureaucracy and president are also weak. The most effective role of the army has been to keep any president away from populist policies. Several Philippine presidents have made reformist gestures to new kinds of constituents, including entrepreneurs and workers, but these have had no legal or structural outcomes. This archipelago republic is not a military dictatorship, but the

---

[22]For more, see Francisco Lara, Jr. and Horacio Morales, Jr., "The Peasant Movement and the Challenge of Democratization," 148.
[23]Eva-Lotta E. Hedman, "The Philippines: Not So Military, Not So Civil," 183.

army has for decades played a major role in thwarting any effort to change its political structure. This is not a feudal system, because there is no effective central authority, but it is a fragmented system in which local bosses have thus far prevented the rise of any new kind of rival.

LOCALISM

Philippine surveys suggest that citizens trust local politicians more than national leaders.[24] In China, the situation is exactly opposite. Surveys show that Chinese tend to like their leaders in distant Beijing better than the local officials, whom they know more closely.[25] Eric Guttierrez in 1994 published a compendium about the backgrounds of all members of the Philippine Congress, finding that many were still from rentier families.[26] A decade later, he published an update, finding that there was some increase in the number in Congress who came from newer economic groups. Many still had close connections with old families, however. Some new politicians, e.g., from a family named Barbers, were from non-rentier backgrounds — in that case, from the Manila Police Department. Several members of that clan advanced into politics all at once, not from a traditional (or an industrial) base but nonetheless in the same style as traditional politicians, taking mayoral, senatorial, and congressional seats. New prestige came from sources outside the economy, and it sometimes led to new politicians who closely emulated the old ones.

Aquino's 1987 Constitution, part II, sec. 26, very hopefully provided that "the State shall prohibit political dynasties as may be

---

[24]Steven Rood, "Decentralization, Democracy, and Development, in *The Philippines: New Directions in Domestic Policy and Foreign Relations*, David G. Timberman, ed. (Singapore: Institute for Southeast Asian Studies and New York: Asia Society, 1998), 127.

[25]Wang Zhengxu, "Political Trust in China," in *Legitimacy: Ambiguities of Political Success or Failure in East and Southeast Asia*, Lynn White, ed. (Singapore: World Scientific Press, 2005), 113–40.

[26]Eric Guttierrez, *The Ties that Bind: A Guide on Family, Business, and Other Interests in the 9th House of Representatives* (Pasig City: Philippine Center for Investigative Journalism, 1994).

defined by law." No definition of a dynasty emerged during her presidency, however. She and her martyred husband came from very well-established landholding families in Tarlac. The next president was Fidel Ramos, whose political career had been built from a base in the army. Ramos was an Ilocano from Pangasinan, a Protestant, and a military technocrat rather than a traditional politician. The clans of the *trapos* generally did not support his election in 1992. Because the president is directly elected from a national constituency, an incumbent to that office with a military background sufficient to reduce the policy effects of *kudeta* may be the likeliest source of structural reform in the Philippine polity, and many intellectual Filipinos rate Ramos's performance more highly than that of any other recent Philippine president. The cumulative power of local leaders over the central one nonetheless remains very great.

Ramos supported a proposal from the Commission on Elections in 1993 that a "dynasty" be defined as "politicians having a third civil degree of consanguinity" or closer (i.e., spouses, parents, grandparents, children, grandchildren, siblings, nephews, and nieces, or the husbands or wives of any of these). The plan was that they and their third-degree relatives by marriage could not simultaneously run for offices in the same legislative district, city, or town. This proposal did not apply to elections in the national constituency, e.g., those for the whole Senate. Opposition to this plan was severe in the House, whose Rules Committee refused to allow debate on it. This is hardly surprising. The Philippine Center for Investigative Journalism calculated that 17 of the 20 committee members actually had relatives who (at that time or earlier) had held political offices for which they would, under such a law, have been unable to run.[27] Philippine politics remained very familial.

The Philippine House has, in recent years, had slightly more members who are bureaucrats, professionals, or entrepreneurs without obvious *trapo* connections. These are a minority, however. Surveys

---

[27]Kent Eaton, "Restoration or Transformation: *Trapos* vs. NGOs in the Democratization of the Philippines," *Journal of Asian Studies* 62:2 (May 2003), 487; also 476 and 481.

showed that in 1992, fully 145 House members (of the 250 total) "belonged to old oligarchic families."[28] By 2001, "nonclan members" of the House were still a minority, 42 percent.[29] Industrialization and commercialization have affected Philippine politics, but this process would have gone further if growth had been quicker.

WEIGHING PORK

Political machines in the Philippines are controlled by locals. Any national leader needs their support — and, in exchange, is expected to allocate money to them.[30] This is the practical definition of any Philippine political party, whose main policy is pork. It is common in many countries for politicians to deliver favors to their constituents, but in the Philippines especially, these are very seldom goods of a public character. They strengthen voters' dependence on specific incumbents, practically never on government in general. So long as local leaders deliver particularistic goods, their other activities are deemed by many voters to be irrelevant. This causes "the electorate in many places repeatedly to elect convicted criminals, underworld characters, and known grafters."[31]

Public spending has limits because there is scant industrial tax base to pay for it. There are weak industrial lobbies to politick for infrastructural spending that would provide external economies to investors. A famous example is in Metro Manila, on the main auto

---

[28]This number was just slightly down from the 169 old-family congressmen (in the 250-member House) in 1987. Renato S. Velasco, "Does the Philippine Congress Promote Democracy?" in *Democratization: Philippine Perspectives*, Felipe V. Miranda, ed. (Quezon City: University of the Philippines Press, 1997), 290.

[29]Sheila S. Coronel, Yvonne Chua, Luz Rimban and Booma Cruz, *The Rulemakers: How the Wealthy and Well-Born Dominate Congress*, (Quezon City: Philippine Center for Investigative Journalism, 2004), 19.

[30]Kawanaka Takeshi, *Power in a Philippine City* (Chiba: Institute of Developing Economies, 2002), 17.

[31]Paul D. Hutchcroft and Joel Rocamora, "Strong Demands and Weak Institutions: Addressing the Democratic Deficit in the Philippines" (essay provided by courtesy of Dr. Rocamora), 3, also relying on work by Emmanuel deDios and Hutchcroft.

route between Quezon City and downtown. The republic has no more important urban traffic artery, but the road is odd (until it is rebuilt): the barrier that separates lanes of cars going in opposite directions has been extended by means of concrete pylons to close off transit on many cross streets. Traffic in the main road thus runs faster without the public expense of an elevated highway. This kind of "Filipino freeway," as local people call it with good humor, has a disadvantage: vehicles needing to travel at ninety degrees to the main road cannot do so, except at a few widely spaced crossings that have traffic lights. The main advantage, in light of the weak finances of this polity, is that the government avoids spending money on a project whose benefits are exclusive to just a few constituents.

Transport difficulties are one of the serious deterrents to profitable enterprise in the Philippines. Such problems will remain unsolved until the government finds a tax base to pay for better and more coherent infrastructure, providing more external economies for many investments. Bangkok, for example, also has had legendary traffic jams, especially during its boom. But growth at that time now means money that the government has used to begin reducing such bottlenecks. Taipei and practically all Chinese provincial capitals (including Shanghai, Nanjing, and Hangzhou in East China) have gone through major traffic crunches too — but now have, and are spending, resources to relieve them. Fragmented polities inhibit both the generation of new money and its use for the public.

The portion of Philippine government spending on private goods is higher than in other countries. Laws have been passed to combat this. For example, art. VI, sec. 14, of the 1987 Philippine Constitution says that no senator or representative may "directly or indirectly be interested financially in any contract with, or in any franchise or special privilege granted by the government, or any subdivision, agency, or instrumentality thereof, including any government-owned or -controlled corporation or a subsidiary, during his term of office." This law has been egregiously honored in the breach. The mechanisms causing the violations are so many and important, they require some presentation.

The 250 Philippine representatives are elected from districts (except for a very few now elected nationally on a party-list system). The 24 senators are elected to six-year terms, 12 of them every two years when there is not a presidential election — by the whole nation as if it were a single district. The cost of senatorial elections, in particular, is large because the constituency is the archipelago's whole adult population — although to win, only a sufficient plurality is needed to put the candidate among the twelve highest vote-getters. In the 1995 election, a senate seat cost at least 10 million pesos. Representative seats were only somewhat less expensive, partly because (as in the U.S. Congress) all bills to appropriate local money start in the House; the 1995 House cost varied between 3 million and 12 million pesos.[32]

By 2004, each Philippine senator cost the taxpayers about 1 million pesos monthly, while representatives cost an average of 500,000 pesos.[33] Each Congress member had a "Priority Development Assistance Fund," to be used at the sole discretion of the member. A Philippine representative had a moderate salary of just 35,000 pesos per month, but the Priority Development Assistance Fund and the Public Works Fund in 2004 totalled 65 million pesos. Published expenses, allowances, and Christmas gifts from the Speaker and from Malacañang, together with foreign travel allocations, could exceed half a million more pesos per representative per month.

More important, the Speaker of the House could legally put into his own discretionary fund any "savings" from other appropriation bills. (The Senate President, as well as some committee chairs, had similar rights.) Many such funds were then returned to Congress members who had voted for the winner during races for the speakership. A legislative staff member claimed that, in one such election, these amounts ran as high as 200,000 pesos for every vote. "And

---

[32]Renato S. Velasco, "Does the Philippine Congress Promote Democracy?" 287.

[33]This amount was at that time, when about 50 pesos (far more than usual) were needed to buy a dollar, was approximately US$20,000 per senator or US$10,000 per representative, monthly.

once the Speaker is in place, ... Congressmen who do not belong to
the ruling coalition, and party-list representatives, are said to receive
50,000 pesos a month, while 'favored' Congressmen reportedly get
double or even triple that."[34] The total size of the Speaker's discretionary kitty is secret, but it is estimated to be in hundreds of millions
of pesos.

A chairperson of any important committee in the Philippine
Congress can also dispose of large funds. Unsurprisingly, positions
on the House Appropriations Committee are valuable to all its
members. A vice-chair, who headed the Appropriations Committee's
subcommittee on agriculture, Rep. Augusto Syjuco (Iloilo), estimated that, "I could get about 200 million pesos a year [in 'projects'] for my district."[35] Posts on the Public Works Committee or
any committee dealing with transport or communication were also
useful for those who wanted control of contracts. The Committee
on Games and Amusements screened applications for franchises
worth millions of pesos. Seats on the Appropriations Committee,
which had 45 members in the 1987 congress after Marcos's demise,
became so coveted that by the 2004 congress the number of
Appropriations Committee members rose to 170 (three quarters of
the entire House).[36] By then, it became unseemly to be a representative without having a seat on Appropriations.

These published figures of the amounts used for pork were
clearly underaccounted: "Government auditors themselves say they
are in the dark over how Congress spends most of its money, in
part because there is hardly any paper trail to help them scrutinize
how lawmakers use public funds. ... On the average, the upkeep of

---

[34]Yvonne Chua, "Fat Salaries, Big Allowances, and Other Perks of Lawmaking,"
Philippine Center for Investigative Journalism website, March 22–24, 2004, http://
www.pcij.org/stories/2004/congress3.html, seen January 21, 2007.
[35]*Ibid.*
[36]Philippine Center for Investigative Journalism, "Representatives Scramble for
Power, Peso, and Privileges," July 26–27, 2004, http://www.pcij.org/sto-
ries/2004/house2.html, seen January 21, 2007.

legislators has risen ten percent every year [in the decade to 2004] since 1994."[37]

The Commission on Audit is a very political agency, hiding details that congressmen do not wish to make known. In 1997, a Presidential Commission Against Graft and Corruption reported that items in the congressional budget "are not liquidated and audited in the same manner as expenses of public funds by all other government officials, where proofs, documents, receipts, contracts, vouchers, and other pertinent documents are required by laws, rules, and regulations, submitted to justify these expenses before the Commission on Audit would pass them in audit."[38] Congressmen often signed receipts for money that they received, but they did not need to prove how the funds were used. In particular, they needed to submit no payrolls of their district staffs. This meant that any local *lider*-canvasser could be paid by the state for work that was private.

An official of the Commission on Audit said frankly that, "The House is a political body. We don't want to get into trouble." Another admitted, "We're scared of congressmen. We're scared of the system. *Babalikan kami* [They'll seek revenge]. We don't want to tolerate corruption, but nothing happens to our reports. We just become subjects of harassment, and other people even make money out of our reports."[39]

About one-fifth of the Philippine government's total procurement budget for 2001 went directly "to the pockets of legislators, officials, and contractors alone." This estimate of the corruption overhead was made by the then-chair of the House Appropriations Committee, Rep.

---

[37]Yvonne Chua, "An Expensive — and Unaccountable — Legislature," Philippine Center for Investigative Journalism website, March 22–24, 2004, http://www.pcij.org/stories/2004/congress2.html, seen January 21, 2007. See also Philippine Centre for Investigative Journalism and Institute for Popular Democracy, *Pork and Other Perks: Corruption and Governance in the Philippines* (Quezon City: Philippine Center for Investigative Journalism, 1998).

[38]Yvonne Chua, "An Expensive — and Unaccountable — Legislature."

[39]*Ibid.* In various quotations of this book, when short Tagalog sentences or phrases are translated in brackets among English sentences, the speakers originally used English for most of their expression but switched temporarily into Pilipino. (This easy alternation is a frequent linguistic phenomenon of oral discourse in many parts of the world, notably including the Philippines.)

Rolando Andaya, Jr. (Camarines Sur). Nobody had exact figures, and this chairman may well have guessed too low. An earlier estimate of 1998, from the Finance and Budget Secretary Salvador Enriquez, was that as much as 45 percent of pork funds went to corrupt "commissions," for example in purchases of medical or educational materials from businesses owned by congress members' crony friends. For infrastructure projects, the portions were somewhat smaller but ran up to 30 percent.[40] Probably about two-fifths of overall government expenditures went into political overheads to maintain incumbents in office.

The votes-for-money syndrome is solidly a part of Philippine *and other* democratic politics. It is an institution. Liberal political scientists and philosophers (or democratic diplomats who answer to elected politicians) still do not incorporate the importance of money into their accounts of "democracy," either what it is or what it should be. In Manila, even the small minority of relatively idealistic party-list House members also had to participate. It had been hoped that the constitutionally few party-list delegates in the House would break *trapo* patterns, but as one of them said, "We can't fight pork because it's institutionalized. *Hinahanap 'yan ng tao* [People look for it]. What we can do is just to look for projects that address the needs of our constituents."[41]

TAX EVASION, LICENSING, AND RACKETEERING

Electoral democracies in general, and the Philippine electoral democracy very extensively, run an anti-democratic danger that elected politicians and many academics neglect: elections abet government connivance in gains by citizens who can use wealth or coercion to control the preferences of other citizens who do not benefit. Common ways to get private control of the public sphere are to buy, scare, or propagandize voters. Biased official licensing, winking at tax evasions, and racketeering result from such elections. These governmental

---

[40]Yvonne Chua and Booma B. Cruz, "Legislators Feed on Pork," Philippine Center for Investigative Journalism web, September 6–7, 2004, http://www.pcij.org/stories/2004/pork2.html, seen January 21, 2007.

[41]Yvonne Chua and Booma B. Cruz, "Pork is a Political, not a Developmental, Tool," Philippine Center for Investigative Journalism web, September 6–7, 2004, http://www.pcij.org/stories/2004/pork.html, seen January 21, 2007.

faults can also arise in polities that lack elections, but liberals have seldom thus far become serious about the extent to which elections promote them.

Substandard construction work that violates government contracts has been very common in the Philippines, as in other developing countries, but democracy has not ended it. As a senator said, "There is simply no way to monitor how well these [contracts] are implemented. If they tell you they will dredge x cubic meters, who will check where the hell that number of cubic meters went? The same with asphalt overlay. Whether it is one centimeter or ten inches, nobody knows." Auditors may be employed to check the work. Then they can be bribed.

> You have the inspector who does the after-project report and gets 0.5 percent of the pork. You have the director who gives his opinion or approves the report, and you go up the ladder. For the Commission on Audit, that must be about 10 percent or 15 percent of the pork all in all. It's a small price to pay for politicians, when you think of the possibility of going to court.[42]

An index of progress in the Philippines, arguably, was the increasing importance of pork for construction projects as distinct from other uses. More of the "development assistance" monies had previously gone to subsidize local rice prices. Assistance to industries remained minimal, because few congressional districts had any notable industries to lobby for infrastructure that could raise, for any new investor, the profitability of start-ups. As late as the Estrada period, "the rice subsidy was the favorite of many congressmen, because they could give away just a few [lots of rice], and then the rest they would sell to rice traders. That became rampant until finally it was stopped because too many legislators could no longer explain where much of the rice was going."[43] It did not go to tillers, but to *lider* middlemen who canvassed for candidates. The market did not fully industrialize pork, but over time more of the corrupt money went to builders, and less went to agricultural middlemen.

The budgets passed by congresses between 1987–92 and 2001–04 rose from 4.6 billion to 11.2 billion pesos. Tax collection to pay for these

---

[42]Yvonne Chua and Booma B. Cruz, "Legislators Feed on Pork."
[43]*Ibid.*

budgets was a big problem. There would have been enough, if more taxpayers had complied with the law. Corrupt officials in the Bureau of Internal Revenue at one point stopped their work, going on strike, to protest a boss who tried to prevent them from taking bribes.[44]

Congress was very slow to pass regulations establishing checks that might keep tax collectors honest. Also, lobbies for sectors such as cigarettes and alcohol prevented a law that would have indexed to inflation the taxes on their products. The lawyers' lobby (with its members in Congress) exempted their profession from the value-added tax levied on other services. Local monopolies were protected; at one point, every independent brewery in the Philippines was bought out by San Miguel. It may be difficult to prove, in any specific instance such as this, an improper use of public trust. But monopolies and oligopolies are numerous in the Philippines, despite the large market size of nearly 100 million people and an elite ideology that claims to favor competitive free markets.[45]

---

[44]Anon., "Democracy as Showbiz," *Economist*, July 1, 2004, http://www.economist. com/printerfriendly.cfm?story_ID=2876966, seen January 21, 2007.

[45]Gaps between liberal models and liberal practice receive attention in this book, but one economic example of that problem is mostly omitted because it is less evident in the four countries studied here than in some smaller East Asian places such as Hong Kong. This is the extent of misleading claims by business elites that they support maximally free markets. Gurus in the Heritage Foundation still declare Hong Kong to be the world's most free economy. They choose to ignore the extent of oligopoly (in banking, groceries, medicines, telecommunications, and other fields). They ignore that the government has subsidized the wage bills of all companies (to increase the city's collective competitiveness) by renting directly to two-fifths of the households. Half the apartments in Hong Kong were built by the government there, which also runs many other fine socialist programs (regulations of transport fares, smoking, medicine, and so forth). The point is not that such programs are bad; it is only that liberals, especially economists, mislead themselves and others when they proclaim their ideology without looking at practice. See Manuel Castells, Lee Goh, and Reginald Y.W. Kwok, *The Shek Kip Mei Syndrome: Public Housing and Economic Development* (London: Pion, 1991), which also refers to Jonathan Schiffer, "The State and Economic Development: A Note on the Hong Kong 'Model'," *International Journal of Urban and Regional Research* 15:3 (1991). Leo Goodstadt, a former head of the government's main think tank, and retired civil servant John Walden have given detailed evidence about this model in local seminars at Hong Kong University's Centre of Asian Studies.

Philippine regulations about many subjects are structured in ways that maximize rent-seeking. Gambling, for example, is illegal — yet cock fighting, the numbers game *jueteng*, and other games like *sakla* and hi-lo, are addictions among many. "Authorities find it more profitable to retain the law, making these networks illegal, and to connive in their continued operation."[46] As Silliman points out, in words that could apply just as well in China as in the Philippines:

> Legislation does not, in and of itself, correct social problems. This is especially the case in the Philippines, where there is routinely a wide gap between what the law says and what people do, where there is a history of policies and programs that go unimplemented. Yet officials often speak and act as if legal prescriptions are sufficient to correct social ills; legal dramas are enacted as if the process makes a difference, and government officials announce with all sincerity that a problem is being addressed because new guidelines or additional regulations have been promulgated.[47]

Politicians are as egregious as social scientists, when failing to distinguish models from reality.

The chairman of the Philippine Charity Sweepstakes Office, Manuel Murato, used his TV talk program, "Dial M" on the government's channel 4, to show a video in which Vice-President Erap Estrada was screened playing baccarat in the Heritage Hotel Casino's Super VIP Room, along with "suspected gambling and drug lord Charlie Ang." Estrada called Murato's move "black propaganda, a smear drive, and a political demolition job." He said President Ramos was behind it. Estrada said that Murato had paid 20 million pesos for the tape. In riposte, Murato announced that if Estrada were elected president (as later happened), he would file impeachment proceedings, partly because of a law against that kind of gambling by public officials and partly on the report that Estrada had accepted 500,000 pesos in chips from a Sindhi businessman who was Ang's brother-in-law. Some found these accusations odd, since Murato also heads a

---

[46] James Clad, *Behind the Myth*, 33.
[47] G. Sidney Silliman, "Human Rights and the Transition to Democracy," in *Patterns of Power and Politics in the Philippines*, James F. Eder and Robert L. Youngblood, eds. (Tempe: Arizona State University Program for Southeast Asian Studies, 1994), 140.

government agency promoting Lotto all over the Philippines.[48] The objection was not to gambling; it merely concerned who would be in charge of gambling profits.

Political ambition can trump social policy even among those who may seem most socially committed. The Hukbalahap communist movement was strong in Nueva Ecija, but it did not make much headway in Pampanga until after its basic military defeat in the early 1950s. At that point, various Huk bands became little more than mafia-like brotherhoods, and they moved into relatively urbanized environments. In that form, some Huks established themselves as racketeers in Pampanga near Clark Air Base, where the U.S. Air Force provided a supply of customers for the bars and massage salons that were run by recent communists. Opportunities affect political ideals everywhere.

EFFORTS TO CONTROL CORRUPTION

The Constitution includes provision for an ombudsman. He files cases on corruption to the Sandiganbayan, a supposedly independent graft court whose members have long fixed terms. The Constitution also legitimates the national Audit Commission. Nobody claims, however, that such provisions have ended corruption in Philippine politics. On the contrary, there is a general consensus among Filipinos that practically all politicians are corrupt.

In December 2002, bureaucrats under President Arroyo proposed to the Philippine Congress a law concerning government procurements, framing the bill as a technical fix to reduce corruption. Congress passed the law, but an experienced interviewee in the Philippines said that, "They didn't know what they were doing." The law required that contracts for procurement be posted on the internet. Collusion among bidders on official contracts became a legal offense. Enforcement of such rules would prove to be more difficult

---

[48]From http://www.electionline98.com.ph, seen July, 1998; but later the website was apparently closed. Bibliographical purism sometimes mixes badly with money politics, because the latter is more serious.

than was their legislation, but this law might later become effective, and others with similar aims can be passed and perhaps even enforced.

When the term of a very corrupt national ombudsman ('a crook,' according to one non-Filipino expert interviewee) ended in 2002, Arroyo appointed a man named Marcelo to this important prosecutorial job. Conviction rates soon doubled, albeit just from 6 to 12 percent of all corruption cases. Marcelo sued several politicians who were widely deemed to be corrupt — but none of the court cases against them involved the president or figures close to her. Corruption was in part an issue to be used against political rivals of the strong.

When news reporters cover corruption in the Philippines, they may put themselves in physical danger. On May 10, 2005, the publisher of a weekly in the town of Dingalan, north of Manila, was shot dead as he sat down to dinner. In his house were 500 copies of his newspaper that included articles on local corruption. Journalists in Manila are somewhat safer, but in rural towns, "bigwigs riled by the words of a scribbler can easily find an assassin (for about 5000 pesos, US$93) to end the matter. ... Another factor, though hardly a justification for murder, is that many local hacks are shysters, given to raking up (or making up) dirt on local dignitaries, and then blackmailing them to keep it under wraps. ... officials have suggested that journalists should carry firearms in order to defend themselves."[49] A Press Freedom Fund of 5 million pesos offers bounties to anybody who gives information that leads to the arrest of journalists' assassins. The dead reporters, however, receive no benefits.

THE INTEGRITY OF ELECTIONS

All of the Philippines, both urban and rural, is divided into small barangays.[50] More than 50,000 of these elected governments cover

---

[49]"Watch What You Write: One Way to Deal with Irritating Reporters," *Economist*, June 18, 2005, 39.

[50]The origin of the word *barangay* reportedly harks back to the name of a kind of Malay house-boat, bringing a whole community together to a new place.

the whole archipelago. Especially in cities, they are often subdivided into separate district or zone barangays, each with its own committee, elected every three years. The lists of barangay (or district and zone) council members are prominently posted on the sides of roads at the barangay limits.

Alexis de Tocqueville, who had no chance to write a book about *Democracy in the Philippines*, would have been intrigued by the extent of local democracy — and by the fact that it tends to legitimate previously existing local elites. Local contracts and prestige go along with council membership. Barangay politicians seldom have strong national party affiliations, and they may not legally run for office under party labels. They often have personal ties to regional or even national leaders, however. These links rather than any policies are, with money, at the center of Philippine politics.

Under a 1991 local government code, the barangays receive funds from central coffers for local projects. Forty percent of the national budget is allotted to provinces, municipalities, and barangays, and the localities decide how to use most of these funds. Political incumbents at all levels in the Philippines are legitimated by handing out this money. All these units, including the barangays, also have the power to impose local taxes. Municipal elections have largely been seen in public as contests between families for prestige. These elections are demonstrably democratic, and their goals have often centered on the material, as well as the status, interests of specific contestants.

Whether the habit of elections has served Filipinos or not, the idea of holding them has long been very popular. After Benigno Aquino's assassination, hundreds of thousands of people marched in 1984 and 1985 — not just against Marcos, but also in favor of holding an election.[51] Some intellectual leaders suggested a boycott of the polls, since they expected Marcos to manipulate the ballot counting (as indeed he tried to do). But few voters honored the boycott. Even Marcos supporters, who in the event turned out to be slightly less than half of the voters, heartily supported the idea of having an election.

---

[51]Benedict J. Tria Kerkvliet, "Contested Meanings of Elections," 157–58.

Voter turnout in the Philippines is often high, between 80 and 85 percent. Three-fifths of all voters live on the heavily populated island of Luzon — and about a quarter of the Luzon voters live in Metro Manila. The Commission on Elections registers candidates, tries to regulate campaigns according to the law, and supervises civilian and party oversight of the vote count. Comelec deputizes teachers, police, and soldiers to watch polls. Most crucially, the Commission counts the ballots and declares the winners.[52] Comelec's integrity is a major topic of public interest in the Philippines. "Social capital" for that cause is extensive, in part because elected representatives control money.

Comelec is famous for its role in the 1986 presidential race that Corazon Aquino won, but attempts to steal elections remain common at local levels too. Noel Cariño should have won his 2001 race to represent the large Manila suburb of Pasig City in Congress, but he lost due to electoral fraud. He appealed to Comelec and then to the relevant congressional committee, which took two and a half years to declare him the winner — and he was sworn into his seat on the very last day of his term.[53]

Another case may have inspired a disgruntled candidate to cause major arson in February 2007, when Comelec's headquarters in Manila were burned. But the Commission had reportedly foreseen such a danger, because it had backed up its important files elsewhere. As in Thailand, when elections give power to people who control money, specific institutions may be needed to mitigate the consequent violence.

The National Movement for Free Elections (Namfrel) is a "civil society" NGO watchdog institution that is supposed to be impartial among candidates, to provide a check against possible corruption in the official Comelec. Namfrel was founded in 1951 with American CIA funds. But the establishment of local election-watching NGOs has become a Philippine habit, not just an import. These groups symbolize

---

[52]David G. Timberman, *The 1992 Philippine Elections* (New York: Asia Society, 1992), 10.
[53]Anon., "Democracy as Showbiz," January 21, 2007.

the importance that many Filipinos attach to elections as liminal events and games that have rules. The results may also have further importance.

There is no shortage of potential leaders wanting Philippine political offices. One of the reasons may be a paucity of companies that might alternatively provide economic networks that ambitious people could lead. Fully 70,000 candidates ran for 17,250 elected positions nationwide in 1992, and numbers for earlier and later years are similarly high. The vast majority of the offices were naturally local, but also on the ballots that year were a new president, vice-president, senators, representatives, and provincial governorships.[54] Representatives are elected every two years (renewable twice). The senatorial terms are six years, renewable once. Elections in the Philippines are not so frequent as in Taiwan, which has just a quarter as many citizens; but even on a per-capita basis, the numbers of Philippine posts, candidates, and voters are greater.

Candidates for the top posts, including senators, are often people whose names the mass media have propagated over the whole archipelago: basketball stars, film personalities, and TV newscasters. Old political families might therefore be expected to play a less prominent role than in the past, but this is not the case. In 2000, the Senate included two Osmeñas, a Magsaysay, and many others with old names. Every senator, having won at least a plurality in a national election already, is a potential president. The term for the top office is six years (except as *kudeta* may affect it). Re-election to a full second presidential term has been constitutionally prohibited after the experience with Marcos, but this is a sensitive issue in Philippine politics. Estrada's first term was unconstitutionally ended — not just because he claimed it was.

A political broker who leads any size of collectivity smaller than the nation, down to the family, is beholden not only to his immediate group but also to the larger unit in which he is a member. In the Philippines, a *lider* is not a top leader. *Lider* means the head of a local

---

[54]David G. Timberman, *The 1992 Philippine Elections* (New York: Asia Society, 1992), 4; also 11.

network. These canvassers are the hinges of the Philippine political system. Eric Wolf writes about such people in another country, where they "stand guard over the critical junctures or synapses of relationships, which connect the local system to the larger whole."[55]

Wooing votes, in any electoral democracy, is a local process. A Filipino politician is expected to attend and give speeches at "KBL": *Kasal* (weddings), *Binyag* (baptisms), and *Libing* (burials).[56] Politicians thus acquire a considerable sacerdotal role; they become like secular priests, and the elections are also rites, not just administrative events. Alejo and her colleagues find that "the ordinary individual" is excluded from politics, even though the logic of representation suggests "a symbolic deference to the ordinary individual's capacity to act politically." This is drama, often farce, but "the political field through the electoral ritual suddenly hails [each person] as a political competent: a voter. ... Elections are just one moment in people's lives. ... They engage in an electoral exercise because they see it as one occasion for asserting their claims (security, jobs, additional government support)."[57]

Free, competitive voting has still not given ordinary people much control of the Philippine government because the money, force, and norms that guide votes are mostly in the hands of old elites that remain cohesive. Alejo's analysis quoted above speaks to her frustrations with democracy as it operates in her country. Votes are not enough to bring the electors better long-term benefits, although many accounts of liberalism suggest they should be. The problem lies in the force and norms of many local political economies that together overpower the national state.

---

[55]Eric R. Wolf, "Aspects of Group Relations in a Complex Society: Mexico," *American Anthropologist* 58 (1956), 1075, quoted in Wolters, *Politics, Patronage and Class Conflict*, 72.

[56]KBL was also the acronym for Marcos's political party, the *Kilusang Babong Lipunan* (New Society Movement). See John T. Sidel, "The Philippines: The Languages of Legitimation," in *Political Legitimacy in Southeast Asia: The Quest for Moral Authority*, Muthiah Alagappa, ed. (Stanford: Stanford University Press, 1995), 146.

[57]Myrna J. Alejo, Maria Elena Rivera, and Noel Inocencio Valencia, *[De]scribing Elections: A Study of Elections in the Lifeworld of San Isidro* (Quezon City: Institute for Popular Democracy, 1996), 70 and 92.

VOTE INDUCEMENTS

Incumbents are usually re-elected, as in many democracies. Politicians deliver material benefits, and they talk to their constituents. These representatives less often talk to each other, deliberating together in public. Many Philippine lawmakers, whom journalists sarcastically call in elegant Spanish the "Comite de Silencio," the Committee of Silence, seldom or never say anything in Congress.[58] They deliver local roads and contracts. Their local allies and canvassers deliver the voters in elections. That exhausts the whole business of politics.

Allocations by legislators from their congressional accounts are discretionary, although the funds often go through state institutions such as hospitals. An auditor noted that some congress members' offices issue "political ID" cards or letters of recommendation, personally signed by legislators, on the basis of which state hospital officials could use pork money to pay the medical expenses of approved constituents.[59]

As a young congressman said, "What we have is an underground governance structure. Congress is largely a private-based sphere, where you outsmart the system of laws. Gift giving validates the fact that *nakisama ka* [you tried to be with the group]. Every congressman expects bonuses. You walk the tightrope daily. You have to know if you should succumb. ... I have a big overhead." A top legislative staffer said that constituents "look at congressmen as if they were banks on wheels, ATM machines." Local fiestas, e.g., on saints' days, are times for canvassing and generosity. "If you have 300 barangays, you give 5000 pesos per fiesta. That's 1.5 million pesos a year. And even then, they curse you and call you a skinflint."[60]

---

[58]Renato S. Velasco, "Does the Philippine Congress Promote Democracy?" 288.

[59]Yvonne Chua and Booma B. Cruz, "Pork is a Political, not a Developmental, Tool," website, January 21, 2007.

[60]Yvonne Chua, "Fat Salaries, Big Allowances," website, March 22–24, 2004. The tendency of U.S. congressmen to equate democracy with elections, overlooking egregiously undemocratic aspects of electoral systems, is compounded because they face somewhat similar challenges.

Surveys suggest that three-tenths of Filipinos who take bribes for votes were inclined to cast their ballots otherwise, had they not been offered money.[61] In the 2001 elections, a congressman from a poor district said that the going rate for each vote was between 1500 and 2000 pesos. "They don't just buy votes. They pay the antis so they will not vote." As in Taiwan and Thailand, the most effective money was given at the last minute, not for long-term development.

> You know, it's useless to have projects. Let's just save the money and then use it at the eleventh hour. ... If you don't do that, when well-funded candidates come in, our projects will be forgotten. Don't count on *utang na loob* [debts of gratitude] from those you've helped. They'll sell you out, because it's the present that's important.[62]

Late payments were the cost-efficient way to bribe voters. "During the final hour, the one who is going to give them fifty pesos, which they can use for their needs, is the one they're going to vote for. What you did prior to that is glossed over. It is the immediacy of the need. ... You have just one flash flood of money; you keep your people poor. It's like a timebomb, and it's scary."

The cost of Philippine elections has been rising. In Marcos's re-election before he declared martial law, he and his presidential rivals collectively spent as much as one-quarter of the national budget. Campaigning has been costly in more normal and recent times, and in local as well as national races.[63] Politicians are expected to take credit by attaching their own names even to small public works projects such as footbridges, barangay halls, or basketball courts. Some of these expenses were financed privately, rather than directly from the

---

[61]It is difficult to know whether this portion should be considered high or low. Frederic Charles Schaffer, "Disciplinary Reactions: Alienation and the Reform of Vote Buying in the Philippines," paper for the American Political Science Association Annual Meeting, 2002, esp. 29.

[62]Yvonne Chua and Booma B. Cruz, "Pork is a Political, not a Developmental, Tool," website, January 21, 2007.

[63]Paul D. Hutchcroft, "Dictatorship, Development, and Plunder: The Regimes of Park Chung Hee and Ferdinand Marcos Compared," paper for the American Political Science Association Annual Meeting, 2002.

public purse. An electoral candidate's campaign budget could include money for immediate goods that constituents might need, such as a medicine with the candidate's name written prominently on the bottle.[64] Subtlety is not the hallmark of these politics.

Vote fraud occurs in many forms: "flying voters" who register and cast ballots in more than one place, the deletion of whole neighborhoods from registration lists, altering the marks on ballots, and stuffing or destroying ballot boxes.[65] Voting "early and often" is a tradition that Philippine monitors try to stanch, and they are not always successful. In Danao City, "even the dead vote." Registration rolls there, during some years, grew faster than the adult population.[66]

Term limits for mayoralties are designed to prevent local leaders from becoming long-term local tyrants. But often male mayors, whom term limits force out of office, run their wives or daughters for election. For example, Mayor Jose Ginez endorsed his wife "Pinky" for the mayoralty of Santa Maria, Bulacan. The same phenomenon appeared in no fewer than four other cities nearby where laws prevented the mayors from running again. They all ran kinswomen instead. Local family politics could become very public in these situations; two of Pinky's rivals for the post also had the surname Ginez.[67] Philippine voters often cast their ballots for candidates with the surnames of their own families. As a rural elector explained, "It's better to elect a relative or a person with a last name the same as yours. They might be long-lost relatives after all." In case of need, it was supposed that kin would have to help.[68]

Another candidate for Mayor of Santa Maria, Domingo Casabar, charged that, "[Jose] Ginez has gunmen. He was acquitted in regional court of the murder of his bodyguard, whose body was found in a rice field. The judge was biased." He said Mr. Ginez was spending

---

[64]Steven Rood, "Decentralization, Democracy, and Development," 114 and *passim*.
[65]David G. Timberman, *The 1992 Philippine Elections*, 13.
[66]Michael Cullinane, "Patron as Client: Warlord Politics and the Duranos of Danao," in *An Anarchy of Families*, 187.
[67]*South China Morning Post*, May 8, 1998, 19.
[68]This San Isidro woman voted for a senatorial candidate solely because his surname was the same as her mother's. Myrna J. Alejo, *et al.*, *[De]scribing Elections*, 42.

400 pesos per vote. "In the day, he campaigns. In the night, he campaigns with his twenty-odd bodyguards."[69]

CHARISMA IN CANDIDATES

Between 1986 and 1992, no fewer than five mayors in Cavite province were murdered by gangland-style assassins. Each of these had previously conflicted with provincial Governor Juanito "Johnny" Remulla. Bullets had been important means of silencing and scaring political rivals in Cavite for decades. Gov. Schwarzenegger, an actor, just talks about terminations. But Gov. Remulla was a man of real action. He "dispatched armed goons, ordered the bulldozing of homes, and engineered the destruction of irrigation canals to expedite the departure of 'squatters' and tenant farmers who were demanding compensation for their removal from lands designated for sale to Manila-based or foreign companies for 'development' into industrial estates."[70] This governor, no friend of labor unions, announced that his province was a "no-strike zone." He sent police to repress nascent workers' associations. Potential labor leaders tended to "disappear."

Political killings of this kind were as salient in democratic periods as during the Japanese and Marcos eras. Remulla's province experienced slow industrialization because of investment from Hong Kong, Taiwan, and Japan into the "Cavite Export Processing Zone," which is near Manila. Some new wealth was created, but the local tradition of political violence kept new money under the control of old-style leaders. Gov. Remulla "was clearly as ruthless as his warlord predecessor Montano," whom Marcos had earlier exiled to centralize control of Cavite under his friend Remulla.

The National Citizens Movement for Free Elections reported, after the 1986 presidential race, that

> In Cavite, armed goons, local officials together with other KBL [Marcos-Remulla] partisans harassed Namfrel volunteers all over the province.

---

[69] *South China Morning Post*, May 8, 1998, 19.
[70] John T. Sidel, *Capital, Coercion, and Crime: Bossism in the Philippines*, (Honolulu: University of Hawaii Press, 1999), 76; see also 53.

Namfrel was denied entry in 164 precincts and KBL partisans roamed around poll precincts intimidating voters, Namfrel volunteers, and opposition workers. Flying voters [those casting ballots in more than one precinct] were prolific, and vote buying was massive. There were suspicions concerning fake ballots. ... Tampering of election returns may have been rampant, as all precinct election returns had erasures. ... Ghost precincts may have been used as reinforcements, as shown by the more than 100% coverage in the Batasan count.[71]

Marcos won with a big margin in Cavite in 1986, although Cory Aquino carried the other southern Tagalog provinces. Coercive methods were common even in this relatively rich part of the Philippines.

Governor Remulla's local political machine collapsed not after 1986, but only after the 1992 presidential election. He made the mistake not just of opposing the winner, Fidel Ramos, but also of splitting his own supporters between Ramos's main rival candidates, Mitra and Cojuangco — who both sent Remulla miniature coffins as appropriate symbolic gifts on his birthday.[72]

From areas of the Philippines that have begun to industrialize, political violence is reported as more severe than in other fast-changing places where guns are harder to obtain (such as Taiwan or East China, though not Thailand). Poorer parts of the archipelago, where rents come more from land than from official or international links, nonetheless also suffered extensive violence. Alan Berlow's reportage on this phenomenon in Negros is especially harrowing.[73] Not all rich parts of the country were like Cavite, and not all poor parts were like Negros — but discussions of democracy that ignore the influence of coercion on voters' preferences and live options are incomplete.

A hundred people died, and another 141 were injured during the 2001 Philippine elections. In the barangay voting the next year, when

---

[71]Quoted in *ibid.*, 72–73.

[72]Do Sicilians have a copyright on such intellectual property? *Ibid.*, 77–78.

[73]Alan Berlow, *Dead Season: A Story of Murder and Revenge on the Philippine Island of Negros* (New York: Pantheon, 1996), describes a cane-growing place that is far poorer than Cavite and devoid of any industry unrelated to this crop — but local violence has dominated politics in impoverished Negros as surely as it does in the more industrial, more centrally connected suburb of Cavite.

merely 76 people were killed, the chair of the monitoring commission said this figure, which he considered low, showed that the elections were "generally peaceful."[74]

Coercive styles of leadership can persist in democracies for decades, even when such leaders do not advertise their power in public. Many voters like leaders who seem strong to the point of violence, although few of these electors would want to call themselves intellectuals. Martial charisma is known in Tagalog as *anting-anting*, and many recognize it as a virtue in politicians (as in Thai *nakleng*). Alfredo Lim, also known as "Dirty Harry," had a slogan as Mayor of Manila: "I don't shoot good men; only bad men."[75] Joseph Erap Estrada acquired has popular fame, which brought him the presidency, as a movie hoodlum. "Erap" is a nickname derived from a word that means "pal" or "buddy." Estrada was a devoted anti-intellectual, and he took pride in his populism. In 1993, he authorized a book of his own mutilations of the English language, *ERAPtions: How to Speak English Without Really Trial*. President Ramos retorted, saying he would launch a book entitled, *Erap Estrada for President and Other Jokes*. When Ramos's term ended, his elected successor was Estrada.

In movies, "Estrada had played policemen, farmers, priests, bus drivers, and an ice cream vendor, though nearly all of his characters ended up in a triumphant bloodbath by the final reel." He was said to have four families (one of them legal). This colorful reputation did not disturb supporters who voted for him. Estrada said he wanted to be president "so that I can get rid of the 'vice' in front of my name."[76]

Despite this style of nonchalance, Erap Estrada had a serious campaign organization. Funding came especially from several Chinese Filipinos who were known to be very rich. Two World Bank economists and a former Supreme Court judge were among his advisors. Estrada's organization involved some elites, although many educated Filipinos detested him (just as Bangkok intellectuals tend to abominate many populist politicians elected in that country). If the violence

---

[74]Frederic Charles Schaffer, "Disciplinary Reactions," 42.

[75]*Time*, December 22, 1997, 20–22.

[76]*Ibid.*, 22.

had only been in movies, they would have been less concerned. Not just the Philippines, but also the "backlands of Brazil" and many parts of Colombia and Mexico, have shown that electoral machines can support themselves coercively for extended periods. Jonathan Fox writes in a study of Mexico that,[77]

> electoral competition can either strengthen or weaken coercive clientelism. ... If elections offer voters alternatives, they can increase clients' leverage over vote-buying patrons, as in Taiwan [but] the threat of electoral competition can also create incentives for elites to limit political choices sharply. ... Where subnational authoritarian regimes survive within nationally competitive electoral systems, the transition can get stuck and fail to cross the threshold to democratic governance.

ELECTIONS AS FIESTAS

Some Filipinos consider that it is part of the national ethos to stress political style over policy substance. "Pleasing the group," *pakikisama* in Tagalog, stresses the importance of smooth personal relations. As Timberman says, this gives Philippine politics "its 'show biz' quality, its reliance on political rituals, and the indulgence of politicians in *palabas* (hyperbole and ostentatious show)."[78] Wurfel asks, "What did the act of registering, of being a candidate's henchman, of voting, or of attending a political rally really mean? Was not the whole electoral process a spectator sport?" He found "the evidence of a higher election turnout in rural than in urban areas, and in local rather than national elections, pointed to the importance of the patron-client relationship

---

[77] Jonathan Fox, "The Difficult Transition from Clientelism to Citizenship," *World Politics* 46 (January 1994), 182–83; see also 155. Fox was, long ago as an undergraduate at Princeton, a student of the author.

[78] "Imelda Marcos once commented to an interviewer that 'Ninoy [Benigno Aquino] was all sauce and no substance.' In response to his wife's observation, Ferdinand Marcos replied: 'Sweetheart, that is the essence of Filipino politics.'" The Tagalog *palabas* is a cognate of Spanish *palabras*, "words," with the connotation "empty words, promises from which nothing comes." For more, see David G. Timberman, *A Changeless Land: Continuity and Change in Philippine Politics* (Armonk: M.E. Sharpe, 1991), 20.

in voting."[79] People wanted leaders whom they considered more charismatic in communities, not just those who were expected to govern well.

An evening of speeches just before a 1992 election in San Isidro, Bataan, was "a political campaign and musical show rolled into one." Local solidarity was so great, as a San Isidro voter admitted, that although the "candidates all come here and talk with us, they know that we are a big clan and that we vote as a bloc." People's obvious enjoyment of electoral competition belied the lopsidedness of the eventual balloting for many posts. The incumbent congressman there showed up at this promotional meeting (*miting de avance*) to give a brief pep talk for his running mates: "Can you imagine a plan for Bataan being pushed through immediately if I have to deal with people I basically disagree with? Just imagine if the elected governor were Tet Garcia. ..."[80] Votes for popular personalities (including this speaker, Congressman Payumo) were often overwhelming. Their rivals, if also popular, might nonetheless win or come very close to winning — as this gubernatorial candidate Garcia did, for example, in Bataan. The campaign evening was mostly devoted to songs, none of which mentioned politics. It was a communal rite, in which candidates vied to make current and personal links with communities.

Alejo and her colleagues found that, "Elections, as sites of political participation, are supposed to be exercises in rational choice. This view assumes that people participate through the ballots on the basis of rational principles such as 'democracy,' party programs, efficiency. ... But the elections in San Isidro present a different picture. People used normative categories, rather than rational ones, indigenous to their situation."[81] The relevant norms were not reasons deducible from any universal description of human nature. Rational choice logics are too broad and unbehavioral to specify the motives of these voters.

---

[79]David Wurfel, *Filipino Politics: Development and Decay* (Ithaca: Cornell University Press, 1988), 40.

[80]Myrna J. Alejo, *et al.*, *[De]scribing Elections*, 36–38 and 40; see also 123.

[81]*Ibid.*, xiii.

TRAPOS REMAIN STRONG

Sixty percent of the representatives in the first post-Marcos legislature came from political families that had long been in politics. The portion did not decrease in later years, even though 1987 constitutional provisions imposed term limits and added House seats that were elected not from geographical districts but from national party lists. Over half the representatives, at least into the 1990s, personally owned agricultural land.[82] Few high politicians lacked kin who were not also elected politicians. If the party-list delegates are omitted from the count, the percentage of "political clan" *trapos* in Congress actually rose in the elections of 2004.[83]

Term limits did not change this situation. A twice-elected senator, who is ineligible for an third term at that point, may run for election to the House — and then two years later may be able to rejoin the Senate. Term limits apply to offices at all medium and high levels in the Philippines, but they do not actually retire many politicians who would like to stay in politics. The three-term constitutional limit churned Congress members somewhat, but it has done little or nothing to change the main type of representative.

Wars, decades, a dictator, and would-be coups have passed over Philippine politics, but many old landowning families have nearly always been in Congress. Four generations of each of the following clans, at the turn of the millennium, had served as lawmakers: Aquinos and Cojuangcos from Tarlac, Osmeñas from Cebu, Romoualdezes from Leyte, and Marcoses (relatively *nouveaux* though they still were) from Ilocos Norte. The families in which three generations had been elected were far more numerous. Their victories in voting were not inevitable but were perennial.

Changes of incumbents do not necessarily mean democracy, although some political scientists suggest such change is the essential

---

[82] Jeffrey M. Riedinger, *Agrarian Reform in the Philippines: Democratic Transitions and Redistributive Reform* (Stanford: Stanford University Press, 1995), 115.

[83] Sheila S. Coronel, "How Representative is Congress?" *Manila Times* website, March 22, 2004, http://www.manilatimes.net/others/special/2004/mar/22/20040322spel.html, seen January 21, 2007.

distinction between dictatorships and democracies.[84] Kerkvliet gives an example: "Considering that the Philippines has a rather long history of incumbents' being defeated and their rivals' being elected, and national and local governments routinely ... changing hands in accordance with ballot outcomes, one might expect that elections have a significant degree of democratic meaning."[85] As he says, this expectation would be hopeful but wrong.

The increased importance of media, along with other factors such as constitutional term limits, encourages marriages between old political families and new celebrities. So a fourth-generation congressman, Julio Ledesma, married movie star Assunta di Rossi. A member of Corazon Aquino's clan married Robert Jaworski, son of a basketball star.[86] Families, not parties, are the main Philippine political organizations. They fare best if they can combine the old and new ways of winning votes.

A 2004 study of all the legislatures since the Malolos Congress of 1898 showed that post-Marcos deputies stayed in office on average *longer* than their predecessors — despite the three-term limit imposed by the 1987 Constitution. Two-thirds of the representatives by 2004 were members of old "political clans." One third of these had parents who had been elected to public offices, another sixth had grandparents who had enjoyed electoral successes. Nearly half were kin of former Congress members. Also, the portion of Congress representatives from old political families rose slightly after Marcos's fall, because wives or children of incumbents can be elected by reliable local political machines as "breakers," after a representative's

---

[84]These analysts do not intend to support a progressive idea that countries move from dictatorship to democracy (they have studied movement in the opposite direction). But that is implicit in a restrictive definition of democracy as requiring a government to lose an election before the regime qualifies as democratic; they do not require a parallel criterion of dictatorial regimes. See Adam Przeworski, Michael E. Alvarez, José Antonio Cheibub and Fernando Limongi, *Democracy and Development: Political Institutions and Well-Being in the World, 1950–1990* (Cambridge: Cambridge University Press, 2000).

[85]Benedict J. Tria Kerkvliet, "Contested Meanings of Elections," 136.

[86]Anon., "Democracy as Showbiz," *Economist*, July 1, 2004.

three terms is served.[87] In a later election, the patriarch can run and win again.

ELITES' ASSETS AND CHARTER CHANGES

The typical legislator's income included money from professional salaries and dividends as well as rents from property. Income from land was, by the turn of the millennium, still important — but of decreasing importance compared with income from commercial activities such as real estate development, banking, stock broking, and white-collar professions. Lawyers, NGO officials, former bureaucrats, and media celebrities were increasingly elected to Congress, but relatively little of these politicians' income came from running industries.

The reported assets of House members in 1992 had been 8 million pesos; but it soared to 22 million pesos by 2001. (Senators' *reported* average net worth rose from 33 million pesos in 1998 to 59 million in 2001, an increase that greatly outpaced inflation.) So the 1987 constitutional changes seldom produced Filipino representatives from new families, even though some scions of old families now had professional (but seldom industrial) careers as well as rent incomes.[88]

During Estrada's term, it had been expected that the Philippines would convene a national convention to change the constitution again. Many ideas were floated for amendments to the governmental structure. A unicameral legislature was mooted, as was a parliamentary system with a premier. It was proposed that if a presidential election resulted in no majority for any candidate (as in recent elections), a run-off between the two candidates with the highest vote counts would give a clearer mandate to rule. Some intellectuals also thought this change would encourage the development of a two-party system,

---

[87]Yvonne Chua, "An Expensive — and Unaccountable — Legislature," website, March 22–24, 2004.

[88]Sheila S. Coronel *et al.*, *The Rulemakers*, with an accompanying data disk, *The Ties that Bind: A Guide to Family, Business, and Other Interests in Congress* (provided to the author by courtesy of Dr. Steven Rood, The Asia Foundation, Makati City).

in which a market-supporting conservative party might vie against a market-regulating reformist party.

Strong Philippine traditions and interests opposed such a change to left-right politics, such as are salient in wealthier democracies. Governance, on these islands, has been kept safe from democracy. A great many proposals have been made in favor of constitutional change with the aim of correcting this problem. The Philippine Institute for Popular Democracy advocates a constitutional convention to create a parliamentary and federal government for the archipelago, while retaining the nationalistic bans on economic or educational activities by foreigners (including non-citizen Chinese who live there).[89] With vintage Filipino humor, "charter change" is popularly called "cha-cha," copying the name of the slightly risqué dance.

Links between constitutional fixes and improvements of governance are uncertain. In light of old elites' dominant local power in most of the islands, federalism would almost surely not make a stronger state. Yet more authority in Manila is exactly what many observers believe the Philippines needs, before the central government will be able to protect less violent forms of competition in local politics. It is documentable that would-be patriotic bans on enterprise by resident "foreigners" over the long term have weakened the Philippine nation. Political sages in Manila (as in Bangkok) have many proposals to alter power relations *within* the government by amending the constitution. But change within the state can probably do little to help the people, if there is continued effective resistance to peaceable competition among nonstate power networks. "Cha-cha" is indeed risky.

If Negros or Ilocos or Tarlac were to become even more independent provinces within a federation, as many would-be reformist Philippine intellectuals advocate, it is not hard to guess the last names of people who would be elected to govern them. This would not end "traditional politics." Decentralization of economic power to risk-taking entrepreneurs would be useful for democracy, if the government in Manila had more such power to disperse. Central regulation, to

---

[89]The Institute's website is at http://www.ipd.org

assure that the labor they exploit is willing rather than unwilling, and that competition between them is fair on economic rather than political grounds, would also help. Until local power holders have to tolerate local rivals, entrepreneurs to create new jobs and workers to take them will not appear out of thin air. Economic development is led, but locally and politically.

Rewriting the national constitution is a solution whose effectiveness depends on having stronger a nation-state than elites have yet permitted in Manila. Cha-cha may seem attractive to legalists who imagine a unified power that does not exist, forgetting the persistence of regional networks that find many resources to support themselves against national reforms. As Thailand's experience with its 1997 constitutional reforms and then Thaksin shows, the national-legalistic approach does not reach far enough into the political economy to solve the problem. If reformers want to fix it — as many local elites in the Philippines do not — what needs amendment is power in the provinces, not charter change in Manila. Factories, especially autonomous small shops, are the factors that would eventually create democratic constraints between central and local powers on these islands, so that more people could benefit. These would lead to translocal businesses and unions.

POLITICAL PARTIES AS FEUDING FAMILIES

Why do strong parties not form in the Philippines? Jeffrey Riedinger suggests possible causes: "dependency relations embodied in patron-client networks, powerful regional elites, private landowner armies, and crosscutting social cleavages that constrain solidarity along class lines."[90] In this context, the procedure of democratic elections can reinforce a substantively anti-democratic political system.

Competitive parties were actually the norm in early years of Philippine national politics. These parties, at odds though they were during elections, had nearly indistinguishable social policies. In 1922–24 and 1937–41, splits and unifications of the Nacionalistas

---

[90] Jeffrey M. Riedinger, *Agrarian Reform in the Philippines*, 13.

between the two most prominent politicians, Manuel Quezon and Sergio Osmeña, coincided with a fluctuation between three- and one-party patterns. The structure of the post-Marcos period has also been kaleidoscopic, with most parties clearly dependent on rising and falling personalities. Parties have remained in flux not just in Manila but at each size of collectivity from provinces to barangay districts, where personality-based factions are scarcely different in structure from national parties. Electoral experience has not created a trend to more unified coalitions in a stable party system.

As Kimura writes, "Elections prompt politicians to make alliances to fight the contests. After the elections, a new political wind starts to blow and changes the alliance system."[91] Such shifts of wind are frequent in the Philippines. Temporary coalitions appear at many levels of collectivity — and they do so simultaneously, most intensely before elections. The networks often become incoherent: A supports B even though B's patron or client may support A's rival. They depend on decisions taken in light of overall expectations of who will win and who will lose, irrespective of personal esteem or policy preferences.

For example, Ruben Umali as Mayor of Lipa had a prospective opponent, Macala, who gave up his race against Umali only because of the mayor's increased power after the latter supported a candidate who was elected to a lucrative seat in Congress. Soon thereafter, however, that congressman split from his former patrons in the Laurel network (including Umali) by grooming a candidate for governor against the Laurels' nominee, Ronaldo Lina, a Lipeño residing in Manila who had weak but direct connections to President Aquino. Because voters almost always prefer their fellow townspeople (*kababyan*), the congressman's support for Lina posed problems for Mayor Umali. He faced an unexpected challenge that he might lose.

> It disgusted Umali to imagine the possibility that he who had campaigned for President Aquino in the special presidential elections might be running as the opposition's candidate, while Lina who had supported Marcos might be proclaimed by Aquino as an administration candidate, and that the

---

[91]Kimura Masataka, *Elections and Politics, Philippine Style*, 204.

"Cory Magic" which brought about the sweeping victory of the ruling coalition in the congressional and senatorial elections might work in favor of Lina. ... After long consideration, he was inclined to take a neutral stance vis-a-vis the gubernatorial contest. However, he decided that in case UNIDO [the Aquino-Laurel party] bolted the ruling coalition, he would quit UNIDO and become an independent candidate to avoid identification with the opposition; otherwise, he would remain with UNIDO.[92]

This mayor was in the Laurel coalition, but his supporters who needed help from another faction did not necessarily desert him. Policy principles were no basis to predict what they would do.

Politics in Batangas, as in other Philippine locales, is thus divided and reassembled frequently, but not in a way that encourages democratic stability. Politics anywhere can be turbulent, but in the Philippines the kaleidoscope turns with particular constancy. The event that stopped the congressman's pressure to persuade Umali to switch from the Laurel group was extraneous, violent, and national: the assassination of the Minister of Local Government, Jaime Ferrer. After that, President Aquino threatened to delay all local elections. Then, at the national level, Aquino and Laurel were reconciled under an agreement providing that Aquino would not intervene in Batangas, leaving that province a "free zone."

Umali nonetheless switched parties, in an emotional speech at a *miting de avance* in Lipa City square, saying that the only reason he did so was to help his fellow Lipeño to be elected governor. At the same time, he denounced the congressman for having supported his rival for mayor. A Laurel clan member appeared at Umali's residence a few days later, saying that their family's UNIDO party had still not withdrawn their certificate of nomination of Umali for mayor. In the event, Umali was re-elected, as was the anti-Laurel nominee for governor. This mayor was later re-elected twice — on each occasion under a different party banner. "In both cases, a new factional configuration emerged, and the relations among the factions and their relations with the national parties had totally changed."[93] This politics

---

[92] *Ibid.*, 216–17.
[93] *Ibid.*, 247.

was chaotic, tumbling randomly and often. At the end of such tales, the conclusion was often determined by an unexpected external event.[94]

The mayor of Lipa, a city representing only ten percent of the Batangas population, could remain aloof from provincial or national politics no more easily than he could remain aloof from the *liders* of his barangay wards. Factional alignments were in flux because political actors at all sizes of collectivity shared the Brownian motion. Democratic procedures alone could not organize these politics, even though freedom of speech prevailed and truly competitive elections were held.

Family-like organizations are the behavioral and modal Philippine parties, even though such families often feud. Carl Landé provides the classic description of Philippine political organization: "The two rival parties in each province ... are held together by dyadic patron-client relationships, extending from great and wealthy political leaders in each province down to lesser gentry politicians in the towns, down further to petty leaders in each village, and down finally to the clients of the latter: the common [people]."[95]

Locally dominant families often disperse their members among the national temporary coalitions that claim to be parties. The Dy clan, long important in Isabela Province of northern Luzon, produced partisans of both Estrada and Arroyo, when those two national leaders were bitter rivals for the presidency.[96] Although family solidarity is important in the Philippines, it is only a potential basis for politics. Leadership of families and conflict with other families catalyzes latent loyalties. Elections are recurrent occasions for such conflict. In

---

[94]Chinua Achebe, *Man of the People* (New York: Anchor, 1988 [orig. 1966]), ends similarly — with an coup not portended in the main plot — because Nigerian grassroots politics have a somewhat similar form.

[95]Carl H. Landé, "Brief History of Political Parties," in *Foundations and Dynamics of Filipino Government and Politics*, Jose Abueva and Raul de Guzman, eds. (Manila: Bookmark, 1969), 156, quoted in Paul D. Hutchcroft and Joel Rocamora, "Strong Demands and Weak Institutions," 4.

[96]Anon., "Democracy as Showbiz," *Economist*, July 1, 2004.

1992, for example, they allowed different groups of Cojuangcos to run against each other and two different factions of Osmeñas to run against each other.[97]

Dominant families can have severe internal splits. In Tarlac, the Cojuangcos have long been powerful, and Marcos's "crony" there was Eduardo "Danding" Cojuangco, a monopolist in coconut oil. Danding was also, however, a first cousin of Corazon Aquino, whose different branch of the Cojuangco clan (and whose Tarlac Development Company) rose after Marcos fell. Corazon Aquino "is said to believe that Danding conspired with Imelda Marcos to order Benigno Aquino's murder."[98]

Ambition for status is the only hardy perennial constant of such politics. The scions of well-placed Philippine families have shown no lack of drive to mobilize votes — except by appealing to voters on the basis of policy issues. One analyst notes the example of "Sergio Osmeña Jr. of Cebu, who was governor, mayor, congressman, and senator. As soon as he captured one office, he began campaigning for the next (sometimes not even completing the term for the position he had), using the office's discretionary funds to help his new quest, until becoming the presidential nominee of the Liberal Party, running against Marcos [but] the man had no shred of genuine concern for any public problem."[99]

Electoral conflict can strengthen family factionalism. Procedural democracy can spur, rather than moderate, violence. As Cullinane says of one warlord clan, "Over the years Durano family life has been punctuated by elections, consumed by the intrigues of electioneering, and sustained by postelection patronage."[100] Families, and candidates within them, prospered best if they won the prestige that accompanied official posts. The resources that brought electoral victory were "guns, goons, and gold," i.e., buying votes and threatening violence

---

[97]Brian Fegan, "Entrepreneurs in Votes and Violence: Three Generations of a Peasant Political Family" in *An Anarchy of Families*, 49.

[98]James Clad, *Behind the Myth*, 30–31.

[99]Benedict J. Tria Kerkvliet, "Contested Meanings of Elections," 140.

[100]Michael Cullinane, "Patron as Client: Warlord Politics and the Duranos of Danao," 187. On vote buying in the 1987 election, 192.

against any opposition. Deo Durano in 1988 ran against his own father for the Danao City mayoralty with promises to change these practices. The son won, later admitting that he had spent 200,000 pesos buying votes. But this was a bargain, since his father had given 7,000,000 pesos to Danao City voters, clearly including many who had cast their ballots for the son.

PRE-INDUSTRIAL POLITICS TRUMPS PLATFORMS

Factions of any kind can be called parties in the Philippines. A careful sample of heads of households were asked in surveys, "With what political party do you identify?" The overwhelming response was: "None." This option usually garnered between 80 and 90 percent, sometimes more. It did so quite uniformly in *each* major part of the country (Metro Manila, the rest of Luzon, the Visayas, and Mindanao), and in *each* major class group. This was attested by at least 14 careful, separate polls taken at different times. Only once, in all these surveys from November 1991 to June 1997 (and confirmed by more recent polls), could any single party claim the loyalty of more than 10 percent of household heads.[101] Filipinos do not think much of, or about, political parties.

At the national level, the oligarchs elected to power have never established political parties with coherent policies or ideologies. No convincing semblance of party government has ever existed in Manila.[102] Rocamora calls Philippine parties "temporary campaign

---

[101]This exception was in the December 1995 survey, when the ruling Lakas/Christian Democratic coalition garnered a still-unimpressive 12 percent, and the loyalty to "none" option plummeted to a still-overwhelming 77 percent. Fully 79 percent of Manila residents at this time said they were loyal to no party — as did 79 percent of both the best-off and worst-off social classes as coded by interviewers on the basis of their types of dwelling (because reported income would be a less reliable index). This was the only poll in which a single party broke the single-digit barrier. This information, or any data with so much careful detail about Philippine elections in the 1990s, comes from the Social Weather Stations, Inc.

[102]For a contrast, praising the stability of the U.S. party system (and claiming that at least in the Democratic case, the party despite a name change is almost as old as the republic), see E.E. Schattschneider, *Party Government* (New York: Holt, Rinehart and Winston, 1942).

organizations, malleable, unstable, with no organizational reality other than what their leaders choose to give them at each specific point in time."[103] After campaigns, parties tend to dissolve.

Arriving at Congress, if representatives are chosen under a different party label than the president, they can — and frequently do — shift with astonishing blitheness into the presidential "party." Their voters are scarcely ever dismayed by this, if the switch means that presidential patronage is added to congressional patronage for the delivery of grants. The weakness of the Filipino party system is highlighted by this phenomenon of "turncoating." When congressional representatives from losing parties coalesce with the new president's party, they receive a greater portion of the spoils that the executive branch can dispense.

Before a presidential election, there is competition among Congress members to prove that they have passed some laws — *any* laws, for the reputation of having done their legislative duties more than because of their policy goals. The most available way for the President to guide this trend is to form a personal alliance with the Speaker. So President-Speaker political partnerships are a frequent (though not constant) pattern.[104] They are important not only because of the House's fiscal powers, but also because the Senate is often populated by would-be presidents who want to undermine the current head of state. Provincial and local leaders also tend to do best when they are allied with the President in Manila — but the reverse is equally true. Presidents must depend on local bosses to deliver votes.[105]

Thai parties have also been unstable, but slightly less so than the Philippine political array, and Thailand has had a shorter experience with competitive democratic elections. Elites in Bangkok had some ideological and policy coherence. So provincial politicians had to

---

[103] Joel Rocamora, "Introduction," in Myrna J. Alejo, *et al.*, *[De]scribing Elections*, xxvii.

[104] Carlos Manuel Lazatín, *The Challenge of Economic Reform in a Democracy* has material about President-Speaker alliances.

[105] John T. Sidel, *Capital, Coercion, and Crime* stresses the dependence of local bosses more than the dependence of the central state but actually provides evidence of both.

coalesce to ensure that majority control of the Diet would rest in their hands, rather than in the hands of Bangkok intellectuals and professionals who conceive political platforms. Thaksin's biggest innovation was that his Thai Rak Thai Party also had real policies. Philippine political parties have seldom supported long-lasting coherent programs. Before Marcos, just two parties had some continuity of name. The Liberals and the Nacionalistas had constituencies that were often indistinguishable in terms of social ideas.

Personal links, not policies, are the lodestones of Filipino politicians. They establish dyadic relations with each other to hel00p them get elected.[106] This pattern also extends downward into low income strata, linking people who have surplus wealth with those who are impoverished. It often bonds people across places. Locally dominant clan networks try to extend their power geographically by electing, as potential allies in provincial or national governments, the rivals of vulnerable dominant clannish networks in other places. So lively politics are the norm, but this system presents voters no long-lasting platforms among which they can effectively choose.

In the 1992 presidential race, candidate Joseph Estrada at first appeared as the nominee of his *Partido ng Masang Pilipino* (Party of the Philippine Masses). Some who were interested in leftist policies supported him. He was certainly a populist. Before the election, he realized he would not win the top office; so he switched to become the vice-presidential candidate of a rightist party instead — without losing many of these supposedly left-leaning supporters, who still voted for him to be vice-president.[107]

To win elections, there is no sure need to be in a party. Shortly before he won the presidency, Fidel Ramos switched parties. His predecessor Corazon Aquino won more because of her martyred husband

---

[106]A classic description is Carl H. Landé, *Leaders, Factions, and Parties: The Structure of Philippine Politics* (New Haven: Yale University Southeast Asia Monograph Series, 1965).

[107]Filomeno V. Aguilar, "Of Cocks and Bets: Gambling, Class Structuring and State Formation in the Philippines," in *Patterns of Power and Politics in the Philippines*, James F. Eder and Robert L. Youngblood, eds. (Tempe: Arizona State University Program for Southeast Asian Studies, 1994), 182.

than because of her party. Ramos's successor Erap Estrada won because of his persona as a film star, not because of his party.

A corollary is that a president whose party coalition has a strong nominal majority in Congress (as Ramos had, for example) may still lack sufficient influence to discipline the representatives and actually make laws. By mid-1993, the Ramos administration had submitted 74 bills to Congress, but only 18 had been passed.[108]

When the Nacionalista mayor of a medium-sized city was refused the renomination of his party, he continued to use the Nacionalista Party's name — and he won, defeating the NP's official candidate. In the next election, he wanted to move up from the mayoralty into Congress. So he switched to the Liberals, challenged the Nacionalista candidate, and lost in the larger district as a whole (although not in his own city). Next he ran for re-election as mayor. For this vote he remained a Liberal, and his main rival claimed to be Nacionalista — this was one of his own former followers, with whom he had fallen out, who now "carried the banner of the NP unofficially." The mayor lost because his own faction had been split. In all these elections, candidates used party labels whether or not they were recognized as nominees by the party organizations. In none of them did parties, as distinguished from informal networks, affect the outcome.[109]

Philippine parties are so vague, some Congress members belong simultaneously to two of them, having "dual citizenship." Caucuses and parties may pretend to coalesce, while their members' actual loyalties remain uncertain. For example, in 2004 the *Kampi*-Liberal party claimed 116 seats in the House, but their rivals said they had only 79.[110] The problem was not that somebody miscounted. It was that these elected representatives needed more contextual information, before deciding what party they should join on any particular occasion.

---

[108] Jeffrey M. Riedinger, *Agrarian Reform*, 208.

[109] Kimura Masataka, *Elections and Politics*, 31.

[110] Philippine Center for Investigative Journalism, "De Venecia's Reign is Challenged," July 26–27, 2004, http://www.pcij.org/stories/2004/house.html, seen January 21, 2007.

The Philippine president and vice-president are elected separately, not necessarily on the same party slate. Voters chose President Estrada, for example, along with Vice-President Gloria Arroyo, who was originally a presidential candidate running against Estrada in the same year until she switched to the VP race where her chances were better. Arroyo was never part of Estrada's camp. It is difficult to write crisply about the social policies or parties of either. In any case, Arroyo won the country's second job at the same time Estrada won the presidency — and when he was pushed out under the threat of a coup, she ascended to the top job.

There is no major pressure to establish policy parties, because ordinary citizens are attracted to the spectacle of conflict itself. Present elites benefit from this habit of not sullying politics with policy. When a survey questionnaire polled Filipinos whether they would prefer a party slate system to their current system of choosing each candidate separately for each office, over 80 percent replied they liked their present practice.[111] In a discussion of this poll result, a Filipino commented that it was natural for people to split their votes, to achieve "balance" in government. Balance between policies, however, is unnecessary because candidates would apparently lose support if they presented clear programs. This trait of electoral democracies is not unique to the Philippines, but democratic theorists might pay it more attention. Ordinary citizens may know what they are doing better than political scientists do, but a job of the latter is to explain why the observed events occur, and no account (including this one) yet adequately does so.

The instability of Filipino parties can be exemplified by many cases. In the 1987 coup attempt by Colonel Honasan against President Aquino, her Vice-President Jose Laurel, Jr., at first took a pro-coup stance. The dispute lasted for several months, after which Aquino and Laurel made an agreement that reconciled their differences and temporarily restored a pretense of unity in their *Lakas ng Bansa* "party."

---

[111]From a 1992 poll conducted by the Social Weather Stations, Inc.; thanks are due to Jeanette M. Ureta for telling the author about this result.

Another case is the history of a candidate who was a godchild of that same Jose Laurel, Jr., scion of the most important family in Batangas. When *Lakas ng Bansa* needed a senatorial candidate in that province, Jose Laurel insisted that the nomination go to his brother, Sotero H. Laurel. This excluded candidate Perez from the possibility of running. So Perez stomped out of *Lakas ng Bansa*, joining other candidates in Batangas: Jose Malvar Villegas, Querubin Makalintal, and Crisanto Gualberto (who was a defeated congressional candidate of *Lakas ng Bansa*). All of them opposed the Laurels' continued dominance. Perez headed this anti-Laurel local coalition, and a congressman who had also been Jose Laurel's godchild became its vice-chairman. Quasi-kin links with the Laurels did not prevent these factional splits. Members of no fewer seven official parties were included in the new local coalition, which was scarcely more temporary than any other party on the archipelago.[112] This was classic Philippine politics. Attempts to challenge dominant local networks are frequent. Occasionally these oppositions win, at least for a while. When they lose, their members switch to the party-factions that won. By then, everybody's social policy stances are diluted.

Disputes about the recipients of public money are the liveliest kind of policy politics. In 2004, Gloria Arroyo engineered somewhat closer control of the House of Representatives. This change was at the expense of her sometime ally, Speaker Jose de Venecia, Jr. She used "a new bloc of legislators well connected to the presidential palace, especially First Gentleman Jose Miguel Arroyo." The president's son, Juan Miguel ('Mikey') Arroyo, was also a newly elected congressman from Pampanga. The issue between President Arroyo and Speaker de Venecia was not open conflict, but it concerned which representatives would receive lucrative committee chairs. In addition to monetary allowances and free staff, "a committee position can also be used to shake down businesses in efforts disguised as 'inquiry in aid of legislation.'"[113]

---

[112]Kimura Masataka, *Elections and Politics*, 144–45.
[113]Philippine Center for Investigative Journalism website, "Representatives Scramble for Power, Peso, and Privileges," July 26–27, 2004.

As Speaker de Venecia said, "For every committee, there is a request from 10 to 15 [representatives for chairmanships]. There are 60 applicants for [12 slots in] the Commission on Appointments."[114] Each of these prebends was worth money. The Appointments Commission includes just twelve members from the House (as well as twelve from the Senate, i.e., fully half of that upper chamber). The irrelevance of parties was highlighted during the tension in 2004 between de Venecia and Arroyo, when Prospero Pichay (Surigao del Sur) vied with Marcelino Libanan (Western Samar) to head the House delegation on Appointments. Pichay switched from *Lakas* to Arroyo's *Kampi* group in hopes of increasing his support, while Libanan, who had previously been with another party close to Arroyo, switched to *Lakas*.[115] Tentative loyalties to major politicians, rather than to parties, were features of these politics.

Regional coalitions occasionally form. For example, when Rep. Herminio G. Teves (Negros Oriental) fought for the chair of the Ways and Means Committee in 2004, he boasted not only that his personal wealth made him the top taxpayer in the House, but also that he had support from other Visayas representatives. Deputy speakerships are sometimes also distributed regionally. In a previous congress, there was one deputy speaker each from Luzon, the Visayas, and Mindanao. None of these personal and regional connections had any obvious link, however, to national policy choices.

Without meaningful parties, according to Samuel Huntington, "elections are just a conservative device which gives a semblance of popular legitimacy to traditional structures and traditional leadership."[116] The Republic of the Philippines provides much documentation for this. Modern social and industrial issues may later lead to policy parties that can add some government to the present electoral fiestas.

---

[114]Philippine Center for Investigative Journalism website, "De Venecia's Reign is Challenged," July 26–27, 2004.

[115]Philippine Center for Investigative Journalism website, "Representatives Scramble for Power, Peso, and Privileges," July 26–27, 2004.

[116]Samuel Huntington, *Political Order in Changing Societies* (New Haven: Yale University Press, 1968), 402.

LINGUISTIC, REGIONAL, RELIGIOUS, OR IDEOLOGICAL GROUPS

Philippine national identity has sometimes been very strong, but so are local identities and supranational ones. Nearly 10 percent of the country's citizens live abroad. Remittances sent back by Overseas Filipino Workers (after they have met their own expenses in foreign lands) are 14 percent of the GNP.[117]

Many Filipinos know a good deal about the world at large, even if they grew up in poor rural areas. A "Statehood U.S.A." movement organized a petition that a reported million Filipinos signed. "Jokes about the long lines for visas at the U.S. Embassy, about hiring former Singapore prime minister Lee Kwan Yew to run the Philippines, and about the likely overwhelming victory of a referendum making the Philippines the fifty-first state are legion."[118] When the current author mentioned to a highly educated Filipino-American that a Chinese trader and pirate king named Li Mahong in 1574 almost expelled the Spanish by attacking Manila to establish his suzerainty over Luzon (as Zheng Chenggong [Koxinga] later did in Taiwan against the Dutch and 'aborigines' there), the sardonic reply was: "Well, things might have turned out better if he'd succeeded."[119]

All Filipinos speak various Malayo-Polynesian languages, but this is scant basis for unity among them. So few Spaniards came to the Philippines that Spanish was never the language of most of the people.

---

[117]A red carpet and special OFW immigration lane at the Manila airport welcome them back because of their major monetary contributions, but they seldom get red-carpet treatment in the foreign places where they work. Jason DeParle, "A Good Provider is Someone who Leaves," *International Herald Tribune*, April 21, 2007, 2.

[118] John T. Sidel, "The Philippines: The Languages of Legitimation," 143.

[119]Taiwan's "aborigines," now one-fiftieth of the island's population but once a large majority, speak Austronesian languages that are related to Filipino languages. Europeans including Spanish (in Taiwan 1626–42) but mainly Dutch (1623–62) strongly encouraged immigration by South Fujian Chinese to Taiwan, thus ending the power of Austronesians on that island. See Tonio Andrade, *How Taiwan Became Chinese: Dutch, Spanish, and Han Colonization in the Seventeenth Century* (New York: Columbia University Press, 2005). Practically all Filipino Chinese come from families that spoke the Minnan (S. Fujian) language, which is also called Taiwanese.

The church had a limited unifying effect, and the colonial government had less. The advent of U.S. administrators weakened the church and scarcely strengthened the secular authorities in Manila. Straits between islands, paralleled by high ranges of volcanoes, provided much continuing basis for localism.[120]

---

[120]Readers may wish more local knowledge of this large country. The Philippines has about 80 administrative provinces, but the most important cultural groups are less numerous. In Luzon, they include the Tagalogs of the Manila region, whose pre-Spanish Muslim court where the Pasig River flows into Manila Bay was less weak than other clan-states on the island. In central Luzon, more recent Tagalog migrants cleared ricelands in Nueva Ecija province and adjacent regions.

The school system, for linguistic as well as nationalistic reasons, is able to propagate Tagalog more easily than English. The main languages of the Philippines are in the Malayo-Polynesian subgroup of Austronesian tongues, even though they are not mutually comprehensible. Youngsters speaking any of them can learn Tagalog/Pilipino somewhat more readily than they can learn unrelated languages. English remains widespread because of its international and economic importance, and ability in English is a major catalyst of the Philippine diaspora. The government in Manila places touristic advertisements in foreign media asking, "What country has more English speakers than England?" (There are several correct answers to this question, but the Philippine Tourist Board has just one of them in mind.)

In north Luzon, the Ilocanos tend to dominate among many groups, not just in the two provinces of Ilocos Norte and Ilocos Sur but also in nearby areas, partly because they have been prominent in the army officer corps. President Fidel Ramos was an Ilocano from the province of Pangasinan at the southern end of the Lingayen Gulf. President Ferdinand Marcos was from Ilocos Norte. North Luzon is also home to various mountain tribes such as the Igorots, and to peoples of the Cagayan Valley on the northeast and other groups on the east coast.

Two further regional groups are notable here because of their contrasting economic habits. The Kapampangans live on the northern edge of Manila Bay, extending inland to an area that was covered in 1991 by ash from the eruption of Mt. Pinatubo. Over many decades, even centuries, Pampanga has been noteworthy on Luzon for somewhat lively entrepreneurship. For example, the Philippines in 2000 had a steep tariff on laundry soap. Villagers in Pampanga found they could repackage the contents of large sacks of Indonesian soap into smaller plastic bags of one kilo each and make a profit selling these domestically. Their price was less than half the cost of the same soap on other Filipino retail markets, mostly because they had smuggled the soap in, to avoid a tariff. Having found a profitable product, Pampanga traders sold it with great verve. An interviewed traveller reports women lining the sides of roads north of Manila, trying to hawk one-kilo bags of detergent. Pampanga has, among all Philippine provinces, the lowest unemployment rate.

The Philippines' diversity of local languages, even though they are all in the same broad language family, has also strengthened political regionalisms.[121] President Quezon in the 1930s complained when he visited Pampanga, just 100 miles north of the capital, that he could not make himself understood until he got a translator to repeat his speeches in Kapampangan.[122]

The spread of Tagalog, a.k.a. Pilipino, from Manila in recent decades has reduced this problem. Only about 24 percent of Filipinos

---

By contrast, the Bicolanos of the island's southern peninsula have the richest ricelands in the whole archipelago. The strikingly beautiful shield volcano Mt. Mayon hovers over Legazpi City, the first major Spanish settlement in the archipelago, refertilizing land with no fewer than 47 large eruptions since records began in 1616, the latest being in 2006. Yet Bikol has the lowest per capita income of any large region in the archipelago (except for parts of Mindanao in the extreme south). Bicolanos are famous in the islands for their religious conservatism, their particularly strong cult of Spanish-style grandees who collect rents but do not stoop to business, and their dignified poverty.

[121]A language "diversity index," on which rather slight changes of value indicate notable differences and portions of speakers are considered, has been estimated by the Ethnologue organization for each of the countries of interest here. This index is highest in the Philippines, at 0.85. It would be higher yet, if the many diverse noncolonial languages there (which are related to Malay-Indonesian, Maori, Hawaiian, Merina-Malgasy, etc.) were not all Austronesian. For the three-fourths of Filipinos who do not normally speak Tagalog in their households, this factor makes study of Tagalog easier than study of non-Austronesian tongues such as English. The diversity index for Thailand is 0.75, largely because of the difference between Lao in the Isan and standard Bangkok Thai (although the language of the South, on the Isthmus of Kra, is closer to Lao than either is to central Thai, as Anthony Diller has shown). In Taiwan, where both Taiwanese-Minnan and Mandarin are very common, the diversity index is 0.49. In mainland China, where four-fifths of the people speak varieties of Mandarin (Beijingese, Hunanese, Sichuanese, etc., dialects that are sometimes barely intelligible with each other) and the other 20 percent speak truly different languages (Shanghainese/Wu/Zhejiangese, Cantonese, Teochiu/Hainanese, Hokkien/Minnan, the Fuzhou language, and Hakka, as well as non-Sinitic Zhuang, Tibetan, etc.), the diversity index is lower because of the enormous population and relative coherence of the Mandarin/Putonghua group, at 0.48. See http://www.ethnologue.com/show_map.asp?name=Philippines

[122]Pampanga in the 1930s, when Quezon made this complaint, was a relatively rich province. Now Tagalog has spread more widely because of schools. But see Benedict Anderson, "Elections and Participation," in *The Politics of Elections in Southeast Asia*, R.H. Taylor, ed. (Washington: Woodrow Wilson Center, 1996), 21–22.

normally speak Tagalog (or one of its approximately seven dialects), and a slightly larger portion speak various kinds of Cebuano, the most common language in the central Visayan islands. Ilocano, Kapampangan, Bicolano, Ilongo-Panayan, and several Mindanao languages are each used in far more than a million households each. Just two tongues, Tagalog and English, are official.[123]

This linguistic situation is one of several factors that has "dispersed power across the archipelago, while concentrating it vertically," as Benedict Anderson notes. "Provincial caciques were assured of more or less equal representation in Manila. A final malignity was the development of this decentralized system of oligarchy in tandem with the failure to create a professional central bureaucracy." This produced in colonial times "a quickly Filipinized state machinery subordinate to congressional oligarchs, both more corrupt than anywhere else in colonial Southeast Asia."[124] It largely survives into the new millennium.

A survey long ago found that language was a more important determinant of Philippine votes than was party.[125] The dominant self-identification of Filipinos is now with the whole country, however, not linguistic or ethnic subgroups (except among Muslims in Mindanao and Sulu). Extensive temporary migration between the

---

[123]Lists of Philippine culture areas elsewhere in this text are political, but careful linguists have also measured the extent of division between seven distinct major groups of languages (one including both Ilocano and Kapampangan together, the majority "Meso-Philippine" group including Tagalog and many Visayan languages together, "Southern Philippine" mostly in Mindanao, "Spanish-based Creole," and small largely Muslim languages called "Sama-Bajaw," "Sulawesi," and "South Mindanao"). They claim to have found 169 living Filipino languages, not including several others which have recently become disused. Diverse people in many parts of this large archipelago of separated islands have their own strong senses of place and often devotion to their own regional patrons and leading families. For more of the precise linguistics, see http://www.ethnologue.com/show_map.asp?name=Philippines\seq=1.

[124]Benedict Anderson, "Elections and Participation," 22

[125]Four languages (in order of the number of households speaking them: Cebuano, Tagalog, Ilongo, and Ilocano) account for two-thirds of the national population, estimated on the basis of a 1969 survey in David Wurfel, *Filipino Politics*, 27, from work by H.A. Averch *et al.*

islands in recent decades has increased this tendency. A candidate who wants votes in any dialect area still does best to campaign in the local tongue.

Religious divisions might become politically more important if tensions between Roman Catholic and Protestant sects increase — as they have in some Latin American countries. In 1994, when Cardinal Sin was dissatisfied with Protestant President Ramos's positions prior to the UN Population Conference in Cairo, he organized a rally of about a million people in Manila, causing the government to stop using contraceptives in its family planning program.[126] El Shaddai is a Catholic evangelistic-millenarian organization with a Hebrew name and with some political importance. It is part of the Roman Catholic organization but has a particularly enthusiastic liturgical style. It is a Roman response to the growth of Protestant sects, including the anti-Catholic Iglesia ni Cristo. Brother Mike Velarde, a preacher in charge of El Shaddai, claimed nine million followers (one tenth of all Filipinos). In the 1998 elections, his advice to his flock was "vote as you wish" — which may have been a sufficient but unofficial acceptance of Erap Estrada, whom Cardinal Sin openly opposed. The Roman Catholic hierarchy's concerns about abortion, in particular, create policy tensions with Philippine intellectuals who know that a reason for the country's slow rise of per-capita income is the high birth rate.

Very general ideologies, not just patronist links, occasionally affect Philippine elections. In the "snap election" of 1986, Marcos's strong authoritarianism contrasted with Cory Aquino's democratic appeals. Voters in the Estrada election were moved either by his populism or by his corruption (or by both, in which case they tended to vote for him). There are many local examples, too.[127] So politicians' personal styles are of import in Philippine elections. Cleavages practically never emerge, however, in labor-capital, left-right terms.

---

[126]Carlos Manuel Lazatín, *The Challenge of Economic Reform in a Democracy*, 19.

[127]Benedict J. Tria Kerkvliet, "Contested Meanings of Elections," 148ff, offers examples all the way from Ilocos Norte at the top of Luzon down to Zamboanga City in Mindanao.

Policy reformism is a recurrent aspect of Philippine presidential politics, but few structural reformers (with the moot exception of Fidel Ramos) have actually been elected. In 1992, Miriam Defensor Santiago laid a claim to the reformist label, but she did not do well at the polls. In 1998, Renato de Villa took up this mantle; de Villa, a previously close colleague of Ramos, had hoped to obtain the ruling party's nomination that went instead to de Venecia. Mere party loyalty, however, was not enough to keep de Villa from running for the presidency against de Valencia (and Estrada, who won). De Villa vowed that he would stamp out corruption. This appeal was greeted, according to many reports, with considerable cynicism by voters.

Raul Roco, another 1998 presidential candidate, also made policy appeals on behalf of women, education for youths in technical fields, and human rights (including deprecations of the military regime in Burma). He founded a Democratic Action Party to work for these policy causes. Roco's effort stirred some enthusiasm among female and young voters. His campaign was like the 1992 campaign of Miriam Defensor Santiago, who six years later was somewhat vulnerable to accusations of corruption herself, such as are common against any candidate in the mudslinging environment of electoral politics. Neither Roco in 1998 nor Santiago in 1992 got close to winning the presidency.

A Citizens' Action Party (*Akbayan*) was founded in 1998, presenting itself as a nonviolent worker and peasant party to oppose *trapos*. It also involved professionals and academics who wanted to counteract the "rightwing populism" of candidates such as Erap Estrada or Fernando Poe, Jr. Such a party, led by intellectuals, would have had no hope of winning even a congressional seat in geographical districts; but it could garner enough votes nationwide to contest the few House places set aside for party lists under the post-Marcos constitution. In 1998, *Akbayan* won a single seat in the House; in 2001, it won two; and by 2004, three seats. It could be effective in some localities. It had less luck winning congressional places than in convincing municipal mayors to join *Akbayan* after their elections.

Its emphasis was on grassroots barangay organization. As its organizers fully realized, this was still a far cry from serious national power.[128]

Reformist candidates in a post-Marcos election in Bataan refused even to shake the hands of voters, on grounds this would have been patronizing traditional politics (*trapo*). They decisively lost.

> What the [reformists] failed to consider is that the people have their own schemes of judging and criticizing a candidate, and that these schemes are predominantly normative. A simple gesture like handshaking means a lot to the people. It signifies one's openness, shared interests, and intention to be in solidarity with the other. It is one moment where the lopsided relations between an ordinary man and a politician level off.[129]

Popular reaction to vote buying is similar. Poor people are understandably willing to accept money, but they do not like the sense that they are being bought.[130]

SOCIOPOLITICAL CAPITAL AND GOVERNANCE QUALITY

Putnam found in Italy that "the quality of governance was determined by longstanding traditions of civic engagement (or its absence). Voter turnout, newspaper readership, membership in choral societies and football clubs — these were the hallmarks of a successful region."[131] Comparing different regions in the Philippines might lead

---

[128] Joel Rocamora, "Impossible is Not So Easy: Party Building and Local Governance in the Philippines" (essay provided by courtesy of the author), *passim*.

[129] Myrna J. Alejo *et al.*, *[De]scribing Elections*, 109.

[130] Likewise in Thailand, Pasuk and Sungsidh write that, money canvassing "is an act of 'giving with compassion,' a gift of good will or *sin nam jai*. ... It is bribery of a sort, but it is not binding on the receiver, who can still take gifts from many candidates and vote however he likes." Pasuk Phongpaichit and Sungsidh Piriyarangsan, *Corruption and Democracy in Thailand* (Chiangmai: Silkworm, 1997), 153, also in Frederic Charles Schaffer, "Disciplinary Reactions," 37.

[131] Robert D. Putnam, "Bowling Alone: America's Declining Social Capital," in *The Global Resurgence of Democracy*, Larry Diamond and Marc F. Plattner, eds. (Baltimore: Johns Hopkins University Press, 1996), 291.

to the same conclusion. But the country as a whole has very high rates of voter turnout, church attendance, and other associational activities, even though the Philippine "quality of governance" is faulty. Putnam cites "mechanisms through which civic engagement and social connectedness produce such results — better schools, faster economic growth, lower crime, and more effective government." Institutional mechanisms, rather than any general lack of "social capital" in associations, are the missing element in the Philippines.[132] Monetary capital, if local elites permitted new entrepreneurs to use it and start modern plants, would go even further in the long run toward good governance.

The Philippines has a plethora of voluntary associations and high civic spirit. Electoral turn-out rates in the Philippines are higher than in any other democracy (except those, like Australia, that fine nonvoters).[133] For example in the 1998 election, 86 percent of eligible voters in the whole nation actually cast ballots.[134] The extraordinary Philippine enthusiasm for voting is hard to explain solely because of material compensations or threats. Vote-buying is at least as common in other polities (for example, Thailand), where turn-outs do not reach Philippine heights (they range in Thai parliamentary elections from 40 to 65 percent). A plausible factor explaining the Philippines' very high turnout is that Filipinos traditionally enjoy watching conflicts. They speak of elections using some phrases applicable to cockfights.

---

[132]Because the term "social capital" refers to organizations of power, usually in local units, it might more precisely be called "sociopolitical capital" (presuming the analogy to economic capital is still needed). Like the term "civil society," which in many cases really refers to uncivil polities, it is not vaguely social at all. These phrases are both used to talk about politics without seeming to do so. They are about power in small collectivities.

[133]This generalization excludes systems that encourage noncompetitive votes, or competitive balloting only at local levels, since such practices make dubious democracies. It also does not include a few systems, such as Australia, that impose legal sanctions against an eligible elector's failure to vote.

[134]Steven Rood, "Elections as Complicated and Important Events in the Philippines," in *How Asia Votes*, John Fu-sheng Hsieh and David Newman, eds. (New York: Chatham House, 2002), 148–50.

These ceremonies perform similar roles, dividing and integrating communities.[135]

Adequate political equality, as Charles Beitz's theory of it shows, is essential to democracy, which depends on "fair terms of participation." These conditions he defines as "those that no citizen has a sufficient reason to refuse to accept, given that everyone shares a desire to come to agreement on some mechanism for participation." Beitz suggests three unfair terms that might give a person valid grounds to protest. One is normal recognition of the citizen's status as an equal member of the polity. A second is "protection against political outcomes that place one's prospects in serious jeopardy (equitable treatment)." The third is "conditions of public deliberation conducive to responsible judgement about public affairs."[136]

By these tests, no actual democracy is close to perfect, and the Philippine democracy is very far from perfect. Its performance on the second and third criteria, in particular, are very weak. In surveys trying to assess "legitimacy" in 51 countries for the 1990s, the Philippine state was seen by its citizens as relatively legitimate. (The archipelago ranked 16 in a set of 51, which included many richer places.) But when the same respondents were asked about "justice," they ranked the Philippine state 45th among the sample's 51.[137]

Because the archipelago has had electoral institutions for most of a century, this situation should be very worrisome for democrats. They generally expect more from the habit of forming governments through competitive balloting. Talk of habituation to democracy, or

---

[135]The current author has seen Filipinos raising cocks for fighting, but he is uncertain how much to see consistencies in Malay-Austronesian culture, or to extend to Luzon the famous argument of Clifford Geertz in "Deep Play: Notes on the Balinese Cockfight," in *The Interpretation of Cultures* (New York: Basic Books, 1973), 412–53. Geertz's main study of an election is *The Social History of an Indonesian Town* (Cambridge: MIT Press, 1965).

[136]Charles R. Beitz, *Political Equality: An Essay in Democratic Theory* (Princeton: Princeton University Press, 1989), xiii. Beitz is a theorist but has told this author he was particularly inspired by the 1986 movement in Manila.

[137]Bruce Gilley, *States and Legitimacy: The Politics of Moral Authority* (Ph.D. dissertation, Politics Department, Princeton University, January 2007), 69.

definitions of democracy that depend on change of incumbents, prove vacuous in these islands. Many theories still fail to note that money and even violence can play major roles in electoral choice.

CLASSES AND STATUS GROUPS

Income inequality is a major phenomenon in the Philippines, and its links to political inequality are many. Market researchers on the archipelago conventionally divide society into five classes, lettered A through E: A for the "super rich," B for the "normal rich," C for small managers and officials, D for the "lower class," and E for the indigent. Exact definitions vary, but the "ABC classes" together account for roughly a tenth of the population, class D for half or three-quarters by varying estimates, and the destitute class E for the remaining two or three tenths.[138] Because of high electoral turnouts, the middle and upper classes cast only a bit more than a tenth of the votes. Successful politicians thus reflect the tastes of poor "D" and penniless "E" classes — but do little for them.

Temario Rivera finds in his country a "unique combination of landed power, bestowed with sociocultural sanctity and enhanced by the fortunes of export agriculture, together with a long tradition of political leadership that distinguishes the landed capitalist segment of the manufacturing bourgeoisie from its newer non-landed corporate segment and Chinese-Filipino component."[139] The latter group is weak, and the "landed capitalist segment" is still attached to land, not just manufacturing.

Scholars have bestowed a host of pejoratives on Philippine capitalism, calling it crony capitalism, bureaucratic capitalism, derivative capitalism, feudal capitalism, booty capitalism, and *ersatz* capitalism. Each of these accolades can be extensively documented. The Philippine bourgeoisie that came out of "import-substitution industrialization" in the 1950s and 1960s can be analyzed in terms of landed, non-landed, and Chinese-Filipino segments that "are constituted by key

---

[138]Frederic Charles Schaffer, "Disciplinary Reactions," and interviews by this author.
[139]Temario C. Rivera, *Landlords and Capitalists*, 39.

families and family alliances that control the top manufacturing corporations."[140] When the Philippine bourgeoisie is discussed as a "class" by analysts such as Rivera, the discourse quickly becomes more specific: about families. Blood is even thicker than sociological abstractions.

The relatively small Philippine middle-income group is becoming more like a class. But there is no guarantee that it is as firm a supporter of democratic procedures as are either the enthusiastic low-income voters or the landowners who can buy or coerce elections and thus capture government. Comparisons of the Filipino middle class with that in other countries, such as Iran, have shown that middle-income people readily support dictators who do not interfere much with their everyday economic activities.[141] Middle classes may become important for the maintenance of democracies, but they can also support authoritarians — and in large part, the Philippine middle class did support Ferdinand Marcos.

What is a "crony"? At least for the period after Marcos, a journalist offers a definition that is almost legally precise: "Someone on the other side of the political fence, who has the misfortune of not having moved his assets out before February 1986." Cronies were the people on whom evidence could be produced, for example, to the Salonga Commission that sought to prosecute those responsible for predations in the Marcos era. Jose Campos was a documentable crony, because he "had the supreme bad luck to leave behind a list, showing all his dummy business operations for Marcos."[142] Structural change of politics, supported by competitive commercial industrialization, is what erodes cronyism.

So the rise of middle-income people may not be enough to support substantive democratization. In the Philippines, the middle class is growing, but the vast majority of people remain poor. A specialist notes that, "The closest Filipino expression to 'new rich' is the pejorative

---

[140] *Ibid.*, 23.

[141] Misgah Parsa, "Entrepreneurs and Democratization: Iran and the Philippines," *Comparative Studies in Society and History* 37:4 (Oct. 1995), 803–30.

[142] James Clad, *Behind the Myth*, 39.

biglang yaman (suddenly rich) which implies that the person so labeled has acquired wealth in an underhand way."[143] Rocamora reports that by 1990, "speculative real estate investments gave Manila and a few other urban centers such as Cebu the look of business centers but contributed little to the country's productive capacity."[144] The elite of the Philippines has increasingly been a bourgeoisie that lives in towns.[145] It engages in services more than production. Lee Kwan Yew and other anti-liberals like to describe the Philippines as the "sick man of Asia" because of its democracy. Yet several Asian democracies have been economic "tigers" — notably India in recent years — so Lee's elitist description is inadequate. The problem is not what the Philippine elite has, but what it discourages. It lacks enough support for innovative, risk-taking entrepreneurs, including Chinese-Filipinos but also "Indio" Filipinos who might start firms.

Recent years have seen an increase in the number of Filipino white-collar professionals. Manila's "Megamall" is reputed to be the world's third-largest shopping center. The capital has at least twenty other large malls too, and Cebu City's mayor claims his metropolis has the world's fourth largest. If traffic jams are an index of middle-class prosperity, either Metro Manila or Cebu City can easily be classed as bourgeois. Expensive townhouses and condominiums, with names like Richeville Mansion and North Olympus, abound in new Philippine residential areas.

The issue is partly ethnic: "To the question 'Who are the new rich?' most non-Chinese-Filipinos respond that they are the Chinese. Many Filipino-Chinese say the same."[146] *Nouveaux riches* exist in the Philippines, but their production scarcely keeps up with their

---

[143]Michael Pinches, "Entrepreneurship, Consumption, Ethnicity, and National Identity in the Making of the Philippines' New Rich," in *Culture and Privilege in Capitalist Asia*, M. Pinches, ed. (New York: Routledge, 1999), 281.

[144]Joel Rocamora, "Lost Opportunities, Deepening Crisis," 217.

[145]Gillian Hart, "Agrarian Change in the Context of State Patronage," in *Agrarian Transformations: Local Processes and the State in Southeast Asia*, Gillian Hart *et al.*, eds. (Berkeley: University of California Press, 1989), 41.

[146]This quotation and several of the examples come from Michael Pinches, "Entrepreneurship, Consumption, Ethnicity ... New Rich," 275–301.

consumption. Michael Pinches had the job of writing a chapter about "The New Rich in the Philippines" for a general book on new bourgeoisies in many Asian countries. He found just a few "layers of people not previously associated with the nation's propertied elite," educated professionals, and "overseas contract workers whose incomes and purchasing power far exceed those of their counterparts employed in the Philippines."[147] These groups exist, but none of them is politically potent yet. There will be more new rich, when Filipinos make more riches.

FUTURE NONSTATE INDUSTRIALIZATION AND STATE DEMOCRATIZATION

Careful survey research suggests that Philippine citizens demand little of their government. They tend to personalize the state as the president. In the late 1980s and early 1990s, even respondents who deemed themselves "poor" and said they had a "low quality of life" and expected "no improvement in the next twelve months" nonetheless tended to rate highly the personalities of their presidents (Aquino and Ramos in these years). These responses were especially numerous early in presidential terms. They had consistently higher rates of political than of economic satisfaction.[148] Felipe Miranda, writing about such polls, claimed that Filipinos have a "compulsive optimism." He describes "the political economy of a prayerful people," not just because practically all of them report praying, but because they evinced "willfully optimistic" hopes for governments that did nothing for them.

Aguilar claims that Philippine "social existence is powerfully perceived and lived as a gamble: stratification is the outcome of *dungan* [spirit] rivalries that confound kin relations and intermingle social categories."[149] Filipinos sometimes criticize themselves by talking

---

[147]*Ibid.*, 106.

[148]Filipe V. Miranda, "Political Economy in a Democratizing Philippines," 173–79.

[149]Filomeno V. Aguilar, *Clash of Spirits: The History of Power and Sugar Planter Hegemony on a Visayan Island* (Honolulu: University Press of Hawaii, 1998), 228.

about a fictional character, Juan Tamad, "Juan the Lazy," who hopes that wealth will befall him through a good marriage or lucky bets. Hard work is not seen as the road to riches. By contrast, Southeast Asian Chinese sometimes criticize themselves for being too nervous, too "fearful of losing" (*pa shu*). They know they have trouble relaxing. They are not content unless they are worrying. These opposite self-criticisms are anecdotes, but they are widespread. They reflect some real laziness and some real discipline.

The trouble with such analyses is not that they are inaccurate. Nor is the trouble that they are culturalist. Instead, the problem is that such analyses tend to be static, not expecting results from structural change including shifts of usual norms. The Philippine future is almost sure to turn out brighter than the recent past, both politically and economically. Such change may come largely from new kinds of nonstate institutions, not from the state or new parties. The importance of these agencies is not limited to what they can do to improve the government.

Careful scholars of Philippine politics suggest that the only way to end oligarchs' rule and make government public is "through the long-term cultivation of stronger and more programmatic political parties."[150] But Thailand's experience suggests a need for this recommendation to be combined with sure separations of powers in government, so that elections legitimate no dictator (no Thaksin or Marcos), and also with an expectation that there might be at least two strong parties: one whose program is broadly pro-poor and pro-worker, and the other, pro-capital and pro-market. Contest between unions and businesses may be essential in industrialized democracies. The first page of Steinberg's comprehensive interpretation of the Philippines notes that, "Filipino society has stamped industrialization with a native label."[151] It is thus far so native that there is scant industry.

A knowledgeable interviewee claimed that there are two kinds of local politicians in the Philippines: those who are best at generating

---

[150]Paul D. Hutchcroft and Joel Rocamora, "Strong Demands and Weak Institutions," 24.
[151]David Joel Steinberg, *The Philippines: A Singular and Plural Place*, third edition (Boulder: Westview, 1994), 1.

money from the central government, and those who are best at controlling illegal activities that generate money. The first of these two groups consists mostly of elected politicians who skim their political networks' revenues from public allocations. This group is held together by family connections and feuds, school and university old ties, and many kinds of fraternities. The second group uses locally institutionalized violence.[152]

There is little taxable income in most Philippine places. So these two options are the only available ways of financing loyalty networks. What industrialization would do — and has done in other parts of East Asia — is to create local tax bases that would begin by financing old politics with new money, but would end by creating new politics. "Manila newspapers frequently feature articles implicating town mayors from various parts of the Philippines in murder, extortion, robbery, illegal gambling, illegal logging, and land grabbing." Officials can do this most often, as Sidel writes, when "the local political economy lends itself to enduring monopolistic or oligopolistic control."[153] But if new entrepreneurs compete to get wealth on their own, not just to obtain more from external sources including the state, then oligarchs lose their previous coercive, financial, and ideological power.

"Democracy is the best political system in all circumstances" was a proposition to which 72 percent of Filipinos agreed in a 2001 poll, even though many realized that their own democracy was not working well.[154] The U.N. Development Programme has published arguments that "deepening democracy" is not just good for economic growth; it is good in itself. It involves building these institutions: (1) political parties and interest groups that represent people, (2) free and fair elections with universal suffrage, (3) a separation of executive, legislative, and judicial powers, (4) NGOs that can monitor both businesses and government, (5) independent media, and (6) civilian

---

[152]See also Joel Rocamora, "Impossible is Not So Easy," 6.

[153]John T. Sidel, *Capital, Coercion, and Crime*, 25 and 27.

[154]Jose Abueva, "Dissatisfaction with the Way Our Democracy Works," in *Towards a Federal Republic of the Philippines: A Reader*, Jose Abueva, ed. (Manila: Center for Social Policy and Governance, 2002), 1–4.

control of the army and police.[155] The Philippines scores relatively well on some of these criteria. But big questions remain about the reasons for Filipino democratic failings that the UNDP criteria highlight: why do the parties not represent people well after the elections? Why do soldiers sporadically threaten civilian leaders with *kudeta*? Why are the state's executive, legislative, and judicial powers all relatively weak (whether separated or not)? The answers to such questions require an analysis that goes beyond formally political institutions. In the Filipino case, the most obvious problem has been the repression of sustained local industrial growth because of local polities that stymie local entrepreneurship. More SMEs would, and probably will, deepen democracy not just in national institutions.

---

[155]United Nations Development Programme, *Human Development Report, 2002: Deepening Democracy in a Fragmented World* (New York: Oxford University Press, 2002).

10

Conclusion: Do Booms Aid Democracy?

What is the relationship, if any, between economic growth and regime types? Seymour Martin Lipset in the 1950s showed that wealth helped sustain democracies.[1] Samuel Huntington in the 1960s warned that the correlation between riches and liberalism, although statistically true for the best-off and poorest countries, was particularly unreliable at middle levels of income per-capita. These are the levels where economic booms tend to occur and where they raise the volume and diversity of demands that governments try to meet.[2] Quick economic progress tends to legitimate whatever kind of regime is in power at the time, but it also temporarily disrupts the immediate connection between growth and fairness, for which liberals in the 1950s had naïvely hoped.

This book emphasizes a factor that moderates, for countries at middle levels of income, the vacillation or "chaos" in the long-term mainly linear relationship between riches and tolerance. This factor is independent legitimacy for local powers that include nonstate entrepreneurs, and later the leaders of workers and poor people. These

---

[1]Seymour Martin Lipset, *Political Man: The Social Bases of Politics* (Baltimore: Johns Hopkins University Press, orig. 1961, expanded ed. 1981).
[2]Samuel Huntington, *Political Order in Changing Societies* (New Haven: Yale University Press, 1968).

catalysts of political development were studied previously by Barrington Moore, and his work has been updated by Reuschmeyer, Stephens, and Stephens.[3] A usual precursor of modern democratization is the eclipse of land-controlling elites in agricultural economies by worker- and capital-associated conflicting elites, whose local power rises in industrial economies. Leaders *may* then decide to channel this normal capital-labor conflict into institutions that can manage it peaceably.[4]

In Taiwan, East China, Thailand, and the Philippines, the move to modern politics and its economic basis (or the prevention of it) has been political, led by both local and national elites for their own reasons. Agrarian changes in Taiwan during the 1950s, and in Sunan during the 1970s, were either encouraged or could not be prevented by the governments. The resulting autonomy in local polities allowed the establishment of SMEs and ignited booms. In Thailand, such autonomy was traditionally already available outside Bangkok, and access to new markets and technologies were by themselves enough to spur the quick development of low-tech industries. In the Philippines, Marcos's land reform and short-stalk rice program reduced the autonomy of rural actors. Changes in the countryside deeply affected industrialization in each of the four places studied here. Agrarian "reforms" may be called by a single name. From a distance, they at first might look rather similar. Seen closely, though, they turn out to be as varied as the Galilean moons. Each of these rural trajectories is fascinating and important for what followed, but each is radically different from each of the others.

---

[3]Barrington Moore, Jr., *Social Origins of Dictatorship and Democracy: Lord and Peasant in the Making of the Modern World* (Boston: Beacon, 1966), followed by Dietrich Rueschmeyer, Eveleyne Huber Stephens, and John D. Stephens, *Capitalist Development and Democracy* (Chicago: University of Chicago Press, 1992).

[4]Such institutions may also, as in India with its strong parliament and the Indian Administrative Service that were imported from Britain, have democratic institutions prior to high per-capita income. Such cases are rare (and India does have many industries).

Commercial industrialization provides institutions for the recruitment of both populist and capitalist interests. In terms of values, it also shapes the norms that underlie any elite decisions to change regime types. Sizeable states that sustain booms tend to pluralize. Business networks gain local power at the expense of the kinds of networks that were previously dominant. If elites in the national polity decide to deal with their own tensions by legitimating elections, such countries may democratize. But electoral procedures alone do not assure governments that serve the people. Factories and stores are the first pilots of substantive democratization, and central state elites may (or may not soon) decide to carry it further.

Because nations are various, because many are small, and because data on quick booms and on democratization beyond elections have scarcely been collected, any worldwide statistical tests of propositions like the ones above must be left to the future. Evidence from the intrinsically interesting four countries at hand suggest reasons why these patterns might hold in general, but the aim here is to compare those places, not to prove any "law" of politics. If others seek more universalism, they can look for it.

CORRUPTION AS A SUBSET OF MONEY POLITICS

New wealth from industrialization tends to create "black money politics" (called *heijin zhengzhi* in Chinese). That pattern has been evident in both East China and Taiwan, as it was also during the period of fastest growth in the U.S., from 1865 to 1929. It has appeared in Thailand and to some extent in the Philippines, where straightforward local violence often substitutes for money as means by which local bosses keep their influence.

Money politics is easier to specify than corruption, although most political scientists start by defining the latter. Melanie Manion uses a definition that summarizes a consensus among many other scholars: "corruption is the *abuse of public office for private gain in violation of rules.*"[5] Much politics can usefully be studied on the basis of such a definition.[6]

The project of this book, however, is somewhat broader. Moral rules in any polity change over time.[7] Also, different norms are supposed to bind actors with greater or lesser legal tightness.[8] Diverse people have diverse senses of what is properly public or private, and official legalisms about this variance do not necessarily match all citizens' understandings. Especially during boom times, when active power networks are often local and private, corruption is common. But uses of money to influence politics are easier to identify. Corruption is just one aspect of money politics, whose origins can partly be traced to the new sources of funds.

---

[5]Melanie Manion, *Corruption by Design* (Cambridge: Harvard University Press, 2004), 5, italics in original.

[6]For example, a recent statistical study suggests that corruption tends to be lower in states that have liberal trade and investment policies as well as effective market regulations, although the size of the state sector in an economy correlates with neither low nor high levels of political corruption. See John Gerring and Strom C. Thacker, "Do Neoliberal Policies Deter Political Corruption?" *International Organization* 59 (Winter 2005), 233–54. So the best response to corruption is a policy of establishing open yet regulated economies — and the issue then changes: Is there enough political support to implement such measures? To find that out, it is necessary to look at the types of links between local and central power networks.

[7]See, for example, Lynn White, "Changing Concepts of Corruption in Communist China: Early 1950s vs. Early 1980s," in *Changes and Continuities in Chinese Communism*, Yu-ming Shaw, ed. (Boulder: Westview Press, 1988), 316–53, or Benjamin N. Nelson, *The Idea of Usury: From Tribal Brotherhood to Universal Otherhood*, No. 3, "History of Ideas" Series (Princeton: Princeton University Press, 1953), about a Renaissance change in the West.

[8]It is possible to disapprove corruptions without saying they all have the same status in consensual rules. Early Christians classed vices in two levels: the seven "cardinal" sins, for which forgiveness would require perfect contrition, and less serious "venial" offenses that any sacrament was believe to absolve. Or to take a political example: Sen. Lowell Weicker (R-Conn) adopted a brilliant line of three standard questions with which to pummel Richard Nixon's cronies, as they came before the Senate committee investigating Watergate corruptions. After verifying that each item of their dubious behavior took place, Weicker pressed them (many were lawyers) for details that could categorize each act as fully "unconstitutional," or simply "illegal," or merely "gross."

Moral dirtiness in public is an important but perceptual object of study. The criteria for specifying it change from time to time. Whenever an accusation of "corruption" is made, it almost always claims that service has been done to a small group or individual that should instead have been done to a larger collectivity. Culturalists sometimes say that collectivist (or Asian) views of choice are more realistic than Western views, because small groups or families socialize the content of each person's preferences. Many liberal writers nonetheless define preferences in an economic style, as a preference for generic "utility," presumed to be the same for all people. Rawls and his followers similarly give preferences "veiled" contents that are generic. Yet corruption is in the eye of the beholder. People identifying with large groups can see corruption in acts that people who identify with smaller groups deem good. Money politics is easier to evidence behaviorally than is corruption. It is simply the use of funds to influence people's decisions. It is often seen as corrupt, but it is a more specific syndrome that can clearly be related to the economic booms that supply the money.

The main problem is the extent to which many legalized uses of money for political ends violate norms of justice. Corruption (by its usual definition) is a symptom, not a cause, of the kind of flexibility in state-business relations that correlates with growth. Economic booms make money more abundant, and encourage corruption. Gunnar Myrdal famously referred to a "folklore of corruption" that emerges where officials can be bribed, and where anyone who ignores this fact is deemed naïve.[9] The extent to which a collective culture of corruption is present largely determines actors' estimates of the likelihood that corrupt acts will give them a high payoff (psychic or material). But the relevant norms vary over time and space, and they are usually generated by nonstate rather than state powers. They also vary not just with the money available, but also with a willingness to take risks that is a major factor producing prosperity. So this book is not about corruption in legal sense, nor is it just about the incentives to

---

[9]Gunnar Myrdal, *Asian Drama*, vol. 2 (New York: Twentieth Century Fund, 1968), 937–58.

individuals that campaigns for cleanliness may bring. Instead, it is about "macro" arrangements of factors that create those climates, one of whose results is to encourage either corruption or rectitude.

Booms do not justify perceived corruption, but they make it temporarily less dangerous to governments as a political issue. For years, as East Asian economies prospered, windfall benefits from subsistence-priced labor serving modern markets could be traded between officials and entrepreneurs. Neither the bureaucrats nor the business people usually felt threatened when engaging in such deals, legal or not. Booms and personalistic politics legitimated them. Booms and elections, combined together, often empowered politicians who were economic gangsters. Then as legislators and judges, they could arrange the rules to legalize any business.

In Taiwan, China, and Thailand during their periods of quick growth, officials tried to push extensive corruption to the "back burner" of the political stove. They could often do so, as long as most people were pleased by becoming richer. In the Philippines, where the lack of a boom became a political issue, academics and journalists excoriated state connivance with "crony capitalists." But these critics were in a national elite that lacked local powers. After the financial crisis of 1997, when many economies suffered, publicists in East Asia have more often denounced money politics (and in China, this also happened earlier during the late-1980s inflation). Booms create cash and corruptions, but recessions from booms or lacks of booms create even more public discourse about the problems.

Anek rues "the paradoxical co-existence of corruption and high economic growth in Thailand."[10] Actually, corruption and growth have usually been found together. Schumpeterian entrepreneurs aim for money, not for fair markets. That is their principle, more than any kind of liberalism is. They thrive best in a fluid environment, with some order but without any single power network (an army, a government bureaucracy, a church, an aristocracy) that can tax or coerce

---

[10]Anek Laothamatas, "From Clientelism to Partnership: Business Government Relations in Thailand," in *Business and Government in Industrializing Asia*, Andrew MacIntyre, ed. (Ithaca: Cornell University Press, 1994), 209.

them heavily. If an authoritarian such as Chiang or Deng or Thaksin or Marcos can dominate the state, then entrepreneurs have a more concentrated group of officials with whom to deal. Taiwan since the 1950s, China since the 1970s, and Thailand during its boom (but not the Philippines) had structures that encouraged microeconomic risk-taking, because the most effective local powers allowed or could not prevent it.

Corruption lubricates growth by letting businesses get around red tape and by linking new groups, both within the state and outside it, to the boom.[11] Corruption channels the support of officials toward growth, even as it also distorts allocative markets. Some modernization writers have regarded corruption as just a short-term phase. Later public practice is expected to become more honest as incomes rise — and empirical evidence for this eventual change can be found. But methods of vote-buying in rich democracies, now including Taiwan, are more subtle and propagandistic than in poorer democracies. Authoritarian regimes can equally use propaganda to reduce perceptions of public wrongdoing.

Transparency International in recent years has calculated a "corruption perception index," using surveys over three-year periods and a sophisticated method that is described on its website. The results of the analyses from 1998 and 2005 are presented below for the four places of greatest interest here. (Also included are notes of other countries that had similar "CPI" scores in those years.) Higher numbers indicate less perceived corruption, on a scale from 1 to 10.

The Philippines and Taiwan were among just seven countries, from the survey of 69, in which more than 70 percent of business respondents said that, "Corruption affects political life to a large extent."[12] In Thailand, more than half had that view. Such a response

[11]Early arguments along these lines range from Colin Leys, "What is the Problem about Corruption?" *Journal of Modern African Studies* 3 (1965), 215–30, to Samuel Huntington, "Modernization and Corruption," in *Political Corruption: Readings in Comparative Analysis*, A.J. Heidenheimer, ed. (New York: Holt, 1970), 479–86.

[12]Transparency International website, http://www.transparency.org/policy_research/surveys_indices/gcb, seen November 1, 2006. The other five were Bolivia, Bosnia, Greece, Israel, and Peru.

Corruption Perception Indices

	Taiwan	Thailand	China	Philippines
2005	**5.9**	**3.8**	**3.2**	**2.5**
(similar score in)	Uruguay	Trinidad	Morocco	Bolivia
1998	**5.3**	**3.0**	**3.5**	**3.3**
(similar score in)	Malaysia	Argentina	Salvador	Ghana

Notes: The 1998 range of surveyed figures was from a high of 10.0 for Denmark to a low of 1.4 for Cameroon. The 2005 range was from 9.7 for Iceland down to 1.7 for Chad. Not all parts of China are equally relevant to the argument in this book. The 1998 figures for Thailand were atypically low, as compared to other years, because of severe malaise due to the financial crisis that first became evident in that country's banks. Countries' scores for earlier years have not been found. Perception surveys are attitudinal, not behavioral. These numbers are based on responses from business people, who were in good positions to make such assessments of each other and of government officials. See http://www.transparency.org/policy_research/surveys_indices/cpi, November 1, 2006.

in the PRC might bring official retribution to the respondent. As Premier Wen Jiabao said in 2007, "The most important cause [of corruption] is excessive concentration of power, and there is no efficient restriction and supervision over it. We therefore need to reform our systems."[13]

When established networks are successful in maintaining order, less coercive sources of power such as money become more important. Tawney notes that English landlords, when the monarchy was weak, had been most interested in maximizing the number of retainers to support them; under weak central governments, they were less interested in maximizing profits from their fields. But when the forceful Tudor bureaucracy "put down private warfare," its better-enforced order made money the main basis for local loyalties.[14] The marketization of land commonly results from a new relation between elites, as stronger central leaders develop more regular relations with local

---

[13]Mark Magnier, "China Creating its own Democracy, Premier Says" *Los Angeles Times,* March 17, 2007, in http://taiwansecurity.org/news/2007/LAT-170307.htm, seen March 19, 2007.

[14]See citation and interpretation of Tawney in Barrington Moore, Jr., *Social Origins of Dictatorship and Democracy,* 6.

ones. This process is propelled in contemporary times by rural factories, which first industrialize previous patterns of rural violence (as has not yet happened in the Philippines but is happening in Thailand and East China) and later modernize the state's ability to maintain order (as on Taiwan). Perceived and behavioral corruption becomes more widespread, at least in these places, when local entrepreneurial leaders glean windfall profits while workers' wages are still near subsistence farming levels. Later, corruption eventually declines.

COERCIVE CONTROLS OF CORRUPTION

Any serious practitioner of corruption must, through bribery or otherwise, make sure of friends in the police. Local coercive agencies are natural partners of businesses that make money by violating or skirting laws, especially laws against the private use of force. Anti-corruption campaigns can bring a political backlash from police.[15] Anti-graft institutions can take serious form if they are created with provisos that they will not go into any but the most serious cases that predate their founding. Commissions against corruption are initiated because of crises, but they can easily be seen as agencies of political vindictiveness, if their focus is on earlier corruptions rather than current and future graft.

The classic problem, from the viewpoint of anti-corruption reformers, is how to police the police. The East Asian jurisdiction with the most effective anti-graft agency is Hong Kong, whose Independent Commission Against Corruption (since 1974 when the British established this bureau to raise the colonial regime's legitimacy) has fought corruption by officials and entrepreneurs alike. This comprehensive approach, tackling the problem together in both public and private

---

[15]This happened, for example, even in Hong Kong after the 1974 establishment of the Independent Commission Against Corruption. By November 1977, a "partial amnesty" was declared, preventing the ICAC from handling any but the most egregious cases predating the amnesty. The author benefitted from discussions of these matters with David Hodson, former head of the Hong Kong Police, and Gerald Osborn, Principal Investigator (operational head) of the ICAC.

power networks, which are linked, has been attempted in few other places — because it inhibits both politicians and businesspeople. Very powerful interests resist any ICAC that is politically independent and can investigate both business and government corruption. The original is worth particular study, because it provides the best template for policy proposals elsewhere.

The Hong Kong ICAC is completely separate from the police, in which many of its early targets were found. Its operations are overseen by a high-level review board of that meets eight times each year. All ICAC officers are on relatively short-term contracts, which are not renewed if there is any whiff of suspicion that their integrity may have been compromised. Stronger institutions of this kind are needed in the Philippines, Thailand, and the rest of China besides Hong Kong, before levels of corruption are likely to drop. Similar agencies in other countries are now generically called ICACs. Singapore's Corrupt Practices Investigation Bureau dates back to 1952, but "the top-level political backing so critical to its success did not develop" until much later.[16] Dubious practices, like any other norm or behavior are path-dependent and resist change. As experiences in many countries have shown, citizens often fail to see their hopes of cleaning corruption implemented quickly, because corruption can give effective leaders great benefits.[17]

---

[16]Michael Johnston, "A Brief History of Anticorruption Agencies," in *The Self-Restraining State: Power and Accountability in New Democracies*, Andreas Schedler, Larry Diamond, and Marc F. Plattner, eds. (Boulder: Lynne Rienner, 1999), 217.

[17]In democracies, patterns of corruption become more than distortions of the political systems; they may become integral parts of those systems. In American politics, for example, many policies have been franchised to small minorities that feel passionately about particular issues and give money to politicians who support their positions. Cuba policy, gun policy, health policy, Middle East policy, and defense procurement policy are well-known examples. The Middle Eastern example has received most attention because of documented Likud support for the U.S. occupation of Iraq, specific war planners' previous connections with Likud, and research by James Petras and Stephen Walt and John Mearscheimer. Data about many such issues are presented by Jacob S. Hacker and Paul Pierson. The pattern is just as evident in gun policy, health policy, abortion policy, Cuba policy, and other fields. Americanists

The privatization of public space is seen by many as an erosion of fundamental notions about equal justice. If each citizen is supposed to have a voice, but if minority money through media propaganda sways many who have not thought about issues from the viewpoint of their whole community, then equality is lessened. Marcin Walecki lists five general conditions in which this pattern most readily emerges[18]:

— intense competition between political factions for state resources;
— poverty, which induces the poor to sell their votes or lessens public funding of public procedures;
— lack of education, which weakens civil transparency and lowers the information diversity in media;
— lack of police or judicial enforcement of laws that regulate the financing of politics; and
— prior capture of the state by monied interests, which keeps the state in those chains.

Further conditions may relate to electoral systems and constitutional protections of the use of money as free "speech." Booms have mixed effects on the conditions of corruption. In the short run, they increase conflict over local control of state resources, but in the long run they reduce poverty. They tend to fund education, but they make

---

in political science have claimed that the causes of this tendency are well understood, and indeed they have been studied for a long time by famous analysts such as David Truman, Robert Dahl, Charles Lindblom, Edward Banfield, and others. But few scholars have proposed effective ways to make the U.S. democracy represent the long-term interests of its whole community more evenly. See Mearscheimer and Walt, "The Israel Lobby," *London Review of Books* 28:6 (March 23, 2006), http://lrb.co.uk/c28/n06/print/mear01_.htm, seen October 24, 2006, Petras, *The Power of Israel in the United States* (New York: Clarity Press, 2006), and on many such topics Hacker and Pierson, *Off Center: The Republican Revolution and the Erosion of American Democracy* (New Haven: Yale University Press, 2005).

[18]This list is lightly edited from Marcin Walecki, "Political Corruption: Democracy's Hidden Disease," *Democracy at Large* 2:4 (2006), 16.

national bureaucracies or elected officials more dependent on monied interests.

Links between money and patronage have been broken in the older democracies partially, but only when severe political crises have forced reform. In the United States before 1883, most nonelective government jobs were presumed to be owed to those who had given money and showed loyalty to the elected officials who could make appointments. The assassination of President James Garfield, by a man who had expected such a job, inspired passage of the Pendelton Act in that year. The first regulation of campaign finance (the Tillman Act of 1907, prohibiting direct corporate contributions to campaigns) was passed because of egregious amounts that had been given to President McKinley's campaign. It took the Teapot Dome Scandal of the early 1920s, in which a Secretary of the Interior gave profitable oil drilling rights to political supporters of the Republican Party, to inspire the Corrupt Practices Act of 1925. These laws, plus the Hatch Acts of 1939 and 1940, after more of the national economy was in government hands, still did not close all loopholes. Outrage at Watergate scandals underlay the 1974 Federal Election Campaign Act and Ethics in Government Act — but by the 2000s, it was clear that "soft money" still determined many elections. Senators McCain and Feingold obtained passage of a Bipartisan Campaign Reform Act that still leaves many ways for lobbyists to buy the government.[19] The Supreme Court chose to weaken that law. Such a history suggests that vigilance against political corruption postdates crises and is very difficult to maintain.

There is such a myriad of means by which money can determine political outcomes — including the outcome of preserving these means — that effective anticorruption reform faces enormous difficulties. It is hard to pass as law. Reform intentions are even harder to enforce. In such respects, antigraft campaigns are like other kinds of democratization: they never succeed more than partially. They are

---

[19]Craig Donsanto, "From Crisis to Reform: A Historical Perspective," *Democracy at Large* 2:4 (2006), 10–11.

historically discontinuous. Public transparency is the prerequisite to lessening corruption, and it depends especially on enforced laws that protect the legitimacy of nonstate expressions by reporters of all interests, not just monied interests.

MONEY CHANGES FACTIONS INTO MODERN POWER NETWORKS

Booms affect community values. They also affect the modal types of local political network. Political relations between two individuals may be mainly vertical or mainly horizontal. Such links can be based on normative traditions of either equality or deference, or on material inducements. Modern growth affects both aspects of these dyadic links: the extent to which they are vertical or equal, and the extent to which their basis is intended-normative or unintended-contextual. Such change tends to make relations more equal — or else vertical only for achieving specific community goals. Theorists such as James Scott describe the gradual transformation in patron-client networks. At first, factions are held together by traditional force and deference. Then come larger political machines that involve provision and protection in exchange for followers' support. Parties in industrialized polities are usually held together by ideologies favoring either labor or capital.[20]

In an early phase, the social or state prestige of a synaptic hinge leader connects smaller with larger networks to generate the leader's wealth. Industrialization then reverses this: money is what brings government posts and social standing, more than vice-versa. Before the advent of modern industry, bureaucratic and local prestige brought more money. Later, wealth keeps score in the prestige game.

---

[20]This expands on James C. Scott, "Corruption, Machine Politics, and Political Development," *American Political Science Review* 63:4 (December 1969), 1142–58 and Scott, "The Erosion of Patron-Client Bonds and Social Change in Rural Southeast Asia," *Journal of Asian Studies* 32:1 (November 1972), 6–37.

Pre-industrial political networks continue into early industrialization and are often called factions. Factions may be defined by four characteristics:

— They do not exist singly; members consciously contrast their own faction with other similar factions.
— They are general conflict groups, relevant to many issues (not just one).
— They are family-like, at least ideally, with patriarchal leaders or a single father figure (seldom a mother figure).
— They are recurrent in systems, even when particular factions disappear.[21]

Factional conflict emerges especially when leaders whose relative status is unclear disagree about appointments to positions of power. In such systems, policies are easier to change than personnel. Conflicts occur less readily when cleavages are between offices, places, or generations, because factions are then less threatening to each others' power.

These networks range from close complex relations (as between members of a family) to links that have scant emotional content (as in markets or bureaucracies). Arghiros calls this a "continuum of personalism." He finds that political largesse in Thailand "is often dispensed outside the context of patron-client relationships," which tend to become "instrumental and short-term, without any personal component ... mediated only by a cash transaction." So "Thai non-kin frequently make fictive use of kinship terms to lend an otherwise

---

[21]As the first and last items on this list suggest, a robust definition of "faction" is not separate from a definition of systems of multiple factions. The list is revised from another version in Ralph W. Nicholas, "Factions: A Comparative Analysis," in *Political Systems and the Distribution of Power*, Michael Banton, ed. (London: Tavistock, 1968), 21–58. That study covers factions among Indian villagers, Iroquois, Ft. Jamieson Ngoni, Fijians, Japanese LDP diet members, and others.

amoral relationship familial morality."[22] The same thing happens often in the Philippines, and also unofficially in China.

Booms make money more important, relative to other sources of prestige, in defining local leaders. Wealth can buy traditional sources of charisma, but only weakly or at high prices. So the new patron-client links tend to be less personalistic. Polite norms of social obligation (e.g., a vote for a payment) survive modernization more robustly than do the traditional emotions that were supposed to underlie them. Traditional factionalism is based on direct face-to-face relations between a leader and followers. Patron-client factionalism that remains common in agricultural communities is different from "machine politics" factionalism in industries and cities.

Rivalry between leaders, e.g., in local elections, often bifurcates traditional political structures into two segments. When a polity has a two-party system at the top, each of the big-collectivity coalitions tries to create links to whichever local faction is largest or most malleable.[23] As industrial sources of wealth become important, and as rural markets for trading grain develop into centers for diversified commerce and local industries, the old form of factionalism faces organizational span-of-influence problems. Patron-client relations are still common among local leaders, but the largest factions grow by attracting followers from other factions or from among people who had not been politicized earlier. So wealth from new factories or stores destabilizes factional arrangements. Networks can also change when a faction leader retires or dies, when fresh types of members are inducted, or when new factional activities create conflicts with previous members.

---

[22]Daniel Arghiros, *Democracy, Development, and Decentralisation in Provincial Thailand* (London: Curzon, 2001), 7–8, and Jeremy Kemp, "The Manipulation of Personal Relations: From Kinship to Patron-Clientage," in *Strategies and Structures in Thai Society*, Han ten Brummelhuis and Jeremy Kemp, eds. (Amsterdam: Anthropological-Sociological Centre, 1984), 55–69, esp. 63.

[23]See Joseph Bosco, "Taiwan Factions: *Guanxi*, Patronage, and the State in Local Politics," in *The Other Taiwan: 1945 to the Present*, Rubinstein and Murray, eds. (Armonk: Sharpe, 1994), 114–44.

Although kin, related by blood, may still be prominent in the leadership of semi-modernized factions, family loyalty loses much of its importance because most members are not kin or even fictive kin.

Such organizations are very common in the machine politics of most medium-sized Asian cities (as they have also been in other contexts, such as American cities in the long boom from 1865 to 1929). They flourish in either electoral democracies or authoritarian systems. So do larger coalitions, whose continuance depends on the constancy of agreement between the faction leaders who comprise them. Blocs of this kind may call themselves political parties, but in pre-industrial situations they are evanescent groups, linked to lineages or leaders rather than social policies. This is the recent situation of parties in Thailand or the Philippines. In places where party systems are weak, the politics of income stratification is less prominent than is conflict between regional leaders. Left-right politics, even when present, is usually trumped by differences based on other sorts of cleavage, especially those imagined in terms of the ultimate kind of status group, the family.[24]

Industrial and marketing potential in countries that still have near-subsistence wages is like a natural resource (oil in the ground, gold in streams, or diamonds in mines). When an onslaught of wealth occurs, the main question becomes: who has access to it? Do elites use it to reconfirm established patronage networks, or instead to mobilize resources for further change? The answer depends partly on whether there is a normalized opposition with which the elites at the time of such a windfall must compete. A comparative study of Iran and Indonesia, referring also to other countries such as Norway, shows that if a regime comes to power before it relies on windfall revenues, it has already had to extend its political structure beyond factions — and in that process, to make concessions to partners or oppositions.[25] Taiwan because of the KMT's ethnic problem after

---

[24]This is based very loosely on the discussion in Kimura Masataka, *Elections and Politics, Philippine Style* (Manila: De La Salle University Press, 1997), 256–63.

[25]Benjamin B. Smith, *Hard Times in the Land of Plenty: Oil Booms and Opposition in Late-Developing States* (Ph.D. dissertation, University of Washington Political Science Department, September 2002), puts this in terms of institutions rather than cleavages.

1947, perhaps China because of 1957 and post-1965 labeled groups, and Thailand because of the 1932 and later military-civilian divisions normalized cleavages that became political. If, however, a regime's creation coincides in time with a windfall, for example a trade boom, then exploiting it can at first strengthen traditional patron-client relations.

The main trouble with the patron-client model is that it is static. It covers some aspects of relations between people, but it does not explain change. The model fails to highlight factors that erode or increase patron-client links of different kinds. As Girling writes about Thailand, "in my view, the concept of patron-client relations... complements as a social theory or model, but does not replace, structural analysis of the production and distribution of wealth, power, and values in modern society. Modernization is one attempt at [such an] analysis."[26]

IS DEMOCRACY AN INTENTION, A RESULT — OR BOTH?

This book concerns democracy mainly insofar as it concerns pluralization, the increase in the variety of social groups that economic expansion creates. That is the local but insufficient usual precursor of democracy. These plural groups are different from factions. They hold together not with family-like bonds, but instead by their members' similarity of socioeconomic roles. The process by which people may become slightly less "semi-sovereign" over government has been everywhere sporadic, slow, and incomplete. But plural groups have abetted that process. It is possible to define democracy as a procedure by which, as Schumpeter put it, "individuals acquire the power to decide by means of a competitive struggle for the people's vote."[27]

---

[26] John Girling, *Interpreting Development: Capitalism, Democracy, and the Middle Class in Thailand* (Ithaca: Cornell Southeast Asian Studies, 1996), 57.

[27] Joseph Schumpeter, *Capitalism, Socialism, and Democracy* (New York: Harper, 1950), 269, quoted, e.g., in Alan M. Wachman, *Taiwan: National Identity and Democratization* (Armonk: M.E. Sharpe, 1994), 33. See also E.E. Schattschneider, *The Semi-Sovereign People: A Realist's View of Democracy in America*, intro. by David Adamany (Hinsdale, IL: Dreyden Press, 1975), to which the next two paragraphs also owe much.

Yet these people almost never govern directly.[28] It is feasible to describe events in which they acquire more or less power to choose their rulers, but it is very difficult to measure how much power (if any) non-leading citizens have.

"Democracy" was a chancy word among libertarians for many years. Many founders of the American republic abhorred it. The most creative political philosopher among them, James Madison, was proud to write in *Federalist No. 63* that the "true distinction" between the United States and ancient republics "lies in the total exclusion of the people, in their collective capacity, from any share" of American rule. Instead, the early U.S. had a government "in which the scheme of representation takes place."[29] This representative republic abolished the difference between peers and commoners, but it definitely did not abolish the difference between governors and citizens. In the nascent American nation, a severely selected portion of the people — so long as they were not female, not young, not landless, and not enslaved — could vote for delegates in half the federal legislature (the House of Representatives), which was with the executive and judicial branches one-sixth of the government. But they could not vote directly for senators, judges, or the president. They could certainly not initiate recalls or referenda.

The word "democracy" remained a pejorative among many elites in the early U.S., but ordinary people rather liked the idea. They began to identify it with their new nationalism. The Founding Fathers could not prevent this phenomenon. A Baptist leader named Elias Smith preached that, "The government adopted here is a democracy. It is well for us to understand this word, so much ridiculed by the international enemies of our beloved country.... My

---

[28]See Robert Michels, *Political Parties: A Sociological Study of the Oligarchical Tendencies of Modern Democracies*, tr. Eden and Cedar Paul (New York: Dover, 1958).

[29]Quoted with interesting commentary in Gordon S. Wood, "Democracy and the American Revolution," in *Democracy: The Unfinished Journey, 508 B.C. to A.D. 1993*, John Dunn, ed. (Oxford: Oxford University Press, 1992), 97.

Friends, let us never be ashamed of democracy!"[30] That is the current American credo too, and this kind of democracy mainly means elections.

"Liberalization" not the same as "democratization," although the processes are related because democratic elections require liberal rights.[31] As more study of Asia might convince political philosophers, liberalism based on individual rights is less realistic than liberalism based on tolerant communal norms. Michael Sandel's political philosophy is consistent with the sustainable insight that individuals come out of communities (at first, their parents). Sandel criticizes rights-based liberalism in a way that would interest Confucians, and alas also Leninists, but he remains realistic enough to stress that ideals of freedom matter in politics. They are actually inseparable from ideals of tolerance. "Despite its powerful appeal, the image of the unencumbered self is flawed. It cannot make sense of our moral experience ... obligations of solidarity, religious duties, and other moral ties that may claim us for reasons unrelated to a choice." Under these natural conditions, especially as modern technologies of linkage affect them, old problems about the integrity of actors that have engaged thinkers from Aristotle to Burke to Weber to Rorty must be combined with modeled ethics of unintended consequences. There are two valid moralities, forever in tension with each other: ethics based on the principles by which an actor understands his or her identity, and an ethics based on expected results from the action.

> Self-government today ... requires a politics that plays itself out in a multiplicity of settings, from neighborhoods to nations to the world as a whole. Such a politics requires citizens who can think and act as multiply-situated selves. The civic virtue distinctive to our time is the capacity to negotiate our way among the sometimes overlapping, sometimes conflicting obligations that claim us, and to live with the tension to which multiple loyalties give rise.... Others can seek refuge in fundamentalism. The hope of our time rests instead with those who can summon the conviction and restraint

---

[30] *Ibid.*, 98.

[31] See James Cotton, "The Limits to Liberalization in Industrializing Asia: Three Views of the State," *Pacific Affairs* 64:3 (Autumn, 1991), 312.

to make sense of our condition and repair the civic life on which democracy depends.[32]

Voting does not ensure substantive democracy. "Pluralization" of a variety of social interests during a modern division of labor does not by itself determine government structures. "Polyarchy" (Dahl's shy tag for democracy) involves both legitimate competition and mass participation, and these are in mutual tension.[33] The conditions that promote democratization also threaten it. By the 1970s and early 1980s, Huntington predicted that democracy would not easily expand in countries that had not been much influenced by Northwest Europe.[34] But soon in Spain and Portugal, then in Eastern Europe and Latin America — haltingly even in Africa and parts of Asia — democracy seemed to be breaking out all over.

This "third wave" of democratization, cresting in 1989–91, seemed to deluge pessimists about liberalism. Following a seminal

---

[32]Sandel's formulation does not justify intolerance or arrogance in tribal wars, such as are particularly obvious in several regions of the world. It meshes well with Weber's insight that a modeled-calculative ethic predicting results is as important in telling what actors do (or should do) as is an ethic based on their identities. Neither rational nor ethical action can be parsed just in terms of value (*Wert*) or of goal (*Zweck*). For the quoted general-local version of how to solve this quandary, see Michael J. Sandel, *Democracy's Discontent: America in Search of a Public Philosophy* (Cambridge: Harvard University Press, 1996), 350–51, also 13. Weber's justly classic statement is in "Politics as a Vocation," in *From Max Weber: Essays in Sociology*, trans. H.H. Gerth and C.W. Mill (New York: Oxford University Press, 1946), 77–128.

[33]See Robert Dahl, *Polyarchy: Participation and Opposition* (New Haven: Yale University Press, 1971) and Samuel Huntington, *Political Order in Changing Societies*. Also, Seymour Martin Lipset, "Some Social Requisites of Democracy: Economic Development and Political Legitimacy," *American Political Science Review* 53 (March 1959), 69–105; and Gabriel Almond and Sidney Verba, *The Civic Culture* (Princeton: Princeton University Press, 1963).

[34]See, for example, Samuel Huntington, "Will More Countries Become Democratic?" *Political Science Quarterly* 99:2 (Summer 1984), 193–218; Huntington answered his title question in the negative. His *The Third Wave: Democratization in the Late Twentieth Century* (Norman: University of Oklahoma Press, 1991) is the most learned apology for an earlier misprediction that a political scientist has ever made.

approach proposed earlier by Dankwart Rustow, many agreed that democratization was "underdetermined" by socioeconomic factors.[35] If the boundaries of a country were unsure (as on Taiwan), or if cultural factors seemed unpropitious (especially if they were also un-Western), then democracy was deemed shaky. Not all such guesses have been proven wrong, and Rustow's stress on the role of political leaders in changing regime types has been robust. He emphasized that an elite decision, followed by a period of testing, is needed for the founding of a liberal regime. He was interested in transitions to democracy; but in fact, his paradigm could as easily be used to model choices by leaderships for any non-democratic regime type too. Some of these have endured in Asia, especially China. In the Philippines, which holds elections, the national elite is relatively regionalized.

An extension of Rustow's interest would be to explore reasons why leaders engage in any such decision, e.g., to have a military coup or to want civilian authoritarians that are strong or weak. Some of the reasons lie in elite concerns that, if they do not act either to channel or repress new rivals, they might be overthrown. Such rivals are threatening if they can mobilize non-elites, for example in new groups created by modernization of the kind that many functionalist essays describe.

Elite fears can lead to democracy. They can also lead to repressions or stronger dictatorships, national or local. Samantha Ravich suggests that the rise of markets contributes to diversification that presents contemporary elites with needs to make such choices.[36] E.E. Schattschneider argued that immigration to cities and industrialization of the work force exacerbates conflicts with which elites must deal.[37] Przeworski and Limongi show that high per-capita income, certainly over a threshold that Thailand and China are approaching, prevents an established democracy from being overthrown. This phenomenon

---

[35]Dankwart Rustow, "Transitions to Democracy," *Comparative Politics* 2:3 (1970), 337–63.

[36]Samatha Ravich, *Marketization and Democracy: East Asian Experiences* (Cambridge: Cambridge University Press, 2000).

[37]E.E. Schattschneider, *The Semi-Sovereign People*.

may result from the increasing social dependence of the most coercive leaders, who are in the military and might make coups.[38]

High incomes imply local political-economic structures that dictatorial regimes cannot coordinate without either more normative resources (e.g., because of public fear of ethnic strife) or more wealth (e.g., from rich economies or oil). Przeworski found that established democracies are less likely to be overthrown if economic growth is faster than five percent. This challenged earlier hypotheses by Mancur Olson and Samuel Huntington that quick growth destabilized democracies.[39] None of these extensions of Rustow's paradigm negates its stress on the importance of elite decisions. They only relate the bases of such decisions to modernity and coercive politics.[40]

What is democratization? For the reasons suggested above, many writers take it to be a decision by authoritarian elites.[41] It is that, but such decisions are not taken in a vacuum, either normative or situational. Democracy defangs populist movements. It tends to demobilize discontents. For the elite, it transforms mass unrest by making representatives responsible for each sector. Do "the people" know what they are doing if they support democratization? It seems they do not exactly know, but they are supposed gradually to benefit in this process. Democracy is always incomplete, a result of previous

---

[38]It may still be true that no democracy has been subverted in any country with a per-capita income higher than during the Argentinean coup of 1975 (US$6,055 then); see Adam Przeworski and Fernando Limongi, "Modernization: Theory and Facts," *World Politics* 49 (January 1997), 159–83, and Adam Przeworski, Michael E. Alvarez, José Antonio Cheibub, and Fernando Limongi, *Democracy and Development: Political Institutions and Well-Being in the World, 1950–1990* (Cambridge: Cambridge University Press, 2000), 98. Calculation of the current threshold is complex, both because of inflation and because some measures of per-capita wealth (e.g., by purchasing power) may be more appropriate than others.

[39]Adam Przeworski *et al.*, *Democracy and Development*, 109.

[40]See Carles Boix and Susan Stokes, "Endogenous Democratization," *World Politics* 55:4 (2003), 517–49.

[41]Examples are in *Transitions from Authoritarian Rule: Tentative Conclusions about Uncertain Democracies*, Guillermo O'Donnell, Philippe C. Schmitter, and Laurence Whitehead, eds. (Baltimore: Johns Hopkins University Press, 1986).

results iterated over time. It depends on both conscious intentions and unintended situations.

Political science scarcely handles fractal or scalar forms yet. Przeworski and his colleagues write clearly but simply that, "Democracy is a system in which parties lose elections.... Whenever in doubt, we classify as democracies only those systems in which incumbent parties actually did lose elections."[42] This is too restrictive a definition of democracy, for many reasons. "Parties" can, as data from the Philippines or Thailand abundantly show, be so fluid that they are not stable institutions. Some places (e.g., Taiwan) had serious inter-party contestation before the executive authority was directly elected or before it changed hands between parties. If democracy should mean substantive service to people, a purely procedural definition does not in any case cover it. Use of Przeworski's narrow definition reduces subjective judgements in observing electoral contestation, but it does not guarantee that democracy is anything more than that. Like Kenneth Arrow's famous proof that there is no ideal way to aggregate interests, this intellectually admirable push for clarity has in this case produced truths that are sure in analytic terms but useless, or at least discouraging, for practice.[43]

Is it necessary to have an alternation of power between parties in the executive for a democracy to exist? An election that an opposition wins (as in the Philippines in 1986, Thailand on several occasions, or Taiwan in 1999) is one index of the extent to which voters may control society's most obvious power organization. But this alternation-in-power definition of democracy misses differences between relatively free systems in which a long-term loose coalition of factions practically always wins elections (Japan), systems in which elections are studiously designed to be no threat to incumbents (China and

---

[42]Adam Przeworski *et al.*, *Democracy and Development*, 15–16.

[43]Contrast the analytic epistemology implicit in Kenneth Arrow, *Social Choice and Individual Values* (New York: Wiley, 1965) with William James, *Essays in Radical Empiricism* (Lincoln: University of Nebraska Presss, 2003 [1912]) and James's *The Meaning of Truth: A Sequel to 'Pragmatism'* (Amherst, NY: Prometheus Books, 1997 [1909]), as well as Rorty's postanalytic approach in Richard Rorty, and Pascal Engel, *What's the Use of Truth?* (New York: Columbia University Press, 2007).

many other cases), and systems in which parties alternate but are socially inchoate (the Philippines or Thailand).

To what extent are regime types (authoritarianism, democracy, or others) adopted for their results, e.g., legitimating policies or settling intra-elite disputes? Or instead, to what extent are regime types adopted for expressive reasons, as ways to construct ideas about collective or individual identities? Are regime types widely supported because of the outcomes they bring, or instead because of the values they are seen to embody? The answer is almost surely: both.

BOOMS AFFECT ELITE DECISIONS

Przeworski claims, "Ideally, we would like to observe something like 'pressures toward transition' and relate them to economic dynamics. But we cannot observe them."[44] Actually, we can try. Such pressures come mostly through local politics (alternative terms such as 'subnational politics' or 'politics at low levels' would imply a power hierarchy that is in practice often inverted). The most relevant economic dynamics may not surely be captured by national aggregates, because industrialization occurs in some locales more than others, and some regions affect wider politics more than others. But these factors touch the cultures of elites, not the attitudes of all people who can more reliably be surveyed. In any case, the foundings of democracies in East Asian nations may present more obstacles than their maintenance after they are founded.

Regime-type change is a rare event, compared to change of incumbents. But it is unnecessary to base a theory of political development solely on national level shifts, or just on shifts from dictatorship to democracy or vice-versa. In Przeworski's main sample, transitions in either direction occur during just 2 percent of the country-years.[45] Yet politics is not stagnant during the other 98 percent

---

[44]Adam Przeworski *et al.*, *Democracy and Development*, 114.

[45]This is computed from Przeworski's Table 2.3: the sum of 49 transitions to democracy plus 39 to dictatorship is divided by 4,126 country-years in all. See *Democracy and Development*, 93; also 115.

of the time. The question becomes: how do socioeconomic changes affect elites' ideas?

Every large rich nation in the current world is unabashedly, unapologetically liberal. But the historical paths of sizeable rich countries to this mix of wealth and democracy have been both bumpy and diverse. Modernization means a great deal in objective terms, despite all the learned abuse that scholars have heaped on this m-word. Socioeconomic modernization is neither a sufficient nor a necessary factor to create democracy, but it correlates very highly with long-term (not short-run) movements toward that regime type. Przeworski misconstrues "modernization theory" by saying, "The basic assumption of this theory is that there is one general process, of which democratization is but the final facet.... The specific causal chains consist in ... a progressive accumulation of social changes that make a society ready to proceed to the final one, democratization."[46] Actually, though, many modernization theorists and some of their critics are clear that history need not end.

Frank Fukuyama took a more positive view than Przeworski of an "end of history," which he saw as "the universalization of Western [*sic*] liberal democracy as the final form of human government."[47] But he was impatient at least. There is no past evidence of a future "final" situation, even if some currently authoritarian countries may later pass through a phase of wanting to be democracies.

The links between modernization and politics are loosely rather than tightly connected. They are dynamic. Norms of elite or non-elite choice change under pressure from unintended aspects of historical developments. "Agency" decisions for or against regime types such as democracy shape sociopolitical changes, just as industrialization, rationalization, education, communication, and other "-tion" trends do. So apparently does an increasing number of non-Americans' expressed distaste for American democracy, whose mistakes give that

---

[46]*Ibid.*, 88–89.
[47]Francis Fukuyama, "The End of History?" *The National Interest* 16 (summer 1989), 4.

regime type a bad name.[48] The test of a theory is the extent to which it helps people by explaining facts. The habit of looking for links between roles and institutions in modern societies is an approach that can account for much of recent politics. But there is no need, when finding these links, to claim that they are frozen, that they cannot break, or that they can mean anything if separated from specific places.

POSTMODERN DEMOCRATIZATION?

Cross-national surveys show that, as modernization by standard measures reaches higher levels, "materialistic" concerns (such as income or hope for more income) give way to "post-materialistic" preoccupations (justice, civil freedom, rights for women and minorities, environmental cleanliness, and others) that erode authoritarian styles of rule. Inglehart finds that indices of subjective "trust" and "well-being" correlate significantly with stable democracy. So does GNP/capita. Those two, normative and situational, may be enough to bring democracy. Other variables, such as organizational networks that Putnam emphasizes, also correlate with that regime type. The organizational variable and assorted possible others (income inequality, ethnolinguistic divisions, or support for revolutionary change or gradual reform, for examples) add very little to GNP/capita and the well-being index as predictors of democratic stability, once a country's elite has decided to compete in elections.[49]

---

[48]This observation may depend on its date, but the Pew Research Center in 2007 surveyed citizens in 47 nations and found that over the previous five years, favorable ratings of the U.S.'s democracy declined in 26 of the 33 countries that showed clear trends. Among all 47, a plurality of respondents in 33 expressed negative views of "American ideas about democracy." See Meg Bortin, "Among Friends and Foes, Distrust of U.S. is Rising," *International Herald Tribune* June 28, 2007, 8.

[49]Inglehart's surveys of subjective values in forty-three societies for 1981 and then for 1990 unfortunately did not cover Taiwan, Thailand, or the Philippines. (China was included, but separate soundings were not taken for the relatively modern East China area, which is the main interest here.) Inglehart's conclusion is that belief sets change in predictable ways during socioeconomic modernization (and during a later stage that he calls 'postmodernization'). These changes of "mass belief systems ... have important economic, political, and social consequences." See Inglehart, *Modernizations and Post-Modernizations: Culture, Economics, and Politics in 43 Countries* (Princeton: Princeton University Press, 1997), 3–4; also 183.

Ronald Inglehart's attitude surveys can be interpreted to suggest that the long-run trend toward populist liberalism in the world will continue "because economic development tends to bring changes in social structure and culture that are favorable to democracy."[50] This is consistent with Przeworski's finding that development makes democracy survive, but because both of these authors rely on statistical tests of socioeconomic or cultural quantities to make their suggestions, rather than also on treatments of the mechanisms of change, neither gets very far toward explaining the dynamics of a process by which development affects regime types. Several recent surveys show that in China especially, "trust" of government at the central rather than local levels is exceptionally high.[51] It is less clear whether this trust encourages democratization, as most theorists have supposed. Rustow argued that a fundamentally impossible-to-resolve issue, a "hot family feud" between inherently distrustful actors (perhaps bosses and workers), was a factor that forced elites to compromise on liberal procedures.

Students of democratization may have paid relatively too much heed to quantifiable data, and too little to institutional evolutions of state and nonstate networks that produce these numbers. Inglehart's finding that "development [is] favorable to democracy," with its associated values of tolerance and trust, may miss the civil violence and distrust that has actually accompanied this transition in many historical cases. Przeworski's almost aesthetic asceticism, shying away from judgements about multiple degrees of democracy in favor of an all-or-nothing "dummy variable" (dictatorship or democracy), defines the process in unrealistically narrow terms: as a top-of-the-system actualized willingness to risk losing an election only. The data and correlations they find are useful, but the political histories of countries are useful too. Mass or elite attitudes of trust, tolerance, and other liberal values help stabilize democracy. They tell far less about the specific dangers and opportunities that leaders see as live.

---

[50]*Ibid.*, 167.

[51]Wang Zhengxu, "Political Trust in China," in *Legitimacy: Ambiguities of Political Success or Failure in East and Southeast Asia*, Lynn White, ed. (Singapore: World Scientific Press, 2005), 113–40. Tang Wenfang has made credible surveys showing high trust among Chinese citizens for top leaders — not just because they advertise themselves so assiduously.

It would be revealing to find common factors that elites consider. Development-by-boom tends to force a predictable set of political considerations on elites. Leaders at times of quick change become aware that resource distributions and non-elite values are in flux. They know their societies are pluralizing. They seek strategies to channel the changes brought by this process. Comparisons of the situations they face in various countries at such times may help to forecast their decisions about regime types.

Borrowing Machiavelli's metaphors to animals, Pareto described "foxes" who seek power through reforms. Economic entrepreneurs and political brokers are of this type. They are essential for making elites adaptable enough to absorb new techniques and fresh blood. Leaders for the opposite norm are conservative "lions." (In other theorists' zoos, conservatives are just hedgehogs — but the fiercer beast is the more accurate simile.) These upholders of the status quo are just as necessary to an overall elite, because they protect its own integral solidarity. They maintain loyalty to country or religion or class — and they justify force to preserve their system of rule whenever this is threatened.[52] Such groups are evident in decaying authoritarian states such as China's, and they also exist in small localities.

Lions have many means of deflecting foxes' pressures to admit new elites. A frequent method is to institute elections but to make the electoral posts powerless.[53] Constitutional means to restrict

---

[52]Niccolò Machiavelli, *The Prince*, intro. Christian Gauss (New York: Mentor, 1955 [orig. 1532]), 92, and Vilfredo Pareto, *The Rise and Fall of the Elites: An Application of Theoretical Sociology* (New York: Arno Press, 1979; orig. 1901). An explicit application of Pareto to Thai political history after 1931 is Joseph J. Wright, Jr., *The Balancing Act: A History of Modern Thailand* (Oakland: Pacific Rim Press, 1991), and it shows that the ideas of the reactionary Italian count can explain a good deal. Pareto's odd writing and terminology, e.g., using the word "residues" for norms, and his arch-conservatism have put his insights about elite circulation out of currency among political scientists, who have neglected what he wrote about the need for creativity.

[53]East Asian examples abound: China's village votes, Hong Kong's geographical elections to half of the Legislative Council, or authoritarian Taiwan's former elections to local posts (and not until 1991–92 to the National Assembly or Legislative Yuan, or until 1996 to the executive).

democracy are many. It is easy to take the people out of populism. Elected patriotic demagogues can do this, as can unelected executives. Appointed members of legislatures, or members chosen by small occupational groups, can be mixed with elected members. Simultaneous majorities within each group may be required to approve any new law. Supermajority voting can be mandated. Multi-member districts can favor representatives of minority parties. Prior executive approval of any bill may be needed, even before legislative debates; and the subjects on which elected members may pass laws can be constitutionally limited. Most usually, crucial power can be allocated to the part of a government that is not elected. Practically all East Asian constitutions provide for several of these methods, and representative democracies elsewhere use many of them too.[54]

Another method is sincere coercion combined with monetary incentives. These methods of gesturing at political modernity while actually thwarting it have been used and continue to be used to varying extents in all democracies. Many conservative elites have pretended "government by the people" while effectively disallowing it.[55] Electoral competition and authoritarian rule can co-exist nationally or locally.

---

[54]Hong Kong's *Basic Law*, together with its Electoral Law, provides a limiting case, because they enshrine the whole panoply of these methods. In Singapore, which because of the danger of ethnic mobilizations has a more justifiably illiberal system, these mechanisms are complemented by the unusually frequent use of libel laws in political cases.

[55]Authoritarian regimes often have accurate information on popular desires, and they sometimes react to meet these. President Chiang Ching-kuo in Taiwan during the early 1980s paid attention to the successes of candidates "outside the party" (i.e., non-KMT, '*dangwai*' local leaders). Even when they won elections in this period, however, they had scant power.

Singapore, with a population between 3 and 4 million only, is a rarity: a rich illiberal state, in which the wealth is not based on mineral extraction. It has received much attention because Lee Kwan Yew, Minister Mentor by his latest title, has philosophized in favor of a modern kind of patronism. The ruling People's Action Party

Among the democratic countries of interest in this book, this combination has been most fully developed in the Philippines; but it is also evident in Thailand. It involves elections in which money or force, paid or organized by economic elites, tends to center politics on personalities rather than policies. This detaches popular influence from electoral mandates as efficiently as constitutional provisions to the same end. In some democracies (late Weimar Germany is a famous case), conservative elites banned parties they disliked. In mainland China, and in Taiwan for some time, the personnel procedures of Leninist parties trumps all other politics. During Taiwan's early boom, this was bolstered by martial law. Democratic elections can be effectively divorced from democratic policy choice.

---

nonetheless holds competitive elections. The PAP uses legal means to discourage opposition, and an electoral law ensures that the PAP's normal portion of the national ballots (two-thirds or more) captures practically all the parliamentary seats. When the portion dips downward, the government responds strongly — in part by adopting better policies. Its votes could, in some future election, conceivably drop below 50 percent. The main restraint on Singapore liberalism is not "Asian" values. It is the potential disaster that would come from any mobilization of Chinese or Muslims against each other. Singapore is a small, ethnically distinct place in a Muslim neighborhood. Lee favors policies that may be wholly rational in a small, ethnically challenged city state. He presents these as universal truths, because that is also the habit of either the liberals or the communists whom he has opposed for years. His son, the current premier, follows similar policies.

Oil sheikdoms with small populations, needing few workers to run the rigs, also have socioeconomic structures that make them irrelevant to the analysis in this book. Some democracies, including several small island states in the Caribbean that have coherent elites strongly committed to parliamentary institutions because of British backgrounds, are likewise incomparable with the places studied here. The reasons for their democracy (as in Barbados) or sometime dictatorship (as in Grenada) are partly exogenous. For various reasons, suggestions in this book do not apply to countries with populations below ten million; and strictly, they apply only to the four important places the book studies. India, Indonesia, Bangladesh, and Pakistan are each so complex and big, they are above this author's pay scale. More important, claims to include them in this book would obscure what it finds about four other places. India's success thus far as a low-income democracy may be a credit to the Indian elite's continuing commitment to ex-British institutions.

The degree of social threat that a national elite feels is almost surely one of the most important domestic factors determining its impulse to authorize or to resist competitive elections. But that relationship is probably bell-shaped: elites allow elections when the threat to themselves is medium-high. They do not call for votes when the threat is very low (when they can keep power without asking electoral consent) or very high (when they expect elections will displace them permanently). One of the reasons for conclusions of the kinds that Przeworski reached while refining Lipset, or as further refined by Boix and Stokes, is the greater difficulty of establishing correlations with bell-shaped rather than with straight-line hypotheses.[56]

ARMED AGENCIES' AMBITIONS

Leonine politicians often bear arms. In all four countries studied in this book, the military has somewhat influenced political decisions — but soldiers have seldom colonized the bureaucracy. In Taiwan, Gen. Chiang Kai-shek and his son (and former intelligence chief) Chiang Ching-kuo were free to appoint civilian technocrats rather than soldiers to ministries, and they ordinarily did so. Military coups have been practically unthinkable in Taiwan since the early 1990s at the latest.[57] Former Gen. Hau Pei-ts'un's 1993 departure from the premiership in favor of Lien Chan seems to have civilianized Taiwan's government permanently.

---

[56]Adam Przeworski and Fernando Limongi, "Modernization: Theory and Facts," 159–83, and Carles Boix and Susan Stokes, "Endogenous Democratization," 517–49.

[57]Since the year of the Japanese Empire's surrender, 1945, coups have also been inconceivable in Japan. In South Korea, Roh Dae Woo's peaceful accession as president with a plurality of the vote in 1988 may be a similar watershed. King Bhumibol's reproof of conservative Gen. Suchinda in 1992 was for many years expected to end Thailand's coups, but Thaksin Shinawatra's electoral corruptions brought another coup a decade and a half later. The merely partial failures of recurrent attempts against presidents Corazon Aquino and Gloria Macapagal Arroyo, and the popularity of coup leaders Honasan and Trillanes who were later elected senators, show that ambitious militarists and many voters still readily conceive coups as legitimate politics in the Philippines.

In China, Communist Party control of the People's Liberation Army was a steady tradition under Mao Zedong and Deng Xiaoping, both of whom had prestige as strategic writers and military commissars, as well as personal connections with high officers. The constitutional equality of China's Military Affairs Commission with its government (the State Council), and the ostensible subordination of both to the Communist Party, institutionalizes the military in rule even though civilians have for years been the top leaders in name and probably in fact. A PRC military coup might have been nearly pointless, because the hierarchal structure of the Leninist party-state and the institutionalized embeddedness of the army deep into politics gives the government a martial cast, even when civilians are in charge.[58]

In Thailand, the "revolution" of 1932 "was actually a military coup planned together with officials ... it cemented the relationship between the bureaucracy and the military. This cooperative relationship has endured."[59] A series of top Thai generals became premiers from the late 1940s into the 1990s, and much money was made from their links to bureaucracies and businesses. But the officers themselves seldom became civilian bureaucrats. Thailand in 2006 had another coup, but it was led by the king and by soldiers who at least proclaimed their commitment to democracy despite their quandary about how to make it meaningful for most Thais.

In the Philippines, both the army and the bureaucracy have been smaller and far weaker than any of the other three countries. Soldiers have often not colonized ministries, in part because the power of those bureaus is so marginal. Especially in the Philippines, militarists instead hold recurrent semi-coups, threatening if not changing the government. These *kudeta* suggest that future successful coups on the archipelago are conceivable. When the central state bureaucracy

---

[58]See Lynn White, "The Liberation Army and the Chinese People," *Armed Forces and Society*, I:3 (May, 1975), 364–83.

[59]James Ockey, "Thailand: The Struggle to Redefine Civil-Military Relations," in *Coercion and Governance: The Declining Political Role of the Military in Asia* (Stanford: Stanford University Press, 2001), 191.

has more power to seize, the generals may become more interested in it. They already are important in many of the islands' local networks.[60]

WHEN ARE MIDDLE-INCOME PEOPLE LIBERAL?

Levels of development and levels of democracy relate to each other, but not directly, because the link operates through elite decisions. Quick, non-gradual development brings to the fore new elites, with which old elites in their own interest deal. Military coups occur in poor countries, but co-optation is the establishment's more usual strategy in countries that the division of labor and increase of money have made more complex. *Nouveaux riches*, when they emerge in large numbers, are often sufficiently pleased to participate in state institutions even if the electoral posts available to them at first carry little power.

Quick growth among small industries and traders, because this prosperity aids the legitimacy of governments, gives established elites reasons to admit new entrepreneurs into socio-political leadership. Top politicians may hope the merchants will remain politically docile. In China, Leninist modes of promotion to leadership in any large organization bolster such control. This appointment system, however, only assures monitoring by a single level higher than the target in China's multi-level administration.[61] A consensus decision rule, "if the agents agree, let it be," allows sharp differences of policy between regions.[62] Over time, localities that have less economic success experience "contagion" and begin to follow the policies of places

---

[60]On Negros, for example, see Alan Berlow, *Dead Season: A Story of Murder and Revenge on the Philippine Island of Negros* (New York: Pantheon, 1996). Local links to the central state are more important when richer built-up areas are studied; see John T. Sidel, "Philippine Politics in Town, District, and Province: Bossism in Cavite and Cebu," *Journal of Asian Studies* 56:4 (November 1997), 947–66.

[61]Pierre-François Landry, *Decentralized Authoritarianism in China: The Communist Party's Control of Local Elites in the Post-Mao Era* (New York: Cambridge University Press, 2008).

[62]Susan L. Shirk, *The Political Logic of Economic Reform in China* (Berkeley: University of California Press, 1993), chap. 7, 116–28.

that prosper, whether they obey central state rules or not.[63] So the Leninist system of scalar governance, a centralist approach to modern organization, prevents the liberal separation of powers while failing to prevent — or enabling — pluralization by places.

Other, slower kinds of growth (of large firms, of agriculture, or of import-substituting industries) may also promote some change. But small and medium firms do so in particular, because they bring really new types of people into local power networks. Industrialization enlarges the middle-income class. It generates ideologists who ascribe traits to the new entrepreneurial class, defining it as a status group too. Economic development generally involves a long period of capital accumulation, during which wages for unskilled workers remain near subsistence. Many in the middle status group like to distinguish themselves from the proletariat. Compassionate patronizers emerge, along with snobs. Middle-income groups claim rights to assign traits to whole nations, whose identity seems increasingly to depend on them.

The bourgeoisies of many countries have been famed for such smugness and nationalism. Sinclair Lewis in his novel *Babbit* offered a caustic view of boosterist civil associations and their chauvinism.[64] In the Philippines, Cullinane writes, such local leaders have created "'burgis projects' — efforts on the part of upper middle-class intellectuals to construct and display Filipino society and culture mainly to themselves."[65] Other writers suggest that voluntary groups are

---

[63]Mary Elizabeth Gallagher, *Contagious Capitalism: Globalization and the Politics of Labor in China* (Princeton: Princeton University Press, 2005; orig. Ph.D. dissertation, Politics Department, Princeton University, 2001).

[64]See Sinclair Lewis, *Babbit* (New York: Harcourt Brace, 1922). Lewis wrote a novel, but he was explicitly interested in local politics and in the psychological effects of boosterism during growth. He described limitations of personality that he found among entrepreneurs during the United States' boom, and he found corollaries of the boom in unsustainable norms of social prestige.

[65]Michael Cullinane, "Burgis Projects in the Post-Marcos Era," *Pilipinas* 21 (1993), 74–76, quoted in Schaffer, *op. cit.*, 40. See also James Ockey, "Creating the Thai Middle Class," in *Culture and Privilege in Capitalist Asia*, Michael Pinches, ed. (New York: Routledge, 1999), 240–45.

"schools of democracy."[66] No sort of civil association is more important, in boom times, than business federations — which can also become schools of stratification.

Many Westerners like to believe that an increase of middle-income people in any country will automatically raise the frequency of demands for democracy. Bourgeois can indeed be cranky citizens — but they are just as likely to support whatever regime is in power. Their rise bolsters governments and oppositions alike. Participation in politics may expand, but the participation is often pro-establishment. Juan Linz refers to "semi-oppositions" that are neither loyal nor disloyal to government elites. There are "groups that are not dominant or represented in the governing group but that are willing to participate in power without fundamentally challenging the regime."[67]

The term "middle class" usually refers to an income category that also becomes a status group. Much theorizing, based on Marx, Weber, Mills, Giddens, and others has made uses of the phrase "middle class" so various that it is still moot. Some writers, such as E. Thompson, want mainly to discuss the historical evolution of the middle class.[68] As Jim Ockey has noted for Thailand, "The prostitute, the university professor, the bank manager, the independent farmer, the owner of a Chinese traditional medicine shop, the police officer, and the soldier are all 'middle class' under various definitions, yet they have little in common."[69] Each of the countries studied in this book nonetheless has an increasing number of middle-rich people, and they have had somewhat comparable effects on these very different polities.

The "middle class," described in terms of either incomes or customs, has many parts: large entrepreneurs, small entrepreneurs, professionals and semi-professionals in academe, journalism, finance, medicine, law, politics, and other fields. As government offices try to

---

[66]Robert D. Putnam, *Bowling Alone* (New York: Simon and Schuster, 2000), 339.

[67]Juan J. Linz, "Opposition to and under an Authoritarian Regime: The Case of Spain," in *Regimes and Oppositions*, Robert Dahl, ed. (New Haven: Yale University Press, 1973), 191.

[68]E.P. Thompson, *The Making of the English Working Class* (Harmondsworth: Penguin, 1968).

[69]Ockey, James, "Creating the Thai Middle Class," 235.

centralize their countries, and businesses try to develop larger markets, the "lower-middle class" of accountants, nurses, and other service aides grows. Urban service workers and clerks have been important in some Asian cities (for example, they were a majority in the Bangkok street demonstrations of 1992). The group of greatest interest is entrepreneurs. They are the agents who increase the "middle class," spreading it into provincial cities, which are an insufficiently studied kind of polity.[70] This extension of pluralized politics outside capitals, albeit not over any nation uniformly, produces an increasingly modern and complex power structure.

If the "middle class" consists of the households whose heads are self-employed or salaried in white collar occupations, this term is not easy to use in political analysis. Scholars who have generalized about the influence of "middle" strata have not reached agreement. Some such as Jürgen Habermas see in the rise of this group a vanguard of "civil society" and modernized politics. Others such as C. Wright Mills follow an Aristotelian tradition, seeing the middle stratum as a resolver of tensions between tycoons and workers. A similar option, taken in this book, is to see these groups as disunited, shifting their support between various kinds of politicians on short-term grounds. They often support a ruling party whether it is authoritarian or democratic, so long as it does not extract too much from them. "Petty bourgeois" shop and factory managers, if they receive official assistance, often have been able to detach local officials from control by the central government. If they do not receive help, local business people can become disgruntled and support opposition parties if these are available. Suburban and rural booms bring the enrichment, and usually the empowerment, of shop-keepers and factory managers.

These local leaders are not the whole middle-income group. So the concept of a middle class is pitched at too high a level of abstraction to be surely useful for many kinds of generalization.

---

[70]"Place promotion" in "entrepreneurial cities" may become the research focus of Meg Rithmire, a graduate student in Government at Harvard. More sociologists and geographers than political scientists have previously explored this phenomenon.

Thailand, for example, had no traditional word for "middle class." The translation *konchanklan*, meaning "people of the middle level," is an adaptation from English. Middle class people might be categorized that way either in terms of their incomes and managerial/ownership roles, or alternatively in Weberian status terms. As Ockey writes, "many traditionally high-status occupations do not allow, either morally or materially, for a lifestyle of high consumption, while many traditionally low-status occupations do."[71] William Skinner, writing before Thailand's boom, found "at least two major middle-class groupings, the Chinese and the Thai." He found a Thai middle class "consisting mainly of those in high-status (government employees, small entrepreneurs, teachers, newspapermen, clerks, secretaries, and so on) … strongly white-collar in flavor," while the Chinese middle class could better be defined in terms of income.[72]

Differences like these in Thailand can be found in Taiwan or China, but not on ethnic bases. The standard translation of "middle class" into Chinese is *zhongchan jieji* (middling-production class), a Marxist concept that suggests a measure of wealth but ignores prestige status. Not just in Mao's time, low-paid government cadres or teachers in China could be relatively high-prestige. In Taiwan, many SME bosses could identify alternatively with bespoke-suited bureaucrats or, just as easily, with down-to-earth betelnut-chewing workers who proudly called themselves "black hands," because dirt under their fingernails showed their economic prowess.[73]

The "middle class" concept is difficult to use precisely, although there are linkages between the income/property and lifestyle/status aspects of the idea. It will not disappear despite all these problems, because — as Barrington Moore famously showed — the increase of such a group, no matter how it is exactly defined, is important for potential evolutions of politics. Groups like the "mobile telephone

---

[71] James Ockey, "Creating the Thai Middle Class," 230.

[72] G. William Skinner, *Chinese Society in Thailand: An Analytical History* (Ithaca: Cornell University Press, 1957), 307–08.

[73] See David D. Yang, "Classing Ethnicity: Class, Ethnicity, and the Mass Politics of Taiwan's Democratization" *World Politics* 59:4 (July 2007), 503–38.

mob" (to use Anek's term for the 1992 pro-democracy protesters in Bangkok) have also appeared in Manila (as 'people power' in 1986), in Taipei (e.g., in the anti-corruption protests of 2006), and in Beijing and Shanghai (the 1989 specter that CCP conservatives are most eager to preclude for the future).

Taiwan's parties have all been led by middle-class professionals and business people, even though the DPP has drawn support from workers and SME bosses who want to identify with them. Suchit characterizes Thailand's "new elites," especially those in the House of Representatives, as "diversified ... wealthy, ruthless, opportunistic, and pragmatic, whose interest in seeking power is based on their quest for personal aggrandizement."[74] This description could be applied to the elites of many democracies. The Philippine middle class has been often pro-authoritarian, both locally and nationally, but it has sometimes been a force for political change.

Many liberal philosophers, in the most refined case John Rawls, present careful myths that tell nothing about the actual emergence of liberal politics. A recent illiberal treatise on Asian political ideas argues that few there see much use in "the principle of keeping the government out of the business of judging the good life.... Instead, East and Southeast Asian political understandings place great value on substantive moral consensus that denies or suppresses moral pluralism and social diversity."[75] This consensus is not just about procedures. In the West too, much happens behind opaque shrouds; not much happens behind mere "veils of ignorance."[76] The admonition not too peek is coy. It is unrealistic. Economically and culturally constructed substantive interests lie behind that curtain, which elites close only if they benefit in terms of their specific situation, beyond any generic rationality that all individuals are supposed to share.

---

[74]Suchit Bunbongkarn, *State of the Nation: Thailand* (Singapore: Institute of Southeast Asian Studies, 1996), 71.

[75]Daniel A. Bell *et al.*, *Towards Illiberal Democracy in Pacific Asia* (New York: St. Martin's Press, 1995), 8.

[76]See John Rawls, *A Theory of Justice* (Cambridge: Harvard University Press, 1971).

In Asia, when elites want to deny or suppress moral pluralism and social diversity, they end up with a great deal of differentiation anyway, because they want rich economies and inadvertently abet a division of labor for that end. The problem is not that there is a philosophical difference between East and West. In fact, each place has a rich store of various specific ideas about order and freedom. The problem is theories that fail to link the notions of the increasing variety of political actors (not just abstracting intellectuals) to the contexts in which they think.

Nonstate power institutions often take pluralistic "civil society" forms, but locally they are not all reformist. Religious and business networks are in many cases rock-ribbed conservative petty tyrannies. They may also express a frustration among local elite traditionalists that plural politics and markets change power relations.[77] The development of local wealth finances old-style patriarchal politics with more resources than civil networks traditionally had. So "civil society" is often uncivil.

It is also, sometimes, an evasive concept. It attempts to describe influence as vaguely social rather than definitely political.[78] Those who unintentionally behave as pluralists in national contexts are often totalists in local structures. They can bring either violence with poverty, or peace with prosperity, as surely as more public tyrants can. Does "civil society" consolidate democracy, as many social scientists have hoped?[79] In some cases it does, but Sheri Berman shows that German civil groups provided major bases for Hitler's totalitarians,

---

[77]See Ernest Gellner, *Conditions of Liberty: Civil Society and its Rivals* (New York: Penguin, 1994), which mentions not only Islam, but also Confucian societies.

[78]See Lynn White, *Unstately Power: Local Causes of China's Intellectual, Legal, and Governmental Reforms* (Armonk: Sharpe, 1999), and Garry Rodan, "Theorizing Political Opposition in East and Southeast Asia," *Political Oppositions in Industrializing Asia*, Garry Rodan, ed. (London: Routledge, 1996), 22, and sources cited there concerning Eastern Europe and South Africa.

[79]See Philippe Schmitter, "Civil Society East and West," in *Consolidating the Third Wave Democracies*, Larry Diamond *et al.*, eds. (Baltimore: Johns Hopkins University Press, 1997), 239–62.

who were elected to overthrow the Weimar democracy.[80] Research by Amaney Jamal suggests that, in the externally fettered politics of the West Bank, many civic associations are just formally pro-democratic. Many support either the ruling authority or else liberation movements that are illiberal but win elections.[81]

The Chinese-Filipina lawyer Amy Chua argues that the dominance of economies by ethnic minorities in many countries, ranging from the Philippines to Russia to Zimbabwe, has — especially when combined with globalist economic policies and electoral traditions — raised dangers of holocausts by majorities.[82] This is the polar opposite

---

[80]Sheri Berman, "Civil Society and the Collapse of the Weimar Republic," *World Politics* 49 (April 1997), 401–29. See related essays in *Beyond Tocqueville: Civil Society and the Social Capital Debate in Comparative Perspective*, Bob Edwards, Michael Foley, and Mario Diani, eds. (Hanover: University Press of New England, 2001).

[81]See important work by Amaney Jamal, *Barriers to Democracy: The Other Side of Social Capital in Palestine and the Arab World* (Princeton: Princeton University Press, 2007), which shows how external — in this case Israeli — oppression can create pro-electoral views that are in substance at least as anti-democratic as are the East Asian examples of electoral money politics raised in this current book. See also another sometime Princetonian (like Berman, Jamal, two D. Yangs, and the present author): Jason Brownlee, *Authoritarianism in an Age of Democratization* (New York: Cambridge University Press, 2007).

[82]Amy Chua, *World on Fire: How Exporting Free Market Democracy Breeds Ethnic Hatred and Global Instability* (New York: Doubleday, 2003) presents an argument that many have avoided because of their intuition that many Jewish intellectuals, with whom they wish to remain friends, regard the tragedies and victories of Jewish history as incomparable. Chua writes about Tutsis and Hutus, Croats and Serbs, Zimbabwean Whites and Blacks, Ibos and other Nigerians, Jews and Russians, Indians and Kenyans, and cases in Latin America. In rather Huntingtonian style, she sees a worldwide clash, Western Whites vs. everyone else (especially Muslims). Conflicts over land figure in several of the instances, as they do in the Middle East. Chua's argument about economic inequality applies less strongly in the most sensitive case, Weimar Germany, than in others (as she indicates). Nothing can justify what Hitler did; but also, the "never again" vow means nothing moral separate from efforts to understand what happened then. Chua's accusations against globalist economic policies are debatable. Perhaps it should be unsurprising that this argument about minorities' economic dominance, and majorities' sometime reaction, should have come from a Chinese-Filipina, apparently not a self-identifying

of liberal toleration. Because Chinese have been relatively accepted in Thailand, this danger is predictably less there than in the Philippines, where the inability of non-Chinese Filipinos to found enterprises may have left roughly half of all assets by value in the hands of an ethnic minority that is just 1 percent of the population.

THE SPECIFIC DIVERSITY OF ECONOMIC AGENTS

Economic managers might be analyzed in four groups: (1) local entrepreneurs, (2) local controllers of land, (3) foreign capitalists, and (4) agents of the state. In Taiwan,

(1) Especially after 1960, manufacturing and commercial entrepreneurs had intrinsically diverse politics. The island's businesses included both mainlanders (such as then ran the government) and Taiwanese (who under Chiang Kai-shek were discouraged from political initiatives, although they were 86 percent of the island's population). Middle-income entrepreneurs of small factories and stores were socially mobile, but at first they were not politically mobile. This group regenerated itself with particular alacrity because of a clear and strong cultural penchant of experienced employees in the island's firms to resign, in hopes of founding independent companies in which they could be the bosses.

(2) As regards control of land, reforms of the early 1950s in Taiwan had been exceptionally thorough. These reforms, engineered by the KMT state for its own political reasons at that time, tended to separate the owners of agricultural land from the owners of industry and commerce.

(3) Foreign capitalists were welcomed by the ROC government for security reasons, and they (along with American advisors and

---

Westerner, although she teaches at Yale Law School. Chua's aunt was murdered in Manila by a Filipino chauffeur with the apparent connivance of this very rich Chinese family's Filipina maids. One murder does not make a holocaust, but Chinese in some southeast Asian countries, probably not including Thailand or Malaysia, should at least read Chua's book.

overseas-educated economists) acquired some influence over policy. Foreigners were important in protecting the island against threats from mainland China.

(4) In sum, the ROC authoritarian state enjoyed considerable autonomy from other groups, both on the island and elsewhere. This government was more independent of local power networks because of the politics that flowed from its insecure external environment and its obvious ethnic-minoritarian weakness.

In East China,

(1) Especially after 1970, local entrepreneurs did not think of themselves as a bourgeoisie, particularly when they were local state cadres and members of the Chinese Communist Party. Nonetheless they had growing control of capital and increased local power because of the boom they created in "village and township enterprises," TVEs, the acronym of that moment for SMEs.

(2) As regards control of paddies, the landlord class had been eliminated in China's relatively violent reforms of the early 1950s, even though some of the new entrepreneurs were aware that their ancestors had owned land that was now pooled in production teams and brigades.

(3) As for foreign capitalists, they were at first completely absent from Jiangnan's (East China's) boom. They entered only *after* strong growth had already been achieved in TVEs, whose Chinese entrepreneurs were ready partners in joint firms.

(4) The PRC state is even more famous than it should be for its strength and autonomy. Chinese industry remained inefficient, in the sense that it lacked dynamic entrepreneurship in many sectors, until conservatives in the central state and localities could not prevent local public and private authorities from taking their own initiatives.

In Thailand,

(1) Practically all manufacturers and traders are Sino-Thais, sometimes imagining that their status creates serious discrimination

against them. But they control most of the country's wealth and now occupy the highest political offices.

(2) They are not Thailand's traditional landowners, and practically none of them work paddies, although some have bought land in recent years as financial speculation. There has never been a major land reform in Thailand, and there has also never been a major land consolidation, such as occurred in the Philippines especially during the Spanish period, so that land has remained divided relatively equally, and tenancy is relatively low.

(3) Thailand's foreign capitalists have been particularly diverse, coming from Japan, the U.S., Europe, China, Taiwan, and elsewhere. The state has been able to establish tax relations with them.

(4) Just as important, bureaucrats and military officers have established rent-extracting relations with domestic capitalists, whose power has increased because money derived from state-licensed monopolies can be used to help elect the politicians who assure that the licenses are issued. The Thai state is more embedded than autonomous, but it has a strong centralist ideology as well as considerable popular prestige on traditional grounds.

In the Philippines,

(1 and 2) Unlike the other three cases, much of the manufacturing bourgeoisie also owns agricultural land.[83] This is a tiny group, relative to the whole population. Local families that collected agricultural rents were often the same as those who owned the few and simple local factories. There are a very few non-landed manufacturers, especially among Chinese-Filipino families, but they do not represent most of the rich or middle-income group. This contrast between the Philippines and the other three cases exists in part because no political coalition for effective wealth-redistributing

---

[83]This analysis is partly indebted to Temario C. Rivera, *Landlords and Capitalists: Class, Family, and State in Philippine Manufacturing* (Quezon City: University of the Philippines Center for Integrative and Development Studies, 1994).

land reform has existed in the islands since land was consolidated during the Spanish colonial era.

(3) As for foreign capitalists, except in some agribusinesses that ally with local landowners, foreigners have been largely excluded by Philippine patriotic protectionism, currency controls, import-substitution policies since 1949, and anti-Chinese politics. Foreign investment has partly gone into companies, often run on a joint basis with Philippine rent-collecting families, that export raw materials, especially food products from Visayas and Mindanao plantations. Future growth is predictable in the areas where it has begun, the west coast of Luzon and Cebu.

(4) Even at many of these locations, the Philippine state is weak for any social purpose in two senses. First, it is fragmented because its American-style structure of checks and balances pits its parts against each other very effectively, its decentralized civil service includes many jobs that are distributed as patronage, and its politicians move easily between unstable parties that do not consistently represent policy options (e.g., along the labor-capital dimension, or along any alternative stable spectrum). Second, regionally based families vie with each other to create a bewitching democratic politics that has scant social content. So various organs of the state are captured by leaders whose agendas are narrow, although the constant conflict among them absorbs rapt public attention.

DEMOCRATIC DEFICIENCIES AND HOPES OF LEGITIMATE CONFLICT

Voting is an insensitive means to aggregate such a variety of specific interests, coming from such assorted economic and social generators. Partly for this reason, democratic elections can produce anti-democratic outcomes. As Jonathan Fox notes, "If there is more to democracy than elections, then there is more to democratization than the transition to elections, but... the dynamics of political transitions toward respect for other fundamental democratic rights is still not well understood."[84]

---

[84] Jonathan Fox, "The Difficult Transition from Clientelism to Citizenship," *World Politics* 46 (January 1994), 151.

This lack of understanding is less consequential among political scientists than among political elites. The Thai political scientist Chai-Anan Samudavanija describes the view of democracy among the absolute monarchs of early 20th century Siam in a way that sounds much like arguments heard now from leaders and intellectuals in the People's Republic of China. As Chai-Anan says of the kings, "Not all of them rejected constitutionalism and democracy as an ideal... desirable and even inevitable, but it was still premature to establish such a system in Siam." He reports four main reasons that were given. (1) There was scant "middle class" in Siam, and bureaucrats opined that "peasants took little or no interest in public affairs." (2) "Parliamentary government was not suitable for the Siamese people...." (3) Democracy was "unlikely to succeed in Siam... the parliament would be entirely dominated by the Chinese [greedy business people]," as has actually happened although they are now also well-assimilated Thais. And (4) "the great bulk of the people of Siam were as yet not trained in political or economic thought."[85] Many stately intellectuals in Beijing, albeit they are not kings, have a similar view of the unwashed masses.

There are good reasons to be wary of elections, but they do not all lie in the educational and economic inadequacies of the masses. Instead, they lie in structures that local and national elites have built to exclude potential rivals from legitimation by this modern means. It is documentable that many elections in new democracies are parodies. Nigeria, the most populous African country, in April 2007 held a presidential election that the International Republican Institute labeled "below acceptable standards" because of voter intimidation, ballot stuffing, and murders. Election observer Madeline Albright opined that, "In a number of places, and in a number of ways, the

---

[85]The last point is especially delicious, because it assumes that "the great bulk of the people" in any democracy "are trained in political and economic thought," or perhaps that those with such training are morally superior to others. See Chai-Anan Samudavanija, who is reporting old views with which he does not agree, "Thailand: A Stable Semidemocracy," in *Politics in Developing Countries: Comparing Experiences with Democracy*, Larry Diamond, Juan Linz, and S.M. Lipset, eds., 2nd edition (Boulder: Rienner, 1990), 272–73.

election process failed the people."[86] This was the first time in Nigerian history that one civilian president, Obasanjo, handed power to another, Umaru Yar'Adua. But the successor was handpicked, and when the electoral rite was held, the link between the specific result and the interests of most Nigerians was very indistinct. In 2000, after an earlier election had brought Nigeria out of a long period of military rule, the Afrobarometer survey showed that 84 percent of the people were satisfied with democracy. By 2005, the portion was down to 25 percent. Fully 70 percent of Nigerians disbelieved, by 2005, that an election could remove objectionable rulers. The masses could be hoodwinked, but it was leaders who did the hoodwinking.

Many democrats hope that the electoral habit itself, rather than broader-based and more local sociopolitical changes, will by its own mechanism make future elections cleaner. Yet this does not happen automatically.[87] Diamond, Plattner, and Schedler made an understatement when they wrote: "Deficiencies of accountability are often more visible, dramatic, and urgent in new than in long-established democracies. But as we know, problems of democratic quality are by no means confined to fledgling democracies."[88] A democracy's age

---

[86]Nigeria has its Independent National Electoral Commission, like ComElec in the Philippines or the National Election Commission in Thailand, but such institutions alone do not solve these problems. Countries such as Uganda or Ethiopia have held elections that Western politicians have deemed respectably fair (although many observers too have reasons to discount the role of money in elections). But in these and other African countries, later elections were accompanied by extensive coercion and vote-buying. For every African election that seems successful, in countries as different as Mauritania or the Democratic Republic of Congo, others held in places like Gabon, Guinea, or Zimbabwe have been documentably flawed. Lydia Polgreen, "Nigerian Vote Another Sign of Africa's Disillusionment with Democracy," *International Herald Tribune*, April 24, 2007, 4.

[87]Elections perform the same role in politics that tests of "error elimination" are supposed to perform in Popper's analytic epistemology — and they work no more substantively for their expected ends. Without more specific hints on the ways in which propositions, tests, preferences, and voters are constructed, this mainstream form of analysis is at least incomplete. See Karl Popper, *The Logic of Scientific Discovery* (London: Routledge, 1959), which is consistent with his kind of liberalism.

[88]"Introduction" by the editors, *The Self-Restraining State*, 2.

may correlate loosely with its "democratic quality," somehow measured, but the Philippines would be far off the line of any such correlation. Old democracies, such as that of the U.S. are also still affected by money politics. Data in this book's Taiwan chapter suggest that electoral uses of money on that rich island have become far subtler than in the early post-authoritarian years. This development is comparable to that of democracies in North America or Europe.

Economic change is the factor that eventually, partially, reduces democratic deficits. Free speech and voting do not by themselves reduce the political inequalities that money makes, nor does time alone. Still, eventual Philippine industrialization is likely to become unpreventable by the traditional elites there. It will sublimate the currently severe democratic deficits, the extensive violence and bribes, into forms that are more psychological.[89] Economic growth does not solve all problems of fairness. It transmogrifies them into new issues, and people like the extra wealth.

Democracy is generally conceived in terms of two concurrent norms: that public contest between electoral candidates is legitimate, and that every adult is able to vote. Without questioning the usefulness of this view, the current book seeks to complement it by pointing out an unintended situation in which leaders gain by espousing these ideals: modern development creates a variety of nonstate power networks that minimize their net costs by finding institutions to manage their disputes. This makes public debate more legitimate even though conservative leaders may abhor the disharmony of views. A second common situation is that such groups can win over their rivals if they mobilize new sources of support from actors who were previously unengaged. So citizens become increasingly involved in politics. Ideas about legitimate contest and participation do not win in politics just because reformist actors find them philosophically pleasing. They emerge from the pluralized place-specific contexts that industrialization brings.

---

[89]See Michel Foucault, *Discipline and Punish: The Birth of the Prison*, trans. Alan Sheridan (New York: Vintage Book, 1977).

THE MODERN FEUD: CAPITAL VS. LABOR

Economic development drives classes that control capital to get along with workers. That process both exploits labor and eventually separates powers, so that executives, lawmakers, judges, investigators, prosecutors, reporters, and others autonomous agents monitor each other "horizontally" as they normalize ways to mediate these conflicts. Mass elections can also monitor officials "vertically," from the bottom that on election day only (a quick saturnalia) becomes the top. But elections work to control government just periodically. Power networks outside the state have legitimate autonomy in a liberal system, including unions, businesses, belief groups, NGOs, and media.

Traditions for both horizontal and vertical interlocking networks in specific countries have usually come from violent and prolonged capital-labor conflicts. In a very few cases (India's national politics), habits that started on the basis of such conflict in other countries travelled surprisingly well.[90] In far more cases, the normalization of legitimate contest is industrial, and it is always incomplete. Capitalists organize early to reap profits while wages are near subsistence. The main practical question is how long they (or their Leninist counterparts) succeed in preventing workers' unionization.

Labor has been politically weak in all four places studied here. Taiwanese, East Chinese, and Thai large units of "civil society," to the extent they are actually autonomous, are overwhelmingly in business. Either elections or Leninist appointments can combine with local greed to consolidate hierarchy in factories and stores. Parochial bosses

---

[90]A democracy eventually needs roots, although many liberal theorists, including Americanists, do not stress how weak these are even in established democracies. Kohli corrects them regarding the main exception: "As long as democracy remains more a gift that a society's leaders give to its people, and less an established framework that dwarfs the leaders, only exceptional leaders are likely to resist the tendency to maintain personal power at the expense of institutional development." Atul Kohli, *Democracy and Discontent: India's Growing Crisis of Governability* (Cambridge: Cambridge University Press, 1990), 390. Historian Ramachandra Guha also warns of weakened local institutions in India's democracy, in *India After Gandhi: The History of the World's Largest Democracy* (New York: HarperCollins, 2007).

establish support for their local rule over long periods of time, but new leaders circulate into local elites more readily as booms begin. Bosses use their posts to extract rents, either legalized or illegal. Some invest their money; others use it mainly for consumption.

What determines the choices these local potentates make? The level of wealth in the locality, political-economic stability or tumult there, and family cultures of entrepreneurship or gentry-hidalgo status are all relevant. The most important factor, however, is the extent to which wealth is plentiful from factories and trading, or less so from agricultural rents or external prebends (usually from governments, sometimes from large corporations). When the political environment allows returns on investments, then rich people naturally tend to invest in whatever economic, social, or political factors they expect to bring returns. They organize workers to make profits under either market or socialist property norms. Ownership (capitalist or communist or mixed) makes less difference than the effective autonomy or suppression of local political networks.

Compared to development, capitalism and socialism are ephemeral. These two ideologies and the politicos who trumpet them respectively support capital-increasing entrepreneurs (for market efficiency) or capital-decreasing public cadres (for market regulation and welfare). Both capitalism and socialism are normative factors of development. They become rhetorics that politicians use to serve party interests while supporting different aspects of modern change. A state in a poor country can do little, and both public and private power networks in rich countries can do much, regardless of the ideologies leaders use to present their economic politics.

The usual hunch of either liberals or Marxists is that the rise of the bourgeoisie is what creates democracies — but this may be wrong. Instead, democracies apparently come from situations in which elites' net losses are minimized by institutionalizing conflict between bourgeois and workers. Barrington Moore's famous finding, "no bourgeoisie, no democracy," does not mean that the existence of a bourgeoisie by itself assures a democracy.[91] Capitalists easily cooperate

---

[91]Barrington Moore, Jr., *Social Origins of Dictatorship and Democracy*, 418.

with authoritarian regimes that prevent unionization and keep labor costs low. Capitalist industrialization is almost surely a conditioning factor toward democracy, but the social classes with the most obvious interest in such a transition are the ones with the most votes: farmers and workers, not capitalists.[92]

Reuschmeyer and the Stephenses found that, "The working class was the most consistently pro-democratic force. The class had a strong interest in effecting its political inclusion, and it was more insulated from the hegemony of dominant classes than the rural lower classes.... The bourgeoisie we found to be generally supportive of the installation of constitutional and representative government, but opposed to extending political inclusion to the lower classes."[93] The best-established democracy among the four places studied here is Taiwan, and David Yang documents that liberal institutions rose in the 1980s there not mainly because of ethnic cleavages but because the DPP could establish itself most easily by mobilizing against its rich KMT rival, using a majoritarian Taiwanese discourse that was politically effective for garnering workers' votes.[94]

Extension of the political franchise does not translate quickly into welfare benefits without a great deal of political struggle.[95] This transition was facilitated in late-authoritarian Taiwan because practically all workers were ethnic Taiwanese and the KMT government was largely run by mainlanders. In reform China, state and now private capitalists have tended to keep welfare budgets low, so that money could go into their investments instead. In Thailand, despite

---

[92]Dietrich Rueschemeyer *et al.*, *Capitalist Development and Democracy*, and Misgah Parsa, "Entrepreneurs and Democratization: Iran and the Philippines," *Comparative Studies in Society and History* 37:4 (Oct. 1995), 803–30.

[93]See Dietrich Rueschemeyer *et al.*, *Capitalist Development and Democracy*, 7–8, although the aim there is to explain democracy.

[94]David D. Yang, "Classing Ethnicity."

[95]T.H. Marshall described the stages by which citizenship expanded in England. At first, only elites were citizens in the sense that they had liberal freedoms to speak and to influence policy. Later, in a second era, all adults received rights to vote. This led, in a third period, to an expansion of welfare. See T.H. Marshall, *Citizenship and Social Class, and Other Essays* (Cambridge: Cambridge University Press, 1950).

universal franchise, industrialization has given far more resources for political organization to elites than to workers. Despite democratic formalities in the Philippines, the capacities of the rentier rich to forestall welfare have trumped the abilities of the needy to get more resources. Lively civil societies, pleas from intellectuals, street demos, and elections all bring scant social result. In the long run, commercial-industrial growth that has recently begun will shape even Philippine politics.

Factories in countries whose populations still spend part of their work time in agriculture at near-subsistence wages easily use "flexible production":[96] the factory-owning capitalists hire labor mainly in agrarian lax seasons, when it is cheap, and can lay off workers in economic periods when their own production is temporarily less profitable. Another kind of "flexible production" occurs when capitalists vary the kinds of jobs their workers do at different times. Either sort describes uses of power (managerial orders) within non-state networks. But the rise of flexible production in early industrialization also affects the state, because factory owners increase their wealth, which is used directly in either bureaucratic or democratic politics. Flexible production lay-offs impede the formation of workers' unions that are a crucial factor for the usual left-right form of politics, seen in all industrial countries that have large populations.

Nostalgia for the stability of pre-industrial patterns can become widespread during booms. Not until modern interests begin to hold larger political networks together, especially as entrepreneurs and workers organize, does politics become more predictable again. The problem of political chaos in the transitional stage is obvious in the Philippines, but it has been observed in many other countries previously.[97] If elite mobility in local politics has been stirred by new

---

[96]See Michael J. Piore and Charles F. Sabel, *The Second Industrial Divide: Possibilities for Prosperity* (New York: Basic Books, 1984). The term "flexible production" is used by scholars such as Frederic Deyo — and recently by constitutional lawyer Michael Dowdle. It has two different but related meanings, which the text explains.

[97]See Jon Elster, *Consequences of Constitutional Choice: Reflections on Tocqueville* (Chicago: University of Chicago Press, 1980).

wealth and new pretensions to social status, then near-term local repressions and later civil liberties are both likely to increase. Modernization does not have wholly unpredictable regime effects in the long run, particularly in sizeable countries whose local politics have been tossed by the experience of quick growth. Democracy depends on "a fairly strong institutional separation of the realm of politics from the overall system of inequality in society."[98] Neither military rule nor civilian money politics assures this division in a stable, institutionalized way — nor does free electoral competition, if votes can be bought. Unresolvable feuds between nonstate interests, especially labor and capital, have been the surest guarantees of stability in actual democracies that need to build strong institutions.

WHAT MAKES A STATE STRONG ENOUGH TO MEDIATE CONFLICT FAIRLY?

Economic development is a bumpy process, not a smooth or continuous one. Shocks are natural in it. After each of them, recovery is led mostly by entrepreneurs who find new technologies and markets. So economies cycle, but not regularly. Pioneering sectors drive each flow. After the inevitable later ebb, different sectors may (if other habits do not dampen the will to innovate) allow the surge of a fresh wave of growth.[99] This theory of economic circulation, set forth by Schumpeter, probably emerged from earlier ideas about elite circulation. Pareto realized that changes from conservative to reformist leaders, even in localities, could threaten large states. In an essay on "The Crumbling of Central Authority," he realized that businesses might erode sovereignties. As a conservative in an age of revolutions, though, he mainly thought that labor unions would do so. Unions might become "exempt from the enforcement of the laws

---

[98]Dietrich Reuschmeyer *et al.*, *Capitalist Development and Democracy*, 41.

[99]See Joseph A. Schumpeter, *The Theory of Economic Development* (New York: Oxford University Press, 1934), *Business Cycles* (New York: McGraw-Hill, 1939), and "The Creative Response in Economic History," *Journal of Economic History* 7:2 (1947), 149–59.

and regulations."[100] But in practice, businesses usually dominate modern states. Such a system functions best if workers' and entrepreneurs' representatives check each other in this stable separation of powers outside the state.

Booms also affect state strength, but the effects are not linear. More growth does not necessarily mean more strength in the state relative to other social networks, nor does it mean less state strength. Different aspects of capability can be considered.[101] Four types of state capability are evidenced by (1) revenues, (2) obedience by lower officials to higher ones rather than to other interests, (3) strong collective state elite norms, and (4) evidence that administration is effective. The first two of these four types deal, respectively, with the unintended situations and intended norms of individuals; the third and fourth deal with the intended norms or the unintended situations of elites considered together as a whole group.[102]

The Philippine government is weakest among the four cases considered in this book. (1) Even during the martial law era, when Marcos extracted more than was officially reported, the Philippine regime's revenues have been relatively low. (2) The personal identification of politicians, especially senators, with the government in Manila has ranged from very weak to violently oppositionist. (3) The elite has been fragmented regionally, so even politicians with national constituencies have strong local bases. (4) State agencies, especially coercive agencies, have often been superseded by local private militias.

---

[100]Vilfredo Pareto, *The Transformation of Democracy*, trans. Renata Girola (New Brunswick: Transaction Books, 1984), 37–54, and quote on 83.

[101]See Eric Nordlinger, "Taking the State Seriously," in *Understanding Political Development*, Myron Wiener and Samuel Huntington, eds. (Boston: Little, Brown, 1987), 353–90. Nordlinger lists four aspects of state strength/weakness: "malleability" by nonstate interests, "vulnerability" to societal unpopularity, "insulation" from a need for civil support, and "resilience" against potential opposition. The list in the text above differs from Nordlinger's but relates to it and may be easier to apply behaviorally.

[102]For a discussion of this kind of framework, which reduces four types to two dimensions, see Lynn White, *Unstately Power: Local Causes of China's Economic Reforms* (Armonk, NY: M.E. Sharpe, 1998), introduction.

The Philippine elite will have to allow entrepreneurs (even if they are Chinese-Filipinos) to change local politics autonomously from the interests of old families, before more democratic fairness emerges from that economic change. This could happen, if local leaders are forced to become less dominant.

A more diverse picture, on these four dimensions of state strength, is offered by places whose countrywide or local leaders have managed to accommodate recent economic booms. In Thailand, East China, and Taiwan, the various kinds of official strength are more mutually corroborative. Still, these states are not all strong in the same ways.

In Thailand,

(1) Revenue collection has been low, allowing capitalists to keep wealth they have partly reinvested. Thai taxes have been slowly regularized over more than a century, since King Chulalongkorn first attempted to extend civilian and military officers into provincial areas, where the tax base later became more modern during the boom.

(2) Much evidence shows identification with the triad of "nation, religion, king" by bureaucrats, soldiers, and even successive generations of Sino-Thai politicians. The ethnic marginality of most entrepreneurs may increase their personal wills to assimilate with Thailand and reject remaining bases of Thai discrimination against them.

(3) The boom has done little, however, to create more unity within the elite. Thai politics remains contentious, factionalized, litigious, sometimes violent, and plagued with scandals. Local and functional leaders' conflicts threaten the state much less than they would if Thailand did not now have a king whose actions during crises in 1992, 1997, and even 2006 further legitimated his power.

(4) Coercive functions that would normally be performed by the state's police have sometimes been performed by quasi-private militias (although less often than in the Philippines). This situation has been complex, because local notables who hire gunmen usually had connections with the government through elected MPs. The integration of these networks was particularly evident

under Thaksin. The franchising of state police and regulatory functions to Thai nonstate parties has been less destructive of the state than it would have been, if many local powers had not embedded themselves in the state.

East China presents a further variation of these patterns:

(1) Official revenues have risen along with the boom; and unofficial local imposts, including many that could be extracted illegally in the semi-market economy, have risen even faster. Local state resources became much greater than those of the central Chinese state, especially in the era from the mid-1980s collapse of official prices to the 1994 tax reform under Zhu Rongji. In this decade of boom, economic growth financed local networks more than they financed the central state.

(2) The traditional Chinese norm that locally prestigious people want to become state officials has remained strong. Party personnel departments now have somewhat less power in nonstate networks than they once had (despite their continuing dominance within the party-state), because jobs are now more widely available in economic units that are autonomous in market operations. Lenin reinvented traditional hinge leadership norms, making them seem modern because he devised a specific way to appoint personnel. If a large poor state lacked the informational resources to hold together as a fully centralized bureaucracy, it could nonetheless at each size of collectivity centralize to one higher level in the system. This gave an impression of unity, because it frightened all but the top cadre. Lenin's scalar approach to government worked in Eastern Europe for a long time. In China too, it will not last forever.

(3) Norms of harmony within local elites, and between them and the state elite, also remain fairly strong — or their weaknesses remain unprofitable to discuss.

(4) The mid-1980s end of Chinese socialism franchised many previous state functions to increasingly "local states," and then to openly private entrepreneurs. Welfare, housing, education, health

care, elder care, and even some security functions are now served privately with varying degrees of effectiveness.

Taiwan, which enjoys a higher per capita income than the other three places studied here, during its fastest boom had a state that was strong in yet different ways:

(1) The ROC in its 1963–73 peak performance period sustained an economic record that by any global comparison was spectacularly successful in both growth and equity. This furnished a strong tax base; and the state collected much money despite some tax evasions.

(2) The civil service has been generally led by technocrats who are even more highly educated than their typical counterparts in reform China. Taiwan's politicians, of many stripes, have striven to identify with their constituents' interests, even when they have used ethnic symbols to represent emerging class and security concerns.

(3) A great deal of disunity has been evident, and extensively publicized though lately decreasing, within Taiwan's elite along islander-mainlander ethnic lines. Fights in parliament dramatized conflicts in this democracy. Islanders' pride in their boom fueled this tension while it lasted.

(4) Although mafias and "black money politics" were evident in Taiwan especially during the periods of fastest economic growth, modern regulatory and coercive functions have now been monopolized by the government.

A rise of central state capacity is an important support of socioeconomic development that may lead, *if* leaders decide for this, to more liberal politics. This kind of strength comes in many forms, and political scientists would do well to explore their variety. A rise of *nonstate* capacity has been equally crucial, as have its types.

TOWARD A POLITICAL SCIENCE THAT INCLUDES NONSTATE CHANGE

The state sector in China was once more important than it has ever been in Thailand, the Philippines, or even Taiwan. Big firms and official agencies nonetheless receive a great deal of analytic attention, because they are better-documented than SMEs. Similarly, the links of farmers and land reforms to industrialization (or its lack) have drawn some academic attention, but not enough. Also, there has been insufficient study of the extent to which booms are bumpy; economies growing quickly over decades may nonetheless show tremendous year-to-year variation. Above all, booms have been presented as mainly economic, not political. When, as in Japan, the government has been crucial in guiding growth, politics has been given credit for the developmental results. But when the relevant leadership has been in small or rural collectivities, as it largely has been in the places this book studies, power has been neglected as a factor of development. Political scientists have been slow to treat influence as political when it is out of the public eye or local. The "literature" on development is too statist and too narrowly economic. Booms are mainly political, and local politics is powerful politics.

Preferences for obvious authorities, and for quantitative work that requires fixed definitions, have hindered understanding in political economy. The epistemological emphasis of most social scientists inherently gives them some conservative bias even if they do not want that. It is revealing that prominent analytic philosophers such as Ludwig Wittgenstein or A.J. Ayer in their mature years recanted their exclusively logical enthusiasms of youth, realizing that "clouds of meaning" are the actual bases for communication, and rejecting the notion that the whole meaning of a proposition must be contained in the procedure by which external observers try to verify it.[103] But their opening has not affected most social scientists' positivism yet. Studies of power will become more cogent when political science returns to

---

[103]Contrast Ludwig Wittgenstein most mature book, *Philosophical Investigations* (New York: Macmillan, 1953) with his less practical *Tractatus Logico-Philosophicus* (London: Routledge, 1974 reprint [orig. 1922]), which has had a deeper and unfortunate effect on political scientists because it provides an ideology (an incomplete one) for managing careers and the "discipline." Or contrast A.J. Ayer, *Language, Truth, and Logic* (New York: Dover, 1952) with Ayer's taped BBC interviews shortly before his death ("Bryan Magee Talks to A.J. Ayer about Frege, Russell, and Modern Logic," videorecording, London: BBC, 1987). Wittgenstein in particular became more circumspect, but most social scientists have not yet understood the reasons.

include research on specific informal institutions and methods of synthesis.

Distanced, positivist proofs that are still *de rigueur* in the profession are tried by models that the researcher has constructed and therefore can understand. Yet these models can be deduced as true only at probability, at less than full confidence. That problem is parallel to the difficulty of the alternative method, the inductive, "soak and poke," synthetic approach, relying on the hope that a social scientist (being human like the subjects of investigation) can try to replicate their perceptions in his or her own head. Since the researcher is not those subjects, however, that method is also unsure. Both approaches produce science, which means knowledge (*scientia*) rather than the method of obtaining it.

The anti-scientific attitude would be to reject either the deductive natural science method or the inductive human science one, before seeing what each can contribute to knowledge. Such repudiations of useful methods are now rife in social studies. Many anthropologists, for instance, now claim that all knowledge about humans must be reducible to intended and changeable notions (especially cultures), and that unintended situations are beyond the range of disciplined thought. Most political scientists, many sociologists, and apparently all economists now have the opposite prejudice: that "interesting" discoveries come only from proving the usual validity of models about unintended situations that generate behavior. Both of these narrow approaches are useful, so neither is justifiable as exclusive.

Because this book is about politics, and because political science (especially among Americanists) has become epistemologically challenged, four anti-scientific biases require explicit refutations.

— No divine tablet commands belief in the validity of explanations only if they are expressed in terms of the processes of individuals. None commands disbelief that explanations can derive the preferences of individuals from the processes of collective groups (such as families, congregations, or nations).
— No divine tablet commands belief in the validity of explanations only if they are expressed in terms of changes in unintended situations.

None mandates disbelief that valid explanations can equally be expressed in terms of intended norms and habits (including institutions).

— None commands disbelief in specific, documentable truths from particular places until they have been processed as valid deductions from general laws that apply everywhere.

— None commands disbelief in specific, evidenced truths from particular times until they have been presented as valid deductions from general laws that apply eternally.

"Methodological individualism" is no stronger in epistemological terms than is methodological collectivism, although perhaps to some it seems more patriotically American or politically liberal. As regards the first and second dubious commandments above: the frequent habit of denigrating "culturalist" explanations in social science has gone so far that most anthropologists, either put off because they were ostracized or perhaps seeing professional advantages in championing an opposite academic fad, no longer call themselves social scientists. Economists and most political scientists unfailingly react as did Hitler's aide Hermann Göring: "When I hear the word 'culture,' I reach for my gun." That is the behavioral law they prove. But this prejudice is, as a method for finding truth, no stronger than the view that human action can be understood only through the interpretation of human meanings. As regards the third and fourth fake commandments above, recent efforts to read space (and geographers) or time (and historians) out of social science apparently relate more to academic institutions' budgeting than to anything that is intellectually defensible.

All serious students of society or politics actually pay close attention to both individuals and groups, both norms and situations. They hope to find both general and specific truths that will benefit people. Professional ideologies should not obstruct this search.[104] Political

---

[104]See Karl Mannheim, *Ideology and Utopia*, which defines ideology as a set of beliefs whose partial untruth its advocates know but hide from themselves, because doing so brings them immediate (not long-term) advantages. It is intellectually wrong to remain silent, when a science is in danger of becoming an ideology.

scientists should not fear to study the intellectual effects of their own disciplinary institutions.

"Bringing the state back in" to political discourse means that socioeconomic factors are no longer treated as mystical spirits, embodied in no actors. Bringing *politics* back in would be an even better idea, because power relations outside the state very strongly affect public decisions. Unstately powers are formed in modern development, and they mingle with the powers of the government.[105] Democratization can be studied in terms of the groups and individuals who initiate it. It also needs to be studied in terms of the contexts that affect their intentions and give them resources. Many actors who shape the state over time are not in it.

TOWARD A POLITICAL SCIENCE THAT INCLUDES SPECIFIC RESEARCH ON PLACES

A distinction between democratic and dictatorial systems is often supposed by political scientists to be the basic frame for discussion of all other differences in comparative politics. But many citizens of China, Thailand, the Philippines, and even Taiwan do not come with this presumption. It is possible to distinguish leaders, parties, and regimes on many grounds: whether they are benign or scary, whether they can foster both freedom and order with prosperity, and whether they represent their country's perceived political culture. Ordinary citizens, unlike most social scientists, are willing to find consequences in cultures.

Bruce Gilley looked at 72 governments at the turn of the millennium to calculate their "legitimacy scores." He used responses to questions about popular views of legal predictability, system support, and consent as measured by tax payments and voting turnouts. A standard

---

[105]"Bringing politics back in" is also a theme of Prof. Ahn Chung-si. See his "Democratization and Political Reform in Korea: Development, Culture, Leadership, and Institutional Change," in *Korea in the Global Wave of Democratization*, Doh Chull Shin, Myeong-han Zho, and Myung Chey, eds. (Seoul: Seoul National University Press, 1994), 177, for example.

number-crunch for these 72 places put Taiwan and China, perhaps surprisingly, just next to each other, both high at ranks 12 and 13.[106] The Philippines also does well in this calculation, ranking 26th. Thailand is not part of the sample, but its government at the time of the 1990s surveys was at least as popular as those of the other three places under study. Ordinary people in these polities, despite their differences, are reasonably content and hopeful.

Prominent among the criteria that citizens use to judge their governments is the issue of whether the regime has fostered wealth for them, even though money is not the sole factor of happiness.[107] At various times and places, both democratic and dictatorial regimes have done well or badly in this respect. The bipartite categorization of all governments as essentially liberal or illiberal has caught some part of political development but fails to catch much of it. The current orthodox emphases in political science are distinctive of the political culture of one nation: America. U.S. scholars did not start out to make their academic discipline a patriotic ideology — and as perhaps this book shows, they have not entirely done so. But they have fostered many versions of the idea that all politics is basically a problem of voting. Only some politics takes that form. Exploiting, hoodwinking/brainwashing, and scaring are also political, as are preaching or inspiring.

In the countries under study here, economic booms had political origins largely in local, nonstate power networks. The wealth that small and medium enterprises created has temporarily strengthened these local polities. They have often been able to buy elections or bureaucrats. In the past, political scientists usually failed to link the

---

[106]Bruce Gilley, *States and Legitimacy: The Politics of Moral Authority* (Ph.D. dissertation, Politics Department, Princeton University, January 2007), Tables 1–3, 23. Taiwan and China had scores of 6.62 and 6.58 respectively; less than top-ranked Denmark at 7.62, but very far from bottom-ranked Russia at 2.27. The scale is from 10 to 0; the methodology is complex and is described in the thesis appendix.

[107]Perry, Elizabeth J., "Chinese Conceptions of 'Rights': From Mencius to Mao — and Now," *Perspectives on Politics*, 6:1 (March 2008), 37–47.

power of business or family networks to governments. When discussing democracy, they have therefore provided an incomplete account of it, especially when explaining how fairness may be delivered by elections. Research on four places cannot fill all the gaps that need to be filled, but it can point to the epistemological hangups that have tended to make professionals think less substantively than they could about modern change.

Readers will want to know what politics to expect from booms in the future. Nobody can be sure. The present author is an optimist and a communitarian liberal. Yet booms can lead to wars, and the mechanisms by which they may engender liberal tolerance are complex. If China were to suffer an economic recession because its banking system had failed (as some have predicted in practically every year since 1989), this could cause a sharp reversion to patriotic centralism, probably under a nationalist and socialist dictator. Elite decisions by individuals are not easy to predict. If China's reformers were all Nelson Mandelas (and if the opposition conservatives showed some flexibility, as F.W. de Klerk did in South Africa's transition to democracy), then the prospects of a more tolerant PRC regime would be bright. That possibility is neither excluded nor certain, on current evidence. Taiwan already has institutions that constrain its leaders. The same logic predicting bumpy progress also applies to Thailand — and to the Philippines, even though certainty is unavailable about what will happen in any of these places. Some social scientists suggest the availability of crystal balls that might let them see future events. General "laws" of political science are hard to find, though, and research on specific places would anyway be necessary for understanding them.

History will not end through any single process. Globalization and democratization occur, but they suggest political agendas that are not final. Intellectuals like to look for simple keys to eternal truth, but happily the world is more complex than that. Post-modern and then post-post-modern forms of politics that nobody yet knows are likely to become more obvious later. It is the prestige of claiming a last analysis, and the power that such truth might legitimate, that makes many thinkers into eschatologists. More important, citizens will continue to press for local and central regimes that are fair to them. Elections will eventually aid their cause, but only if these are combined with other liberal institutions that optimize the balances among many public and private powers.

SOURCES

Aside from books and articles, other essential bases for this study were interviews in Taipei, Shanghai, various Zhejiang cities especially during a 2006 trip, Bangkok and Chiangmai in Thailand, Manila and Quezon City in the Philippines, Hong Kong, Princeton, and elsewhere. Interviewees have been cited among the acknowledgements, near the title page, and I am very thankful to them. Chinese authors' names are recorded as in normal text, and Thai authors are alphabetized by their personal names (as they are usually cited in Thai writing and conversation). Books or articles comparing different Southeast Asian countries, or comparing Taiwan and China, are listed appropriately with other comparative books.

This bibliography alphabetizes East Asian authors, unless they individually prefer Western names, as they are cited when people speak. So Thai personal names go first, and Chinese, Japanese, or Korean family names go first (without commas, since that order is normal in ordinary speech). In the text, short references to people follow the same rule. Until Chinese begin referring to Zedong Mao, or Thais to Shinawatra without his main name, these procedures are less counterintuitive. Names of persons and places in mainland China are offered in pinyin romanization. Those in Taiwan are offered (unless authors' or maps' common usage is different) in the island's most frequent romanization, the Wade–Giles system, omitting hyphens except in personal names. The bibliography is categorized first according to the four main places studied in this book, then according to three additional lists of comparative sources: one comparing Asian countries, a second on globalist issues (including democratization, corruption, and SMEs), and a third on sources that explicitly or implicitly stress epistemological issues in the study of politics.

SOURCES ON TAIWAN

Amsden, Alice H., "The State and Taiwan's Economic Development," in *Bringing the State Back In*, Peter Evans, Dietrich Rueschemeyer, and Theda Skocpol, eds. (Cambridge: Cambridge University Press, 1985), pp. 78–106.

Andrade, Tonio, *How Taiwan Became Chinese: Dutch, Spanish, and Han Colonization in the Seventeenth Century* (New York: Columbia University Press, 2005).

Anon., "Poll: 70 Percent Want to Start Own Businesses to Pursue Fortune, Self-Fulfillment," *Taiwan Update* 5:5, May 10, 2004, p. 9.

Arrigo, Linda Gail [wife of DPP leader Shih Ming-teh], "From Democratic Movement to Bourgeois Democracy: The Internal Politics of the Taiwan Democratic Progressive Party in 1991," in *The Other Taiwan: 1945 to the Present*, Rubinstein, Murray, ed. (Armonk: Sharpe, 1994), pp. 145–82.

Arthorpe, R., "The Burden of Land Reform in Taiwan: An Asian Model Reanalyzed," *World Development* 7 (1979), pp. 519–30.

Bain, Irene, *Agricultural Reform in Taiwan: From Here to Modernity?* (Hong Kong: Chinese University Press, 1993).

Biggart, Nicole Woolsey, and Gary Hamilton, "On the Limits of a Firm-Based Theory to Explain Business Networks: The Western Bias of Neoclassical Economics," in *The Economic Organization of East Asian Capitalism*, Marco Orrù, Nicole Woolsey Biggart, and Gary Hamilton, eds. (Thousand Oaks: Sage, 1997), pp. 33–54.

Bosco, Joseph, "Taiwan Factions: *Guanxi*, Patronage, and the State in Local Politics," in *The Other Taiwan: 1945 to the Present*, Rubinstein, Murray, ed. (Armonk: Sharpe, 1994), pp. 114–44.

Bush, Richard C., *Untying the Knot: Making Peace in the Taiwan Strait* (Washington: Brookings Institution Press, 2005).

Cabestan, Jean-Pierre, "From Missiles to Missives," *China Perspectives* 17 (June–July 1998), pp. 22–29.

Cabestan, Jean-Pierre, "The KMT, a Minority Party," *China Perspectives* 15 (January–February 1998), pp. 38–48.

Ch'ü Ming, *2010 nian liangan tongyi: Zhonggong maixiang haiquan shidai* (Unification of the Two Shores in 2010: The Era When Chinese Communism Leaps to Sea Power) (Taipei: Jiuyi, 1995).

Chan, Gordon Hou-sheng, "The Relationship of Social Security System to Economic Development, with Special Reference to Hong Kong, Singapore, and Taiwan," *Journal of Sociology* (National Taiwan University) No. 13 (1979), pp. 139–50.

Chang Mau-Kuei, "Middle Class and Social and Political Movements in Taiwan," in *Discovery of the Middle Classes in East Asia*, Michael Hsiao Hsin-huang, ed. (Taipei: Ethnology Institute, Academia Sinica, 1994), pp. 121–76.

Chang Mau-kuei, "Toward an Understanding of the *Sheng-chi Wen-ti* in Taiwan," in *Ethnicity in Taiwan*, Chen Chung-min, *et al.*, eds. (Taipei: Institute of Ethnology, Academia Sinica, 1994).

Chang Mau-kuei, *Shehui yundong yu zhengzhi juanhua* (Taipei: Guojia Zhengce Yanjiu Ziliao Zhongxin, 1989).

Chen Chung-min, *Upper Camp: A Study of a Chinese Mixed Cropping Village in Taiwan* (Taipei: Institute of Ethnology, Academia Sinica, 1977).

Chen Ming-tong and Lin Chi-wen, *"Taiwan difang xuanju de qiyuan yu guojia shehui guanxi juanbian* (The Origins of Taiwan District Elections and Changes in State-Society Relations)," in *Liangan jiceng xuanju yu zhengzhi shehui bianqian* (Basic Level Elections and the Transformation of Political Society on the Two Shores [Mainland and Taiwan]), Chen Ming-tong and Zheng Yongnian, eds. (Taipei: Yuedan, 1998), pp. 23–70.

Chen Ming-tong, *"Jitseng xuanju, difang paixi yu wailai zhengquan de shengcun fazhan moshi: Dui Taiwan zhengzhi minzhuhua de chongxin pinggu* (Elections at the Basic Level, Regional Factions and the Survival Development Pattern of a Foreign Regime: A Reappraisal of the Democratization of Taiwan Politics)," in *Liangan jiceng xuanju yu zhengzhi shehui bianqian* (Basic Level Elections and the Transformation of Political Society on the Two Shores [Mainland and Taiwan]), Chen Ming-tong and Zheng Yongnian, eds. (Taipei: Yuedan, 1998), pp. 3–22.

Chen Ming-tong, *Paixi zhengzhi yu Taiwan zhengzhi bianqian* (Factional Politics and Change in Taiwan Politics) (Taipei: Yuedan, 1995).

Chen Shih-meng, *et al.*, *Jiegou: Dang-guo ziben zhuyi: Lun Taiwan guanying shiye zhi minguan hua* (Disintegrating KMT-State Capitalism: A Closer

Look at Privatizing Taiwan's State- and Party-Owned Enterprises [trans. in original]) (Taipei: Chengshe Baogao, 1991).

Chen Yi-yan and Huang Li-ch'iu, *Xuanju xingwei yu zhengzhi fazhan* (Voting Behavior and Political Development) (Taipei: Liming Wenhua, 1992).

Cheng Jui-cheng, *et al.*, *Jiegou: Guangbo meiti* (Deconstruction of [Taiwan's] Broadcast Media) (Taipei: Chengshe Baogao, 1993).

Cheng Tun-jen and Chou Tein-cheng, "Informal Politics in Taiwan," in *Informal Politics in East Asia*, Lowell Dittmer, Fukui Haruhiro, and Peter Lee, eds. (New York: Cambridge University Press), pp. 42–65.

Cheng Tun-jen and Hsu Yung-ming, "Issue Structure, DPP Factionalism, and Party Realignment" (Durham, NC: Working Papers in Taiwan Studies, 1994).

Cheng Tun-jen and Stephan Haggard, "Regime Transformation in Taiwan: Theoretical and Comparative Perspectives," in *Political Change in Taiwan*, Cheng Tun-jen and Stephan Haggard, eds. (Boulder: Lynne Rienner, 1992), pp. 1–32.

Cheng Tun-jen, "Taiwan in Democratic Transition," in *Driven by Growth: Political Change in the Asia-Pacific Region*, James Morley, ed. (Armonk: M.E. Sharpe, 1993), pp. 193–218.

Chu, J.J., "Taiwan: A Fragmented 'Middle' Class in the Making," in *Culture and Privilege in Capitalist Asia*, Michael Pinches, ed. (New York: Routledge, 1999), pp. 207–24.

Chu Yin-wah, "Democracy and Organized Labor in Taiwan: The 1986 Transition," *Asian Survey* 36:5 (May 1996), pp. 495–510.

Chu Yin-wah, "Ideology and Organization in the Oppositional Movements of Taiwan and South Korea," unpublished paper from the author, Department of Sociology, University of Hong Kong, 1997.

Chu Yun-han, "*Cong dangguo tizhi dau zhipeixing yidang tizhi: Guomindang yu Taiwan de minzhu juanxing* (From a Party-State System to a Dominant One-Party System: The Kuomintang and Taiwan's Democratic Transformation)," in *Liangan jiceng xuanju yu zhengzhi she-hui bianqian* (Basic Level Elections and the Transformation of Political Society on the Two Shores [Mainland and Taiwan]), Chen Ming-tong and Zheng Yongnian, eds. (Taipei: Yuedan, 1998), pp. 261–86.

Chu Yun-han, "Social Protests and Political Democratization in Taiwan," in *The Other Taiwan: 1945 to the Present*, Rubinstein, Murray, ed. (Armonk: Sharpe, 1994), pp. 99–113.

Chu Yun-han, "State Structure and Economic Adjustment in the East Asian Newly Industrializing Countries," in *Business and Government in*

Industrializing Asia, Andrew MacIntyre, ed. (Ithaca: Cornell University Press, 1994), pp. 247–62.

Chu Yun-han, "Taiwan's Unique Challenges," in *Democracy in East Asia*, Larry Diamond and Eric Plattner, eds. (Baltimore: Johns Hopkins University Press, 1998), pp. 133–46.

Chu Yun-han, "The Realignment of Business-Government Relations and Regime Transition in Taiwan," in *Business and Government in Industrializing Asia*, Andrew MacIntyre, ed. (Ithaca: Cornell University Press, 1994), pp. 113–143.

Chu Yun-han, "The State and the Development of the Automobile Industry in South Korea and Taiwan, in *The Role of the State in Taiwan's Development*, Joel D. Aberbach, *et al.*, eds. (Armonk: Sharpe, 1994), pp. 125–69.

Chu Yun-han, *Crafting Democracy in Taiwan* (Taipei: National Policy Research Institute, 1992).

Chyu Li-ho and Douglas C. Smith, "Secondary Academic Education," in *The Confucian Continuum: Educational Modernization in Taiwan*, Douglas C. Smith, ed. (New York: Praeger, 1991), pp. 99–166.

Cohen, Myron L, *House United, House Divided: The Chinese Family in Taiwan* (New York: Columbia University Press, 1976).

Cole, Allan B., "The Political Roles of Taiwanese Entrepreneurs," *Asian Survey* 7 (September 1967), pp. 645–54.

Contemporary Taiwan, special issue of *China Quarterly* 148 (December 1996).

Contending Approaches to the Political Economy of Taiwan, Edwin A. Winckler and Susan Greenhalgh, ed. (Armonk: Sharpe, 1988).

Copper, John F., *Taiwan's Mid-1990s Elections* (Westport, Conn.: Praeger, 1998).

Dessus, Sébastien, Jia-Dong Shea, and Mau-Shan Shi, *Chinese Taipei* [a.k.a. Taiwan]*: The Origins of the Economic "Miracle"* (Paris: OECD, 1995).

Diamond, Norma, *K'un Shen: A Taiwan Village* (New York: Holt, Rinehart, and Winston, 1969).

Difang shehui (Local Society), Tunghai University East Asia Socioeconomic Research Center, ed. (Taipei: Lianjing, 1997).

Discovery of the Middle Classes in East Asia, Michael Hsiao Hsin-huang, ed. (Taipei: Ethnology Institute, Academia Sinica, 1994).

Domes, Jürgen, "Political Differentiation in Taiwan: Group Formation within the Ruling Party and the Opposition, 1979–1980," *Asian Survey* 21:10 (October 1981), pp. 1011–28.

Economic Development in Taiwan, Kowie Chang, ed. (Taipei: Cheng Chung Book Co., 1968).

Feng Hua-nong, *Taiwan de zhongji mingyun* (The Determinative Fate of Taiwan [trans. in orig.]), (Taipei: Shengzhi, 1996).

Fields, Karl, "Strong States and Business Organization in Korea and Taiwan," in *Business and the State in Developing Countries* Sylvia Maxfield and Ben Ross Schneider, eds. (Ithaca: Cornell University Press, 1997), pp. 122–50.

Gallin, Bernard, "Land Reform in Taiwan: Its Effect on Rural Social Organization and Leadership," *Human Organization* 22 (Summer 1963), pp. 109–12.

Gallin, Rita S., and Bernard Gallin, "Hsin Hsing Village, Taiwan: From Farm to Factory," in *Chinese Landscapes: The Village as Place*, Ronald G. Knapp, ed. (Honolulu: University of Hawaii Press, 1992), pp. 279–94.

Gates, Hill, "Small Fortunes: Class and Society in Taiwan," in *Taiwan: Beyond the Economic Miracle*, Dennis Simon and Y.M Kao, eds. (Armonk: Sharpe, 1992), pp. 169–86.

Geldenhuys, Deon, *Isolated States: A Comparative Analysis* (Cambridge: Cambridge University Press, 1990).

Ger Yeong-kuang, *Zhengdang zhengzhi yu minzhu fazhan* (Party Politics and Democratic Development) (Taipei: Guoli Kongjun Daxue, 1996).

Gold, Thomas B., "Colonial Origins of Taiwanese Capitalism," in *Contending Approaches to the Political Economy of Taiwan*, Edwin A. Winckler and Susan Greenhalgh, eds. (Armonk: Sharpe, 1988), pp. 101–20.

Gold, Thomas B., "Entrepreneurs, Multinationals, and the State," in *Contending Approaches to the Political Economy of Taiwan*, Edwin A. Winckler and Susan Greenhalgh, eds. (Armonk: Sharpe, 1988), pp. 175–205.

Gold, Thomas B., *State and Society in the Taiwan Miracle* (Armonk: M.E. Sharpe, 1986).

Greenhalgh, Susan, "De-Orientalizing the Chinese Family Firm," *American Ethnologist* 21:4 (1994), pp. 746–75.

Greenhalgh, Susan, "Families and Networks in Taiwan's Economic Development," in *Contending Approaches to the Political Economy of Taiwan*, Edwin A. Winckler and Susan Greenhalgh, eds. (Armonk: Sharpe, 1988), pp. 224–45.

Guiheux, Gilles, "Enterprises, Entrepreneurs, and Social Networks in Taiwan," in *Politics in China: Moving Frontiers*, Françoise Mengin and Jean-Louis Rocca, eds. (New York: Palgrave Macmillan, 2002), pp. 187–211.

Guiheux, Gilles, *Les grands entrepreneurs privés à Taiwan: la main visible de la prospérité* (Paris: Phénix, 2003).

Guofang baipishu (National Defense White Paper), Taiwan Research Foundation National Defense Research Small Group, ed. (Taipei: Taiwan Yanjiu Jijinhui, 1992).

Haggard, Stephan, and Chien-Kuo Pang, "The Transition to Export-Led Growth in Taiwan," in *The Role of the State in Taiwan's Development*, Joel D. Aberbach, *et al.*, eds. (Armonk: Sharpe, 1994), pp. 47–89.

Hamilton, Gary, "Organization and Market Processes in Taiwan's Capitalist Economy," in *The Economic Organization of East Asian Capitalism*, Marco Orrù, Nicole Woolsey Biggart, and Gary Hamilton, eds. (Thousand Oaks: Sage, 1997), pp. 237–96.

Hamilton, Gary, *Chinese Capitalism: The Organization of Chinese Economics* (London: Routledge, 2002).

Ho Shuet Ying, *Taiwan: After a Long Silence the Emerging New Unions of Taiwan* (Hong Kong: Asia Monitor Research Centre, 1990).

Ho Yhi-min, "The Production Structure of the Manufacturing Sector and its Distribution Implications," *Economic Development and Cultural Change* 28:2 (January 1980), pp. 321–43.

Ho, Samuel P.S., "Decentralized Industrialization and Rural Development: Evidence from Taiwan," *Economic Development and Cultural Change* 28:1 (1979), pp. 77–96.

Hood, Steven J., *The Kuomintang and the Democratization of Taiwan* (Boulder: Westview, 1997).

Hsiao Chuan-cheng, *Taiwan diqu de xin chongshang zhuyi* (Neo-mercantilism in the Taiwan Area) (Taipei: Guojia Zhengce Yanjiu Ziliao Zhongxin, 1989).

Hsiao Hsin-huang, "Normative Conflicts in Contemporary Taiwan," chapter for *Normative Conflicts: The Frontiers of Social Cohesion*, Bertelsman Science Foundation, Germany, May 1996.

Hsiao Hsin-Huang, "The Rise of Social Movements and Civil Protests," in *Political Change in Taiwan*, Tun-jen Cheng and Stephan Haggard, eds. (Boulder: Lynne Rienner, 1992), pp. 57–72.

Hsiao Hsin-huang, *Government Agricultural Strategies in Taiwan and South Korea: A Macrosociological Assessment* (Taipei: Institute of Ethnology, Academia Sinica, 1981).

Hsiao Hsin-huang, *et al.*, *Longduan yu boxiao: Weiquan zhuyi de zhengzhi jingji fenxi* (Monopoly and Exploitation: A Political-Economic Analysis of Authoritarianism) (Taipei: Taiwan Yanjiu Jijinhui, 1989).

Hsiao Hsin-huang, L. Milbrath, and R. Weller, "Antecedents of an Environmental Movement in Taiwan," in *Capitalism, Nature, Socialism* 6:3 (September 1995), pp. 91–104.

Hsiao Hsin-huang, Michael, and Alvin Y. So, *Taiwan-Mainland Economic Nexus: Socio-Political Origins, State-Society Impacts, and Future Prospects* (Shatin: Hong Kong Chinese University, Institute of Asia-Pacific Studies Occasional Paper No. 37, 1994).

Hsieh, John Fuh-shen, and Emerson M.S. Niou, "Salient Issues in Taiwan's Electoral Politics" (Durham, NC: Working Papers in Taiwan Studies, 1994).

Hsiung Ping-Chun, *Living Rooms as Factories: Class, Gender, and the Satellite Factory System in Taiwan* (Philadelphia: Temple University Press, 1996).

Hsü Chieh-lin, *Zhengdang zhengzhi de zhixu yu lunli* (Platforms and Principles in the Politics of [Taiwan's] Parties) (Taipei: Guojia Zhengce Yanjiu Zhongxin, 1997).

Hsü Huo-yen, "*Taiwan de xuanju yu shehui fenqi jiegou: Zhengdang jingzheng yu minzhuhua* (Elections and the Structure of Social Differences in Taiwan: Political Party Competition and Democratization)," in *Liangan jiceng xuanju yu zhengzhi shehui bianqian* (Basic Level Elections and the Transformation of Political Society on the Two Shores [Mainland and Taiwan]), Chen Ming-tong and Zheng Yongnian, eds. (Taipei: Yuedan, 1998), pp. 127–168.

Hsü Jui-hsi, *Zhengshang guanxi jiedu* (Understanding Political-Commercial Relations [in Taiwan]) (Taipei: Yuanliu Chubanshe, 1991).

Hu Fu and Chu-yun Han, "Electoral Competition and Political Democratization," in *Political Change in Taiwan*, Cheng Tun-jen and Stephan Haggard, eds. (Boulder: Lynne Rienner, 1992), pp. 177–206.

Huang Shu-ming, *Agricultural Degradation: Changing Community Systems in Rural Taiwan* (Washington DC: University Press of America, 1981).

Huang, Mab, *Intellectual Ferment for Political Reforms in Taiwan, 1971–1973* (Ann Arbor: University of Michigan Papers in Chinese Studies, 1976).

Hughes, Christopher, *Taiwan and Chinese Nationalism: National Identity and Status in International Society* (London: Routledge, 1997).

Hwang, Y. Dolly, *The Rise of a New World Economic Power: Postwar Taiwan* (New York: Greenwood, 1991).

In the Shadow of China: Political Developments in Taiwan Since 1949, Steve Tsang, ed. (Honolulu: University of Hawaii Presss, 1993), esp. article by Hu Fu.

Industrialization and the State: The Changing Role of the Taiwan Government in the Economy, 1945–1998, Li-min Hsueh, Chen-kuo Hsu, and Dwight H. Perkins, eds. (Cambridge: Harvard Institute for International Development, 2001).

Jacobs, J. Bruce, "Recent Leadership and Political Trends in Taiwan," *China Quarterly* 45 (January-March 1971),

Jacobs, J. Bruce, *Local Politics in a Rural Chinese Cultural Setting: A Field Study of Mazu Township, Taiwan* (Canberra: Contemporary China Centre, ANU, 1980).

Johnson, Marshall, "Classification, Power, and Markets: Waning of the Ethnic Division of Labor on Taiwan," in *Taiwan: Beyond the Economic Miracle*, Dennis Simon and Ying-mau Kao, eds. (Armonk: Sharpe, 1992), pp. 69–97.

Jordan, David K., and Daniel L. Overmyer, *The Flying Phoenix: Aspects of Chinese Sectarianism in Taiwan* (Princeton: Princeton University Press, 1986).

Kerr, George H., *Formosa Betrayed* (Boston: Houghton Mifflin, 1965).

Kuan Ta-kung, *Xuanju zhandou jiqi* (Instruments of Electoral Struggle) (Taipei; Pingshi, 1995).

Kuo Cheng-tian, "Private Governance in Taiwan," (Durham, NC: Working Papers in Taiwan Studies, 1994).

Lai Tse-han, Ramon H. Myers, and Wei Wou, *A Tragic Beginning: The Taiwan Uprising of February 28, 1947* (Stanford: Hoover Institution Press, 1991).

Leng Shao-chuan and Lin Cheng-yi, "Political Change on Taiwan: Transition to Democracy?" *China Quarterly* 136 (December 1993), pp. 805–39.

Leng Tse-kang, *The Taiwan-China Connection* (Boulder: Westview, 1996).

Lerman, Arthur J., "National Elite and Local Politician in Taiwan," *American Political Science Review* 71:4 (1977), pp. 1406–22.

Lerman, Arthur J., *Political, Traditional, and Modern Economic Groups, and the Taiwan Provincial Assembly* (Ph.D. dissertation, Politics Department, Princeton University, 1972).

Lerman, Arthur J., *Taiwan's Politics: The Provincial Assemblyman's World* (Washington: University Press of America, 1979).

Li Hui-jung, *Taiwan zhengzhi guancha* (Observations on Taiwan Politics) (Taipei: Qianwei, 1997).

Liangan jiceng xuanju yu zhengzhi shehui bianqian (Basic Level Elections and the Transformation of Political Society on the Two Shores [Mainland and Taiwan]), Chen Ming-tong and Zheng Yongnian, eds. (Taipei: Yuedan, 1998).

Lin Cheng-yi, "The Taiwan Factor in Asia-Pacific Regional Security," in *North-East Asian Regional Security: The Role of International Institutions* T. Inoguchi and G. Stillman, eds. (Tokyo: United Nations University Press, 1995), pp. 98–117.

Lin Gang, "Taiwan's Power Reconfiguration and its Impact on Cross-Strait Relations," *Journal of Chinese Political Science* 6:1 (Spring 2000), pp. 17–36.

Lin Pin-yan, *Taiwan Dianli Zhushihui fazhan shi* (History of the Development of the Taiwan Power Company, Inc.) (Taipei: Taiwan Dianli Zhushihui She Ziliao Zhongxin, 1997).

Lin Wan-I, "Labor Movement and Taiwan's Belated Welfare State," *Journal of International and Comparative Social Welfare* 7:1 (1992), pp. 31–44.

Liu Fu-shan, *Building a Farmers' Organization in a Developing Country: The Taiwan Experience* (Taipei: Maw Chang Book Co., 1995).

Liu I-chou, "Generational Divergence and Party Image among the Taiwan Electorate," *Issues and Studies* 31:2 (February 1995), pp. 87–114.

Liu I-Chou, "Public Attitudes on the Unification Issue and Presidential Preference in Taiwan," paper for a conference at the Centre of Asian Studies, University of Hong Kong, February 1996.

Liu Li-wei, *The Growth and Transformation of Small and Medium Enterprises in Taiwan: Reassessment and Analysis from a Spatial Perspective* (Ph.D. Dissertation, Cornell University, 2000).

Liu, Alan P.L., *The Phoenix and the Lame Lion: Modernization in Taiwan and Mainland China, 1950–1980* (Stanford: Hoover Institute Press, 1989).

Lo Chih-cheng, "Taiwan: The Remaining Challenges," in *Coercion and Governance: The Declining Political Role of the Military in Asia* (Stanford: Stanford University Press, 2001), pp. 143–64.

Lü Ronghai, *Zhonghua Taiwan guolian* (United Republics of China and Taiwan [trans. in original]) (Taipei: Shinian hui, 1995).

Mark, Lindy Li, *Taiwanese Lineage Enterprises: A Study of Familial Entrepreneurship* (Ph.D. dissertation, Anthropology Department, University of California, Berkeley, 1972).

Marsh, Robert M., *The Great Transformation: Social Change in Taipei, Taiwan, Since the 1960s* (Armonk: M.E. Sharpe, 1996).

Martz, John, "Taiwanese Campaigning and Elections, 1991: An Outsider's View," *Studies in Comparative International Development* 27:2 (Summer 1992), pp. 84–94.

McBeath, Gerald A., *Wealth and Freedom: Taiwan's New Political Economy* (Aldershot: Ashgate, 1998).

Mendel, Douglas, *The Politics of Formosan Nationalism* (Berkeley: University of California Press, 1970).

Mengin, Françoise, "Taiwanese Politics and the Chinese Market: Business's Part in the Formation of a State, or the Border as a Stake of Negotiations," in *Politics in China: Moving Frontiers*, Françoise Mengin and Jean-Louis Rocca, eds. (New York: Palgrave Macmillan, 2002), pp. 232–57.

Moody, Peter, *Political Change on Taiwan: Ruling Party Adaptability* (New York: Praeger, 1992).

Numazaki Ichiro, "The Role of Personal Networks in the Making of Taiwan's *Guanxiqiye* (Related Enterprises)," in *Asian Business Networks*, Gary G. Hamilton, ed. (Berlin: de Gruyter, 1996), pp. 71–86.

Olson, Gary L., *U.S. Foreign Policy and the Third World Peasant* (New York: Praeger, 1974).

Page, Richard C., *Aiding Development: The Case of Taiwan, 1949–65* (Ph.D. dissertation, Politics Department, Princeton University, 1967).

Political Change in Taiwan, Cheng Tun-jen and Stephan Haggard, eds. (Boulder: Lynne Rienner, 1992).

Ravich, Samatha, "Taiwan: The Bringing In of New Elites," in *Marketization and Democracy: East Asian Experiences*, Samantha Ravich, ed. (Cambridge: Cambridge University Press, 2000), pp. 95–136.

Rigger, Shelley, "Electoral Strategies and Political Institutions in the Republic of China on Taiwan," *Fairbank Center Working Papers*, No. 1. (Cambridge: Harvard University Fairbank Center, 1993).

Rigger, Shelley, "Mobilizational Authoritarianism and Political Opposition in Taiwan," in *Political Oppositions in Industrializing Asia*, Garry Rodan, ed. (London: Routledge, 1996), pp. 300–22.

Rigger, Shelley, "Social Science and National Identity: A Critique," *Pacific Affairs* 72:4 (Winter 1999–2000), pp. 537–52.

Rigger, Shelley, *From Opposition to Power: Taiwan's Democratic Progressive Party* (Boulder: Rienner, 2001).

Rigger, Shelley, *Politics in Taiwan: Voting for Democracy* (New York: Routledge, 1999).

Sautedé, Eric, "New Majority, New Faces," *China Perspectives* 15 (January-February 1998), pp. 49–51.

Selya, Roger M., *The Industrialization of Taiwan: Some Geographic Considerations* (Jerusalem: Jerusalem Academic Press, 1974).

Shea Jia-Dong and Ya-Hwei Yang, "Taiwan's Financial System and the Allocation of Investment Funds," in *The Role of the State in Taiwan's Development*, Joel D. Aberbach, *et al.*, eds. (Armonk: Sharpe, 1994), pp. 193–230.

Shen Min, *Taihai zhanzheng da yuyan* (Predictions about War in the Taiwan Strait) (Taipei: Dujia, 1997).

Shieh Gwo-shyong, *"Boss" Island: The Subcontracting Network and Micro-entrepreneurship in Taiwan's Development* (New York: P. Lang, 1992).

Shih Chih-yu, *Houxiandai de guojia rentong* (Post-Modern State Identity) (Taipei: Shijie Shuju, 1995).

Shyu Huoyan, "Reasoning and Choice in Taiwan's Gubernatorial Election," paper for a conference at the Centre of Asian Studies, University of Hong Kong, February 1996.

Skoggard, Ian A., *The Indigenous Dynamic in Taiwan's Postwar Development: The Religious and Historical Roots of Entrepreneurship* (Armonk: Sharpe, 1996).

Sun Chin-ming (Gen.), "Taiwan: Toward a Higher Degree of Military Professionalism," in *Military Professionalism in Asia: Conceptual and Empirical Perspectives*, Muthiah Alagappa, ed. (Honolulu: East-West Center, 2001), pp. 61–76.

Tai Hung-chao, "The Political Process of Land Reform," in *The Political Economy of Development*, Norman T. Uphoff and Warren F. Ilchman, eds. (Berkeley: University of California Press, 1972), pp. 295–303.

Taiwan de guojia yu shehui (State and Society in Taiwan), Hsiao Hsin-huang and Hsu Cheng-guang, eds. (Taipei: Dongda, 1996).

Taiwan shehui li de fenxi (An Analysis of Social Forces in Taiwan), Chang Ching-han, ed. (Taipei: Tahsüeh Tsungk'an, 1971).

Taiwan Statistical Data Book (Taipei: ROC Statistical Bureau, 1976).

Taiwan xinxing shehui yundong (Taiwan's Emerging Social Movements), Hsü Cheng-kuang and Sung Wen-li, eds. (Taipei: Juliu, 1992).

Taiwan's Electoral Politics and Democratic Transition, Tien Hung-mao, ed. (Armonk: M.E. Sharpe, 1996).

Taiwan's Future, Yung-Hwan Jo, ed. (Tempe: Arizona State University Center for Asian Studies, 1974).

The Other Taiwan: 1945 to the Present, Rubinstein, Murray, ed. (Armonk: Sharpe, 1994).

The Role of the State in Taiwan's Development, Joel D. Aberbach, *et al.*, eds. (Armonk: Sharpe, 1994).

Tien Hung-mao and Cheng Tun-jen, "Crafting Democratic Institutions in Taiwan," *The China Journal* 37 (June 1997), pp. 1–30.

Tien Hung-mao, "Taiwan's Evolution Toward Democracy: A Historical Perspective," in *Taiwan: Beyond the Economic Miracle*, Dennis Simon and Y.M Kao, eds. (Armonk: Sharpe, 1992), pp. 3–24.

Tien Hung-mao, *The Great Transition: Political and Social Change in the ROC* (Stanford: Hoover Institution, 1988).

Wachman, Alan, "Competing Identities in Taiwan," in *The Other Taiwan: 1945 to the Present*, Rubinstein, Murray, ed. (Armonk: Sharpe, 1994), pp. 17–80.

Wade, Robert, *Governing the Market: Economic Theory and the Role of Government in East Asian Industrialization* (Princeton: Princeton University Press, 1990).

Wang Chin-shou, "*Guomindang houxuanjen maipaio jiqi de jianli yu yunzuo: Yijiujiusan nian Fengmang xianzhang xuanju de gean yanjiu*" (The Establishment and Use of Instruments for KMT Candidates Buying Votes: A Case Study of the 1993 Magistrate's Election in Fengmang [fictitious name, real place] County), paper seen in August 1997.

Wang Jenn-hwan, *Shei tongzhi Taiwan?* (Who Controls Taiwan?) (Taipei: Juliu, 1996).

Wang Jianmin, *Taiwan heishehui neimu* (Behind the Curtain of Taiwan's Black Societies) (Beijing: Xinhua, 2002).

Wang Tso-jung, *Fuliguo bushi meng: Jingji gongping yu guoji jingji* (A Welfare State Isn't a Dream: Economic Equality and International Economics) (Taipei: Shibao, 1996).

Wang Yi-hsiang, *Bu liuxue de shehui geming: Wo weishenma yao changzhu Gongdang* (Bloodless Social Revolution: Why I support the Labor Party) (Taipei: Jiubo, 1989).

Wei Yung, "The Modernization Process in Taiwan: An Allocative Analysis," *Asian Survey* 16 (March 1976), pp. 249–69.

Wennerlund, Pelle, *Taiwan: In Search of the Nation* (Stockholm: Department of Chinese, Stockholm University, 1977).

White Paper on Small and Medium Enterprises in Taiwan, 2001, Li Min-hsueh, *et al.*, eds. (Taipei: Small and Medium Enterprise Administration, Ministry of Economic Affairs).

White, Lynn T. III, "Taiwan's External Relations: Identity vs. Security," in *The International Relations of Northeast Asia*, Samuel S. Kim, ed. (Lanham: Rowman & Littlefield, 2002), pp. 301–30.

White, Lynn T. III, "The Political Effects of Resource Allocations in Taiwan and Mainland China," *The Journal of the Developing Areas* 15 (October 1980), pp. 43–66.

Winckler, Edwin A., "Elite Political Struggle, 1945–1985," in *Contending Approaches to the Political Economy of Taiwan*, Edwin A. Winckler and Susan Greenhalgh, eds. (Armonk: Sharpe, 1988), pp. 151–74.

Winn, Jane Kaufman, and Tang-Chi Yeh, "Relational Practices and the Marginalization of Law: Informal Financial Practices of Small Businesses in Taiwan," *Law and Society Review* 28:2 (1994), pp. 193–232.

Wolf, Margery, *The House of Lim* (New York: Appleton, Century, Crofts, 1968).

Woo Wing Thye, and Liang-Yn Liu, "Taiwan's Persistent Trade Surpluses: The Role of Underdeveloped Financial Markets," in *The Role of the State in Taiwan's Development*, Joel D. Aberbach, *et al.*, eds. (Armonk: Sharpe, 1994), pp. 90–112.

Wu Hui-lin and Chou Tein-chen, "Small and Medium Enterprises and Economic Development in Taiwan," *Industry of Free China* 69:3 (1988), pp. 15–30.

Wu Jaushieh, "*Wenming de chongtu huoer wenming? Ping Han Yandun 'Wenming chongtu lun*'" ("Clash of Civilizations, or Civilization? A Critique of Huntington's 'Clash of Cultures'), *Wenti yu yanjiu* (Issues and Studies, Chinese edition) 36:5 (May 1997), pp. 67–75.

Wu Jaushieh, *Taiwan's Democratization: Forces Behind the New Momentum* (Hong Kong: Oxford University Press, 1995).

Wu Nai-Teh and Lin Chia-Long, "Democratic Consensus and Social Cleavage: The Role of the Middle Class in Political Liberalization in Taiwan," in *Discovery of the Middle Classes in East Asia*, Michael Hsiao Hsin-huang, ed. (Taipei: Ethnology Institute, Academia Sinica, 1994), pp. 201–18.

Wu Nai-teh, "Forming a New Nation: Ethnic Identity and Liberalism in Taiwanese Nationalism," paper for XVII World Congress, IPSA, Seoul, August 1997.

Wu Nai-teh, *The Politics of a Regime Patronage System: Mobilization and Control within an Authoritarian System* (Ph.D. Dissertation, University of Chicago, Political Science Department, 1987). This is the most widely cited, and duly respected, unpublished book on Taiwan politics.

Wu Yongping, "Rethinking the Taiwanese Developmental State," *China Quarterly* 183 (2004), pp. 91–114.

Wu Yongping, *A Political Explanation of Economic Growth: State Survival, Bureaucratic Politics, and Private Enterprises in the Making of Taiwan's Economy, 1950–1985* (Cambridge: Harvard University Press, 2005).

Wu Yu-shan, "Nationalism, Democratization, and Economic Reform: Political Transition in the Soviet Union, Hungary, and Taiwan" (Durham, NC: Working Papers in Taiwan Studies, 1994).

Wu Yuan-li, *Income Distribution in the Process of Economic Growth of the Republic of China* (Baltimore: University of Maryland School of Law, 1977).

Yang, David D., "The Bases of Political Legitimacy in Late Authoritarian Taiwan," in *Legitimacy: Ambiguities of Political Success or Failure in East and Southeast Asia*, Lynn White, ed. (Singapore: World Scientific Press, 2005), pp. 67–112.

Yang, David D., "Classing Ethnicity: Class, Ethnicity, and the Mass Politics of Taiwan's Democratization", *World Politics* 59:4 (July 2007), 503–38.

Zhang Mau-kuei, *Shehui yundong yu zhengzhi juanhuan* (Social Movements and Political Transformation) (Taipei: Guoji Zhengce Yanjiu Zhongxin, 1989).

SOURCES ON CHINA

Angle, Stephen C., "Must We Choose Our Leaders? Human Rights and Political Participation in China," *Journal of Global Ethics* 1:2 (2005), pp. 177–96.

Ba Xian Xianwei Yanjiushi (Research Office of the Ba County Party Committee), "Jia jiti xingcheng yuanyin zoushi chutan" (The Causes for the Rise of Fake Collectives), *Nongcun jingji* (Rural Economics) 2 (February 1993), pp. 13–14.

Bernstein, Thomas, and Lu Xiaobo, "Taxation Without Representation: Peasants, the Central and Local States in Reform China," *China Quarterly* 163 (September 2000), pp. 742–63.

Bianco, Lucien, *The Origins of the Chinese Revolution, 1915–1949* (Stanford: Stanford University Press, 1971).

Birney, Mayling E., *Can Local Elections Contribute to Democratic Progress in Authoritarian Regimes? Exploring the Political Ramifications of China's Village Elections* (Ph.D. dissertation, Yale University Department of Political Science, 2007).

Bruun, Ole, *Business and Bureaucracy in a Chinese City: An Ethnography of Private Business Households in Contemporary China* (Berkeley: Institute of East Asian Studies, University of California, Berkeley, 1993).

Chan Kam Wing, "Post-1949 Urbanization Trends and Policies: An Overview," in *Urbanizing China*, Gregory Eliyu Guldin, ed. (Westport: Greenwood Press, 1992), pp. 41–63.

Chan, Anita, "Boot Camp at the Shoe Factory; Where Taiwanese Bosses Drill Chinese Workers to Make Sneakers for American Joggers," *Washington Post*, November 3, 1996, p. C1.

Chan, Anita, "The Changing Ruling Elite and Political Opposition in China," in *Political Oppositions in Industrializing Asia*, Garry Rodan, ed. (London: Routledge, 1996), pp. 161–87.

Chan, Anita, and Jonathan Unger, "Grey and Black: The Hidden Economy of Rural China," *Pacific Affairs* 55:3 (1982), pp. 452–71.

Chen Fang, *Tiannü: Shizhang yaoan* (The Wrath of God: A Mayor's Severe Crime [English trans. on orig. paperback cover, also marked *dalu jinshu*, "prohibited book on the mainland"]) (Taipei: Yuanjing, 1997).

Chen Yuan-tsung, *Dragon's Village: A Novel of Revolutionary China* (New York: Pantheon, 1980).

Cheung, Anthony B.L., "Bureaucrats-Enterprise Negotiation in China's Enterprise Reform at the Local Level: Case Studies in Guangzhou," *Journal of Contemporary China* 14:45 (November 2006), pp. 695–720.

Chhibber, Pradeep K., and Samuel Eldersveld, "Local Elites and Popular Support for Economic Reform in China and India," *Comparative Political Studies* 33:3 (April 2000), pp. 350–73.

Child, John, and Xu Xinzhong, "The Communist Party's Role in Enterprise Leadership at the High Water of China's Economic Reform," (Beijing: China-EC Management Institute Working Paper, September 1989).

China 2000: Emerging Business Issues, Lane Kelley and Yadong Luo, eds. (Thousand Oaks, CA: Sage, 1999).

China's Rational Entrepreneurs: The Development of the New Private Business Sector, Barbara Krug, ed. (London: RoutledgeCurzon, 2004).

China's Rural Industry: Structure, Development, and Reform, Lin Qingsong and William Byrd, eds. (New York: Oxford University Press for the World Bank, 1990).

China, Modernization, and the Goal of Prosperity: Government Administration and Economic Policy in the Late 1980s, Kate Hannan, ed. (Cambridge: Cambridge University Press, 1995).

Chinese Nationalism, Unger, Jonathan, ed. (Armonk: Sharpe, 1996).

Chinese Rural Development: The Great Transformation, William L. Parish, ed. (Armonk: M.E. Sharpe, 1985).

Choi Eun-Kyong, *Building the Tax State in China: Center and Region in the Politics of Welfare Extraction, 1994–2003* (Ph.D. dissertation, Politics Department, Princeton University, 2006).

Chûgoku no toshika to nôson kensetsu (Chinese Urbanization and Rural Construction), Kojima Reeitsu ed. (Tokyo: Ryûkei Shosha, 1978).

Conner, Alison W., "To Get Rich is Precarious: Regulation of Private Enterprise in the People's Republic of China." *Journal of Chinese Law* 5:1 (Spring 1991), pp. 1–57.

Cui Zhiyuan, "Epilogue: A Schumpeterian Perspective and Beyond," in *China: A Reformable Socialism*, Gan Yang and Cui Zhiyuan, eds. (New York: Oxford University Press, 1995), pp. 145–68.

Deng Xiaoping, "*Gaige de buzi yao jia kuai*" (To Speed up Reforms), in *Shierda yilai zhongyao wenjian xuanbian* (Selected Important Documents since the Twelfth Plenum), pp. 1444–49.

Deng Xiaoping, *Selected Works of Deng Xiaoping, 1975–1982* (Beijing: Foreign Languages Press, 1984).

Dickson, Bruce J., *Red Capitalists in China: The Party, Private Entrepreneurs and Prospects for Political Change* (New York: Cambridge University Press, 2003).

Ding Xueliang, "Informal Privatization through Internationalization: The Rise of Nomenklatura in China's Offshore Businesses," *British Journal of Political Science* 30:1 (January 2000), pp. 121–46.

Domes, Jürgen, *Socialism in the Chinese Countryside: Rural Societal Policies in the People's Republic of China, 1949–1979*, trans. Margritta Wendling (London: C. Hurst, 1980).

Donnithorne, Audrey, "Comment: Centralization and Decentralization in China's Fiscal Management," *China Quarterly*, 66 (June 1976), pp. 328–39.

Duihua Foundation, *Political and Religious Crime in Zhejiang Province*, Occasional Publication # 20 (San Francisco: Duihua Foundation, December 2005).

Dutton, Michael R., *Policing and Punishment in China: From Patriarchy to "the People"* (Cambridge: Cambridge University Press, 1992).

Edin, Maria, "State Capacity and Local Agent Control in China: CCP Cadre Management from a Township Perspective," *China Quarterly* 173 (March 2003), pp. 35–52.

Esherick, Joseph, "Ten Theses on the Chinese Revolution," *Modern China* 21:1 (1995), pp. 45–75.

Evans, Grant, "The Southern Chinese Borders: Still a Frontier," in *Politics in China: Moving Frontiers*, Françoise Mengin and Jean-Louis Rocca, eds. (New York: Palgrave Macmillan, 2002), pp. 215–31.

Fabre, Guilhem, "Le réveil de Shanghaï: Stratégies Économiques 1949–2000" ('The Awakening of Shanghai: Economic Strategies, 1949–2000'), *Le courrier des pays de l'est*, No. 325 (January 1988), pp. 3–40.

Fei Xiaotong and Luo Yanxian, *Xiangzhen jingji bijiao moshi* (Comparative Model of the Village and Town Economy) (Chongqing: Chongqing Chuban She, 1988).

Fei Xiaotong, "Foreword," in *Urbanizing China*, Gregory Eliyu Guldin, ed. (Westport: Greenwood Press, 1992), p. ix.

Fei Xiaotong, *"Xiao shangpin, da shichang"* (Small Commodities, Big Market), in *Fei Xiaotong xuanji* (Selected Works of Fei Xiaotong) (Tianjin: Tianjin Renmin Chubanshe, 1988), pp. 364–83.

Fei Xiaotong, *Fei Xiaotong lun xiao chengzhen jianshe* (Fei Xiaotong on the Construction of Small Cities and Towns) (Beijing: Qunyan Chuban She, 2000).

Fewsmith, Joseph, "Chambers of Commerce in Wenzhou Show Potential, Limits of 'Civil Society' in China," Zhejiang University Conference on "The Development of the Non-State Sector, Local Governance, and Sustainable Development in China," June 24–25, 2006, vol. 1, pp. 81–91.

Fewsmith, Joseph, "Formal Structures, Informal Politics, and Political Change in China," in *Informal Politics in East Asia*, Lowell Dittmer, Fukui Haruhiro, and Peter Lee, eds. (New York: Cambridge University Press), pp. 141–64.

Fewsmith, Joseph, Review of "Leninger's" *Disan zhi yanjing kan Zhongguo* (Looking at China Through a Third Eye), *Journal of Contemporary China* 7 (Fall 1994), pp. 100–04.

Forster, Keith, "The 1982 Campaign Against Economic Crime in China," *Australian Journal of Chinese Affairs* 14 (1985), pp. 1–19.

Forster, Keith, *Rebellion and Factionalism in a Chinese Province: Zhejiang 1966–1976* (Armonk: M.E. Sharpe, 1990).

Forster, Keith, *Zhejiang Province in Reform* (Sydney: Wild Peony, 1998).

Francis, Corinna-Barbara, "Quasi-Public, Quasi-Private Trends in Emerging Market Economies: The Case of China," *Comparative Politics* (April 2001), pp. 275–93.

Gallagher, Mary Elizabeth, *Contagious Capitalism: Globalization and the Politics of Labor in China* (Princeton: Princeton University Press, 2005; orig. Ph.D. dissertation, Politics Department, Princeton University, 2001).

Gallagher, Mary Elizabeth, "Reform and Openness: Why Chinese Economic Reforms Have Delayed Democracy," *World Politics* 54 (April 2002), pp. 338–72.

Gates, Hill, *China's Motor: A Thousand Years of Petty Capitalism* (Ithaca: Cornell University Press, 1996).

Gilley, Bruce, "The Yu Zuomin Phenomenon: Entrepreneurs and Politics in Rural China," in *The New Entrepreneurs of Europe and Asia: Patterns of Business Development in Russia, Eastern Europe, and China*, Victoria E. Bonnell and Thomas B. Gold, eds. (Armonk: Sharpe, 2002), pp. 66–82.

Gilley, Bruce, *Model Rebels: The Rise and Fall of China's Richest Village* (Berkeley: University of California Press, 2001).

Gold, Thomas, "Guerrilla Interviewing Among the *Getihu*," in *Unofficial China: Popular Culture and Thought in the People's Republic*, Perry Link, *et al.*, eds. (Boulder: Westview, 1989), pp. 175–92.

Goodman, David S.G., "The New Middle Class," in *The Paradox of China's Post-Mao Reforms*, Merle Goldman and Roderick MacFarquhar, eds. (Cambridge: Harvard University Press, 1999), pp. 241–61.

Goodman, David S.G., "The People's Republic of China: The Party-State, Capitalist Revolution, and New Entrepreneurs," in *Culture and Privilege in Capitalist Asia*, Michael Pinches, ed. (New York: Routledge, 1999), pp. 225–44.

Gore, Lance, *Market Communism: The Institutional Foundation of China's Post-Mao Hyper-Growth* (Hong Kong: Oxford University Press, 1998).

Green, Elizabeth, *Land Reform in China* (B.A. thesis, Princeton University, East Asian Studies Department, 1977).

Grove, Linda, *A Chinese Economic Revolution: Rural Entrepreneurship in the Twentieth Century* (Lanham: Rowman and Littlefield, 2006).

Guldin, Gregory, *What's a Peasant to Do? Village becoming Town in Southern China* (Boulder: Westview, 2001).

Guo Zhenying, Lu Jian, Song Ning, and Zhang Tai, "China's Changing Ownership Structure," *Social Sciences in China* 2 (Spring, 1993) pp. 178–93.

Guowuyuan nongcun fazhan yanjiu zhongxin bangongshi (Rural Development Research Center of the State Council), "*Guowuyuan bangongting guanyu zhizhi jiajia qianggou he tiji shougou yanye de tongzhi*" (State Council Ban on Price Rises, Snap Purchases, and Raised Grading of Tobacco), September 1, 1987, in *Nongcun zhengce wenjian xuan, 1985–89* (Selected Documents on Agricultural Policy, 1985–89) (Beijing: Zhongyang Dangxiao Chubanshe, 1987)

Guowuyuan yanjiushi geti siying jingji diaochazu (State Council Investigation Team on the Individual and Private Economy), *Zhongguo de geti he siying jingji* (China's Individual and Private Economy) (Beijing: Gaige Chubanshe, 1990).

Hannan, Kate, *Industrial Change in China: Economic Restructuring and Conflicting Interests* (London: Routledge, 1998).

Harding, Harry, *China's Second Revolution: Reform After Mao* (Washington: Brookings Institution, 1987).

He Baogang, "The Theory and Practice of Chinese Grass-Roots Governance: Five Models," Zhejiang University Conference on "The Development of the Non-State Sector, Local Governance, and Sustainable Development in China," June 24–25, 2006, vol. 1, pp. 56–80.

He Zengke, "A Study on the Institutional Barriers on the Development of Civil Society in Current China," Zhejiang University Conference on "The Development of the Non-State Sector, Local Governance, and Sustainable Development in China," June 24–25, 2006, vol. 1, pp. 40–55.

Heberer, Thomas, *Private Entrepreneurs in China and Vietnam: Social and Political Functioning of Strategic Groups*, trans. Timothy J. Gluckman (Leiden: Brill, 2003).

Hodder, Rupert N. W., "China's Industry — Horizontal Linkages in Shanghai," *Transactions of the Institute of British Geographers* 15 (1990), pp. 487–503.

Hodder, Rupert N. W., "Exchange and Reform in the Economy of Shanghai Municipality: Socialist Geography under Reform," *Annals of the Association of American Geographers* 83:2 (1993), pp. 303–19.

Honig, Emily, *Creating Chinese Ethnicity: Subei People in Shanghai, 1850–1980* (New Haven: Yale University Press, 1992).

Hu Heli, "1988 nian woguo zujin jiazhi de gusuan" (The Estimation of Chinese Rent-Seeking in 1988), *Jingji shehui tizhi bijiao*, 5 (1989), pp. 10–15.

Huang, Philip C. C., *The Peasant Family and Rural Development in the Yangzi Delta, 1350–1988* (Stanford: Stanford University Press, 1990).

Ishida Hiroshi, *Chûgoku nôson keizai no kiso kôzô: Shanhai kinkô nôson no kôgyôka to kindaika no ayumi* (Rural China in Transition: Experiences of Rural Shanghai toward Industrialization and Modernization) (Kyôto: Kôyô Shobô, 1991).

Jeffery, Lyn, "Marketing Civility, Civilizing the Market: Multilevel Marketing's Challenge to the State," in *The New Entrepreneurs of Europe and Asia: Patterns of Business Development in Russia, Eastern Europe, and China*, Victoria E. Bonnell and Thomas B. Gold, eds. (Armonk: Sharpe, 2002), pp. 325–46.

Johnson, Chalmers A., *Peasant Nationalism and Communist Power: The Emergence of Revolutionary China, 1937–1945* (Stanford: Stanford University Press, 1962).

Johnston, Alastair Iain, *Social States: China in International Institutions, 1980–2000* (Princeton: Princeton University Press, 2008).

Kelliher, Daniel, *Peasant Power: The Era of Rural Reform, 1979–1989* (New Haven: Yale University Press, 1993).

Kennedy, Scott, "The Stone Group: State Client or Market Pathbreaker?" *China Quarterly* 152 (December 1997), pp. 746–77.

Kennedy, Scott, *The Business of Lobbying in China* (Cambridge: Harvard University Press, 2005).

Kim Icksoo, "Accession into the WTO: External Pressure for Internal Reforms," *Journal of Contemporary China* 11:32 (August 2002), pp. 433–58.

Knapp, Ronald G., "Cangpo Village, Zhejiang: A Relic with a Future?" in *Chinese Landscapes: The Village as Place*, Ronald G. Knapp, ed. (Honolulu: University of Hawaii Press, 1992), pp. 173–88.

Kraus, Willy, *Private Business in China: Revival between Ideology and Pragmatism*, trans. Erich Holz (Honolulu: University of Hawaii Press, 1991).

Kung, James Kai-sing, "The Role of Property Rights in China's Rural Reforms and Development," in *China's Developmental Miracle: Origins, Transformations, and Challenges*, Alvin So, ed. (Armonk: M.E. Sharpe, 2001), pp. 58–78.

Kung, James Kai-sing, and Yiu-fai Lee, "So What if there is Income Inequality? The Distributive Consequence of Nonfarm Employment in Rural China," *Economic Development and Culture Change* 50:1 (October 2001), pp. 19–46.

Kwok, Reginald Yin-wang, "Urbanization Under Economic Reform," in *Urbanizing China*, Gregory Eliyu Guldin, ed. (Westport: Greenwood Press, 1992), pp. 65–85.

Lam, Danny K.K., and Ian Lee, "Guerrilla Capitalism and the Limits of Statist Theory," in *The Evolving Pacific Basin in the Global Political Economy: Domestic and International Linkages*, Cal Clark and Steven Chan, eds. (Boulder: Rienner, 1992), pp. 107–24.

Landry, Pierre-François, *Decentralized Authoritarianism in China: The Communist Party's Control of Local Elites in the Post-Mao Era* (New York: Cambridge University Press, 2008).

Lau Chung-ming, Hang-yue Ngo, and Clement Kong-wing Chow, "Private Businesses in China: Emerging Environment and Managerial Behavior," in *China 2000: Emerging Business Issues* (Thousand Oaks, CA: Sage, 1999), pp. 25–48.

Lee Ching Kwan, "Three Patterns of Working-Class Transitions in China," in *Politics in China: Moving Frontiers*, Françoise Mengin and Jean-Louis Rocca, eds. (New York: Palgrave Macmillan, 2002), pp. 62–91.

Lee, Peter Nan-shong, "Bureaucratic Corruption During the Deng Xiaoping Era," *Corruption and Reform* 5:5 (1990), pp. 29–47.

Lee, Yok-shiu F., "Rural Transformation and Decentralized Urban Growth in China," in *Urbanizing China*, Gregory Eliyu Guldin, ed. (Westport: Greenwood Press, 1992), pp. 89–118.

Li Cheng, *China's Leaders: The New Generation* (Lanham: Rowman and Littlefield, 2001).

Li Cheng and Lynn T. White III, "Elite Transformation and Modern Change in Mainland China and Taiwan," *China Quarterly* 121 (March 1990), pp. 1–35.

Li Cheng and Lynn T. White III, "The Sixteenth Central Committee of the Chinese Communist Party: Emerging Patterns of Power Sharing," in *China's Deep Reform: Domestic Politics in Transition*, L. Dittmer and G. Liu, eds. (Boulder: Rowman and Littlefield, 2006), pp. 81–118.

Li, Linda Chelan, "The Prelude to Government Reform in China? The 'Big Sale' in Shunde," *China Information* 18:1 (2004), pp. 29–65.

Lieberthal, Kenneth, and Michel Oksenberg, *Policymaking in China: Leaders, Structures, and Processes* (Princeton: Princeton University Press, 1988).

Lieberthal, Kenneth, *Governing China* (New York: Norton, 1995 and later editions).

Lin Yi-min, *Between Politics and Markets: Firms, Competition, and Institutional Change in Post-Mao China* (Cambridge: Cambridge University Press, 2001).

Liu Jixin, "*Woguo feigong youzhi qiye ji qunti jiben xianzhuang*" (Nonstate Entrepreneurs and Their Basic Conditions), *Shehuixue yanjiu* (Sociological Research) 6 (June 1992), pp. 13–20.

Liu Xinwu, *Jumping into the Sea: From Academics to Entrepreneurs in South China* (Lanham: Rowman and Littlefield, 2001).

Liu Yia-ling, "Reform from Below: The Private Economy and Local Politics in the Rural Industrialization of Wenzhou," *China Quarterly* 130 (June 1992), pp. 293–316.

Liu, Alan P.L., "The Politics of Corruption in the People's Republic of China," *American Political Science Review* 77 (September 1983), pp. 602–23.

Liu, Alan P.L., "The Wenzhou Model of Development and China's Modernization," *Asian Survey* 32:8 (August 1992), pp. 696–711.

Lu Ding, *Entrepreneurship in Suppressed Markets: Private-Sector Experience in China* (New York: Garland, 1994).

Lü Xiaobo, *Organizational Involution and Official Deviance: A Study of Cadre Corruption in China, 1949–93* (Ph.D. Dissertation, University of California at Berkeley, Political Science, 1994).

Lu Xueyi and Li Peilin, *Zhongguo shehui fazhan baogao* (Report on China's Social Development) (Shenyang: Liaoning Renmin Chubanshe, 1991).

Luo Yadong, J. Justin Tan, and Oded Shenkar, "Township and Village Enterprises in China: Strategy and Environment," in *China 2000: Emerging Business Issues*, Lane Kelley and Yadong Luo, eds. (Thousand Oaks, CA: Sage, 1999), pp. 3–24.

Ma Rong, "The Development of Small Towns and their Role in the Development of China," in *Urbanizing China*, Gregory Eliyu Guldin, ed. (Westport: Greenwood Press, 1992), pp. 119–53.

Ma Shu-Yun, "Understanding China's Reform: Looking Beyond Neoclassical Explanations," *World Politics* 52 (July 2000), 586–603.

Ma Zhongdong, "Social-Capital Mobilization and Income Returns to Entrepreneurship: The Case of Return Migration in Rural China," *Environment and Planning* 34 (2002), pp. 1763–84.

MacFarquhar, Roderick, and Michael Schoenhals, *Mao's Last Revolution* (Cambridge: Harvard University Press, 2006).

Malhotra, Angelina, "Shanghai's Dark Side: Army and Police Officers are Once Again in League with Vice," *Asia, Inc.* 3:2 (February 1994), pp. 32–39.

Malik, Rashid, *Chinese Entrepreneurs in the Economic Development of China* (Westport: Praeger, 1997).

Manion, Melanie, "Corruption by Design: Bribery in Chinese Enterprise Licensing," *Journal of Law, Economics, and Organization* 12:1 (1996), pp. 167–95.

Manion, Melanie, "Democracy, Community, Trust: The Impact of Elections in Rural China," *Comparative Political Studies* 39:3 (April 2006), pp. 301–24.

Manion, Melanie, "The Electoral Connection in the Chinese Countryside," *American Political Science Review* 90 (December 1996), pp. 736–48.

Manion, Melanie, *Corruption by Design: Building Clean Government in Mainland China and Hong Kong* (Cambridge: Harvard University Press, 2004).

Market Forces in China: Competition & Small Business, The Wenzhou Debate, Peter Nolan and Dong Fureng, eds. (London: Zed Books, 1990).

Marton, Andrew M., *China's Spatial Economic Development: Restless Landscapes in the Lower Yangzi Delta* (New York: Routledge, 2000).

Meaney, Connie Squires, "Market Reform in a Leninist System: Some Trends in the Distribution of Power Strategy and Money in Urban China," *Studies in Comparative Communism* 22:2–3 (Summer–Autumn 1989), pp. 203–20.

Meskill, John, *Gentlemanly Interests and Wealth on the Yangtze Delta* [in medieval times] (Ann Arbor: Association for Asian Studies, 1994).

Miao Zhuang, *"Zhidu bianqian zhong de gaige zhanlüe xuanze wenti"* (The Problem of Choosing Reform Strategies for System Change), *JJYJ* 10 (October 1992), pp. 72–79.

Mobrand, Erik Johan, *Internal Migration and Urban Conflict in Chinese and South Korean Industrialization* (Ph.D. Dissertation, Politics Department, Princeton University, 2006).

Moore, Thomas G., *China in the World Market: Chinese Industry and International Sources of Reform in the Post-Mao Era* (New York: Cambridge University Press, 2002, and Ph.D. Dissertation, Politics Department, Princeton University, 1995).

Morgan, Stephen L., "City-Town Enterprises in the Lower Changjiang (Yangtze) River Basin" (M.A. Thesis in Asian Studies, University of Hong Kong, 1987).

Mote, Frederick W., and Lynn White, "Political Structure," in *The Modernization of China*, Gilbert Rozman, ed. (New York: Free Press, 1981), pp. 255–351.

Mulvenon, James, "China: Conditional Compliance," in *Coercion and Governance: The Declining Political Role of the Military in Asia* (Stanford: Stanford University Press, 2001), pp. 317–35.

Murphy, Rachel, *How Migrant Labor is Changing Rural China* (Cambridge: Cambridge University Press, 2002).

Murphy, Rachel, "Returning Migration, Entrepreneurship, and Local State Corporatism in Rural China: The Experience of Two Counties in Southern Jiangxi," *Journal of Contemporary China* 9:24 (2000), pp. 231–47.

Nathan, Andrew J., and Shi Tianjian, "Cultural Requisites for Democracy in China: Findings from a Survey," *Daedalus* (Spring 1993), pp. 95–123.

Nathan, Andrew J., *China's Crisis: Dilemmas of Reform and Prospects for Democracy* (New York: Columbia University Press, 1990).

Nathan, Andrew J., *Chinese Democracy* (Berkeley: University of California Press, 1985).

Naughton, Barry, "Implications of the State Monopoly over Industry and Its Relaxation," *Modern China* 18 (January 1992), pp. 14–41.

Nolan, Peter, and Robert F. Ash, "China's Economy on the Eve of Reforms," *China Quarterly* 144 (December 1995), pp. 980–98.

Nongyebu Jingji Zhengce Yanjiu Zhongxin (Economic Policy Research Center of the Ministry of Agriculture), *Zhongguo nongcun: Zhengce yanjiu beiwanglu* (Rural China: Policy Research Backgrounder), (Beijing: Nongye Chubanshe, 1988).

O'Brien, Kevin J., *Reform Without Liberalization: China's National People's Congress and the Politics of Institutional Change* (New York: Cambridge University Press, 1990).

Ogden, Suzanne, *Inklings of Democracy in China* (Cambridge: Harvard University Press, 2002).

Oi, Jean C., "Fiscal Reform and the Economic Foundations of Local State Corporatism in China," *World Politics* 45:1 (October 1992), pp. 99–126.

Oi, Jean C., "The Role of the Local State in China's Transitional Economy," *China Quarterly* 144 (December 1995), pp. 1132–49.

Oi, Jean C., and Scott Rozelle, "Elections and Power: The Locus of Decision-Making in Chinese Villages," in *Elections and Democracy in Greater China*, Larry Diamond and Ramon Myers, eds. (Oxford: Oxford University Press, 2001), pp. 513–39.

Oi, Jean C., *Rural China Takes Off: Institutional Foundations of Economic Reform* (Berkeley: University of California Press, 1999).

Ostergaard Clemens and Christina Petersen, "Official Profiteering and the Tiananmen Square Demonstrations in China," *Corruption and Reform* 6:2 (1991), pp. 87–107.

Paltiel, Jeremy T., "China: Mexicanization or Market Reform," in *The Illusive State: International and Comparative Perspectives*, James A. Caporaso, ed. (Newbury Park, CA: Sage, 1989), pp. 255–78.

Parris, Kristen D., *Local Society and the State: The Wenzhou Model and the Making of Private Sector Policy in China* (Ph.D. Dissertation, Political Science, Indiana University, 1991).

Parris, Kristen D., "Entrepreneurs and Citizenship in China," *Problems of Post-Communism* 46 (January–February 1999), pp. 43–61.

Parris, Kristen D., "Local Initiative and Local Reform: The Wenzhou Model of Reform," *China Quarterly* 134 (June 1993), pp. 242–63.

Parris, Kristen D., "The Rise of Private Business Interests," in *The Paradox of China's Post-Mao Reforms*, Merle Goldman and Roderick MacFarquhar, eds. (Cambridge: Harvard University Press, 1999), pp. 262–82.

Paying for Progress: Public Finance, Human Welfare, and Inequality in China, Vivienne Shue and Christine Wong, eds. (Abingdon: Routledge, 2006).

Pearson, Margaret M., "The Janus Face of Business Associations in China: Socialist Corporatism in Foreign Enterprises," *Australian Journal of Chinese Affairs* 31 (January 1994), pp. 25–46.

Pearson, Margaret M., *China's New Business Elite: The Political Consequences of Economic Reform* (Berkeley: University of California Press, 1997).

Pei Minxin, *China's Trapped Transition: The Limits of Developmental Autocracy* (Cambridge: Harvard University Press, 2006).

Perry, Elizabeth J., "Chinese Conceptions of 'Rights': From Mencius to Mao — and Now," *Perspectives on Politics* 6:1 (March 2008), 37–47.

Perry, Elizabeth J., "Labor Divided: Sources of State Formation in Modern China," in *State Power and Social Forces*, Joel S. Migdal, Atul Kohli, and Vivienne Shue, eds. (New York: Cambridge University Press, 1994), pp. 143–73.

Perry, Elizabeth J., *Shanghai on Strike: The Politics of Chinese Labor* (Boulder: Westview, 1995).

Perry, Elizabeth J., and Li Xun, *Workers in the Cultural Revolution* (Boulder: Westview, 1996).

Politics in China: Moving Frontiers, Françoise Mengin and Jean-Louis Rocca, eds. (New York: Palgrave Macmillan, 2002).

Prime, Penelope B., "Industry's Response to Market Liberalization in China: Evidence from Jiangsu Province," *Economic Development and Cultural Change* 41:1 (1992), pp. 23–50.

Putterman, Louis, "Institutional Boundaries, Structural Change, and Economic Reform in China," *Modern China* 18 (January 1992), pp. 3–13.

Qian Yingyi, "How Reform Worked in China," *In Search of Prosperity: Narratives on Economic Growth*, Rodrik Dani, ed. (Princeton: Princeton University Press, 2003), pp. 297–333.

Qin Hui, "Dividing the Big Family Assets," *New Left Review* 20 (March–April 2003), pp. 83–110.

Reynolds, Bruce, *Reform in China: Challenges and Choices* (Armonk: M.E. Sharpe, 1987).

Riskin, Carl, "Small Industry and the Chinese Model of Development," *China Quarterly* 73 (March 1977), pp. 145–73.

Rocca, Jean-Louis, "'Three at Once': The Multidimensional Scope of Labor Crisis in China," in *Politics in China: Moving Frontiers*, Françoise Mengin and Jean-Louis Rocca, eds. (New York: Palgrave Macmillan, 2002), pp. 3–30.

Rocca, Jean-Louis, "Corruption and its Shadow: An Anthropological View of Corruption in China," *China Quarterly* 130 (June 1992), pp. 402–16.

Rubin, Vitaly A., *Individual and State in Ancient China: Essays on Four Chinese Philosophers*, trans. Steven I. Levine (New York: Columbia University Press, 1976).

Ruf, Gregory A., "Collective Enterprise and Property Rights in a Sichuan Village: The Rise and Decline of Managerial Corporatism," in *Property Rights and Economic Reform in China*, Jean C. Oi and Andrew Walder, eds. (Stanford: Stanford University Press, 1999), pp. 27–48.

Ruf, Gregory, *Making a Socialist Village in West China, 1921–91* (Stanford: Stanford University Press, 1998).

Rural Small-Scale Industry in the People's Republic of China, Dwight Perkins, ed. (Berkeley: University of California Press, 1977).

Sands, Barbara N., "Decentralizing and Economy: The Role of Bureaucratic Corruption in China's Economic Reforms," *Public Choice* 65:1 (1990), pp. 85–91.

Schurmann, Franz, *Ideology and Organization in Communist China* (Berkeley: University of California Press, 1966).

Sheehan, Jackie, *Chinese Workers: A New History* (London: Routledge, 1992).

Shi Tianjian, "Cultural Impacts on Political Trust: A Comparison of Mainland China and Taiwan," *Comparative Politics* 33:4 (2001), pp. 401–19.

Shirk, Susan L., *The Political Logic of Economic Reform in China* (Berkeley: University of California Press, 1993).

Shue, Vivienne, "Global Imaginings, the State's Quest for Hegemony, and the Pursuit of Phantom Freedom in China," in *Globalization and Democratization in Asia*, Katarina Kinvall and Kristina Jonsson, eds. (London: Routledge, 2002), pp. 210–29.

Shue, Vivienne, "State Power and Social Organization in China," in *State Power and Social Forces: Domination and Transformation in the Third World*, Joel Migdal, Atul Kohli, and Vivienne Shue, eds. (Cambridge: Cambridge University Press, 1994).

Shue, Vivienne, *The Reach of the State: Sketches of the Chinese Body Politic* (Stanford: Stanford University Press, 1988).

Siu, Helen F., *Agents and Victims in South China: Accomplices in Rural Revolution* (New Haven: Yale University Press, 1989).

Smart, Alan, "Gifts, Bribes, and *Guanxi*: A Reconsideration of Bourdieu's Social Capital," *Cultural Anthropology* 8:3 (August 1993), pp. 388–408.

Smyth, Russell, "Recent Developments of Rural Enterprise Reform in China," *Asian Survey* (August 1998), pp. 784–800.

Social Connections in China: Institutions, Culture, and the Changing Nature of Guanxi, Thomas Gold, Doug Guthrie and David Wank, eds. (New York: Cambridge University Press, 2002).

Solinger, Dorothy J., *Contesting Citizenship in Urban China: Peasant Migrants, the State, and the Logic of the Market* (Berkeley: University of California Press, 1999).

Solinger, Dorothy J., "Despite Decentralization: Disadvantages and Dependence in the Inland and Continuing Central Power in Wuhan," *China Quarterly* 145 (March 1996), pp. 1–34.

Solinger, Dorothy J., "Labor in Limbo: Pushed by the Plan toward the Mirage of the Market," in *Politics in China: Moving Frontiers*, Françoise Mengin and Jean-Louis Rocca, eds. (New York: Palgrave Macmillan, 2002), pp. 31–61.

Su Ya and Jia Lusheng, *Shei lai chengbao? Zhongguo jingji xianzhuang toushi* (Who is Going to Contract? An Analysis of China's Economic Situation) (Guangzhou: Huacheng Chuban She, 1990).

Sun Yan, *Corruption and Market in Contemporary China since Economic Reform* (Ithaca: Cornell University Press, 2004).

The Changing Meanings of Citizenship in Modern China, Merle Goldman and Elizabeth J. Perry, eds. (Cambridge: Harvard University Press, 2002).

The New Entrepreneurs of Europe and Asia: Patterns of Business Development in Russia, Eastern Europe, and China, Victoria E. Bonnell and Thomas B. Gold, eds. (Armonk: Sharpe, 2002).

The Paradox of China's Post-Mao Reforms, Merle Goldman and Roderick MacFarquhar, eds. (Cambridge: Harvard University Press, 1999).

Thireau, Isabelle, and Hau Linshan, "Power beyond Instituted Power: Forms of Mediation Spaces in the Chinese Countryside," in *Politics in China: Moving Frontiers*, Françoise Mengin and Jean-Louis Rocca, eds. (New York: Palgrave Macmillan, 2002), pp. 157–86.

Thun, Eric, *Changing Lanes in China: Foreign Direct Investment, Local Governments, and Auto Sector Development* (New York: Cambridge University Press, 2006).

Tsai, Kellee S., "Capitalists without a Class: Political Diversity among Private Entrepreneurs in China," http://www.jhu.edu/~polysci/faculty/tsai/capitalists.pdf, posted August 5, 2002.

Tsai, Kellee S., *Back-Alley Banking: Private Entrepreneurs in China* (Ithaca: Cornell University Press, 2002).

Unger, Jonathan, "'Bridges': Private Business, the Chinese Government, and the Rise of New Associations," *China Quarterly* 147 (September 1996), pp. 795–819.

Unger, Jonathan, "'Rich Man, Poor Man': The Making of New Classes in the Countryside," in *China's Quiet Revolution: New Interactions Between State and Society*, David S. G. Goodman and Beverley Hooper, eds. (New York: St. Martin's, 1994), pp. 43–63.

Unger, Jonathan, and Anita Chan, "China, Corporatism, and the East Asian Model," *Australian Journal of Chinese Affairs* 33 (1995), pp. 29–54.

Urbanizing China, Gregory Eliyu Guldin, ed. (Westport: Greenwood Press, 1992).

Veeck, Gregory, "Suburban Weigang, Jiangsu: A Transformed Village," in *Chinese Landscapes: The Village as Place*, Ronald G. Knapp, ed. (Honolulu: University of Hawaii Press, 1992), pp. 211–20.

Walder, Andrew G., "Zouping in Perspective," in *Zouping in Transition: The Process of Reform in Rural North China*, A.G. Walder, ed. (Cambridge: Harvard University Press, 1998), pp. 1–31.

Walder, Andrew, *Communist Neo-Traditionalism: Work and Authority in Chinese Industry* (Berkeley: University of California Press, 1986).

Waley, Arthur, *Three Ways of Thought in Ancient China* (London: Allen and Unwin, 1939).

Wang Hongying, *Weak State, Strong Networks: The International Dynamics of Foreign Investment in China* (New York: Oxford University Press, 2001, and Ph.D. Dissertation, Politics Department, Princeton University, 1996).

Wang Shiyuan, Li Xiuyi, and Yang Shijiu, *Zhongguo gaige daquan* (Encyclopedia of China's Reforms) (Dalian, Liaoning: Dalian Renmin Chubanshe, 1992).

Wang Xiaoqiang, Bai Nanshen, Liu Chang, Song Lina, and Zhao Xiaodong, "*Nongcun shangpin shengchan fazhan de xin dongxiang*" (New Trends in

Developing the Production of Rural Commodities), *Nongcun jingji shehui* (Rural Chinese Economy and Society), Vol. 3 (Beijing: Zhishi Chuban She, 1985), pp. 69–93.

Wang Xu, *Mutual Empowerment of State and Peasantry: Village Self-Government in Rural China* (Ph.D. dissertation, Politics Department, Princeton University, 2001).

Wang Yu-Qing, *Venturing Out: The Emergence of Domestic Entrepreneurs in Chinese Hybrid Economy* (Hong Kong: Science and Education Publishers, 2005).

Wang Zhengxu, "Political Trust in China," in *Legitimacy: Ambiguities of Political Success or Failure in East and Southeast Asia*, Lynn White, ed. (Singapore: World Scientific Press, 2005), pp. 113–40.

Wank, David L., "The Making of China's Rentier Entrepreneur Elite: State, Clientelism, and Power Conversion, 1978–1995," in *Politics in China: Moving Frontiers*, Françoise Mengin and Jean-Louis Rocca, eds. (New York: Palgrave Macmillan, 2002), pp. 118–40.

Weller, Robert P., *Resistance, Chaos, and Control in China: Taiping Rebels, Taiwanese Ghosts, and Tiananmen* (Seattle: University of Washington Press, 1994).

Weller, Robert P., *Unities and Diversities in Chinese Religion* (Seattle: University of Washington Press, 1987).

White, Lynn T. III, "Changing Concepts of Corruption in Communist China: Early 1950s vs. Early 1980s," in *Changes and Continuities in Chinese Communism*, Yu-ming Shaw, ed. (Boulder: Westview Press, 1988), pp. 316–53.

White, Lynn T. III, "Future Fortunes vs. Present People in China's Richest Cities," in *Social Policy Reform in Hong Kong and Shanghai: A Tale of Two Cities*, in Linda Wong, Lynn White, and Gui Shixun, eds. (Armonk: M.E. Sharpe, 2004), pp. 239–56.

White, Lynn T. III, "Shanghai's Polity in Cultural Revolution," in *The City in Communist China*, John W. Lewis, ed. (Stanford: Stanford University Press, 1971), pp. 325–70.

White, Lynn T. III, "Shanghai-Suburb Relations, 1949–1966," in *Shanghai: Revolution and Development in an Asian Metropolis*, Christopher Howe, ed. (Cambridge: Cambridge University Press, 1981), pp. 241–68.

White, Lynn T. III, "The Cultural Revolution as an Unintended Result of Administrative Policies," in *New Perspectives on the Cultural Revolution*, W. Josephs, C. Wong, and D. Zweig, eds. (Cambridge: Harvard University Press, 1991), pp. 83–104.

White, Lynn T. III, "The Liberation Army and the Chinese People," *Armed Forces and Society*, I:3 (May, 1975), 364–83.

White, Lynn T. III, "The Political Effects of Resource Allocations in Taiwan and Mainland China," *The Journal of the Developing Areas* 15 (October 1980), pp. 43–66.

White, Lynn T. III, "The Road to Urumchi: Approved Institutions in Search of Attainable Goals," *China Quarterly* 79 (October 1979), pp. 481–510.

White, Lynn T. III, "Workers' Politics in Shanghai." *Journal of Asian Studies* XXVI:1 (November 1976), pp. 99–116.

White, Lynn T. III, *Careers in Shanghai: The Social Guidance of Personal Energies in a Developing Chinese City 1949–1966* (Berkeley and Los Angeles: University of California Press, 1978).

White, Lynn T. III, *Policies of Chaos: The Organizational Causes of Violence in China's Cultural Revolution* (Princeton: Princeton University Press, 1989).

White, Lynn T. III, *Shanghai Shanghaied? Uneven Taxes in Reform China* (Hong Kong: University of Hong Kong Centre of Asian Studies, 1989).

White, Lynn T. III, *Unstately Power: Local Causes of China's Economic Reforms* (Armonk, NY: M.E. Sharpe, 1998).

White, Lynn T. III, *Unstately Power: Local Causes of China's Intellectual, Legal, and Governmental Reforms* (Armonk, NY: M.E. Sharpe, 1999).

White, Lynn T. III, and Li Cheng, "China Coast Identities: Region, Nation, and World," in *China's Quest for National Identity*, Lowell Dittmer and Samuel Kim, eds. (Ithaca: Cornell Univ. Press, 1993), pp. 154–93.

Whiting, Susan H., *Power and Wealth in Rural China: The Political Economy of Institutional Change* (New York: Cambridge University Press, 2001).

Wolf, Margery, "Chinese Women: Old Skills in a New Context," in *Woman, Culture, and Society*, Rosaldo, Michelle Z. and Louise Lamphere, eds. (Stanford: Stanford University Press, 1974), pp. 157–72.

Wong, Joseph C., "Zhouzhuang, Jiangsu: A Historic Market Town," in *Chinese Landscapes: The Village as Place*, Ronald G. Knapp, ed. (Honolulu: University of Hawaii Press, 1992), pp. 139–50.

Woo Wing Thye, "The Real Reasons for China's Growth," *The China Journal* 41 (January 1999), pp. 115–37.

Xu Yuanming and Ye Ding, *Tangqiao gongye hua zhi lu* (The Way to Industrialization in Tangqiao), (Shanghai: Shanghai Shehui Kexue Yuan Chuban She, 1987).

Yan Yunxiang, "The Impact of Rural Reform on Economic and Social Stratification in a Chinese Village," *Australian Journal of Chinese Affairs* 27 (January 1992), pp. 1–24.

Yang Dali L., *Calamity and Reform in China* (Stanford: Stanford University Press, 1996 [orig. a Ph.D. Dissertation, Politics Department, Princeton University, 1993]).

Yang Dali L., *Remaking the Chinese Leviathan: Market Transition and the Politics of Governance in China* (Stanford: Stanford University Press, 2005).

Yang Minchuan, "Reshaping Peasant Culture and Community: Rural Industrialization in a Chinese Village," *Modern China* 20:2 (April 1994), pp. 157–79.

Yang, Mayfair Mei-hui, *Gifts, Favors, & Banquets: The Art of Social Relationships in China* (Ithaca: Cornell University Press, 1994).

Yao Shuntian, "Privilege and Corruption: The Problem of China's Socialist Market Economy," *American Journal of Economics and Sociology* 61:1 (January 2002) pp. 279–99.

Ye Min, *Embedded State: Foreigners, Diasporas, and the Economic Transitions of China and India* (Ph.D. Dissertation, Politics Department, Princeton University, 2007).

Yep, Ray, "Bringing the Managers In: A Case of Rising Influence of Enterprise Managers in Rural China," *Issues and Studies* 36:4 (July–August 2000), pp. 132–65.

Yep, Ray, *Manager Empowerment in China: Political Implications of Rural Industrialization in the Reform Era* (London: RoutledgeCurzon, 2003).

You Ji, "China: From Revolutionary Tool to Professional Military," in *Military Professionalism in Asia: Conceptual and Empirical Perspectives*, Muthiah Alagappa, ed. (Honolulu: East-West Center, 2001), pp. 111–36.

Young, Susan, *Private Business and Economic Reform in China* (Armonk: Sharpe, 1995).

Zhang Jianjun, "State Power, Elite Relations, and the Politics of Privatization in China's Rural Industry: Different Approaches in Two Regions [Wuxi and Wenzhou]," *Asian Survey* 48:2 (March–April 2008), pp. 215–38.

Zhang Jinjiang, "*Shixi 'jiti' mingyi xia de siren qiye*" (A Preliminary Analysis of Private Enterprises that Call Themselves 'Collective'), *Chongqing shehui kexue* (Chongqing Social Sciences) 1 (January 1988), pp. 60–64.

Zheng Yongnian, *Globalization and State Transformation in China* (Cambridge: Cambridge University Press, 2004).

Zheng Yongnian, "The State, Firms, and Corporate Social Responsibility in China," Zhejiang University Conference on "The Development of the

Non-State Sector, Local Governance, and Sustainable Development in China," June 24–25, 2006, Vol. 1, pp. 184–99.

Zhong Yang, "Dissecting Chinese County Governmental Authorities," Zhejiang University Conference on "The Development of the Non-State Sector, Local Governance, and Sustainable Development in China," June 24–25, 2006, vol. 1, pp. 487–516.

Zhongguo gongye jingji tongji ziliao, 1986 (Statistical Materials on China's Industrial Economy, 1986) (Beijing: Zhongguo Tongji Chubanshe, 1987).

Zhongguo nongcun tongji nianjian, 1992 (Yearbook of Chinese Rural Statistics, 1992), ed. Rural Data Group of the State Statistics Bureau (Beijing: Zhongguo Tongji Chubanshe, 1992).

Zhongguo qinggong ye nianjian, 1992 (China Light Industry Yearbook, 1992), ed. Research Center on Light Industry (Beijing: Zhongguo Qinggong Ye Nianjian Chuban She, 1992).

Zhou, Kate Xiao, *How the Farmers Changed China*, (Boulder: Westview, 1996, and Ph.D. Dissertation, Politics Department, Princeton University, 1994).

Zhou, Kate Xiao, and Lynn White, "Quiet Politics and Rural Enterprise in Reform China," *The Journal of the Developing Areas* 29 (July 1995), pp. 461–90.

Zweig, David, "Peasants, Ideology, and New Incentive Systems: Jiangsu Province, 1978–81," in *Chinese Rural Development: The Great Transformation*, William L. Parish, ed. (Armonk: M.E. Sharpe, 1985), pp. 141–63.

Zweig, David, "Rural Industry: Constraining the Leading Growth Sector in China's Economy," in Joint Economic Committee, *China's Economic Dilemmas in the 1990s: The Problems of Reforms, Modernization, and Interdependence* (Washington: Government Printing Office, 1991), pp. 418–36.

Zweig, David, *Freeing China's Farmers: Rural Restructuring in the Reform Era* (Armonk: M.E. Sharpe, 1997).

SOURCES ON THAILAND

Abonyi, George, and Bunyraraks Ninsananda, *Thailand: Development Planning in Turbulent Times* (North York, Ont.: University of Toronto-York University, 1989).

Agrarian Transformations: Local Processes and the State in South-east Asia, Gillian Hart, *et al.*, eds. (Berkeley: University of California Press, 1989).

Albritton, Robert B., and Thawilwadee Bureekul, "The Role of Civil Society in Thai Electoral Politics," paper for the American Political Science Association Annual Meeting, 2002.

Ammar Siamwalla, "Can a Developing Democracy Manage its Macroeconomy? The Case of Thailand," in *Thailand's Boom and Bust: Collected Papers*, Ammar Siamwalla, *et al.*, eds. (Bangkok: Thailand Development Research Institute Foundation, 1997), pp. 63–75.

Ammar Siamwalla, "The Thai Economy: Fifty Years of Expansion," in *Thailand's Boom and Bust: Collected Papers*, Ammar Siamwalla, *et al.*, eds. (Bangkok: Thailand Development Research Institute Foundation, 1997), pp. 1–20.

Anan Ganjanapan, "Control of Labor in a Thai Village," in *Agrarian Transformations: Local Processes and the State in Southeast Asia*, Gillian Hart, *et al.*, eds. (Berkeley: University of California Press, 1989), pp. 98–122.

Anderson, Benedict, "Murder and Progress in Modern Siam," *New Left Review* 181 (1990), pp. 33–48.

Anderson, Benedict, "Withdrawal Symptoms: Social and Cultural Aspects of the October 6 Coup," *Bulletin of Concerned Asian Scholars* (July-September 1977), pp. 13–30.

Anek Laothamatas, "Business and Politics in Thailand: New Patterns of Influence," *Asian Survey* 28:4 (April 1988), pp. 451–70.

Anek Laothamatas, "Development and Democratization," in *Democratization in Southeast and East Asia*, Anek Laothamatas, ed. (Chiang Mai: Silkworm Books, 1997), pp. 1–20.

Anek Laothamatas, "From Clientelism to Partnership: Business Government Relations in Thailand," in *Business and Government in Industrializing Asia*, Andrew MacIntyre, ed. (Ithaca: Cornell University Press, 1994), pp. 195–215.

Anek Laothamatas, "Tale of Two Democracies: Conflicting Perceptions of Elections and Democracy in Thailand," in *The Politics of Elections in Southeast Asia*, R.H. Taylor, ed. (Washington: Woodrow Wilson Center, 1996), pp. 201–23.

Anek Laothamatas, *Business Associations and the New Political Economy of Thailand: From Bureaucratic Polity to Liberal Corporatism* (Singapore: Institute of Southeast Asian Studies [also Westview], 1992).

Arghiros, Daniel, "Political Reform and Civil Society at the Local Level: Thailand's Local Government Reforms," in *Reforming Thai Politics*, Duncan McCargo, ed. (Singapore: Institute of Southeast Asian Studies, 2002), pp. 223–46.

Arghiros, Daniel, *Democracy, Development, and Decentralisation in Provincial Thailand* (London: Curzon, 2001).

Arghiros, Daniel, *Political Structures and Strategies: A Study of Electoral Politics in Contemporary Rural Thailand* (Hull: University of Hull Centre for South-East Asian Studies, 1995).

Battersby, Paul, "Border Politics and the Broader Politics of Thai International Relations in the 1990s," *Pacific Affairs* 71:4 (Winter 1998), pp. 473–90.

Bello, Walden, Shea Cunningham, and Li Kheng Poh, *A Siamese Tragedy: Development and Disintegration in Modern Thailand* (Bangkok: White Lotus, 1998).

Bidhya Bowornwathana, "Thailand: Bureaucracy Under Coalition Governments," in *Civil Service Systems in Asia*, John P. Burns and Bidhya Bowornwathana, eds. (Cheltenham: Elgar, 2001), pp. 281–318.

Biggs, Tyler, Peter Brimble, and Donald Snodgrass, *Rural Industry and Employment Study: A Synthesis Report* (Rural Industries and Employment Project, Thailand Development Research Institute, 1990).

Bowie, Alasdair, and Danny Unger, *The Politics of Open Economies: Indonesia, Malaysia, the Philippines, and Thailand* (Cambridge: Cambridge University Press, 1997).

Bowie, Katherine Ann, *Rituals of National Loyalty: An Anthropology of the State and the Village Scout Movement in Thailand* (New York: Columbia University Press, 1997).

Brimble, Peter, David Oldfield, and Manusavee Monsakul, "Policies for SME Recovery in Thailand," in *The Role of SMEs in National Economies in East Asia*, Charles Harvie and Boon-Chye Lee, eds. (Cheltenham: Edward Elgar, 2002), pp. 202–37.

Brown, Andrew, *Labour, Politics, and the State in Industrializing Thailand* (New York: RoutledgeCurzon, 2004).

Callahan, William A., and Duncan McCargo, "Vote Buying in Thailand's Northeast: The July 1995 General Election," *Asian Survey* 36:4 (April 1996), pp. 376–92.

Callahan, William A., *Imagining Democracy: Reading "The Events of May" [1992] in Thailand* (Singapore: Institute of Southeast Asian Studies, 1998).

Callahan, William A., *Pollwatching, Elections, and Civil Society in Southeast Asia* (Aldershot: Ashgate, 2000).

Chai-Anan Samudavanija and Parichart Chotiya, "Beyond Transition in Thailand," in *Democracy in East Asia*, Larry Diamond and Eric Plattner, eds. (Baltimore: Johns Hopkins University Press, 1998), pp. 147–67.

Chai-Anan Samudavanija and Sukhumband Paribatra, "Thailand: Liberalization without Democracy," in *Driven by Growth: Political Change in the*

Asia-Pacific Region, James Morley, ed. (Armonk: M.E. Sharpe, 1993), pp. 119–41.

Chai-Anan Samudavanija, "Economic Development and Democracy," in *Thailand's Industrialization and its Consequences*, Medhi Krongkaew, ed. (New York: St. Martin's, 1995), pp. 235–50.

Chai-Anan Samudavanija, "Thailand: A Stable Semidemocracy," in *Politics in Developing Countries: Comparing Experiences with Democracy*, Larry Diamond, Juan Linz, and S.M. Lipset, eds. 2nd edition (Boulder: Rienner, 1990), pp. 271–312.

Chai-Anan Samudavanija, *The Thai Young Turks* (Singapore: Institute of Southeast Asian Studies, 1982).

Chalongphob Sussangkarn, *The Thai Labour Market: A Study of Seasonality and Segmentation* (Bangkok: Thai Development Research Institute, 1987).

Chantavanich, Supang, "From Siamese-Chinese to Chinese-Thai: Political Conditions and Identity Shifts among the Chinese in Thailand," in *Ethnic Chinese as Southeast Asians*, Leo Suryadinata, ed. (Singapore: Institute for Southeast Asian Studies, 1997), pp. 232–66.

Christensen, Scott R., Ammar Siamwalla, and Pakorn Vichyanond, "Institutional and Political Bases of Growth-Inducing Policies in Thailand," in *Thailand's Boom and Bust: Collected Papers*, Ammar Siamwalla, *et al.*, eds. (Bangkok: Thailand Development Research Institute Foundation, 1997), pp. 21–52.

Christensen, Scott R., and Ammar Siamwalla, *Beyond Patronage: Tasks for the Thai State* (Bangkok: Thailand Development Research Institute Foundation, 1993).

Connors, Michael K., *Democracy and National Identity in Thailand* (London: RoutledgeCurzon, 2003).

Cooper, Donald F., *Thailand: Dictatorship or Democracy?* (Montreux: Minerva Press, 1995).

Corbitt, Brian, "T-BIRD Rural Development Projects in Northeast Thailand," in *Development Dilemmas in the Mekong Region*, Bob Stensholt, ed. (Clayton: Monash Asia Institute, 1996), pp. 36–41.

Crispin, Shawn W., "Thaksin's New Deal," *Far Eastern Economic Review*, August 1, 2002, pp. 36–38.

Cushman, Jennifer, *Family and State: The Formation of a Sino-Thai Mining Dynasty, 1797–1932* (Singapore: Oxford University Press, 1992).

Dhiravegin, Likhit, *Thai Politics: Selected Aspects of Development and Change* (Bangkok: Tri-Sciences Publishing House, 1985).

Dobbin, Christine, *Asian Entrepreneurial Communities: Conjoint Communities in the Making of the World-Economy, 1570–1940* (Richmond, Surrey: Curzon, 1996).

Doner, Richard F., and Anek Laothamatas, "Thailand: Political and Economic Gradualism," in *Voting for Reform: Political Liberalization, Democracy, and Economic Adjustment*, Stephan Haggard and Steven B. Webb, eds. (Oxford: Oxford University Press, 1994), pp. 411–52.

Doner, Richard F., and Ansil Ramsay, "Competitive Clientelism and Economic Governance: The Case of Thailand," in *Business and the State in Developing Countries*, Sylvia Maxfield and Ben Ross Schneider, ed. (Ithaca: Cornell University Press, 1997), pp. 233–76.

Douglass, Clyde Michael, *Regional Integration on the Capitalist Periphery: The Central Plains of Thailand, 1855–1980* (The Hague: Institute of Social Studies, 1984).

Durrenberger, E. Paul, *State Power and Culture in Thailand* (New Haven: Yale Southeast Asian Studies, 1996).

Embree, John F., "Thailand: A Loosely Structured Social System," *American Anthropologist* 52:2 (1950), pp. 191–93.

Estler, Otte, *Der Beitrag kleiner und mittlerer Unternehmen zum Entwicklungs-prozess Thailands* (The Contribution of SMEs to Thailand's Development) (Hamburg: Institut für Asienkunde, 1998).

Feder, Gershon, *et al.*, *Land Rights and Farm Productivity in Thailand* (Baltimore: Johns Hopkins University Press, 1988).

Fry, Gerald, "Thailand's Political Economy: Change and Persistence," in *The Evolving Pacific Basin in the Global Political Economy: Domestic and International Linkages*, Cal Clark and Steven Chan, eds. (Boulder: Rienner, 1992), pp. 83–106.

Gagliardi, Jason, "From Drugs and Bugs to Thugs," *South China Morning Post*, May 25, 2003, p. 12.

Girling, John, *Interpreting Development: Capitalism, Democracy, and the Middle Class in Thailand* (Ithaca: Cornell Southeast Asian Studies, 1996).

Girling, John, *Thailand: Society and Politics* (Ithaca: Cornell University Press, 1981).

Government and Politics of Thailand, Sosakdi Xuto, ed. (Singapore: Oxford University Press, 1987).

Handley, Paul, "More of the Same? Politics and Business, 1987–96," in *Political Change in Thailand: Democracy and Participation*, Kevin Hewison, ed. (London: Routledge, 1997), pp. 94–113.

Hanks, Lucien M., "Merit and Power in the Thai Social Order," *American Anthropologist* 46 (1982), pp. 1247–61.

Hart, Gillian, "Agrarian Change in the Context of State Patronage," in *Agrarian Transformations: Local Processes and the State in Southeast Asia*, Gillian Hart, *et al.*, eds. (Berkeley: University of California Press, 1989), pp. 31–49.

Henderson, Jeffrey, "Uneven Crises: Institutional Foundations of East Asian Economic Turmoil," *Economy and Society* 28:3 (1999), pp. 327–68.

Hewison, Kevin, "Emerging Social Forces in Thailand: New Political and Economic Roles," in *Culture and Privilege in Capitalist Asia*, Michael Pinches, ed. (New York: Routledge, 1999), pp. 137–62.

Hewison, Kevin, "Of Regimes, State, and Pluralities: Thai Politics Enters the 1990s," in *Southeast Asia in the 1990s: Authoritarianism, Democracy, and Capitalism*, Kevin Hewison, Richard Robison, and Garry Rodan, eds. (St. Leonards, NSW: Allen & Unwin, 1993), pp. 159–90.

Hewison, Kevin, "Political Oppositions and Regime Change in Thailand," in *Political Oppositions in Industrializing Asia*, Garry Rodan, ed. (London: Routledge, 1996), pp. 72–94.

Hewison, Kevin, *Bankers and Bureaucrats: Capital and the Role of the State in Thailand*, Monograph 34 (New Haven: Yale University, Southeast Asia Center, 1989).

Hewison, Kevin, *Power and Politics in Thailand* (Manila and Wollongong: Journal of Contemporary Asia Publishers, 1989).

Hewison, Kevin, and Andrew Brown, "Labour and Unions in an Industrialising Thailand," *Journal of Contemporary Asia* 24:4 (December 1994), pp. 483–514.

Hewison, Kevin, and Maniemai Thongyou, *The New Generation of Provincial Business People in Northeastern Thailand* (Perth: Asia Research Centre, Murdoch University, 1993).

In the Mirror, Benedict Anderson and Ruchira Mendiones, eds. (Bangkok: DK Book House, 1985).

Jackson, Peter A., *Buddhism, Legitimation, and Conflict: The Political Functions of Urban Thai Buddhism* (Singapore: Institute for Southeast Asian Studies, 1989).

Jansen, Karel, "Thailand: The Next NIC?" *Journal of Contemporary Asia* 21:1 (1991), pp. 13–30

Jansen, Karel, *Finance, Growth, and Stability: Financing Economic Development in Thailand, 1960–1985* (Aldershot: Ashgate, 1990).

Ji Ungpakorn, *The Struggle for Democracy and Social Justice in Thailand* (Bangkok: Arom Pongpangan Foundation, 1997).

Johnston, David B., "Bandit, *Nakleng*, and Peasant in Rural Thai Society," *Contributions to Asian Studies* 15 (1980), pp. 90–101.

Kemp, Jeremy, "The Manipulation of Personal Relations: From Kinship to Patron-Clientage," in *Strategies and Structures in Thai Society*, Han ten Brummelhuis and Jeremy Kemp, eds. (Amsterdam: Anthropological-Sociological Centre, 1984).

Kermel-Torrès, Dorayne, *Atlas of Thailand: Spatial Structure and Development* (Chiang Mai: Silkworm Books, 2004).

Keyes, Charles F., *Isan: Regionalism in Northeastern Thailand* (Ithaca: Cornell Southeast Asian Studies, 1997).

Keyes, Charles F., *Thailand: Buddhist Kingdom as Modern Nation-State* (Boulder: Westview, 1987).

Khamsing Srinawk, *The Politician and Other Thai Stories* (Kuala Lumpur: Oxford University Press, 1973).

Kirby, Andrew, "State, Local State, Context, and Spatiality: A Reappraisal of State Theory," in *The Illusive State*, J.A. Caporaso ed. (Newberry Park: Sage, 1989), pp. 204–26.

Kraiyudt Dhiratayakinant, "Public-Private Sector Partnership in Industrialization," in *Thailand's Industrialization and its Consequences*, Medhi Krongkaew, ed. (New York: St. Martin's, 1995), pp. 99–115.

Kramol Tongdhamachart, *Toward a Political Party Theory in Thai Perspective* (Singapore: Maruzen Asia, 1982).

Krannich, Ronald L., *Mayors and Managers in Thailand: The Struggle for Political Life in Administrative Settings* (Athens: Ohio University Center for International Studies, 1978).

Krirkkiat Phipatseritham and Yoshihara Kunio, *Business Groups in Thailand* (Singapore: Institute of Southeast Asian Studies, 1983).

Krongkaew, Medhi, "The Political Economy of Decentralization in Thailand," *Southeast Asian Affairs* (1995), pp. 343–61.

Kuhonta, Erik Martinez, *The Political Foundations for Equitable Development in Malaysia and Thailand* (Ph.D. Dissertation, Politics Department, Princeton University, 2003).

Kuhonta, Erik Martinez, and Alex M. Mutebi, "Thaksin Triumphant: The Implications of One-party Dominance in Thailand," *Asian Affairs* 33:1 (Spring 2006), pp. 39–54.

Kulick, Elliott, and Dick Wilson, *Thailand's Turn: Profile of a New Dragon* (New York: St. Martin's, 1992).

Laird, John, *Money Politics, Globalisation, and Crisis: The Case of Thailand* (Singapore: Graham Brash, Ltd., 2000).

Laird, John, *Proposals for Constitutional Reform: Thailand in the 21st Century* (Bangkok: John Laird at Craftsman Press, 1997).

Lim, E.R., *et al.*, *Thailand: Toward a Development Strategy of Full Participation* (Washington: World Bank, 1980).

Lissak, Moshe, *A Socio-Political Hierarchy in a Loose Social Structure: The Structure of Stratification in Thailand*, forward by S.N. Eisenstadt (Jerusalem: Jerusalem Academic Press, 1973).

London, Bruce, and Kristine L. Anderson, "Rural-Urban Hierarchy and National Development: The Role of Elites in the Distribution of Scarce Resources to the Thai Hinterland," *Social Science Quarterly* 67 (1986) pp. 545–60.

London, Bruce, *Metropolis and Nation in Thailand: The Political Economy of Uneven Development* (Boulder: Westview, 1980).

Lynch, Daniel C., "International 'Decentering' and Democratization: The Case of Thailand," *International Studies Quarterly* 48 (2004), pp. 339–62.

MacIntyre, Andrew, "Business-Government Relations in Industrializing East Asia: South Korea and Thailand," (Nathan: Centre for the Study of Australian-Asia Relations, Griffith University, Australia-Asia Paper No. 53, 1990).

Maniemai Thongyou, "Sub-contracting Industry in Rural Villages: Fish-nets in Rural Thailand," Working Paper (Hong Kong: City University of Hong Kong, Southeast Asia Research Center, June 2001).

McCargo, Duncan, "Thailand's Political Parties: Real, Authentic, and Actual" in *Political Change in Thailand: Democracy and Participation*, Kevin Hewison, ed. (London: Routledge, 1997), pp. 114–31.

McCargo, Duncan, *Chamlong Srimuang and the New Thai Politics* (London: Hurst, 1997).

McCargo, Duncan, *Politics and the Press in Thailand* (London: Routledge, 2001).

McCargo, Duncan, *Reforming Thai Politics* (Singapore: Institute of Southeast Asian Studies, 2002).

Missingham, Bruce, "Local Bureaucrats, Power, and Participation," in *Political Change in Thailand*, Kevin Hewison, ed. (London: Routledge, 1997), pp. 149–62.

Moerman, Michael, *Agricultural Change and Peasant Choice in a Thai Village* (Berkeley: University of California Press, 1968).

Money and Power in Provincial Thailand, Ruth McVey, ed. (Singapore: Institute for Southeast Asian Studies, 2000).

Morell, David L., *Power and Parliament in Thailand: The Futile Challenge* (Ph.D. Dissertation, Woodrow Wilson School, Princeton University, 1974).

Morell, David L., and Chai-Anan Samudavanija, *Political Conflict in Thailand: Reform, Reaction, Revolution* (Cambridge: Oelgeschlager, 1981).

Mulder, Niels, *Thai Images: The Culture of the Public World* (Chiangmai: Silkworm Books, 1997).

Murray, David, *Angels and Devils: Thai Politics from February 1991 to September 1992 — A Struggle for Democracy?* (Bangkok: White Orchid Press, 1996).

Muscat, Robert J., *Thailand's 1992 Elections: Economic Growth and Political Change* (New York: Asia Society, 1992).

Muscat, Robert J., *The Fifth Tiger: A Study of Thai Development Policy* (Armonk: Sharpe, 1994).

Mutebi, Alex M., *Revealed Preferences for Locally Provided Public Goods and Services: Experiments from Four Thailand Towns* (Ph.D. Dissertation, Woodrow Wilson School, Princeton University, 2000).

Neher, Clark D., "Democratization in Thailand," *Asian Affairs* 21:4 (Winter 1995), pp. 195–09.

Neher, Clark D., "Political Corruption in a Thai Province," *Journal of Developing Areas* 7:4 (1977), pp. 484–89.

Nelson, Michael H., *Central Authority and Local Democratization in Thailand* (Bangkok: White Lotus Press, 1998).

Nipon Poapongsakorn, "Rural Industrialization: Problems and Prospects, in *Thailand's Industrialization and its Consequences*, Medhi Krongkaew, ed. (New York: St. Martin's, 1995), pp. 116–42.

Ockey, James, *Business Leaders, Gangsters, and the Middle Class: Societal Groups and Civilian Rule in Thailand* (Ph.D. Dissertation, Government Department, Cornell University, 1992).

Ockey, James, "*Chaopho*: Capital Accumulation and Social Welfare in Thailand," *Crossroads* 8 (1993), pp. 48–77.

Ockey, James, "Creating the Thai Middle Class," in *Culture and Privilege in Capitalist Asia*, Michael Pinches, ed. (New York: Routledge, 1999), pp. 230–49.

Ockey, James, "Political Parties, Factions, and Corruption in Thailand," *Modern Asian Studies* 28:2 (1994), pp. 251–77.

Ockey, James, "Thailand: The Struggle to Redefine Civil-Military Relations," in *Coercion and Governance: The Declining Political Role of the Military in Asia*, Muthiah Alagappa, ed. (Stanford: Stanford University Press, 2001), pp. 187–208.

Ockey, James, "Thailand in 2007," *Asian Survey* 48:1 (January–February 2008), pp. 20–28.

Onchan Tongroj, "Informal Rural Finance in Thailand," in *Informal Finance in Low-Income Countries*, Dale W. Adams and Delbert A. Fitchett, eds. (Boulder: Westview, 1992), pp. 103–17.

Parichart Chotiya, "The Changing Role of Provincial Business in the Thai Political Economy," in *Political Change in Thailand: Democracy and Participation*, Kevin Hewison, ed. (London: Routledge, 1997), pp. 251–64.

Paritta Chalermpow Koanantakool, "Thai Middle-class Practice and Consumption of Traditional Dance: 'Thai-ness' and High Art," in *Local Cultures and the "New Asia": The State, Culture, and Capitalism ion Southeast Asia*, C.J.W.-L. Wee, ed. (Singapore: Institute for Southeast Asian Studies, 2002), pp. 217–39.

Pasuk Phongpaichit and Chris Baker, "Power in Transition: Thailand in the 1990s," in *Political Change in Thailand: Democracy and Participation*, Kevin Hewison, ed. (London: Routledge, 1997), pp. 21–41.

Pasuk Phongpaichit and Chris Baker, *Thai Capital after the 1997 Crisis* (Chiangmai: Silkworm Books, 2008).

Pasuk Phongpaichit and Chris Baker, "Thailand's Brutal Campaign in the Name of a Drug War," *International Herald Tribune*, May 27, 2003, p. 7.

Pasuk Phongpaichit and Chris Baker, *Thailand's Boom and Bust* (Chiangmai: Silkworm Books, 1998).

Pasuk Phongpaichit and Chris Baker, *Thailand's Boom!* (North Sydney: Allen and Unwin, 1996).

Pasuk Phongpaichit and Chris Baker, *Thailand's Crisis* (Singapore: Institute for Southeast Asian Studies, 2000).

Pasuk Phongpaichit and Chris Baker, *Thailand: Economy and Politics* (Kuala Lumpur: Oxford University Press, 1995).

Pasuk Phongpaichit and Chris Baker, *Thaksin: The Business of Politics in Thailand* (Chiangmai: Silkworm Books, 2004).

Pasuk Phongpaichit and Sungsidh Piriyarangsan, *Corruption and Democracy in Thailand* (Chiangmai: Silkworm, 1997).

Pasuk Phongpaichit, "Civilizing the State: State, Civil Society, and Politics in Thailand," Wertheim Lecture (Amsterdam: Centre for Asian Studies, 1999).

Pasuk Phongpaichit, Sungsidh Piriyarangsan, and Nualnoi Theerat, *Guns, Girls, Gambling, and Ganja [marijuana & drugs]: Thailand's Illegal Economy and Public Policy* (Chiangmai: Silkworm, 1998).

Peleggi, Maurizio, *Thailand: The Worldly Kingdom* (London: Reaktion Books, 2007).

Phillips, Herbert P., "The Election Ritual in a Thai Village," *Journal of Social Issues* 14 (September 1958), pp. 36–58.

Phillips, Herbert P., *Thai Peasant Personality: The Patterning of Interpersonal Behavior in the Village of Bang Chan* (Berkeley: University of California Press, 1965).

Political Change in Thailand: Democracy and Participation, Kevin Hewison, ed. (London: Routledge, 1997).

Political Reform in Thailand: From Representative Democracy towards Participatory Democracy, "Krasuang Kantangprathet," ed. (Bangkok: News Division, Information Department, Ministry of Foreign Affairs, 1997).

Pradit Charsombut, *Provincial Industry Labor Market* (Bangkok: Thailand Development Research Institute, 1990).

Prince of Songkla University, *Farming Systems Research and Development in Thailand* (Haad Yai: Thai-French Farming Systems Research Project, 1988).

Prizzia, Ross, *Thailand in Transition: The Role of Oppositional Forces* (Honolulu: University of Hawaii Press, 1985).

Prudhisan Jumbala and Maneerat Mitprasat, "Mobilization, Movement Formation, and Politicization: Environment-Related Cases from Southern Thailand," *Journal of Social Sciences* 28:3 (April 1994), pp. 93–105.

Prudhisan Jumbala, *Nation-Building and Democratization in Thailand: A Political History* (Bangkok: Chulalongkorn University Social Research Institute, 1992).

Quah, Jon S.T., "Combating Corruption in South Korea and Thailand," in *The Self-Restraining State: Power and Accountability in New Democracies*, Andreas Schedler, Larry Diamond, and Marc F. Plattner, eds. (Boulder: Lynne Rienner, 1999), pp. 245–56.

Richardson, Harry W., "Towards a National Urban Development Strategy in Thailand," in *Equity with Growth? Planning Perspectives for Small*

Towns in Developing Countries, H.D. Kammeier and P. Swan, eds. (Bangkok: Asian Institute of Technology, 1984), pp. 110–33.

Riggs, Fred W., *Thailand: The Modernization of a Bureaucratic Polity* (Honolulu: East-West Center Press, 1966).

Samporn Sangchai, *Some Observations on the Elections and Coalition Formation in Thailand, 1976* (Singapore: Institute of Southeast Asian Studies, 1976).

Seri Phongphit, *Back to the Roots: Village and Self-Reliance in a Thai Context* (Bangkok: Rural Development Documentation Center, 1986).

Siamwalla, Ammar, "The Thai Rural Credit System and Elements of a Theory: Public Subsidies, Private Information, and Segmented Markets," in *The Economics of Rural Organization: Theory, Practice, and Policy*, Karla Hoff, Avishay Raverman, and Joseph E. Stiglitz, eds. (New York: Oxford University Press for the World Bank, 1993), pp. 154–85.

Siffin, William, *The Thai Bureaucracy: Institutional Change and Development* (Honolulu: East-West Center Press, 1966).

Skinner, G. William, "Change and Persistence in Chinese Culture Overseas: A Comparison of Thailand and Java," in *Change and Persistence in Thai Society: Essays in Honor of Lauriston Sharp*, Skinner, ed. (Ithaca: Cornell University Press, 1975).

Skinner, G. William, "Chinese Assimilation and Thai Politics," *Journal of Asian Studies* 16 (February 1957), pp. 237–50, reprinted in *Southeast Asia: The Politics of National Integration*, John T. McAlister, ed. (New York: Random House, 1973).

Skinner, G. William, "Overseas Chinese Leadership: Paradigm for a Paradox," in *Leadership and Authority: A Symposium*, Gehan Wijeyewardene, ed. (Singapore: University of Malaya Press, 1968), pp. 191–203.

Skinner, G. William, *Chinese Society in Thailand: An Analytical History* (Ithaca: Cornell University Press, 1957).

Skinner, G. William, *Leadership and Power in the Chinese Community of Thailand* (Ithaca: Cornell University Press, 1958).

Somboon Suksamrann, *Military Elite in Thai Politics: Brief Bibliographical Data on the Officers in the Thai Legislature* (Singapore: Institute for Southeast Asian Studies, 1984).

Somchai Jitsuchon, "Sources of Thailand's Economic Growth, A Fifty-Years Perspective, 1950–2000," in http://www.gdnet.org/pdf/jitsuchon.pdf, seen July 19, 1983.

Somchai Phatharathanunth, "Civil Society and Democratization in Thailand: A Critique of Elite Democracy," in *Reforming Thai Politics*, Duncan McCargo, ed. (Copenhagen: Nordic Institute of Asian Studies, 2002), pp. 125–42.

Somsak Tambunlertchai, *et al.*, *Small- and Medium-Scale Industries in Thailand and Subcontracting Arrangements* (Tokyo: Institute of Developing Economies, 1986).

Somsak Tambunlertchai, *A Profile of Provincial Industries* (Bangkok: Thailand Development Research Institute, 1990).

Somsak Tambunlertchai, *Changes in the Industrial Structures and the Role of Small and Medium Industries in Asia: The Case of Thailand* (Tokyo: Institute of Developing Economies, 1986).

State Power and Culture in Thailand, E. Paul Durrenberger, ed. (New Haven: Yale University Southeast Asia Studies Center, 1996).

Stifel, Laurence D., "Patterns of Land Ownership in Central Thailand During the Twentieth Century," *Journal of the Siam Society* 64:1 (January 1976), pp. 237–74.

Stowe, Judith A., *Siam Becomes Thailand: A Story of Intrigue* (Honolulu: University Press of Hawaii, 1991).

Structural Adjustment and Policy Reform: Impacts on Small and Medium Enterprises in Asian Economies (report of a 1990 seminar in Chiangmai), Bruce M. Koppel, ed. (Tokyo: Asian Productivity Organization and Honolulu: East-West Center, 1990).

Suchit Bunbongkarn, "Elections and Democratization in Thailand," in *The Politics of Elections in Southeast Asia*, R.H. Taylor, ed. (Washington: Woodrow Wilson Center, 1996), pp. 184–200.

Suchit Bunbongkarn, *State of the Nation: Thailand* (Singapore: Institute of Southeast Asian Studies, 1996).

Suchit Bunbongkarn, *The Military in Thai Politics, 1981–86* (Singapore: Institute of Southeast Asian Studies, 1987).

Suehiro Akira, "Capitalist Development in Postwar Thailand: Commercial Bankers, Industrial Elite, and Agribusiness Groups," in *Southeast Asian Capitalists*, Ruth McVey, ed. (Ithaca: Southeast Asia Program, Cornell University, 1992), pp. 35–64.

Sukhumband Paribatra and Kitti Limskul, *Thailand After the Election: Politics and Economics* (Singapore: Institute of Southeast Asian Studies, 2001).

Sungsidh Phiriyarangsan and Kanchada Poonpanich, "Labor Institutions in an Export-oriented Country: A Case Study of Thailand," in *Workers,*

Institutions, and Economic Growth in Asia, G. Rodgers, ed. (Geneva: International Institute of Labour Studies, 1994), pp. 211–53.

Supachai Manusthaidool, "Thailand," in *Labour and Industrial Relations in Asia* (Melbourne: Longman Cheshire, 1994), pp. 241–69.

Surachart Bamrungsuk, "Thailand: Military Professionalism at the Crossroads," in *Military Professionalism in Asia: Conceptual and Empirical Perspectives*, Muthiah Alagappa, ed. (Honolulu: East-West Center, 2001), pp. 77–92.

Surin Maisrikrod, *Thailand's Two General Elections of 1992: Democracy Sustained* (Singapore: Institute of Southeast Asian Studies, 1992).

Surin Maisrikrod and Duncan McCargo, "Electoral Politics: Commercialisation and Exclusion," in *Political Change in Thailand: Democracy and Participation*, Kevin Hewison, ed. (London: Routledge, 1997), pp. 132–48.

Thailand's Boom and Bust: Collected Papers, Ammar Siamwalla, *et al.*, eds. (Bangkok: Thailand Development Research Institute Foundation, 1997).

Thailand's Industrialization and its Consequences, Medhi Krongkaew, ed. (New York: St. Martin's, 1995).

The Informal Sector in Thai Economic Development, Pasuk Phongpaichit and Shigeru Itoga, eds. (Tokyo: Institute for the Developing Economies, 1992).

The Thai Economy in Transition, Peter G. Warr, ed. (Cambridge: Cambridge University Press, 1993).

Thitinan Phonsudhirak, "Thailand: Democratic Authoritarianism," in *Southeast Asian Affairs, 2003* (Singapore: ISEAS, 2003).

Thongchai Winichakul, *Siam Mapped: A History of the Geo-Body of a Nation* (Honolulu: University of Hawaii Press, 1994).

Torelli, Hans B., and Gerald D. Sentell, *Consumer Emancipation and Economic Development: The Case of Thailand* (Greenwich: JAI Press, 1982).

Tower, Ivory [pseud. of Ammar Siamwalla], "Mexico 1994 versus Thailand 1997," in *Thailand's Boom and Bust: Collected Papers*, Ammar Siamwalla, *et al.*, eds. (Bangkok: Thailand Development Research Institute Foundation, 1997), pp. 53–62.

Turton, Andrew, "Local Powers and Rural Differentiation," in *Agrarian Transformations: Local Processes and the State in Southeast Asia*, Gillian Hart, *et al.*, eds. (Berkeley: University of California Press, 1989), pp. 70–97.

Turton, Andrew, "People of the Same Spirit: Local Matrikin Groups and their Cults," *Mankind* 14 (1984), pp. 272–85.

Turton, Andrew, "Thailand: Agrarian Bases of State Power," in *Agrarian Transformations: Local Processes and the State in Southeast Asia*, Gillian Hart, *et al.*, eds. (Berkeley: University of California Press, 1989), pp. 53–69.

Ueda Yoko, *Local Economy and Entrepreneurship in Thailand: A Case Study of Nakhon Ratchasima* (Kyoto: Kyoto University Press, 1995).

Unger, Danny, *Building Social Capital in Thailand: Fibers, Finance, and Infrastructure* (Cambridge: Cambridge University Press, 1998).

Warr, Peter G. and Bhanupong Nidhiprabha, *Thailand's Macroeconomic Miracle: Stable Adjustment and Sustained Growth* (Washington: World Bank, 1996).

Warr, Peter, "Boom, Bust, and Beyond," in *Thailand Beyond the Crisis*, P. Warr, ed. (London: RoutledgeCurzon, 2004).

Wilson, David A., *Politics in Thailand* (Ithaca: Cornell University Press, 1962).

World Bank, "Thailand: Rural Growth and Employment" (Washington: World Bank, 1984).

World Bank, "Thailand: Towards a Development Strategy of Full Participation" (Washington: World Bank, 1980).

Wright, Joseph J., Jr., *The Balancing Act: A History of Modern Thailand* (Oakland: Pacific Rim Press, 1991).

Wyatt, David, *A Short History of Thailand* (New Haven: Yale University Press, 1984).

Zimmerman, Robert F., *Reflections on the Collapse of Democracy in Thailand* (Singapore: Institute of Southeast Asian Studies, 1978).

SOURCES ON THE PHILIPPINES

Abao, Carmela, "Dynamics among Political Blocs in the Formation of a Political Party," in *Philippine Democracy Agenda*: vol. 3, *Civil Society Making Civil Society*, Miriam Coronel Ferrer, ed. (Quezon City: Third World Studies Center, University of the Philippines, 1997), pp. 271–88.

Abenir, Luis E., and Pedro Laylo, Jr., "Monitoring Recent National Elections in the Philippines: The SWS 1992 and 1995 Surveys" (Diliman: Social Weather Stations Occasional Paper, 1997).

Abenir, Luis E., and Pedro R. Laylo, Jr., "The 1995 Senatorial Election Surveys" (Diliman: Social Weather Stations Bulletin, 1996).

Abinales, Patricio N., *Images of State Power: Essays on Philippine Politics from the Margins* (Diliman: University of the Philippines Press, 1998).

Abinales, Patricio N., *State and Society in the Philippines* (Lanham: Rowman and Littlefield, 2005).

Abrenica, Ma. Joy, *Building the Capital Goods Sector: An Agenda for Development* (Quezon City: Philippine Center for Policy Studies, n.d., c. 1993).

Abueva, Jose, "Dissatisfaction with the Way Our Democracy Works," in *Towards a Federal Republic of the Philippines: A Reader*, Jose Abueva, ed. (Manila: Center for Social Policy and Governance, 2002).

Adams, Dale W., H.Y. Chen and M.B. Lamberte, "Differences in Uses of Rural Financial Markets in Taiwan and the Philippines," *World Development* 21:4 (April 1993), pp. 555–63.

Aguilar, Filomeno V., "Of Cocks and Bets: Gambling, Class Structuring and State Formation in the Philippines," in *Patterns of Power and Politics in the Philippines*, James F. Eder and Robert L. Youngblood, eds. (Tempe: Arizona State University Program for Southeast Asian Studies, 1994), pp. 147–96.

Aguilar, Filomeno V., *Clash of Spirits: The History of Power and Sugar Planter Hegemony on a Visayan Island* (Honolulu: University Press of Hawaii, 1998).

Aguilar, Filomeno V., *Landlessness and Hired Labour in Philippine Rice Farms* (Swansea: Centre for Development Studies, 1981).

Alejo, Myrna J., Maria Elena P. Rivera, and Noel Inocencio P. Valencia, *[De]scribing Elections: A Study of Elections in the Lifeworld of San Isidro* (Quezon City: Institute for Popular Democracy, 1996).

An Anarchy of Families: State and Family in the Philippines, Alfred W. McCoy, ed. (Madison: University of Wisconsin Center for Southeast Asian Studies, 1993).

Anderson, Benedict, "Cacique Democracy in the Philippines: Origins and Dreams," *New Left Review* 169 (May–June 1988), pp. 3–31.

Ang See, Teresita, "People of the Philippines vs. Crimes," in *Philippine Democracy Agenda*, vol. 2, *State-Civil Society Relations in Policy-Making*, Marlon A. Wui and Ma. Glenda S. Lopez, eds. (Quezon City: Third World Studies Center, University of the Philippines, 1997), pp. 125–39.

Ang See, Teresita, "The Ethnic Chinese as Filipinos," in *Ethnic Chinese as Southeast Asians*, Leo Suryadinata, ed. (Singapore: Institute for Southeast Asian Studies, 1997), pp. 158–210.

Ang See, Teresita, and Go Bon Juan, *The Ethnic Chinese in the Philippine Revolution* (Manila: Kaisa Para Sa Kaunlaran, 1996).

Angeles, Jocelyn Vicente, "The Naga City Urban Poor Federation and Pro-Poor Ordinances and Policies, in *Philippine Democracy Agenda*: vol. 2, *State-Civil Society Relations in Policy-Making*, Marlon A. Wui and Ma. Glenda S. Lopez, eds. (Quezon City: Third World Studies Center, University of the Philippines, 1997), pp. 97–112.

Angeles, Leonora C., "Grassroots Democracy and Community Empowerment: The Political Requirements of Sustainable Poverty Reduction in Asia," paper for the conference on "Democracy and Civil Society: Challenges and Opportunities in Asia," Queen's University, Montreal, August 2000.

Angeles, Leonora C., "The Political Dimension in the Agrarian Question: Strategies of Resilience and Political Entrepreneurship of Agrarian Elite Families in a Philippine Province," *Rural Sociology* 64:4 (December 1999), pp. 667–92.

Arroyo, Dennis M., "Emerging Cracks in the Political Machine" (Diliman: Social Weather Stations Bulletin, 1992).

Arroyo, Dennis M., "Midway in the Race for the Presidency" (Diliman: Social Weather Stations Bulletin, 1997).

Arroyo, Dennis M., "Selected Personal Characteristics which May Affect the Chances of National Candidates in 1992" (Diliman: Social Weather Stations Bulletin, 1991).

Arroyo, Dennis M., "Surveys of Satisfaction with Democracy, 1991–95" (Diliman: Social Weather Stations Bulletin, 1995).

Assessing People's Participation in Governance: The Case of Itogon Municipality, Steven Rood, ed. (Baguio: University of the Philippines College Baguio, Cordillera Studies Center, 1993).

Balisacan, Arsenio M., "Getting the Story Right: Growth, Redistribution, and Poverty Alleviation in the Philippines," *Philippine Review of Economics and Business* 34:1 (June 1997), pp. 1–37.

Balisacan, Arsenio M., "Rural Growth Linkages, Poverty, and Income Distribution," *Philippine Review of Economics and Business* 29:1 (June 1992), pp. 62–85.

Balisacan, Arsenio M., Fuwa Nobuhiko, and Margarita H. Debuque, "The Political Economy of Philippine Rural Development Since the 1960s," in http://www.chiba-u.ac.jp/mkt/philippines.pdf, seen July 19, 1983.

Barreveld, Dirk J., *Erap Ousted: People Power versus Chinese Conspiracy?.... How the Philippine Nation Almost Became a Victim of a Chinese*

Conspiracy to Turn the Country into a Gambling and Entertainment Paradise, With a Blueprint for Survival (Mandaue City, Cebu: Arcilla Travel Guides, 2001).

Batara, John, *The Comprehensive Agrarian Reform Program: More Misery for the Philippine Peasantry* (Manila: Ibon Philippines Databank and Research Center, 1996).

Bautista, Luz A., Joy L. Casuga, and Gerardo A. Sandoval, "Public Opinion Surveys and Local Governance: The Quezon City 1993–96 Surveys" (Diliman: Social Weather Stations Occasional Paper, 1997).

Bello, Walden, and John Gershman, "Democratization and Stabilization in the Philippines," *Critical Sociology* 17:1 (1990), pp. 35–56.

Belmonte, Patricia A., "Opinion Surveys about Term Limits" (Diliman: Social Weather Stations Bulletin, 1997).

Berlow, Alan, *Dead Season: A Story of Murder and Revenge on the Philippine Island of Negros* (New York: Pantheon, 1996).

Berner, Erhard, and Rüdiger Korff, *Dynamik der Burökratie und Konservatismus der Unternehmer: Strategische Gruppen in Thailand und den Philippinen* (The Dynamics of Bureaucracy and the Conservatism of Entrepreneurs: Strategic Groups in Thailand and the Philippines), *Internationales Asienforum* 22:3–4 (November 1991), pp. 287–305.

Betrayals of the Public Trust: Investigative Reports on Corruption, Sheila S. Coronel, ed. (Quezon City: Philippine Center for Investigative Journalism, 2000).

Bionat, Marvin P., *How to Win (or Lose) in Philippine Elections* (Pasig City: Anvil Publishing, 1998).

Boudis, Howarth E. and Lawrence J. Haddad, *Agricultural Commercialization, Nutrition, and the Rural Poor: A Study of Philippine Farm Households* (Boulder: Lynne Rienner, 1990).

Boyce, James K., *The Political Economy of Growth and Impoverishment in the Marcos Era* (Quezon City: Ateneo de Manila University Press, 1993).

Bray, Francesca, *The Rice Economies: Technology and Development in Asian Societies* (Berkeley: University of California Press, 1986).

Broad, Robin, *Unequal Alliance: The IMF, the World Bank, and the Philippines* (Berkeley: University of California Press, 1988 [and in original form, a Princeton University Woodrow Wilson School Ph.D. thesis]).

Canlas, Mamerto, Mariano Miranda, and James Putzel, *Land, Poverty, and Politics in the Philippines* (Quezon City: Claretian Publications, 1988).

Cariño, Theresa Chong, *Chinese Big Business in the Philippines: Political Leadership and Change* (Singapore: Times Academic Press, 1998).

Carroll, John J., S.J., "Growth, Agrarian Reform, and Equity: Two Studies [in Bulacan and Bikol]," in *Second View from the Paddy*, Antonio J. Ledesma, *et al.*, eds. (Manila: Institute of Philippine Culture, Ateneo de Manila University, 1983), pp. 15–23.

Casper, Gretchen, *Fragile Democracies* [esp. the Philippines]: *Legacies of Authoritarian Rule* (Pittsburgh: University of Pittsburgh Press, 1995).

Castillo, Gelia T., *All in a Grain of Rice* (Laguna: Southeast Asian Regional Center for Research in Agriculture, 1975).

Castillo, Gelia T., *How Participatory is Participatory Development? A Review of the Philippine Experience* (Manila: Philippine Institute for Development Studies, 1983).

Casuga, Joy L., "Perceived Honesty and Ethical Standards of People from Various Occupations" (Diliman: Social Weather Stations Bulletin, 1995).

Causes of Poverty: Myths, Facts, and Policies, Arsenio M. Balisacan and Shigeaki Fujisaki, eds. (Quezon City: University of the Philippines Press, 1999).

Chikiamco, Calixto V., *Reforming the System: Essays on Political Economy* (Manila: Orange Publications and Kalikasan Press, 1992).

Choice, Growth, and Development: Emerging and Enduring Issues, Emmanuel S. de Dios and Raul V. Fabella, eds. (Quezon City: University of the Philippines Press, 1996).

Chu, Hung M., Evan Leach, and Russell Manuel, "Cultural Effect and Strategic Decision among Filipino Entrepreneurs," http://www.icsb. org/pbs/98icsb/j010.htm.

Chua, Yvonne T., *Robbed: An Investigation of Corruption in Philippine Education* (Quezon City: Philippine Center for Investigative Journalism, 1999).

Citizen Participation in Local Governance: Experiences for Thailand, Indonesia, and the Philippines, Joel Rocamora, *et al.*, eds. (Manila: Institute for Popular Democracy, 2004).

Compadre Colonialism: Studies on the Philippines under American Rule, Norman G. Owen, ed. (Ann Arbor: Center for South and Southeast Asian Studies, 1971).

Contract Growing: Intensifying TNC [Transnational Corporation] Control in Philippine Agriculture, Antonio J. Tujan, Jr., ed. (Manila: IBON Foundation, 1998).

Coronel, Sheila S., "How Representative is Congress?" http://www.pcij.org/ stories/2004/congress.html, Philippine Center for Investigative Journalism Web, November 12, 2006.

Coronel, Sheila S., Yvonne Chua, Luz Rimban, and Booma Cruz, *The Rulemakers: How the Wealthy and Well-Born Dominate Congresss*,

(Quezon City: Philippine Center for Investigative Journalism, 2004), with accompanying data disk, *The Ties that Bind: A Guide to Family, Business, and Other Interests in Congress* (provided to the author by courtesy of Dr. Steven Rood, The Asia Foundation, Makati).

Cullinane, Michael, "Burgis Projects in the Post-Marcos Era," *Pilipinas* 21 (1993), pp. 74–76.

Cullinane, Michael, "Patron as Client: Warlord Politics and the Duranos of Danao," in *An Anarchy of Families: State and Family in the Philippines*, Alfred W. McCoy, ed. (Madison: University of Wisconsin Center for Southeast Asian Studies, 1993), pp. 163–242.

Cullinane, Michael, *Ilustrado Politics: Filipino Elite Responses to American Rule, 1898–1908* (Manila: Ateneo de Manila Press, 2004).

Danguian-Vitug, Marites, *Kudeta: The Challenge to Philippine Democracy*, Rigoberto Tiglao, ed. (Quezon City: Philippine Center for Investigative Journalism, 1990).

Day, Beth, *The Philippines: Shattered Showcase of Democracy in Asia* (intro. by Carlos P. Romulo, Sec. of Foreign Affairs) (New York: M. Evans, 1974).

Dayag-Laylo, Carijane C., "Filipino Perceptions on the Social Reform Agenda" (Diliman: Social Weather Stations Bulletin, 1997).

de la Cruz, Edwin S., "Litigants' Perceptions of Court Decisions: A Case Study of a Workers' Community in Malabon," in *Philippine Democracy Agenda*: vol. 1, *Democracy and Citizenship in Filipino Political Culture*, Maria Serena I. Diokno, ed. (Quezon City: Third World Studies Center, University of the Philippines, 1997), pp. 239–54.

Decentralization Towards Democratization and Development, Raul P. de Guzman and Mila A. Reforma, eds. (Manila: Eastern Regional Organization for Public Administration, 1993).

Democratization: Philippine Perspectives, Felipe B. Miranda, ed. (Quezon City: University of the Philippines Press, 1995).

Doner, Richard, "Politics and the Growth of Local Capital in Southeast Asia: Auto Industries in the Philippines and Thailand," in *Southeast Asian Capitalists*, Ruth McVey, ed. (Ithaca: Southeast Asia Program, Cornell University, 1992), pp. 191–218.

Doronila, Amando, *The State, Economic Transformation, and Political Change in the Philippines, 1946–1972* (Singapore: Oxford University Press, 1992).

Eaton, Kent, "Restoration or Transformation: *Trapos* vs. NGOs in the Democratization of the Philippines," *Journal of Asian Studies* 62:2 (May 2003), pp. 469–96.

Eder, James F., *A Generation Later: Household Strategies and Economic Change in the Rural Philippines* (Quezon City: Ateneo de Manila University Press, 2000).

Endriga, Jose N., "The National Civil Service System of the Philippines," in *Civil Service Systems in Asia*, John P. Burns and Bidhya Bowornwathana, eds. (Cheltenham: Elgar, 2001), pp. 212–48.

Entrepreneurship and Small Enterprises Development: The Philippine Experience, Arnulfo F. Itao and Myrna R. Co, eds. (Quezon City: University of the Philippines Institute for Small Scale Industries, 1979).

Esguerra, Emmanuel F., and Richard F. Meyer, "Collateral Substitutes in Informal Financial Markets in the Philippines," in *Informal Finance in Low-Income Countries*, Dale W. Adams and Richard Meyer, eds. (Boulder: Westview, 1992), pp. 149–64.

Fabella, Raul V., "Strategic Household Behavior in Labor Surplus Economies," *Philippine Review of Economics and Business* 28:2 (December 1991), pp. 119–26.

Feder, Ernest, *Perverse Development* (Quezon City: Foundation for Nationalist Studies, 1983).

Fegan, Brian, "Accumulation on the Basis of an Unprofitable Crop," in *Agrarian Transformations: Local Processes and the State in Southeast Asia*, Gillian Hart, *et al.*, eds. (Berkeley: University of California Press, 1989), pp. 159–78.

Fegan, Brian, "Between the Lord and the Law: Tenants' Dilemmas," in *View from the Paddy: Empirical Studies of Philippine Rice Farming and Tenancy*, Frank Lynch, ed., *Philippine Sociological Review*, 20:1–2 (January/April 1972), pp. 113–28.

Fegan, Brian, "Entrepreneurs in Votes and Violence: Three Generations of a Peasant Political Family" in *An Anarchy of Families: State and Family in the Philippines*, Alfred W. McCoy, ed. (Madison: University of Wisconsin Center for Southeast Asian Studies, 1993), pp. 33–108.

Fegan, Brian, "The Philippines: Agrarian Stagnation Under a Decaying Regime," in *Agrarian Transformations: Local Processes and the State in Southeast Asia*, Gillian Hart, *et al.*, eds. (Berkeley: University of California Press, 1989), pp. 125–43.

Florintino-Hofileña, Chay, *News for Sale: The Corruption of the Philippine Media* (Quezon City: Philippine Center for Investigative Journalism and Center for Media Freedom and Responsibility, 1998).

Formilleza, Liezl S., "Comparing Enterprise Development in the Philippines and China," *Currents: Newsletter of the Philippine-China Development Resource Center* 11:1 (January–June 2000), pp. 24–27.

Fox, Jonathan, "Editor's Introduction," in *The Challenge of Rural Democratization: Perspectives from Latin America and the Philippines*, Jonathan Fox, ed. (London: Frank Cass, 1990), pp. 1–13.

From Marcos to Aquino: Local Perspectives on Political Transition in the Philippines, Benedict J. Kerkvliet and Rasil Mojares, eds. (Quezon City: Ateneo de Manila University Press, 1992).

Ghate, Prabhu B., "Lending to Micro Enterprises through NGOs in the Philippines," *Financial Landscapes Reconstructed: The Fine Art of Mapping Development*, Frits Bouman, *et al.*, eds. (Boulder: Westview, 1994), pp. 125–41.

Gills, Barry, Joel Rocamora, and Richard Wilson, "Low Intensity Democracy," in *Low Intensity Democracy: Political Power in the New World Order*, Barry Gills, Joel Rocamora, and Richard Wilson, eds. (Boulder: Pluto Press, 1993), pp. 3–34.

Gonzalez, Eduardo T. and Magdalena L. Mendoza, *Governance in Southeast Asia: Issues and Options* (Makati: Philippine Institute for Development Studies, 2003).

Gruta, Eileen M., "Review of Government Performance in 1994: Grades from the People's Perspective" (Diliman: Social Weather Stations Bulletin, 1995).

Guidote, Tony, "1998 Presidentiables, Part II: Socio-Demographic Profile of Public Opinion" (Diliman: Social Weather Stations Bulletin, 1996).

Guerrero, Linda Luz B., and Rumelia Mañgalindan, "The Chineseness of Filipinos: The SWS December 1996 National Survey" (Diliman: Social Weather Stations Bulletin, 1997).

Guttierez, Eric, *The Ties that Bind: A Guide on Family, Business, and Other Interests in the 9th House of Representatives* (Pasig City: Philippine Center for Investigative Journalism, 1994).

Hawes, Gary, "Marcos, His Cronies, and the Philippines' Failure to Develop," in *Southeast Asian Capitalists*, Ruth McVey, ed. (Ithaca: Southeast Asia Program, Cornell University, 1992), pp. 145–60.

Hawes, Gary, "Theories of Peasant Revolution: A Critique and Contribution from the Philippines," *World Politics* 42:2 (1990), pp. 261–98.

Hawes, Gary, *The Philippine State and the Marcos Regime* (Ithaca: Cornell University Pres, 1987).

Hawes, Gary, and Liu Hong, "Explaining the Dynamics of the Southeast Asian Political Economy: State, Society, and the Search for Economic Growth," *World Politics* 45:4 (July 1993), pp. 629–60.

Hedman, Eva-Lotta E., "The Philippines: Not So Military, Not So Civil," in *Coercion and Governance: The Declining Political Role of the Military in Asia* (Stanford: Stanford University Press, 2001), pp. 165–86.

Hicks, George L. and Geoffrey McNicoll, *Trade and Growth in the Philippines: An Open Dual Economy* (Ithaca: Cornell University Press, 1971).

Hicks, George L., and S. Gordon Redding, "Culture and Corporate Performance in the Philippines: The Chinese Puzzle," *Philippine Review of Economics and Business* 19 (1982), pp. 199–215.

Hollnsteiner, Mary Racelis, *The Dynamics of Power in a Philippine Municipality* (Quezon City: Community Development Research Council, University of the Philippines, 1963).

Hossain, Mahabub, "Economic Development in the Philippines: A Frustrated Take-Off?" *Philippine Review of Economics and Business* 33:1 (June 1996), pp. 88–118.

Hutchcroft, Paul D., *Booty Capitalism: The Politics of Banking in the Philippines* (Quezon City: Ateneo de Manila University Press, 1998) [orig. "Predatory Oligarchy, Patrimonial State: The Politics of Domestic Commercial Banking in the Philippines," Ph.D. Dissertation, Political Science Department, Yale University, 1993]).

Hutchcroft, Paul D., "Booty Capitalism: Business-Government Relations in the Philippines," in *Business and Government in Industrializing Asia*, Andrew MacIntyre, ed. (Ithaca: Cornell University Press, 1994), pp. 216–43.

Hutchcroft, Paul D., "Colonial Masters, National Politicos, and Provincial Lords: Central Authority and Local Autonomy in the American Philippines, 1900–1913," *Journal of Asian Studies* 59:2 (2000), pp. 277–306.

Hutchcroft, Paul D., "Dictatorship, Development, and Plunder: The Regimes of Park Chung Hee and Ferdinand Marcos Compared," paper for the American Political Science Association Annual Meeting, 2002.

Hutchcroft, Paul D., "Obstructive Corruption: The Politics of Privilege in the Philippines," in *Rents, Rent-seeking, and Economic Development: Theory and Evidence in Asia*, Mushtaq H. Kahn and K.S. Jomo, eds. (New York, Cambridge University Press, 2000), pp. 207–47.

Hutchcroft, Paul D., "Oligarch and Cronies in the Philippine State: The Politics of Patrimonial Plunder," *World Politics* 43 (April 1991), pp. 414–50.

Hutchcroft, Paul D., "Sustaining Economic and Political Reform: The Challenges Ahead," in *The Philippines: New Directions in Domestic Policy and Foreign Relations*, David G. Timberman, ed. (Singapore: Institute for Southeast Asian Studies and New York: Asia Society, 1998), pp. 23–48.

Hutchcroft, Paul D., and Joel Rocamora, "Strong Demands and Weak Institutions: Addressing the Democratic Deficit in the Philippines" (essay provided by courtesy of Dr. Rocamora).

Hutchcroft, Paul D., *Deciphering Decentralization: Central Authority and Local Bosses in the Philippines and Beyond* (New York: Cambridge University Press, forthcoming).

Hutchison, Jane, "Class and State Power in the Philippines," in *Southeast Asia in the 1990s: Authoritarianism, Democracy, and Capitalism*, Kevin Hewison, Richard Robison, and Garry Rodan, eds. (St. Leonards, NSW: Allen & Unwin, 1993), pp. 191–212.

Ibon Workers Desk, *The Philippine Garment and Textile Industries* (Manila: Ibon Foundation, 2001).

Impact of the East Asian Financial Crisis Revisited, Shahid Khandker, ed. (Makati: Philippine Institute for Development Studies, 2002).

Kaplan, Paul F., and Cynthia Hsien Huang, "Achievement Orientation of Small Industrial Entrepreneurs in the Philippines," *Human Organization* 33:2 (Summer 1974), pp. 173–82.

Karaos, Anna Marie A., "Democracy and Citizenship among Urban Middle Class Families," in *Philippine Democracy Agenda*: vol. 1, *Democracy and Citizenship in Filipino Political Culture*, Maria Serena I. Diokno, ed. (Quezon City: Third World Studies Center, University of the Philippines, 1997), pp. 113–32.

Kawanaka Takeshi, *Power in a Philippine City* [Naga City, Bikol] (Chiba: Institute of Developing Economies, 2002).

Kerkvliet, Benedict J. Tria, "Contested Meanings of Elections in the Philippines," in *The Politics of Elections in Southeast Asia*, R.H. Taylor, ed. (Washington: Woodrow Wilson Center, 1996), pp. 136–63.

Kerkvliet, Benedict J. Tria, *Everyday Politics in the Philippines: Class and Status Relations in a Central Luzon Village* (Berkeley: University of California Press, 1990).

Kessler, Richard J., *Rebellion and Repression in the Philippines* (New Haven: Yale University Pres, 1989).

Kikuchi Yasushi, *Uncrystallized Philippine Society: A Social Anthropological Analysis* (Quezon City: New Day Publishers, 1991).

Kimura Masataka, *Elections and Politics, Philippine Style: A Case in Lipa* (Manila: De La Salle University Press, 1997).

Koike Kenji, "Group Management of Business Groups in the Philippines," in *Philippine Business Leaders*, in Perla Q. Makil, *et al.*, eds. (Tokyo: Institute of Developing Economies, 1983), pp. 30–49.

Koike Kenji, "The Reorganization of *Zaibatsu* Groups under the Marcos and Aquino Regimes," *East Asian Cultural Studies* 28:1–4 (1989), pp. 127–43.

Landé, Carl H., *Leaders, Factions, and Parties: The Structure of Philippine Politics* (New Haven: Yale University Southeast Asia Monograph Series, 1965).

Landé, Carl H., *Post-Marcos Politics: A Geographical and Statistical Analysis of the 1992 Presidential Elections* (Singapore: Institute of Southeast Asian Studies, 1996).

Landé, Carl H., *Southern Tagalog Voting, 1946–63: Political Behavior in a Philippine Region* (DeKalb: Northern Illinois University Center for Southeast Asian Studies, 1973).

Laquian, Aprodicio, and Eleanor, *Joseph Ejercito "Erap" Estrada: The Centennial President* (Diliman: College of Public Administration, University of the Philippines, 1998).

Lara, Jr., Francisco, and Horacio Morales, Jr., "The Peasant Movement and the Challenge of Democratization in the Philippines," in *The Challenge of Rural Democratization: Perspectives from Latin America and the Philippines*, Jonathan Fox, ed. (London: Frank Cass, 1990), pp. 143–57.

Larkin, John A., *The Pampangans: Colonial Society in a Philippine Province* (Berkeley: University of California Press, 1972).

Lazatín, Carlos Manuel, *The Challenge of Economic Reform in a Democracy: The Philippines and Thailand in the 1990s* (Princeton University Senior Thesis, Woodrow Wilson School, 1999).

Lee-Chua, Queena N., *Successful Family Businesses: Dynamics of Five Filipino Business Families* (Quezon City: Ateneo de Manila University Press, 1997).

Lewis, Henry T., *Ilocano Rice Farmers: A Comparative Study of two Philippine Barrios* (Honolulu: University of Hawaii Press, 1971).

Lim-Mangada, Ladylyn, "Grooming the Wards: Dynamics Between a Political Party and Community Groups," in *Philippine Democracy Agenda*: vol. 3, *Civil Society Making Civil Society*, Miriam Coronel

Ferrer, ed. (Quezon City: Third World Studies Center, University of the Philippines, 1997), pp. 259–70.

Low Intensity Democracy: Political Power in the New World Order, Barry Gills, Joel Rocamora, and Richard Wilson, eds. (Boulder: Pluto Press, 1993).

Lund, Susan-Marie, *Informal Credit and Risk-Sharing Networks: Empirical Evidence from the Philippines* (Ph.D. dissertation, Stanford University, 1996).

Lynch, Frank, S.J., *Social Class in a Bikol Town* (Chicago: Philippine Studies Program, Anthropology Department, University of Chicago, 1959).

Machado, Kit G., "From Traditional Faction to Machine: Changing Patterns of Political Leadership in the Rural Philippines," *Journal of Asian Studies* 33:4 (August 1974), pp. 523–47.

Mackie, Jamie, "Changing Patterns of Chinese Big Business in Southeast Asia," in *Southeast Asian Capitalists*, Ruth McVey, ed. (Ithaca: Southeast Asia Program, Cornell University, 1992), pp. 161–90.

Mackie, Jamie, and Bernardo Villegas, "The Philippines: Still an Exceptional Case?" in *Driven by Growth: Political Change in the Asia-Pacific Region*, James Morley, ed. (Armonk: M.E. Sharpe, 1993), pp. 142–60.

Magno, Alexander R., *Kasaysayan: The Story of the Filipino People, vol. 9, A Nation Reborn* (Manila: Reader's Digest, 1998).

Mangahas, Mahar, "Democracy and Economic Progress: The Filipino People's Perspective," paper for XIII World Congress of Sociology, Germany, 1994.

Mangahas, Mahar, "Lotto, Jueteng, and Cockfighting" (Diliman: Social Weather Stations Bulletin, 1996).

Mangahas, Mahar, "Making a 'True' Filipino" (Diliman: Social Weather Stations Bulletin, 1996).

Mangahas, Mahar, "Pinoy [Filipino] Voters, Incorporated" (Diliman: Social Weather Stations Bulletin, 1995).

Mangahas, Mahar, "Public Opinion about Public Officials" (Diliman: Social Weather Stations Occasional Paper, 1995).

Mangahas, Mahar, "SWS Surveys on Self-Rated Poverty" (Diliman: Social Weather Stations Bulletin, 1997).

Mangahas, Mahar, "The Divine Word College-Tagbilaran/Social Weather Stations Bohol Poll 1" (Diliman: Social Weather Stations Bulletin, 1997).

Mangahas, Mahar, "The Government's Pop Charts: Personalities" (Diliman: Social Weather Stations Bulletin, 1995).

Mangahas, Mahar, "The Popular Call for Government Spending" (Diliman: Social Weather Stations Bulletin, 1996).

Mangahas, Mahar, "Why the Vatican Likes Filipino Catholics" (Diliman: Social Weather Stations Bulletin, 1997).

McCoy, Alfred W., "An Anarchy of Families: The Historiography of State and Family in the Philippines," in *An Anarchy of Families: State and Family in the Philippines*, Alfred W. McCoy, ed. (Madison: University of Wisconsin Center for Southeast Asian Studies, 1993), pp. 1–32.

McCoy, Alfred W., "Rent-Seeking Families and the Philippine State: A History of the Lopez Family," in *An Anarchy of Families: State and Family in the Philippines*, Alfred W. McCoy, ed. (Madison: University of Wisconsin Center for Southeast Asian Studies, 1993), pp. 429–536.

McCoy, Alfred W., *Closer than Brothers: Manhood at the Philippine Military Academy* (New Haven: Yale University Press, 1999).

Miranda, Felipe B., "A Higher Budget for a Truly More Capable, Modern AFP [Armed Forces of the Philippines]" (Diliman: Social Weather Stations Bulletin, 1995).

Miranda, Felipe B., "The Philippine Military at the Crossroads of Democratization" (Diliman: Social Weather Stations Occasional Paper, 1996).

Miranda, Filipe V., "Political Economy in a Democratizing Philippines: A People's Perspective," in *Democratization: Philippine Perspectives*, Felipe V. Miranda, ed. (Quezon City: University of the Philippines Press, 1997), pp. 153–228.

Mitchell, Bernard, and John Ravenhill, "Beyond Product Cycles and Flying Geese: Regionalization, Hierarchy, and the Industrialization of East Asia," *World Politics* 47 (1995), pp. 171–209.

Modina, Rolando B., and A.R. Ridao, *IRRI Rice: The Miracle that Never Was* (Quezon City: ACES Foundation, 1987).

Montes, Manuel F., "The Private Sector as the Engine of Philippine Growth: Can Heaven Wait?" *Journal of Far Eastern Business* 1:3 (Spring 1995), pp. 132–47.

Murray, Francis J., Jr., "Land Reform in the Philippines: An Overview," in *View from the Paddy: Empirical Studies of Philippine Rice Farming and Tenancy*, Frank Lynch, ed., *Philippine Sociological Review* 20:1–2 (January/April 1972), pp. 151–68.

Nowak, Thomas C., and Kay A. Snyder, "Economic Concentration and Political Change in the Philippines," in *Studies in Local Political Change: The Philippines Before Martial Law*, Benedict J. Kerkvliet, ed. (Honolulu: University of Hawaii Press, 1974), pp. 153–242.

Organizing for Democracy: NGOs, Civil Society and the Philippine State, G. Sidney Silliman and Lela G. Noble, eds. (Honolulu: University of Hawaii Press, 1998).

Oshima, Harry T., "Changes in Philippine Income Distribution in the 1970s," *Philippine Review of Economics and Business* 20:3–4 (September–December, 1983), pp. 281–90.

Owen, Norman G., *Prosperity without Progress: Manila Hemp and Material Life in the Colonial Philippines* (Berkeley: University of California Press, 1983).

Owen, Norman G., *The Bikol Blend: Bikolanos and their History* (Quezon City: New Day Publishers, 1999).

Paez, Patricia Ann V., "State-Civil Society Relations in Policy-Making: Focus on the Legislative," in *Philippine Democracy Agenda*: vol. 2, *State-Civil Society Relations in Policy-Making*, Marlon A. Wui and Ma. Glenda S. Lopez, eds. (Quezon City: Third World Studies Center, University of the Philippines, 1997), pp. 33–80.

Pahilanga-de los Reyes, Romana, and Frank Lynch, "Reluctant Rebels: Leasehold Converts in Nueva Ecija," in *View from the Paddy: Empirical Studies of Philippine Rice Farming and Tenancy*, Frank Lynch, ed., *Philippine Sociological Review* 20:1–2 (January/April 1972), pp. 7–78.

Parsa, Misagh, "Entrepreneurs and Democratization: Iran and the Philippines," *Comparative Studies in Society and History* 37:4 (October 1995), pp. 803–30.

Patterns of Power and Politics in the Philippines: Implications for Development, James Eder and Robert Youngblood, eds. (Tempe: Arizona State University Program for Southeast Asian Studies, 1994).

Pearse, Andrew, *Seeds of Plenty, Seeds of Want: Social and Economic Implications of the Green Revolution* (Oxford: Clarendon Press, 1980).

Pertierra, Raul, *Religion, Politics, and Rationality in a Philippine Community* (Quezon City: Ateneo de Manila University Press, 1988).

Philippine Centre for Investigative Journalism and Institute for Popular Democracy, *Boss: 5 Case Studies of Local Politics in the Philippines* (Pasig City: Philippine Center for Investigative Journalism, 1995).

Philippine Centre for Investigative Journalism and Institute for Popular Democracy, *Pork and Other Perks: Corruption and Governance in the Philippines* (Pasig City: Philippine Center for Investigative Journalism, 1998).

Philippine Centre for Investigative Journalism and Institute for Popular Democracy, *Patrimony: 6 Cases on Local Politics and the Environment in the Philippines* (Pasig City: Philippine Center for Investigative Journalism, 1996).

Philippine Democracy Agenda: vol. 1, *Democracy and Citizenship in Filipino Political Culture*, Maria Serena I. Diokno, ed.; vol. 2, *State-Civil Society Relations in Policy-Making*, Marlon A. Wui and Ma. Glenda S. Lopez, eds.; and vol. 3, *Civil Society Making Civil Society*, Miriam Coronel Ferrer, ed. (Quezon City: Third World Studies Center, University of the Philippines, 1997).

Philippine Human Development Report, 2000 (n.p. [Manila]: Human Development Network and UNDP, 2000).

Pinches, Michael, "Entrepreneurship, Consumption, Ethnicity, and National Identity in the Making of the Philippines' New Rich," in *Culture and Privilege in Capitalist Asia*, M. Pinches, ed. (New York: Routledge, 1999), pp. 275–301.

Pinches, Michael, "The Philippines' New Rich: Capitalist Transformation amidst Economic Gloom," in *Culture and Privilege in Capitalist Asia*, Michael Pinches, ed. (New York: Routledge, 1999), pp. 105–36.

Pinches, Michael, "The Working Class Experience of Shame, Inequality, and People Power in Tatalon, Manila," in *From Marcos to Aquino: Local Perspectives in Political Transition in the Philippines*, Benedict J. Kerkvliet and Resil B. Majares, eds. (Honolulu: University Press of Hawaii, 1991), pp. 166–86.

Pingali, Prabhu L., *et al.*, "Prospects for Rice Yield Improvement in the Post-Green Revolution Philippines," *Philippine Review of Economics and Business* 27:1 (June 1990), pp. 85–106.

Prystay, Cris, "Small Loans and Hard Work Spark Entrepreneurial Spirit," *Asian Business* 32:12 (December 1996), pp. 62–69.

Putzel, James, *A Captive Land: The Politics of Agrarian Reform in the Philippines* (Manila: Ateneo de Manila University Press, 1992).

Ranis, Gustav, Frances Stewart, and Edna Angeles-Reyes, *Linkages in Developing Economies: A Philippine Study* (San Francisco: ICS Press, 1990).

Reconsidering the East Asian Economic Model: What's Ahead for the Philippines?, Eduardo T. Gonzalez, ed. (Pasig City: Development Authority of the Philippines, 1999).

Riedinger, Jeffrey M., *Agrarian Reform in the Philippines: Democratic Transitions and Redistributive Reform* (Stanford: Stanford University Press, 1995).

Rivera, Temario C., *Landlords and Capitalists: Class, Family, and State in Philippine Manufacturing* (Quezon City: University of the Philippines Center for Integrative and Development Studies, 1994).

Rivera, Temario C., *Philippines: State of the Nation* (Singapore: Institute of Southeast Asian Studies, 1996).

Rocamora, Joel, "Impossible is Not So Easy: Party Building and Local Governance in the Philippines" (essay provided by courtesy of the author).

Rocamora, Joel, "Lost Opportunities, Deepening Crisis: The Philippines under Cory Aquino," in *Low Intensity Democracy: Political Power in the New World Order*, Barry Gills, Joel Rocamora, and Richard Wilson, eds. (Boulder: Pluto Press, 1993), pp. 195–225.

Rodil, Ma. Cristina G., "Philippine Centennial Celebration" (Diliman: Social Weather Stations Bulletin, 1997).

Rodolfo, Kelvin S., *Pinatubo and the Politics of Lahar* (Quezon City: University of the Philippines Press, 1995).

Rodriguez, Edgard, and Albert Berry, "SMEs and the New Economy: Philippine Manufacturing in the 1990s," in *The Role of SMEs in National Economies in East Asia*, Charles Harvie and Boon-Chye Lee, eds. (Cheltenham: Edward Elgar, 2002), pp. 136–57.

Roman, Emerlinda R., *et al.*, *Management Control in Chinese-Filipino Enterprises* (Quezon City: Center for Integrative and Development Studies, U.P., 1996).

Rood, Steven, "Decentralization, Democracy, and Development, in *The Philippines: New Directions in Domestic Policy and Foreign Relations*, David G. Timberman, ed. (Singapore: Institute for Southeast Asian Studies and New York: Asia Society, 1998), pp. 111–36.

Rood, Steven, "Elections as Complicated and Important Events in the Philippines," in *How Asia Votes*, John Fu-sheng Hsieh and David Newman, eds. (New York: Chatham House, 2002), pp. 148–50.

Rutten, Rosanne, *Artisans and Entrepreneurs in the Rural Philippines* (Amsterdam: VU University Press, 1990).

Saito, Katrine Anderson, and Delano P. Villanueva, "Transaction Costs of Credit to the Small-Scale Sector in the Philippines," *Economic Development and Cultural Change* 29:3 (April 1981), pp. 631–40.

Santiago, Miriam Defensor, *Cutting Edge: The Politics of Reform in the Philippines* (Mandaluyong City: Woman Today Publications, 1994).

Satake, Masaaki, *People's Economy: Philippine Community-Based Industries and Alternative Development* (Kagawa: Shikoku Gakuin University, 2003).

Schaffer, Frederic Charles, "Disciplinary Reactions: Alienation and the Reform of Vote Buying in the Philippines," paper for the American Political Science Association Annual Meeting, 2002.

Scipes, Kim, *KMU [Kilusang Mayo Uno]: Building Genuine Trade Unionism in the Philippines, 1980–1994* (Quezon City: New Day Publishers, 1996).

Seagrave, Sterling, *The Marcos Dynasty* (New York: Harper and Row, 1988).

Sermeno, Donna A., *Circumventing Agrarian Reform: Cases of Land Conversion* (Manila: Institute on Church and Social Issues, 1994).

Sidel, John T., "Philippine Politics in Town, District, and Province: Bossism in Cavite and Cebu," *Journal of Asian Studies* 56:4 (November 1997), pp. 947–66.

Sidel, John T., "The Philippines: The Languages of Legitimation," in *Political Legitimacy in Southeast Asia: The Quest for Moral Authority*, Muthiah Alagappa, ed. (Stanford: Stanford University Press, 1995), pp. 136–69.

Sidel, John T., "Walking in the Shadow of the Big Man: Justiniano Montano and Failed Dynasty Building in Cavite, 1935–1972," in *An Anarchy of Families: State and Family in the Philippines*, Alfred W. McCoy, ed. (Madison: University of Wisconsin Center for Southeast Asian Studies, 1993), pp. 109–62.

Sidel, John T., *Capital, Coercion, and Crime: Bossism in the Philippines* (Honolulu: University of Hawaii Press, 1999).

Silliman, G. Sidney, "Human Rights and the Transition to Democracy," in *Patterns of Power and Politics in the Philippines*, James F. Eder and Robert L. Youngblood, eds. (Tempe: Arizona State University Program for Southeast Asian Studies, 1994), pp. 103–46.

Sison, A.J.G., "Business and Culture in the Philippines: A Story of Gradual Progress," *Issues in Business Ethics* 13 (1999), pp. 145–66.

Sison, Jose Ma., and Julieta da Lima, *Philippine Economy and Politics* (Manila?: Aklat ng Bayan Publishing House, 1998).

Social Weather Stations Staff, "Public Opinion on Prominent Political Personalities" (Diliman: Social Weather Stations Occasional Paper, 1992).

Social Weather Stations Staff, "Public Reactions to the August 28, 1987, Coup Attempt" (Diliman: Social Weather Stations Occasional Paper, 1988).

Stauffer, Robert B., *The Political Economy of Refeudalization* [also published as *The Philippines Under Marcos: Failure of Transnational Developmentalism*]

(Sydney: University of Sydney Transnational Corporations Research Project, 1983).

Steinberg, David Joel, *The Philippines: A Singular and Plural Place* (Boulder: Westview, 1994).

Tharun, G., "From Waste to Money: Promoting Profitable Bioconversion Technology among Rural Entrepreneurs in the Philippines and Thailand," *Industry and Environment* 17:3 (1994), pp. 30–37.

The Aquino Government and the Question of Ideology, Raul J. Bonoan, S.J., et al., eds. (Quezon City: Phoenix Publishing House, 1987).

The Challenge of Rural Democratization: Perspectives from Latin America and the Philippines, Jonathan Fox, ed. (London: F. Cass, 1990).

The Philippine Economy: Alternatives for the 21st Century, Dante B. Canlas and Shigeaki Fujisaki, eds. (Diliman: University of the Philippines Press, 2001).

The Philippine Economy: Development, Policies, and Challenges, Arsenio Balisacan and Hal Hill, eds. (Manila: Ateneo De Manila University Press, 2003).

The Philippines: New Directions in Domestic Policy and Foreign Relations, David G. Timberman, ed. (Singapore: Institute for Southeast Asian Studies and New York: Asia Society, 1998).

The Revolution Falters: The Left in Philippine Politics after 1986, Patricio Abinales, ed. (Ithaca: Cornell Southeast Asia Program, No. 15, 1996).

Thompson, Mark R., "Off the Endangered List: Philippine Democratization in Comparative Perspective," *Comparative Politics* 28:2 (January 1996), pp. 179–205.

Thompson, Mark R., *The Anti-Marcos Struggle: Personalistic Rule and Democratic Transition in the Philippines* (New Haven: Yale University Press, 1995).

Thompson, W. Scott, "Observations on the Philippine Road to NIChood," in *The Philippine Road to NIChood*, W. Scott Thompson and Wilfredo Villacorta, eds. (Manila: De la Salle University and Social Weather Stations, 1996), pp. 54–68.

Tiglao, Rigoberto, "Gung-ho in Manila," *Far Eastern Economic Review*, February 15, 1990, pp. 68–72.

Timberman, David G., *A Changeless Land: Continuity and Change in Philippine Politics* (Armonk: M.E. Sharpe, 1991).

Timberman, David G., *The 1992 Philippine Elections* (New York: Asia Society, 1992).

Umehara Hiromitsu, "Green Revolution for Whom?" in *Second View from the Paddy*, Antonio J. Ledesma *et al.*, eds. (Manila: Institute of Philippine Culture, Ateneo de Manila University, 1983), pp. 24–40.

Velasco, Renato S., "Does the Philippine Congress Promote Democracy?" in *Democratization: Philippine Perspectives*, Felipe V. Miranda, ed. (Quezon City: University of the Philippines Press, 1997), pp. 281–302.

View from the Paddy: Empirical Studies of Philippine Rice Farming and Tenancy, Frank Lynch, ed., *Philippine Sociological Review* 20:1–2 (January/April 1972), pp. 3–274.

Vitug, Marites Dañguilan, *Power from the Forest: The Politics of Logging* (Pasig City: Philippine Center for Investigative Journalism, 1993).

Wolters, O. Willem, *History, Culture, and Region in Southeast Asian Perspectives*, rev. ed. (Ithaca: Cornell University Southeast Asia Program, 1999).

Wolters, O. Willem, *Politics, Patronage, and Class Conflict in Central Luzon* (The Hague: Institute of Social Studies, 1983).

Wurfel, David, *Filipino Politics: Development and Decay* (Ithaca: Cornell University Press, 1988).

Yoshihara Kunio, *Philippine Industrialization: Foreign and Domestic Capital* (Quezon City, Ateneo de Manila University Press, 1985).

Yuson, Alfred A., *FVR, Sin, Erap, Jawô, and Other Peeves* [F.V. Ramos, Cardinal Sin, Estrada, Jaworski....] (Pasig City: Anvil Publishing, 1997).

Zhuang Guotu, *Cong Feilübin Huaren dui Fujian Jinjiang, Xiamen he Nan'an de jiaoyu sunceng kan dongnan Ya Huaren yu Zhongguo guanxi de shehui nioudai* (Social Links between the Ethnic Chinese of ASEAN and China: The Case of Educational Donations by Filipino Chinese to Fujian's Jinjiang, Xiamen, and Nan'an), in *China and Southeast Asia: Changing Socio-Cultural Interactions, Zhongguo yu dongnan Ya: Shehui wenhua zhi hudong ji qi bianqian* (bilingual book), Melissa G. Curley and Hong Liu, eds. (Hong Kong: Centre of Asian Studies, 2002), pp. 123–34.

COMPARATIVE ASIAN SOURCES

Agrarian Transformations: Local Processes and the State in Southeast Asia, Gillian Hart, *et al.*, eds. (Berkeley: University of California Press, 1989).

Amsden, Alice H., *Asia's Next Giant: South Korea and Late Industrialization* (New York: Oxford University Press, 1989).

Amsden, Alice H., *The Rise of the Rest: Challenges to the West from Late-Industrializing Economies* (New York: Oxford, 2003).

Anderson, Benedict, "Elections and Participation," in *The Politics of Elections in Southeast Asia*, R.H. Taylor, ed. (Washington: Woodrow Wilson Center, 1996), pp. 12–33.

Ayal, Eliezer B., "The Role of the Chinese Minorities in the Economic Development of Southeast Asian Countries," in *Elites, Minorities, and Economic Growth*, Elise S. Brezis and Peter Temin, eds. (Amsterdam: Elsevier, 1999), pp. 149–60.

Bardhan, Pranab, "Dominant Proprietary Classes and India's Democracy," in *India's Democracy: An Analysis of Changing State-Society Relations*, Atul Kohli, ed. (Princeton: Princeton University Press, 1988), pp. 214–24.

Barron, Patrick, *et al.*, *Understanding Local Level Conflict in Developing Countries: Theory, Evidence, and Implications from Indonesia* (Social Development Paper No. 19) (Washington: World Bank, December 2004).

Barth, Fredrik, *Political Leadership Among Swat Pathans* (London: Athlone Press, 1959).

Bellah, Robert, *Tokugawa Religion* (New York: Free Press, 1957).

Bowie, Alasdair, and Danny Unger, *The Politics of Open Economies: Indonesia, Malaysia, the Philippines, and Thailand* (New York: Cambridge University Press, 1997).

Bruch, Mathias, and Ulrich Hiemenz, *Small- and Medium-Scale Industries in the ASEAN Countries: Agents or Victims of Economic Development?* (Boulder: Westview, 1984).

Business and Government in Industrializing Asia, Andrew MacIntyre, ed. (Ithaca: Cornell University Press, 1994).

Callahan, William A., *Cultural Governance in Pacific-Asia* (London: Routledge, 2006).

Callahan, William A., *Contingent States: Greater China and Transnational Relations* (Minneapolis: University of Minnesota Press, 2004).

Castells, Manuel, Lee Goh, and Reginald Y.W. Kwok, *The Shek Kip Mei Syndrome: Public Housing and Economic Development* (London: Pion, 1991).

Chang Ha-Joon, *Kicking the Ladder: Development Strategy in Historical Perspective* (London: Anthem Press, 2002).

Cheah Hock-Beng, "From Miracle to Crisis and Beyond: The Role of Entrepreneurship and SMEs in Asia," in *Globalisation and SMEs in East*

Asia, Charles Harvie and Boon-Chye Lee, eds. (Cheltenham: Edward Elgar, 2002), pp. 225–52.

China and Southeast Asia: Changing Socio-Cultural Interactions, Zhongguo yu dongnan Ya: Shehui wenhua zhi hudong ji qi bianqian (bilingual book), Melissa G. Curley and Hong Liu, eds. (Hong Kong: Centre of Asian Studies, 2002).

Chua Beng-Huat, *Political Legitimacy and Housing: Stakeholding in Singapore* (London: Routledge, 1997).

Civil Service Systems in Asia, John P. Burns and Bidhya Bowornwathana, eds. (Cheltenham: Elgar, 2001).

Civil Society in Southeast Asia, Lee Hock Guan, ed. (Singapore: Institute of Southeast Asian Studies, 2004).

Clad, James, *Behind the Myth: Business, Money, and Power in Southeast Asia* (London: Hyman, 1989).

Compton, Robert W., Jr., *East Asian Democratization: The Impact of Globalization, Culture, and Economy* (Westport, CT: Greenwood Press, 2000).

Confucian and Economic Development: An Oriental Alternative? Tai Hung-chao, ed. (Washington: Washington Institute for Values in Public Policy, 1989).

Cotton, James, "The Limits to Liberalization in Industrializing Asia: Three Views of the State," *Pacific Affairs* 64:3 (Autumn, 1991), pp. 311–27.

Crouch, Harold, and James Morley, "The Dynamics of Political Change," in *Driven by Growth*, J. Morley, ed. (Armonk: M.E. Sharpe, 1999), pp. 277–310.

Culture and Privilege in Capitalist Asia, Michael Pinches, ed. (New York: Routledge, 1999).

Dana, Leo Paul, *Entrepreneurship in Pacific Asia: Past, Present and Future* (Singapore: World Scientific, 1999).

Designer Genes: I.Q., Ideology, and Biology, Chee Heng Leng and Chee Khoon, eds. (Petaling Jaya: Institute for Social Analysis, 1984).

Deyo, Frederic C., *Beneath The Miracle: Labor Subordination in The New Asian Industrialism* (Berkeley: University of California Press, 1989).

Deyo, Frederic C., *The Political Economy of the New Asian Industrialism* (Ithaca: Cornell University Press, 1987).

Driven by Growth, James Morley, ed. (Armonk: M.E. Sharpe, 1999).

Economic Development and Cooperation in the Pacific Basin: Trade, Investment, and Environmental Issues, Hiro Lee and D. Roland-Holst, eds. (New York: Cambridge University Press, 1998).

Elections as Popular Culture in Asia, Beng Huat Chua, ed. (London: Routledge, 2007).

Emerging Pluralism in Asia and the Pacific, David Y.H. Wu, *et al.*, eds. (Hong Kong: HK Institute of Asia Pacific Studies, 1997).

Entrepreneurship and SMEs in Southeast Asia, Denis Hew and Loi Wee Nee, eds. (Singapore: Institute of Southeast Asian Studies, 2004).

Ethnic Chinese as Southeast Asians, Leo Suryadinata, ed. (Singapore: Institute for Southeast Asian Studies, 1997).

Evans, Grant, *Lao Peasants Under Socialism* (New Haven: Yale University Press, 1990).

Frankel, Francine R., *India's Green Revolution: Economic Gains and Political Costs* (Princeton: Princeton University Press, 1971).

Geertz, Clifford, *Agricultural Involution* (Berkeley: University of California Press, 1971).

Gilley, Bruce, *States and Legitimacy: The Politics of Moral Authority* (Ph.D. dissertation, Politics Department, Princeton University, January 2007).

Globalisation and SMEs in East Asia, Charles Harvie and Boon-Chye Lee, eds. (Cheltenham: Edward Elgar, 2002).

Gomez, Edmund Terence, *Chinese Business in Malaysia: Accumulation, Accommodation, and Ascendence* (London: Curzon, 1999).

Guha, Ramachandra, *India After Gandhi: The History of the World's Largest Democracy* (New York: HarperCollins, 2007).

Hall, Chris, "Profile of SMEs and SME Issues in East Asia," in *The Role of SMEs in National Economies in East Asia*, Charles Harvie and Boon-Chye Lee, eds. (Cheltenham: Edward Elgar, 2002), pp. 21–49.

Harvie, Charles, "China's SMEs: Their Evolution and Future Prospects in an Evolving Market Economy," in *The Role of SMEs in National Economies in East Asia*, Charles Harvie and Boon-Chye Lee, eds. (Cheltenham: Edward Elgar, 2002), pp. 50–88.

Harvie, Charles, "The Asian Financial and Economic Crisis and its Impact on Regional SMEs," in *Globalisation and SMEs in East Asia*, Charles Harvie and Boon-Chye Lee, eds. (Cheltenham: Edward Elgar, 2002), pp. 10–42.

Harvie, Charles, and Boon-Chye Lee, "East Asian SMEs: Contemporary Issues and Developments," in *The Role of SMEs in National Economies in East Asia*, Charles Harvie and Boon-Chye Lee, eds. (Cheltenham: Edward Elgar, 2002), pp. 1–20.

Heine-Geldern, Robert F., *Concepts of State and Kingship in Southeast Asia* (Ithaca: Southeast Asia Program, Cornell University, 1956).

Hill, Ronald, *Southeast Asia: People, Land, and Economy* (Crows Nest, NSW: Allen and Unwin, 2002).

How East Asians View Democracy, Yun-han Chu, Larry Diamond, Andrew J. Nathan, and Doh Chull Shin, eds. (New York: Columbia University Press, 2008).

Hsiao Hsin-huang, Michael, "An East Asian Development Model: Empirical Explorations," in *In Search of an East Asian Development Model*, Peter Berger and Michael Hsiao, eds. (New Brunswick: Transaction Press, 1988), pp. 12–25.

In Search of Southeast Asia: A Modern History, Joel Steinberg, ed. (Honolulu: University of Hawaii Press, 1987).

India's Democracy: An Analysis of Changing State-Society Relations, Atul Kohli, ed. (Princeton: Princeton University Press, 1988).

Johnson, Chalmers A., *MITI and the Japanese Miracle: The Growth of Industrial Policy, 1925–1975* (Stanford: Stanford University Press, 1982).

Kohli, Atul, and Vivienne Shue, "State Power and Social Forces: On Political Contention and Accommodation in the Third World," in *State Power and Social Forces: Domination and Transformation in the Third World*, Joel S. Migdal, Atul Kohli, and Vivienne Shue, eds. (New York: Cambridge University Press, 1994).

Kohli, Atul, *Democracy and Discontent: India's Growing Crisis of Governability* (Cambridge: Cambridge University Press, 1990).

Kohli, Atul, *State-Directed Development: Political Power and Industrialization in the Global Periphery* (Cambridge: Cambridge University Press, 2004).

Krugman, Paul, "The Myth of Asia's Miracle: A Cautionary Fable," http://web.mit.edu/krugman/www/myth.html, seen March 20, 2007.

Kuhonta, Erik Martinez, *The Political Foundations for Equitable Development in Malaysia and Thailand* (Ph.D. Dissertation, Politics Department, Princeton University, 2003).

Legitimacy: Ambiguities of Political Success or Failure in East and Southeast Asia, Lynn White, ed. (Singapore: World Scientific Press, 2005).

Li Cheng and Lynn T. White III, "Elite Transformation and Modern Change in Mainland China and Taiwan," *China Quarterly* 121 (March 1990), pp. 1–35.

Local Cultures and the "New Asia": The State, Culture, and Capitalism in Southeast Asia, C.J.W.-L. Wee, ed. (Singapore: Institute for Southeast Asian Studies, 2002).

McVey, Ruth, "The Materialization of the Southeast Asian Entrepreneur," in *Southeast Asian Capitalists*, Ruth McVey, ed. (Ithaca: Southeast Asia Program, Cornell University, 1992), pp. 7–34.

Mallet, Victor, *The Trouble with Tigers: The Rise and Fall of Southeast Asia* (New York: Harper Collins, 1999).

McQueen, Humphrey, "Repressive Pluralism," in *Emerging Pluralism in Asia and the Pacific*, David Y.H. Wu, *et al.*, eds. (Hong Kong: HK Institute of Asia Pacific Studies, 1997), pp. 3–28.

Military Professionalism in Asia: Conceptual and Empirical Perspectives, Muthiah Alagappa, eds. (Honolulu: East-West Center, 2001).

Mobile Phones, McDonalds, and Middle-Class Revolution, Richard Robison and David S.G. Goodman, ed. (London: Routledge, 1996).

Myrdal, Gunnar, *Asian Drama*, vols. 1 and 2 (New York: Twentieth Century Fund, 1968).

Neher, Clark D., and Ross Marlay, *Democracy and Development in Southeast Asia: The Winds of Change* (Boulder: Westview, 1995).

Ng, Stephen, and Samuel Ho, "Business Transformation Strategy for Small and Medium Enterprises," *International Conference on ISO 9000, ISO 9000 and Total Quality Management*, Samuel K.M. Ho, ed. (Hong Kong: Baptist University Press, 1998), pp. 130–37.

Oshima, Harry T., "Labor Force Explosion and the Labor-Intensive Sector in Asian Growth," *Economic Development and Cultural Change* 19 (January 1971), pp. 161–83.

Palmer, Ingrid, *The New Rice in Indonesia* (Geneva: UN Research Institute for Social Development, 1977).

Pearse, Andrew, *Seeds of Plenty, Seeds of Want* (Oxford: Oxford University Press, 1981).

Perry, Elizabeth J., *Putting Class in its Place: Worker Identities in East Asia* (Berkeley: University of California Institute of East Asian Studies, 1996).

Political Legitimacy in Southeast Asia: The Quest for Moral Authority, Muthiah Alagappa, ed. (Stanford: Stanford University Press, 1995).

Political Oppositions in Industrializing Asia, Garry Rodan, ed. (London: Routledge, 1996).

Political Party Systems in East and Southeast Asia, Wolfgang Sachsenroder and Ulrike Frings, eds. (Aldershot: Ashgate, 1998).

Recalling Local Pasts: Autonomous History in Southeast Asia, Sunait Chutintaranon (Chiang Mai: Silkworm Books, 2002).

Rodan, Garry, "Singapore: Emerging Tensions in the 'Dictatorship of the Middle Class,'" *Pacific Review* (1992), pp. 370–81.

Rutten, Mario, *Rural Capitalists in Asia: A Comparative Analysis of India, Indonesia, and Malaysia* (New York: RoutledgeCurzon, 2003).

Sangren, P. Steven, "Traditional Chinese Corporations: Beyond Kinship," *Journal of Asian Studies* 43:3 (1984), pp. 391–415.

Schiffer, Jonathan, "The State and Economic Development: A Note on the Hong Kong 'Model'," *International Journal of Urban and Regional Research* 15:3 (1991).

Scott, James C. and Benedict J. Kerkvliet, "How Traditional Rural Patrons Lose Legitimacy: A Theory with Special Reference to Southeast Asia," in *Friends, Followers, and Factions: A Reader in Political Clientelism*, Steffen W. Schmidt, *et al.*, eds. (Berkeley: University of California Press, 1977).

Siegel, James T., *A New Criminal Type in Jakarta: Counter-Revolution Today* (Durham: Duke University Press, 1998).

Slater, Daniel, "Where Were the Workers? Communal Elites and Mass Mobilization in Southeast Asia's Democratization Struggles," paper at American Political Science Association Annual Meeting, 2004.

Southeast Asia in Political Science: Theory, Region, and Qualitative Analysis, Erik Martínez Kuhonta, Dan Slater, and Tuong Vu, eds. (Stanford: Stanford University Press, 2008).

Southeast Asia in the 1990s: Authoritarianism, Democracy, and Capitalism, Kevin Hewison, Richard Robison, Garry Rodan, eds. (St. Leonards, NSW: Allen & Unwin, 1993).

Southeast Asian Chinese and China: The Political Economic Dimension, Leo Suryadinata, ed. (Singapore: Academic Times Press, 1995).

Southeast Asian Identities: Culture and the Politics of Representation in Indonesia, Malaysia, Singapore, and Thailand, Joel S. Kahn, ed. (New York: St. Martin's, 1998).

Southeast Asian Capitalists, Ruth McVey, ed. (Ithaca: Southeast Asia Program, Cornell University, 1992).

The Chinese Triangle and the Future of the Asia-Pacific Region, Hsiao Hsin-huang and Alvin Y. So, eds. (Boulder: Westview, 1995).

Thayer, Nathaniel, *How the Conservatives Rule Japan* (Princeton: Princeton University Press, 1969).

The East Asian Region: Confucian Heritage and its Modern Adaptation, Gilbert Rozman, ed. (Princeton: Princeton University Press, 1991).

The Economic Organization of East Asian Capitalism, Marco Orrù, Nicole Woolsey Biggart, and Gary Hamilton, eds. (Thousand Oaks: Sage, 1997).

The Local Political System in Asia, Ahn Chung-si, ed. (Seoul: Seoul National University Press, 1987).

The Political Dimensions of the Asian Crisis, Uwe Johannen, *et al.*, eds. (Singapore: Select Books, 2000).

The Political Economy of Southeast Asia, Gary Rodan, Kevin Hewison, and Richard Robison, eds. (Melbourne: Oxford University Press, 1997).

The Political Economy of the New Asian Industrialism, Frederic C. Deyo, ed. (Ithaca: Cornell University Press, 1987).

The Politics of Democratization: Generalizing East Asian Experiences, Edward Friedman, ed. (Boulder: Westview, 1994).

The Role of SMEs in National Economies in East Asia, Charles Harvie and Boon-Chye Lee, eds. (Cheltenham: Edward Elgar, 2002).

The Triadic Chord: Confucian Ethics, Industrial East Asia and Max Weber, Tu Wei-ming, ed. (Singapore: Institute of East Asian Philosophy, 1987).

Vatikiotis, Michel R. J., *Political Change in Southeast Asia* (London: Routledge, 1996).

Vogel, Ezra, *The Four Little Dragons: The Spread of Industrialization in East Asia* (Cambridge: Harvard University Press, 1991).

Wang Gungwu, "The Study of Chinese Identities in Southeast Asia," in *The Changing Identities of Chinese in Southeast Asia*, Jennifer Cushman and Wang Gungwu, eds. (Hong Kong: Hong Kong University Press, 1988), pp. 15–30.

Wang Gungwu, "Power, Rights, and Duties in Chinese History," *The Australian Journal of Chinese Affairs* 3 (1980), pp. 1–26.

Wang Gungwu, *The Chinese Overseas: From Earthbound China to the Quest for Autonomy* (Cambridge: Harvard University Press, 2000).

Weber, Max, *The Religion of China: Confucianism and Taoism* (Glencoe: Free Press, 1951).

Wheatley, Paul, *Nagara and Commandery* (Chicago: University of Chicago Press, 2003).

World Bank, *The East Asian Miracle: Economic Growth and Public Policy* (New York: Oxford University Press, 1993).

Yao Souchou, *Confucian Capitalism: Discourse, Practice, and the Myth of Chinese Enterprise* (London: RoutledgeCurzon, 2002).

Yoshihara Kunio, *Asia per Capita: Why National Incomes Differ in East Asia* (London: Curzon Press, 2000).

Yoshihara Kunio, *Building a Prosperous Southeast Asia: From Ersatz to Echt Capitalism* (Richmond, Surrey: Curzon Press, 1999).

Yoshihara Kunio, *The Rise of Ersatz Capitalism in Southeast Asia* (Singapore: Oxford University Press, 1988).

GLOBALIST SOURCES (MANY ABOUT DEMOCRACY, SMES, & CORRUPTION)

Achebe, Chinua, *A Man of the People* (New York: Anchor, 1988 [orig. 1966]).

Are Small Firms Important? Their Role and Impact, Zoltan J. Acs, ed. (Boston/Dordrecht: Kluwer Academic, 1999).

Barndt, William T., *Executive Assaults in South America (1979–2006)* (Ph.D. Dissertation, Politics Department, Princeton University, 2007).

Barro, Robert J., and Xavier Sala-i-Martin, "Convergence," *Journal of Political Economy* 100:2 (1992), pp. 223–50.

Bates, Robert H., *States and Markets in Tropical Africa: The Political Basis of Agricultural Policy* (Berkeley: University of California Press, 1981).

Bell, Daniel A., *East Meets West: Human Rights & Democracy in East Asia* (Princeton: Princeton University Press, 2000).

Berman, Sheri, "Civil Society and the Collapse of the Weimar Republic," *World Politics* 49 (April 1997), pp. 401–29.

Bermeo, Nancy, *Ordinary People in Extraordinary Times: The Citizenry and the Breakdown of Democracy* (Princeton: Princeton University Press, 2003).

Bermeo, Nancy, "Redemocratization and Transition Elections: A Comparison of Spain and Portugal," *Comparative Politics* 19 (1987), pp. 307–22.

Beyond Tocqueville: Civil Society and the Social Capital Debate in Comparative Perspective, Bob Edwards, Michael Foley, and Mario Diani, eds. (Hanover: University Press of New England, 2001).

Bialer, Seweryn, *Stalin's Successors: Leadership, Stability and Change in the Soviet Union* (New York: Cambridge University Press, 1980).

Billig, Michael, *Banal Nationalism* (London: Sage, 1995).

Boix, Carles, and Susan Stokes, "Endogenous Democratization," *World Politics* 55:4 (2003), pp. 517–49.

Boone, Catherine, "The Making of a Rentier Class: Wealth Accumulation and Political Control in Senegal," *Journal of Development Studies* 26:3 (1990), pp. 425–29.

Brownlee, Jason, *Authoritarianism in an Age of Democratization* (New York: Cambridge University Press, 2007) [esp. Middle East, orig. a Princeton dissertation].

Brus, Wlodzmierz, "Political Pluralism and Markets in Communist Systems," in *Pluralism in the Soviet Union*, Susan G. Solomon, ed. (New York: St. Martin's, 2003), pp. 108–30.

Business and the State in Developing Countries, Sylvia Maxfield and Ben Ross Schneider, eds. (Ithaca: Cornell University Press, 1997).

Butler, David, Howard Penniman, and Austin Ranney, "Introduction," in D. Butler, *et al.*, eds. *Democracy at the Polls* (Washington: American Enterprise Institute, 1981).

Campbell, Angus, Philip Converse, Warren Miller, and Donald Stokes, *The American Voter* (New York: Wiley, 1960).

Cardoso, Fernando, and Enzo Faletto, *Dependency and Development in Latin America* (Berkeley: University of California Press, 1979).

Centeno, Miguel Angel, "Between Rocky Democracies and Hard Markets: Dilemmas of the Double Transition," *Annual Review of Sociology* 20 (1994), pp. 125–47.

Chaudry, Kiren Aziz, "Economic Liberalization and the Lineages of the Rentier State," *Comparative Politics* 27:1 (1994), pp. 125.

Chua, Amy, *World on Fire: How Exporting Free Market Democracy Breeds Ethnic Hatred and Global Instability* (New York: Doubleday, 2003).

Collier, Ruth Berins, and David Collier, "Inducements vs. Constraints: Disaggregating 'Corporatism,'" *American Political Science Review* 73 (1979), pp. 967–86.

Corruption in the American Political System, Larry L. Berg, *et al.*, ed. (Morristown: General Learning Press, 1976).

Dahl, Robert A., *Polyarchy* (New Haven: Yale University Press, 1971).

Dahlberg, Kenneth, *Beyond the Green Revolution: The Ecology and Politics of Global Agricultural Development* (New York: Plenum Press, 1979).

Deininger, Klaus, and Lyn Squire, "A New Data Set Measuring Income Inequality," *World Bank Economic Review* 10:3 (1996), pp. 565–91.

Di Palma, Giuseppi, *To Craft Democracies* (Berkeley: University of California Press, 1990).

Diamond, Larry, "The Democratic Rollback: The Resurgence of the Predatory State," *Foreign Affairs* (March–April 2008), pp. 36–48.

Diamond, Larry, Juan Linz, and Seymour Martin Lipset, "Introduction: What Makes for Democracy?" in *Politics in Developing Countries: Comparing*

Experiences with Democracy, Diamond, Linz, and Lipset, eds., 2nd edition (Boulder: Rienner, 1995), pp. 1–38.

Dogan, Mattei, and John Higley, "Elites, Crises, and Regimes in Comparative Analysis," in *Elites, Crises, and the Origins of Regimes*, Dogan and Higley, ed. (Lanham: Rowman and Littlefield, 1998), pp. 3–28.

Doner, Richard F., "Limits of State Strength: Toward an Institutionalist View of Economic Development," *World Politics* 44 (April 1992), pp. 398–431.

Doner, Richard F., and Eric Hershberg, "Flexible Production and Political Decentralization in the Developing World: Elective Affinities in the Pursuit of Competitiveness," *Studies in Comparative International Development* 34:1 (Spring 1999), pp. 45–82.

Donsanto, Craig, "From Crisis to Reform: A Historical Perspective," *Democracy at Large* 2:4 (2006), pp. 10–11.

Elites, Crises, and the Origins of Regimes, Mattei Dogan and John Higley, eds. (Lanham: Rowman and Littlefield, 1998).

Elites, Minorities, and Economic Growth, Elise S. Brezis and Peter Temin, eds. (Amsterdam: Elsevier, 1999).

Entrepreneurship, Economic Growth, and Social Change, David Schak, ed. (Brisbane: Griffith University Centre for the Study of Australian-Asian Relations, 1994).

Evans, Peter B., "Predatory, Developmental, and Other Apparatuses: A Comparative Political Economy Perspective on the Third World State," *Sociological Forum* 4:4 (1989), pp. 561–87.

Evans, Peter B., "State Structures, Government-Business Relations, and Economic Transformation," in *Business and the State in Developing Countries*, Sylvia Maxfield and Ben Ross Schneider, eds. (Ithaca: Cornell University Press, 1997), pp. 63–87.

Evans, Peter B., and James Rauch, "Bureaucracy and Growth: A Cross-National Analysis of the Effects of 'Weberian' State Structures on Economic Growth," *American Sociological Review* 64:5 (October 1999), pp. 748–65.

Evans, Peter B., *Embedded Autonomy: States and Industrial Transformation* (Princeton: Princeton University Press, 1995).

Evans, Peter B., *Dependent Development: The Alliance of Multinational, State, and Local Capital in Brazil* (Princeton: Princeton University Press, 1979).

Fenno, Richard F., Jr., *Home Style: House Members in their Districts* (New York: Harper Collins, 1978).

Frentzel-Zagorska, Janina, "Patterns of Transition from a One-Party State to Democracy in Poland and Hungary," in *The Development of Civil Society in Communist Systems*, Robert F. Miller, ed. (Sydney: Allen & Unwin, 1992), pp. 40–64.

Friedberg, Aaron L., *In the Shadow of the Garrison State: America's Anti-Statism and its Cold War Grand Strategy* (Princeton: Princeton University Press, 2000).

Gastil, Raymond D., *Freedom in the World: Political Rights and Civil Liberties* (New York: Freedom House, 1980 and 1990).

Gellner, Ernest, *Conditions of Liberty: Civil Society and its Rivals* (New York: Penguin, 1994).

Gerring, John, and Strom C. Thacker, "Do Neoliberal Policies Deter Political Corruption?" *International Organization* 59 (Winter 2005), pp. 233–54.

Haas, Ernst B., *Nationalism, Liberalism, and Progress: The Rise and Decline of Nationalism* (Ithaca: Cornell University Press, 1997).

Hacker, Jacob S., and Paul Pierson, *Off Center: The Republican Revolution and the Erosion of American Democracy* (New Haven: Yale University Press, 2005).

Haggard, Stephan, and Robert Kaufman, *The Political Economy of Democratic Transitions* (Princeton: Princeton University Press, 1995).

Haggard, Stephan, *Pathways from the Periphery: The Politics of Growth in the Newly Industrializing Countries* (Ithaca: Cornell University Press, 1990).

Harris, John, and Michall Todaro, "Migration, Unemployment, and Development: A Two-Sector Analysis," *American Economic Review* 60:1 (March 1970), pp. 126–42.

Hellman, Joel, "Winners Take All: The Politics of Partial Reform in Post-Communist Transitions," *World Politics* 50:2 (1990), pp. 203–34.

Hirschman, Albert O., *Rival Views of Market Society* (Cambridge: Harvard University Press, 1992).

Horowitz, Donald L., "Comparing Democratic Systems," *Journal of Democracy* 1:4 (Fall 1990), pp. 73–79.

Huntington, Samuel P., "Modernization and Corruption," in *Political Corruption: Readings in Comparative Analysis*, A.J. Heidenheimer, ed. (New York: Holt, 1970), pp. 479–86.

Huntington, Samuel P., *Political Order in Changing Societies* (New Haven: Yale University Press, 1968).

Inglehart, Ronald, *Modernizations and Post-Modernizations: Culture, Economics, and Politics in 43 Countries* (Princeton: Princeton University Press, 1997).

Inkeles, Alex, and David Smith, *Becoming Modern: Individual Change in Six Developing Countries*, (London: Heinemann, 1974).

Institutions and the Role of the State, Leonardo Burlamaqui, Ana C. Castro, and Ha-Joon Chang, eds. (London: Edward Elgar, 2001).

Jamal, Amaney, *Barriers to Democracy: The Other Side of Social Capital in Palestine and the Arab World* (Princeton: Princeton University Press, 2007).

Johnston, Michael, "A Brief History of Anticorruption Agencies," in *The Self-Restraining State: Power and Accountability in New Democracies*, Andreas Schedler, Larry Diamond, and Marc F. Plattner, eds. (Boulder: Lynne Rienner, 1999), pp. 217–26.

Jones, Charles I., *Introduction to Economic Growth*, second edition (New York: W.W. Norton, 2002).

Justman, Moshe, and Mark Gradstein, "The Democratization of Political Elites and the Decline in Inequality in Modern Economic Growth," in *Elites, Minorities, and Economic Growth*, Elise S. Brezis and Peter Temin, eds. (Amsterdam: Elsevier, 1999), pp. 205–20.

Katz, Richard S., "Intraparty Preference Voting," *Electoral Laws and their Consequences*, B. Grofman and A. Lijphart, eds. (New York: Agathon Press, 1986), pp. 85–103.

Key, V.O., *Southern Politics in State and Nation* (New York: Knopf, 1949).

Klitgaard, Robert, *Controlling Corruption* (Berkeley: University of California Press, 1988).

Kotkin, Stephen, *Armageddon Averted: The Soviet Collapse, 1970–2000* (New York: Oxford University Press, 2001).

Krueger, Anne O., "The Political Economy of Rent-Seeking Society," *American Economic Review* 64 (June 1974), pp. 291–303.

Kuznets, Simon, "Economic Growth and Income Inequality," *American Economic Review* 45:1 (1955), pp. 1–28.

Lamounier, Bolivar, "Authoritarian Brazil Revisited: The Impact of Elections on the Abertura," in *Democratizing Brazil: Problems of Transition and Consolidation*, Alfred Stepan, ed. (New York: Oxford University Press, 1989), pp. 43–79.

Landes, David S., *The Unbound Prometheus: Technological Change and Industrial Development in Western Europe from 1750* (Cambridge: Cambridge University Press, 1969).

Lenin, V.I., *The Lenin Anthology*, Robert C. Tucker, ed. (New York: Norton, 1975).

Lewis, Sinclair, *Babbit* (New York: Harcourt Brace, 1922).

Lewis, W. Arthur, "Economic Development with Unlimited Supplies of Labour," *The Manchester School of Economic and Social Studies* (1954), pp. 139–91.

Leys, Colin, "What is the Problem about Corruption?" *Journal of Modern African Studies* 3 (1965), pp. 215–30.

Lieberman, Evan S., *Race and Regionalism in the Politics of Taxation in Brazil and South Africa* (Cambridge: Cambridge University Press, 2003).

Lipset, Seymour Martin, "Some Social Requisites of Democracy: Economic Development and Political Legitimacy," *American Political Science Review* 53 (March 1959), pp. 69–105

McFaul, Michael, "State Power, Institutional Change, and the Politics of Privatization in Russia," *World Politics* 47:2 (1995), 210–43.

Mankiw, Gregory, David Romer, and David Weil, "A Contribution to the Empirics of Economic Growth," *Quarterly Journal of Economics* (May 1992), pp. 407–37.

Melucci, Alberto, *Nomads of the Present: Social Movements and Industrial Needs in Contemporary Society* (London: Radius, 1989).

Michels, Robert, *Political Parties: A Sociological Study of the Oligarchical Tendencies of Modern Democracies*, trans. Eden and Cedar Paul (New York: Dover, 1958).

Moran, J., "Democratic Transitions and Forms of Corruption," *Crime, Law, and Social Change* 36:4 (December 2001), pp. 379–93.

Mosca, Gaetano, *The Ruling Class* (New York: McGraw-Hill, 1939).

Nye, Joseph S., "Corruption and Political Development: A Cost-Benefit Analysis," *American Political Science Review* 61:2 (1967), pp. 417–27.

Pareto, Vilfredo, *The Transformation of Democracy*, trans. Renata Girola (New Brunswick: Transaction Books, 1984 [orig. 1921]).

Piore, Michael J., and Charles F. Sabel, *The Second Industrial Divide: Possibilities for Prosperity* (New York: Basic Books, 1984).

Przeworski, Adam, "Democracy as a Contingent Outcome of Conflicts," in *Constitutionalism and Democracy*, Jon Elster and Rune Slagstad, eds. (Cambridge: Cambridge University Press, 1988), pp. 59–81.

Przeworski, Adam, "Some Problems in the Study of the Transition to Democracy," in *Transitions from Authoritarian Rule: Comparative*

Perspectives, G. O'Donnell, *et al.*, eds. (Baltimore: Johns Hopkins University Press, 1986), pp. 47–63.

Przeworski, Adam, and Fernando Limongi, "Modernization: Theory and Facts," *World Politics* 49 (January 1997), pp. 159–83.

Przeworski, Adam, Michael E. Alvarez, José Antonio Cheibub, and Fernando Limongi, *Democracy and Development: Political Institutions and Well-Being in the World, 1950–1990* (Cambridge: Cambridge University Press, 2000).

Putnam, Robert D., with Robert Leonardi and Raffaella Y. Nanetti, *Making Democracy Work: Civic Traditions in Modern Italy* (Princeton: Princeton University Press, 1993).

Rae, Douglas, *The Political Consequences of Electoral Laws* (New Haven: Yale University Press, 1967).

Reeve, Andrew, and Alan Ware, *Electoral Systems: A Comparative and Theoretical Introduction* (London: Routledge, 1992).

Regimes and Oppositions, Robert A. Dahl, ed. (New Haven: Yale University Press, 1973).

Remmer, Karen L., "Exclusionary Democracy," *Studies in Comparative International Development* 20:4 (Winter 1985–86), pp. 64–85.

Roeder, Philip G., *Red Sunset: The Failure of Soviet Politics* (Princeton: Princeton University Press, 1993).

Rostow, Walt W., *Theorists of Economic Growth from David Hume to the Present: With a Perspective on the Next Century* (New York: Oxford University Press, 1990).

Rostow, Walter W., "The Take-Off into Self-Sustained Growth," *Economic Journal* 66 (March 1956), pp. 25–48.

Rustow, Dankwart, "The Study of Elites: Who's Who, When, and How," *World Politics* 18 (October 1965–July 1966), pp. 690–717.

Rustow, Dankwart, "Transitions to Democracy," *Comparative Politics* 2:3 (1970), pp. 337–63.

Samuels, Richard J., *The Business of the Japanese State: Energy Markets in Comparative Perspective* (Ithaca: Cornell University Press, 1987).

Sandel, Michael J., *Democracy's Discontent: America in Search of a Public Philosophy* (Cambridge: Harvard University Press, 1996).

Sartori, Giovanni, *Parties and Party Systems: A Framework for Analysis* (Cambridge: Cambridge University Press, 1976).

Schattschneider, E.E., *Party Government* (New York: Holt, Rinehart and Winston, 1942).

Schedler, Andreas, "Conceptualizing Accountability," in *The Self-Restraining State: Power and Accountability in New Democracies*, Andreas Schedler, Larry Diamond, and Marc F. Plattner, eds. (Boulder: Lynne Rienner, 1999), pp. 13–28.

Schmitter, Philippe C., and Terry Lynn Karl, "What Democracy Is ... And Is Not," in *The Global Resurgence of Democracy*, Larry Diamond and Marc F. Plattner, eds. (Baltimore: Johns Hopkins University Press, 1996), pp. 49–62.

Schmitter, Philippe, "Civil Society East and West," in *Consolidating the Third Wave Democracies*, Larry Diamond, *et al.*, eds. (Baltimore: Johns Hopkins University Press, 1997), pp. 236–62.

Schmitter, Phillippe C., "The Consolidation of Democracy and Representation of Social Groups," *American Behavioral Scientist* 35 (1992), pp. 422–49.

Schumpeter, Joseph A., "The Creative Response in Economic History," *Journal of Economic History* 7:2 (1947), pp. 149–59.

Schumpeter, Joseph A., *Business Cycles* (New York: McGraw-Hill, 1939).

Schumpeter, Joseph A., *The Theory of Economic Development* (New York: Oxford University Press, 1934).

Schumpeter, Joseph, *Capitalism, Socialism, and Democracy* (London: George Allen and Unwin, 1943).

Scott, James C., "Corruption, Machine Politics, and Political Development," *American Political Science Review* 63:4 (December 1969), pp. 1142–58.

Scott, James C., *Comparative Political Corruption* (Englewood Cliffs: Prentice-Hall, 1972).

Sharlet, Robert, "Stalinism and Soviet Legal Culture," in *Stalinism: Essays in Historical Interpretation*, Robert C. Tucker, ed. (New York: Norton, 1977), pp. 155–79.

Shefter, Martin, *Patronage and its Opponents: A Theory and some European Cases* (Ithaca: Cornell University Western Societies Program, 1977).

Skeldon, Ronald, *Migration and Development: A Global Perspective* (Harlow: Longman, 1997).

Smith, Benjamin B., *Hard Times in the Land of Plenty: Oil Booms and Opposition in Late-Developing States* (Ph.D. dissertation, University of Washington Political Science Department, September 2002).

Smith, Thomas C., *Native Sources of Japanese Industrialization, 1750–1920* (Berkeley: University of California Press, 1988).

Snyder, Jack, *From Voting to Violence: Democratization and Nationalist Conflict* (New York: Norton, 2000).

Solnick, Steven, "The Breakdown of Hierarchies in the Soviet Union and China: A Neoinstitutional Perspective," *World Politics* 48:2 (1996), pp. 209–38.

Sørensen, Georg, *Democracy, Dictatorship, and Development: Economic Development in Selected Regimes of the Third World* (Basingstoke: Macmillan, 1991).

Steen, Anton, and Vladimir Gel'man, *Elites and Democratic Development in Russia* (London: Routledge, 2003).

The Role of Parliaments in Curbing Corruption, Rick Stapenhurst, Niall, Johnston, and Riccardo Pelizzo, eds. (Washington: World Bank, 2006).

The Self-Restraining State: Power and Accountability in New Democracies, Andreas Schedler, Larry Diamond, and Marc F. Plattner, eds. (Boulder: Lynne Rienner, 1999).

Thompson, E. P., *The Making of the English Working Class* (Harmondsworth: Penguin, 1968).

Touraine, Alain, "Democracy: From a Politics of Citizenship to a Politics of Recognition," in *Social Movements and Social Classes*, Louis Maheu, ed. (London: Sage, 1995), pp. 258–75.

Transitions from Authoritarian Rule: Tentative Conclusions about Uncertain Democracies, Guillermo O'Donnell, Philippe C. Schmitter, and Laurence Whitehead, eds. (Baltimore: Johns Hopkins University Press, 1986).

Treisman, Daniel, "The Causes of Corruption: A Cross-National Study," *Journal of Public Economics* 76 (June 2000), pp. 399–457.

United Nations Development Programme, *Human Development Report, 2002: Deepening Democracy in a Fragmented World* (New York: Oxford University Press, 2002).

Varese, Federico, "Transition to the Market and Corruption in Post-socialist Russia," *Political Studies* 45:3 (1997), pp. 579–96.

Walecki, Marcin, "Political Corruption: Democracy's Hidden Disease," *Democracy at Large* 2:4 (2006), pp. 16–19.

Wang Xu, "Mutual Empowerment of State and Peasantry: Grassroots Democracy in Rural China," *World Development* 25 (September 1997), pp. 1431–42.

Warren, Mark E., *Democracy and Association* (Princeton: Princeton University Press, 2000).

Whitehead, Lawrence, "A Comparative Perspective on Democratization," in *Poverty, Prosperity, and the World Economy*, G. Helleiner, *et al.*, eds. (London: Macmillan, 1996).

Wolf, Eric R., "Aspects of Group Relations in a Complex Society: Mexico," *American Anthropologist* 58 (1956), pp. 1085–78.

Yashar, Deborah J., *Contesting Citizenship in Latin America: The Rise of Indigenous Movements and the Postliberal Challenge* (Cambridge: Cambridge University Press, 2005).

Young, Crawford, *The Politics of Cultural Pluralism* (Madison: University of Wisconsin Press, 1976).

SOURCES SHOWING METHODS TO FIND TRUTH ABOUT POLITICS

Alinsky, Saul D., *Rules for Radicals: A Practical Primer for Realistic Radicals* (New York: Vintage, 1989 [1971]).

Arrow, Kenneth, *Social Choice and Individual Values* (New York: Wiley, 1963).

Ayer, A. J., *Language, Truth, and Logic* (New York: Dover, 1952).

Ayer, A. J., "Bryan Magee Talks to A. J. Ayer about Frege, Russell, and Modern Logic," videorecording (London: BBC, 1987).

Banfield, Edward, with Laura Fasano Banfield, *The Moral Basis of a Backward Society* (New York: Free Press, 1958).

Bendix, Reinhard, *Max Weber: An Intellectual Portrait* (New York: Doubleday, 1960).

Biko, Steve, "Black Consciousness and the Quest for a True Humanity," *I Write What I Like* (Chicago: University of Chicago Press, 2002 [1969–72]), pp. 87–98.

Bourdieu, Pierre, and Löic J. D. Wacquart, *An Invitation to Reflexive Sociology* (Chicago: University of Chicago Press, 1992).

Bourdieu, Pierre, *Language and Symbolic Power* (Cambridge: Polity Press, 1991).

Bourdieu, Pierre, *The Logic of Practice* (Cambridge: Cambridge University Press, 1992).

Chua Beng-Huat, *Communitarian Ideology and Democracy in Singapore* (London: Routledge, 1995).

Culture Matters: How Values Shape Human Progress, Lawrence E. Harrison and Samuel P. Huntington, eds. (New York: Basic Books, 2000).

Dahl, Robert A., *Modern Political Analysis* (Englewood Cliffs: Prentice-Hall, 1963).

Douglas, Mary, *Purity and Danger: An Analysis of Concepts of Pollution and Taboo* (New York: Praeger, 1966).

Eisenstadt, S. N., and L. Roniger, *Patrons, Clients and Friends: Interpersonal Relations and the Structure of Trust in Society* (Cambridge: Cambridge University Press, 1984).

Elkins, David, and Richard Simeon, "A Cause in Search of its Effect, or What Does Political Culture Explain?" *Comparative Politics* 11 (January 1979), pp. 127–46.

Elster, Jon, *Consequences of Constitutional Choice Reflections on Tocqueville* (Chicago: University of Chicago Press, 1980).

Emmerson, Donald K., "Southeast Asia in Political Science: Terms of Enlistment," in *Southeast Asia in Political Science: Theory, Region, and Qualitative Political Science*, Erik Martínez Kuhonta, Dan Slater, and Tuong Vu, eds. (Stanford: Stanford University Press, 2000), pp. 302–24.

Foucault, Michel, *Discipline and Punish: The Birth of the Prison*, trans. Alan Sheridan (New York: Vintage Book, 1977).

Fox, Jonathan, "The Difficult Transition from Clientelism to Citizenship," *World Politics* 46 (January 1994), pp. 151–84.

Fukuyama, Francis, *The End of History and the Last Man* (London: Hamish Hamilton, 1992).

Fukuyama, Francis, "The End of History?" *The National Interest* 16 (summer 1989), pp. 3–18.

Gaventa, John, *Power and Powerlessness: Quiescence and Rebellion in an Appalachian Valley* (Urbana: University of Illinois Press, 1980).

Geertz, Clifford, "Deep Play: Notes on the Balinese Cockfight," in *The Interpretation of Cultures* (New York: Basic Books, 1973), pp. 412–53.

Geertz, Clifford, *The Social History of an Indonesian Town* (Cambridge: MIT Press, 1965).

Gramsci, Antonio, *Selections from the Prison Notebooks* (New York: Lawrence and Wishart, 1971).

Granovetter, Mark, "Economic Action and Social Structure: The Problem of Embeddedness," *American Journal of Sociology* 91 (November 1985), pp. 481–510.

Greenfeld, Liah, *Nationalism: Five Roads to Modernity* (Cambridge: Harvard University Press, 1992).

Habermas, Jürgen, *The Structural Transformation of the Public Sphere: An Inquiry into a Category of Bourgeois Society* (Cambridge: Polity Press, 1989).

Hayek, Friedrich August von, "The Pretence of Knowledge," Nobel Prize Acceptance Speech, at http://nobelprize.org/nobel_prizes/economics/.

Hirschman, Albert O., "Changing Tolerance for Income Inequality in the Course of Economic Development," *World Development* 1:12 (1973), pp. 24–36.

Hirschman, Albert O., *Exit, Voice, and Loyalty* (Cambridge: Harvard University Press, 1970).

Hirschman, Albert O., "The Search for Paradigms as a Hindrance to Understanding," in *A Bias for Hope*, Hirschman, ed. (New Haven: Yale University Press, 1971), pp. 342–60.

Huang, Peter H., and Wu Ho-Mou, "More Order without More Law: A Theory of Social Norms and Organizational Cultures," *Journal of Law, Economics, and Organization* 10:2 (1994), pp. 390–406.

Huntington, Samuel P., "The Clash of Civilizations?" *Foreign Affairs* 72:3 (Summer 1993), pp. 12–49.

Huntington, Samuel P., "The West: Unique, not Universal," *Foreign Affairs* 75:6 (November/December 1996), pp. 28–46.

Huntington, Samuel P., *The Clash of Civilizations and the Remaking of World Order* (New York: Simon Schuster, 1996).

In Search of Prosperity: Narratives on Economic Growth, Rodrik, Dani, ed. (Princeton: Princeton University Press, 2003).

James, William, *Essays in Radical Empiricism* (Lincoln: University of Nebraska Presss, 2003 [1912]).

James, William, *The Meaning of Truth: A Sequel to 'Pragmatism'* (Amherst, NY: Prometheus Books, 1997 [1909]).

Krugman, Paul, "The Rise and Fall of Development Economics," from *Rethinking the Development Experience: Essays Provoked by the Work of Albert O. Hirschman*, Lloyd Rodwin and Donald A Schön, eds. (Washington: Brookings Institution, 1994), pp. 39–58.

Lamont, Michèle, *Money, Morals, and Manners: The Culture of the French and the American Upper-Middle Class* (Chicago: University of Chicago Press, 1992).

Leheny, David, *Think Global, Fear Local: Sex, Violence, and Anxiety in Contemporary Japan* (Ithaca: Cornell University Press, 2006).

Levi, Carlo, *Christ Stopped at Eboli* (Cristo si è fermato a Eboli), trans. Frances Frenaye (London: Penguin, 1982).

Lieberman, Evan S., "Nested Analysis as a Mixed-Method Strategy for Comparative Research," *American Political Science Review* 99:3 (August 2005), pp. 435–52.

Lipset, Seymour Martin, *Political Man: The Social Bases of Politics* (Baltimore: Johns Hopkins University Press, orig. 1961, expanded ed. 1981).

Lukes, Steven, *Power: A Radical View* (London: Macmillan, 1974).

Machiavelli, Niccolò, *The Prince*, intro. Christian Gauss (New York: Mentor, 1955 [orig. 1532]).

MacKinnon, Barbara, *American Philosophy: A Historical Anthology* (Albany: SUNY Press, 1985).

Mannheim, Karl, *Ideology and Utopia: An Introduction to the Sociology of Knowledge* (London: Routledge, 1936).

Marshall, T.H., *Citizenship and Social Class, and Other Essays* (Cambridge: Cambridge University Press, 1950).

Mink, Louis O., "The Autonomy of Historical Understanding," *History and Theory* 5 (1965), pp. 24–47.

Moore, Barrington, Jr., *Social Origins of Dictatorship and Democracy: Lord and Peasant in the Making of the Modern World* (Boston: Beacon, 1966).

Nationalism and Rationality, Albert Breton, *et al.*, eds. (New York: Cambridge University Press, 1995).

Nelson, Benjamin N., *The Idea of Usury: From Tribal Brotherhood to Universal Otherhood*, No. 3, "History of Ideas" Series (Princeton: Princeton University Press, 1953).

Nicholas, Ralph W., "Factions: A Comparative Analysis," in *Political Systems and the Distribution of Power*, Michael Banton, ed. (London: Tavistock, 1968), pp. 21–58.

Nicholas, Ralph W., "Segmentary Factional Political Systems," in *Political Anthropology*, Marc J. Swartz, *et al.*, eds. (Chicago: Aldine, 1966).

Nordlinger, Eric, "Taking the State Seriously," in *Understanding Political Development*, Myron Wiener and Samuel P. Huntington, eds. (Boston: Little, Brown, 1987), pp. 353–90.

Ortega y Gasset, José, *What is Knowledge?* (Albany: SUNY Press, 2001).

Pareto, Vilfredo, *The Rise and Fall of the Elites: An Application of Theoretical Sociology* (New York: Arno Press, 1979; orig. 1901).

Parsons, Talcott, "Power and Social System," in *Power*, Steven Lukes, ed. (New York: New York University Press, 1986).

Pierson, Paul, "Big, Slow-Moving, and … Invisible: Macro-Social Processes in Contemporary Political Science," in *Comparative Historical Analysis in the Social Sciences,* James Mahoney and Dietrich Rueschmeyer, eds. (New York: Cambridge University Press, 2003), pp. 177–207.

Piven, Frances Fox, and Richard A. Cloward, *Poor People's Movements: Why They Succeed, How They Fail* (New York: Vintage, 1979).

Polanyi, Karl, *The Great Transformation: The Social and Economic Origins of our Time* (New York: Rinehart, 1944).

Political Science: The State of the Discipline, Ira Katznelson and Helen V. Milner, eds. (New York: Norton, 2002).

Popper, Karl, *The Logic of Scientific Discovery* (London: Routledge, 1959).

Putnam, Robert D., "Bowling Alone: America's Declining Social Capital," in *The Global Resurgence of Democracy,* Larry Diamond and Marc F. Plattner, eds. (Baltimore: Johns Hopkins University Press, 1996), pp. 290–303.

Rawls, John, *A Theory of Justice* (Cambridge: Harvard University Press, 1971).

Rethinking Social Inquiry: Diverse Tools, Shared Standards, Henry E. Brady and David Collier, eds. (Lanham: Rowman and Littlefield, 2004).

Rorty, Richard, and Pascal Engel, *What's the Use of Truth?* (New York: Columbia University Press, 2007).

Rueschmeyer, Dietrich, Evelyne Huber Stephens, and John D. Stephens, *Capitalist Development and Democracy* (Chicago: University of Chicago Press, 1992).

Schattschneider, E. E., *The Semi-Sovereign People: A Realist's View of Democracy in America,* intro. by David Adamany (Hinsdale, IL: Dreyden Press, 1975).

Schmitter, Philippe, "Still the Century of Corporatism?" *Review of Politics* 1 (January 1974), pp. 85–128.

Scott, James C., "The Erosion of Patron-Client Bonds and Social Change in Rural Southeast Asia," *Journal of Asian Studies* 32:1 (November 1972), pp. 6–37.

Scott, James C., *Domination and the Arts of Resistance: Hidden Transcripts* (New Haven: Yale University Press, 1990).

Scott, James C., *Weapons of the Weak: Everyday Forms of Peasant Resistance* (New Haven: Yale University Press, 1985).

Sen, Amartya, *Development as Freedom* (New York: Alfred Knopf, 1999).

Slaughter, Anne-Marie, *The Idea That Is America* (New York: Basic Books, 2007).

Stark, David, *Heterarchy: Asset Ambiguity, Organizational Innovation, and the Postsocialist Firm* (Ithaca: Cornell School of Industrial and Labor

Relations Working Paper 96-21, 1996), also http://www.ilr.cornell.edu/depts/cahrs/downloads/pdfs/workingpapers/WP96-21.pdf.

Swire, Peter M., *The Onslaught of Complexity: Information Technologies and Developments in Legal and Economic Thought* (Senior Thesis, Woodrow Wilson School, Princeton University, 1980).

Tilly, Charles, "War Making and State Making as Organized Crime," in *Bringing the State Back In*, Peter Evans, *et al.*, eds. (Cambridge: Cambridge University Press, 1985), pp. 169–91.

Truman, David B., *The Governmental Process: Political Interests and Public Opinion*, 2nd ed. (New York: Knopf, 1971 [1st ed., 1951]).

Viroli, Maurizio, *For Love of Country* (Oxford: Clarendon, 1995).

Weber, Max, *The Protestant Ethic and the Spirit of Capitalism* (London: George Allen and Unwin, 1976).

Weber, Max, "Politics as a Vocation," in *From Max Weber: Essays in Sociology*, trans. H.H. Gerth and C.W. Mill (New York: Oxford University Press, 1946), pp. 77–128.

Wittgenstein, Ludwig, *Philosophical Investigations* (New York: Macmillan, 1953).

Wittgenstein, Ludwig, *Tractatus Logico-Philosophicus* (London: Routledge, 1974 reprint [orig. 1922]).

Woolf, Virginia, *Three Guineas* (New York: Harcourt, 1938), pp. 85–114.

Wolin, Sheldon S., *Politics and Vision* (Boston: Little, Brown, 1960).

Name Index

Subject Index

Africa, 38*fn78*, 56, 59*fn116*, 148, 554, 579–580

agriculture

banking and, 72–73, 235–239, 275

capitalism and, 144, 237–238, 251. *See also* capitalism

cooperatives and, 209, 268

democratization and, 29, 218, 536, 551, 586

economy of scale and, 17

exports, 528, 568. *See specific products, countries*

fertilizer and, 17, 71, 83, 104, 160–173, 232, 252–257

government and, 69, 168, 353. *See also specific governments*

Green Revolution. *See* Green Revolution

import substitution and, 568

involution and, 17

industrialization and, 70, 91, 144, 166, 237, 344, 352. *See also* industrialization

land reform and. *See* land reform

migrant workers and, 345–348

modernization and, 237, 559. *See also* Green Revolution

nonstate autonomies and, 9–16

peasants and. *See* peasants

plantations and, 16*fn39*, 23, 165, 206, 220, 230, 266

productivity, 17, 104*fn4*, 105, 107, 165, 170, 184, 231, 241

registrations, 349

rice and. *See* rice farming

rural farms, 70, 91, 106, 140, 163, 220, 234, 239, 251

slash-and-burn methods, 17, 220

sharecropping, 234

SMEs and, 87

www.ingramcontent.com/pod-product-compliance
Lightning Source LLC
Chambersburg PA
CBHW050326270326
41926CB00016B/3338